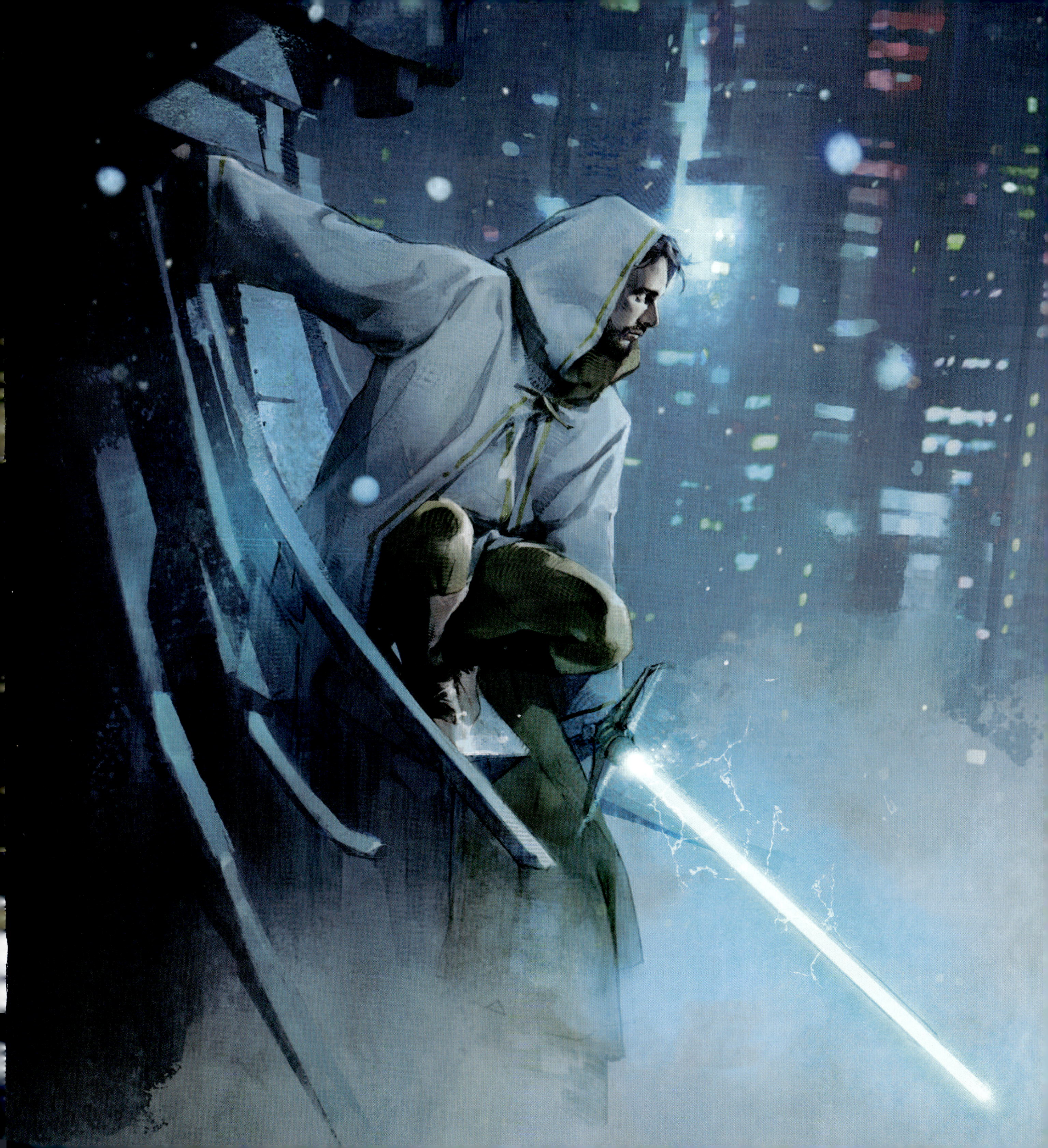

THE ART OF

STAR WARS
THE HIGH REPUBLIC

VOLUME I: LIGHT OF THE JEDI

KRISTIN BAVER

ABRAMS, NEW YORK

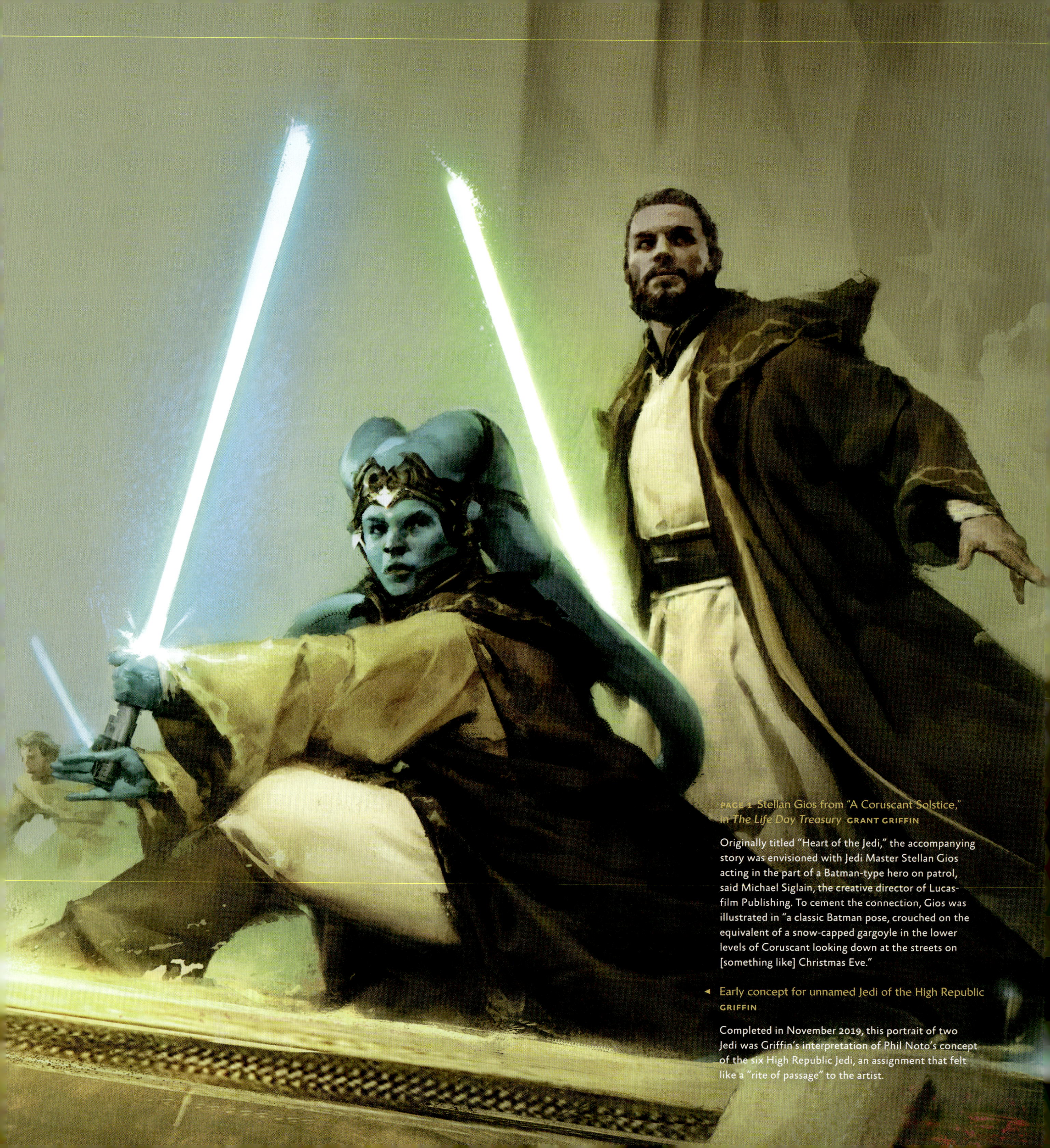

PAGE 1 Stellan Gios from "A Coruscant Solstice," in *The Life Day Treasury* GRANT GRIFFIN

Originally titled "Heart of the Jedi," the accompanying story was envisioned with Jedi Master Stellan Gios acting in the part of a Batman-type hero on patrol, said Michael Siglain, the creative director of Lucasfilm Publishing. To cement the connection, Gios was illustrated in "a classic Batman pose, crouched on the equivalent of a snow-capped gargoyle in the lower levels of Coruscant looking down at the streets on [something like] Christmas Eve."

◂ Early concept for unnamed Jedi of the High Republic GRIFFIN

Completed in November 2019, this portrait of two Jedi was Griffin's interpretation of Phil Noto's concept of the six High Republic Jedi, an assignment that felt like a "rite of passage" to the artist.

CONTENTS

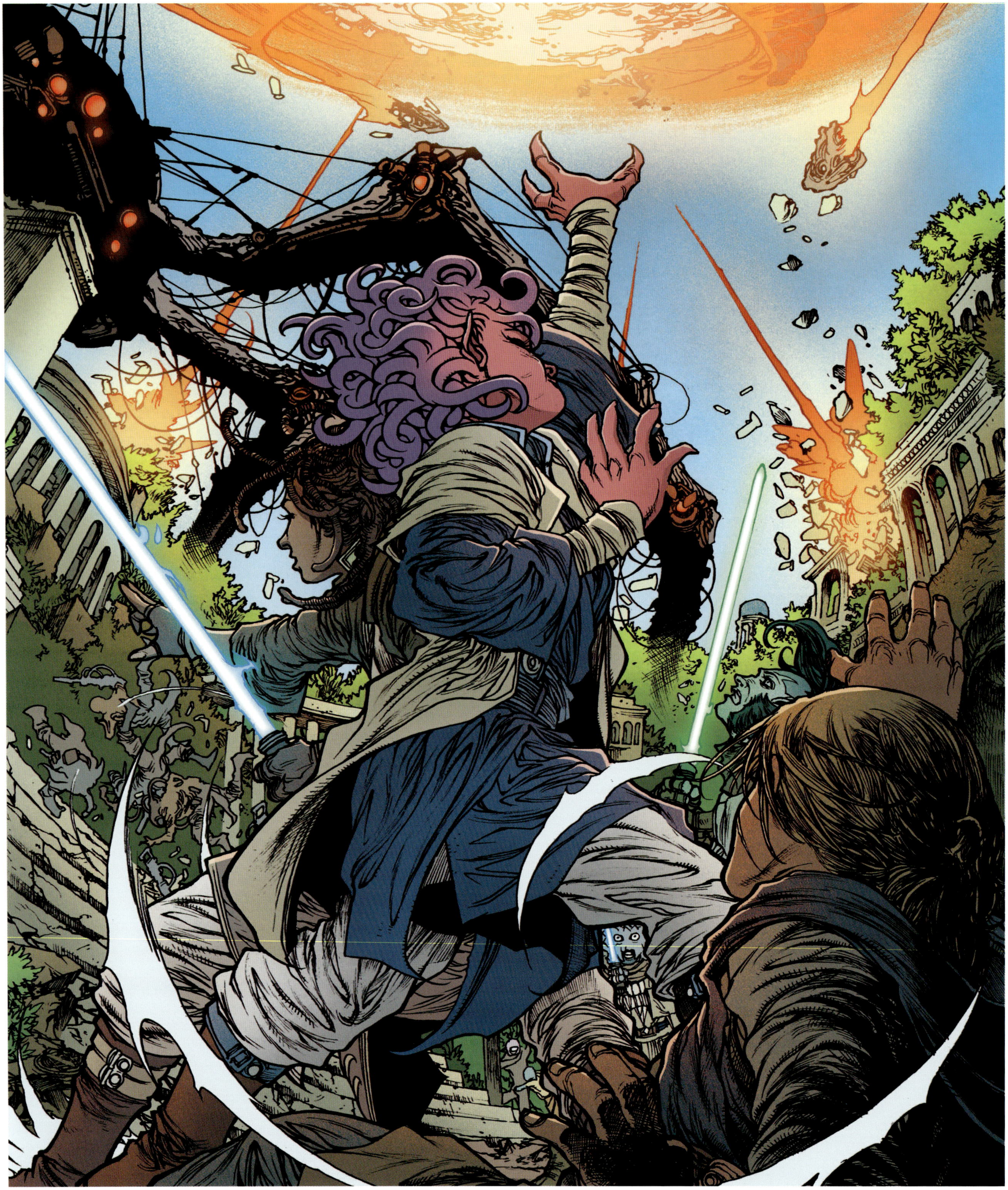

WHO'S WHO

Troy Alders
Lucasfilm art director

Ario Anindito
Concept and Marvel artist

Petur Antonsson
Illustrator, Lucasfilm Press

Giorgio Baroni
Concept artist

John Bell
Concept artist

Joshua Bitzer
Concept artist

Pascal Blanché
Concept artist

Steve Blank
Director of Franchise Content & Strategy, Lucasfilm

Nick Brokenshire
Concept and IDW artist

Adrienne Brown
Concept artist

Ryan Church
Concept supervisor

James Clyne
Design supervisor, ILM

Fausto de Martini
Concept artist

Glyn Dillon
Costume concept artist

Max Dunbar
Concept artist

Jason Eaton
Model maker

Roberto Fernández Castro
Concept artist

Warren Fu
Concept artist

Claudia Gray
Author

Grant Griffin
Book illustrator

Matt Griffin
Illustrator

Kiri Hart
Former Lucasfilm Senior Vice President of Development

Kurt Hartman
Design manager, Disney Publishing Worldwide

Jennifer Heddle
Executive editor, Lucasfilm Publishing

Pablo Hidalgo
Senior creative executive, Lucasfilm Story Group

Justina Ireland
Author

Jama Jurabaev
Illustrator

Georges Jeanty
Concept and Marvel artist

Joe Johnston
Star Wars original trilogy ILM art director

Jama Jurabaev
Concept artist

Kyle Kao
Model photographer

Kathleen Kennedy
Lucasfilm president

Gonzalo Kenny
Concept artist

Soyoung Kim
Designer, Disney Publishing Worldwide

Steve Kurth
Illustrator, concept artist

Grace Lee
Concept artist

Łukasz Liszko
Book illustrator

David López
Marvel artist

George Lucas
Star Wars creator

Giada Marchisio
Concept artist

Iain McCaig
Concept artist

Ralph McQuarrie
Star Wars original trilogy production illustrator/ Concept artist

Manny Mederos
Disney Publishing Worldwide illustration manager and concept artist

Joseph Meehan
Concept artist

Mark Morales
Marvel artist

Phil Noto
Concept and Marvel artist

Daniel José Older
Author

Jose Perez III
Star Wars: Tales from the Galaxy's Edge director

Tara Phillips
Disney Press artist

Scott Piehl
Design director, Disney Publishing

Diogo Saito
Concept artist

Mizuki Sakakibara
Viz Media manga artist

Ornella Savarese
Concept artist

Cavan Scott
Author

Elisa Serio
Concept artist

Michael Siglain
Creative director, Lucasfilm Publishing

Robert Simpson
Senior editor, Lucasfilm Publishing

Will Sliney
Marvel artist

Charles Soule
Author

Rachael Stott
Concept artist

Phil Szostak
Creative art manager, Lucasfilm

Thom Tenery
Concept artist

Jeffrey Thomas
Disney Publishing Worldwide illustration manager and concept artist

Erik Tiemens
Concept supervisor

Harvey Tolibao
Concept and IDW artist

TomatoFarm
Illustration agency

Chris Voy
Art director, ILM

Dave Wachter
Concept and Marvel artist

James Waugh
Lucasfilm Senior Vice President, Franchise Content & Strategy

Evan Whitefield
Concept artist, ILM

Jason Wojtowicz
Senior designer, Lucasfilm Franchise Content Creative

MinJi Yoon
Concept artist

Stephen Zavala
Art director, ILM

Leigh Zieske
Designer, Lucasfilm Publishing

◂ Page from IDW's *Star Wars: The High Republic Adventures* #1
HARVEY TOLIBAO (PENCILER) AND REBECCA NALTY (COLORIST)

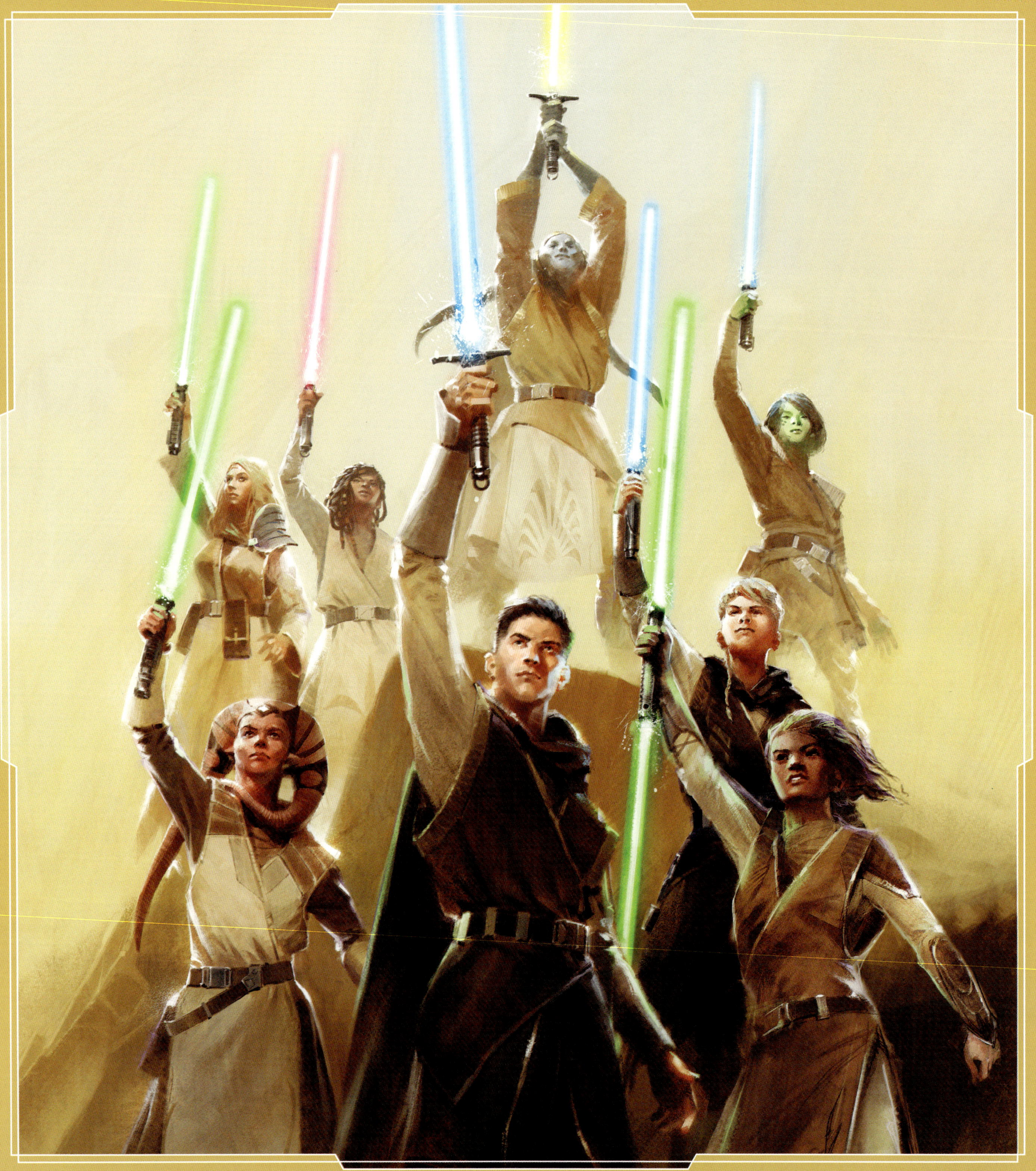

FOREWORD

STAR WARS: THE HIGH REPUBLIC was an unknown quantity for Lucasfilm. Originally pitched as a way to push our publishing offerings beyond our films and give more creative freedom to our authors and editors, it seemed the perfect plan to expand our storytelling opportunities. But the key would be finding the right authors—and the right story.

A powerful and diverse group of current *Star Wars* authors including Claudia Gray, Justina Ireland, Daniel José Older, Cavan Scott, and Charles Soule provided us with a foundation for the golden age of the Jedi and, more importantly, what might possibly scare them.

But as with film production, the story needed to be visualized before it could be fully executed. A team of exceptional artists—including the iconic Iain McCaig—came together under Lucasfilm's direction to deliver an all-new era that takes the tenets of *Star Wars* and interprets them in both traditional and original ways. It pulls from classic *Star Wars* art, such as Ralph McQuarrie's beautiful concept paintings, and is influenced by everyone from Caravaggio to Andrew Wyeth. It draws inspiration from iconic science fiction, horror, and adventure films to classic literature and comic books. The scale is epic and the struggles are personal. At its core, it remains true to what George Lucas first put to screen in 1977. As you'll see, the concept illustrations and artwork that appear in these pages are thoughtful, deliberate, and inspiring.

The success of *The High Republic* is a testament to all of the hard work that the authors and artists have poured into it. Their accomplishments are all the more impressive given the state of the world when the initiative was launched, squarely in the middle of a global pandemic amid political and social unrest. These stories allow fans and readers of all ages to see themselves in *Star Wars* and to find both personal moments and grand adventures that they can truly call their own.

Behind the scenes, Michael Siglain and the publishing team, James Waugh and the franchise story team, and art director Troy Alders have helped to usher in this incredible, exciting, and emotional new direction for Lucasfilm. I can't wait to see where *The High Republic* goes next.

For light and life!

Kathleen Kennedy
President, Lucasfilm

◂ Concept art created for the official announcement of *Star Wars: The High Republic*, February 2020 GIORGIO BARONI

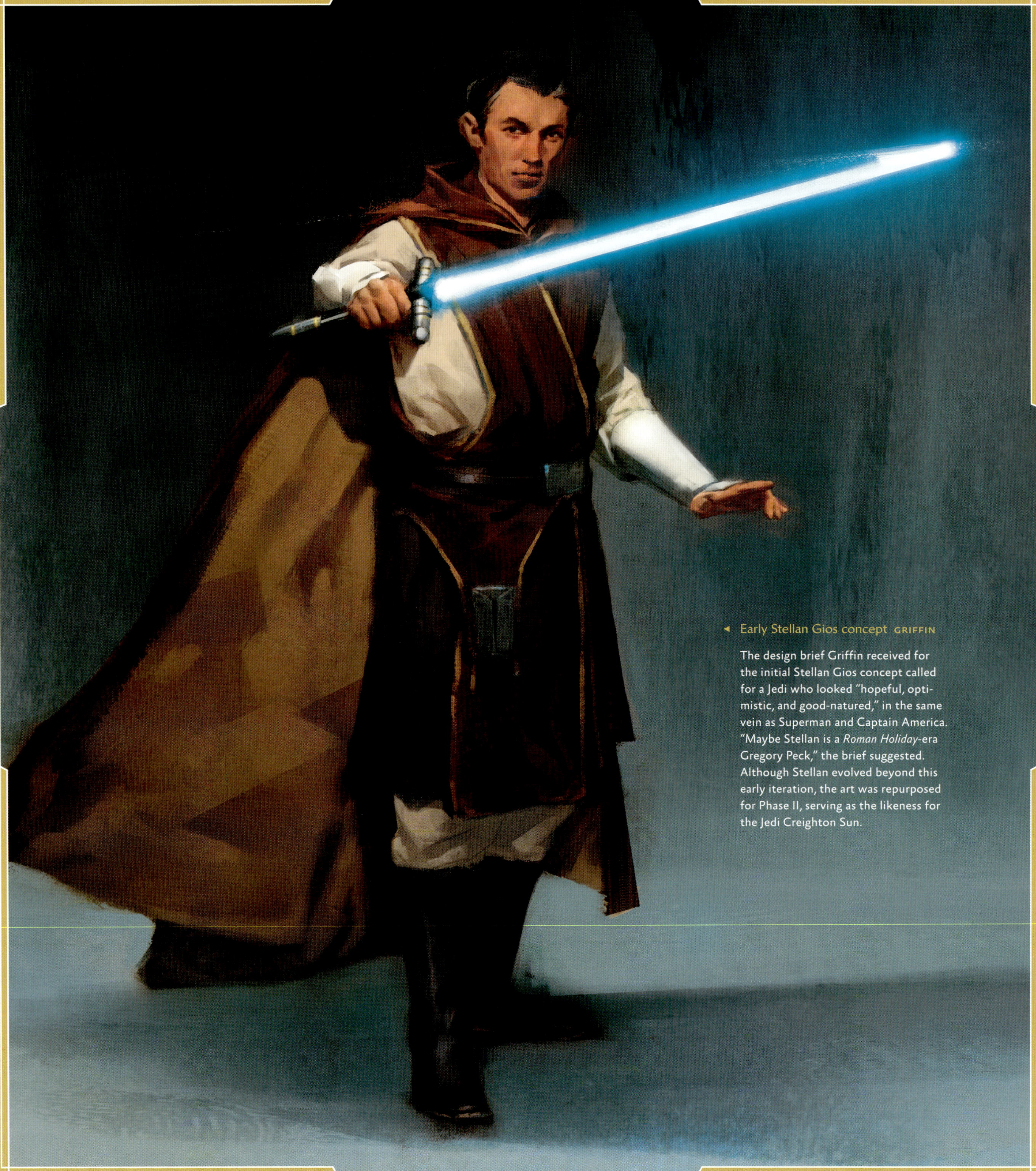

◂ Early Stellan Gios concept GRIFFIN

The design brief Griffin received for the initial Stellan Gios concept called for a Jedi who looked "hopeful, optimistic, and good-natured," in the same vein as Superman and Captain America. "Maybe Stellan is a *Roman Holiday*-era Gregory Peck," the brief suggested. Although Stellan evolved beyond this early iteration, the art was repurposed for Phase II, serving as the likeness for the Jedi Creighton Sun.

INTRODUCTION

"WE ARE ALL THE REPUBLIC."

This rallying cry, heard throughout *Star Wars: Light of the Jedi*—the debut novel in The High Republic initiative—is more than just a political slogan. And when the book arrived in January 2021, it was somehow the exact sentiment we needed in our own world.

I had spent much of those first nine months of the COVID-19 global pandemic working from the safety of my apartment, a job that required the recording of a weekly *Star Wars* news video that felt as if it were being transmitted into the abyss. Sitting on a makeshift set—an old bookcase repurposed and decorated with my own collection of action figures, books, and collectibles—I pushed away the anxiety of the sudden lockdown and the fear of the virus and tried to smile through it. The Thursday episodes of *This Week! In Star Wars* weren't groundbreaking in the grand scheme of things, but they gave me a feeling of near normalcy. And just as *Star Wars* has done for nearly fifty years, it provided a tether to the community of other *Star Wars* fans, a much-needed sense of connection to the outside world, even on days I felt isolated.

At the same time, High Republic architects around the world, including the artists that have defined the appearance of the new era, were working in tandem via virtual meetings and emailed sketches, coming together at a time when many cities all-but shutdown. The arrival of The High Republic, like the Skywalker saga before it and countless other *Star Wars* stories told through animation, live-action television, books, and video games, was itself a beacon of hope. The beauty of storytelling is the way it allows us to process our emotions, examine our darkest fears, and broach impossibly complex and divisive topics with, in the case of *Star Wars*, the safety net of otherworldly creatures, laser swords, and heroes imbued with the power of the Force. The first stories set in the golden age of the Jedi were written before the pandemic reared its beastly head, yet the messages within these tales strike true. In the moments we feel most vulnerable and helpless due to our own Earthly circumstances, stories like these can aid us in searching our feelings and encourage us to seek out glimmers of hope, come together in solidarity, and learn to let go of all that remains out of our control.

The golden age of the Jedi and their defense of the Republic in its glory days, characterized by gleaming white robes accented in literal gold, is not without its battles. Although this Jedi Order is still centuries from the fall from grace that will see the peacekeeping Force-users become generals in the Clone Wars, they still struggle with defending against attackers while remaining in the light. And some lose control in their dance with the darkness. The lifelong quest for balance in all things can be interrupted and upended by emotional attachments and feelings of love or seething hate.

Ultimately, the Jedi are far from perfect even in their prime, and that's precisely why they resonate with us. They are Wookiee and Duros, human and Twi'lek, and countless other alien species from around the galaxy. They feel the Force like a song, like the sea, and in countless other interpretations, echoing the multitudes of religions and faiths in our own world, bound by similar archetypes, yet divergent. They are the best of us, striving for unity in an imperfect galaxy, buoyed by hope even when they feel crushed by the weight of the world and its unfairness. They are relatable in their humanity, individuals in search of connection and empathy.

In a time of uncertainty, fear, detachment, and despair, *The High Republic* in its grandeur is a reminder of togetherness, idealism, unity, and hope. And as Padawan Bell Zettifar tells himself while trying to do the impossible during the attack on the Republic Fair on Valo, the message we must carry forward is this: We are not alone.

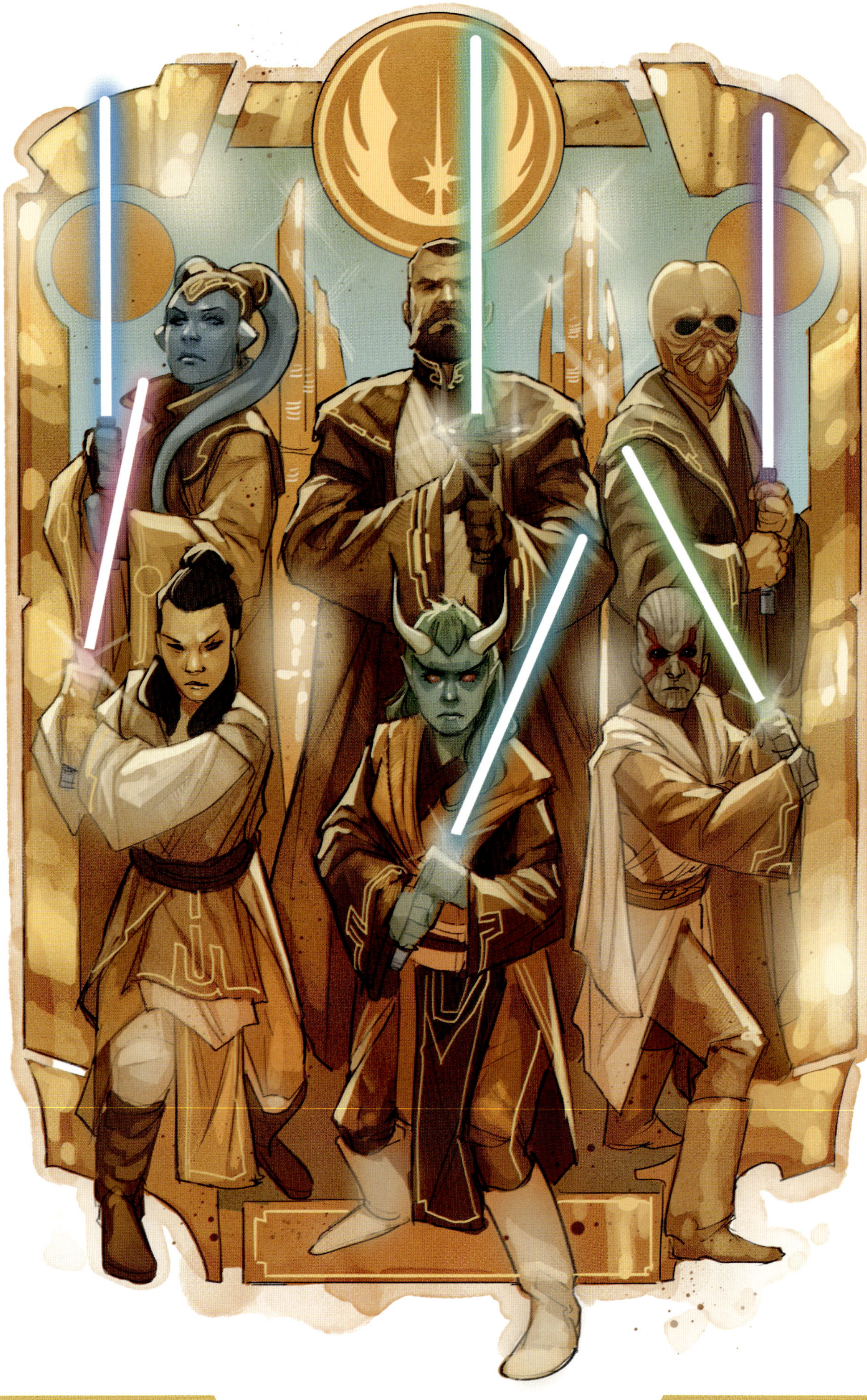

First concept for Jedi of the High Republic
"This was actually the last one that I worked on after doing designs for a few other story concepts and characters. It was presented to me as a grand, regal piece showing the Jedi Renaissance. I also believe it was the first time I saw the title, 'High Republic.' I used some aliens and designs that were left over from my initial Jedi-lineup piece. I leaned heavily into the Golden-Age/Excalibur aesthetic, with a dash of samurai."
PHIL NOTO

CHAPTER 1
THE INSPIRATION

WHAT SCARES THE JEDI?

This was the question author Cavan Scott posed to a room full of fellow writers, publishing colleagues, Lucasfilm executives, and Story Group members on September 26, 2018. It was the third day of the inaugural Authors' Summit, code-named Project Luminous, at Skywalker Ranch, and the moment that sparked what would come to be known as *Star Wars: The High Republic*.

"It was such a profound question because there are multiple ways to answer it," said Lucasfilm Publishing creative director Michael Siglain. "That was really the light bulb moment, and the answer is not, so far, what readers think it is. And that's the beauty of it."

As early as November 2014, Siglain had been dreaming of a multimedia publishing initiative, encouraged by then–Story Group development leader Kiri Hart and Lucasfilm president Kathleen Kennedy. With the Disney acquisition on October 30, 2012, Lucasfilm's publishing projects had pivoted to books and comics that supported new productions including the *Star Wars* sequel trilogy, with predominantly canonical stories that thoughtfully bridged the gaps between films to expand on the origin stories of existing characters.

But Siglain envisioned an ambitious standalone storytelling epic that could break new ground while taking a page from the company's history. Starting in 2015, he began to test his idea, seeding publishing storylines focused on small events with galaxy-spanning impacts and introducing new characters, in an attempt to push the boundaries of *Star Wars* publishing. However, his grand vision more closely resembled a project that had been released twenty years prior, in 1996. Just before the debut of the Special Editions of the original trilogy and the rollout of the *Star Wars* prequels, Lucasfilm introduced *Shadows of the Empire,* a post–Episode V tale that introduced the world to a new hero in Dash Rendar and a new antagonist with the nefarious Black Sun criminal syndicate led by Prince Xizor. Not only did *Shadows* bridge the time between *Star Wars: The Empire Strikes Back* and *Star Wars: Return of the Jedi* through a cohesive web of books, games, and toys, the campaign effectively reignited the *Star Wars* fandom's passion.

By the time the contingent of great minds were meeting in the Tech Building at Skywalker Ranch in late September 2018, Lucasfilm was at a similar juncture, in the midst of preparing for the end of the Skywalker saga and a new beginning in live-action television. "Once the timing was right—as we knew we were ending the Skywalker saga—we were given the approval to go forward with this ambitious publishing initiative," said Siglain. Lucasfilm executives and creatives conceptually understood what they hoped to achieve, but their vision still needed to be refined. As Lucasfilm president Kathleen Kennedy put it in a welcome letter to those in attendance: "This three-day workshop has been something that I've wanted to see happen for a long time—bringing terrific talent together to explore bold directions, new characters, and fresh concepts that can invite, surprise, and delight an entire new generation of *Star Wars* fans." For Siglain, Kennedy's support was a license to experiment with publishing. Books and comics had long been a vital source of galaxy-expanding stories that added depth to existing characters and timelines. This was something different. "Kathy challenged us, specifically, to be bold, and that fueled us as we went into the first retreat at the Ranch."

On the first day of the summit, across the Atlantic, the Main Unit for *Star Wars: The Rise of Skywalker* was shooting

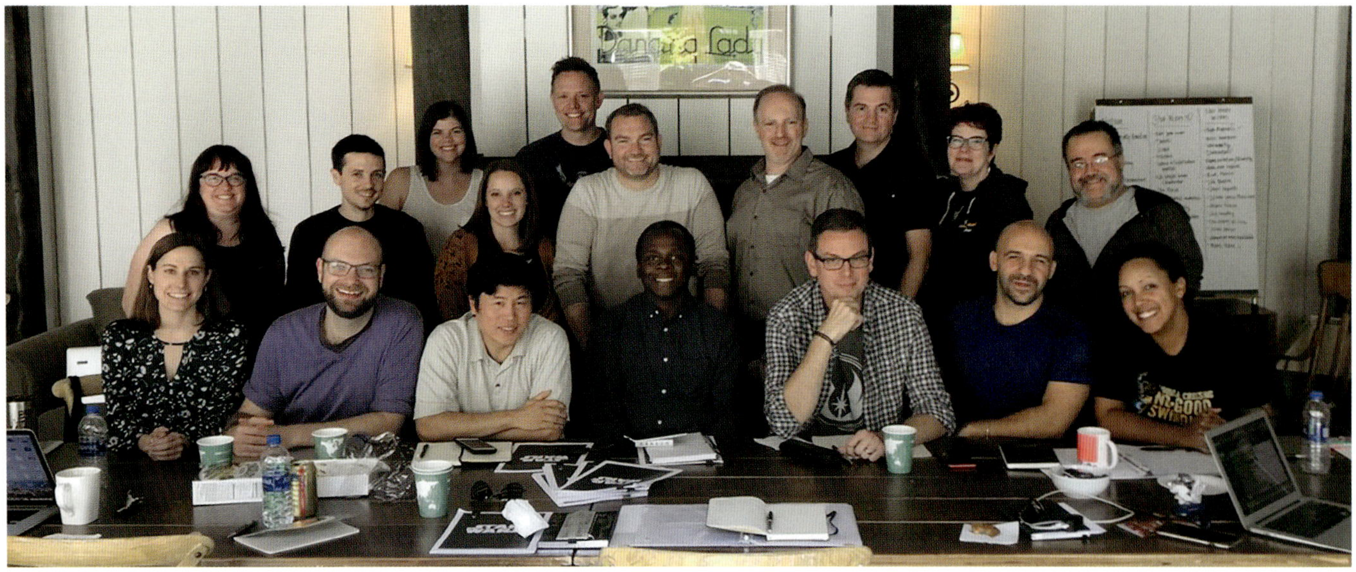

The five authors and members of Lucasfilm publishing and Story Group gather for the first Summit session at Skywalker Ranch. (Left to right) Front row: Kelsey Sharpe, Steve Blank, Leland Chee, Robert Simpson, Cavan Scott, Daniel José Older, Justina Ireland. Back row: Jennifer Heddle, Matt Martin, Caitlin Kennedy, Samantha Holland, Brett Rector, James Waugh, Michael Siglain, Charles Soule, Claudia Gray, and Pablo Hidalgo.

scenes at the Resistance base on Ajan Kloss, including General Leia Organa's quarters, on Stage 5 at Pinewood Studios outside London. At the same time in Los Angeles, Carl Weathers was in his second costume fitting to play disgraced magistrate Greef Karga and the gleaming metallic armor for Pedro Pascal's titular character in *The Mandalorian* was ready for action at the beginning of production on the first *Star Wars* live-action TV series.

On September 24, 2018, just north of San Francisco, Siglain gathered members of Lucasfilm Story Group, Franchise Development, Publishing, and five all-star authors—Cavan Scott, who worked in the time-bending universe of *Doctor Who* and penned the *Star Wars* audio drama *Dooku: Jedi Lost*; Charles Soule, who wrote a thrilling final act for one of the most recognizable X-Men with Marvel's *Death of Wolverine* and told the origin story of Ben Solo's fall to darkness with *The Rise of Kylo Ren*; Claudia Gray, creator of the supernatural vampire romance series *Evernight*, who introduced a fresh perspective to the events of the original trilogy in *Lost Stars* and brought Leia's story full circle with her novel *Bloodline;* Daniel José Older, whose alternate history reimagined dinosaurs on the streets of Civil War–era New York in *Dactyl Hill Squad* and who reunited Han Solo and Lando Calrissian in *Last Shot*; and Justina Ireland, creator of the darkly subversive *Dread Nation* series, which posited an end to slavery via the undead, and author of *Spark of the Resistance*—around a table inside the Stable House Conference Room at Skywalker Ranch. The five writers were mostly strangers, although some had crossed paths on the convention circuit and Older had recently moved not far from Gray in New Orleans.

"For the scope of what we wanted this to be—our own corner of the galaxy, the idea of something that was going to be new, yet very authentically *Star Wars*, something that could be shared from generation to generation—we knew that we had to bring people in who had very different points of view and very different strengths," Siglain said. The structure and collaborative nature of the initiative is unlike anything that has come before it for *Star Wars*. Although they would weave a tapestry of interlocking stories in multiple waves of books and comics, each would ultimately be constructed to be consumed either on its own as a fully encompassed story or as part of the greater whole. And throughout the multi-year process, the diverse pool of creators would be given equal standing. "This initiative works because of everyone's love of *Star Wars* and because everyone has had a voice in the project and a seat at the table," said Siglain. That extended from the five core authors to Lucasfilm employees and beyond to include every artist and individual editor who touched one of the tales.

At the outset, the group of story architects spent the day discussing what they loved most about storytelling in general, including authentic world building that held emotional relevance to the real world, and *Star Wars* specifically, from the basic building blocks of good-versus-evil to the iconic lightsaber, a weapon with a sound, shape, and color like no other. "We started to put up on a whiteboard themes, ideas, characters, and locations, whatever it was that resonates with people personally," recalled Lucasfilm Story Group member Steve Blank. "And you started to see and inherently understand some of these core tenets that you want to make sure are foundational to a new era. We started with that as our foundation: what are these principle tenets that resonate for each of us as creatives in this room that we want to make sure we're carrying forward? What are the most important things we want to preserve?"

Then they began to give voice to what they longed to explore in the galaxy, freely scribbling ideas and sketching their most imaginative whims. A trio of dinosaurs with lightsabers for horns was briefly given life on a whiteboard, and Soule suggested a baby version of Yoda—more than a year before Grogu would be revealed to the world as a young version of the same species. "That was a joke pitch," Soule said. "I presented it as, 'Baby Yodas are huge, and they get smaller as they grow.' [My daughter] drew a little cartoon of old Yoda telling a baby Yoda to go to bed and the baby is like, 'I'm not going to do that.' Basically, 'What are you going to do? I'm seven hundred pounds.'"

"We knew that we needed to craft it in such a way that it would feel like *Star Wars*, and to do that, we needed to dissect *Star Wars*," said Siglain. "We know what [creator George Lucas] put into it, what he was pulling from and what inspired him. But what inspires us?" The answer would span the classic tales of King Arthur and his knights, Humphrey Bogart's surprising pivot from gangster roles to leading man in a romantic drama, and modern-day storytelling, including *Star Wars* mythology itself. "It was important for us to look at it objectively and say, 'OK, what do we love? What do we want to see? What doesn't work? What are we not seeing enough of? What can be done better?' You know, 'What do we not touch?' One of the other important things was to keep that mystery. The beautiful thing about *Star Wars* is that it's not all explained. Growing up, [filling in those elements] was up to me."

If Siglain's gamble succeeded, the story anchoring the new interconnected multimedia initiative stood to open up new storytelling opportunities beyond the page, allowing publishing to evolve into an incubator for new characters and eras that could later appear in games or on screen, a role reversal for the department typically tasked with sustaining interest between tentpole projects and big-screen movies that nevertheless honored the genesis of all stories in film, games, and television. As Kennedy put it: "It all starts with the word."

In the evenings, the authors and creatives gathered for dinner at nearby restaurant Rancho Nicasio and later settled in for a round of Manhattans and more discussion around one of the Main House's fireplaces. "I hadn't realized [Skywalker Ranch] was a place that is very, very specifically designed to enhance creativity, to foster it, to make you feel like this is a place where you can wander and dream and imagine anything," said Gray. "It's very comforting. It's very beautiful, but in a very understated way that isn't pulling a whole lot of attention to itself." Even the rooms at the Ranch's private inn are named for creative geniuses, an eclectic mix from silent film comedian Buster Keaton to architect and designer Frank Lloyd Wright, author John Steinbeck to acclaimed Japanese filmmaker Akira Kurosawa.

Each participant had been given homework before the Summit's start, a list of films to watch or rewatch. At the top of Siglain's list for inspiration was *Casablanca*, a personal love story that expertly balances a small event amid a sprawling backdrop. "In my opinion, this—and not *Citizen Kane*—is the greatest American film ever made," Siglain wrote in an email to the Summit participants. "Though in 1942, it was just another movie, and that's part of its brilliance." He recommended they watch or rewatch *The Godfather* Parts I and II for "a powerful and epic story told over decades"; *Star Trek II: The Wrath of Khan* for an interpersonal tale that worked as well for *Star Trek* aficionados as it did for newcomers; and *It's a Mad, Mad, Mad, Mad World*, which stood out for two reasons. "The first, is that it has an inciting incident that sets off multiple parallel storylines that grow and grow with more guest stars than you can shake a stick at," Siglain noted at the time. "They all come together in the end, which is not unlike what we're trying to do. The second reason I picked this is to remember to add humor, both to your writing and to your outlook on this initiative." Siglain encouraged the authors to try to capture the hope inherent in *Superman* (1978), the epic journey and shocking heartbreak of *The Poseidon Adventure* (1972) and *Planet of the Apes* (1968), and the delicate balance of serious fear, ancient wisdom, and playful banter in *Star Wars: The Empire Strikes Back*. On the second night of the Summit, the writers gathered in the darkened Stag Theater, the Ranch's deluxe 300-seat screening venue with plush turquoise upholstered seats surrounded by art deco design elements and a deluxe audio system carefully designed by the experts at Skywalker Sound, to watch *Star Wars: A New Hope*, a reminder of where it all began. Whatever they created had to fit seamlessly into Lucas's original vision and everything that has come since. "It really brought us all back to the heart of what we do and why we do it," said Lucasfilm executive editor Jennifer Heddle, "which is a really great starting point for going forward."

The workshop culminated in five individual pitches, one from each author, including a detailed exploration of the ancient Jedi. "[The summit] was very friendly," recalled Older. "Not in a corny way, but people supporting each other and respecting each other enough to disagree. I remember there being very little ego in the room, and that's a rare and special thing." Although none of the individual ideas would ultimately be chosen, elements of each can be found threaded throughout, with Scott's core sentiment, an exploration of fear itself, and his flagship Marvel comic forming the backbone of Phase I: Light of the Jedi.

IN JANUARY 2019, Siglain called upon celebrated artist Phil Noto to illustrate each of the five story ideas—the first concept art produced for Project Luminous—a rarity for an initiative not immediately destined for a visual medium. "Basically, I called in a favor," Siglain said. "Phil and I worked together at DC Comics. I was (and am) a massive fan of Phil's art, and Phil's a massive *Star Wars* fan, so the stars aligned and it all came together in the nick of time."

"It sounded very exciting, but there was a catch in that because of the scheduling and approvals, it needed to be all done in about two weeks," Noto recalled. "Lucky for me, I had enough time in-between comic jobs to take it on." To date, Noto has worked on several Marvel *Star Wars* comic series as both cover and interiors artist, illustrating comics featuring Darth Vader, Chewbacca, and Poe Dameron, among others. "Getting to create villains, aliens, and ships alongside the established icons was truly the best of both worlds." For the pitch art that would form the bedrock of *The High Republic*, a visualization from which the story and design would evolve and grow, Siglain advised the artist to incorporate filigree into the Jedi robes. "I asked him to make them distinctive, with a pinstripe or some such subtle design element," Siglain said. "I gave him a quick brief and he was off to the races. Once again, he didn't disappoint."

Over the next four months, The High Republic took shape. The authors began meeting in weekly video calls and exchanged daily text messages, sharing story ideas, recipes, and pet photos. Inspired by a quote from Episode IV: *A New Hope*—Obi-Wan Kenobi's evocative description of a

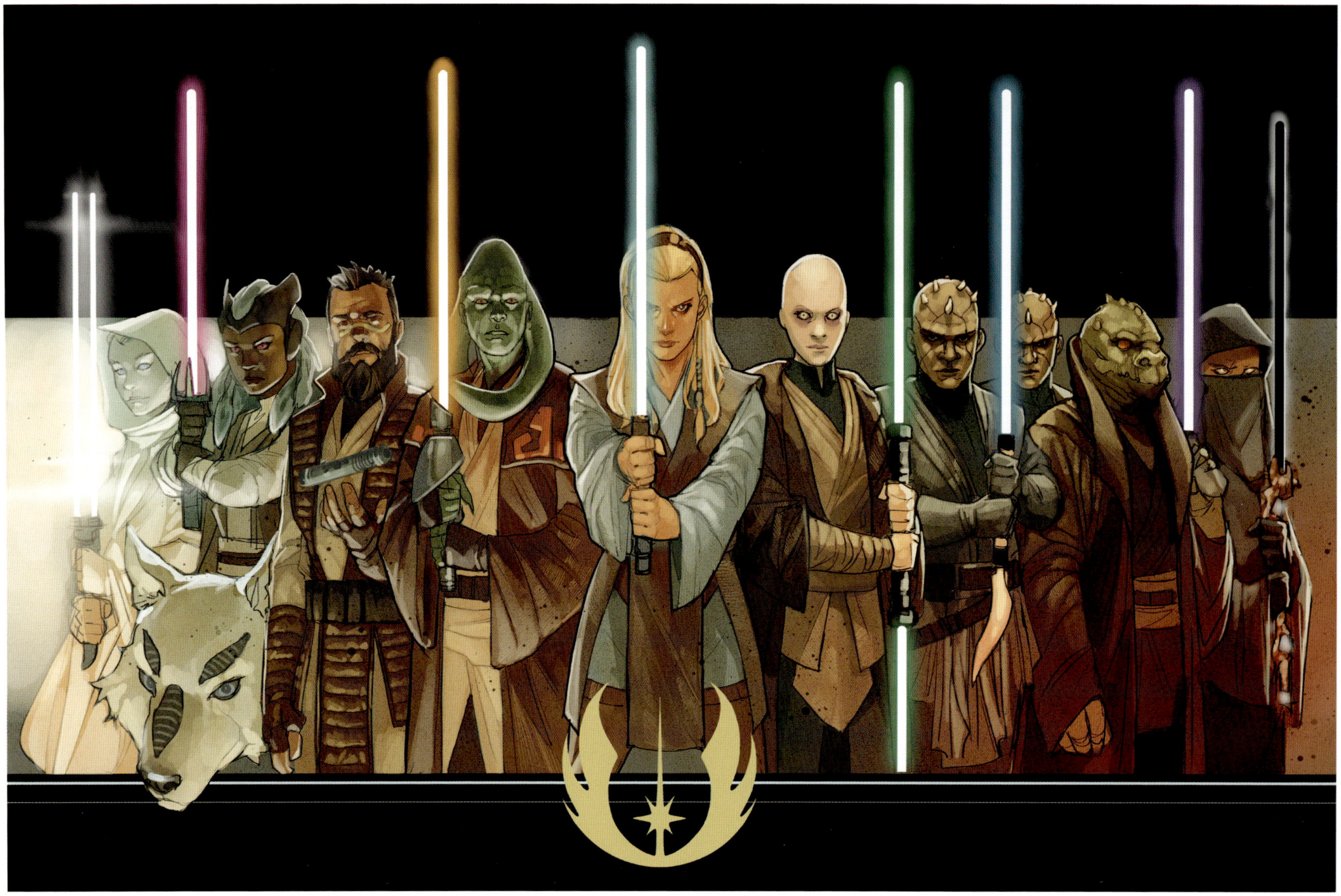

▲ Initial concept art for Charles Soule's pitch "The line-up was initially referred to as the Nine Disciplines. I picked some of my favorite aliens, leaning toward the more obscure ones, and tried to find a good balance of human and alien to keep it interesting. It was fun to put a Trandoshan in there. The lightsaber colors were chosen for their aesthetic in terms of the composition. The tuning-fork white saber was the result of trying to do something different from all the previous lightsaber designs." NOTO

thousand generations of Jedi Knights acting as guardians of peace and justice—by the time the second three-day Project Luminous summit was held starting March 13, 2019, the driving concept had been solidified. The High Republic would explore a bold new era in *Star Wars* lore about 300 years prior to the events of *Star Wars: The Phantom Menace*, populated by a disparate group of new Jedi, Republic citizens, and foes, free of many of the constraints of existing characters and timelines. Pulling from Arthurian legends of Camelot and the Knights of the Round Table, a romantic N.C. Wyeth oil painting called *Lesby* hanging in the Skywalker Ranch library that caught Gray's eye, and the classic films that had set the tone for the story to come, The High Republic set out to construct the grandeur of the Republic and the Jedi Order as they'd never been seen before. The name was somewhat accidentally coined by James Waugh, Lucasfilm's vice president of Franchise Content & Strategy. "I was really just looking at a way to demark time," he said. "And then it stuck."

Understanding that *Star Wars* storytelling is inherently visual—a shape language taking cues from Earthbound cultures and cinematic storytelling, transformed by Lucas into something uniquely its own—Siglain brought in more concept artists to illustrate the legion of new characters, from the Wookiee Jedi Burryaga to the benevolent Chancellor Lina Soh; new species, such as the rocklike Vintian nicknamed Geode and the vicious Drengir; as well as design the overall look of the unexplored era. Executives created mood boards for the Jedi, the Republic, the Starlight Beacon, and the Nihil, pulling in paintings by the original *Star Wars* concept artist Ralph McQuarrie as well as mixed media from other films, fine art, and real-world photography to convey the right tone. "Seeing that visual representation helped to keep everyone focused and on the same page," Siglain said. "And Ralph McQuarrie was on every page. It all starts with—and comes back to—Ralph's art." Concepts had to feel new while also blending in the architecture, fashion, and ships that populated the *Star Wars* prequels, the closest known chronological touchstone point in-universe.

The process was collaborative and cyclical. Noto's initial concept art resonated with Scott in particular, who took a lineup of nine Jedi archetypes and immediately began to

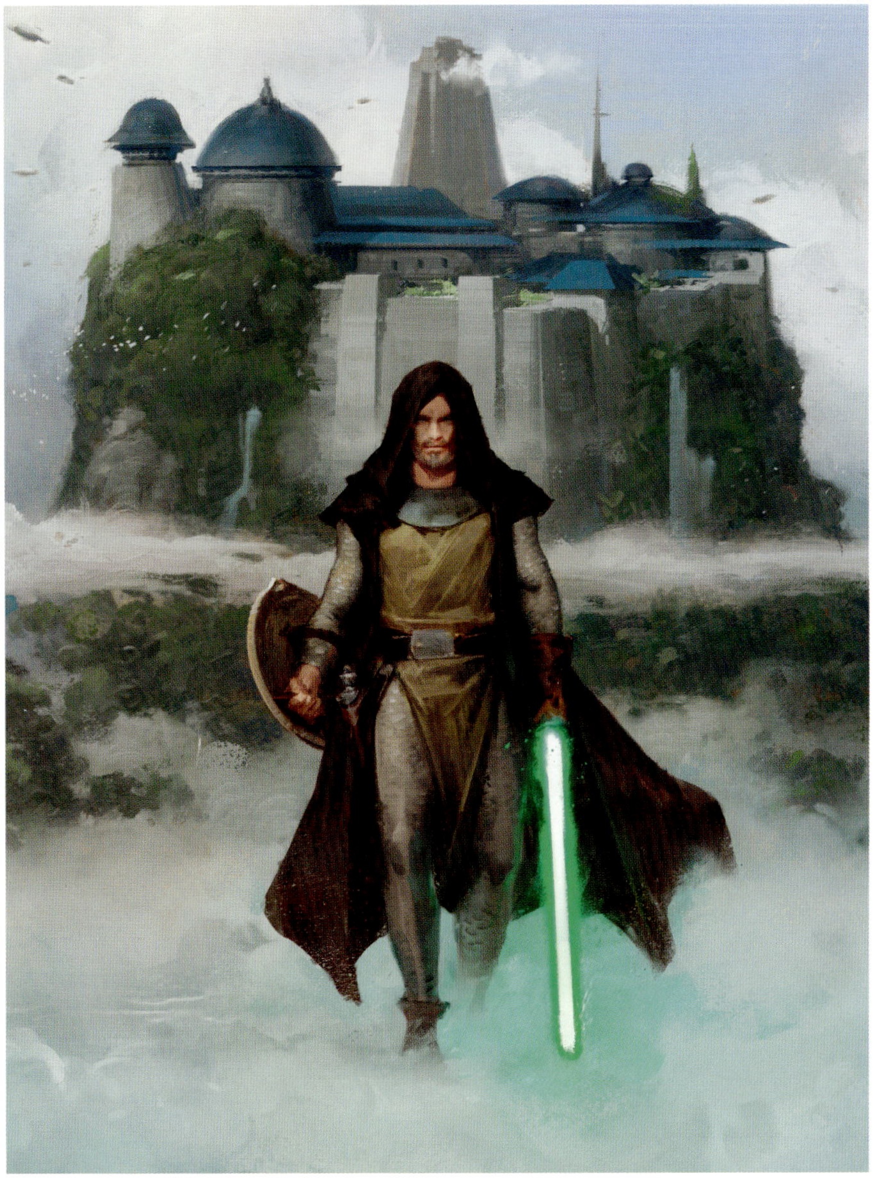

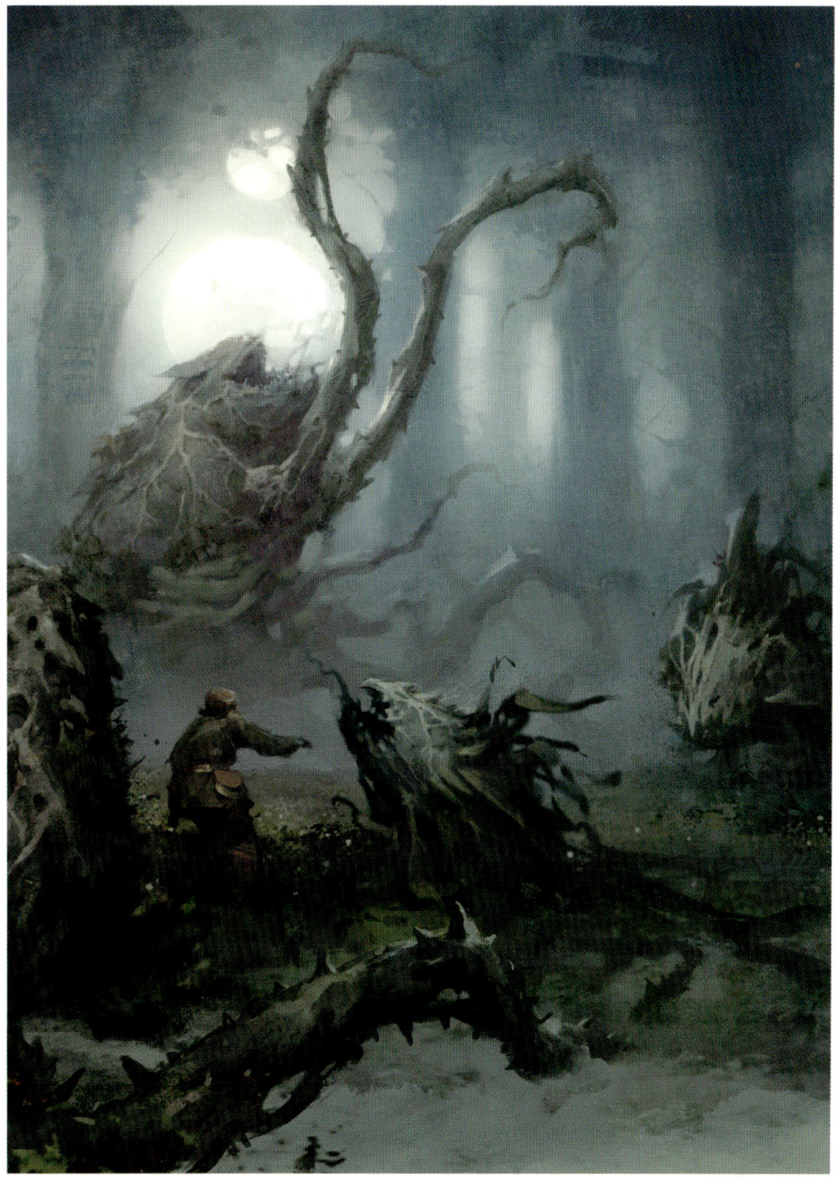

▲ The Wanderer GRIFFIN

Griffin's earlier work in *Star Wars: Myths & Fables* showcased his ability to reimagine the Jedi as legendary knights in a more classical sense.

◄ Drengir from *Star Wars: Dark Legends* GRIFFIN

come up with backstories for the Force-wielders based on their likenesses. "That wasn't even the intention," said Heddle. "But that's what ended up happening because what Phil gave us was so inspiring. What he came up with was so good that once the authors saw it, they wanted to write to those characters."

As new characters emerged in text, in June 2019, Siglain called upon *Star Wars* artist Grant Griffin, whose stunning paintings had previously illustrated *Star Wars: Myths & Fables*, to begin working on five initial pieces of art including a Jedi explorer and their ragtag crew of adventurers, a Force cult, and the first incarnation of the Nihil—villains that fused British punk rock fashion with Viking sensibilities. The following month, Iain McCaig, the renowned concept artist who designed both Queen Padmé Amidala and Darth Maul for *The Phantom Menace*, lent his expertise to the project with a portfolio of captivating and energized line art that riffed off broad ideas to give the era shape and continuity to the "space nouveau" of Amidala's reign. "It was really an organic, fluid approach," said Lucasfilm senior designer Jason Wojtowicz, who helped guide the artists with design briefs, while still allowing them the freedom to thrive creatively.

Publicly, Project Luminous remained shrouded in mystery. First teased at *Star Wars* Celebration Chicago in April 2019, with the authors named during Lucasfilm's Publishing Panel at New York Comic Con on October 4, 2019, Star Wars: The High Republic wasn't officially unveiled until a launch event at Walt Disney Studios in Burbank on February 24, 2020. The special panel was hosted by comedian and *Star Wars* voice actor Bobby Moynihan, an intimate, invite-only press conference that truly revealed The High Republic to the world. In a striking counterpoint to months of dismal world events to come, the first glimpse into the prime of the Jedi Order and the Galactic Republic showcased an era of hope, the golden age of the Jedi with lightsabers held aloft in unity, and a gilded age of prosperity for the galaxy at large.

A mere nine days later, Governor Gavin Newsom would declare a state of emergency in California as COVID-19 spurred a worldwide pandemic. Ultimately the release of the first books and comics for the High Republic were delayed until January 2021.

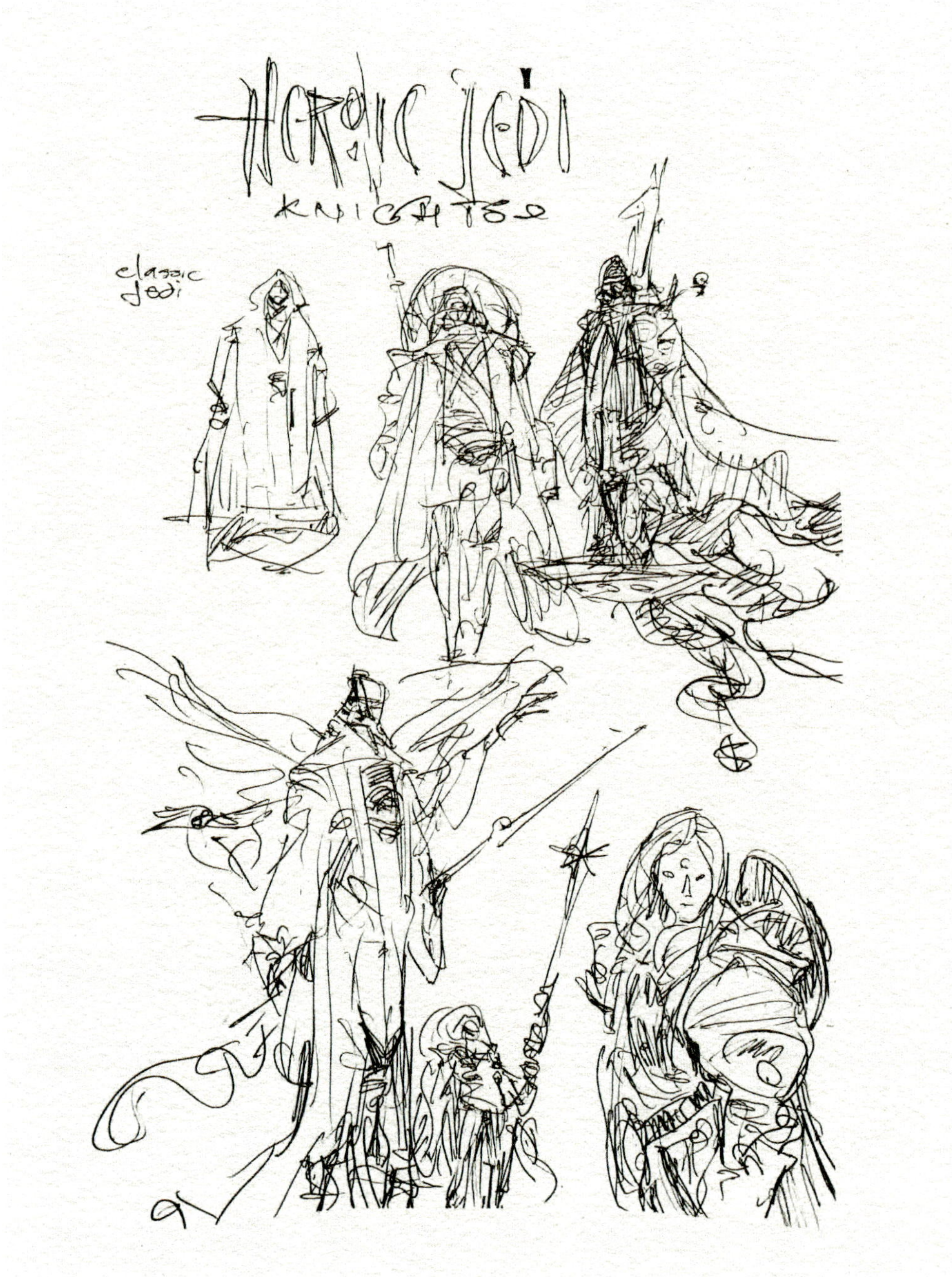

▲ Initial quick sketch of the Jedi of the High Republic, July 2019 "How do we show good people? Knights weren't necessarily good people from certain perspectives. They were bullies and terrible, arrogant superstars. And I thought, well, how fun is that if this is the height of the Jedi and they are literally superstars? When they walk down the street, it's the equivalent of seeing an angel walk by and people just want to touch their robes, but they're friendly. They're not aloof and cold like they were in *The Phantom Menace*. We used to joke that they'd become an old man smoking club or something, but suppose they genuinely cared, and they would walk down the street so they can see people and interact with them and connect.

When I scribble, I don't worry about what it looks like. I truly don't. There was no reference. There was no looking in mirrors or anything. You just draw. I would never have shown these to George [Lucas]." IAIN McCAIG

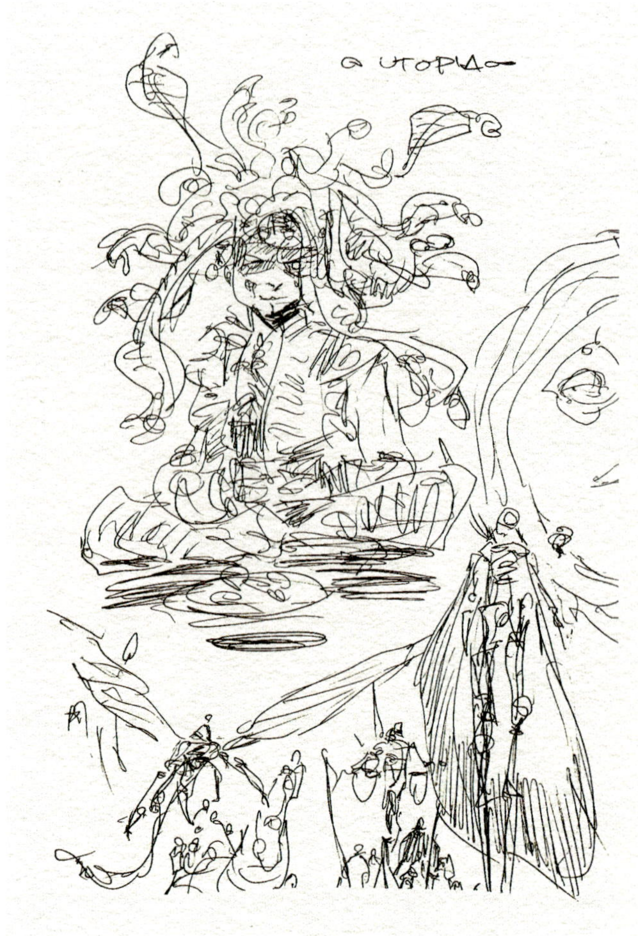

▲ Initial quick sketch of the High Republic as a utopia, July 2019 "Any mythological creature works in *Star Wars* if you put a floating droid beside it or you make it part machine. I always wanted to put Medusa in *Star Wars*; I've tried in every single film. Male or female, I don't care, but I want to do the character. So I thought, well, let's make one of the Jedi or a Force user or even just a kid on the street a Medusa.

I remembered out of nowhere that in Flemish culture they would wade through their fields on stilts to do their farming. I just remember the image of farmers on stilts, so there are Jedi walking down the street on stilts." McCAIG

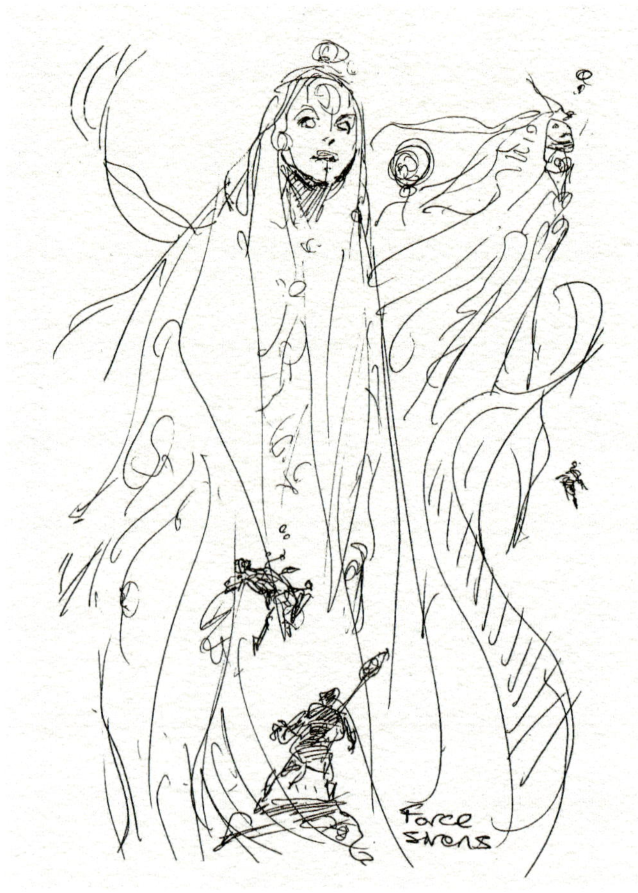

► Concept sketch for Force sirens, July 2019 McCAIG

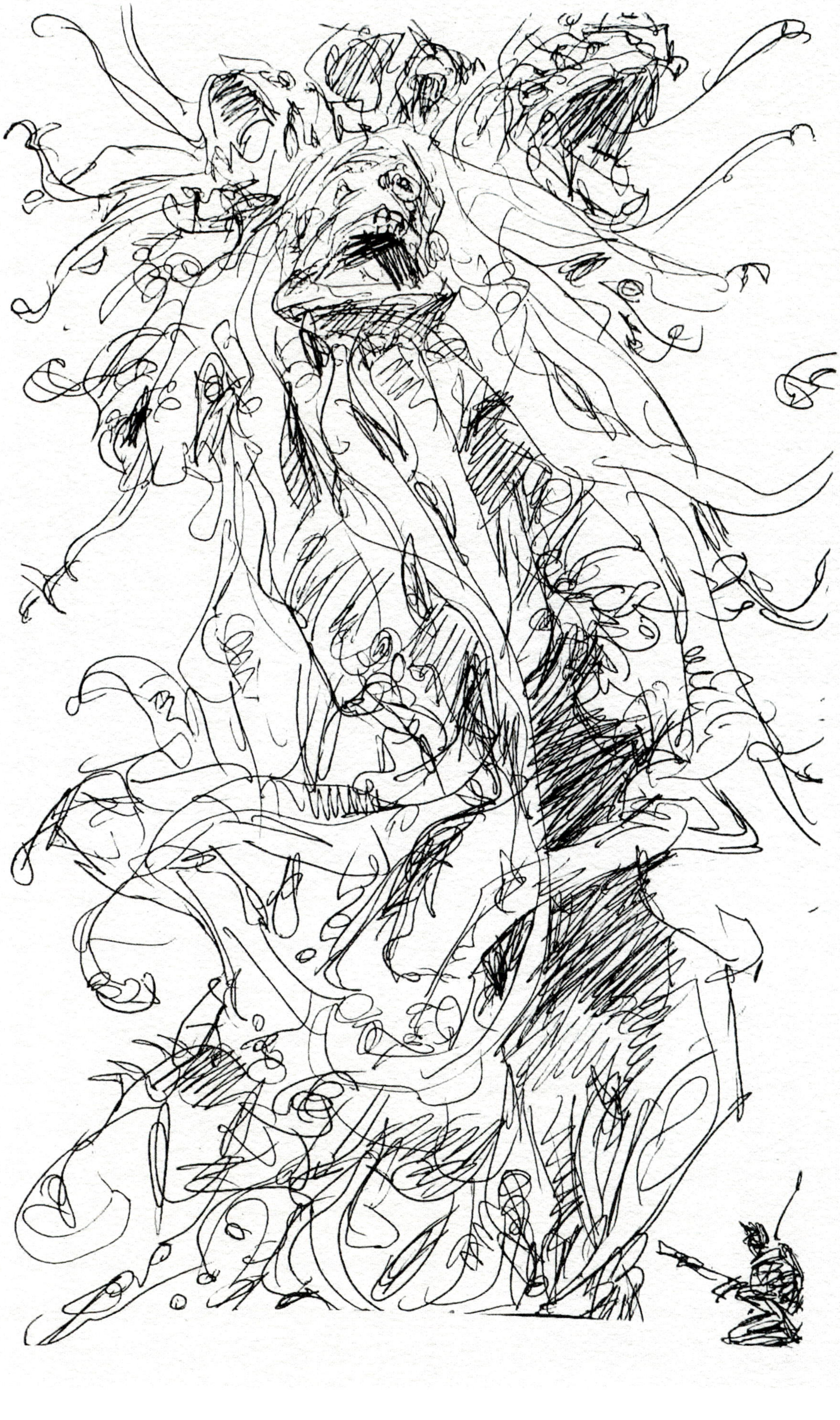

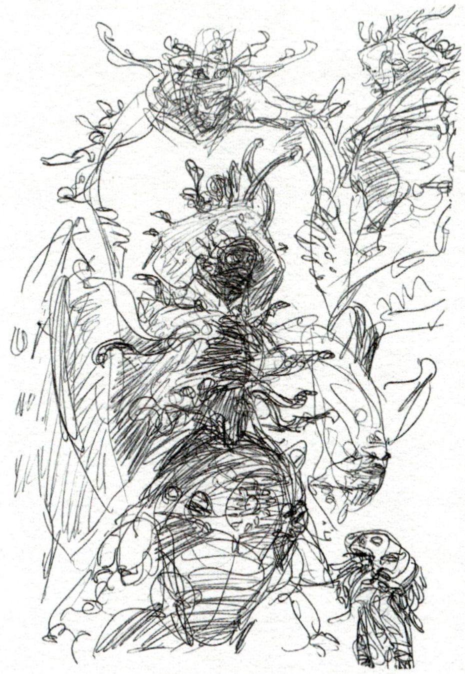

▲ Sketch of a monster, July 2019 "Horror films really took off in the 1920s and '30s because we fought a war that was horrible and terrifying beyond words. Monster movies—*Frankenstein*, *The Wolf Man*, *The Phantom of the Opera*, *Dracula*—came out and allowed people to process that in some ways. So this is parts of bodies, parts of things that shouldn't be on a character. I just wanted weird shapes that made you feel like you want to run away." MCCAIG

◄ Sketch of the Force made manifest, July 2019 "[I drew] a planet where the Force bubbles up out of the ground, like the steam vents down in the Mariana Trench at the bottom of the ocean or like lava coming out of a volcano. The Force, by coming through the earth, literally manifests itself up in the air and it can't keep a shape because it's everything. Here's the thing about the Force—maybe it's just my interpretation of it, but I thought it was something George [Lucas] told us back on *The Phantom Menace*: There was no light [versus] dark side of the Force. The dark side is part of the Force. What keeps it in balance is saying no to it, allowing it to do what it does, to warn and to frighten and to guide us through our dark emotions, and then you're using all of the Force, not just one little piece, which is where the dark side always goes wrong. They're only using a piece of it. But what [the Jedi are] calling the light side is the entirety of the Force. So, let's see a place where the Force is manifest and it's everything. It's good, it's bad, and it changes every second. It can't hold the form because it's just so exuberant with life and imagination." MCCAIG

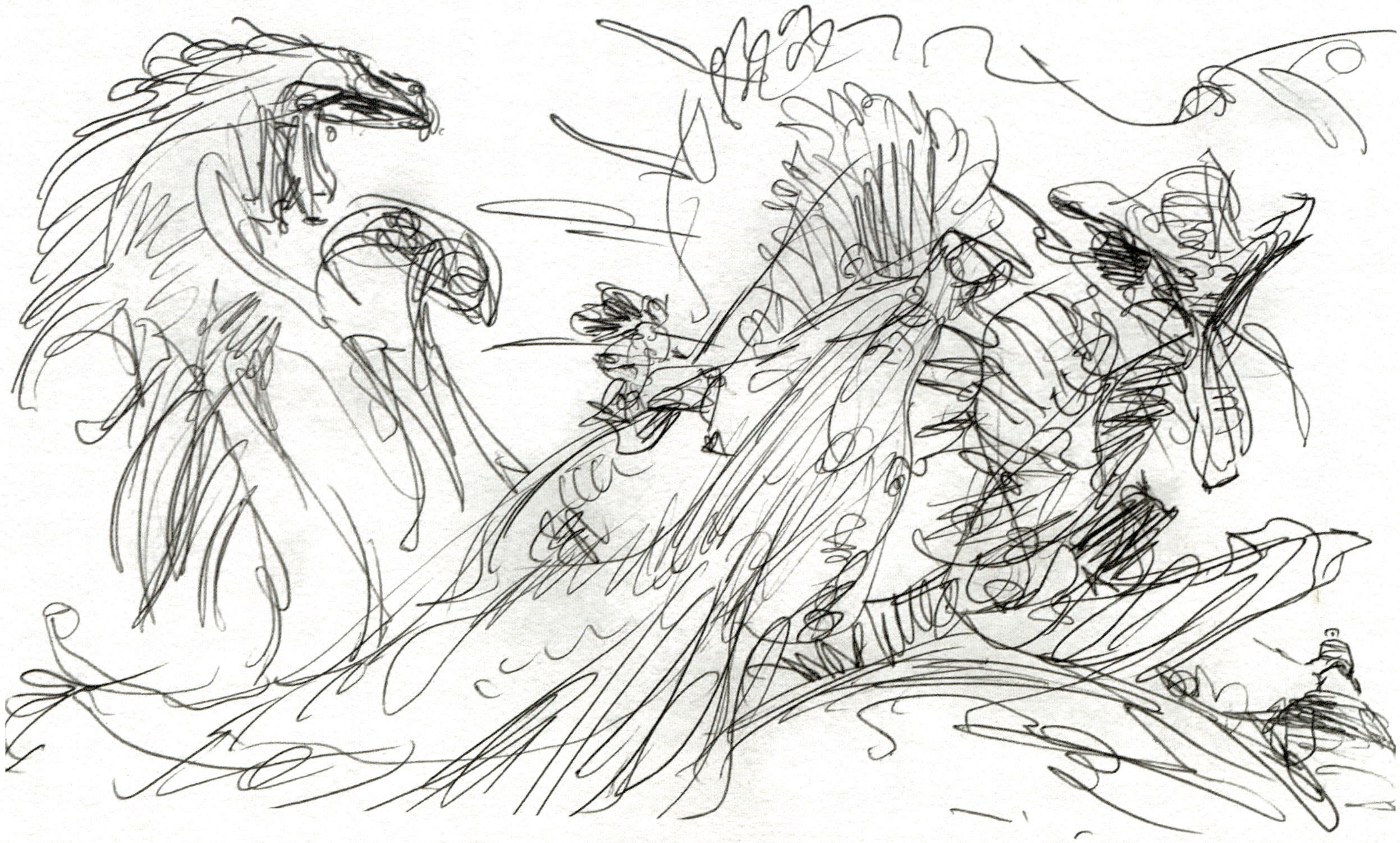

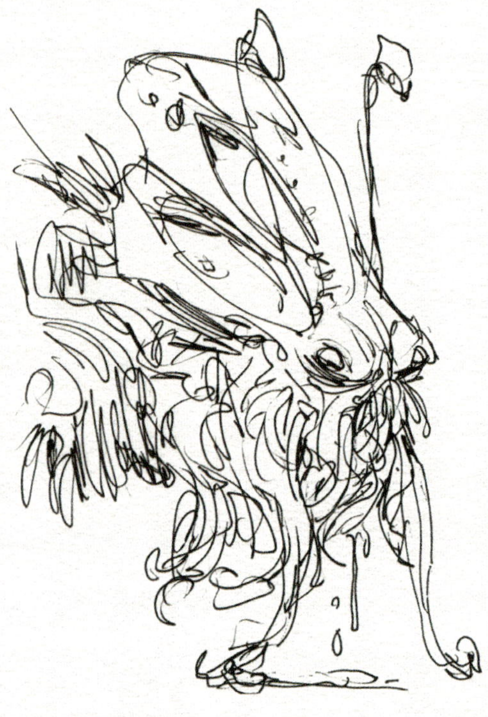

▲ Sketch of a Hydra monster, July 2019
"The Hydra is a philosophical problem. There's too many things attacking you at once. What do you do? I wanted the Jedi to have to confront something with multiple heads." McCAIG

◄ Sketch of an oracle, July 2019 "I didn't want everything to be monstrous and harmful. And this one isn't. This is the Gandalf of the big, snarly, drippy monster creatures. He's like those lovely Labradors that you never want to have in the back seat when you're in the front because they lean over and drool all over you and it's just disgusting. But they're lovable. So I wanted something that was lovable but also terrifying. Just because something is subjectively ugly does not mean that it's evil, which is a good message. The hairy [Wookiee] boy is actually one of the loveliest characters you'll ever meet, even though he can pull your arms out from the sockets." McCAIG

► Sketch of a Jedi with oracle "This is a Jedi consulting with a creature who is showing him visions. [The creature] is a great storyteller; it literally transforms as it tells the story. There's even a severed head of a Jedi or implying something like that up above. It's showing him what will happen if he's not careful." McCAIG

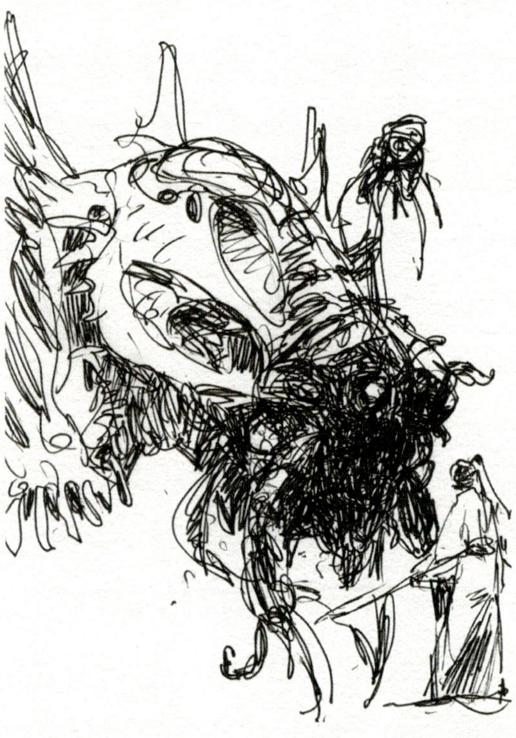

▸ Initial concept art for Cavan Scott's pitch "I threw the mohawk in there to change it up a bit from the past iterations of Jedi haircuts and looked at some artist interpretations of [the Celtic queen] Boudica for inspiration for the Force-Vampire Queen." NOTO

"If you look on Keeve's [left] eye you've got the beginning of the Nihil markings. At this point, she's not a Jedi. She is someone who has walked away from the Jedi Order." CAVAN SCOTT

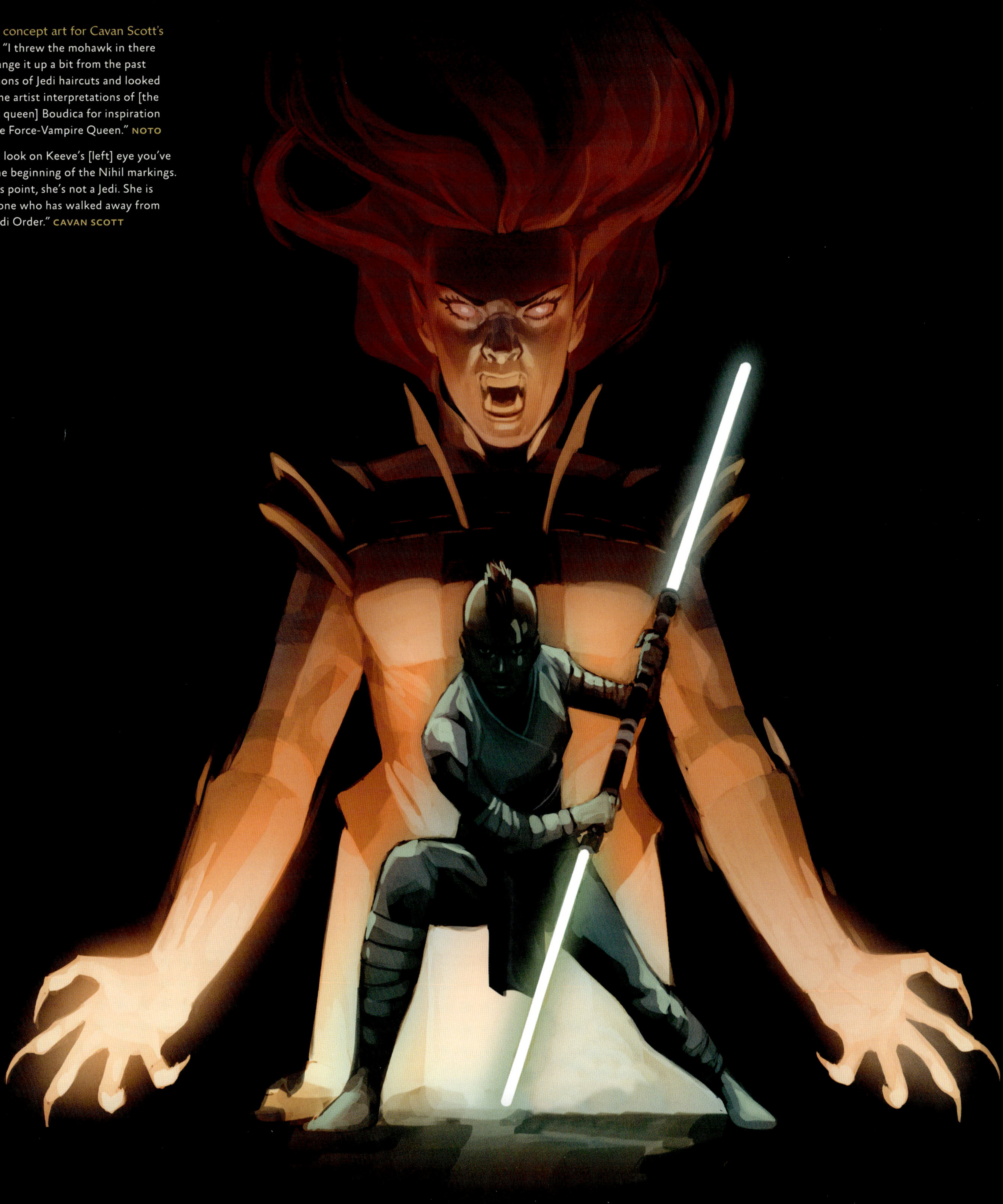

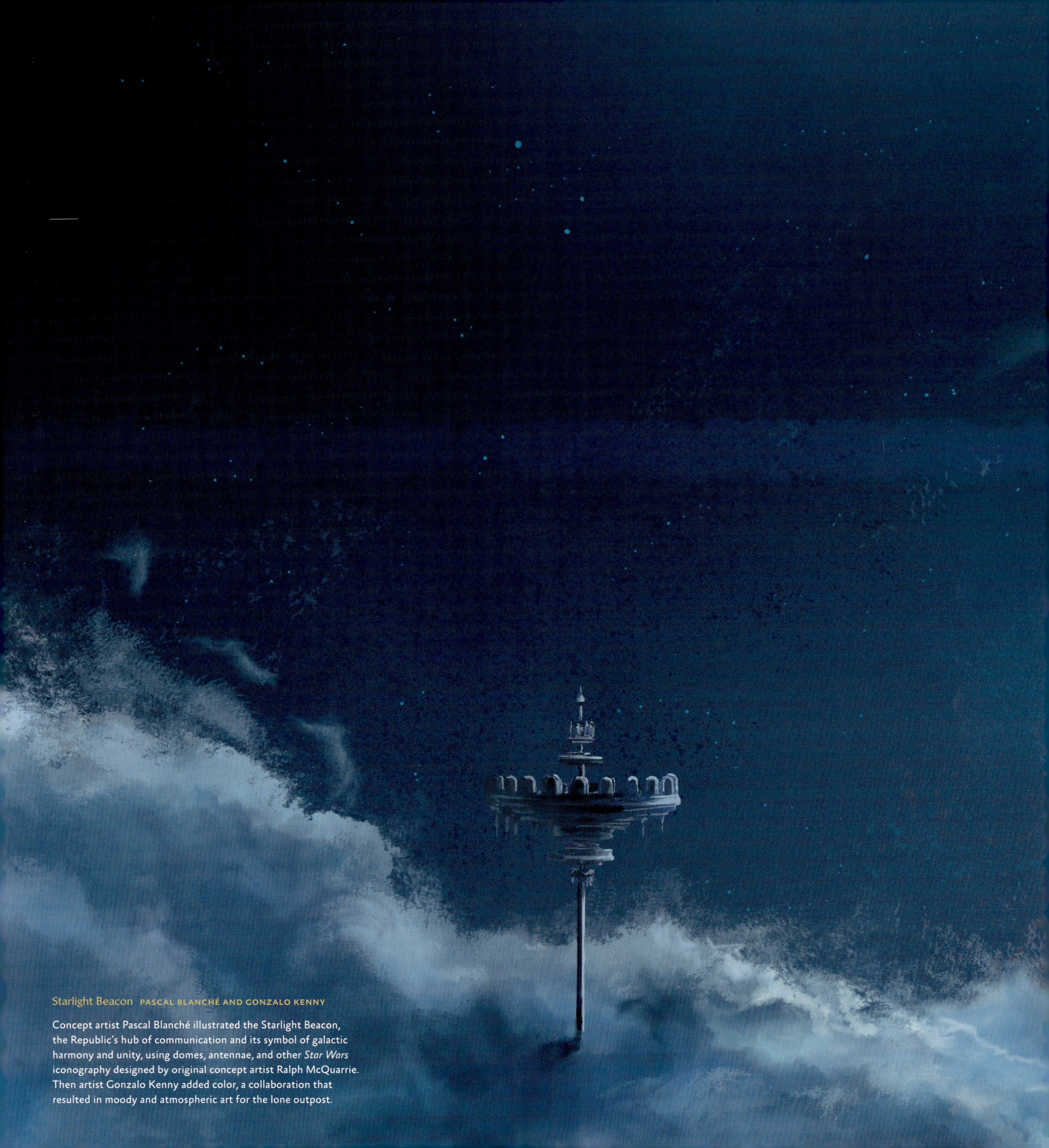

Starlight Beacon PASCAL BLANCHÉ AND GONZALO KENNY

Concept artist Pascal Blanché illustrated the Starlight Beacon, the Republic's hub of communication and its symbol of galactic harmony and unity, using domes, antennae, and other *Star Wars* iconography designed by original concept artist Ralph McQuarrie. Then artist Gonzalo Kenny added color, a collaboration that resulted in moody and atmospheric art for the lone outpost.

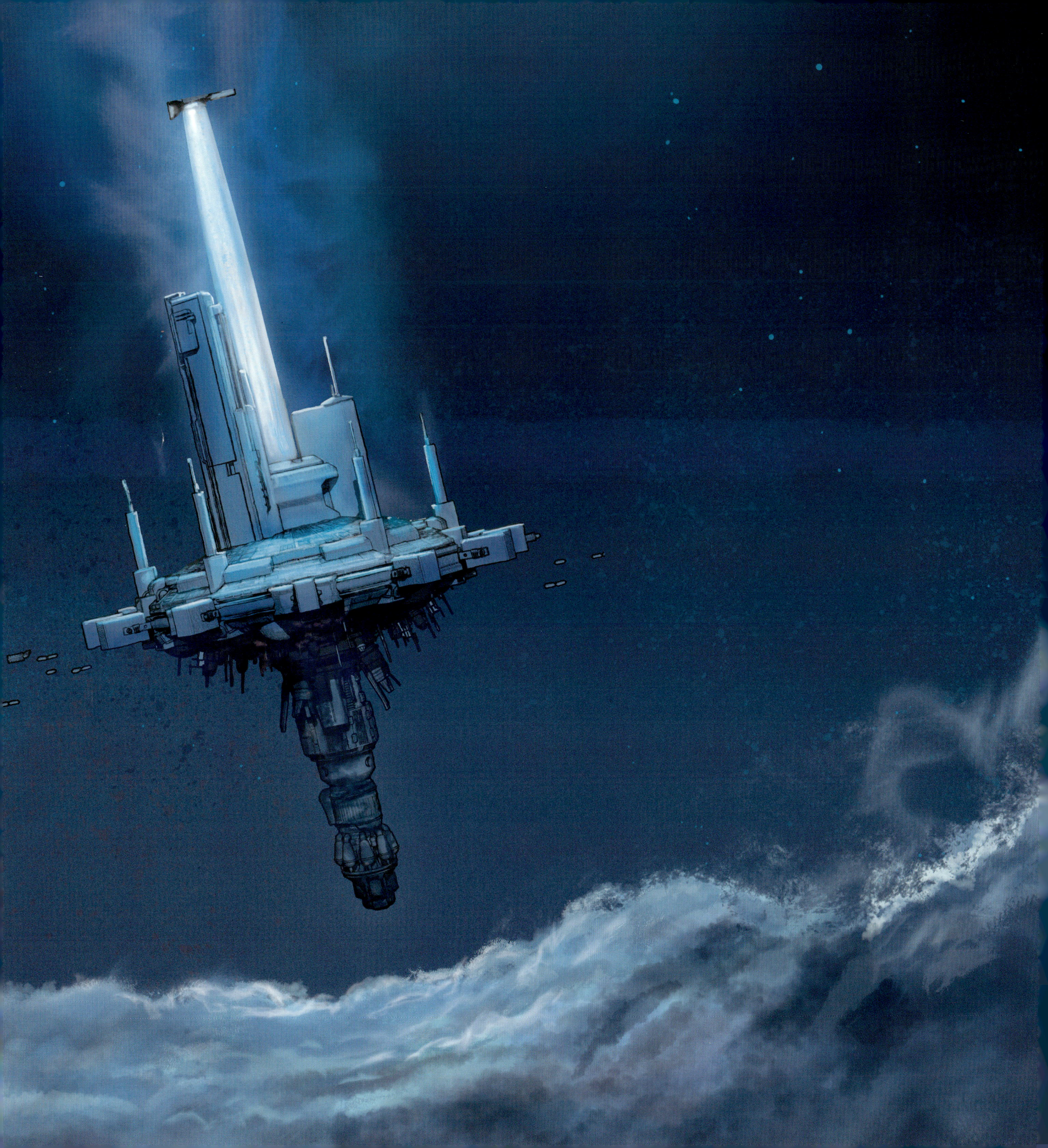

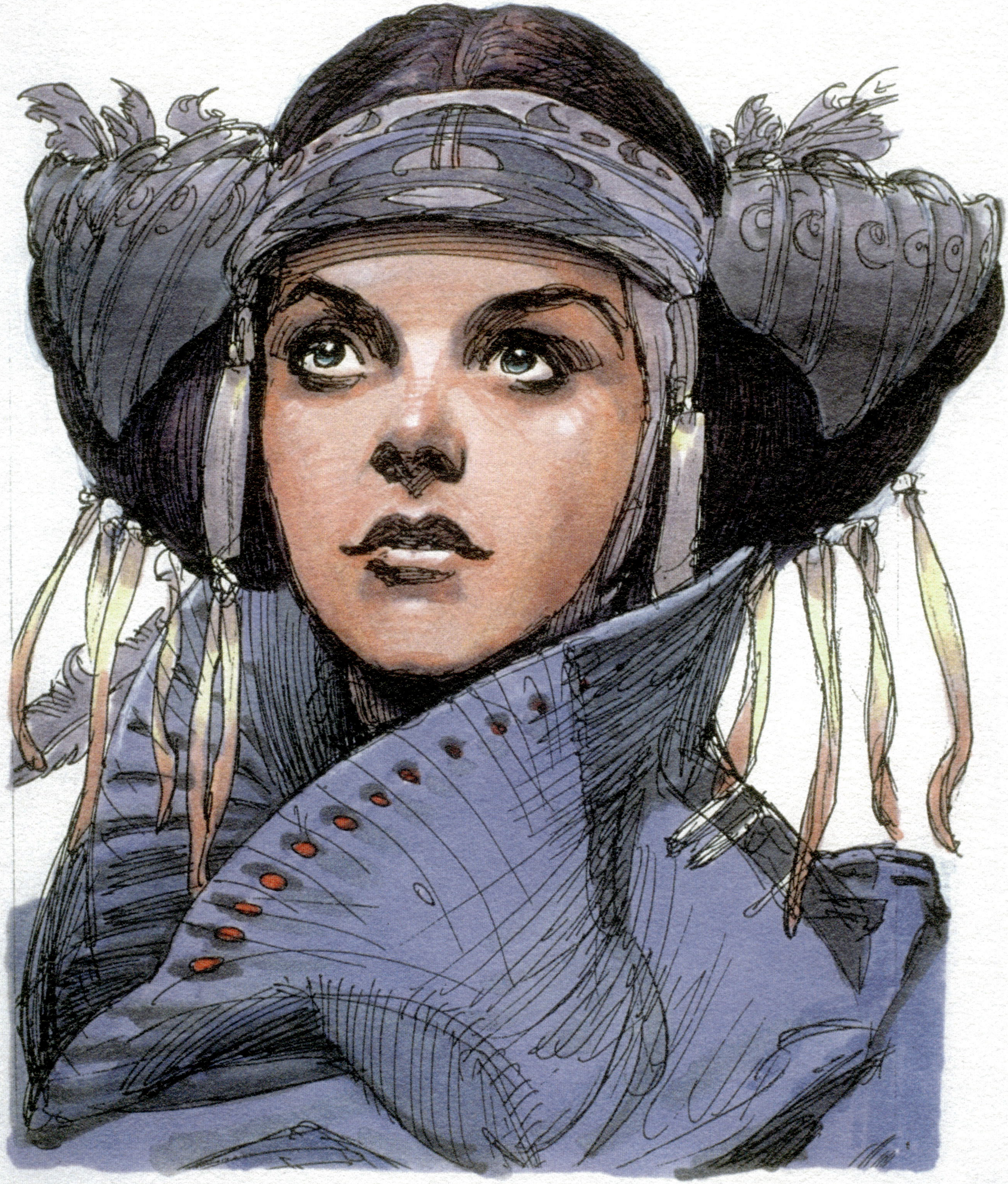

IAIN McCAIG

INTRODUCING CONCEPT ARTIST Iain McCaig into the early pool of artists defining The High Republic was a veritable stroke of genius. On July 15, 2019, McCaig paid a visit to Lucasfilm headquarters in the Presidio—a 1,500-acre swath of green space in San Francisco that once housed a military post—producing a flurry of sketches over just two days. McCaig's contribution was both a significant milestone for the initiative and an invaluable means of connecting the new era to all that had come before. First hired to work on *Star Wars* in 1995 as part of the small team working with George Lucas to tell the story of young Anakin Skywalker's fall to darkness, McCaig worked as a concept artist on all three *Star Wars* prequel films, *The Phantom Menace, Attack of the Clones*, and *Revenge of the Sith*; notably, his designs for Queen Padmé Amidala and Darth Maul—one beauty, the other beast—cemented the look of two characters central to Anakin's journey in the Force, steeped in subtle cultural references from around the world and across hundreds of years of human history. On screen, McCaig donned the white armor of a stormtrooper for a cameo scene filmed as part of the Special Edition of *The Empire Strikes Back*, while behind the scenes he continued to work on concepts for additional aliens added to Jabba the Hutt's palace in the Special Edition of *Star Wars: Return of the Jedi* and returned years later to provide concepts for *Star Wars: The Force Awakens*, *Solo: A Star Wars Story*, and the Disney+ *Obi-Wan Kenobi* series. As an artist who has touched every era of the franchise, McCaig is uniquely suited to the task of incorporating the heart and soul of *Star Wars* storytelling into his designs.

Beyond his impressive résumé, for the artist himself it was an honor to contribute to a medium he values even more than film. "I love films with a passion, but it doesn't even compare with how much I love books," McCaig said, seated in front of a bookshelf lined with some of his favorites, including a copy of *Doré's Illustrations for "Paradise Lost"* that he's had since childhood. That interpretation of John Milton's epic poem exploring the biblical fall of man set McCaig on a lifelong pursuit to redefine the power of virtuousness after feeling that the people depicted in heaven looked flat-out bored. "Even as a kid, I thought, *No, that ain't right*. Heroes are flawed and strange people, too," McCaig said. "Heroic action is a moment, and everyone can reach for that, [but] good has to be that really powerful thing you *want* to do. It's been a life quest of mine to try and make powerful-good stronger than powerful-evil." The pursuit has been a difficult one for McCaig. "You can't cheat and make evil less to make good more. And the problem with designing good and evil is that evil is easier to draw—much easier to draw—because evil is a corruption of good."

Michael Siglain was skeptical that an artist of McCaig's caliber, with years of blockbuster theatrical credits to his name, would be interested in the publishing-driven project. "It was one of those 'We could never get him!' situations,"

◄ Padmé Amidala handmaiden concept "When I was designing [for *The Phantom Menace*] there was no pressure really on Darth Maul to be any kind of icon. He was just a new Sith Lord. And as for Queen Amidala, it didn't matter to me and still doesn't if anyone made her the main character. She was *my* main character. She was the strength of the whole movie. And I needed something that could stand up to a Darth Maul.

With good characters, it very often comes down to an expression. A character who's fearful and yet going forward, you can tell that they're determined and resolute, and yet they're not ignorant of the risk. That's heroic. And that's the look on every drawing I ever did of Padmé. No matter how fearful she was, you can tell that she's going to do [the right thing], whether it's going to kill her or not." McCAIG

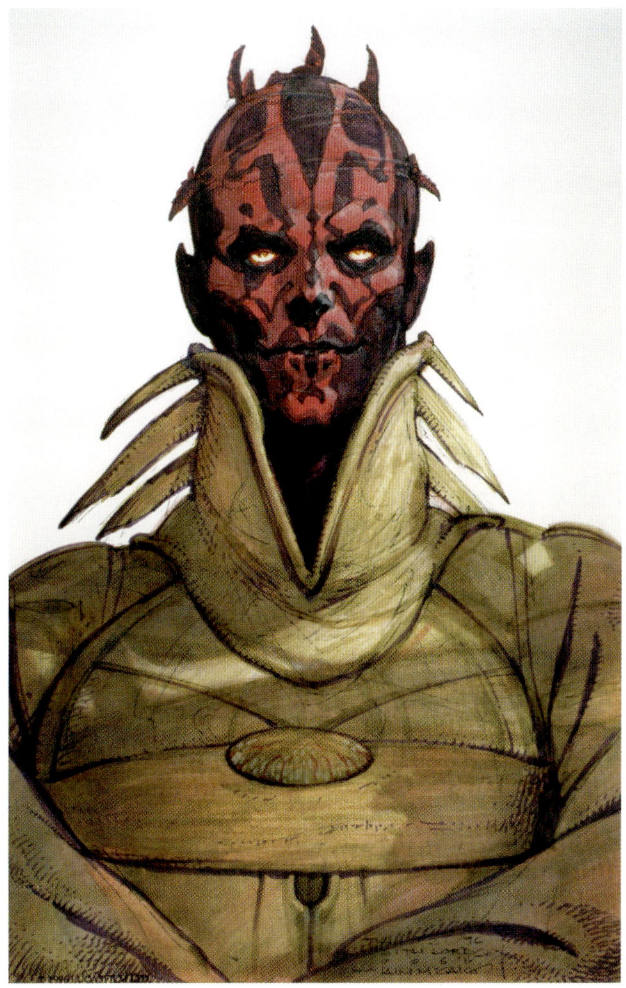

► Darth Maul McCAIG

Siglain recalled. But when Lucasfilm art director Troy Alders and Siglain made the call to inquire, McCaig was overjoyed. "I would take that call any day," McCaig said. "Michael said, 'Well, we're going to do a time period that hasn't been touched. It's essentially *Star Wars* meets H. P. Lovecraft, but we're going to cross that with a sort of Arthurian saga.' I'm in. You mentioned all my favorite things. I'm not a giant H. P. Lovecraft fan, but I am a monster fan. You know, *Frankenstein* is my favorite book in the world."

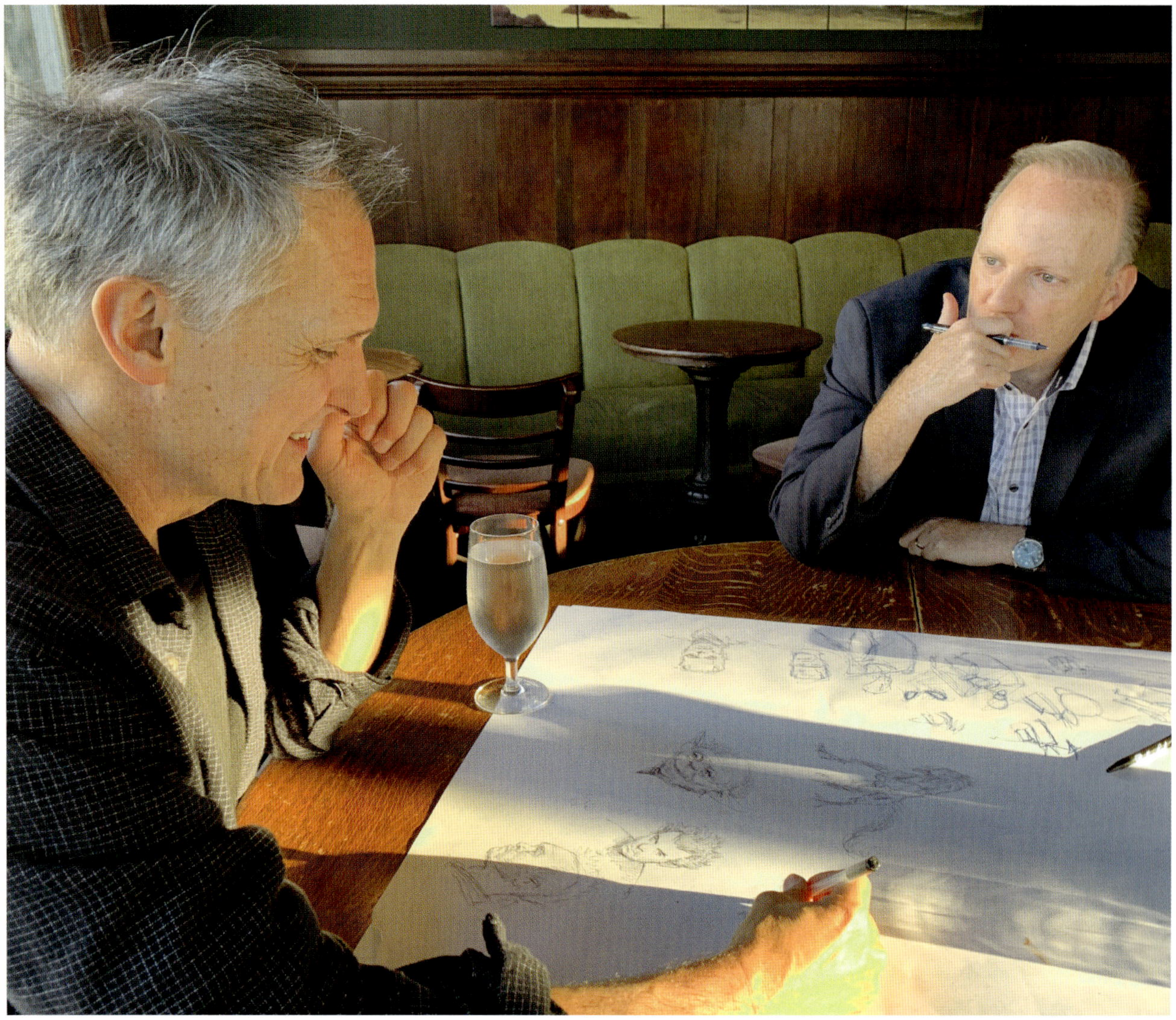

During a two-day trip to San Francisco, Iain McCaig produced dozens of sketches, including character studies scrawled on the white paper table coverings at Balboa Cafe. Here, McCaig, left, and Michael Siglain continue to collaborate at the local eatery as the evening sets in.

McCaig drew on his fascination with the shadowline—an artist's term that means the place between the light and the dark, which, in McCaig's estimation, is "the most interesting place to set stories"—and a predilection for monster movies, classic myth, and unparalleled experience with *Star Wars* visual design. "I didn't do anything until I came down to that meeting and I could just open my mind," McCaig said. Among his earliest pieces for the project, he sketched a Yoda-like alien with a pointy goatee, a Jedi with a broadsword, and a legion of terrifying creatures that seem to shriek from the page. "There's this piece of me that loves monsters, but [these designs are] in this universe, and I can't tell you how much fun that was. You know, it was cathartic," McCaig said. "I have known King Arthur and those legends longer than *Star Wars*—way longer. They're fascinating to me because they come from so many different places, and you get a lot of different flavors. And what I love about it is that the women are as interesting and powerful as the men. I always get very wary of things that are skewed one way or the other."

McCaig drew dozens of loose concepts in a small conference room at Lucasfilm headquarters during the day, then retired, as the evening set in, to the Balboa Cafe, nearby at Greenwich and Fillmore streets, where he, Alders, and Siglain continued to talk and sketch on the white paper tablecloths. "That was so fun. I love it when people draw together, whether they can or not doesn't matter," McCaig said.

The resulting illustrations showcase a design evolution that Alders called "nouveau meets deco." Initial concepts, created at the same time the authors were creating their own characters, reimagined the Merlin of Arthurian myth as a Force-wielding sage and monstrous creatures plucked from the artist's own nightmares. "It looks like the natural progression of maybe how [the *Star Wars* galaxy] would have been before," Alders said. "Just graphically . . . [it] feels authentic."

Afterward, McCaig returned home to Canada to finalize his pieces, sharpening the details on some of his favorites and using his son as a model for his ideal heroic Jedi of the period. "When you layer in someone like Iain McCaig," said Siglain, "and you say, 'OK, Iain, here's the basic story, can you take it a little bit further?' What he did gave us so much to work off of."

McCaig's first sketches were drafted without restrictions and marked the first time the artist showed his initial work to his collaborators, "because I knew Troy and I trust Mike and we needed to communicate fast," McCaig said. "I could scribble a whole bunch of these and then just share them right away. They let it be blue-sky. 'Draw whatever you want. If you have questions, we're down the hall,'" McCaig recalled. "It was really important to me, and I've always said this every time we go into a *Star Wars* meeting without George [Lucas], where we're trying to figure out what would George do? It was one of the most rewarding things in the world to work with George, it really was. And it was important that [The High Republic] was true to what I thought George would want, and it was a joy to come down and do it. It was the opposite of work, you know, because you open the paper, you open your mind, you just put it down on the page."

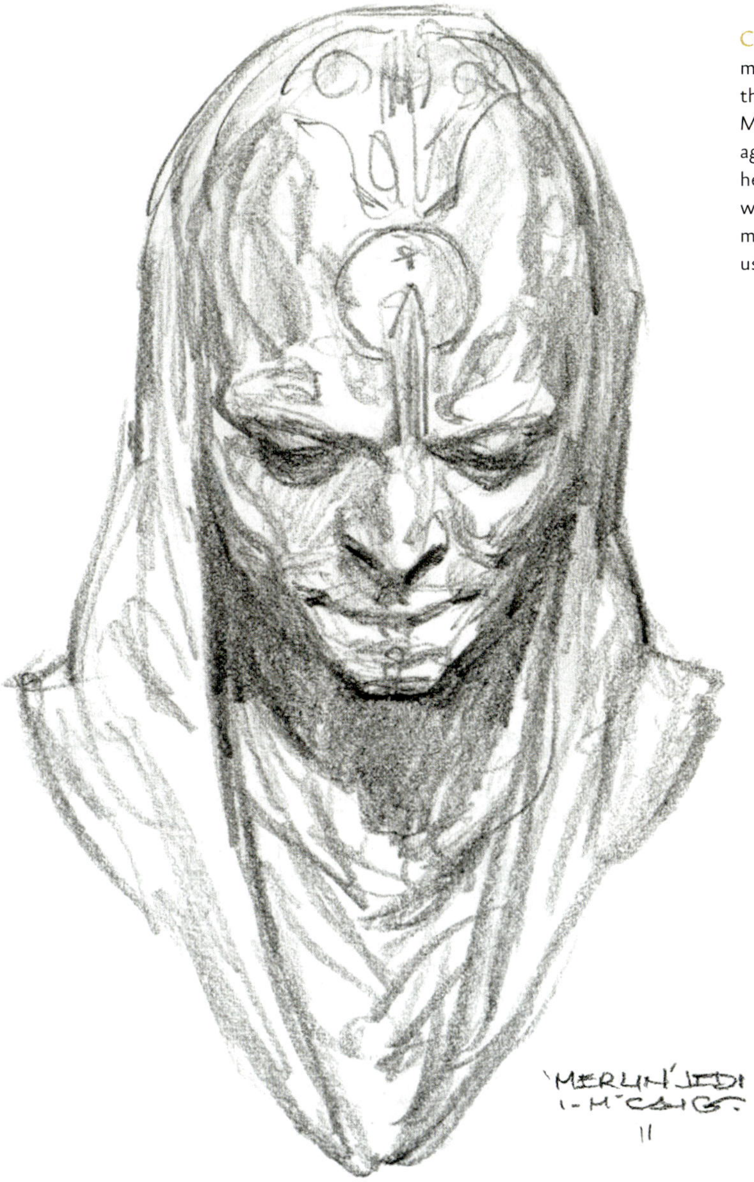

Concepts of a Merlin-like character "This is my son as Merlin the Jedi. If we're going to do the Arthurian saga, then you have to have Merlin. Merlin was not a knight. Merlin had his own agenda. Merlin was doing things for reasons that he thought were good for the world. And yet he was a very flawed character, depending on which mythology you go to. He's not a Jedi; he's a Force-user. He uses the Force in his own way." McCAIG

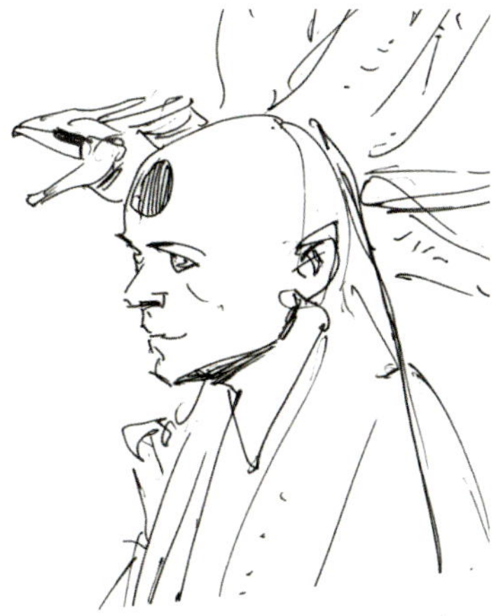

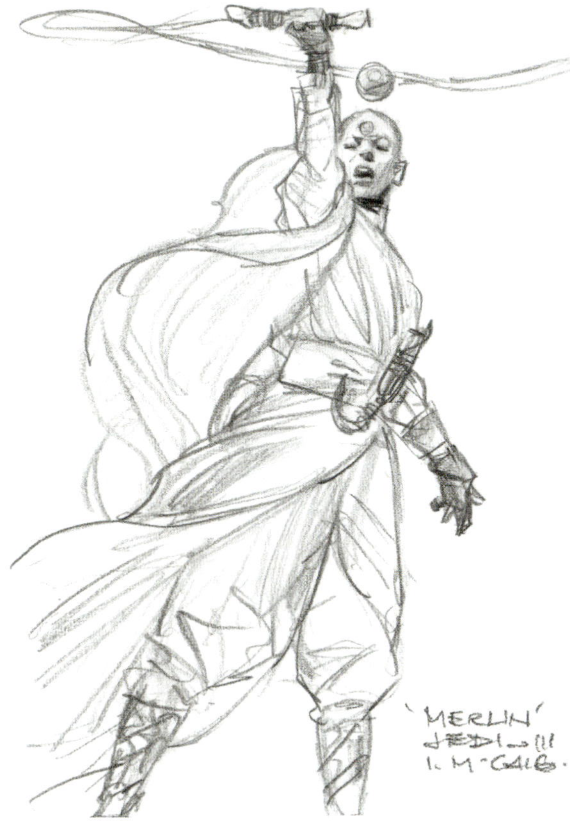

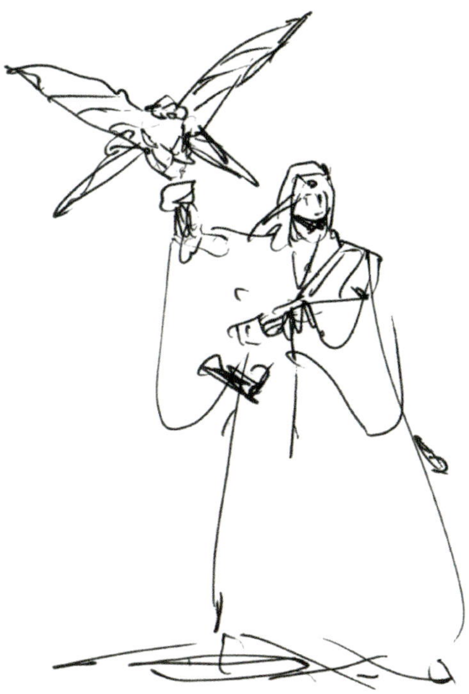

◄ Initial sketch of a Merlin-like character McCAIG

It takes McCaig about a minute to get down a loose sketch like this, but the elegant simplicity of his line work conveys the energy of a man and a four-winged beast.

► Concept of a Merlin-like character McCAIG

The circular marking on the Merlin Jedi's head and the floating black orb are homages to artist Jean "Moebius" Giraud. "Moebius was my bedrock for *Star Wars*. He synthesized cultures; I learned that from him," McCaig said. "And as a thank you, I do two things. He has characters where he puts something on their forehead, so I put a dot. And he has a character who has a floating black thing above his head. I've never known what that is, but every once in a while, I put it there. For me, that's a manifestation of you outside . . . but it's not actually there. It's just allowing you to see a bit of your soul or a bit of your power."

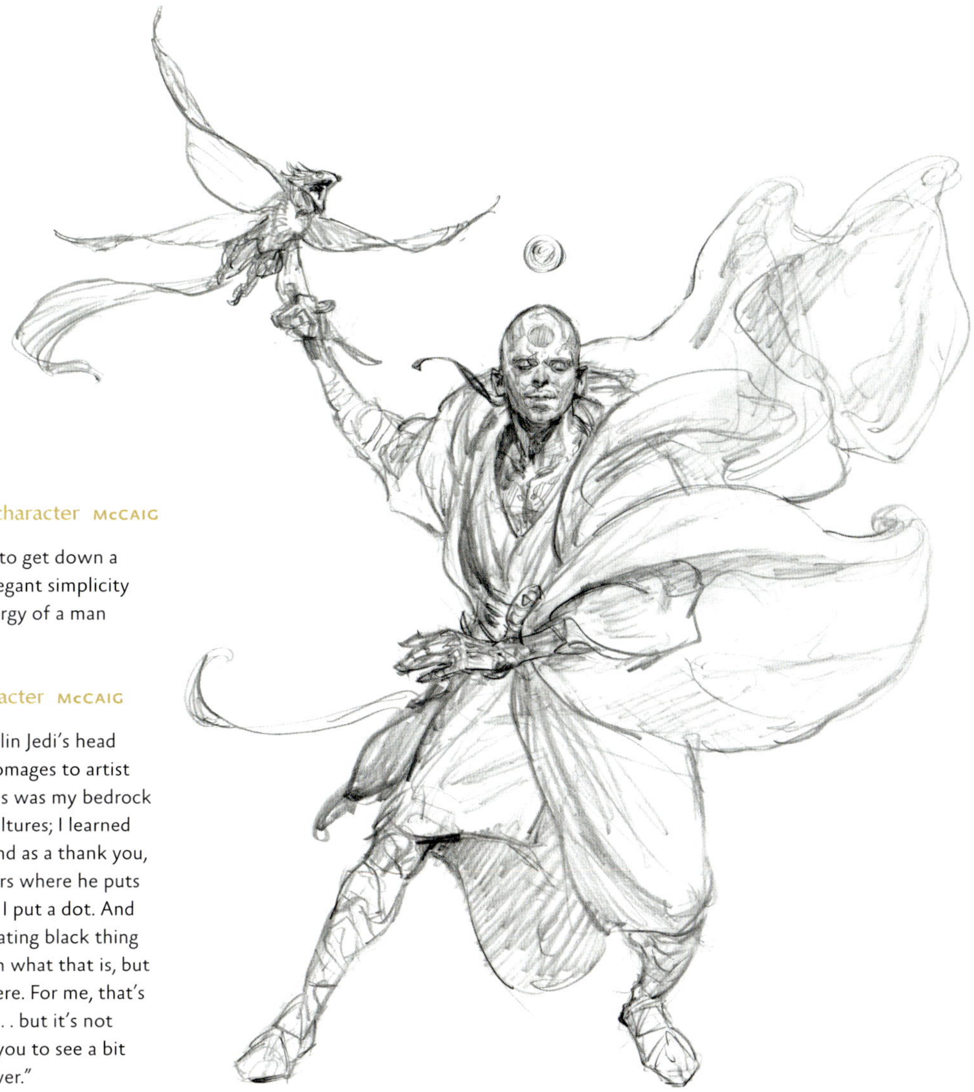

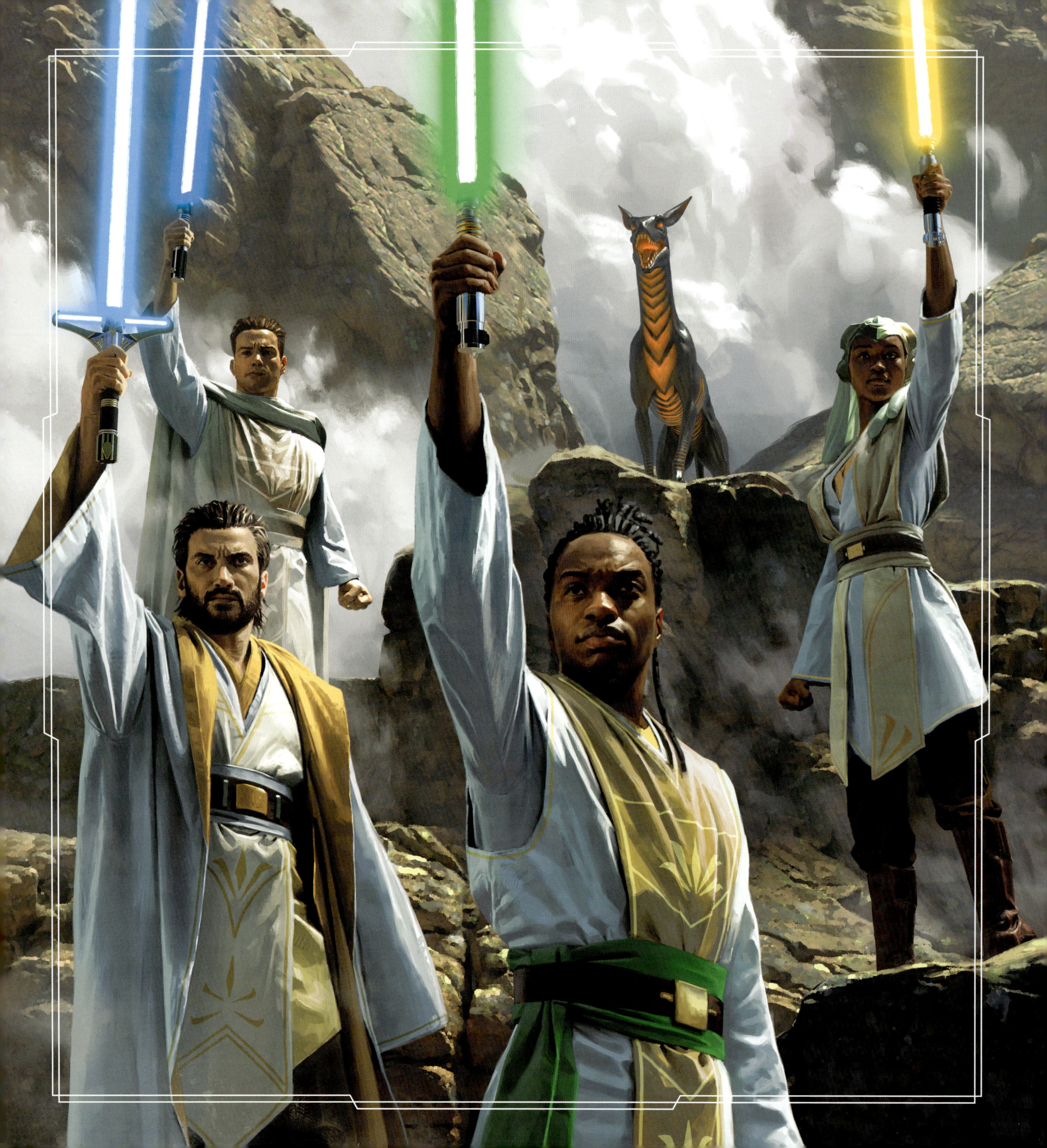

CHAPTER 2
THE JEDI

IN CONTRAST to the knights of the prequel era—an order so blinded by righteousness that its members failed to see, amid the chaos of war, the rise of the Sith and their own downfall—the architects of The High Republic set out to realize the apex of the Jedi Order with a humanistic slant. Early in the Summit discussions, the Jedi emerged as a key focus of the stories the authors were eager to tell. "We kept circling around the Jedi because some argue that that is absolutely the DNA of *Star Wars*," said Lucasfilm Story Group senior creative executive Pablo Hidalgo. "It's hard to do a *Star Wars* without acknowledging the presence or absence of the Jedi, that's for sure. It tells you where you are in the galaxy."

Star Wars storytellers had previously explored the ancient Jedi times with *Knights of the Old Republic*, an initiative that covered video games and books, but The High Republic was altogether different. "It's not legions of Jedi battling legions of Sith in grand wars," said Hidalgo. "It was more Jedi at their height. And what does that mean?"

The new class of Jedi were conceived to embody Obi-Wan Kenobi's poetic phrasing, "guardians of peace and justice," inspired by European mythological legends of knights in shining armor pledged to preserve the greater good and wielding broadswords to slay dragons and defend other noble causes. "Everyone is coming in on the ground floor, and that was one of the beauties and one of the challenges," Lucasfilm Publishing creative director Michael Siglain said. "We wanted to start this off with a bang, literally, with 'the Great Disaster,' this massive event, and the Jedi come in and save the day. We get to see the Jedi as true heroes."

The overall design aesthetic reimagined not only the individuals in the Jedi Order, but the galaxy as a whole. "It's *Star Wars* at its most classic, but dialed back 200 years and seen through a Renaissance-like lens," Siglain said. Lucasfilm's foremost experts in design and continuity—including Troy Alders, Phil Szostak, and Pablo Hidalgo—were called in to provide a critical eye, a crucial role in establishing a look that felt entirely organic. "They drilled down to the core of what makes *Star Wars*, then aged it back and made sure that each design had a truly archetypal and authentically *Star Wars* look and feel."

Although wardrobe changes were uncommon among the Jedi of the prequel and original trilogy eras, storytellers envisioned this incarnation in an array of robes. "Visually, we wanted the High Republic era to be instantly distinguishable from [all known eras]," said Siglain. "We still wanted the Jedi to be iconically Jedi, and still adorned in their trademark robes, but we also wanted to reflect the golden age of the Jedi." Formal affairs, like the dedication of the Starlight Beacon space station, called for pristine dress whites, with Council members in golden tabards and other adornments to designate their status. While on duty defending the Republic, robes of brown fabric and leather were conceived, a better fit for combat and surviving on lawless Outer Rim worlds. Hidalgo is credited with suggesting that designers borrow the pattern from the floor of the Coruscant Jedi Temple, as seen in the prequel films, to tie things together, echoing the same motif on the High Republic Jedi tabards. "It wasn't until the Temple design element was integrated that it really snapped into focus," said senior designer Jason Wojtowicz. "That element, I think, was really the thing that we had been looking for."

"The High Republic, in relation to the prequels, is an older time technologically, but I think it's potentially a more enlightened time," said Lucasfilm executive editor Jennifer

◂ Variant cover of *Star Wars: The High Republic: The Rising Storm* JOSEPH MEEHAN

Heddle. "It's more evolved thinking in some ways. It's like the Jedi Order devolves while the technology evolves. [Visually,] their clothes are a little fancier, and they're a little more celebratory. Even just the fact that we have temple attire and mission attire, I think, is interesting, because it suggests this divide that maybe didn't exist so much later on."

"You had these slick gold robes with adornments that was the Jedi Council at their height," said Lucasfilm art director Alders. "You also had these explorers, quite weathered and very rugged, like we've never seen before. I think that's what made it real. You had the two polar opposites, a super-polished Council and then the Jedi that were just out there on the range."

After the second Summit, artists worked with the initiative's five writers to begin the uncommon assignment of visually interpreting the bold new era beyond what was required for book covers, comic book pages, and merchandising. The artistic renditions cemented the look, providing a starting point should appearances in other media follow, and helping to ensure that characters who appeared in text and illustration were easily identifiable across the board.

Early design briefs called for a "Jedi Texas Ranger," an idea that can be traced all the way back to George Lucas himself. James Waugh, Lucasfilm's vice president of Franchise Content & Strategy, learned of the phrase in passing from the *Star Wars* creator's foremost student, Dave Filoni, who collaborated with Lucas on *Star Wars: The Clone Wars* before helming other *Star Wars* animation and helping Jon Favreau to steer *The Mandalorian* and *The Book of Boba Fett*. According to Filoni, whenever he questioned the roots of the Jedi Order, "George would tell him that Jedi were kind of like Texas Rangers in the way they resolved issues," Waugh said. "It was an off-the-cuff conversation with Dave in my office, as those things would happen. Didn't really go deeper than that. But I just remember glomming onto that idea." Concept artist Grant Griffin refined the idea and brought the Jedi Texas Ranger to fruition by giving the Jedi a holster for their lightsabers, a concept that pays homage to the Western roots of the franchise. "That one simple design decision brought the past and the future together in a visually cool and interesting way," Siglain said.

Inspired by Phil Noto's concept art, author Cavan Scott and his fellow writers began to formulate backstories and names for the characters represented in the lineup of ten Jedi. "A lot of things were triggered by the art, and a lot of the art was triggered by that first set of proposals that came out of the first Summit," recalled Lucasfilm Publishing senior editor Robert Simpson. A Trandoshan with a stiff leather collar and red eyes served as proto-Sskeer. "He was literally the first character, other than Keeve, I created for this," Scott said. An Umbaran with dual white blades needed little alteration to become Orla Jareni. "The one that really drew me in would be Orla," added author Claudia Gray. "She wound up playing a big part in *Into the Dark* as she clearly is a creature slightly apart. She follows her own path. And it's evident from this first moment, isn't it?"

A Twi'lek sparked the creation of Estala Maru, although the Jedi's species would evolve to Kessurian. "I did become a little bit obsessed with going through and creating a bio for all of them," Scott said, although some remain a mystery to readers, characters that may be written into future tales. "All the Jedi look so different, you know, and the attitude of them just opened up for me the idea of the Jedi we were creating at this time period—there wasn't a uniformity."

These Jedi at their peak are selfless and brave, connected to each other and to the Force; they're curious about the complexities of emotion rather than bent on containing and silencing those impulses. Scott looked to the Stoics and the Knights Templar to help guide him, pulling from historical records that told of Templar warriors breaking their vows. "The other Templars wouldn't drag them in front of the master of the temple, but would just take them aside and say, 'If you're going to do this, can you not rub it in everyone's faces because other people might start doing it as well?' Or, you know, 'Are you sure you should be doing this? And if you've made that choice, think about what it means for the Order.' I think that's how the Jedi would have been as well. So, we have Jedi who are perhaps not as celibate as other Jedi. And there's nothing wrong [with that]."

In fact, creator George Lucas himself subscribed to the same idea while creating the prequel era. In an interview with the BBC ahead of the release of *Star Wars: Attack of the Clones*, which famously focused on Anakin Skywalker and Padmé Amidala's budding-yet-forbidden romantic entanglement, Lucas noted that Jedi were permitted to have sex. "Jedi Knights aren't celibate," he said at the time. "The thing that is forbidden is attachments—and possessive relationships."

Beyond the Jedi Order's doctrines, Scott found creative freedom in exploring the core of human emotions present in even the most alien Jedi. "It's a chance to explore the fact these are people, and they all have emotions that we can recognize, and that's why we love them. We love Luke not because he's a Jedi Master, but because he spends most of his life making big mistakes and then having to get over them. That's why he's the hero that he is." Sskeer and Elzar Mann in particular exemplify that duality, respected Jedi Masters who still find themselves keeping secrets and, at times, living in fear.

PART OF THE INHERENT ALLURE of the High Republic Jedi Order is the diverse range of Padawans, knights, and masters, a mix of alien species not typically found among their ranks and, more importantly, a dichotomy of race, sexual orientation, and gender diversity among the human Jedi, all with their own unique lightsaber hilts and expressions of the Force itself. "*Star Wars* should reflect the real world," said author Charles Soule. "It's a galaxy far, far away, but it's being consumed by people who are in *this* galaxy, and everybody wants to see themselves in a story."

"I know diversity came up really early," added author Justina Ireland. "I don't know who said it, but for me, that's always going to be an important thing, because I was the Black kid who grew up and I got Lando. . . . Representation is super important. I remember how excited I was when Mace

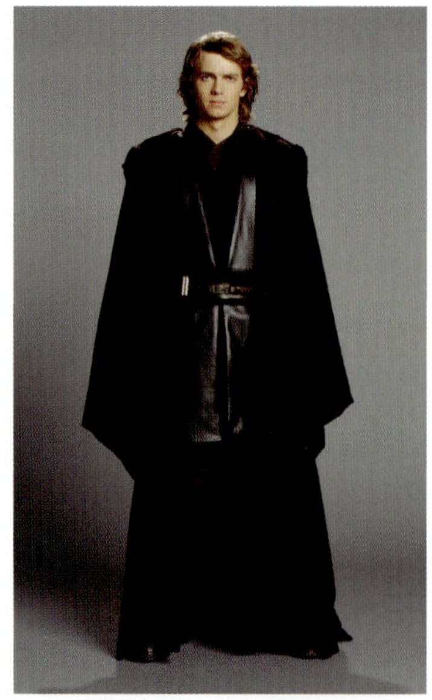

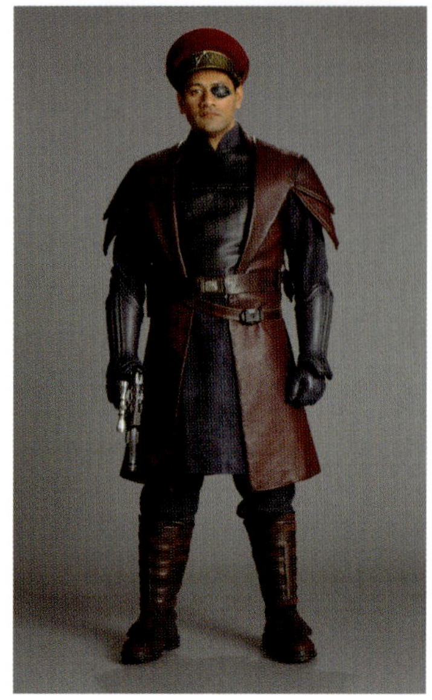

▲ "While their temple attire is their dress blues, and a sign of how the Galactic Renaissance that stems from Phase II has influenced the Jedi [in Phase I], their mission attire is for when they're out in the field," said Siglain. "We wanted them to dress for action, like a knight, in the sense that they need to be prepared for whatever they may face out in the galaxy, with heavy, leather-like tabards over their everyday attire." Designers took inspiration from Anakin Skywalker's costume in *Revenge of the Sith*, along with costumes worn by Naboo's Captain Typho in both *Revenge of the Sith* and *Attack of the Clones*. Starting with those garments, artists worked backward to define the mission apparel with the added protection of wrist guards and a removable comlink, what Siglain called "a genius design element" from artist Diogo Saito.

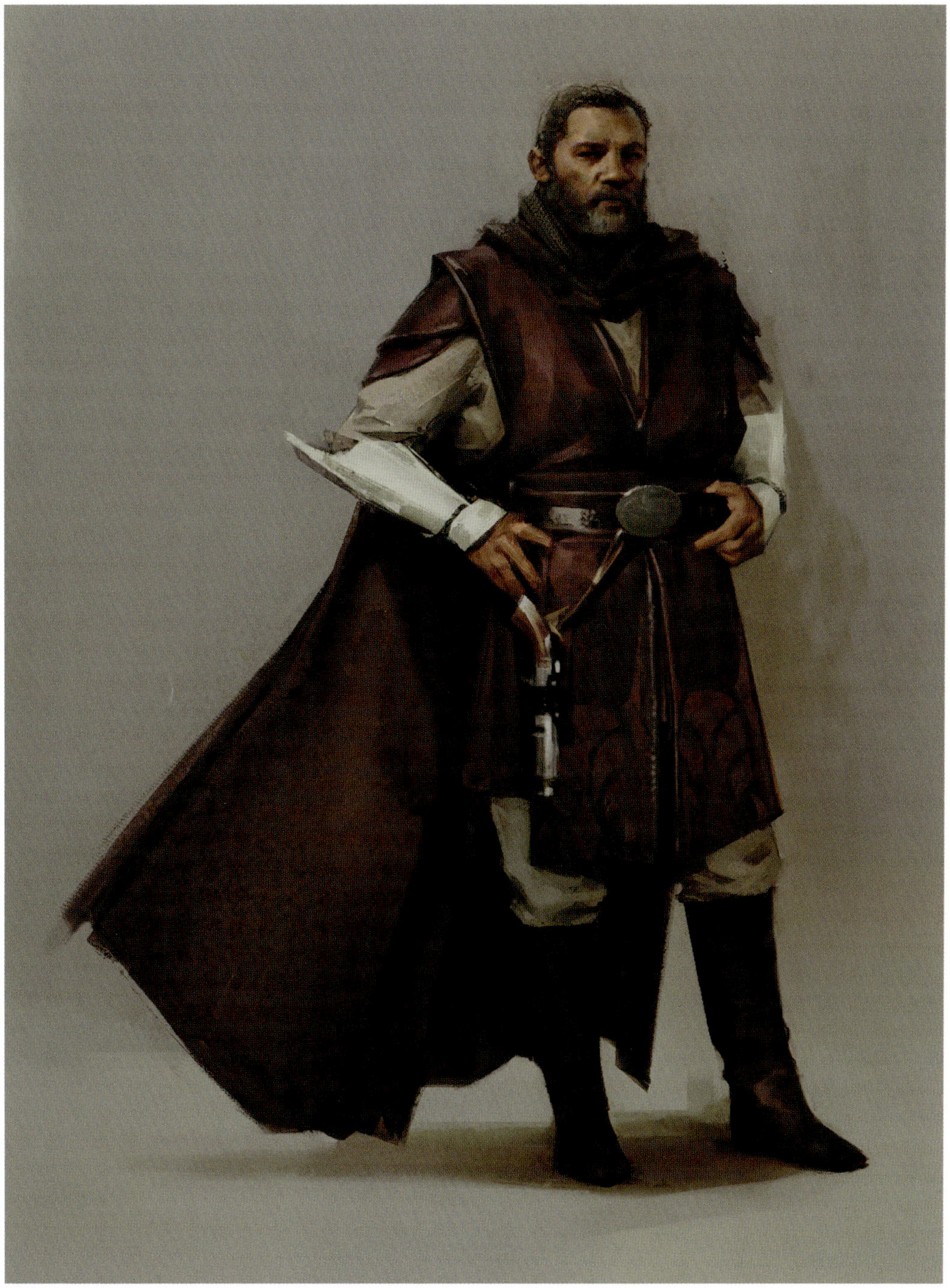

◂ Jedi Texas Ranger, November 2020 "I love this guy. I'm a big fan of all of the old spaghetti Westerns and that kind of swagger and personality—like he grew up within the Jedi but has been on the outskirts of deep space and is that fatherly figure that you rely on that's a little gruff but looks out for everyone. I just wanted to give him that gunslinger vibe. To hearken back to the prequels, it was taking the leather that Anakin [Skywalker] rocks and then adding more armor to it, combined with the Naboo soldiers. This one gave way to more of the functional action suits that you see now on Avar Kriss and Sskeer. A lot of these elements stuck, but they just got more detailed with the layering of the armor.

I think my claim to Jedi design elements is the low-hanging saber. I don't think that has been done before, and it just made sense that he would have a low-hanging, six-shooter vibe. As you get more in the future, things become more streamlined and functional, and it just makes sense that the lightsaber clips directly on the belt. But maybe in an earlier era, it was just the fashion of the day to have that low-hanging saber." GRIFFIN

Windu came on screen. I was just like, 'There's a Black Jedi? They're not just on Cloud City?'"

For IDW's comic series set in the era, author Daniel José Older created a class of students for his all-ages comic led by Padawan Lula Talisola, a gay, dark-skinned Jedi who slept with a headscarf, a detail that resonated for its authenticity. His comic series in particular was a chance to showcase a group of young Jedi growing, maturing, and changing both physically and emotionally. In hindsight, the comic is largely informed by Older's own life changes, as he wrote it on the cusp of becoming a new father. "It's so much about parents, so much about watching kids grow up," he said. "How do you love and let go? That's what every parent has to figure out."

From the beginning, Older set out to pen a queer love story as the emotional center of the series. "Before I even started writing, it was always going to be a love story," Older said. "Issue one is called 'Collision Course,' and the collision course is Lula and Zeen [Mrala]. It's a pun because there's giant rocks falling on a planet, but it's also about these two lives and the gravitational pull bringing them together." Although Older hoped fans would root for the two young girls to fall in love with each other, the fan art and fervent shipping—when readers are vocally in favor of two characters ending up in a romantic relationship long before the canon decrees it—that followed surprised him. "Whether that's the Force or love or both, what's the difference? It's up to the reader. The second that they met, their lives changed dramatically in the best way, and that also brings so much complication." With Talisola, Older explored one Jedi's search for identity in a changing world. "Lula is the person that wants to be a Jedi Knight more than anything else. That's always been her goal. But it's growing pains, and part of Lula's conflict is that she's in love with her best friend, and she's not supposed to be in love with people. But it's also that she's growing up and she's coming to understand the world in a new way. She's seeing different dynamics, and she's not disenchanted with the Jedi Order, but it does give her pause. She really is, like many teenagers, just feeling removed from herself and the things she thought she knew about herself. Her whole identity is in crisis in a very real way from trauma, from life, from war, and just from being a teenager."

Older was adamant that the love story arc should be dealt with directly, leaving no question in the readers' minds about how Lula and Zeen felt. It's a welcome, straightforward approach to queer culture that has too frequently been ignored. "It's so often just been the opposite of that," Older said. "For so long it was nonexistent—across fantasy, across literature, across *Star Wars*, in everything. And then when [creators] finally started doing it, we did it very sloppily or just with too much vagueness or trying to hint at it. I have no tolerance for that type of stuff. I think it's really cowardly. [In the past,] creators have failed queer fans by not providing accurate representation or *any* representation."

That erasure makes even less sense in the context of a galaxy far, far away from our own. "In *Star Wars*, as far as we know, there isn't homophobia," Older added. "And I think that's a really amazing opportunity to show two girls in love and have it not be about their struggle within their society. They have to struggle with it for other reasons, but not because they're girls. It was a great opportunity to just show the joy of love between two people of the same gender. There's no reason for there to be so few [queer people] in space." As soon as Older confirmed Lula and Zeen's mutual feelings, the fan art supporting their love exploded, he added. "Which is so beautiful. I just love that all of High Republic Twitter is rooting for these two teenage girls to just love each other. And they were. And they get to."

The arc also allows Lula's struggle to be explored in parallel to Kantam Sy, who along with twins Terec and Ceret is among the first nonbinary Jedi in *Star Wars* lore. "I knew I wanted a nonbinary Jedi in a role that would really grow and matter," Older said. "In *Midnight Horizon*, there's so much complexity and depth going back into their backstory and having them really be an action hero. As little as we see nonbinary [characters], it's even rarer that we see nonbinary badass action heroes, right?"

NOT EVERY FACE WAS NEW. Given the timeline, Master Yoda was brought into the storytelling through IDW Publishing's all-ages comic, a slightly spryer version of the beloved and wizened Jedi. "Any new expansion to *Star Wars* has to carefully walk the line on how much reinvention there is versus how much familiarity there is," Hidalgo noted, resulting in many conversations on the green-skinned sage. "Yoda is one of our sacred characters, and changing him up too much is a perilous thing. He's also about 900 years old when we first meet him on-screen, so the idea of only going back a small percentage of his life span suggests that he shouldn't be too radically different. If this was set 800 years ago, I can see there being an opportunity to reimagine him. But that's not where our story is set." Also already seated on the Jedi Council were Oppo Rancisis and Yarael Poof, who first debuted as background characters encircling young Anakin Skywalker in the Council chambers in *Star Wars: The Phantom Menace*.

As the authors finalized character descriptions and storylines for the first wave of books and comics, more artists got involved to finesse the design aesthetic, often with multiple artists working in tandem to refine individual characters. "It's kind of like a weird game of *Star Wars* Telephone," remarked Grant Griffin, who was admittedly daunted by being handed a sketch from Iain McCaig. "The guy just lives and breathes storytelling, and his personality is extremely infectious, and he just kind of explodes creativity," Griffin said. "You can see his fingerprints on everything he touches."

Manuscript writers worked in a similarly collaborative fashion, creating some characters in committee and trading others in a relay race between stories and media. Soule was responsible for creating the Twi'lek Jedi Loden Greatstorm for *Light of the Jedi*, but it was Scott who wrote the Jedi's bitter end in *The Rising Storm*, and Older who penned the investigation into his demise in Marvel's *Trail of Shadows*, a detective story that bears a striking resemblance to elements of Scott's original story pitch. Scott created the Jedi Sskeer, but it was Soule who introduced the character to the world and gave him his first physical battle scar. "Charles said to me, 'What can I do to him?' We knew he had to have damage, you know?" Scott recalled. "And I said, 'Whatever you want, just make it gnarly.' So he sliced his arm off because it's *Star Wars*."

For Ireland, the creation of the characters is where the world building really began. "I think what really unlocked it that summer was we came up with our character base list," Ireland said. Together, the Jedi Order began to take shape. Ireland notably added Vernestra Rwoh into the mix early on, describing the precocious Padawan-turned-Jedi Knight through her outward appearance as well as character traits to help artists compose the final designs. "I tend to see the character in my head. And so, for most of my stuff, most of the characters I created, the concept art came after I'd written the story. For Vernestra, we knew who she was, but we didn't get any concept art until after I'd already written and turned in the book." Even then, initial sketches didn't quite match the description of the Mirialan's facial tattoos, a stack of diamonds on the outside of her eyes.

"A lot of decisions of which characters went where grew out of what kind of stories you want to tell about the human experience," added Simpson. "Dealing with what it means to enter into this way of life from a very young age and staying with it your entire life. You go through moments of learning and moments of mastery and moments of rediscovery that you don't know everything you think you know, moments of sheer panic and that wonderful idea of the student teaching the master something."

AFTER CONTRIBUTING A FEW DESIGNS and ideas early on, concept artist Jeffrey Thomas, an illustration manager with Disney Publishing, was brought back on during the spring of 2020 to work on solidifying character concepts. Thomas's personal penchant for weaponry came through in his inventive designs for new lightsaber hilts, deadly accessories, and a blaster nicknamed "Beti." To represent the golden age of the Order, he explored more ornate hilts and elegant decorations, using the previously established Temple Guards as a guiding light and working backward. Still, creators were cautious about taking the lightsaber too far from the classic design, although the impulse was, at times, difficult to resist. "The lightsaber as-is is one of the coolest devices ever imagined," Hidalgo said, and it's enticing for fans and creators alike to want a unique interpretation to call their own. "The concern is, if *everyone* makes a special lightsaber, then no one really has a special lightsaber. It detracts from the original, which is already special. Given that the lightsaber also has such a spiritual component to it too, we had to be wary of the compulsion to bling out the blades too much."

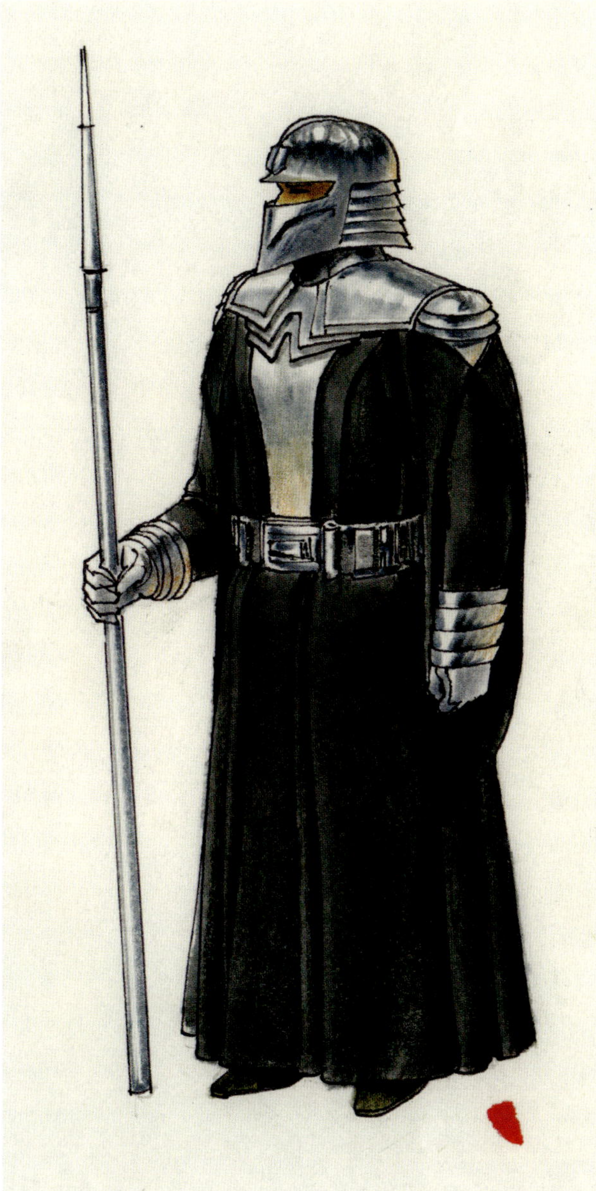

"And given that this is a golden age without massive, galactic wars, we wanted to focus on the weapon of the Jedi really as a tool," Siglain added. "It's something used in both a preventative way—just taking their sabers out of their holsters should be enough to end a threat—and in a teachable way, as the Jedi use their sabers to train and duel to better themselves."

Also that spring, Marvel Comics hired Ario Anindito to illustrate the interiors for the first run of *Star Wars: The High Republic*. On July 9, 2020, Anindito and Scott met for the first time virtually, in a Zoom video call that lasted for hours. The two talked about their shared love of horror movies and monsters, as well as the art of telling stories through comic books. Anindito had turned down an earlier offer to illustrate a Marvel *Star Wars* project—his deep love for the franchise at war with his own self-doubts about being up to the challenge of illustrating ships and droids. After a fellow artist, Alan Quah, heard about his predicament, he gifted Anindito a book on *Star Wars* ships and machines. "So you will not have any reason to say no to *Star Wars* again," Anindito recalled Quah telling him. "And I took it to my heart." He later accepted the call to illustrate pages for Marvel's *Star Wars Annual* #4, published in May 2018, but being assigned to *The High Republic* was something of a second chance. "I'm honored to be chosen," Anindito said. "I feel like Anakin. Ario *Anakindito*." Art revisions for Scott and Anindito's first issue came in just under the wire, with Keeve's hair drastically changing from relaxed and straight into a curly, natural coif after the line work on the first full issue and a handful of variant covers had already been completed. "This is a Jedi that's out to save people," Lucasfilm designer Leigh Zieske pointed out. "I don't think she had the time to press her hair while people were shouting for help."

On July 31, 2020, Older and artist Harvey Tolibao had their first virtual conversation to collaborate on IDW's all-ages comic run, *Star Wars: The High Republic Adventures*. Older had been sketching ideas since the Summit meetings. "That's how I've figured stuff out [since I was] a kid," Older said. "I always had a sketchbook with me, and that was how I would make sense of the world." Another artist, Max Dunbar, took the initial design pass at Padawan newcomers Lula Talisola, Qort, and Farzala, but it was Tolibao who reimagined the trio in their final form. The son of a Filipino artist who hand-drew and painted plywood movie posters for the cinema in their hometown of Mindanao when Tolibao was a child, the illustrator learned early that capturing the precise lines of the *Millennium Falcon* was no less important than perfecting an actor's likeness. Inspiration for the series was varied. A legendary healer from Older's days working as a paramedic in New York City—a man who self-identified as Buckets of Blood even on the official radio frequency—was an early candidate for a character, while Tolibao drew on his affinity for the works of Czech art nouveau painter Alphonse Mucha, French cartoonist and illustrator Jean "Moebius" Giraud, and renowned Swiss artist H. R. Giger.

At the midpoint of *Star Wars: The High Republic Adventures*, artist Toni Bruno took over for a time, aging the core teenage Padawans up about a year to reflect their physical transformation as time marched forward and they matured as a result of the events in the galaxy, before Tolibao finished the run.

"What is really important about the Jedi Order at this time is that they're not at war," said Older. "They're not constantly under attack or on the defensive. And we see such a variety in their understanding of the Force, how they use it, how they feel it, how it moves through them, how they understand it, and then also their own roles and what it means to the question of attachment, what it means to be a Jedi, and what it means to die. All these questions are so complicated and philosophical and fascinating."

"The Jedi aren't machines, and they're not emotionless, and they should never be emotionless," added Scott. "What they should be is controlled. They are passionate, but they control it, and the passion never goes away. Half the reason we love characters is because they are struggling with things. For me, the most believable and the most basic emotion for lots of people, myself included, is fear, because it's driven us as a species. It's basic fight or flight, and Jedi would have to make that choice every day."

The inherent conflict of storytelling and a Jedi Order gripped by fear and the threat of the Nihil also meant not every character would survive Phase I. Although the Starlight Beacon's destruction was a plot point from early on in the planning process, the individual Jedi who met their demise in the path of the Nihil was a cause for much spirited debate in the virtual writer's room sessions. Stellan Gios survived the first draft of *The Fallen Star*, Claudia Gray told SyFy Wire, "but it wasn't working, and Stellan's story wasn't working." She quickly realized Gios, the so-called polestar in the friendship trifecta of Avar Kriss and Elzar Mann, a character who had selflessly been leading by the book, needed to make a sacrifice for the story to resonate. "I realized [Stellan] has to make a bigger sacrifice for that story to land the way it's supposed to. And for the station's death, as much as we love the station, and as much as Starlight Beacon is a symbol, you don't feel it emotionally the way you feel a character. You just don't." Other prominent Jedi, including Burryaga and Lula Talisola, were left with a cliffhanger ending, missing in action as the Starlight Beacon met its fiery end.

▲ Sketch for the Emperor's Royal Guard RALPH McQUARRIE

This stoic knight, originally envisioned to flank the Emperor in *Return of the Jedi*, served as inspiration on a mood board along with Pre-Raphaelite and Arthurian scenes early in the ideation phase of The High Republic's design.

► Concept of an Arthurian Jedi "If we're going to do the Arthurian Saga in any form, we need the Round Table and we need the knights, so presumably there has to be a King Arthur or Queen Arthur, a once and future king. There's always, somewhere in the DNA of a drawing I do, a real person, one that has a quality that embodies this kind of character. And for me, both the Merlin and the King Arthur, were my son. He's got this moral center . . . and he can move so beautifully, and he's just such a gracious soul. So he went out on the porch and posed for everybody in the Round Table. This is him being hopeful and actually knowing how to use that lightsaber. It's an Excalibur sort of lightsaber. It was after *The Force Awakens*, but I wanted a different kind of guard." McCAIG

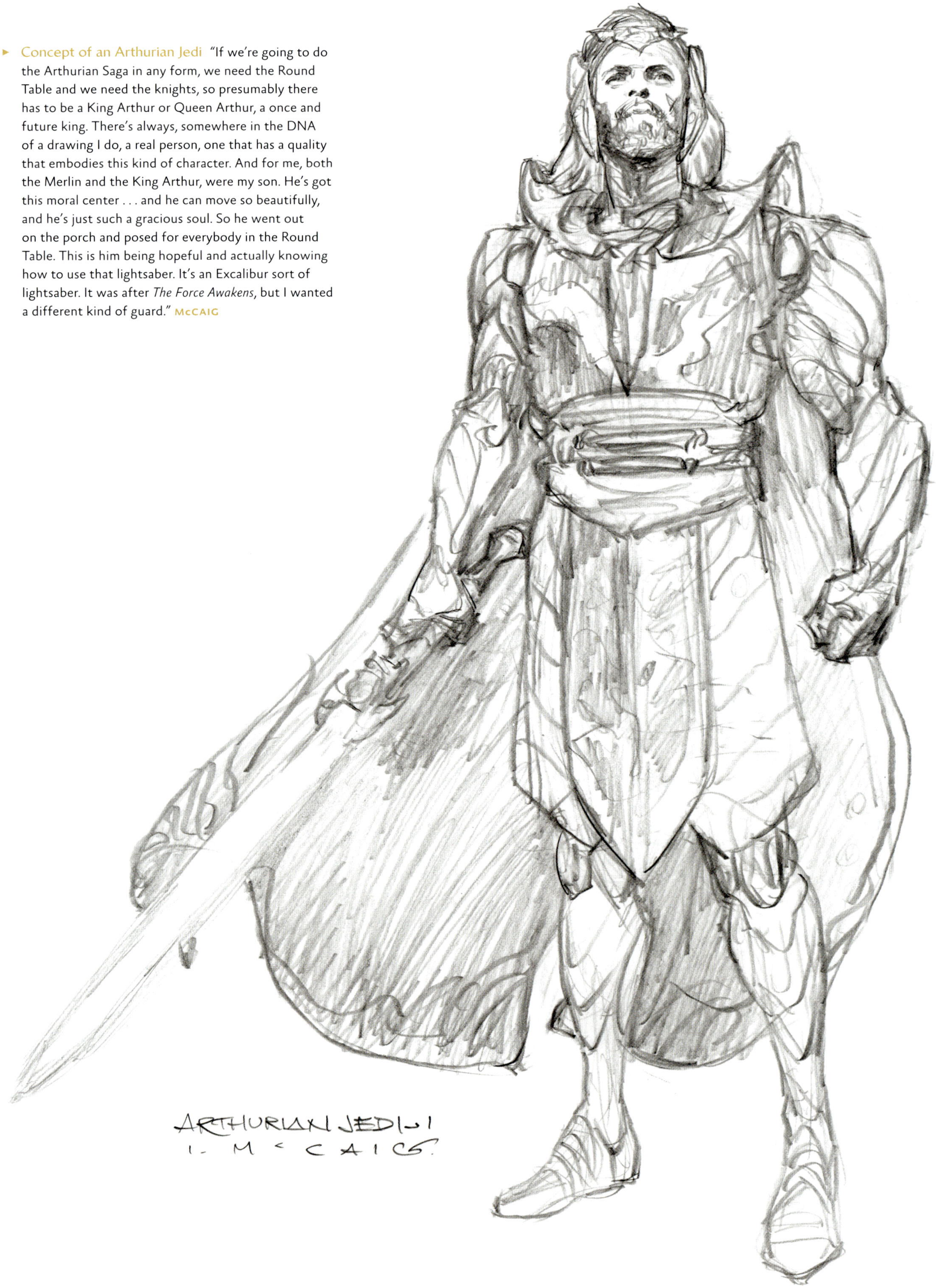

► Concept of a female Jedi
"I wanted someone who was very clearly capable as a fighter, but unlike a lot of the big bully knights, she's grace and dignity as well. More like how a martial artist would do it rather than a big thundering knight in armor." McCAIG

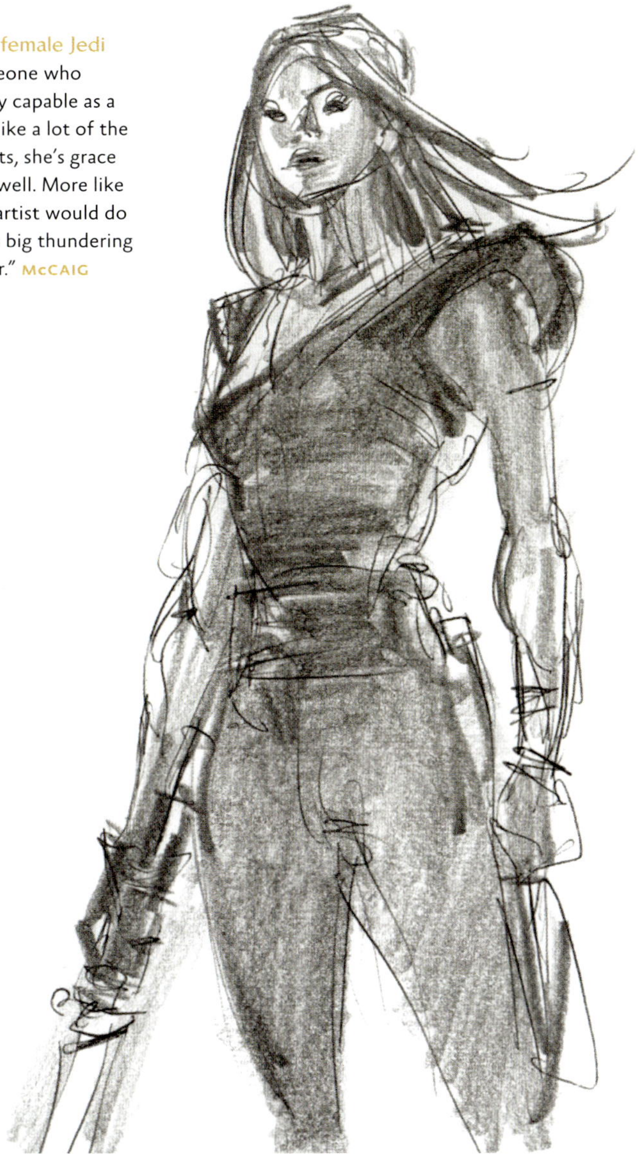

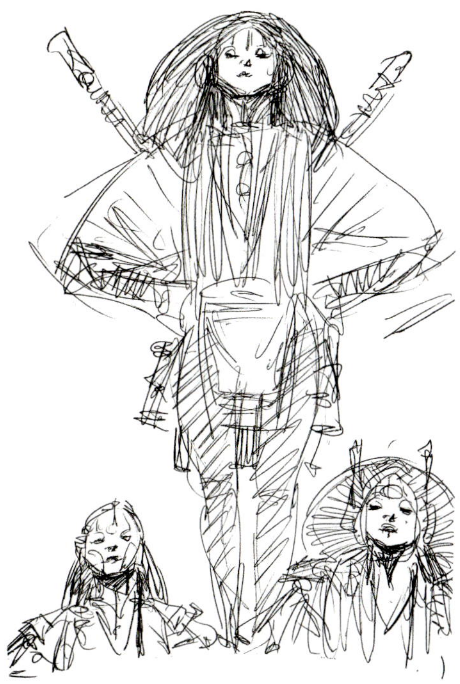

◄ Loose study, July 2019 "Why don't we show the origin of where some of those [galactic fashion] styles came from? Some of the early but more primitive versions might end up being more elaborate going back in time. Things are hand-made and maybe more symbolic and ornamental. This is the high point, so maybe they were even more outrageous than Queen Amidala. Of course, that's who I was thinking of." McCAIG

► Concept of a warrior with shield, July 2019
"Using angel iconography, if the shield comes up behind the head like that, it's not a literal halo, but it gives the same impression of the halo. She has her two swords; it has a little clip on the back, you pull sideways and it disconnects. It's important to know that stuff because people will ask you, 'What is this?' I got that a lot on the prequels. George would hold up my drawings and go, 'OK, and do you know how that works or is that just a squiggle?' And most of the time it was just a squiggle, but I would make stuff up [like] the dress with the lights at the bottom. Poor Trisha [Biggar, the costume designer]. She had to actually figure this stuff out." McCAIG

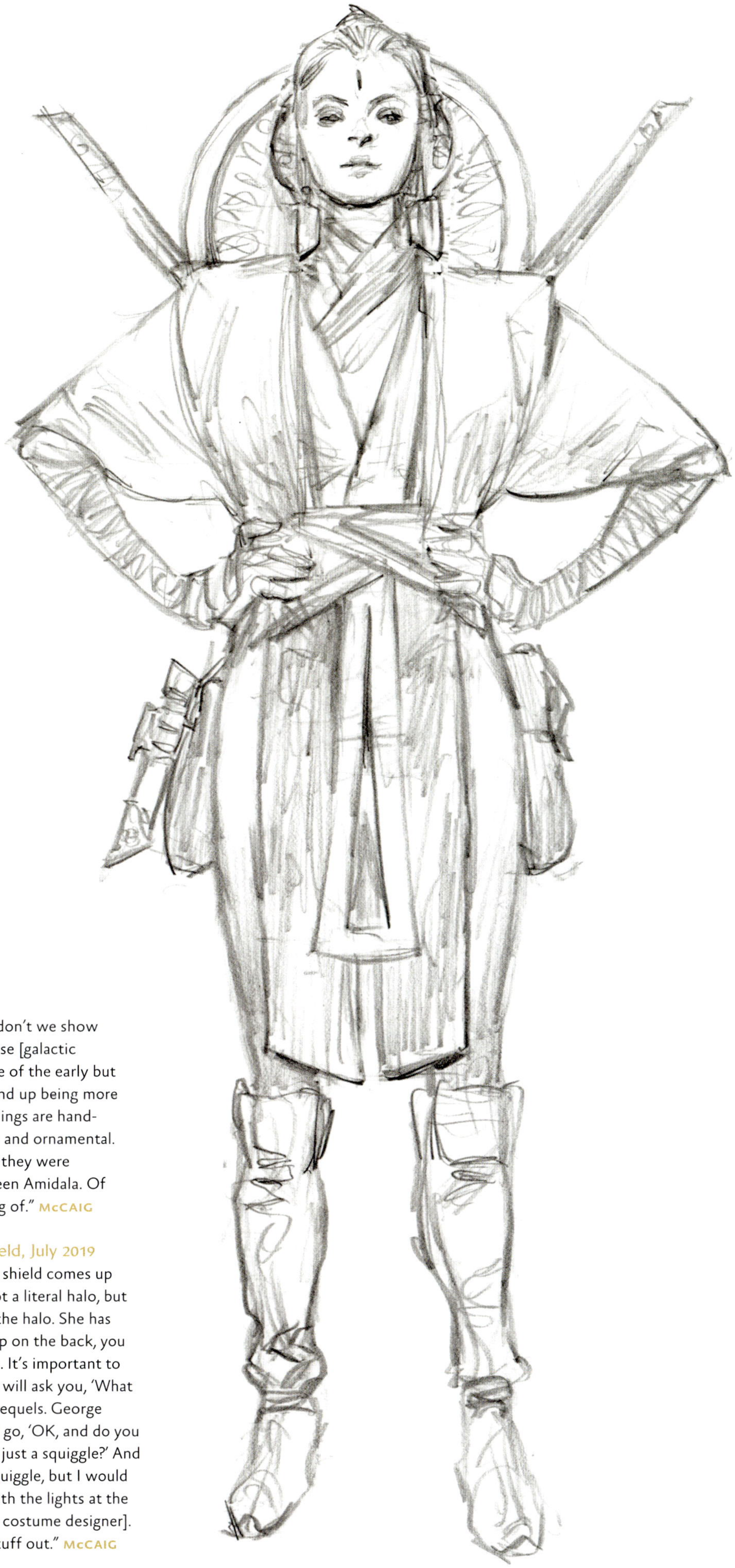

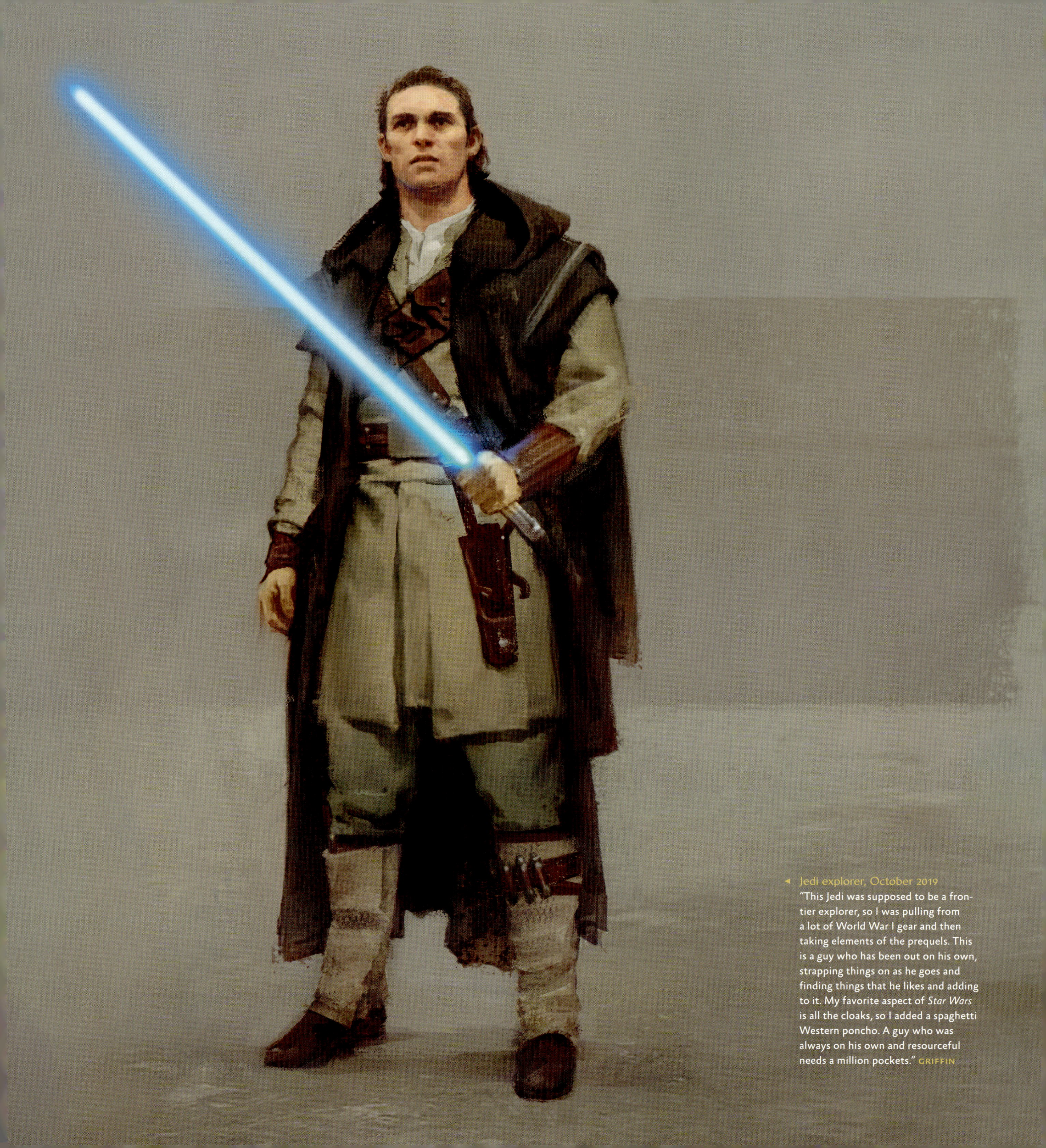

◂ Jedi explorer, October 2019
"This Jedi was supposed to be a frontier explorer, so I was pulling from a lot of World War I gear and then taking elements of the prequels. This is a guy who has been out on his own, strapping things on as he goes and finding things that he likes and adding to it. My favorite aspect of *Star Wars* is all the cloaks, so I added a spaghetti Western poncho. A guy who was always on his own and resourceful needs a million pockets." GRIFFIN

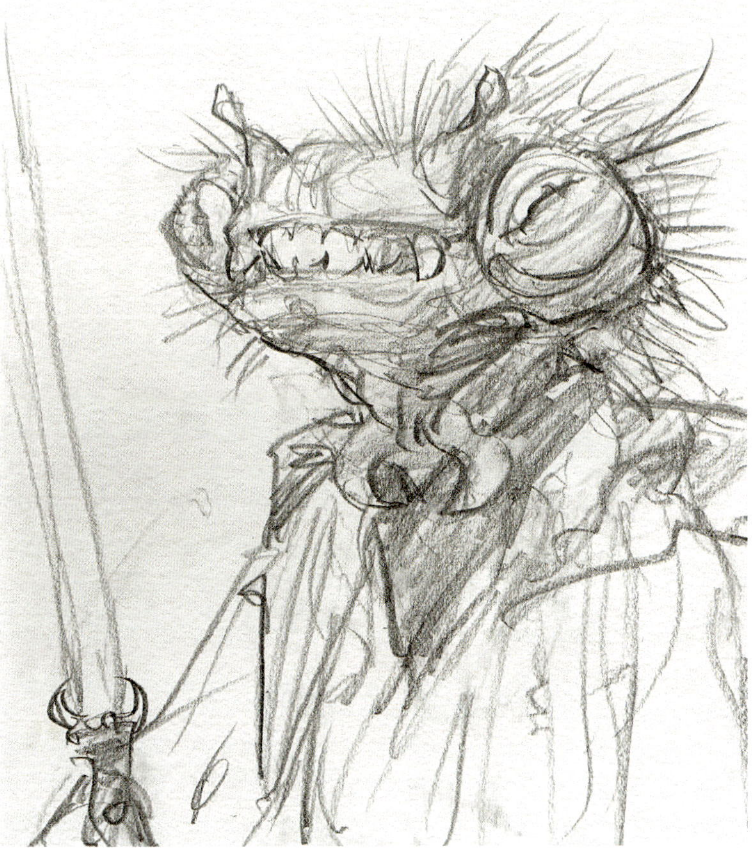

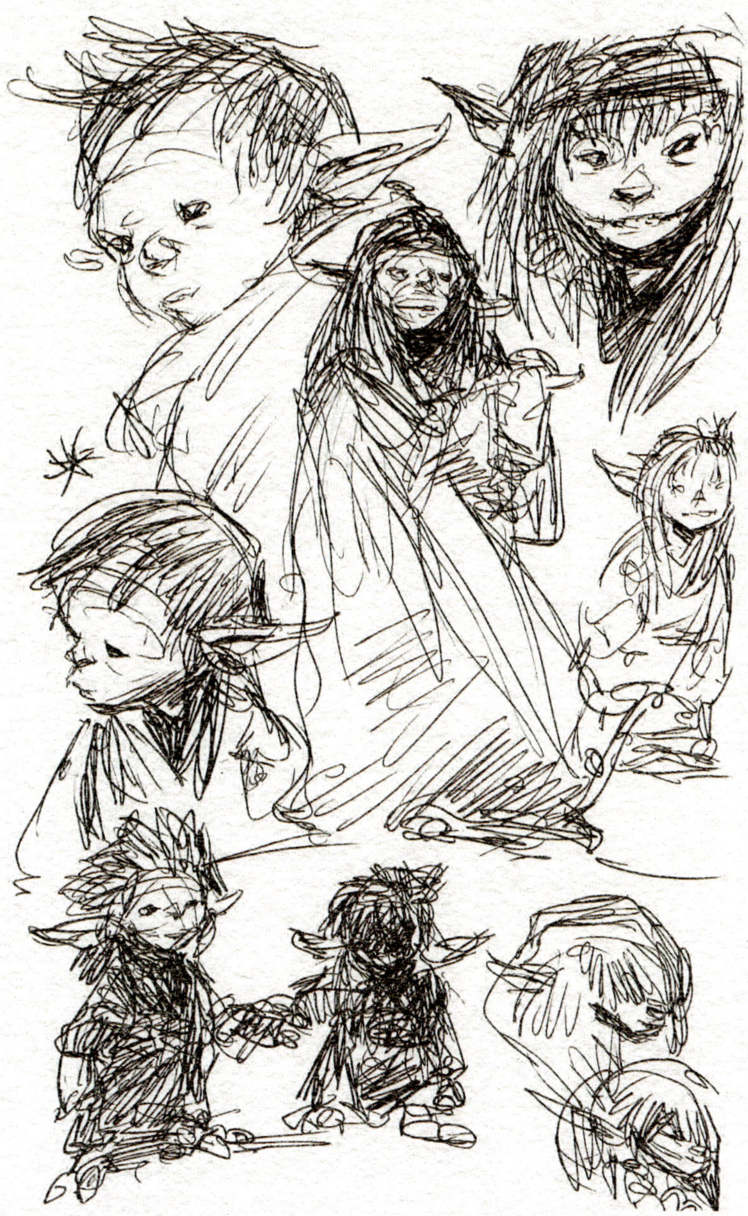

▲ Sketch of a fly-like Jedi, July 2019 "Every once in a while we just need to honor *The Fly*, which is such a great movie. This is Fly Jedi. [I was] trying to use something that's so ugly no one wants to hang out with him and yet he's a Jedi." McCAIG

► Musings on children of the Yoda species, July 2019 McCAIG

▼ Loose sketch of a Yoda-like alien, July 2019 McCAIG

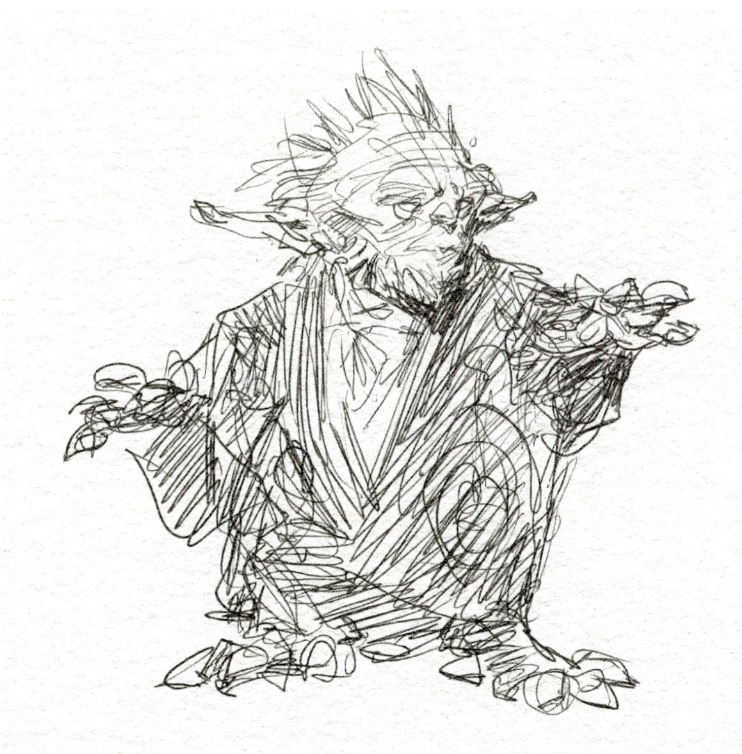

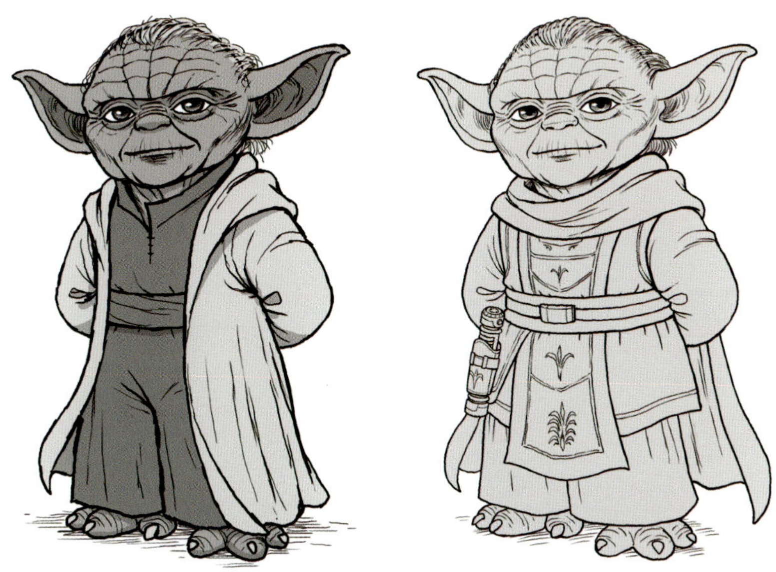

▲ Concept for Yoda PETUR ANTONSSON

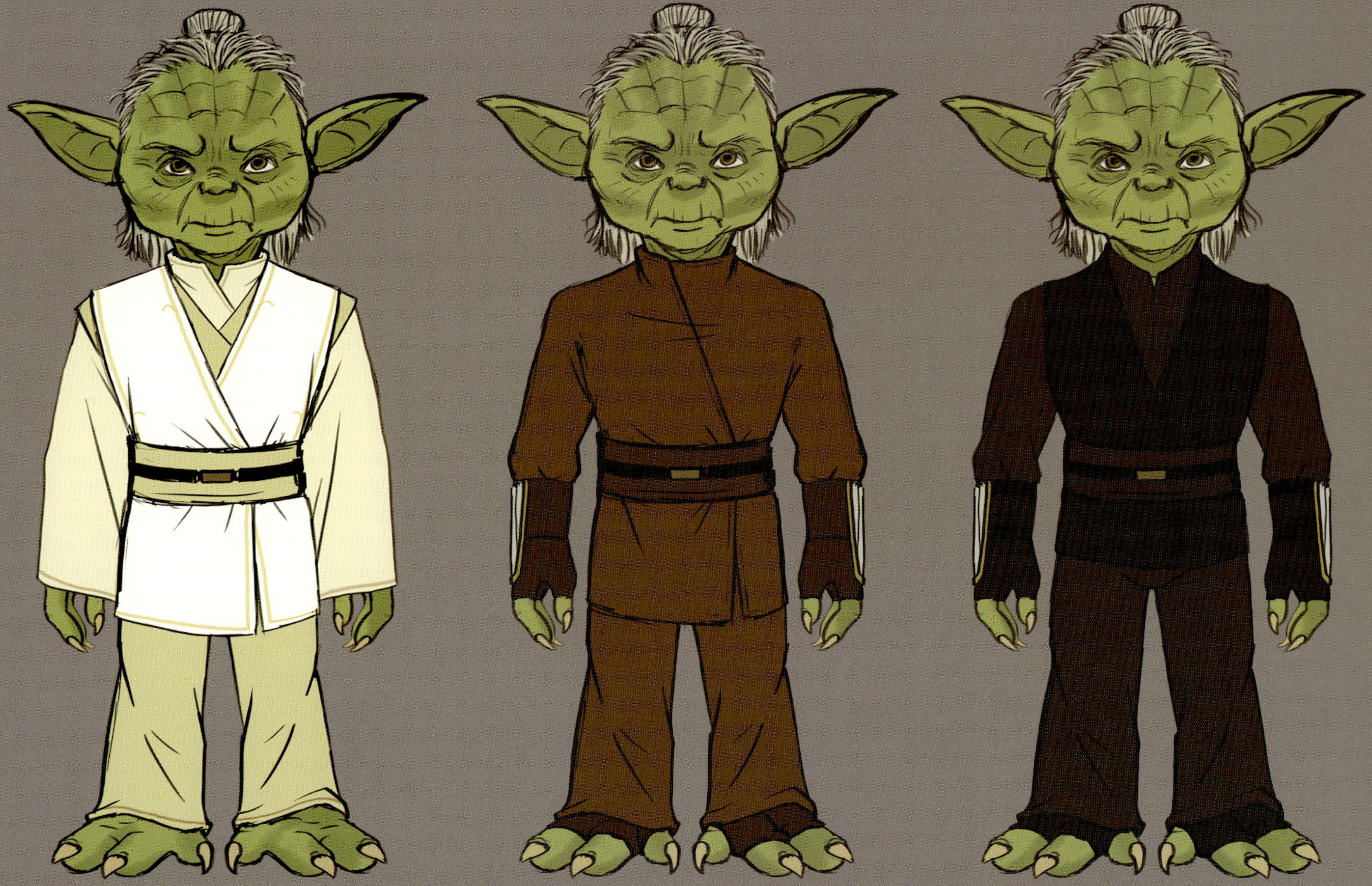

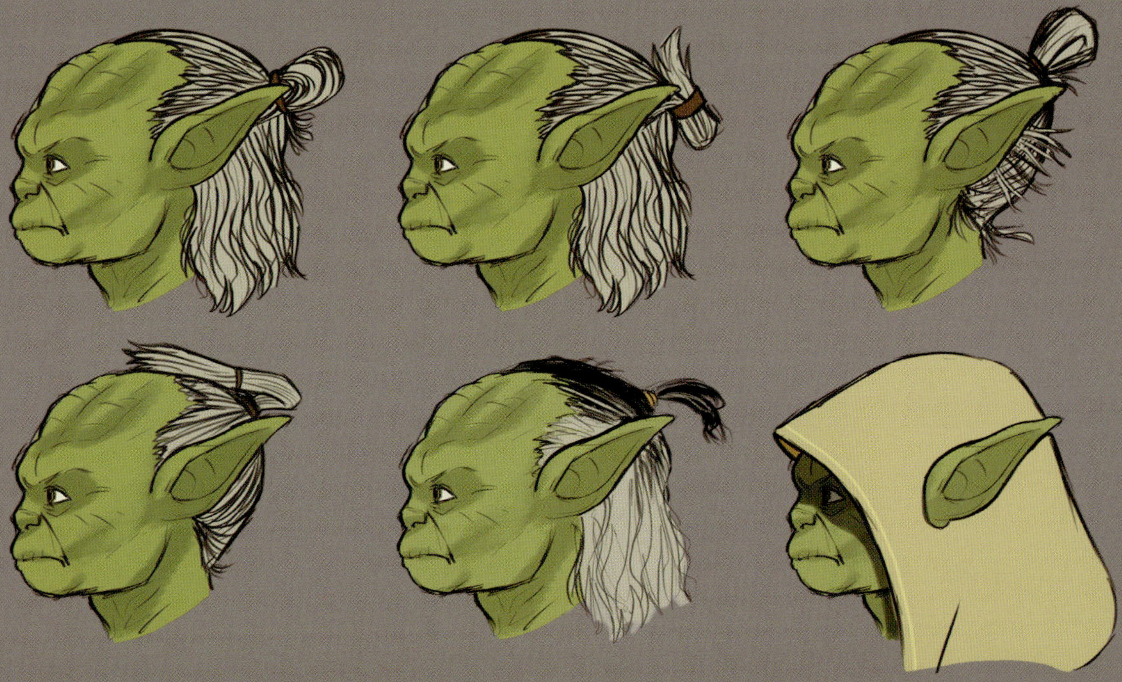

▲ **Master Yoda attire concepts** "This is a hybrid of the normal Jedi attire, Luke Skywalker's *Return of the Jedi* outfit, and then Yoda. I remember looking at Yoda in *Attack of the Clones* when he's about to fight Count Dooku and you actually get to see him fully. His outfit has a straight seam down the center, and I angled the seam to try and make him seem younger and hipper." JEFFREY THOMAS

◄ **Master Yoda hair study** "They wanted to redesign Yoda for this to be distinctly High Republic era, but they didn't want to go too crazy. Before I had any kind of limitations, I thought it would be cool if he did something more stylish with his hair. The one that I think I liked the most was the first one because it was just a simple kind of samurai topknot, going back to kind of what George Lucas was thinking with his inspiration from [Akira] Kurosawa." THOMAS

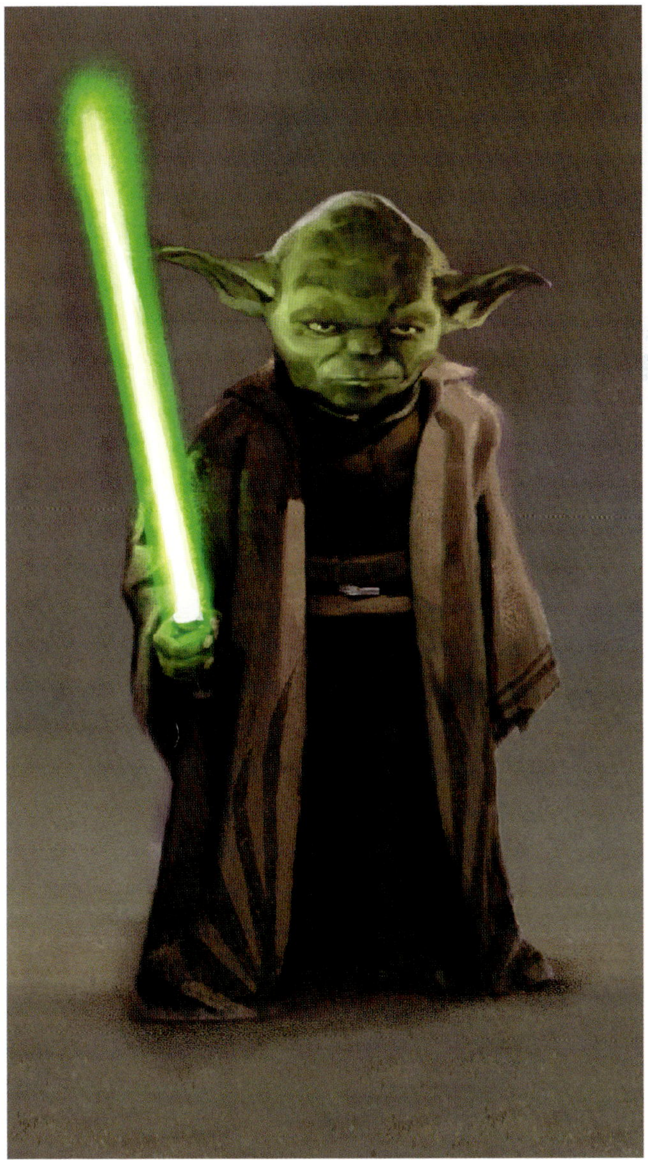

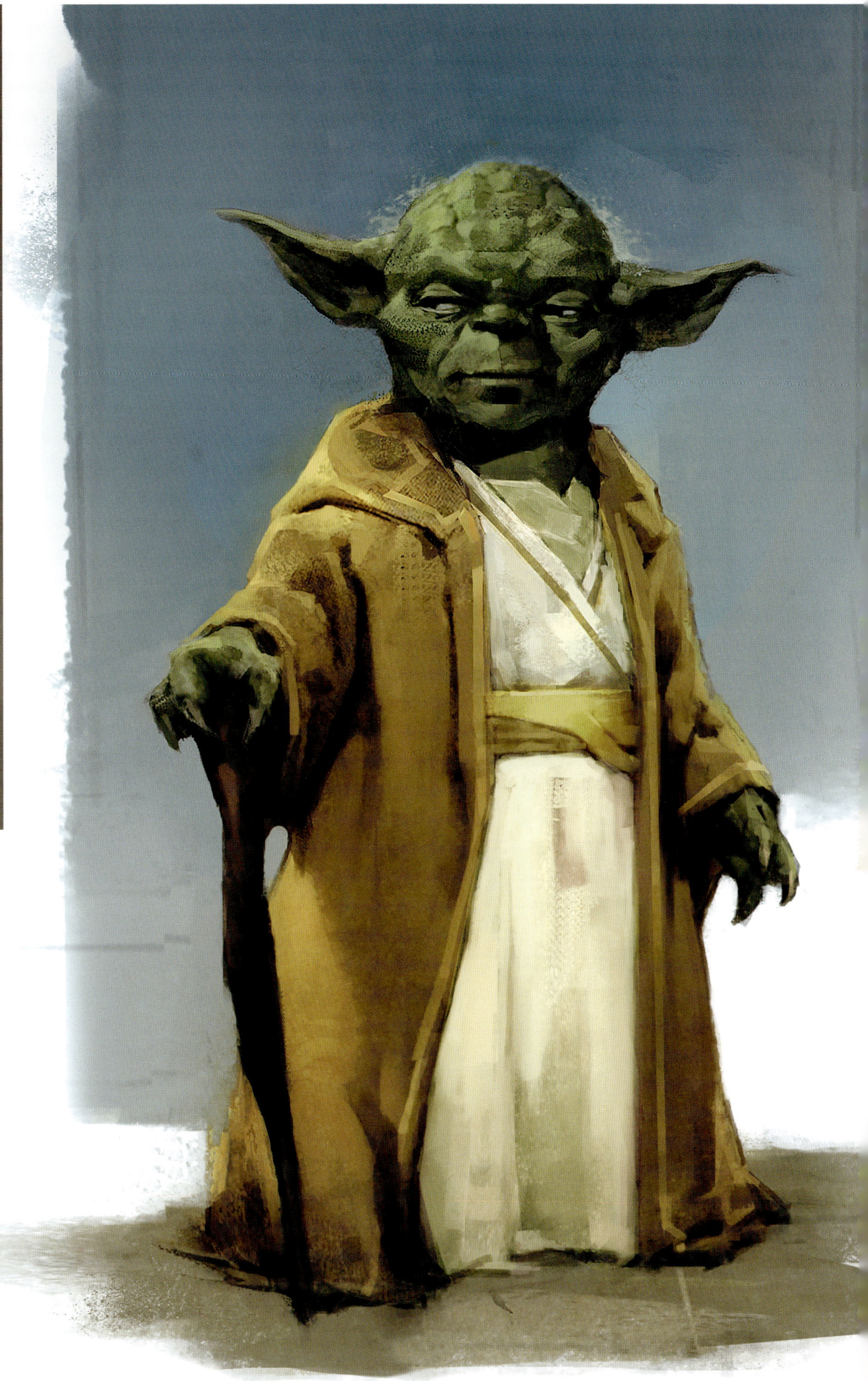

▲ Grandmaster Yoda in mission attire "For a younger Yoda, I was keeping those elements of his bone structure and chiseling them out a little bit, smoothing some areas, but leaving those timeless wrinkles in the forehead. I had some versions where he had more hair, but he kind of looked like [American politician] Bernie Sanders." GRIFFIN

► Grandmaster Yoda in formal robes GRIFFIN

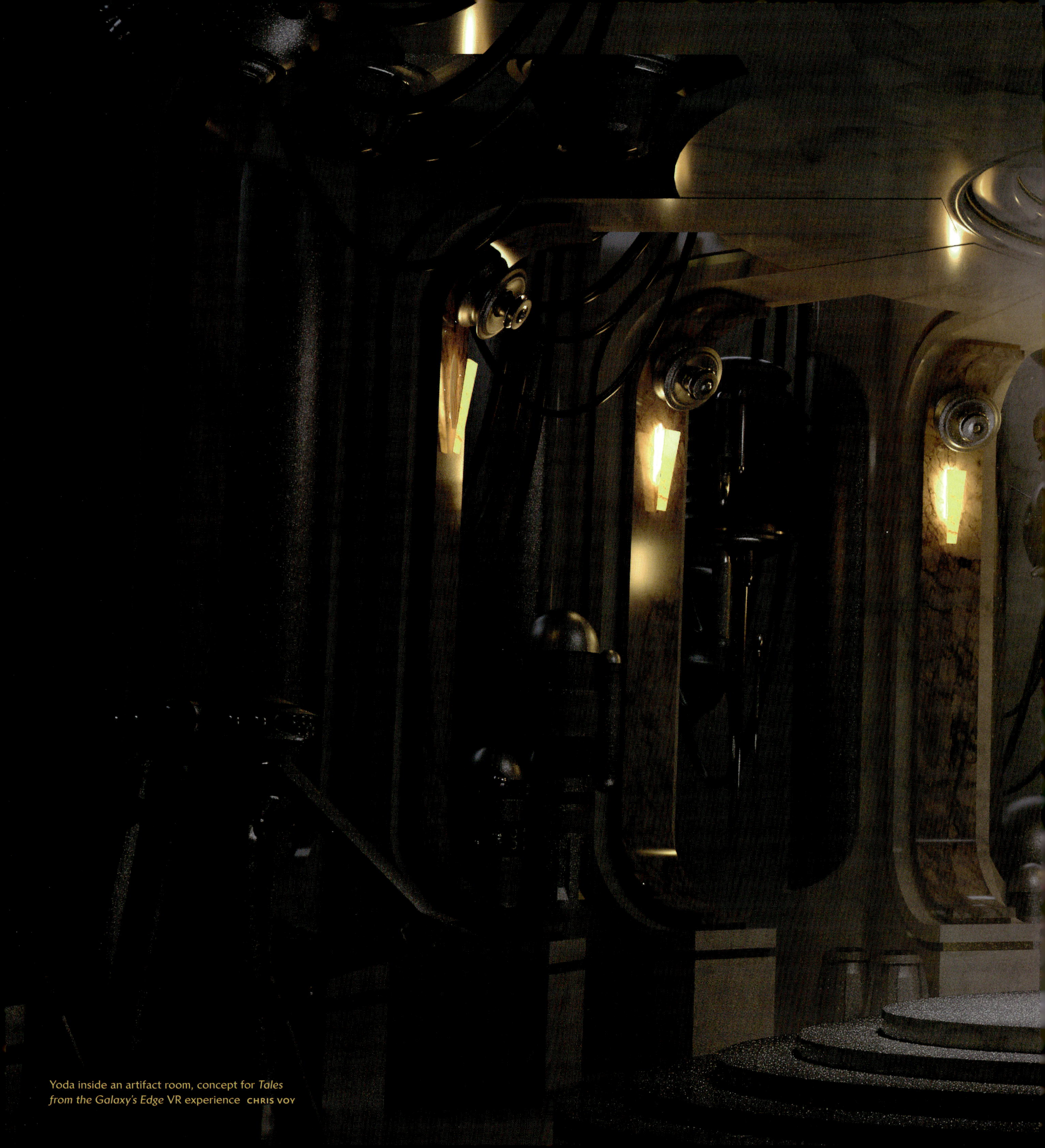

Yoda inside an artifact room, concept for *Tales from the Galaxy's Edge* VR experience CHRIS VOY

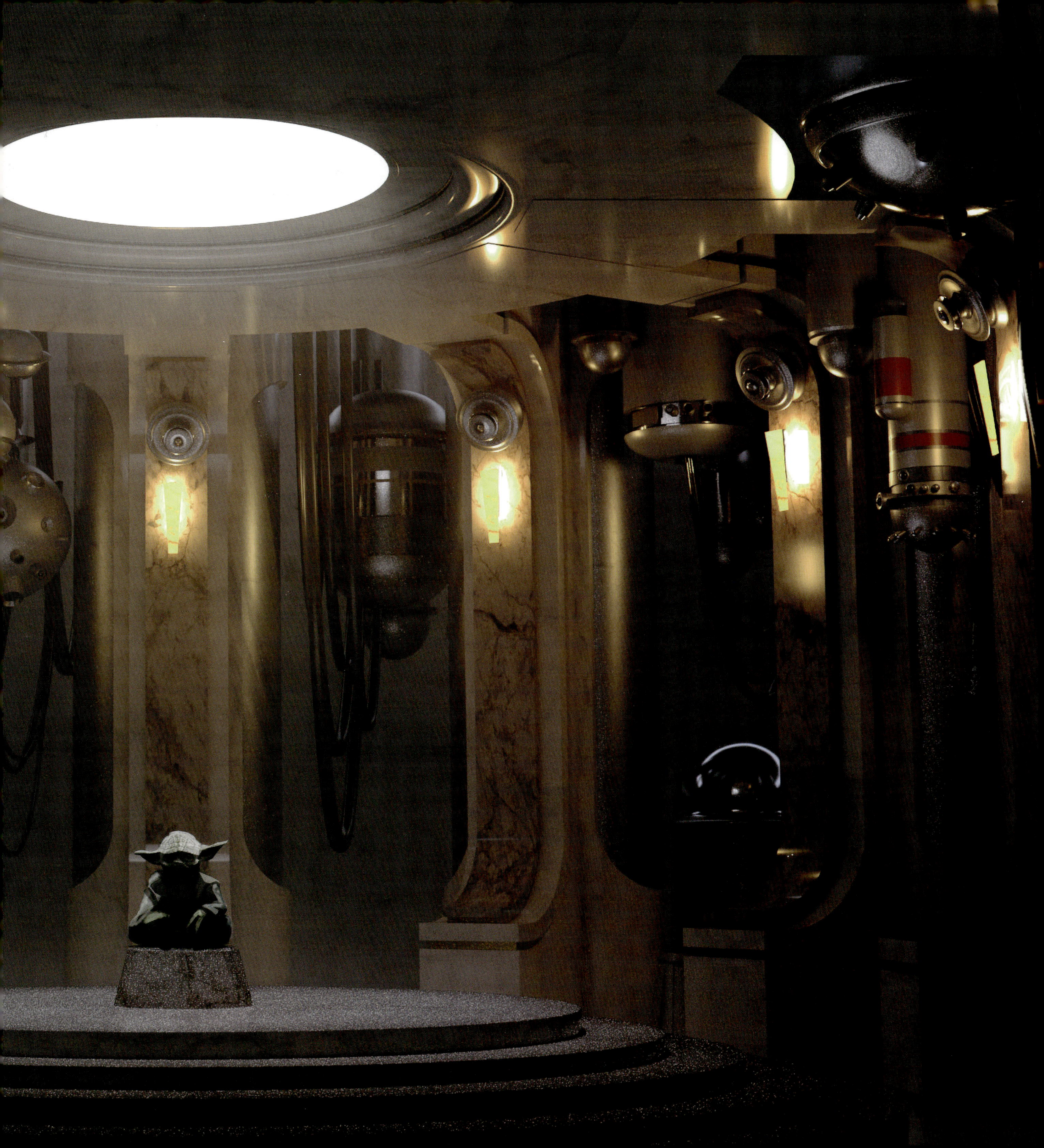

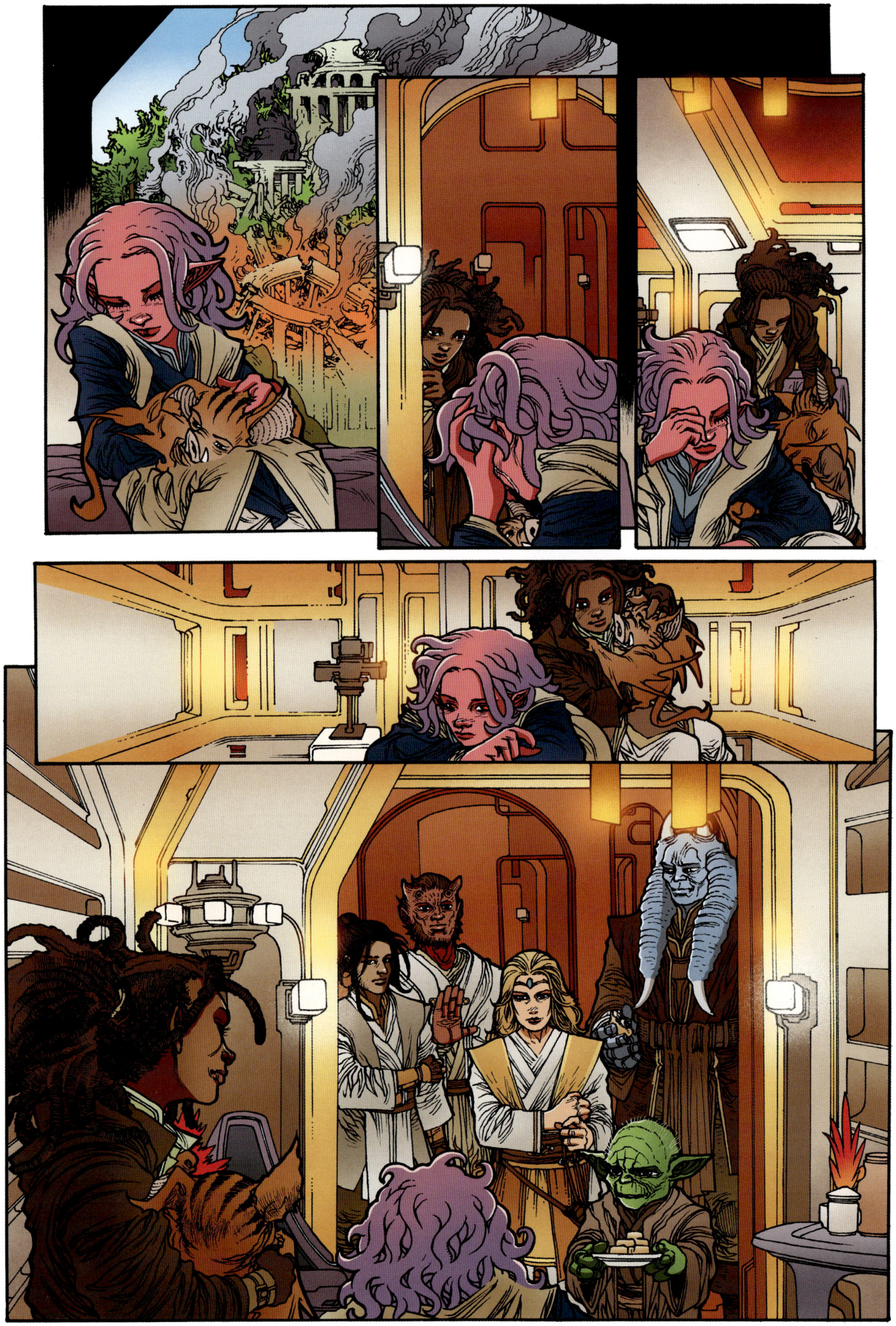

◂ Page from IDW's *Star Wars: The High Republic Adventures* #3
TOLIBAO (PENCILER) AND NALTY (COLORIST)

"We got Yoda's first badass scene [in the comic], and that gives it the *Star Wars* feel a little bit, but the comic still has heart for all the kids. When people are like, 'Oh, Yoda baked muffins?!' Everyone gets so hyped."
TOLIBAO

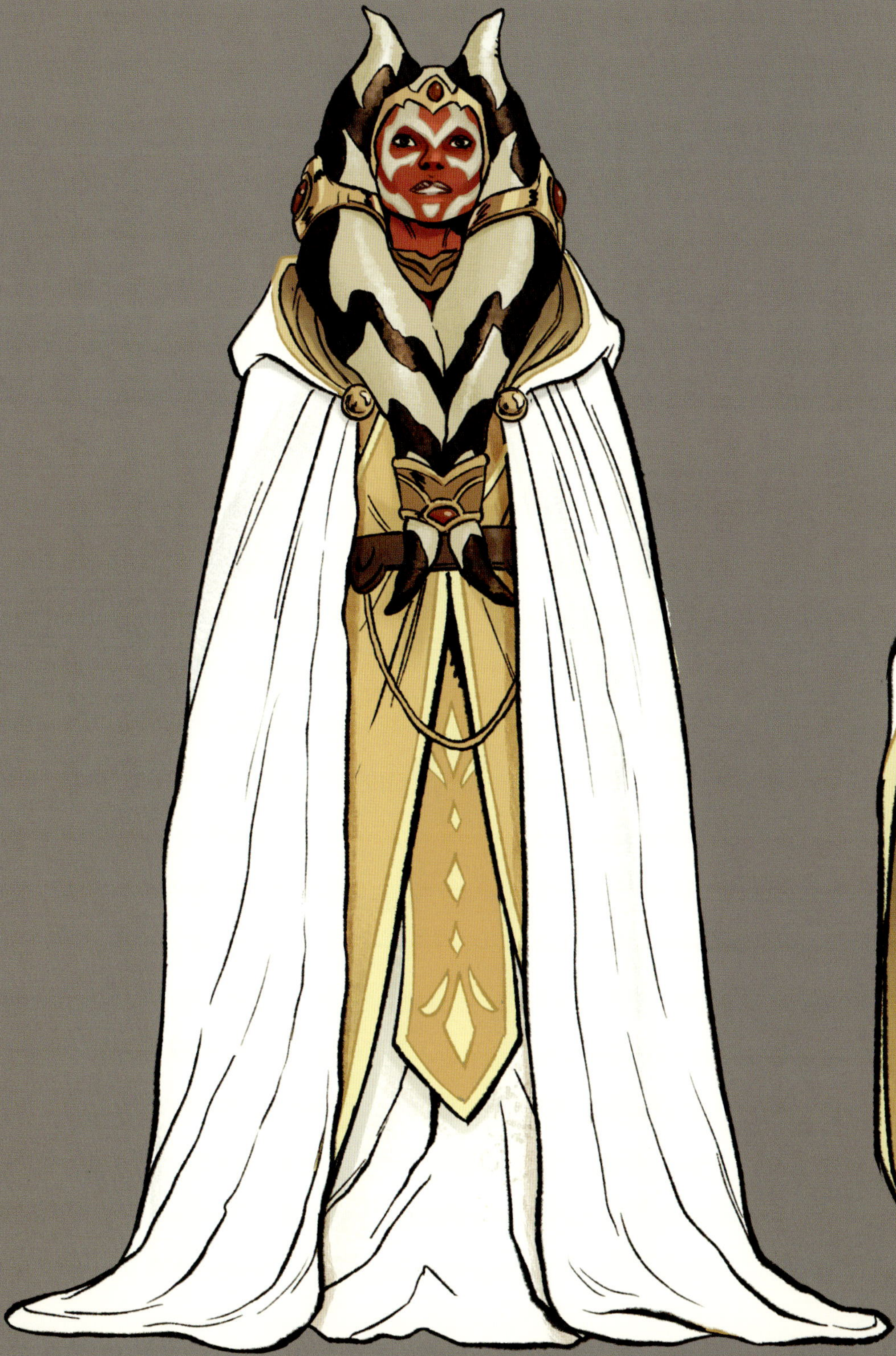

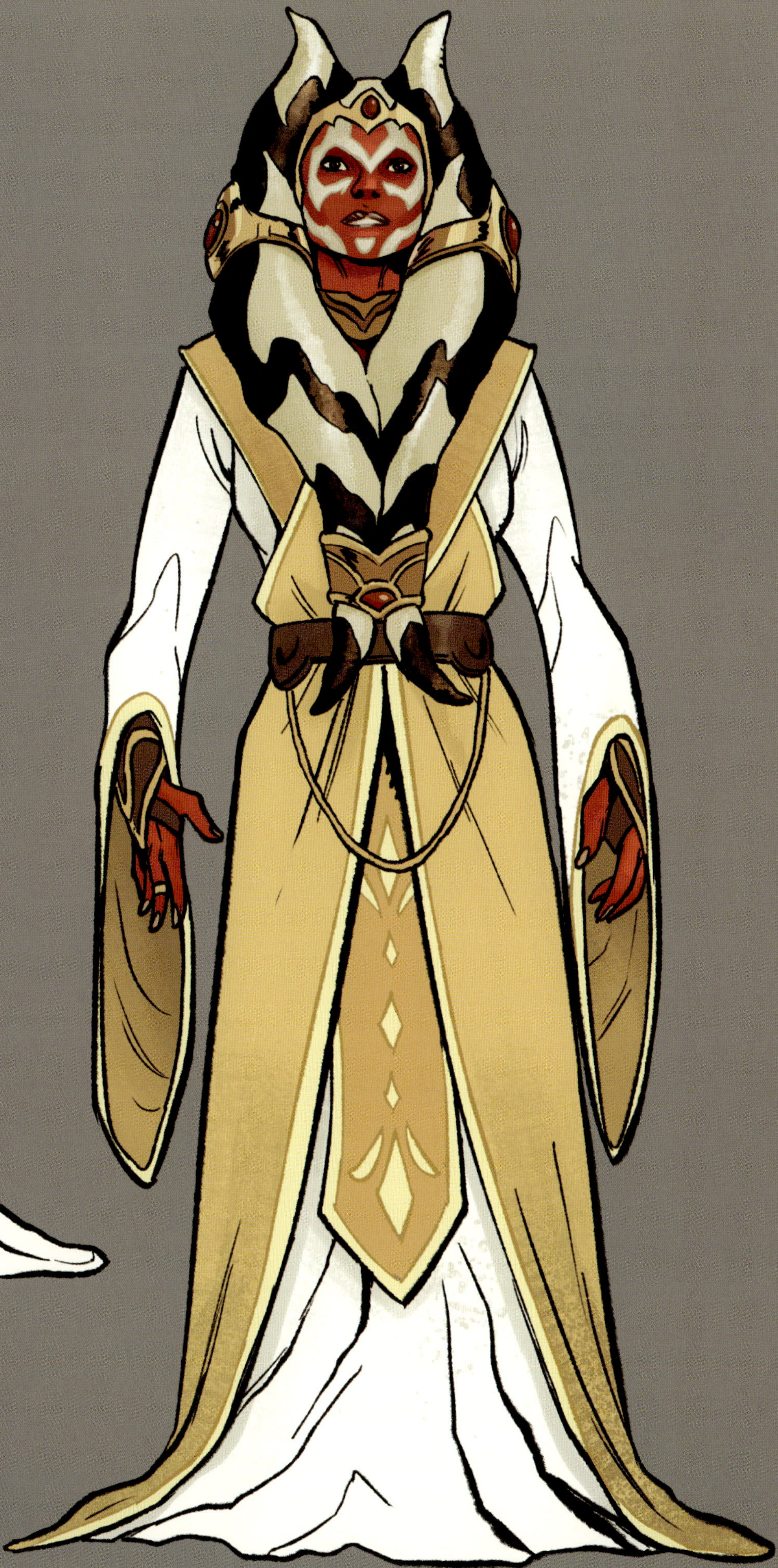

▲ Grandmaster Jora Malli, February 2021 ORNELLA SAVARESE

"It was a great design and pretty iconic and different. Any time we see a Togruta [like Ahsoka Tano] or any alien species that there's a major character of, there's a desire by some artists to kind of lean toward the look of that character. We needed to push away from what's already been seen." PHIL SZOSTAK

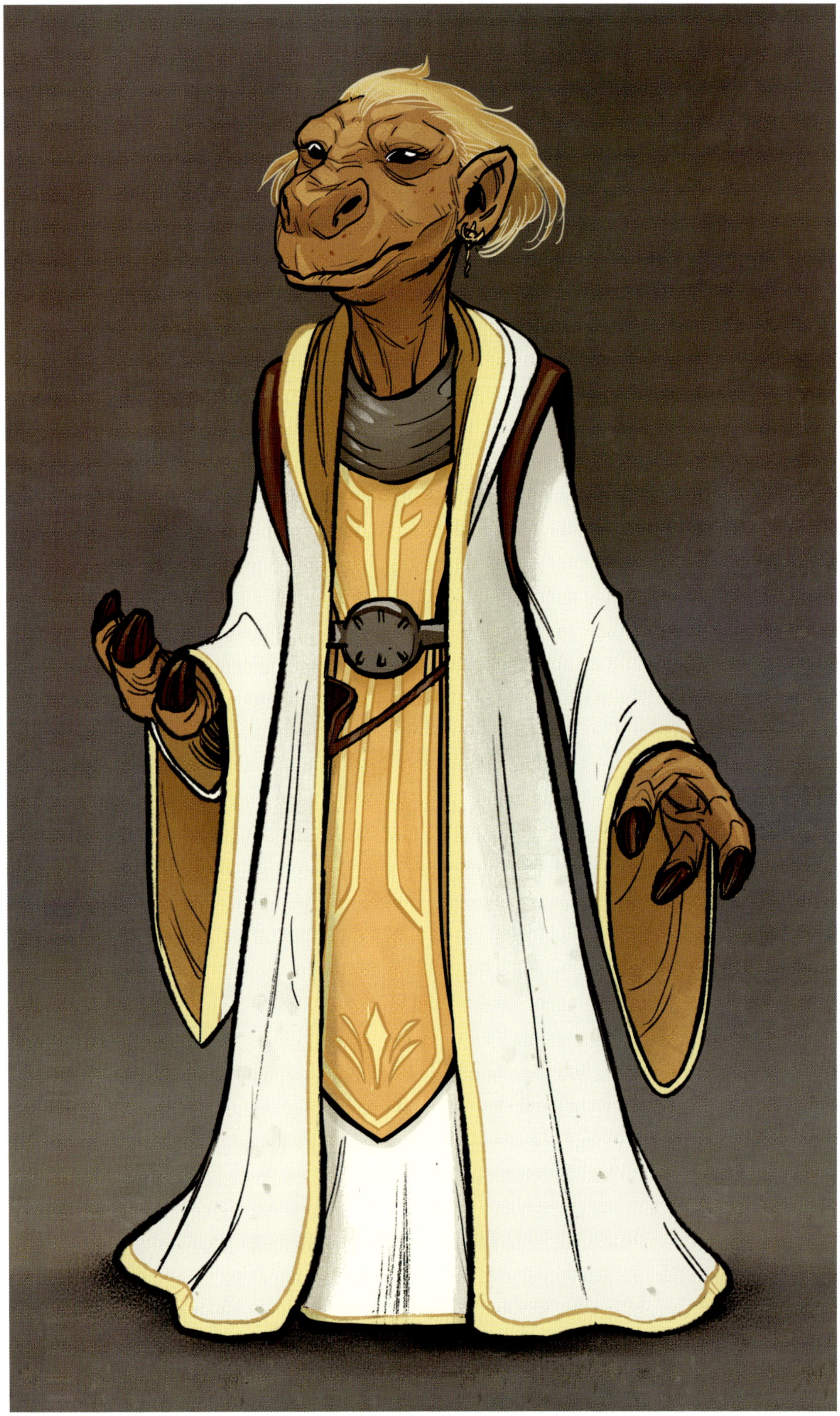

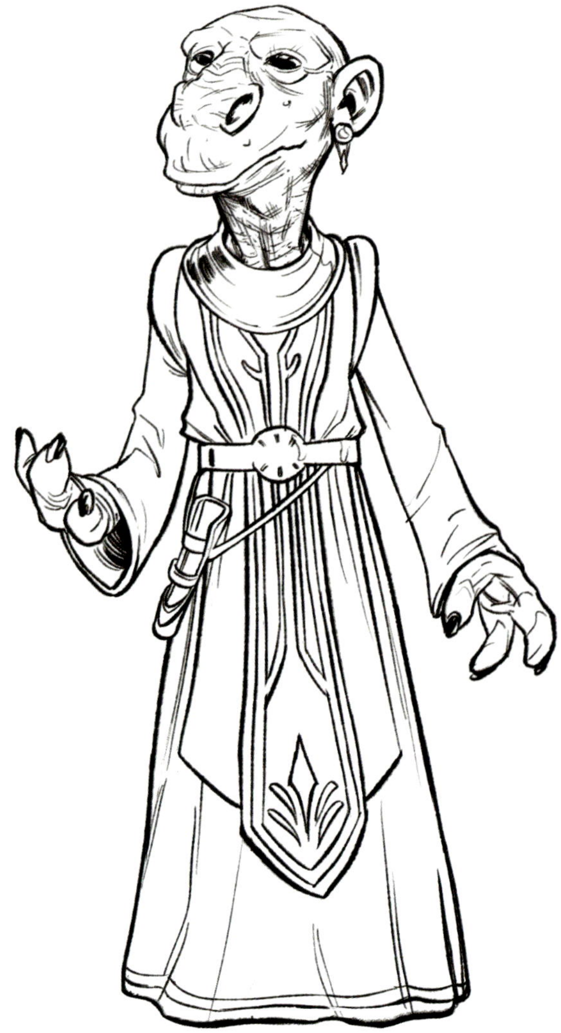

▲ Early concept of Grandmaster Adampo, February 2021 SAVARESE

The same species as the legacy background alien known as Yak Face in *Star Wars: Return of the Jedi*, Adampo was envisioned as a Yarkoran. "For the initial illustration, the head was too large, and it got reduced by like 20 percent," said Szostak, who combed through photo reference in the Lucasfilm archive, some of which has never been released, to help the artist ensure the appropriate proportions.

◂ Final design of Grandmaster Adampo, May 2021 SAVARESE

► Early concept of Grandmaster Keaton Murag, February 2021
SAVARESE

"It was a lot of back and forth coming from this one trying to nail down his age. He looked great, but, you know, we just we kept making him too young, then we gradually aged him up." THOMAS

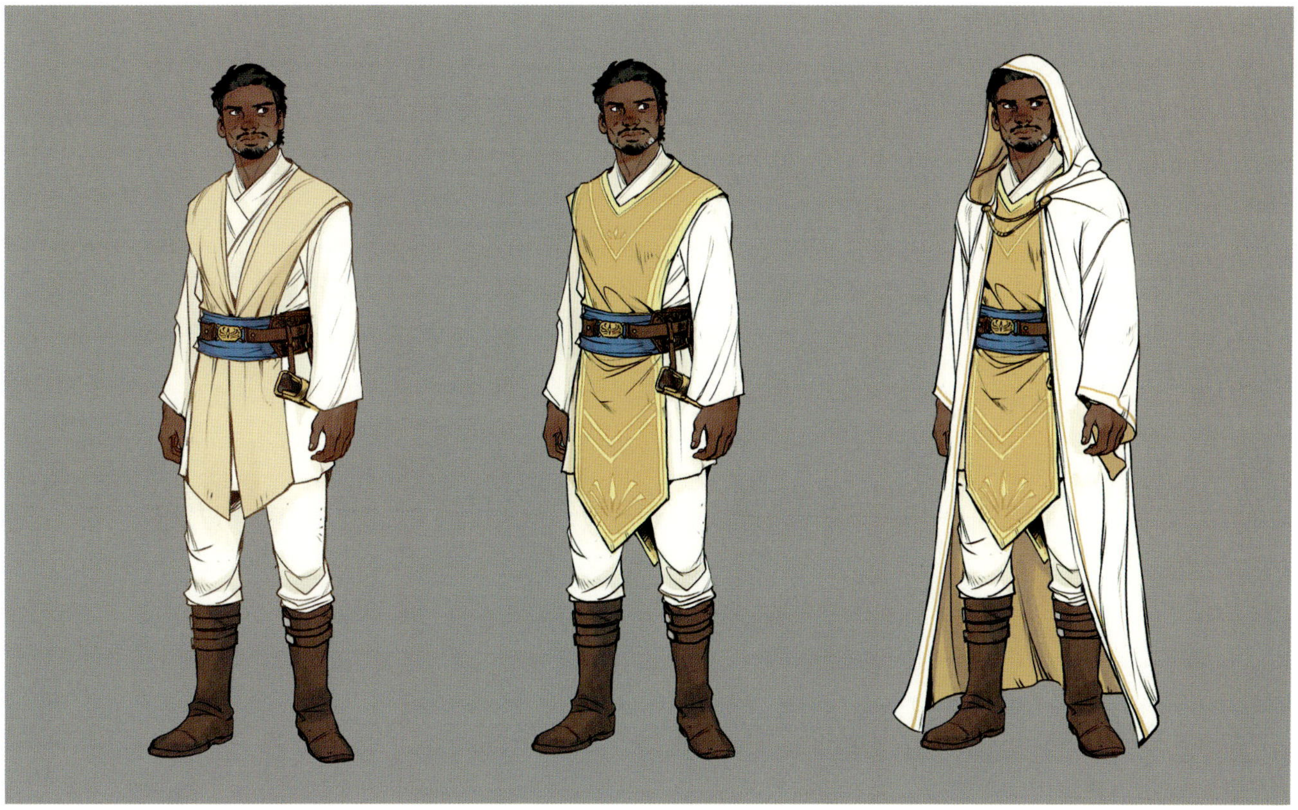

▼ Final design of Grandmaster Keaton Murag, June 2021
SAVARESE

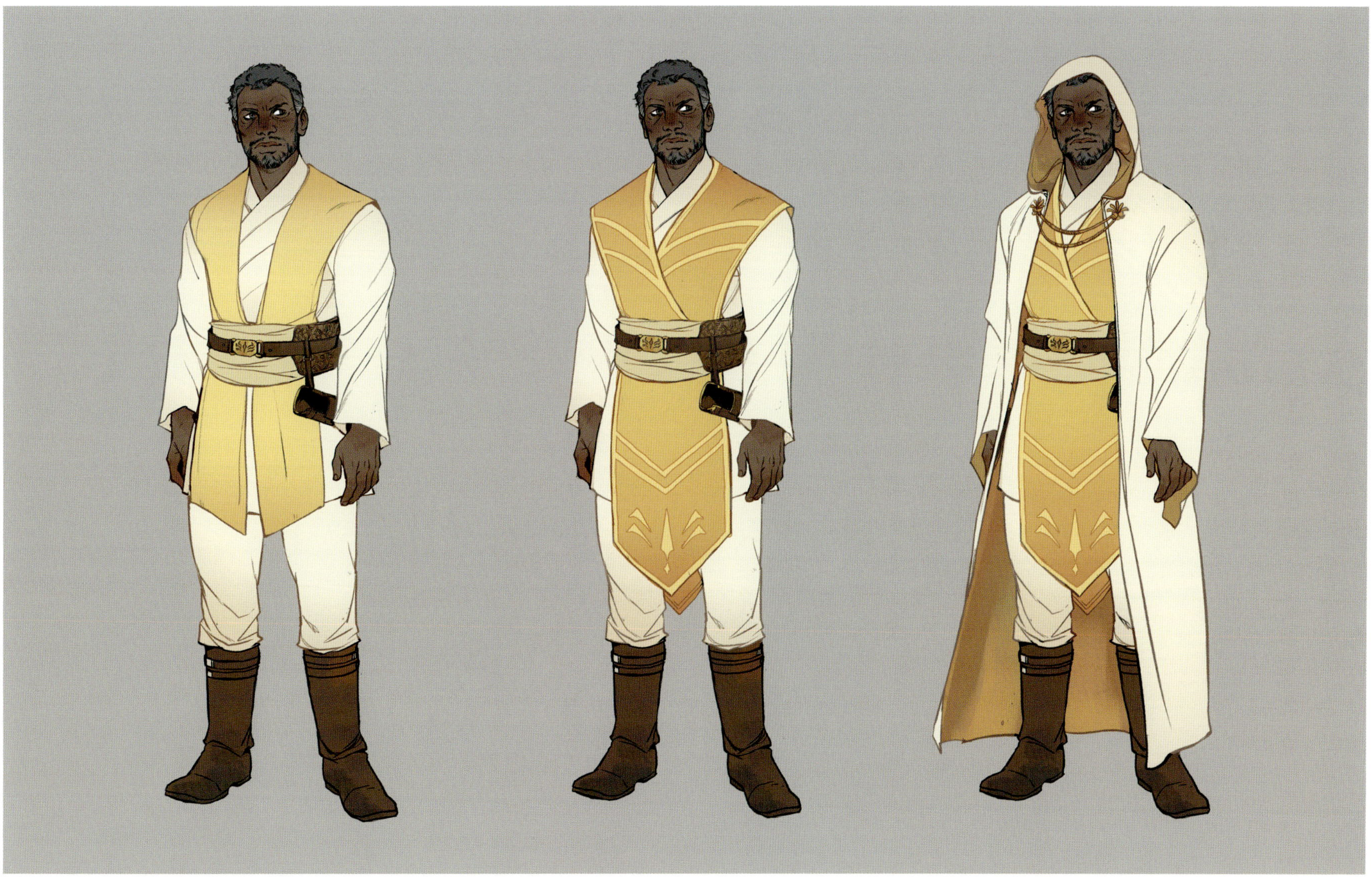

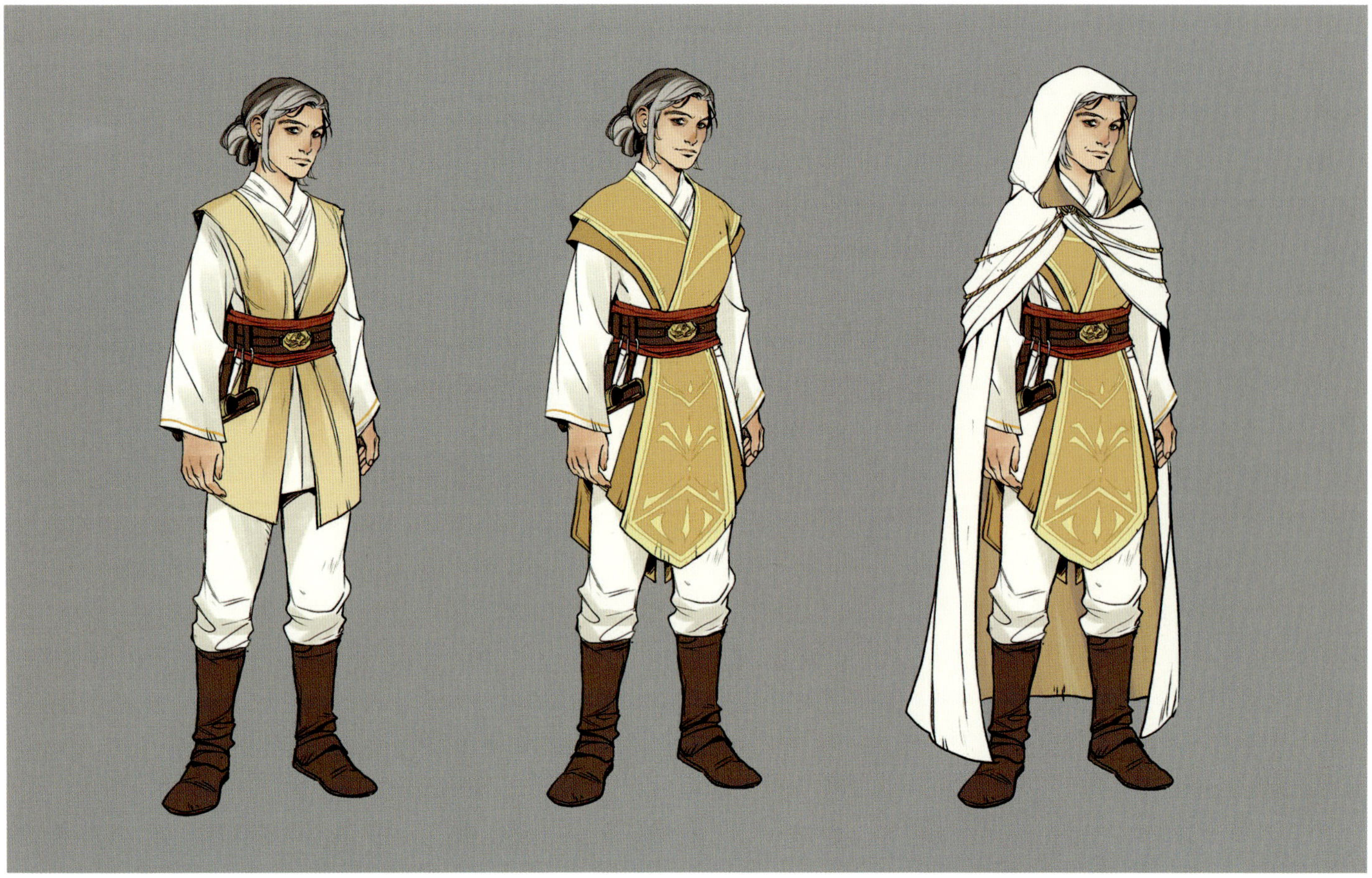

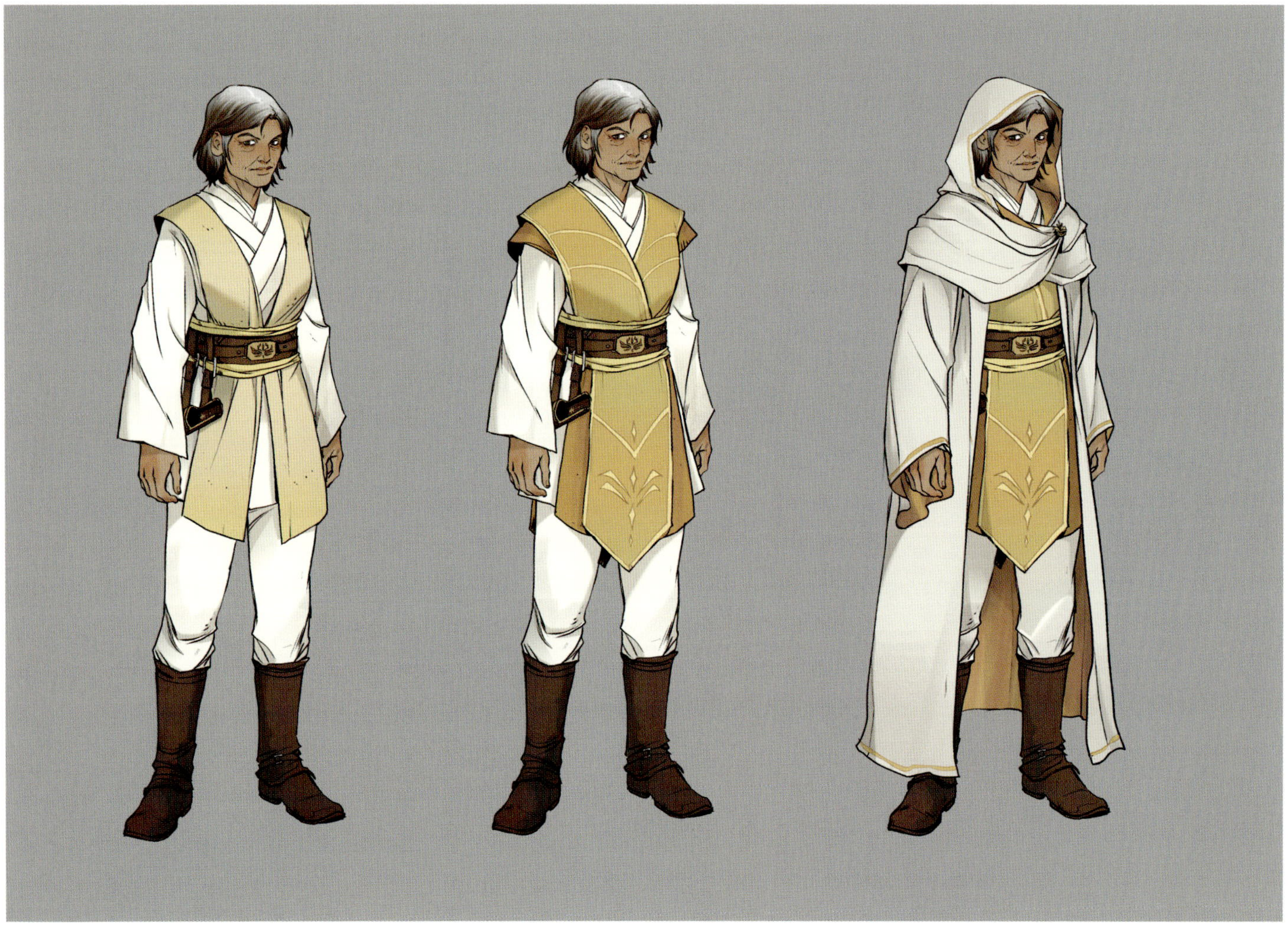

◂ Younger concept and final design of Ada-Li Carro, February and June 2021 SAVARESE

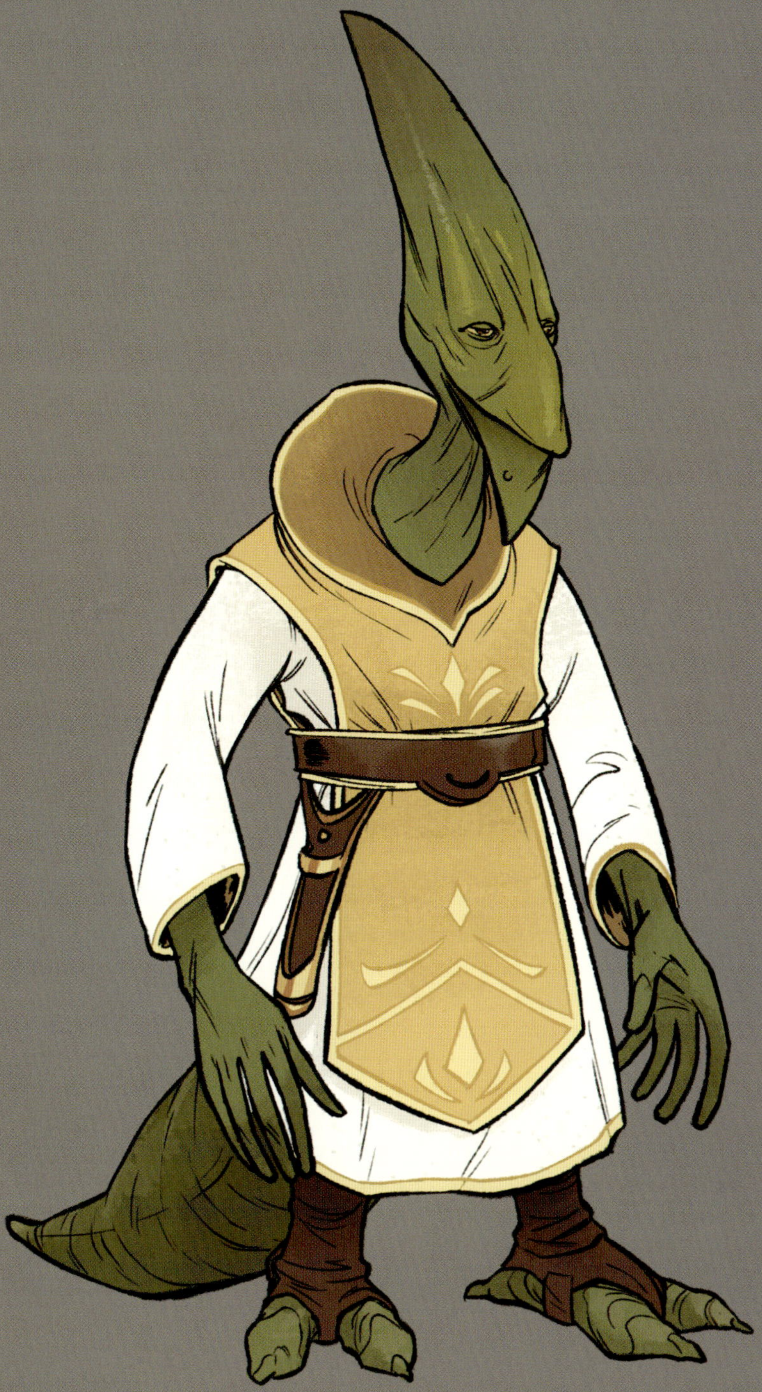

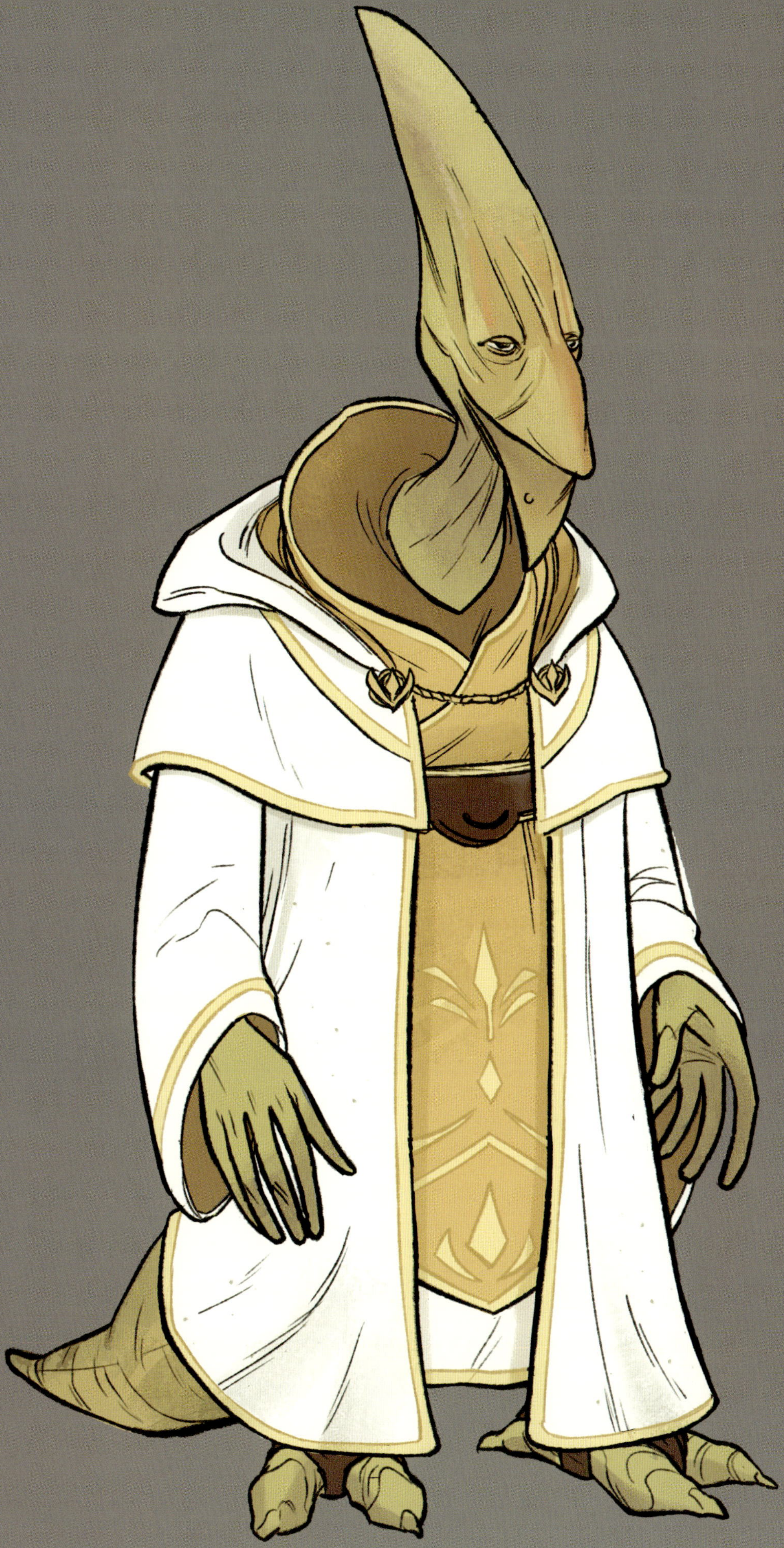

▲ Early concept of Grandmaster Lahru, February 2021 SAVARESE

"Anx is a pretty obscure alien species. There's one watching the race on Tatooine [in Episode I], and I think there's another in the Senate. The character was much taller and proportionally different than is often believed out there in the world. In Episode I, they are taller and less stubby with longer legs than typically depicted." SZOSTAK

► Final design of Grandmaster Lahru, May 2021 SAVARESE

To help differentiate from other green-skinned Council members and better match earlier on-screen aliens of the same species, Szostak suggested the artist make the skin tone a creamy yellow and white.

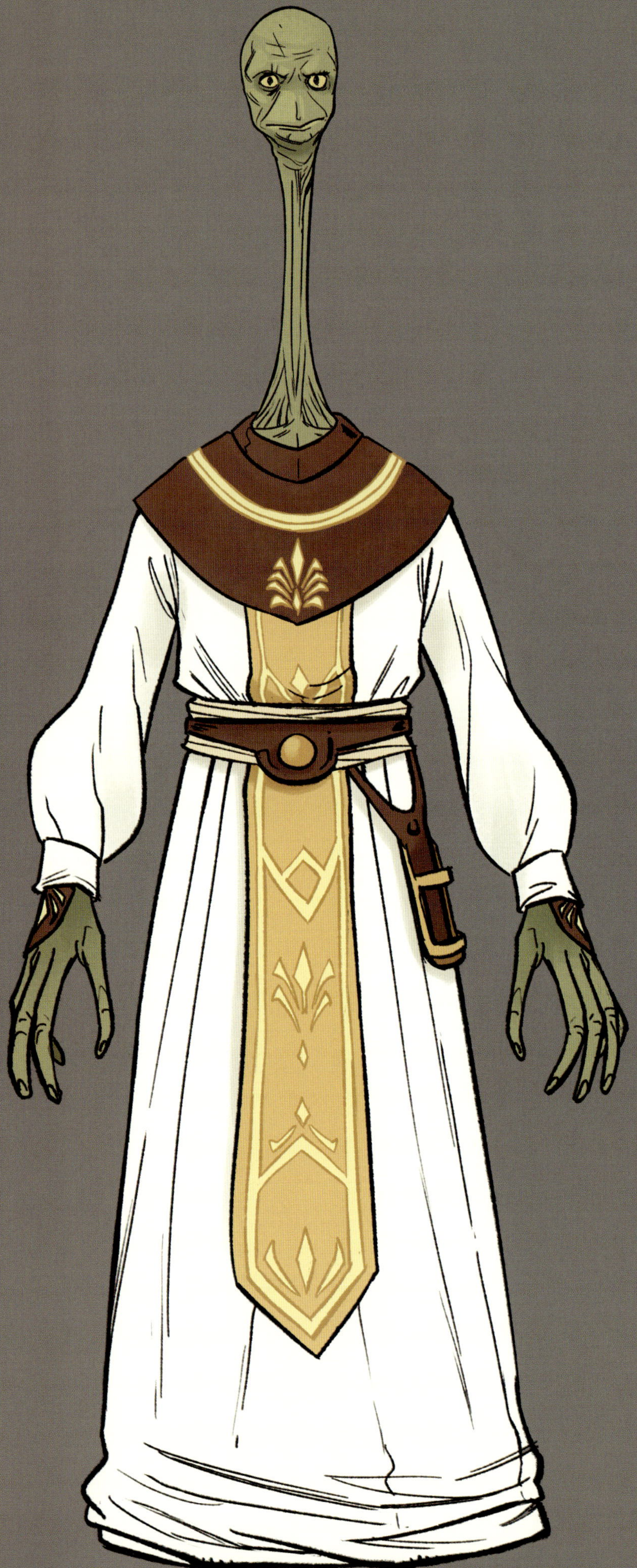

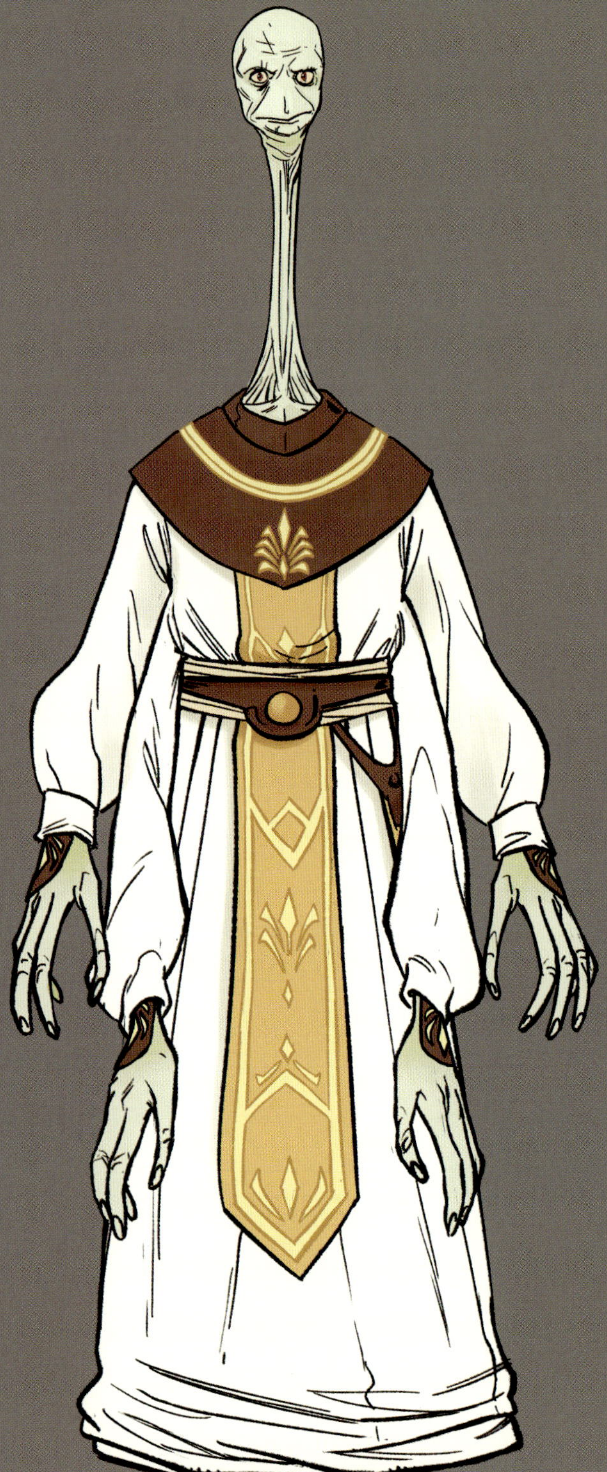

▲ Final design of Grandmaster Yarael Poof, July 2021 SAVARESE

◂ Early concept of Grandmaster Yarael Poof, February 2021 SAVARESE

"We didn't realize that he was supposed to have four arms until the end." THOMAS

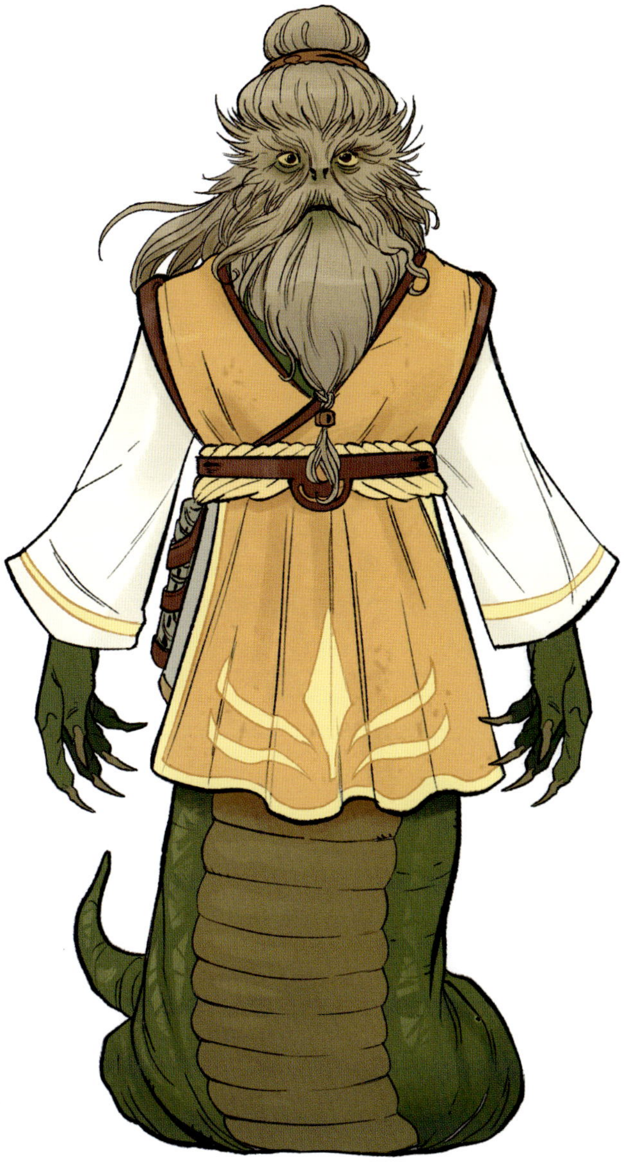

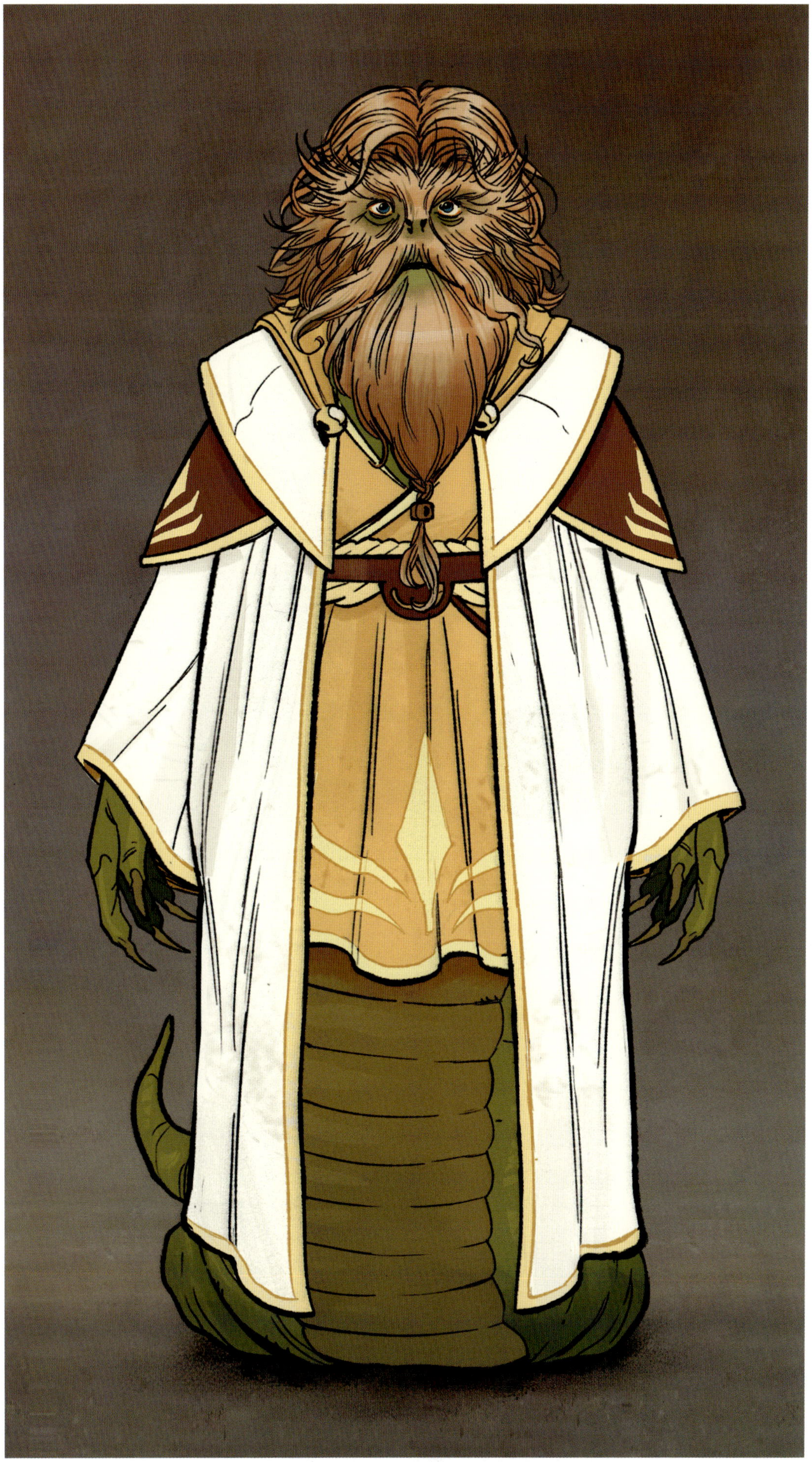

▲ Early concept of Grandmaster Oppo Rancisis, February 2021 SAVARESE

[Pablo] Hidalgo first suggested and sketched an idea to de-age Oppo Rancisis, with Szostak taking inspiration from the strawberry-blond highlights in the original puppet's hair to posit a shift in coloration. "What if during the High Republic he hadn't adopted the hair bun yet, and it was more Sam Elliott in *Roadhouse*?" Hidalgo asked.

► Final design of Grandmaster Oppo Rancisis SAVARESE

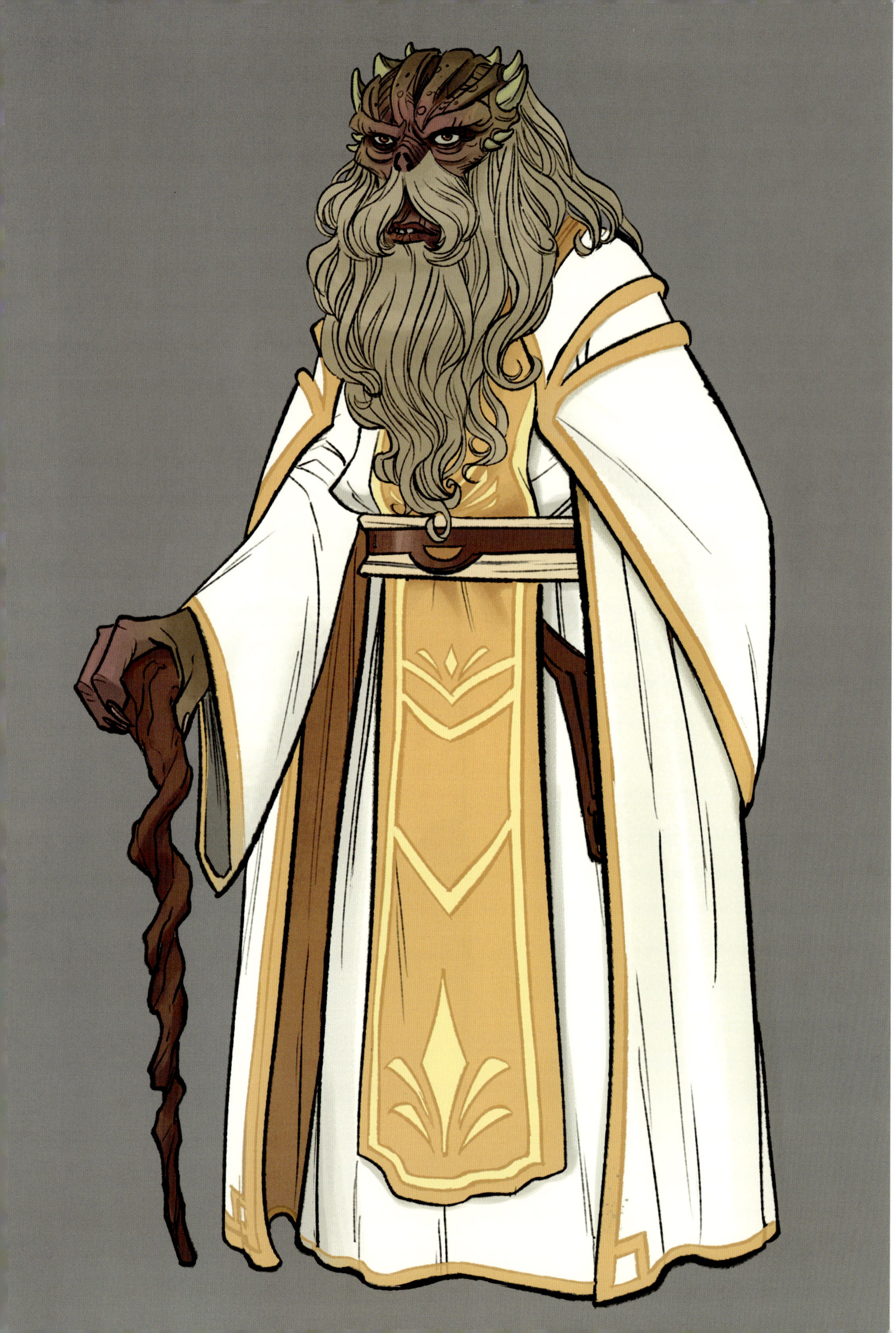

◂ Final design of Grandmaster Pra-Tre Veter, May 2021
ARIO ANINDITO

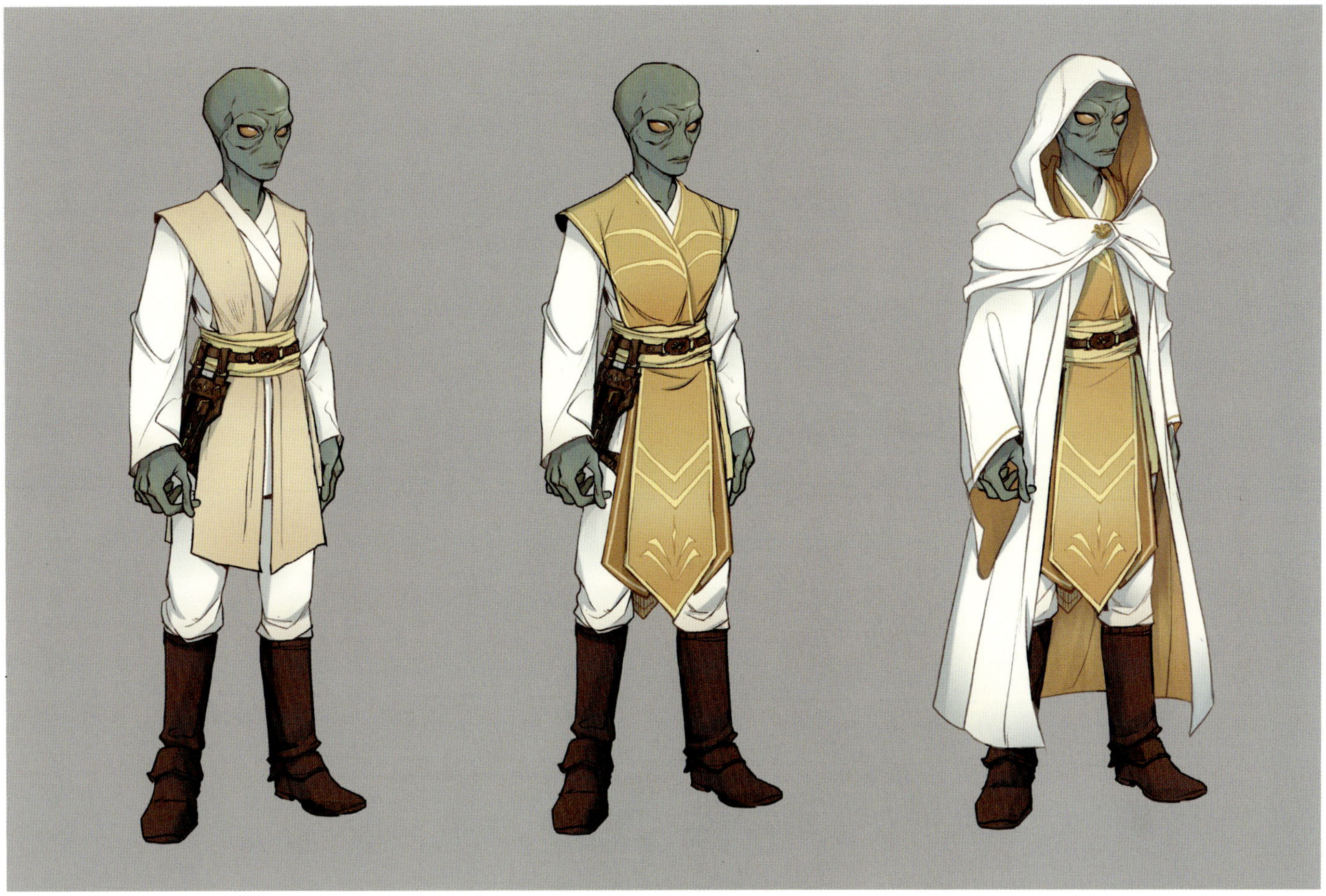

▸ Final design of Grandmaster Rana Kant, May 2021 SAVARESE

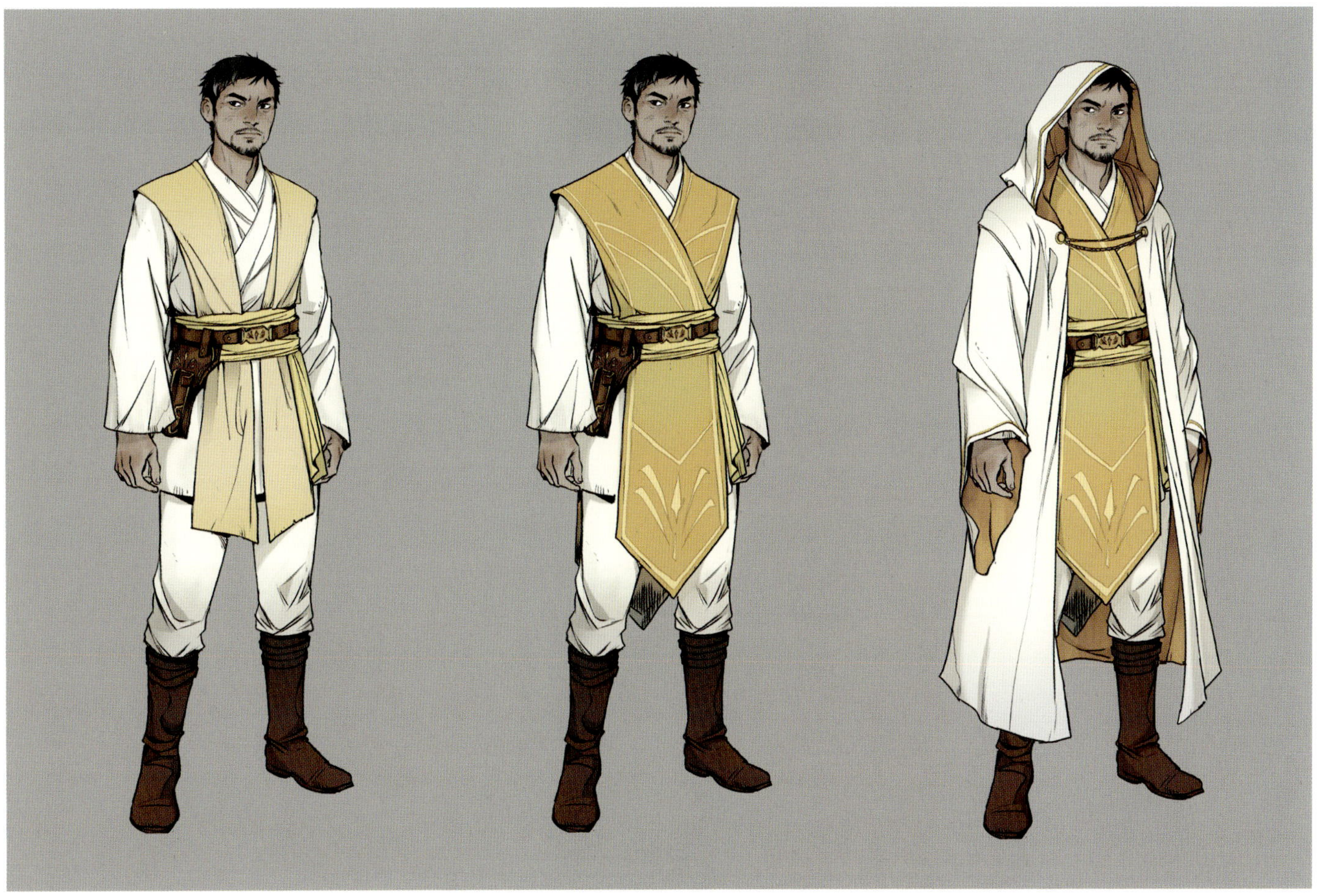

▸ Final design of Grandmaster Ry Ki Sakka, May 2021 SAVARESE

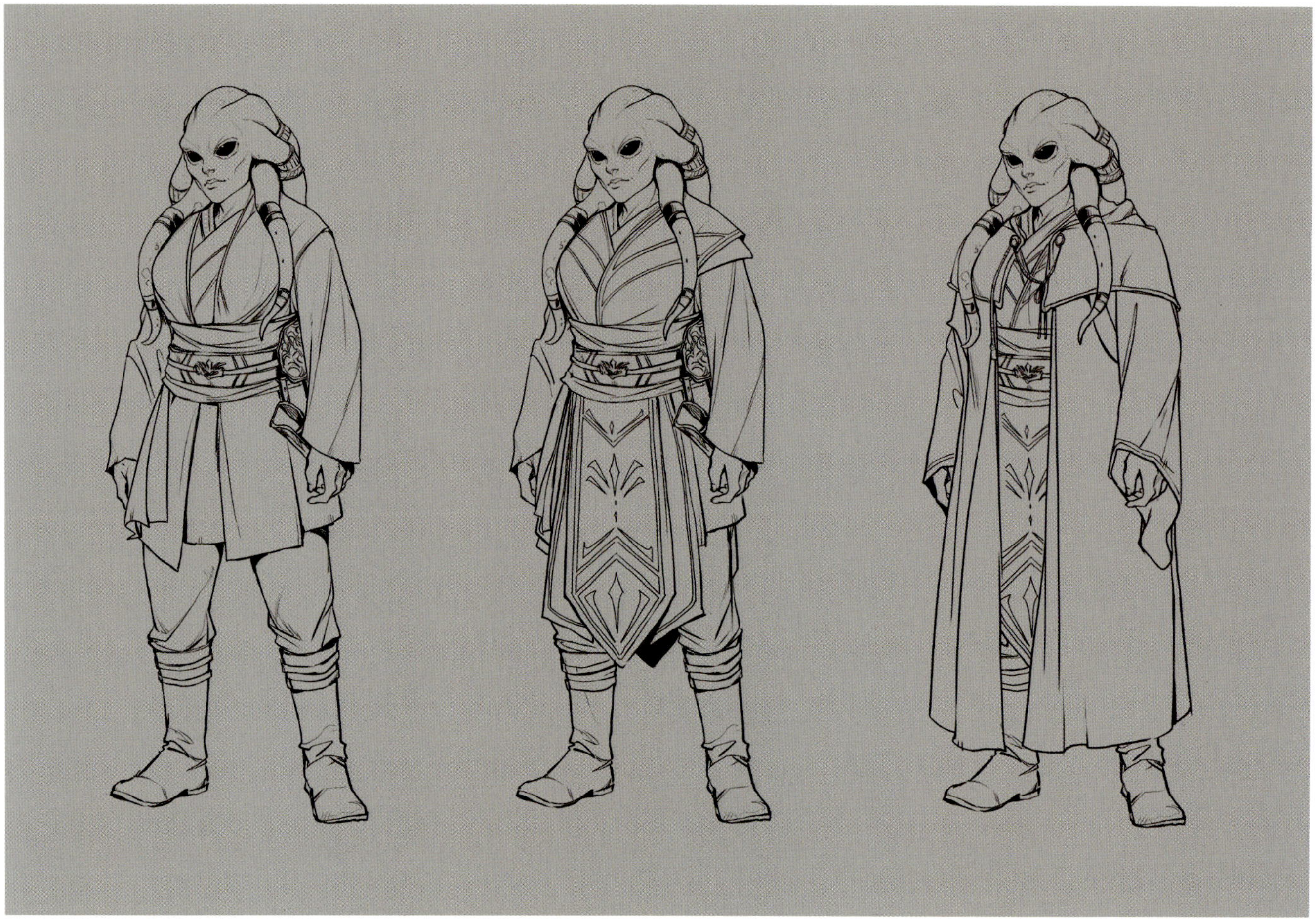

◂ Early concept of Grandmaster Soleil Agra, February 2021 SAVARESE

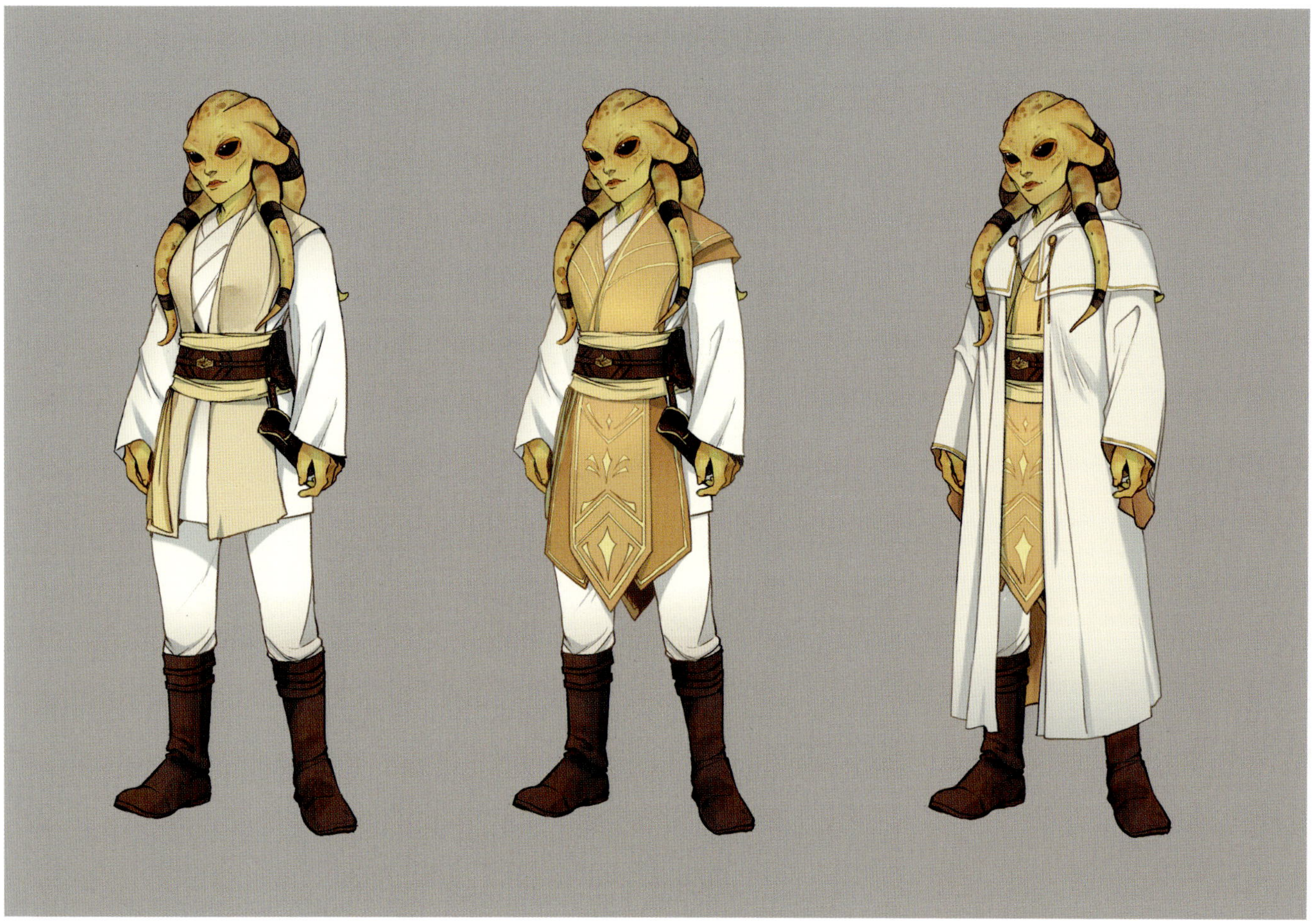

◂ Final design of Grandmaster Soleil Agra, February 2021 SAVARESE

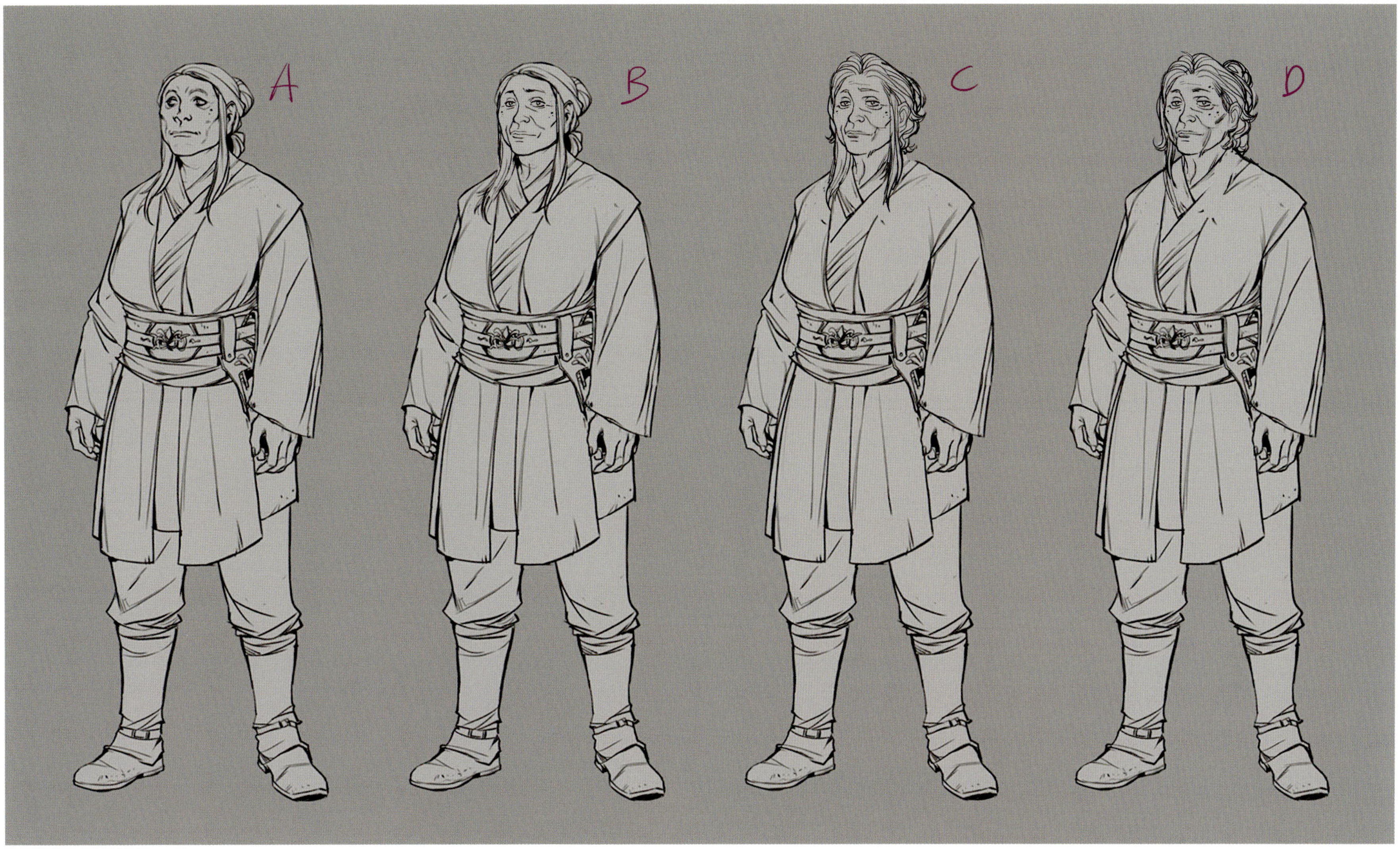

▲ Early concepts of Grandmaster Teri Rosason, February 2021 SAVARESE

"Something George [Lucas] was always very good about historically—not just with the Jedi—was everyone having a silhouette and a color pattern that's just very distinctive. And I think Michael [Siglain] was really pushing to make her one of the most elderly of the Council members to set her further apart from the other human Jedi on the Council." SZOSTAK

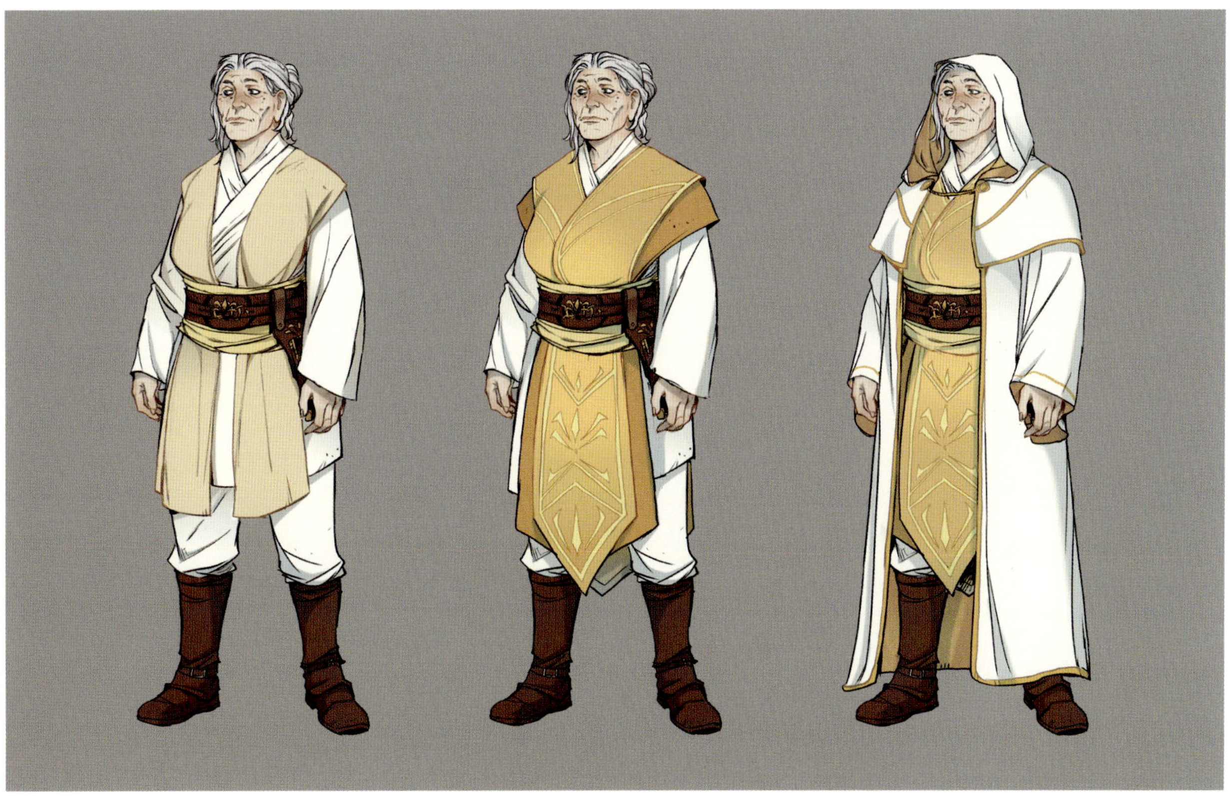

► Final design of Grandmaster Teri Rosason, May 2021 SAVARESE

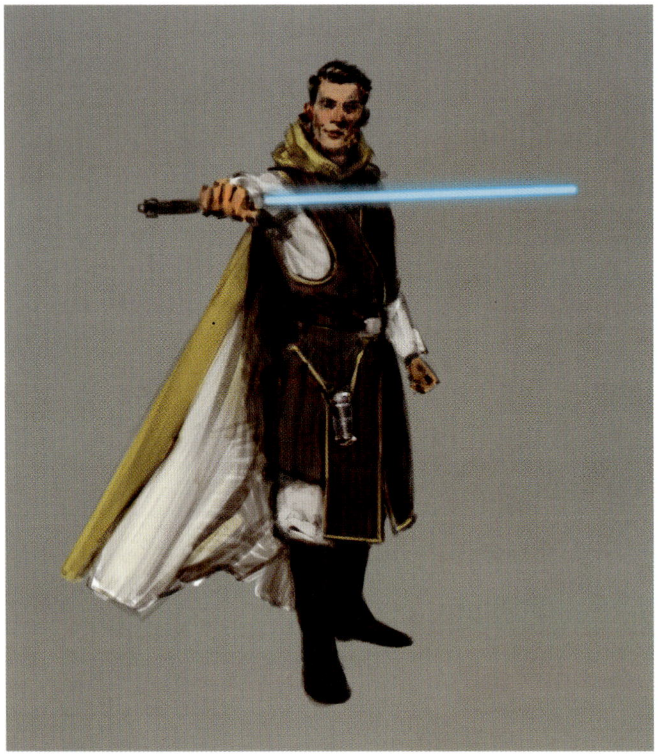

▲ Early concepts of Stellan Gios, November 2019 BARONI

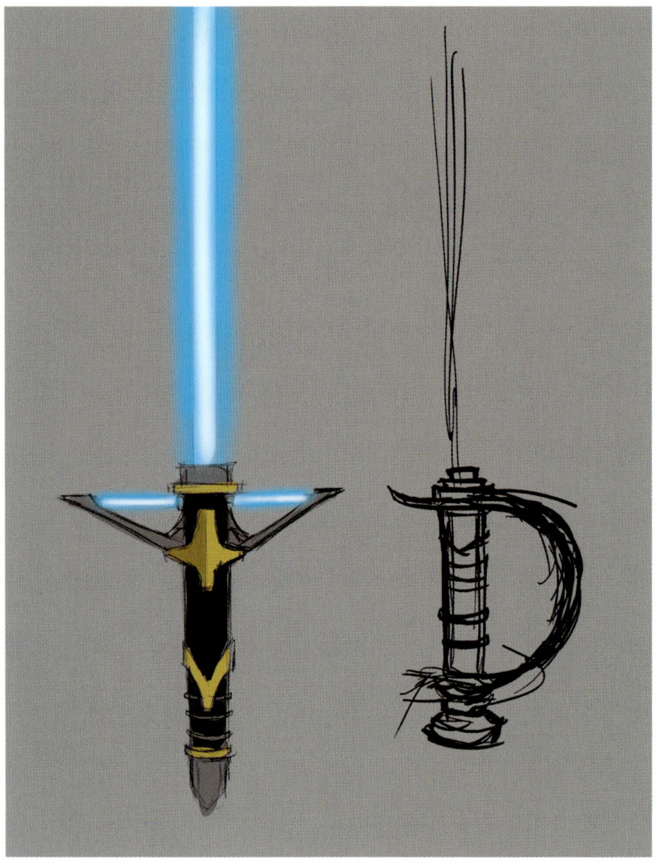

▲ Initial sketch for the lightsaber of Stellan Gios, April 2020
"When I was first told I was going to actually get to work on the High Republic, it was during the pandemic. I had an idea for a lightsaber cross guard, which combined the design of Kylo Ren's with that of a traditional cross guard. During our meeting, I did a quick twenty-second sketch. I really like the idea of Kylo Ren's lightsaber, but it always bugged me that I felt like he would cut himself up." THOMAS

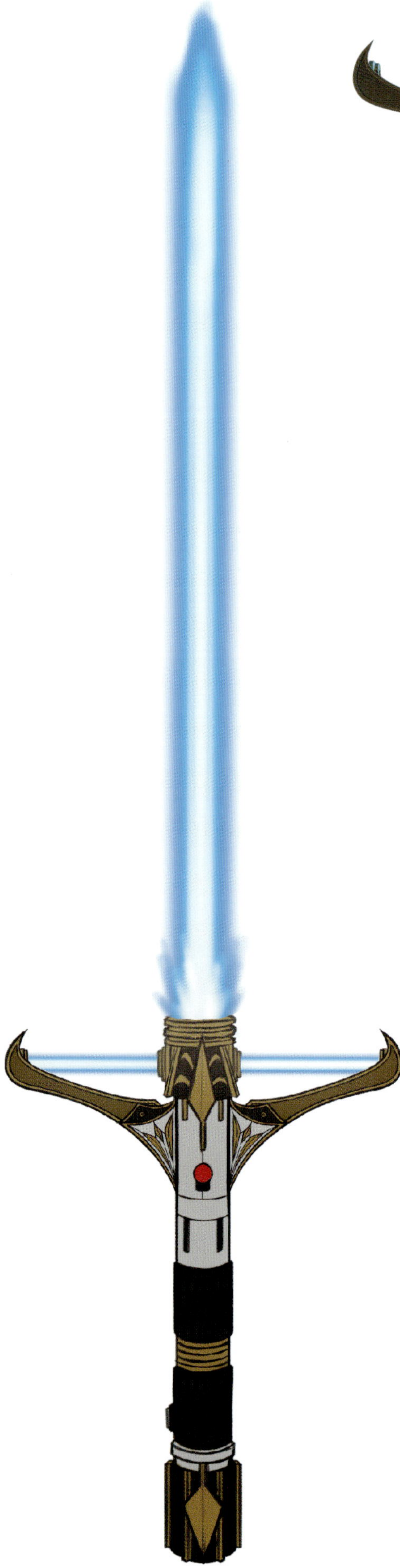

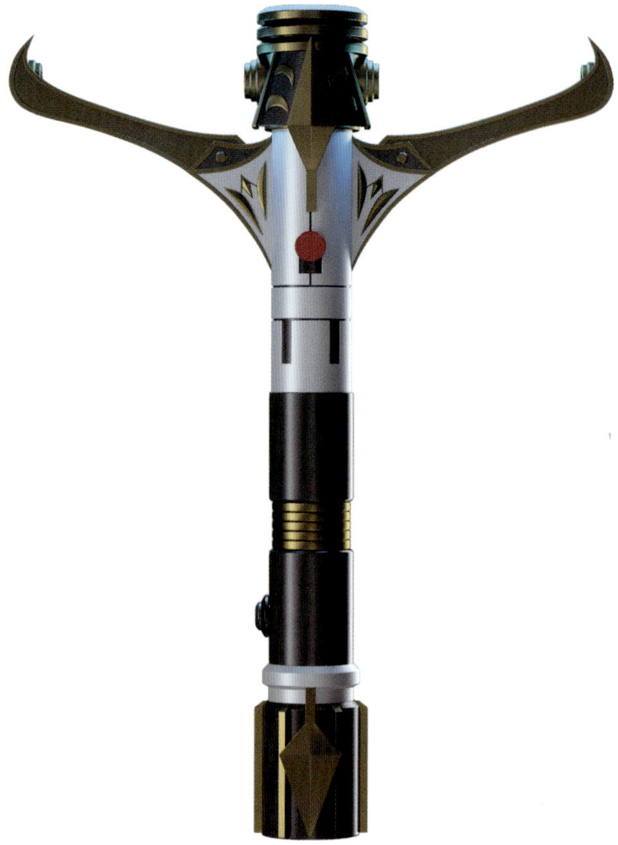

▲ Lightsaber hilt design for Stellan Gios ŁUKASZ LISZKO

▼ Lightsaber holster design for Stellan Gios THOMAS

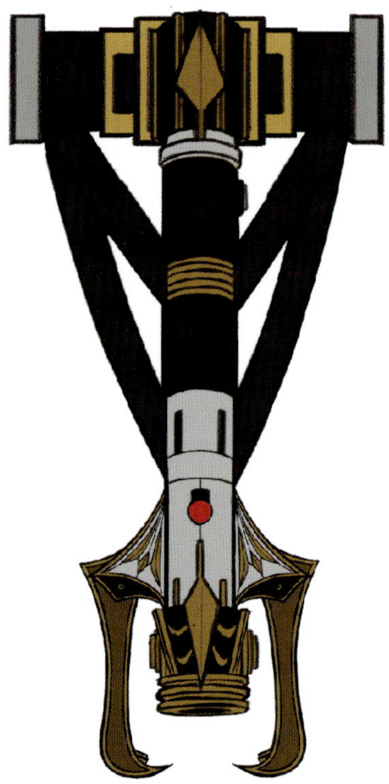

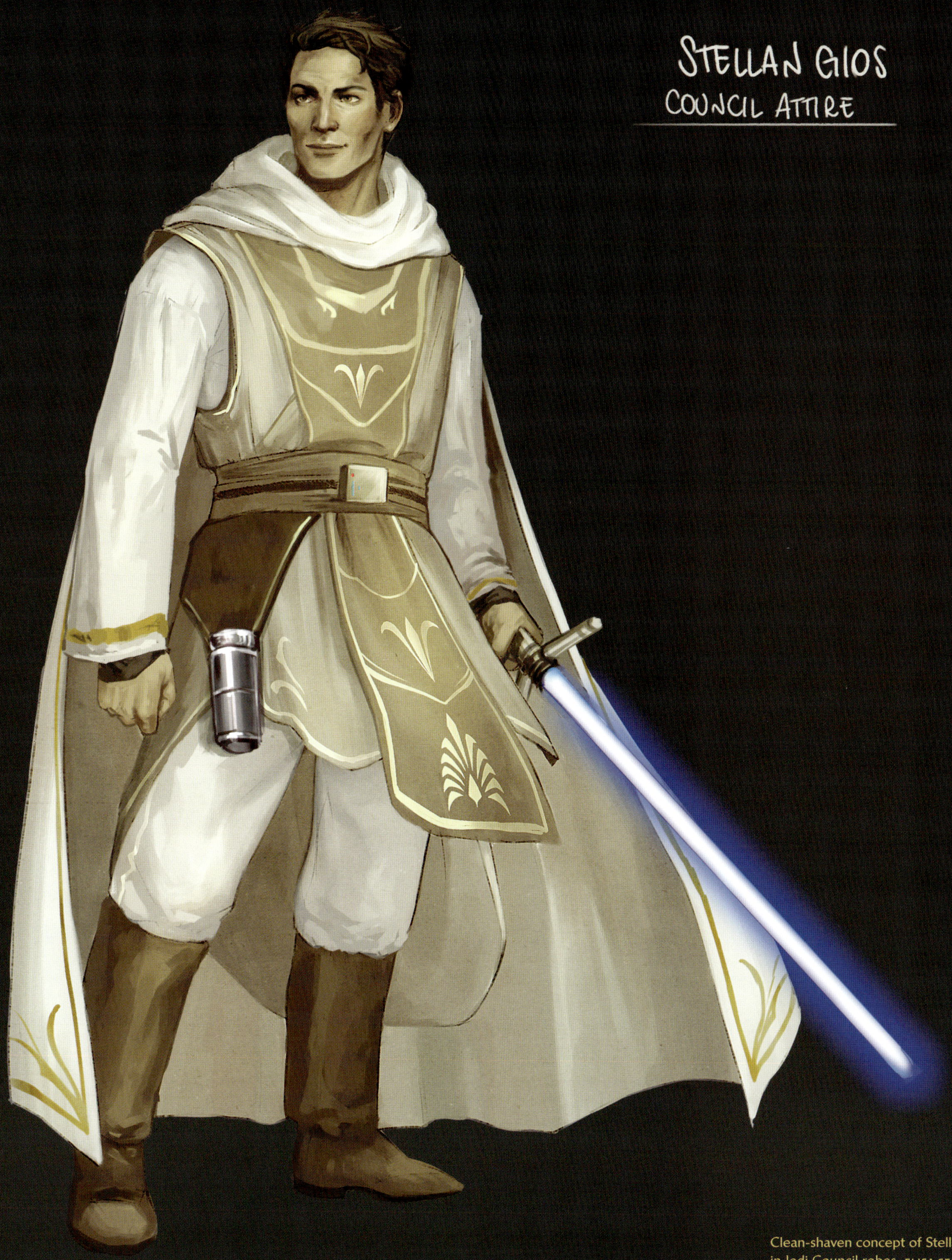

Clean-shaven concept of Stellan Gios in Jedi Council robes ELISA SERIO

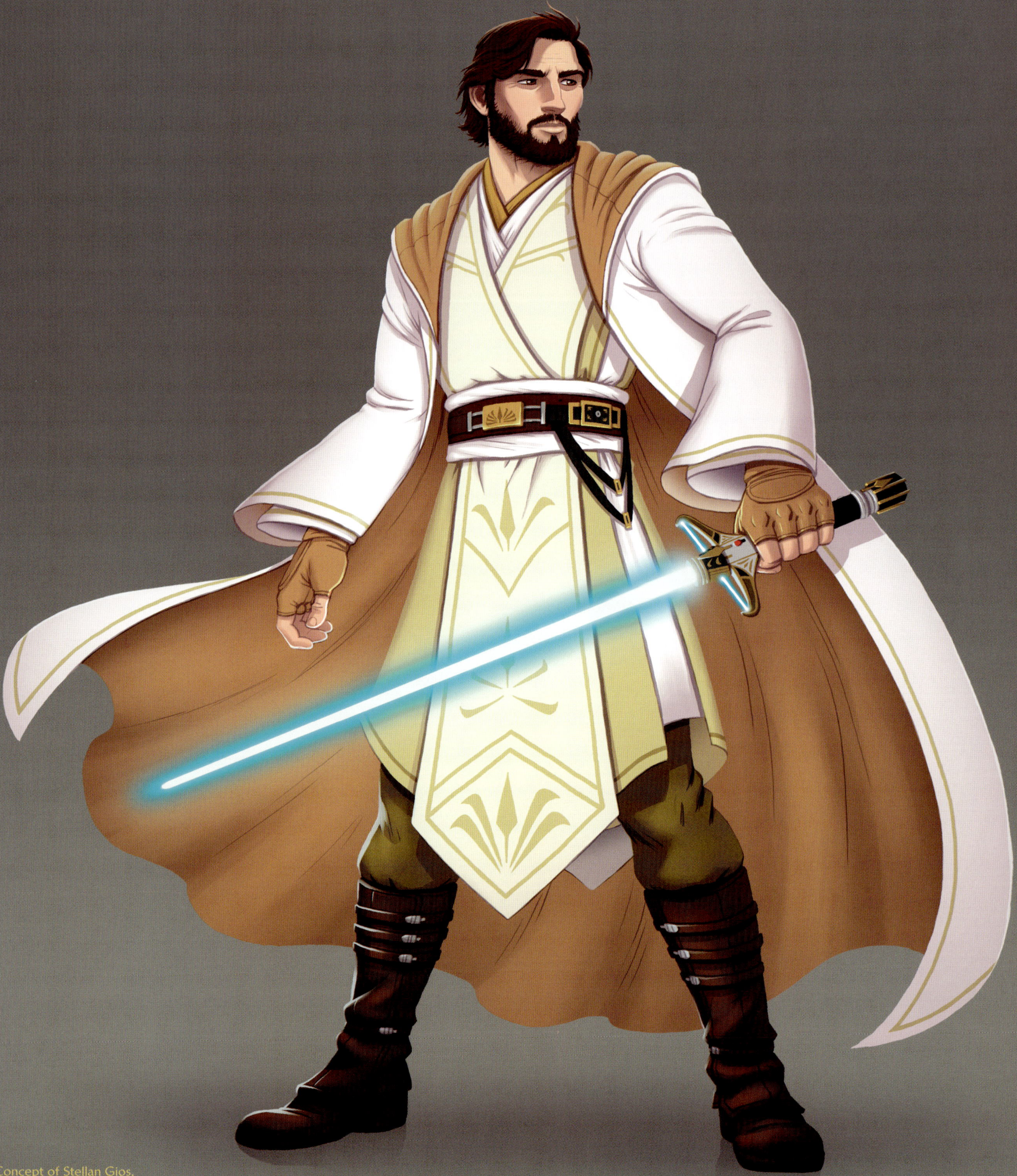

Concept of Stellan Gios,
September 2020 ANTONSSON

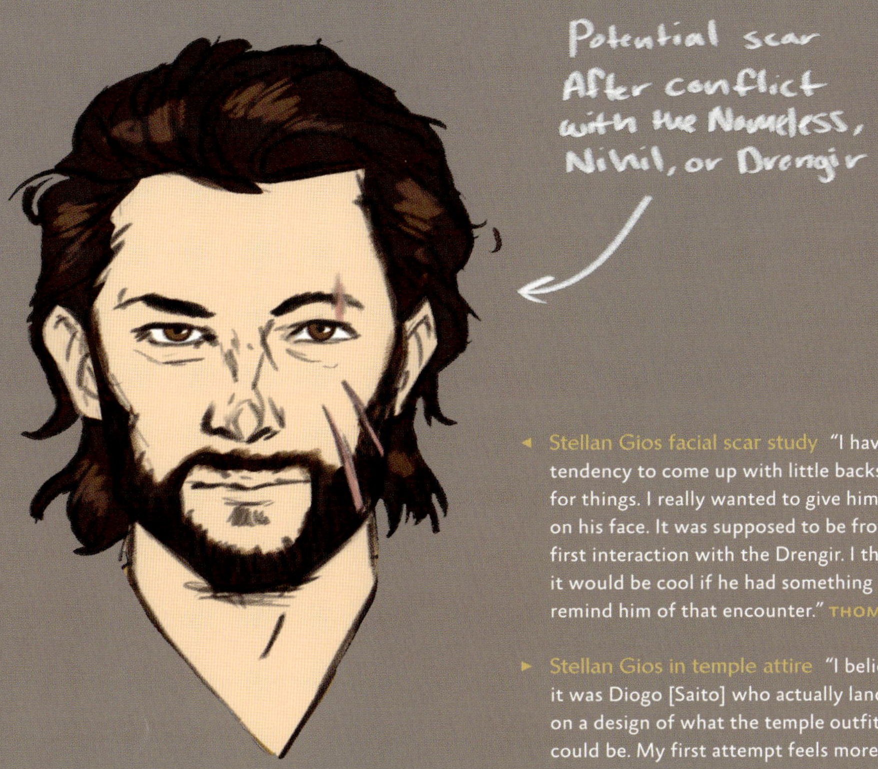

◄ Stellan Gios facial scar study "I have a tendency to come up with little backstories for things. I really wanted to give him a scar on his face. It was supposed to be from his first interaction with the Drengir. I thought it would be cool if he had something to remind him of that encounter." THOMAS

► Stellan Gios in temple attire "I believe it was Diogo [Saito] who actually landed on a design of what the temple outfits could be. My first attempt feels more like a Catholic priest or something like a Knight Templar." THOMAS

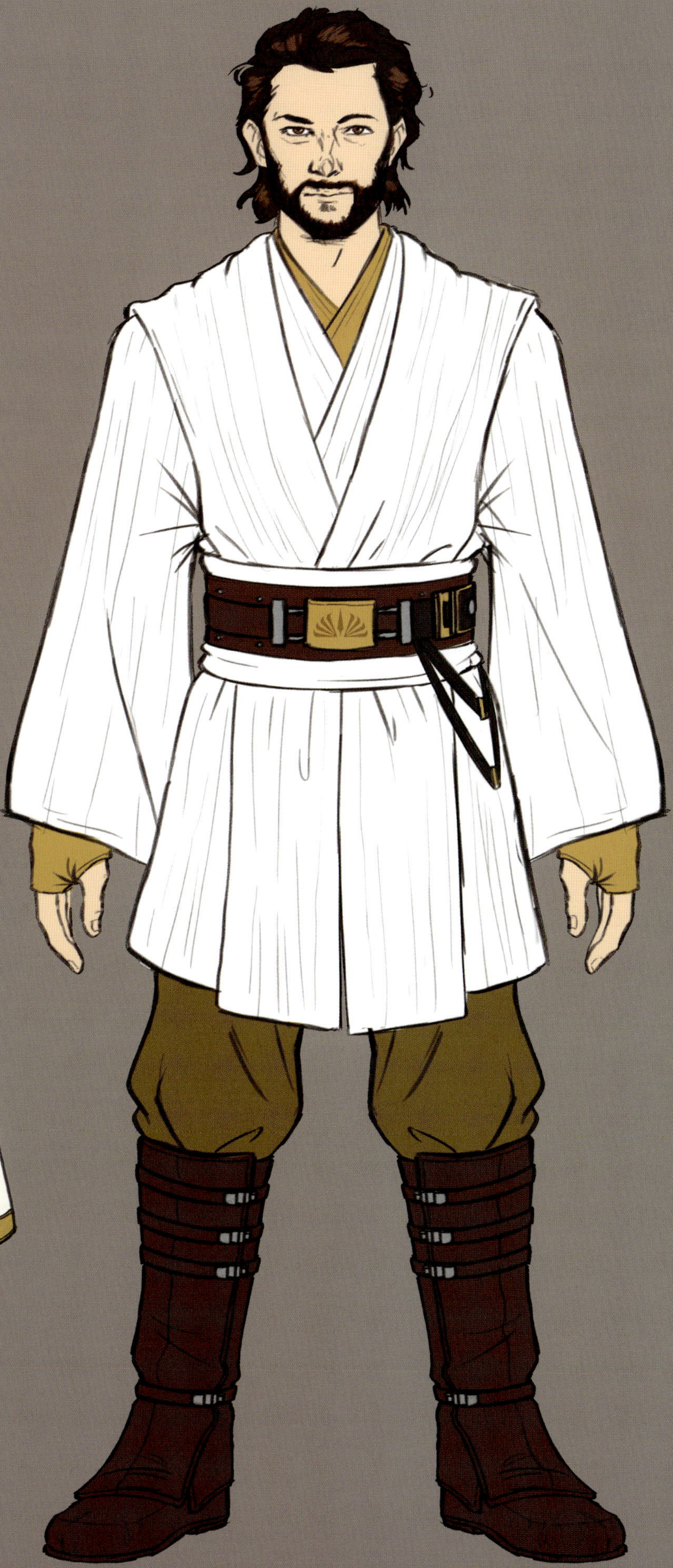

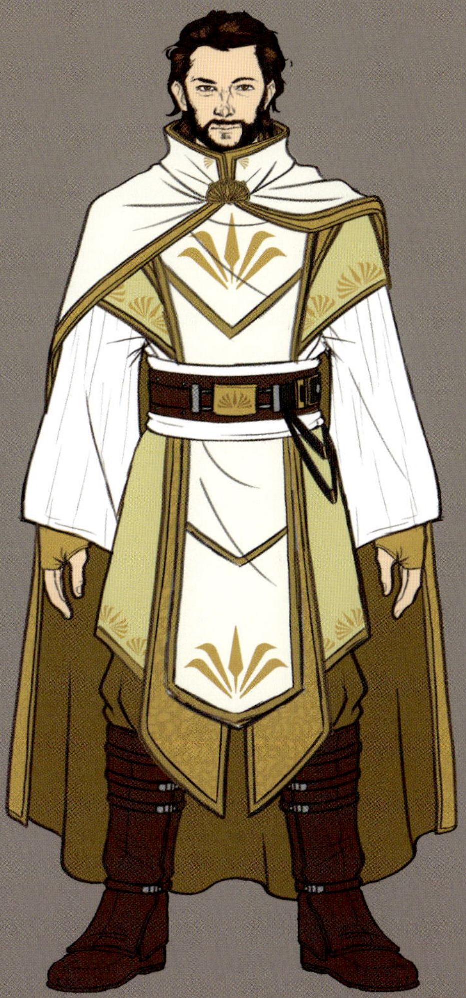

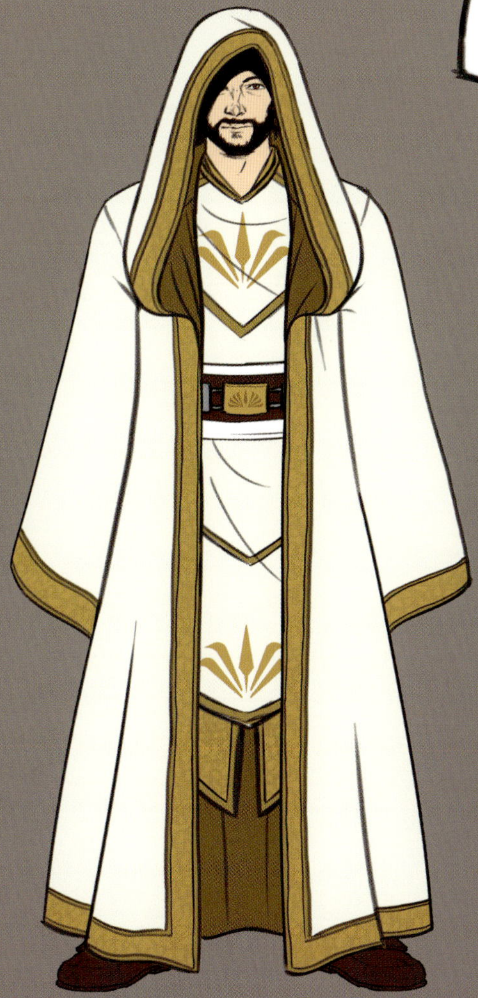

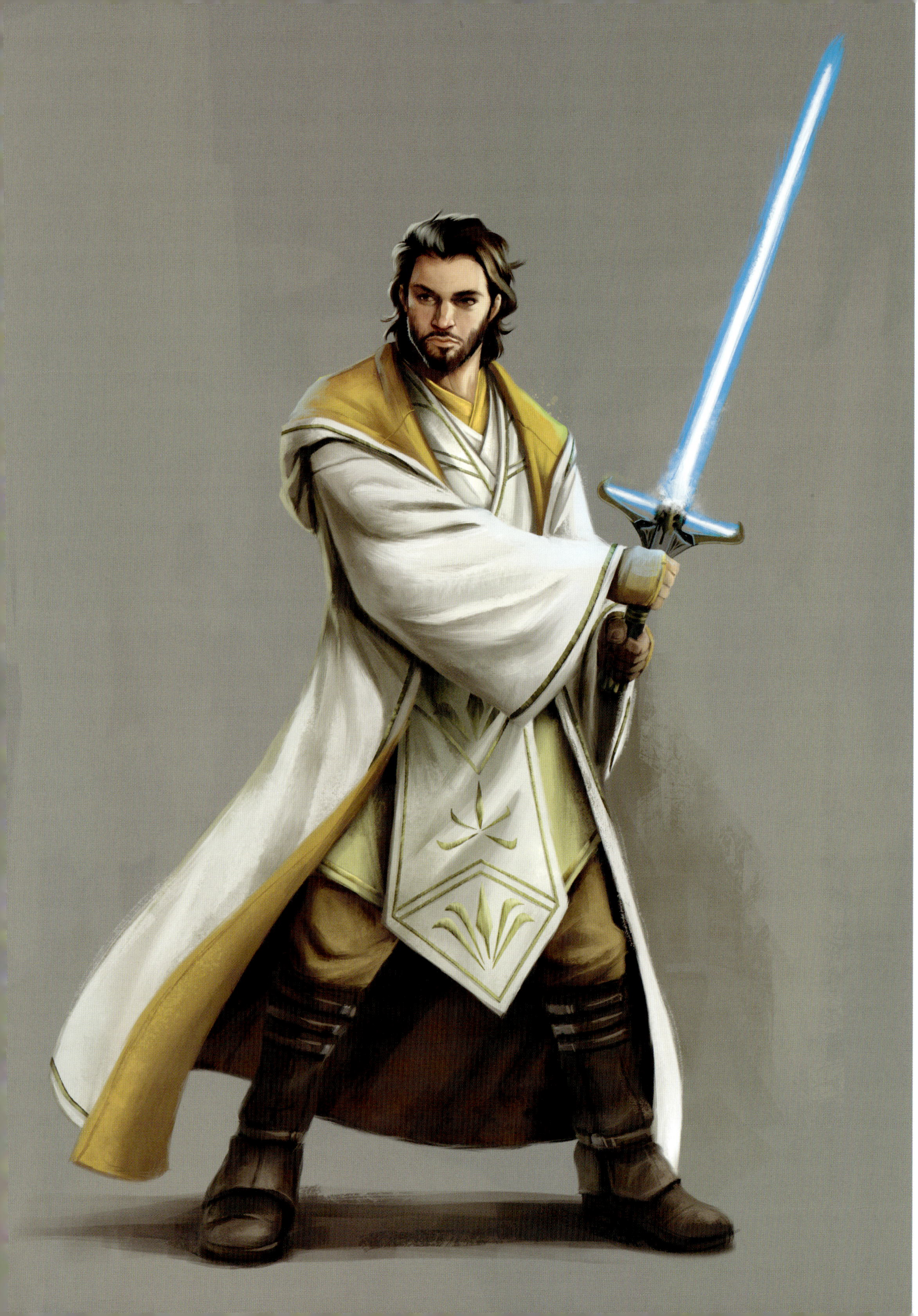

◂ Concept of Jedi Council member Stellan Gios DIOGO SAITO AND ADRIENNE BROWN

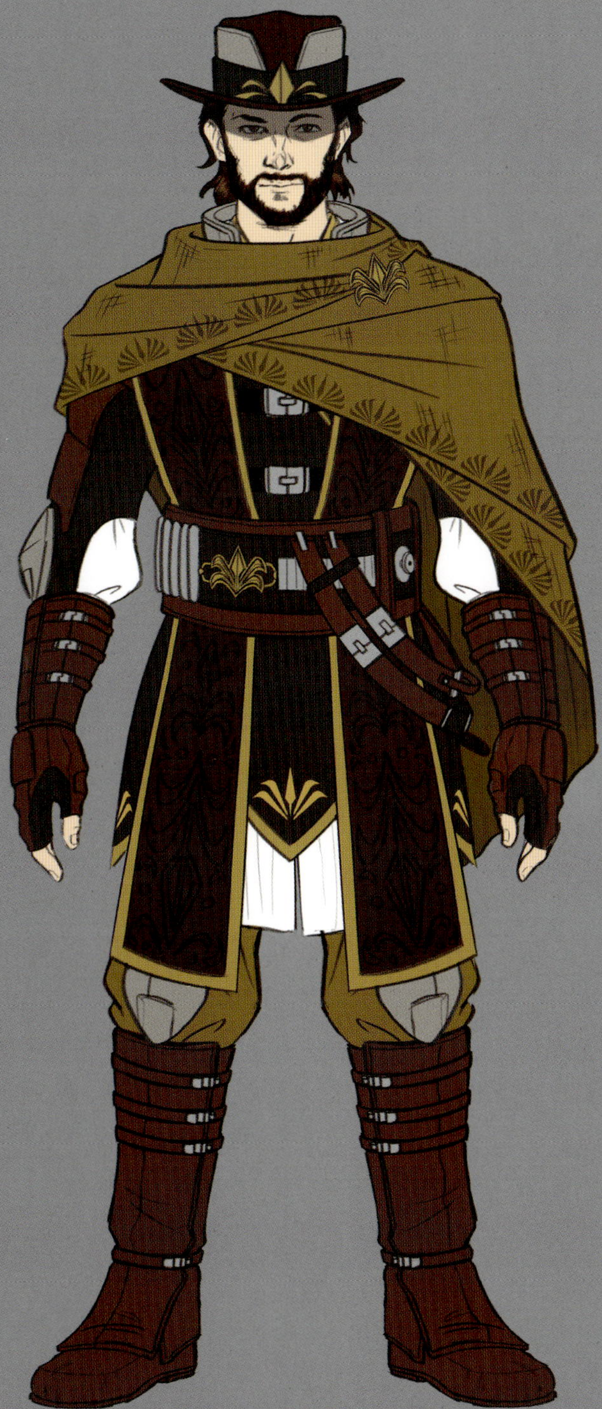

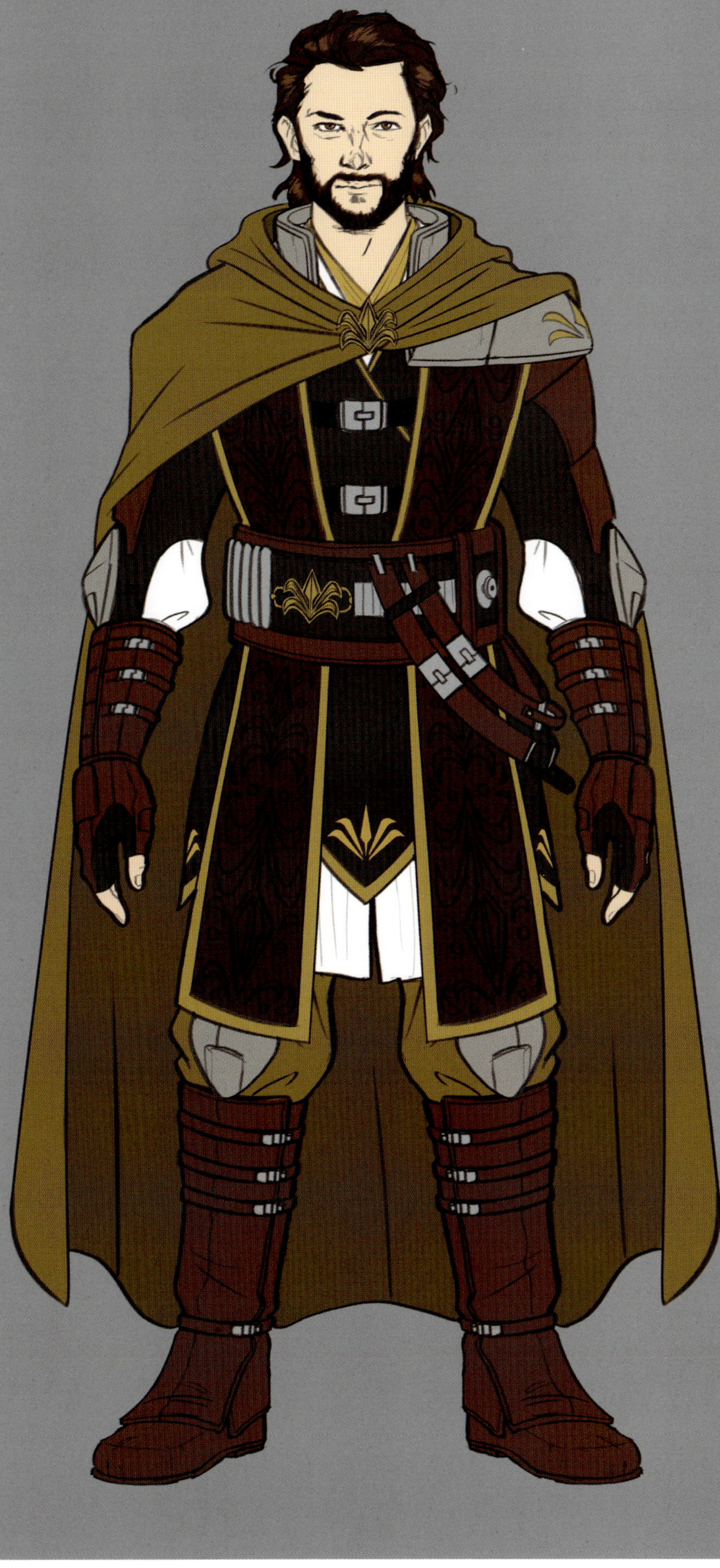

▲ Stellan Gios in Western gear "For Stellan, I actually designed his face and, for some reason, gunslinger came to mind. I really like Cad Bane [the bounty hunter in *Star Wars: The Clone Wars* and *The Book of Boba Fett*], and since he's someone that has a cowboy hat in the *Star Wars* universe already, it wouldn't be too crazy to try and do that. It was a little too far, though." THOMAS

▸ Stellan Gios in mission attire "This was supposed to kind of evoke more of a Robin Hood kind of feel." THOMAS

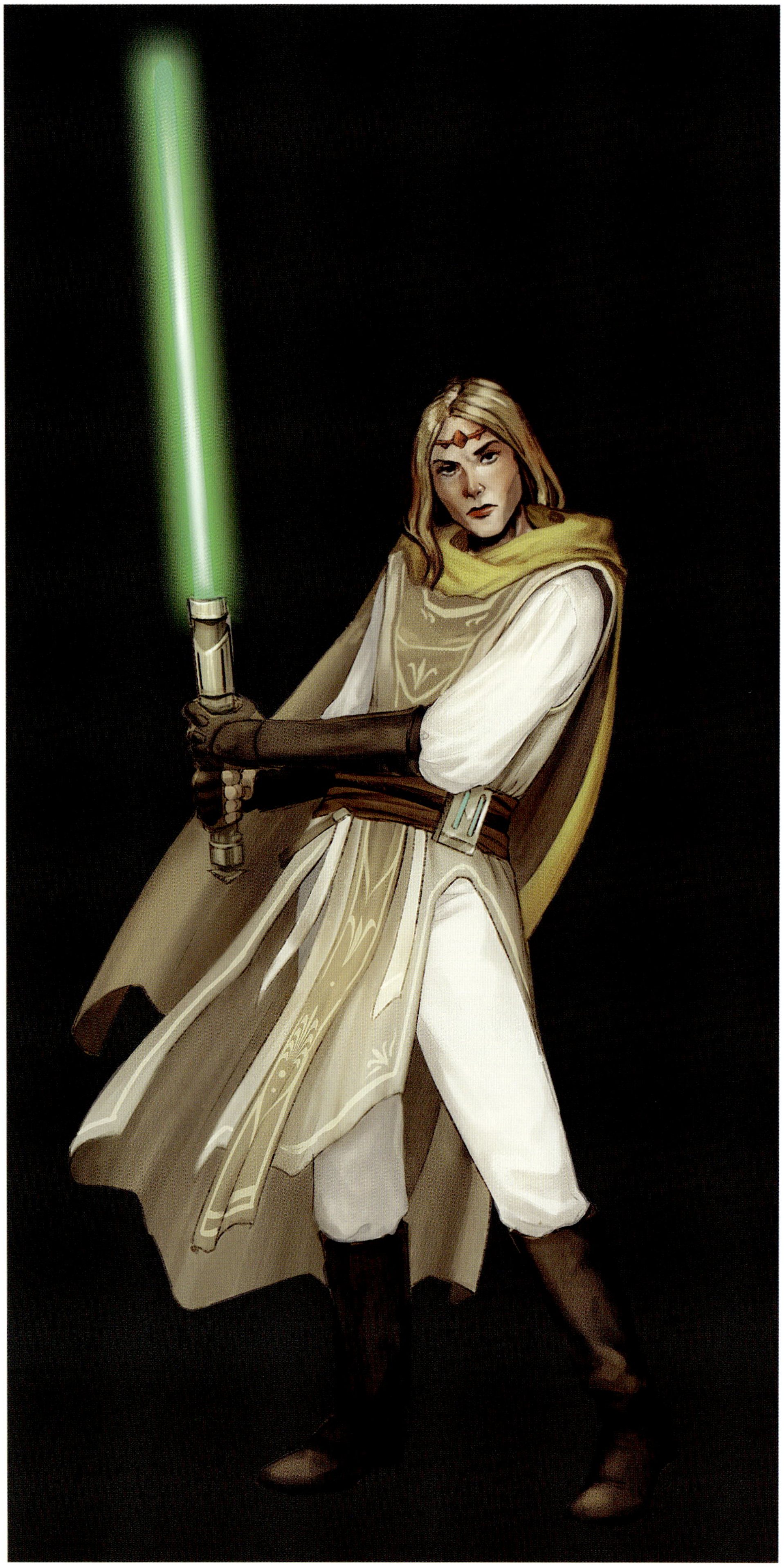

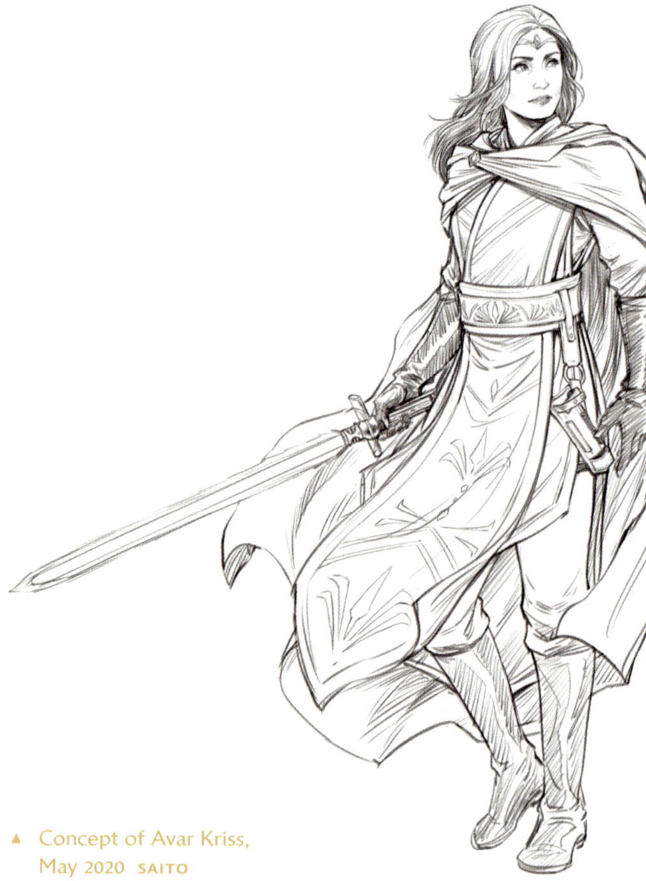

▲ Concept of Avar Kriss, May 2020 SAITO

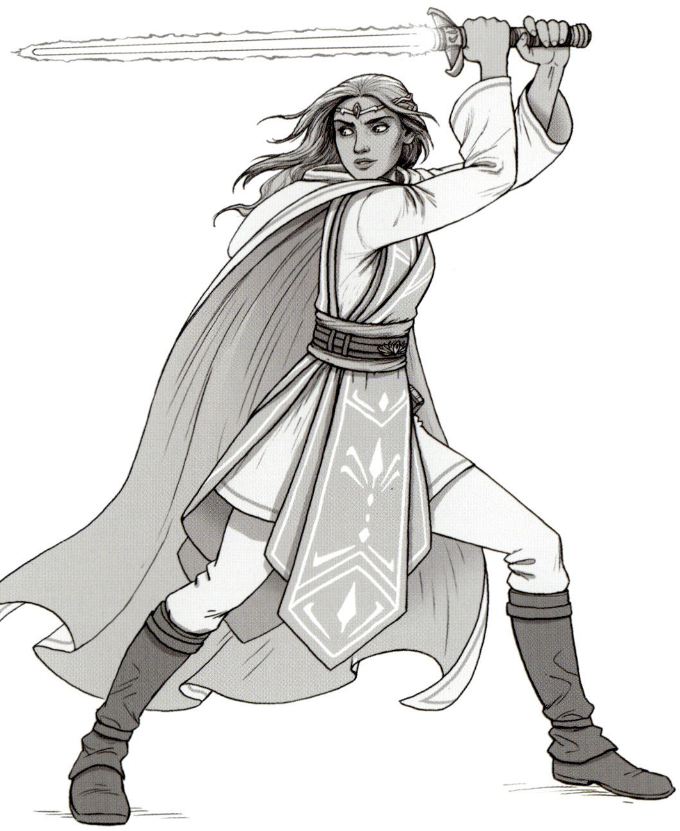

▲ Concept of Avar Kriss, August 2020 ANTONSSON

◂ Early concept of Avar Kriss SERIO

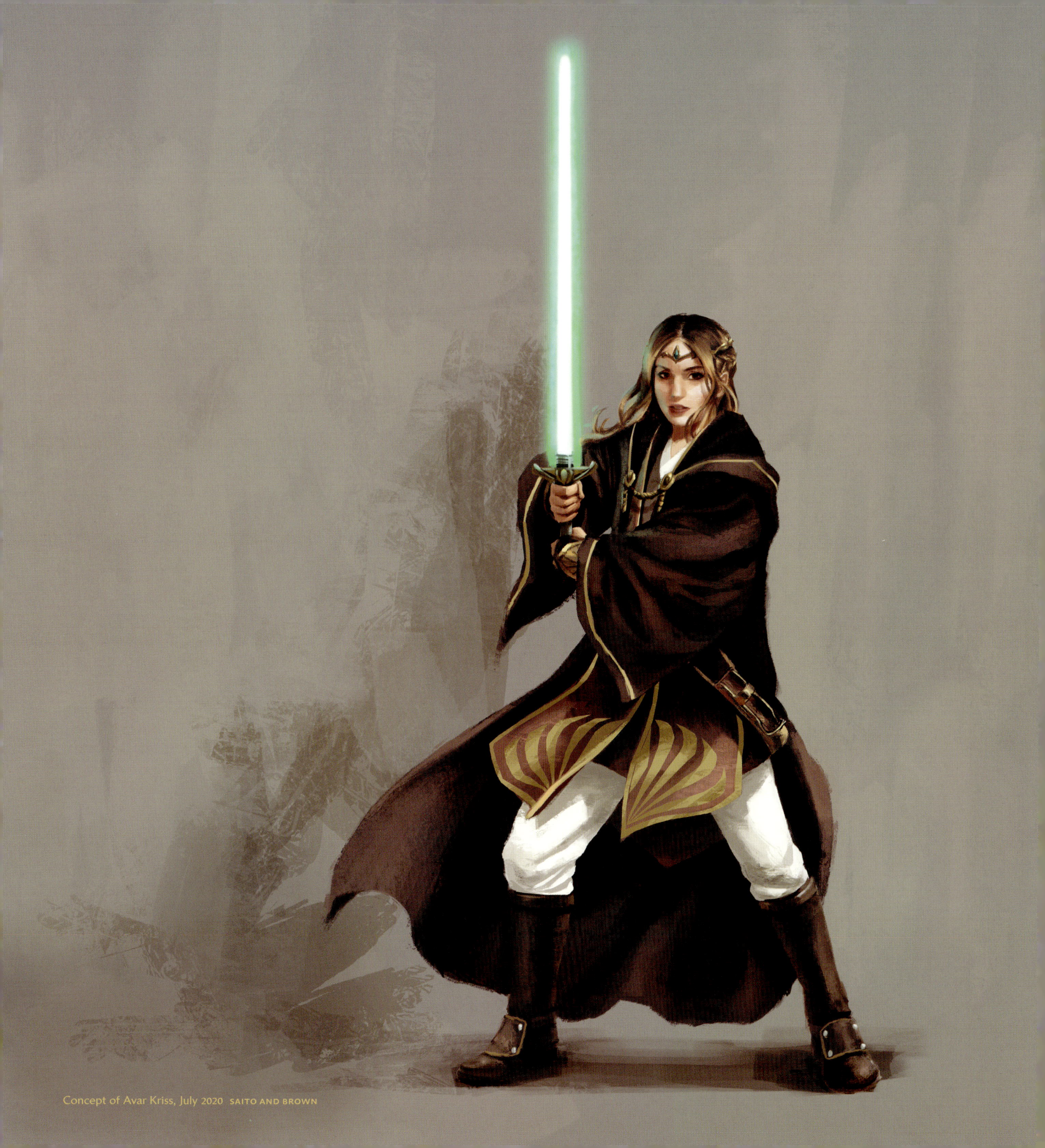

Concept of Avar Kriss, July 2020 SAITO AND BROWN

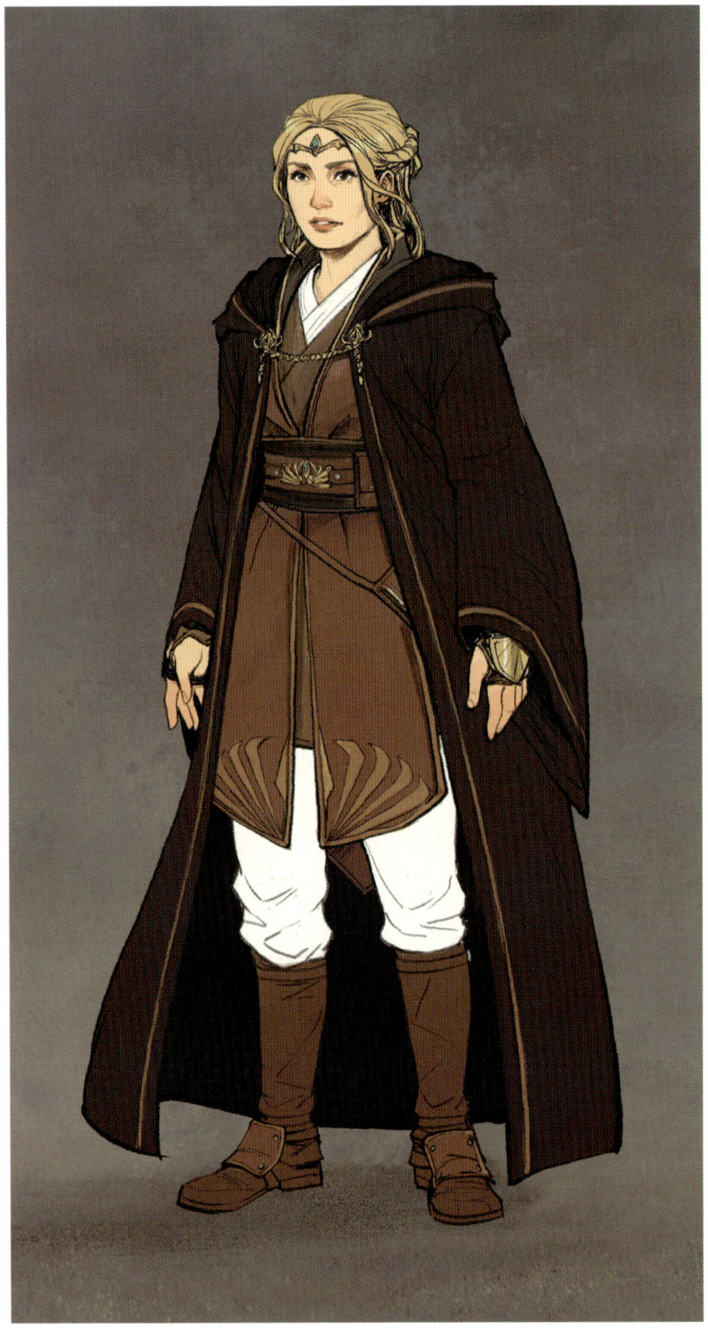

▲ Final design of Avar Kriss mission gear SAITO

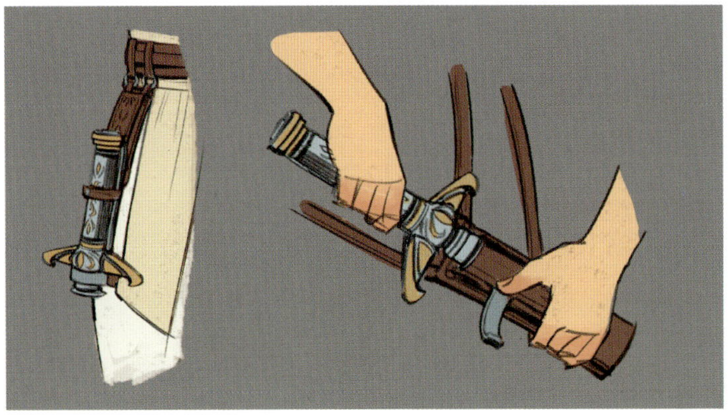

▲ Concept of Avar Kriss's lightsaber holster SAITO

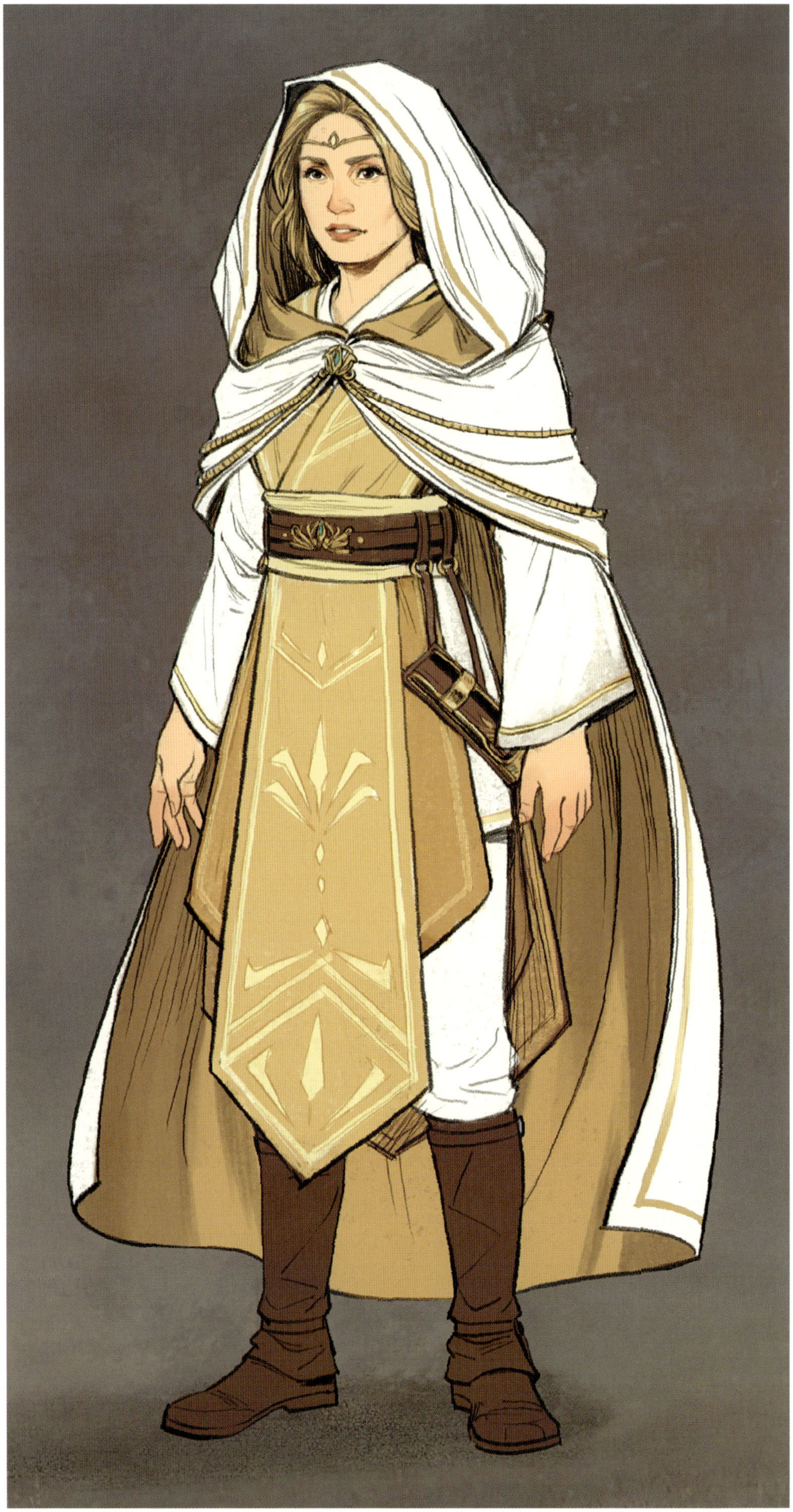

► Final designs of Avar Kriss formal attire SAITO

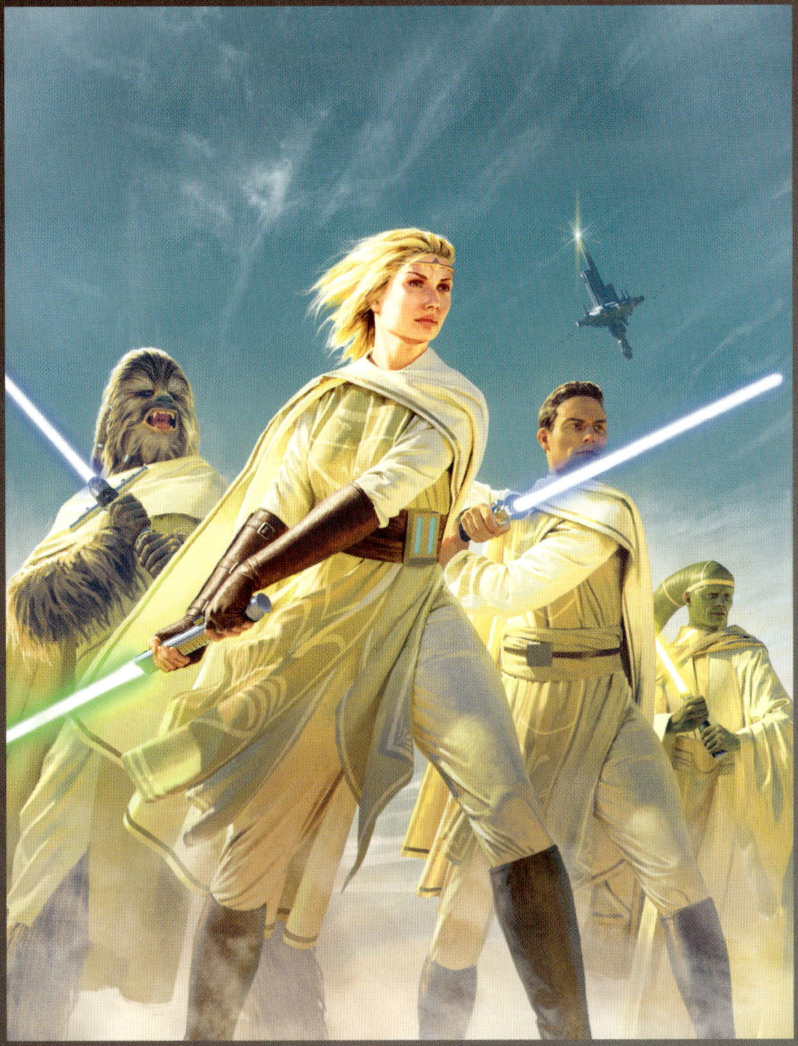

▲ Cover art for *Star Wars: Light of the Jedi* MEEHAN

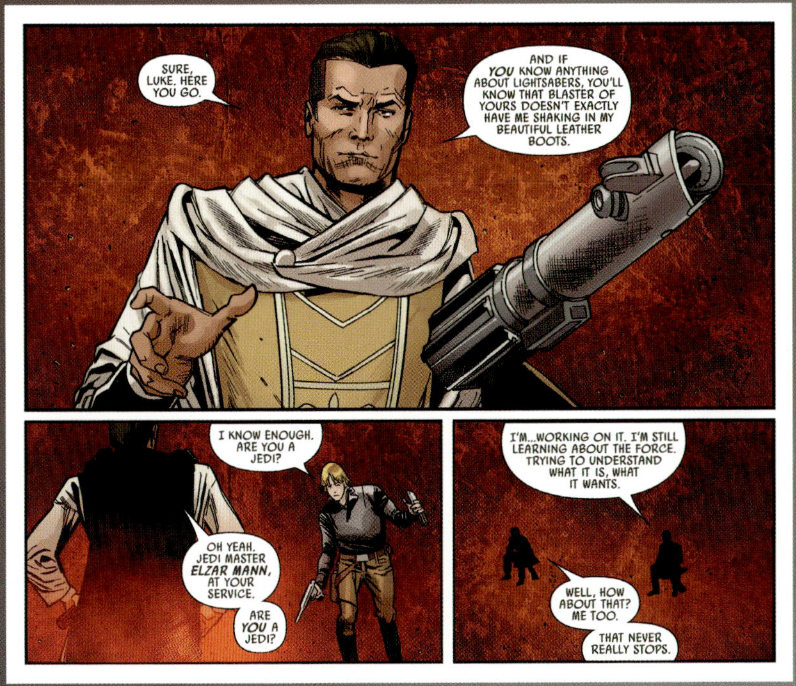

▲ Panels from Marvel's *Star Wars* (2020) #20 MARCO CASTIELLO (PENCILER), RACHELLE ROSENBERG (COLORIST), AND VC'S CLAYTON COWLES (LETTERER)

▸ Final concept of Elzar Mann TOMATOFARM

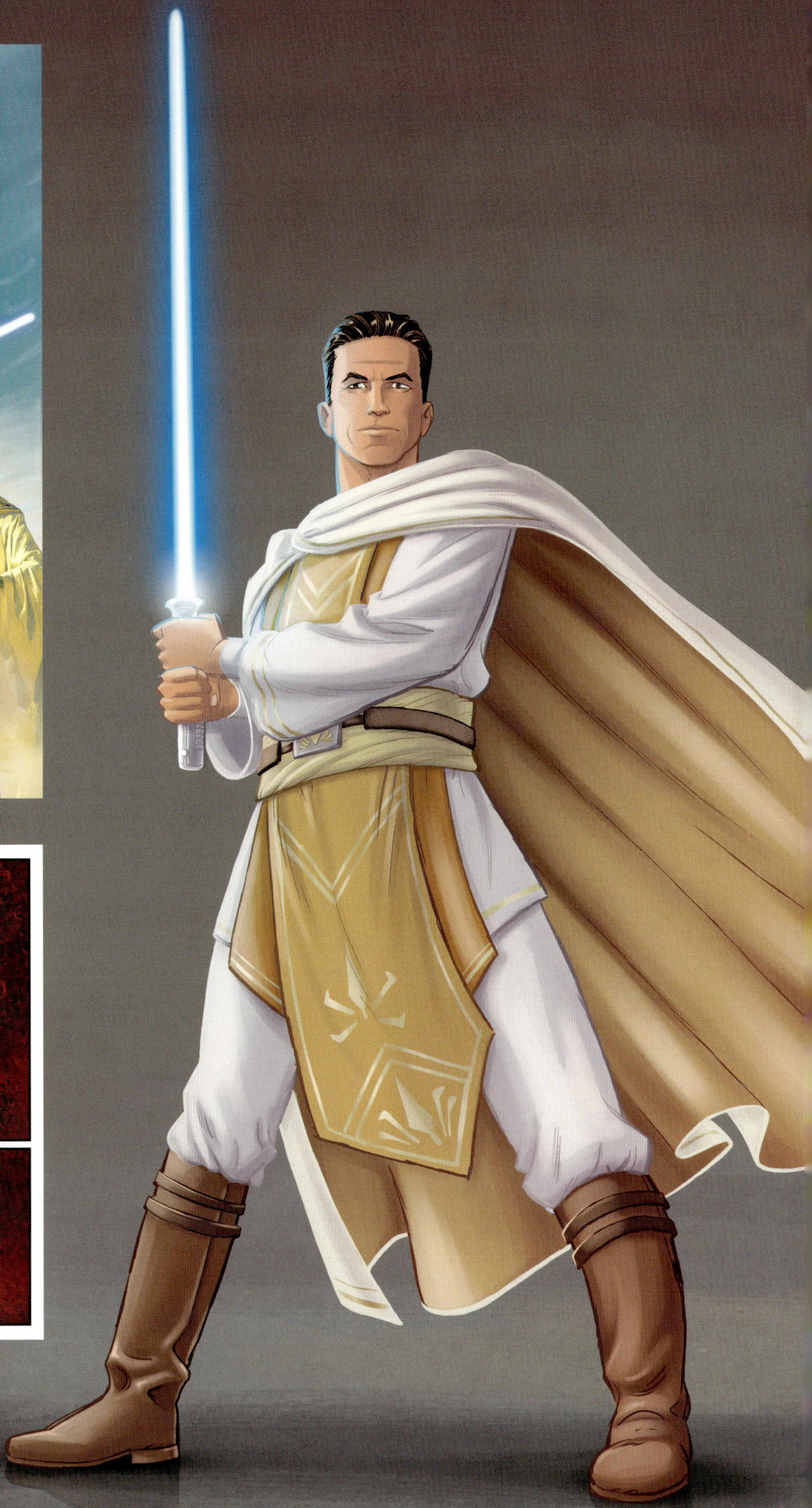

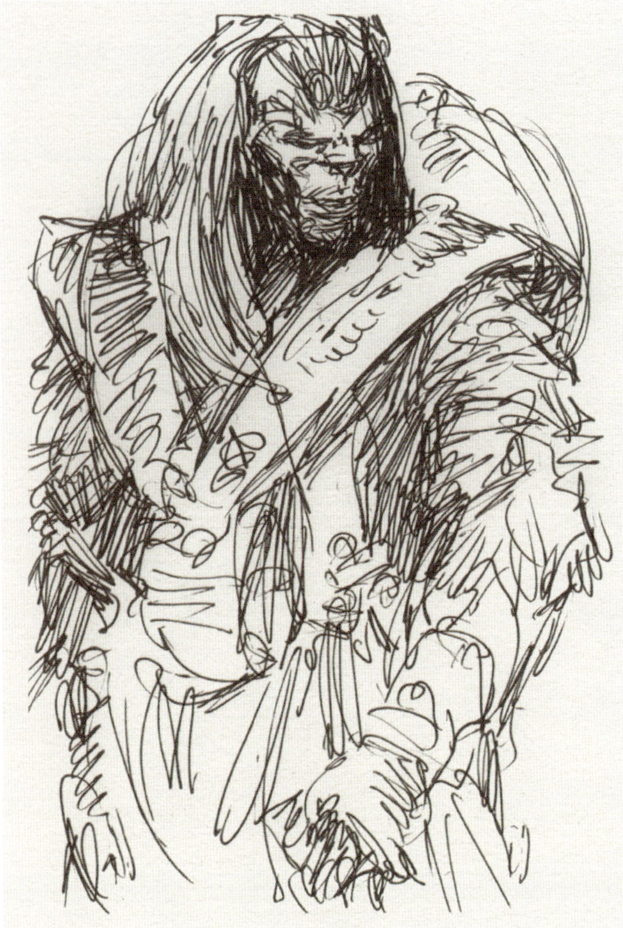

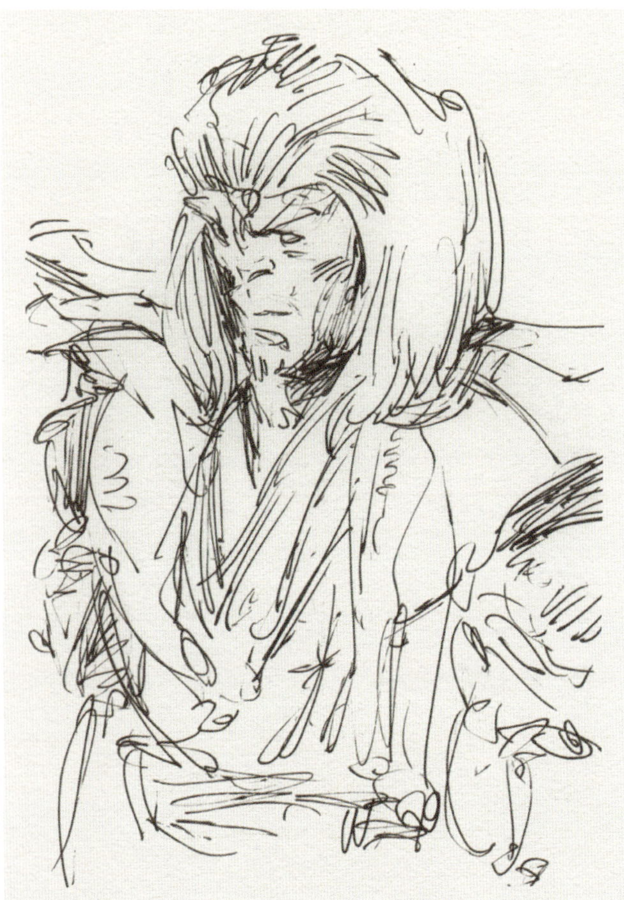

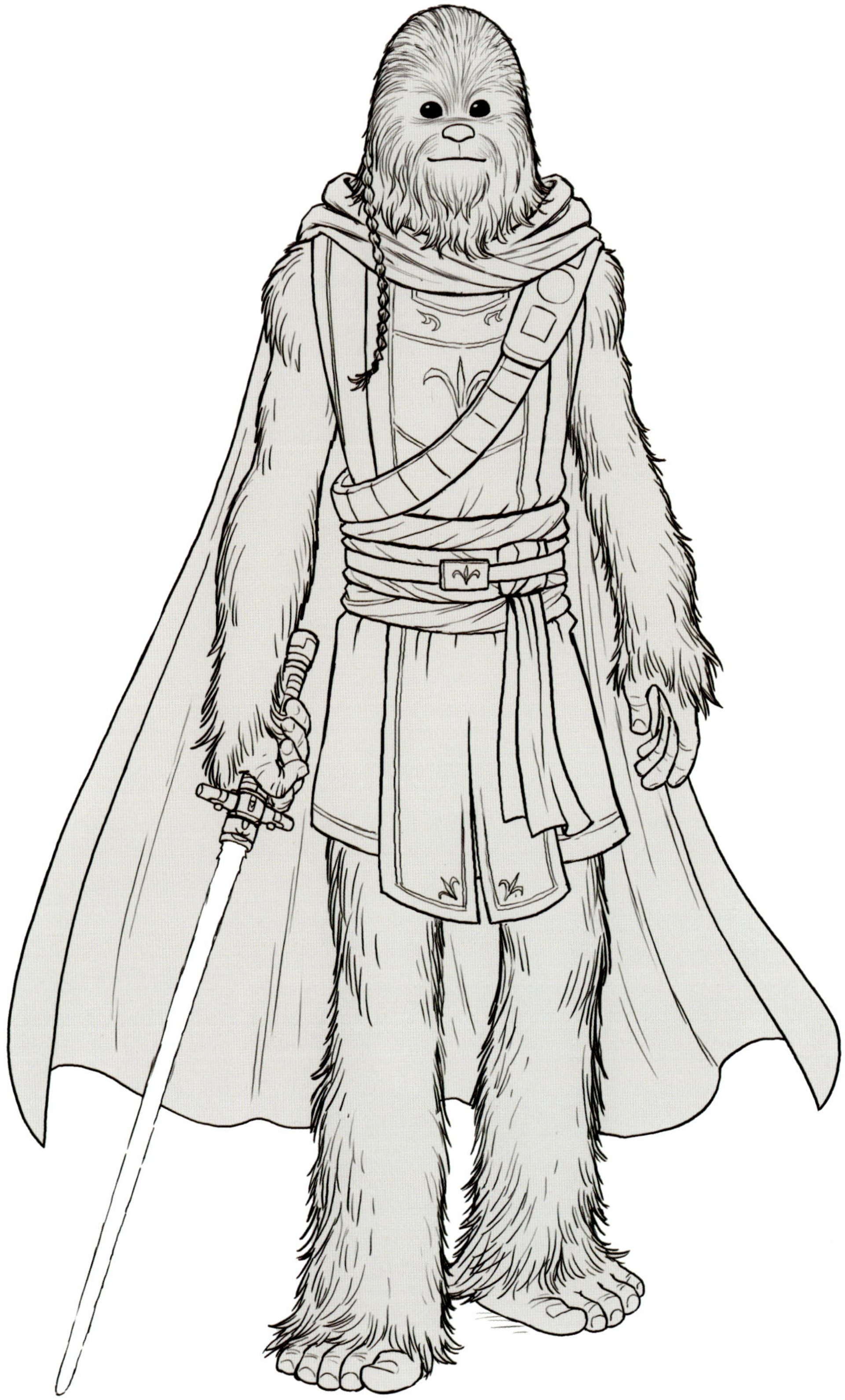

◂ Concepts of Lancelot as a Wookiee "I love Wookiees, I confess. In my heart, I get all these feelings of love toward Wookiees, and I try to express that in the drawing, but there's no story that went with this. It goes to the collaborators, and they come back with [Burryaga]. I mean, a Wookiee who has the greatest empathy? Oh, thank you. Thank you. Thank you. That's a beautiful thing." McCAIG

▴ Concept of Burryaga, May 2020 ANTONSSON

"Burryaga is young for a Wookiee. His fur is not as dark. In the initial brief for him, I describe him as basically being like a golden retriever color. And he needs to be smiling. [Details] like that can go a really, really long way in terms of the way you see and approach a character like that." CHARLES SOULE

► Burryaga KURT HARTMAN

Author Charles Soule first introduced the Wookiee Jedi as Burryaga Aggabury, but he's since dropped the surname. "He's just Burryaga, like Cher or Sting," said Siglain.

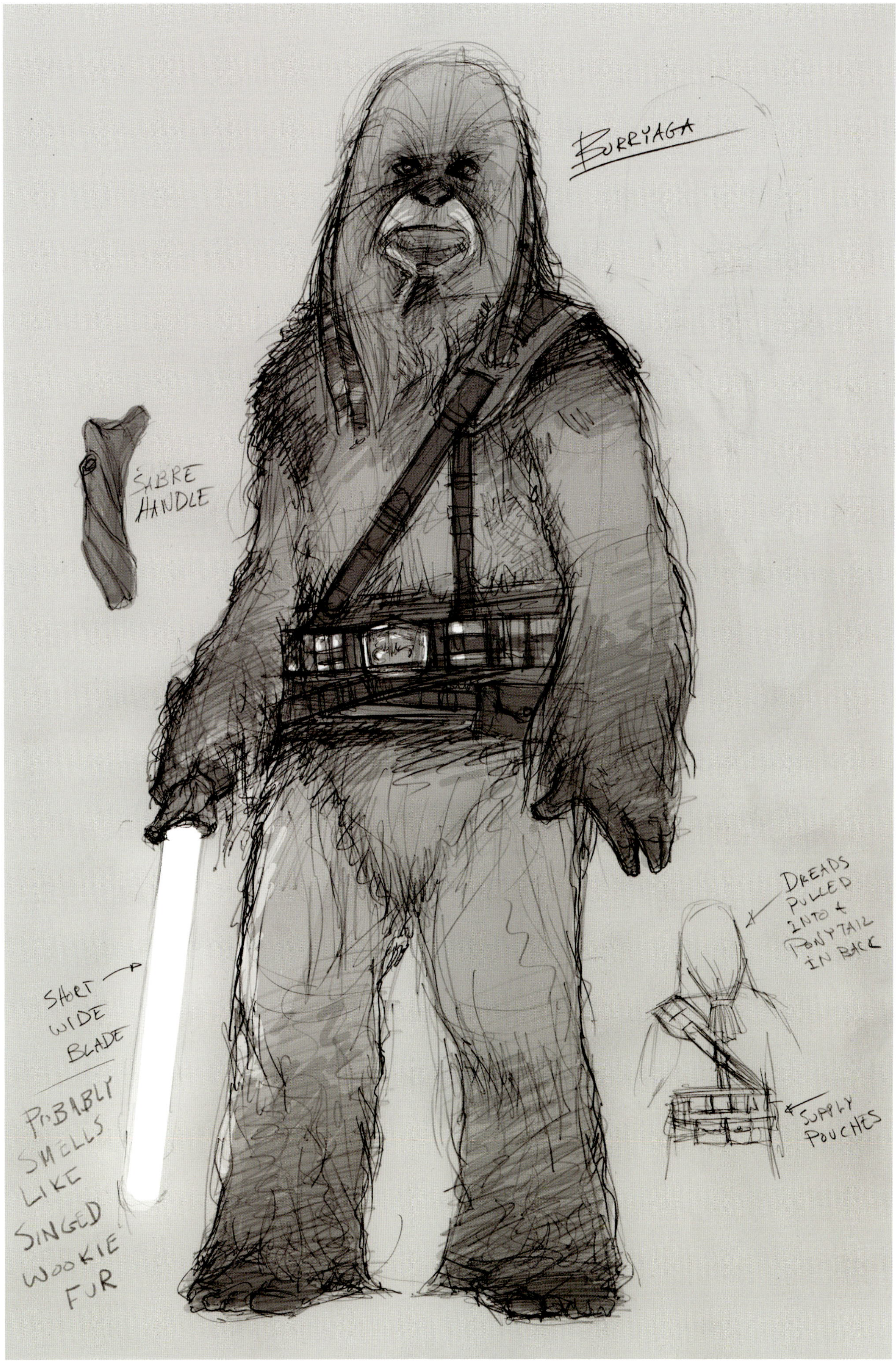

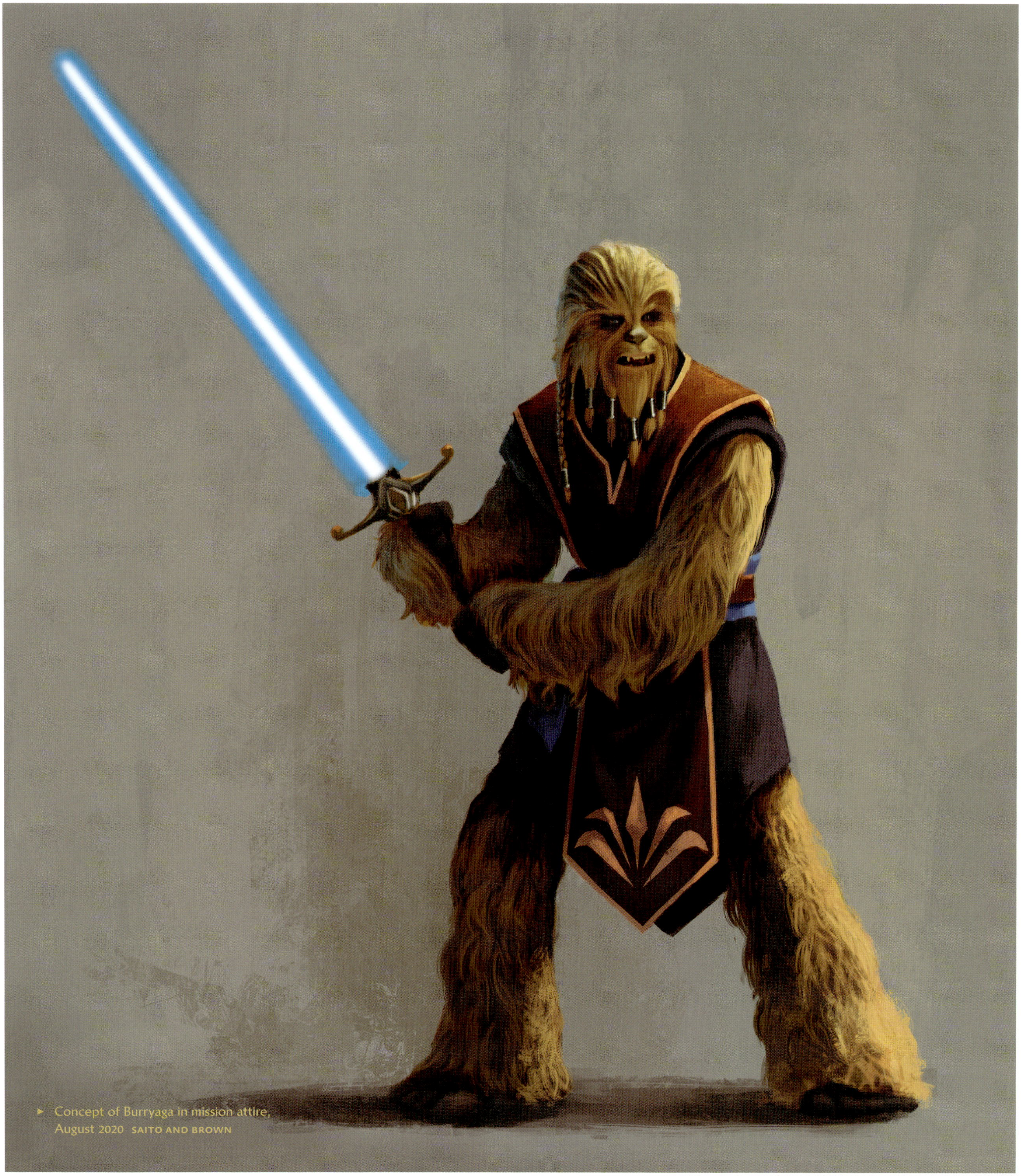

▸ Concept of Burryaga in mission attire, August 2020 SAITO AND BROWN

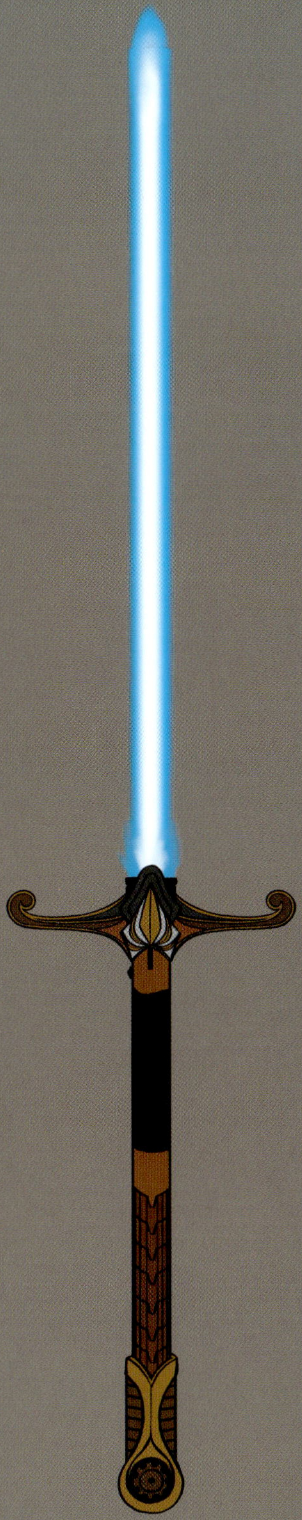

▲ Burryaga's lightsaber, August 2020 "I remember wanting the lightsaber to reflect Kashyyyk and Wookiee culture, which is why it's a more organic-looking lightsaber. I also had an idea—I wasn't entirely sure of his fighting style—for a shorter one. Then, if he wanted a broad sword, the hilt would extend, you know, for Wookiee-sized hands. They ended up really liking how it looked extended and just wanted to keep it like that all the time." THOMAS

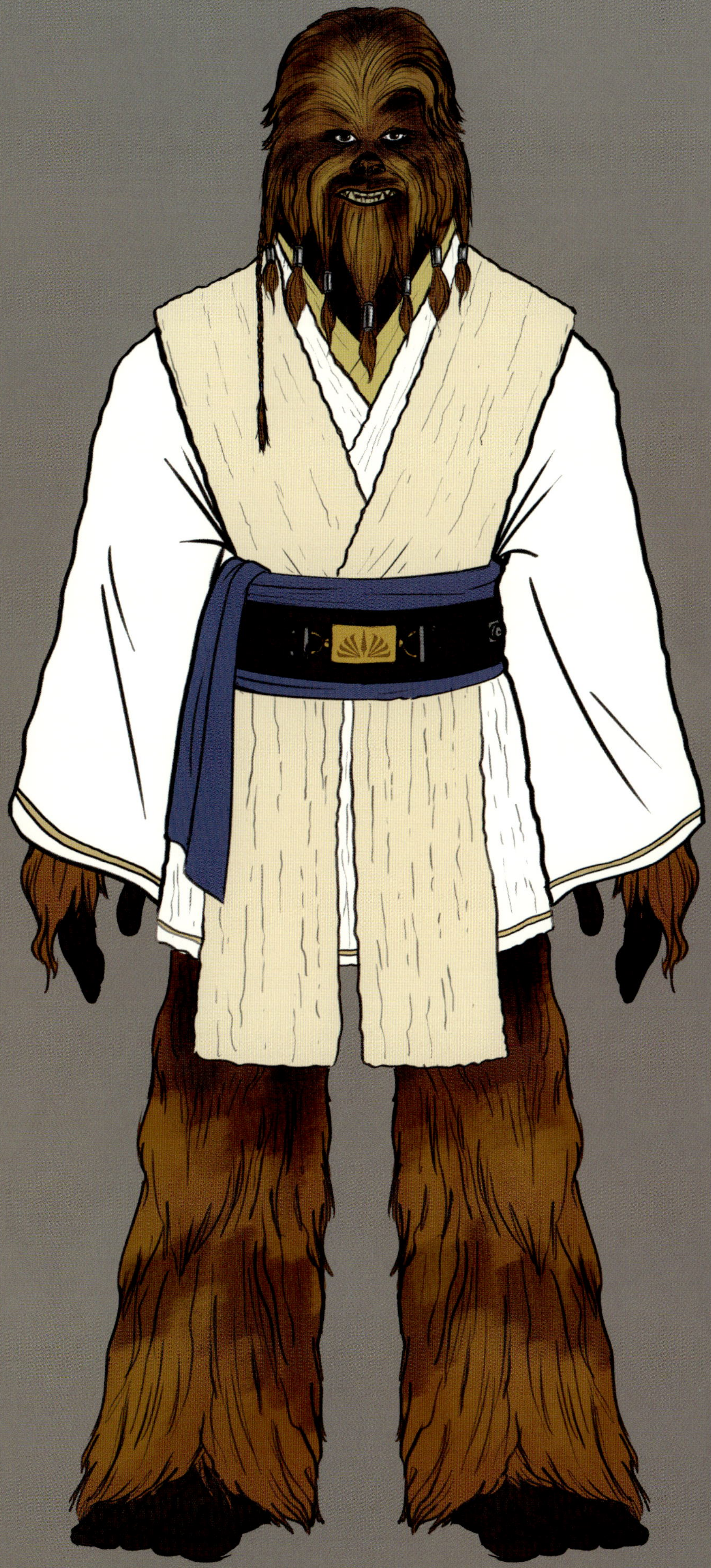

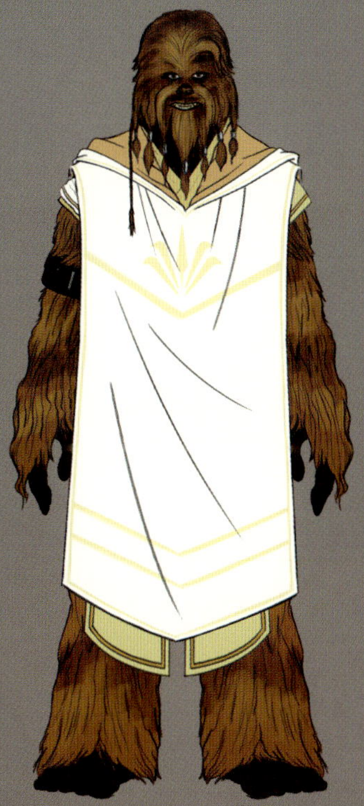

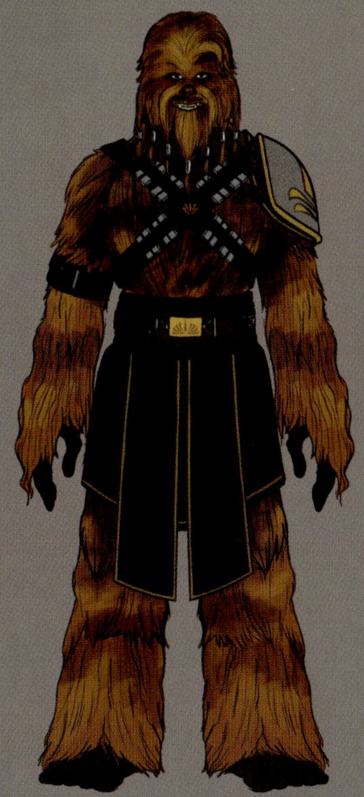

▲ Burryaga concepts, June 2020 "I tried to make a younger Wookiee. I thought a flip of hair would age him down." THOMAS

◄ Burryaga concepts, May 2020 THOMAS

Colored sashes were incorporated into some designs to denote a Jedi's Padawan status, although the typical braid designation was also used. Each sash corresponded to the character's lightsaber and added a color accent to the design.

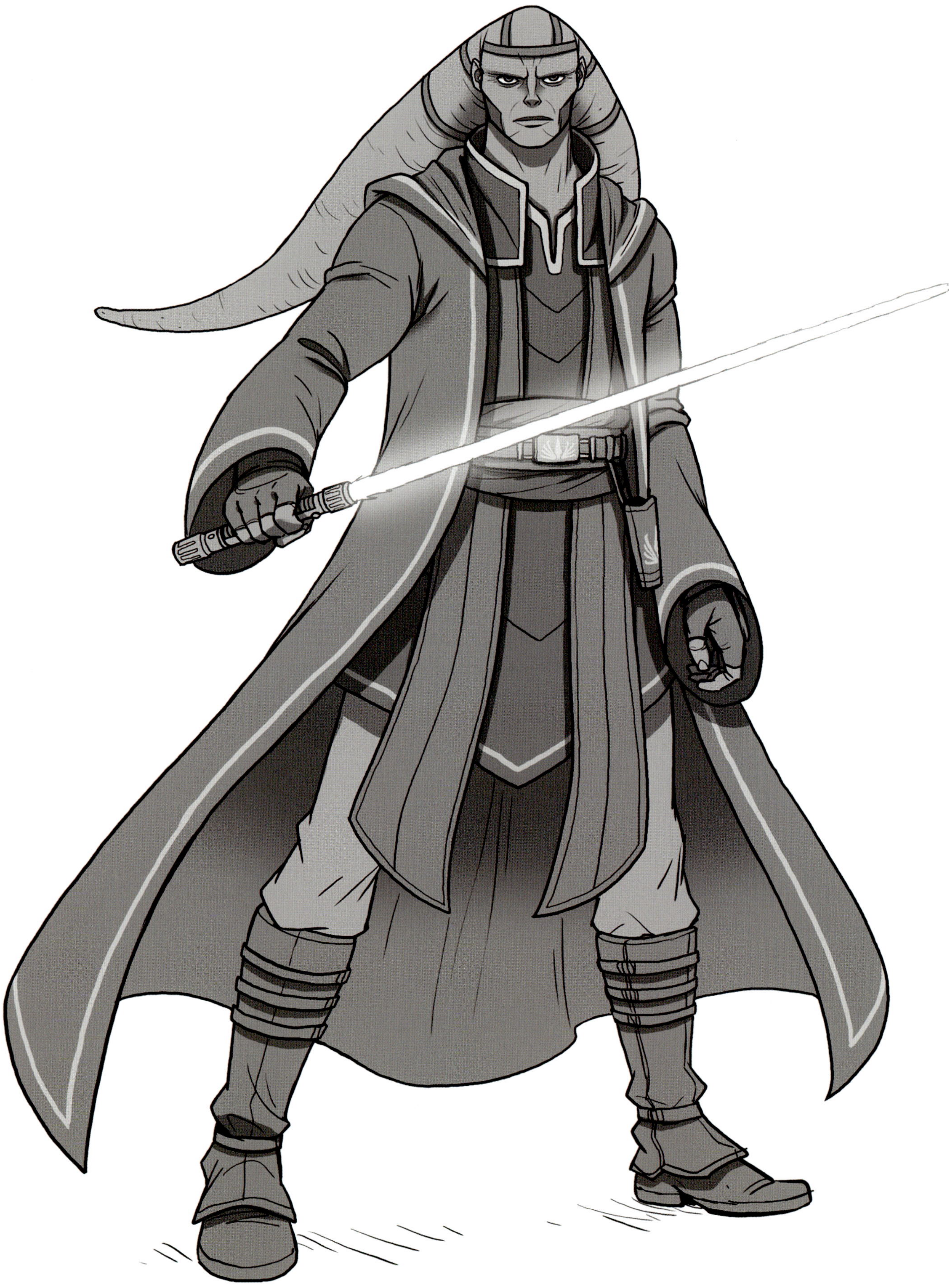

◂ Early Loden Greatstorm sketch, July 2020 ANTONSSON

▸ Final Loden Greatstorm design SERIO

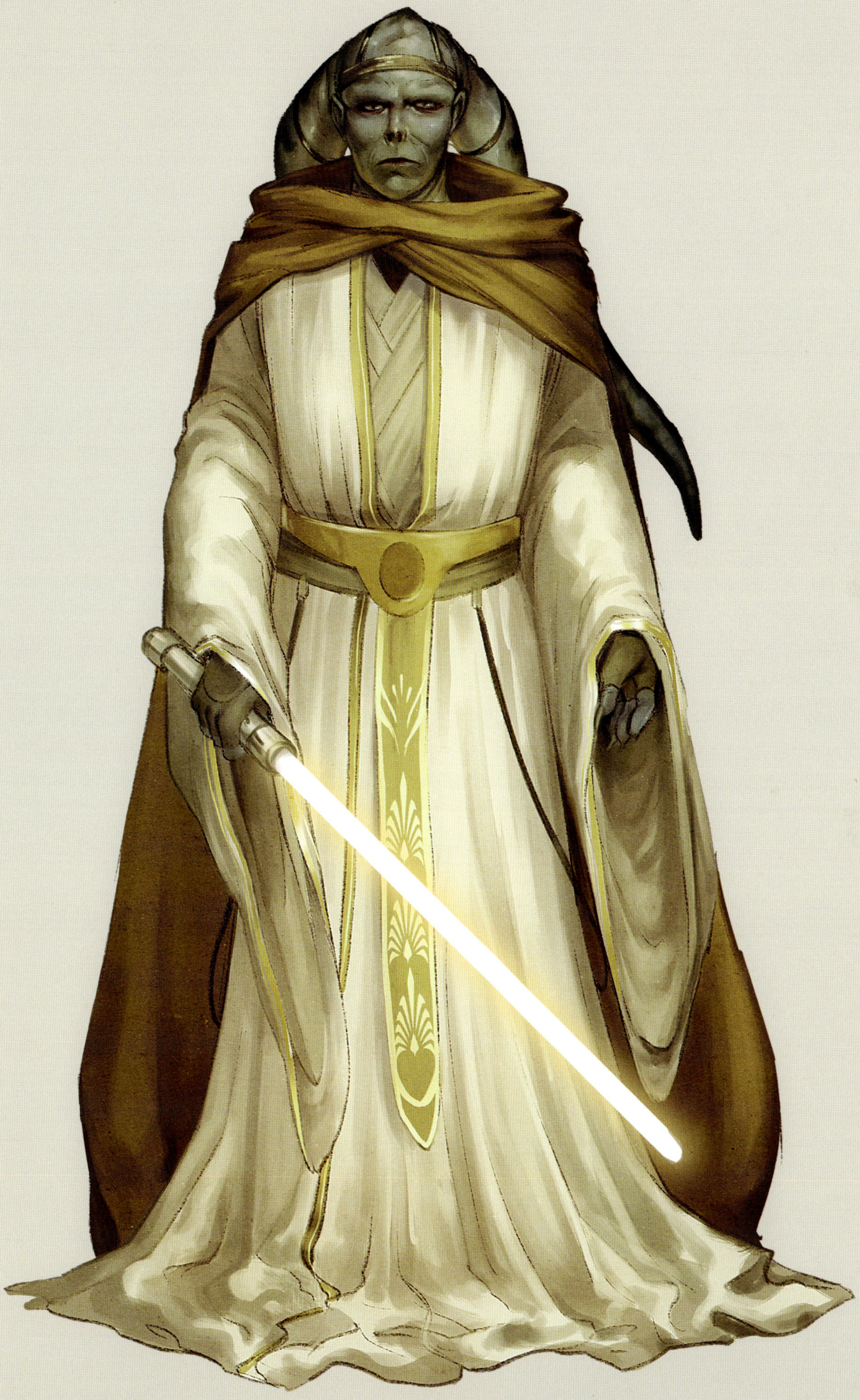

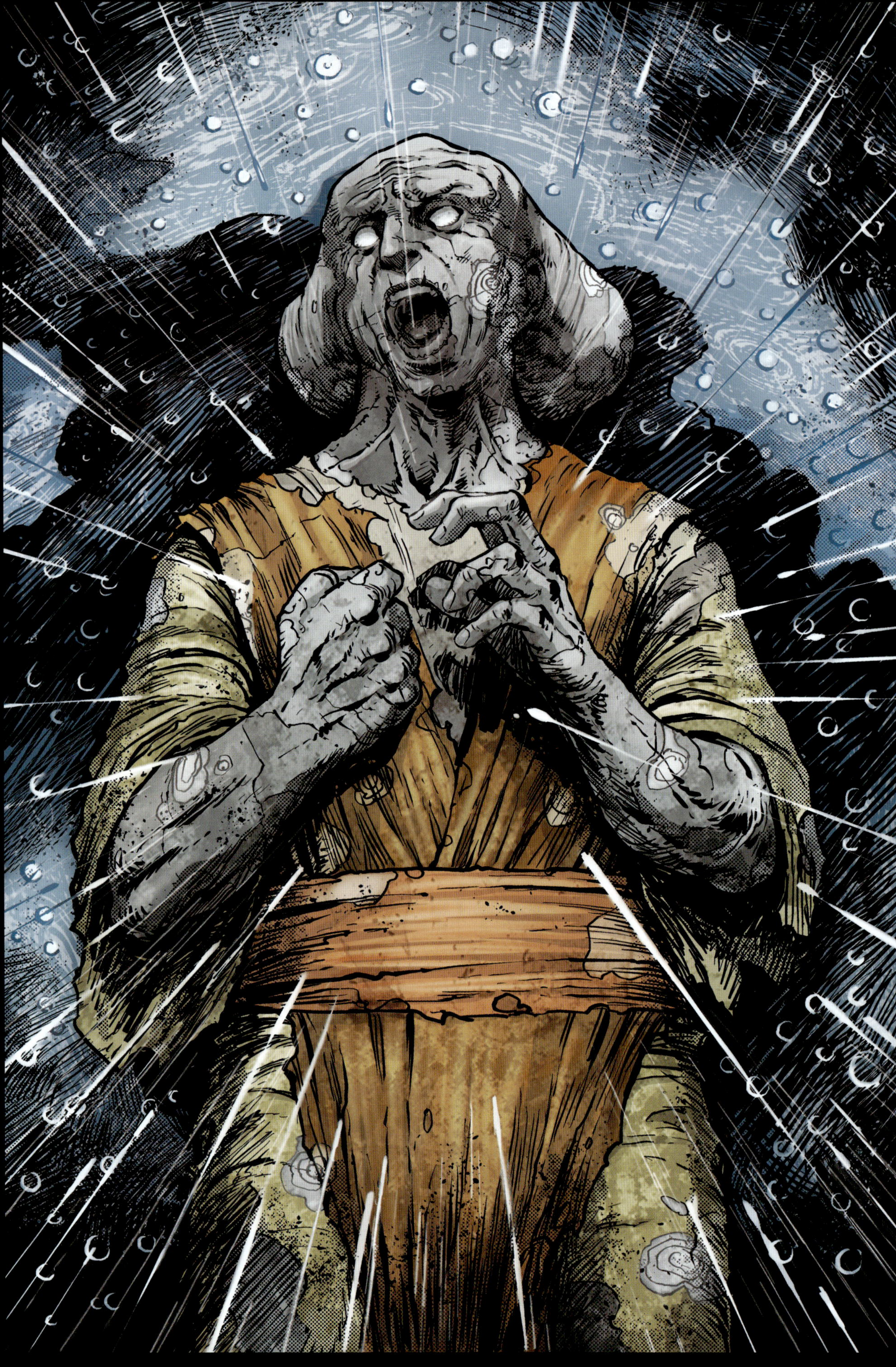

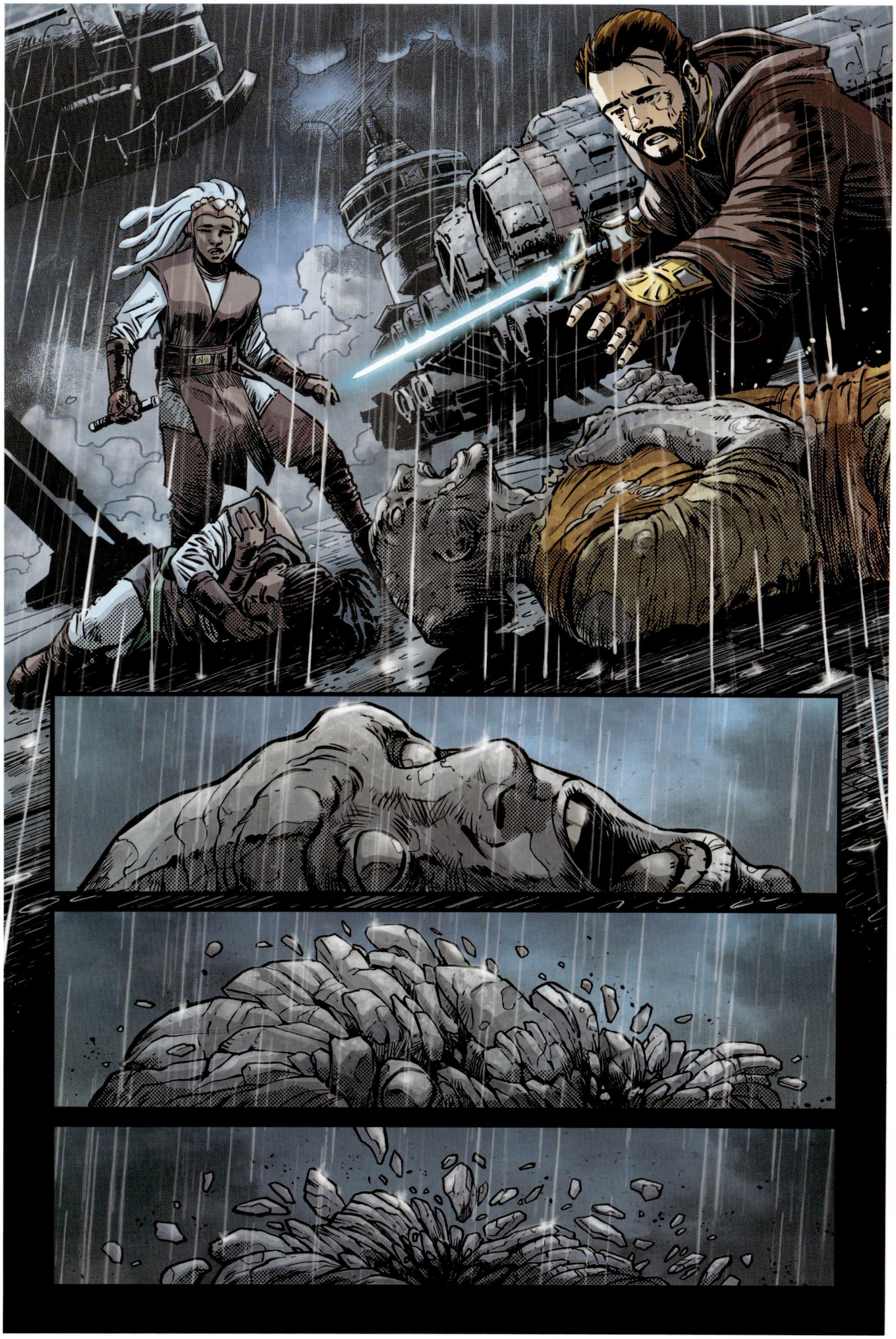

◂▸ Demise of Loden Greatstorm from Marvel's *Star Wars: The High Republic: Trail of Shadows* #1
DAVE WACHTER (PENCILER) AND GIADA MARCHISIO (COLORIST)

"Cavan Scott killed off Loden Greatstorm. I knew that it was coming, and I knew that it was going to be intense, but the reason that beat works in *The Rising Storm*, in part, is because you love Loden. And one of the reasons you love Loden is because of what he does in *Light of the Jedi*. I had to do my job so Cavan could do his job. But at the same time, it still hits me, too."
SOULE

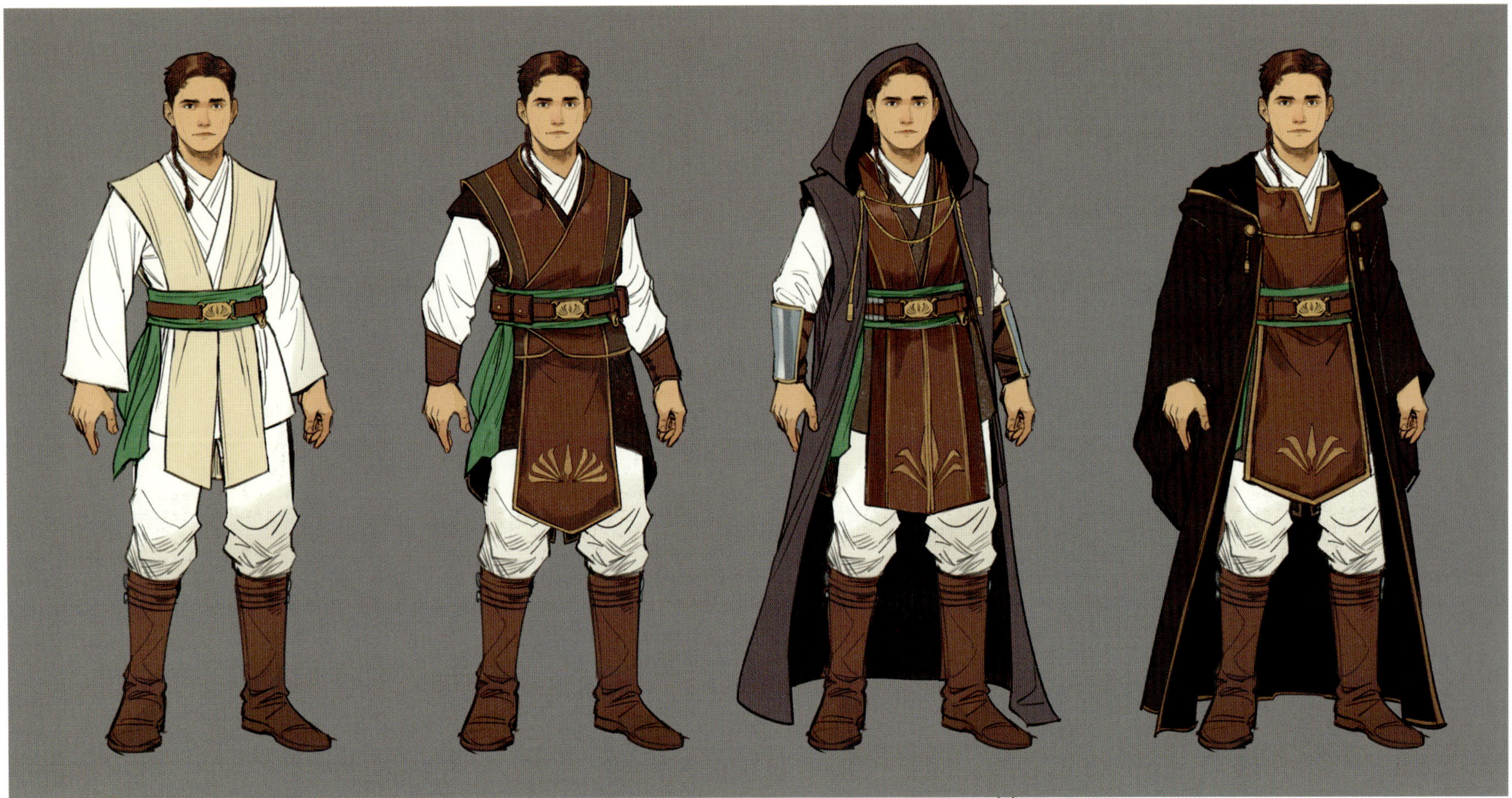

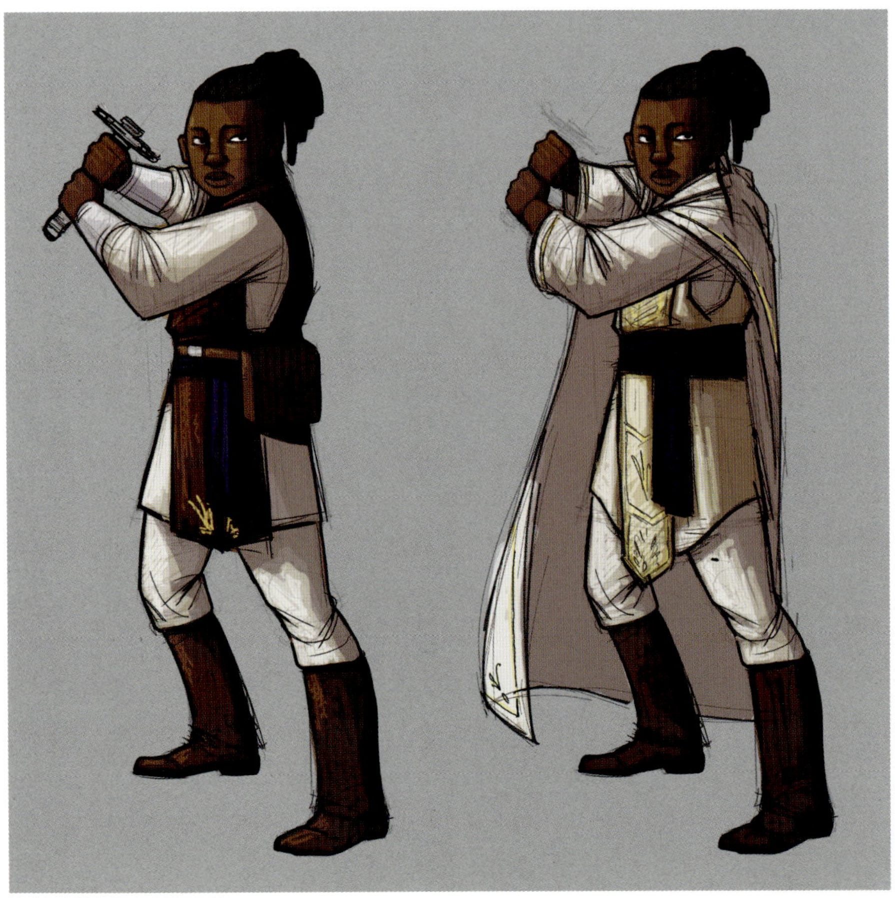

▲ Early Bell Zettifar concept, March 2020 HARTMAN

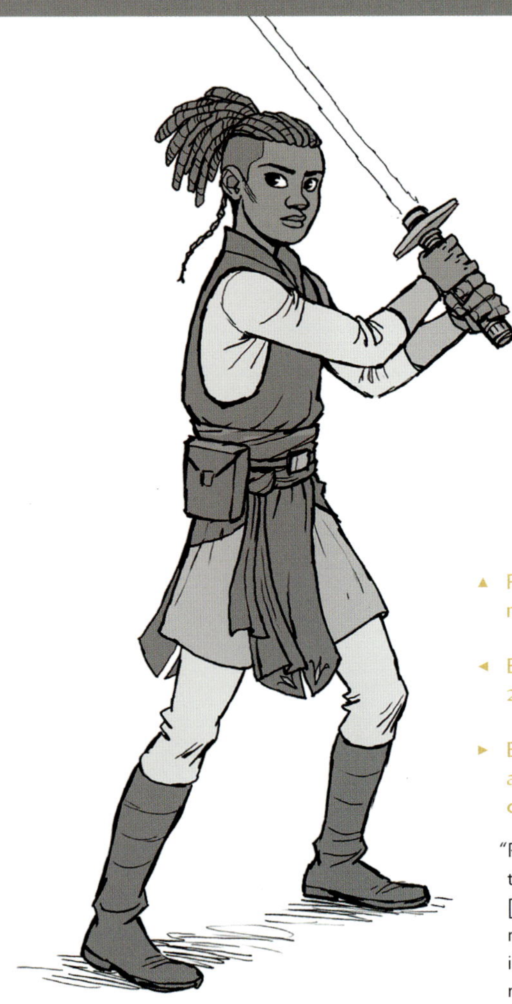

▲ Final concept for Reath Silas mission attire SAITO

◄ Early Bell Zettifar sketch, March 2020 ANTONSSON

► Early Bell Zettifar concepts with and without blue sash, June 2020 GRACE LEE

"Part of our guiding light the whole time was that everybody should be [represented] in the story, so Bell reflects that. He has dreadlocks, which is something that I don't think we've really seen before in *Star Wars*." SOULE

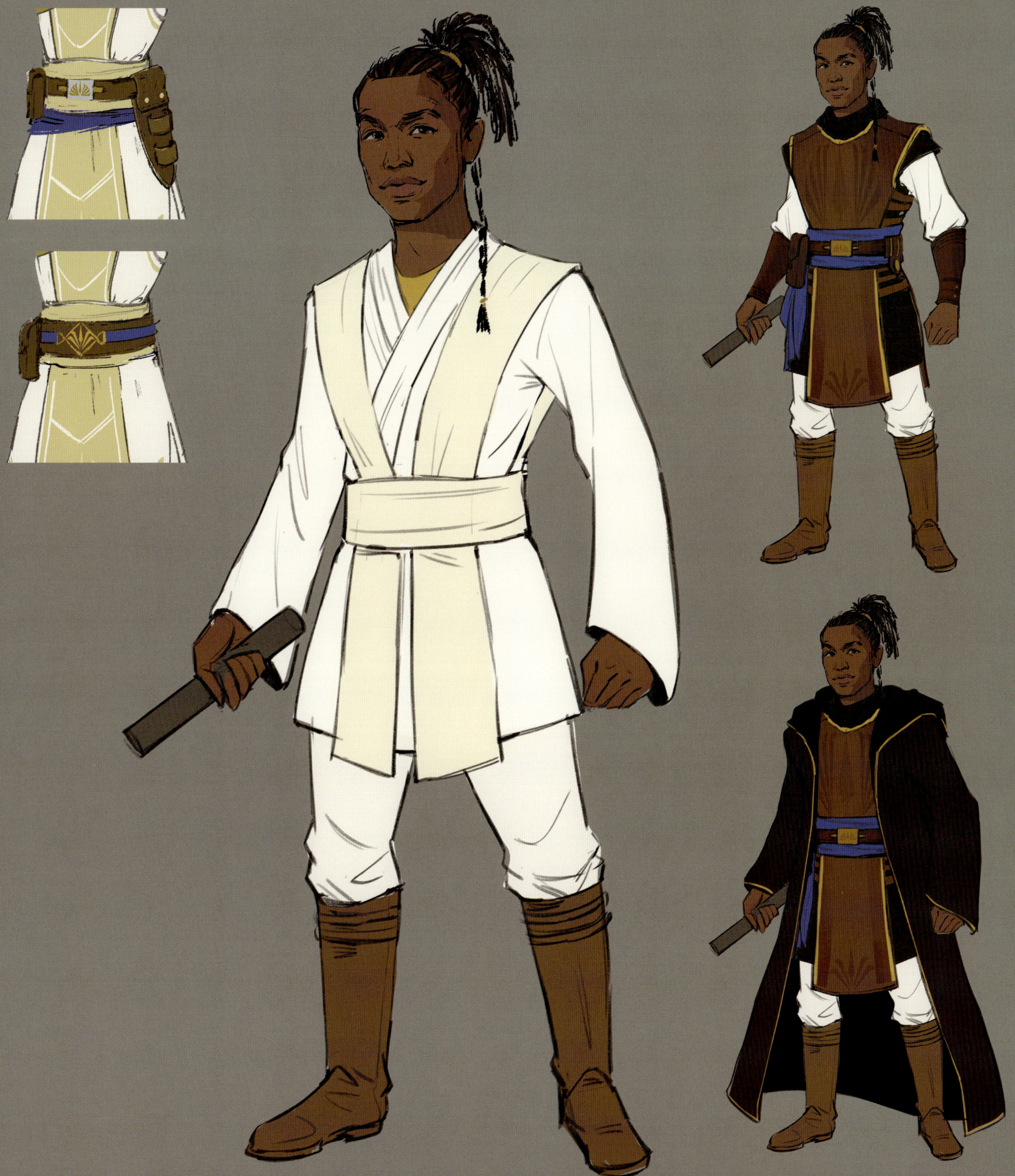

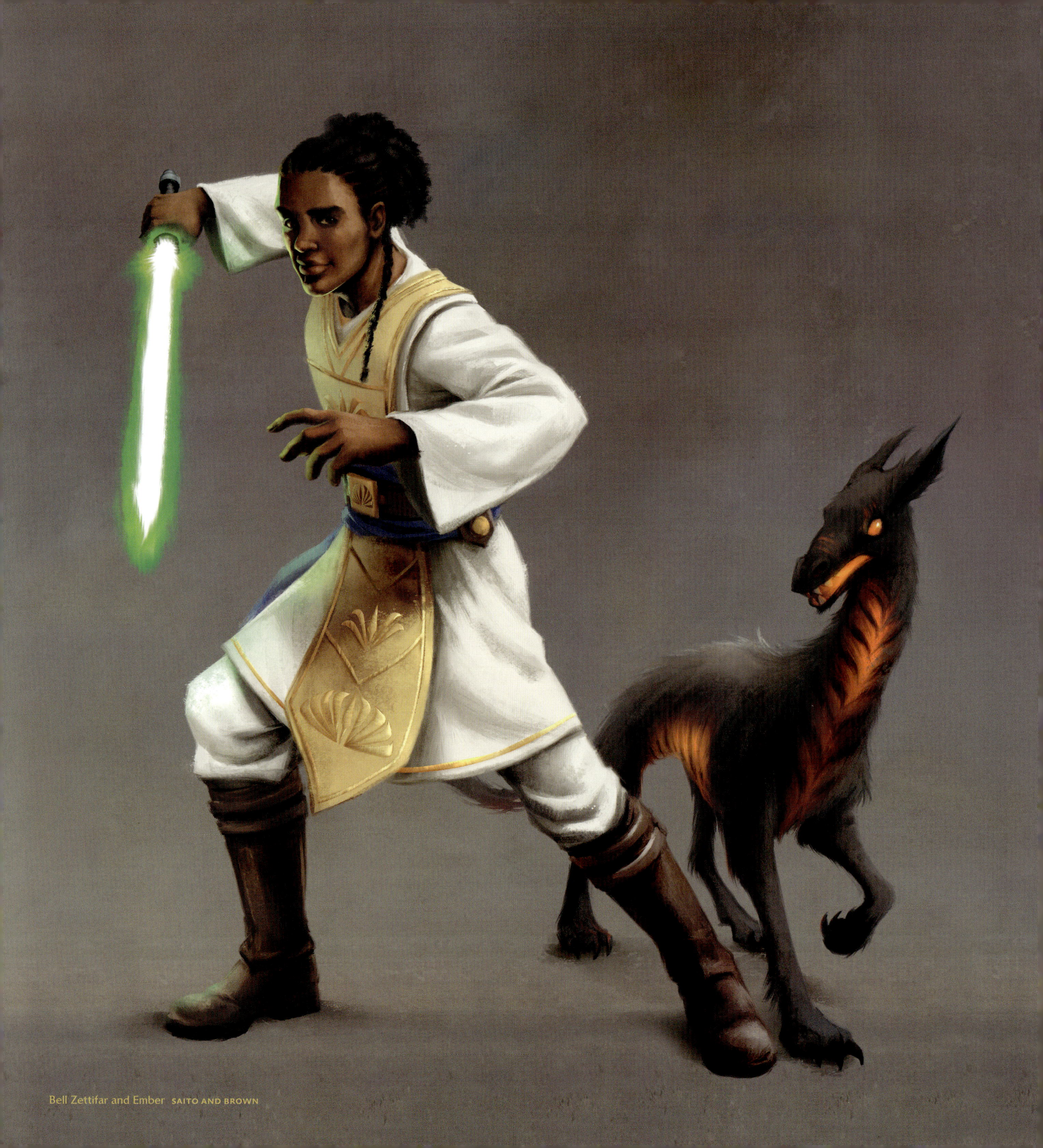

Bell Zettifar and Ember SAITO AND BROWN

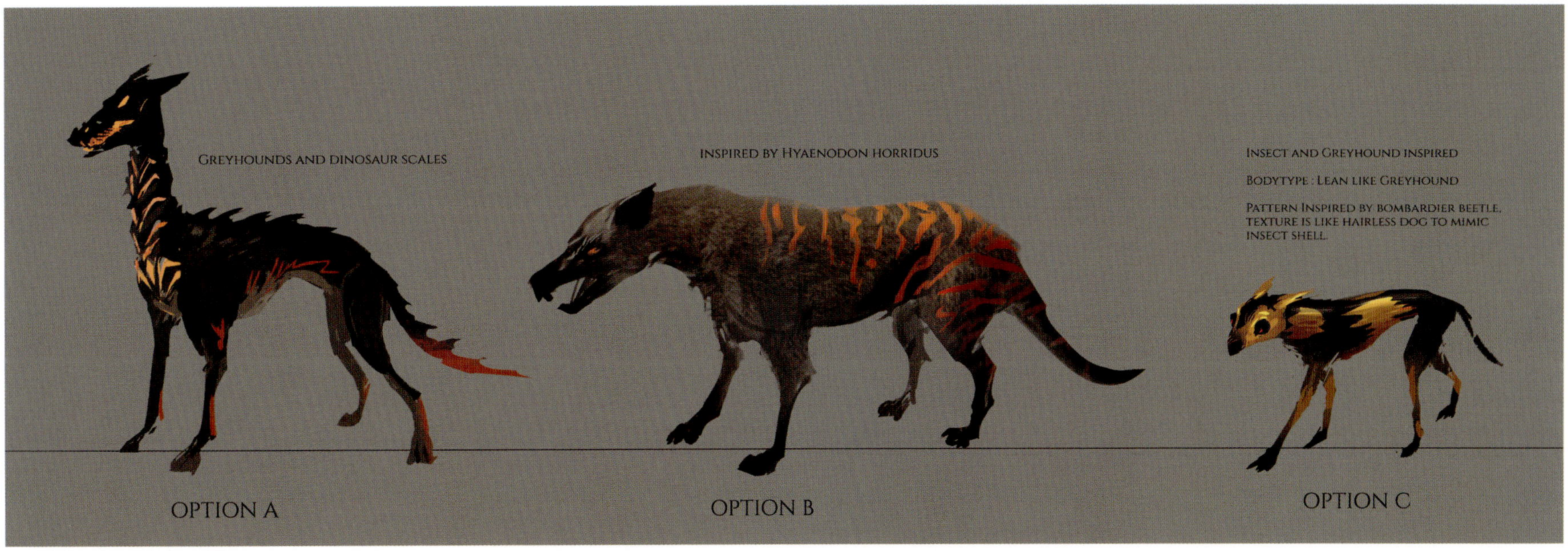

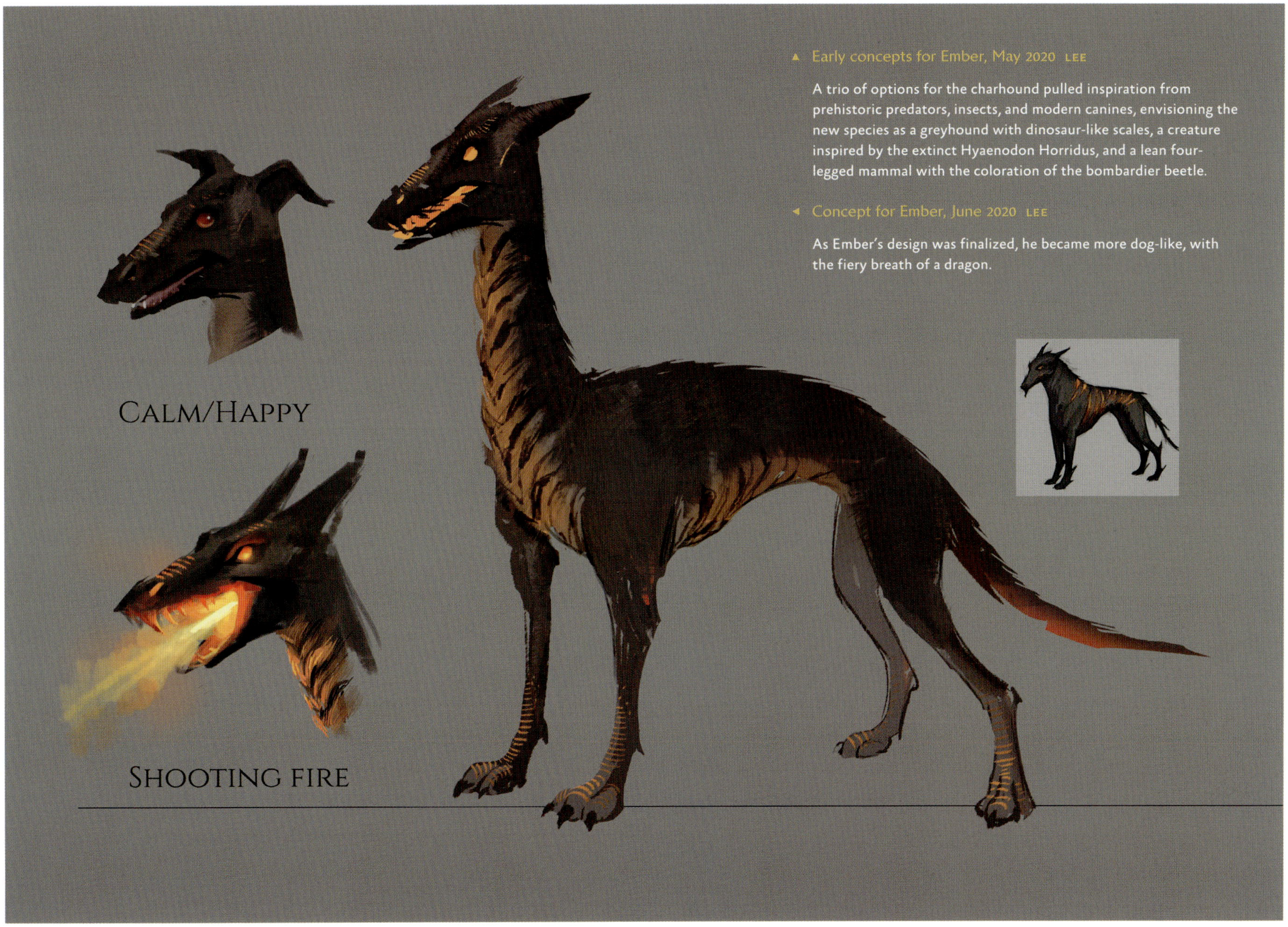

▲ Early concepts for Ember, May 2020 LEE

A trio of options for the charhound pulled inspiration from prehistoric predators, insects, and modern canines, envisioning the new species as a greyhound with dinosaur-like scales, a creature inspired by the extinct Hyaenodon Horridus, and a lean four-legged mammal with the coloration of the bombardier beetle.

◄ Concept for Ember, June 2020 LEE

As Ember's design was finalized, he became more dog-like, with the fiery breath of a dragon.

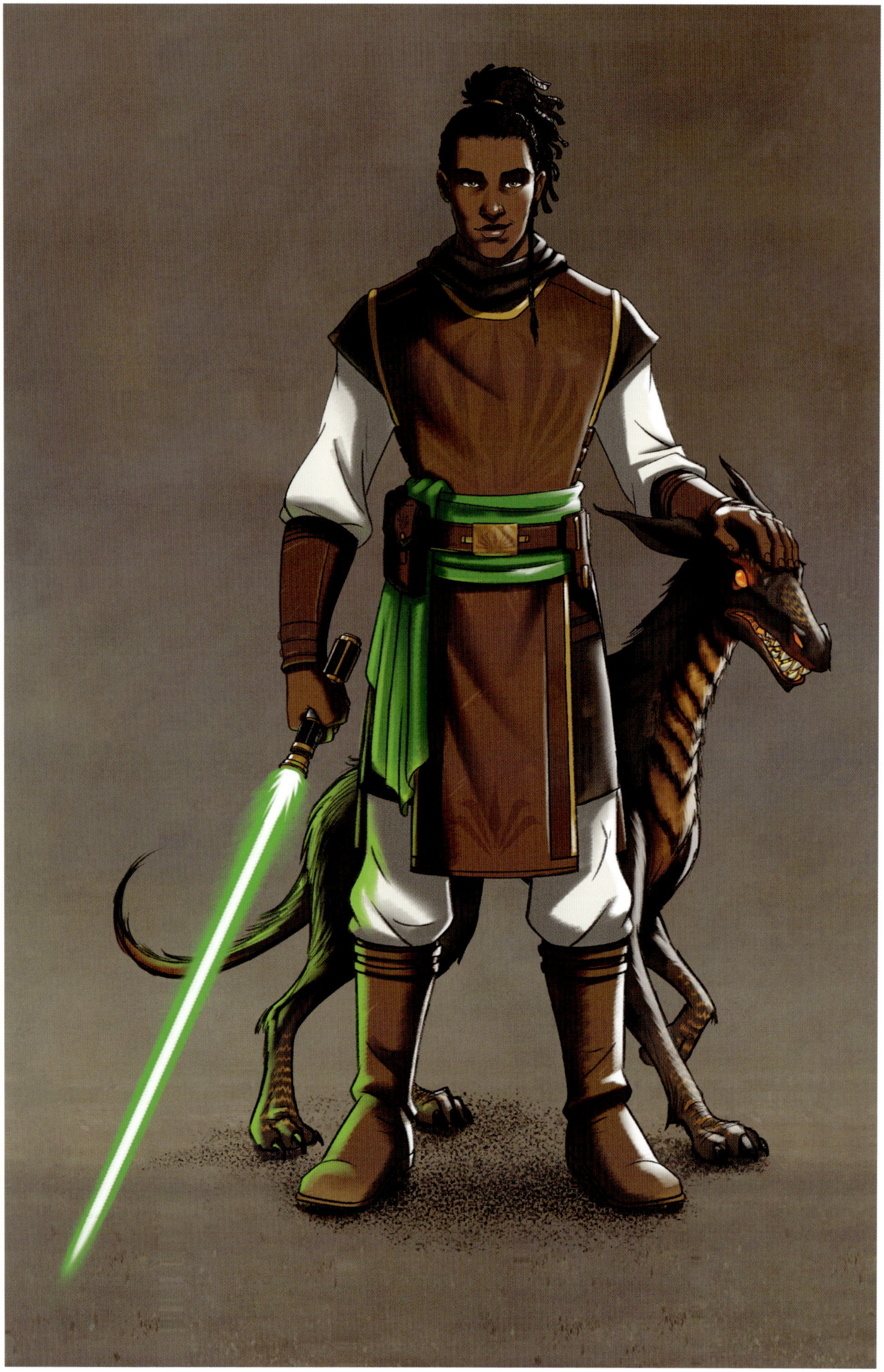

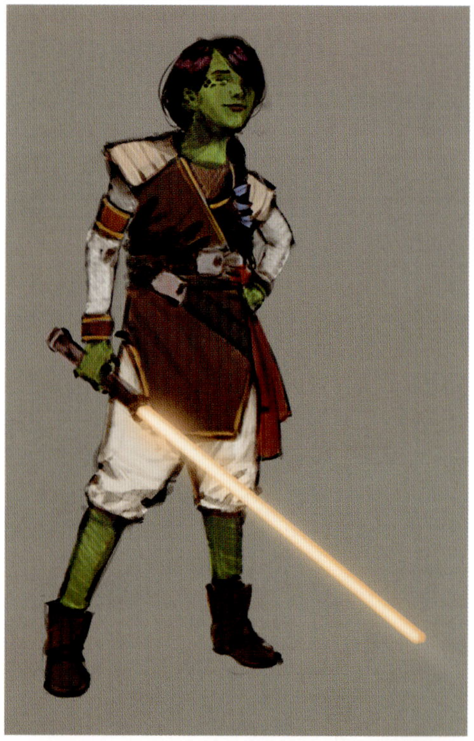

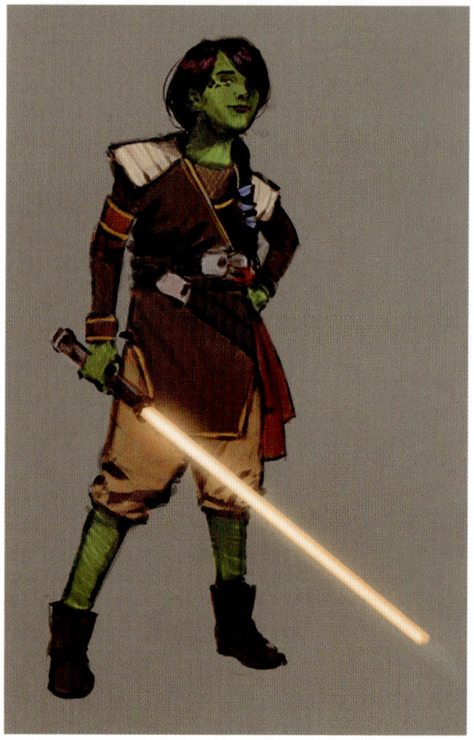

▲ Early concept of Vernestra Rwoh, November 2019 BARONI

◄ Final concept of Bell and Ember, October 2020 THOMAS

Thomas refined Bell's facial features, giving the young Jedi on the cusp of knighthood a more mature bone structure and a lopsided smirk, then turned his attention to the lightsaber hilt, which in Lee's version [see page 73] had been a simple placeholder cylinder reminiscent of the lead pipe in the board game *Clue*. "He killed Colonel Mustard," Thomas joked.

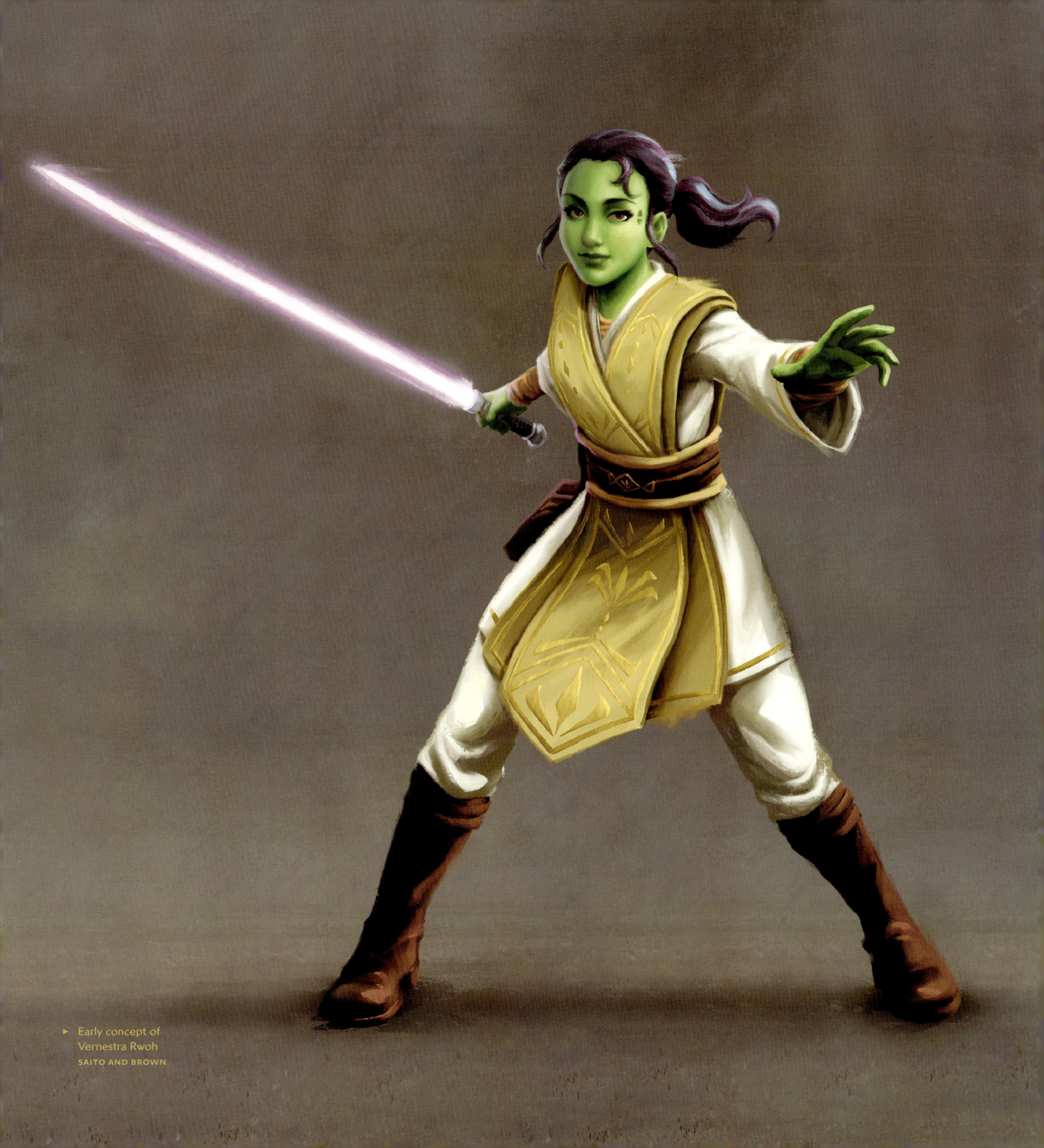

Early concept of Vernestra Rwoh
SAITO AND BROWN

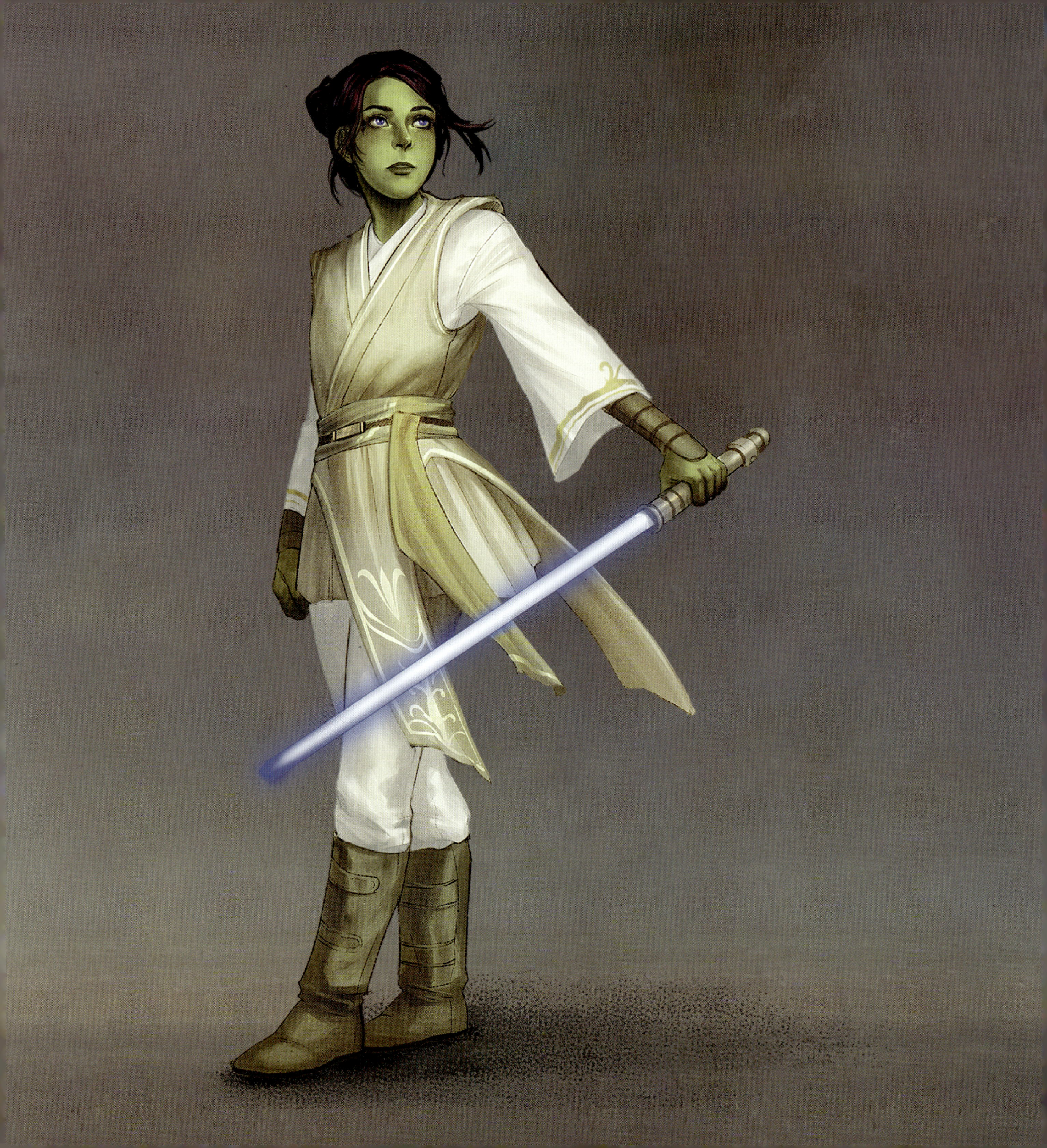

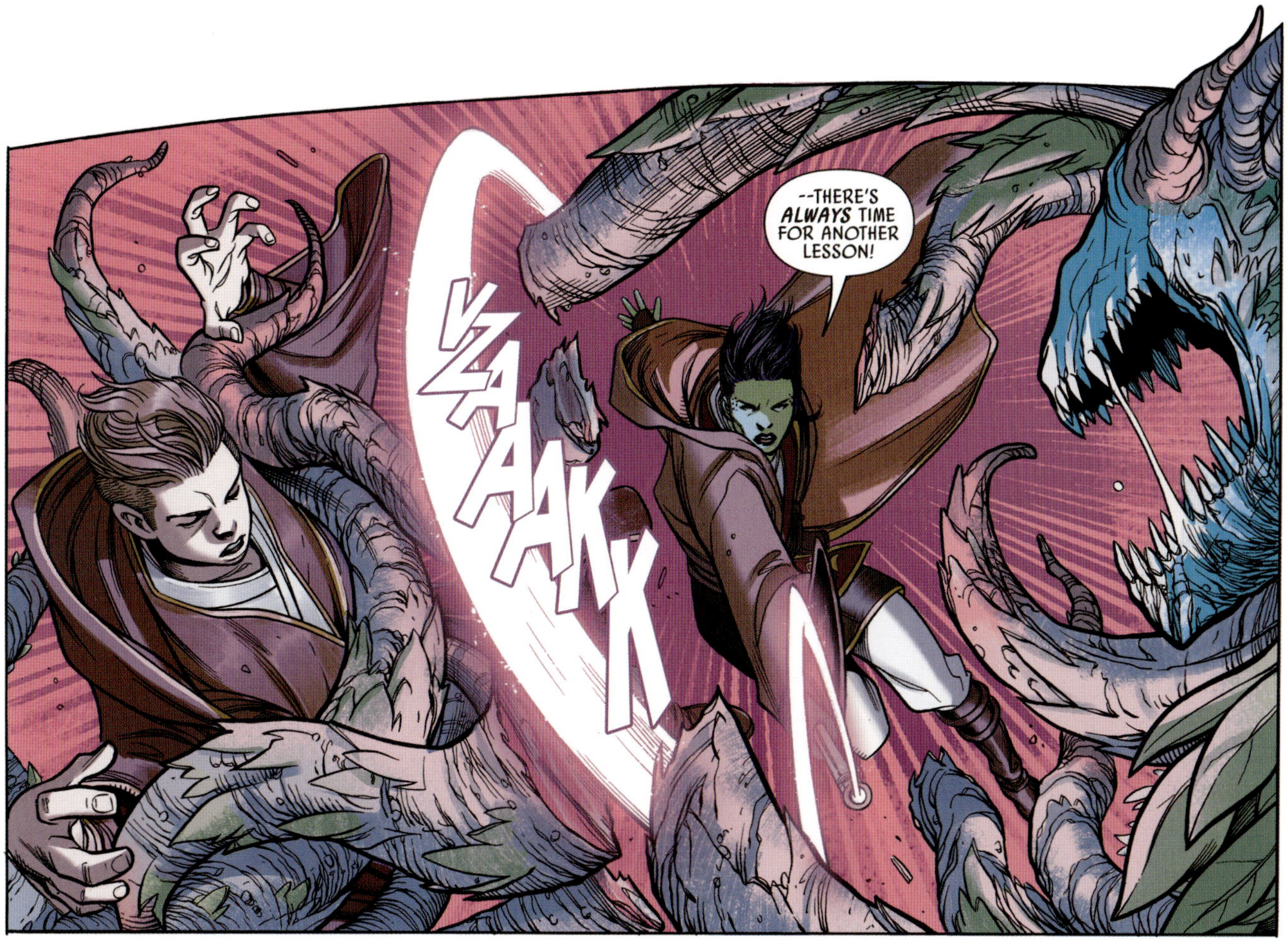

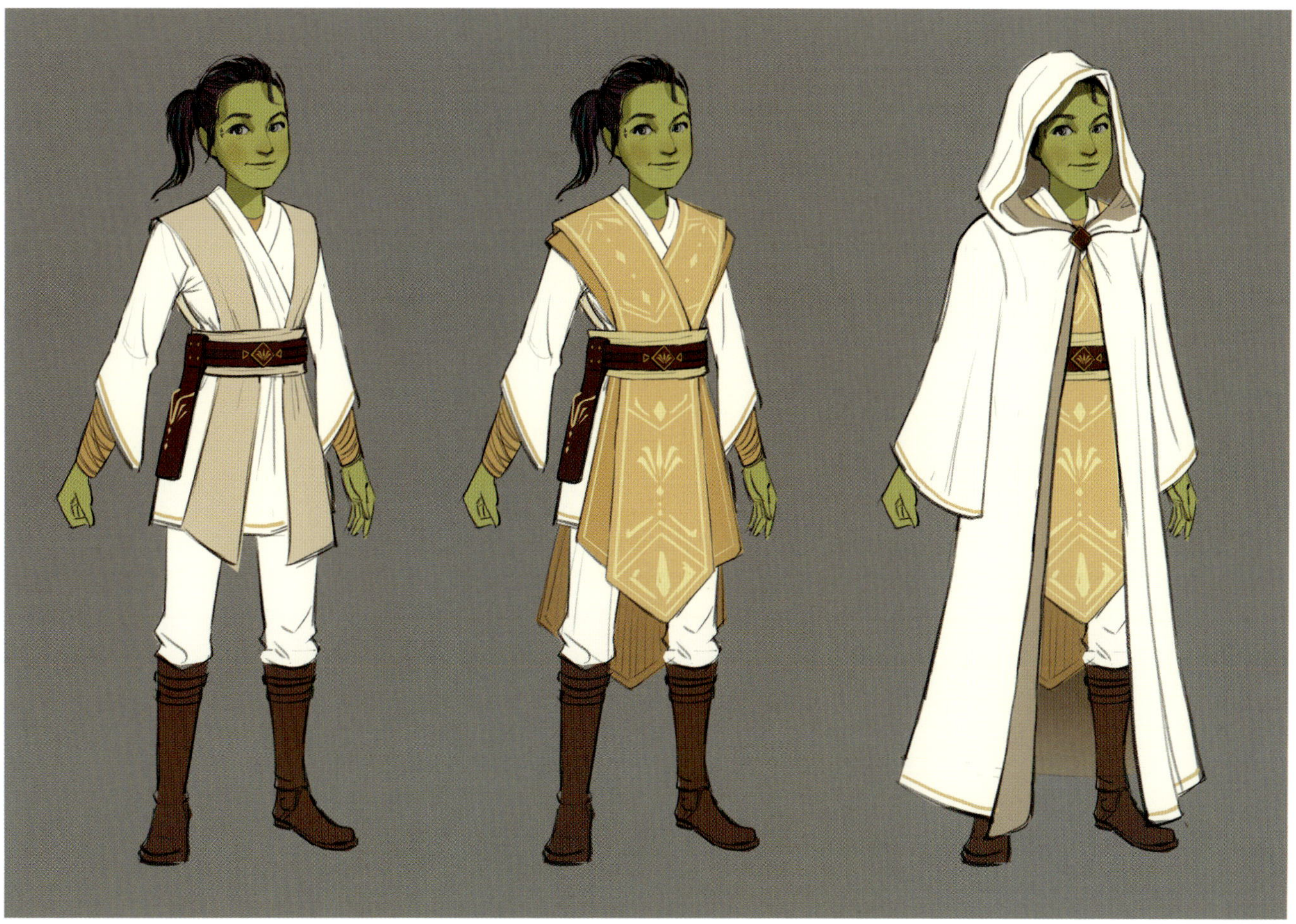

◂ Panel from Marvel's *Star Wars: The High Republic* #5 showcasing Vernestra Rwoh's light whip ANINDITO (PENCILER), MARK MORALES (INKER), ANNALISA LEONI (COLORIST), AND VC'S ARIANA MAHER (LETTERER)

"Everybody tries to create a new lightsaber. 'Here's our nunchaku lightsaber.' That's not what this is. With [Vernestra's light whip], the story reason was very much something I insisted on." JAMES WAUGH

▸ Final designs of Vernestra Rwoh LEE

◂ Final design of Vernestra Rwoh SERIO

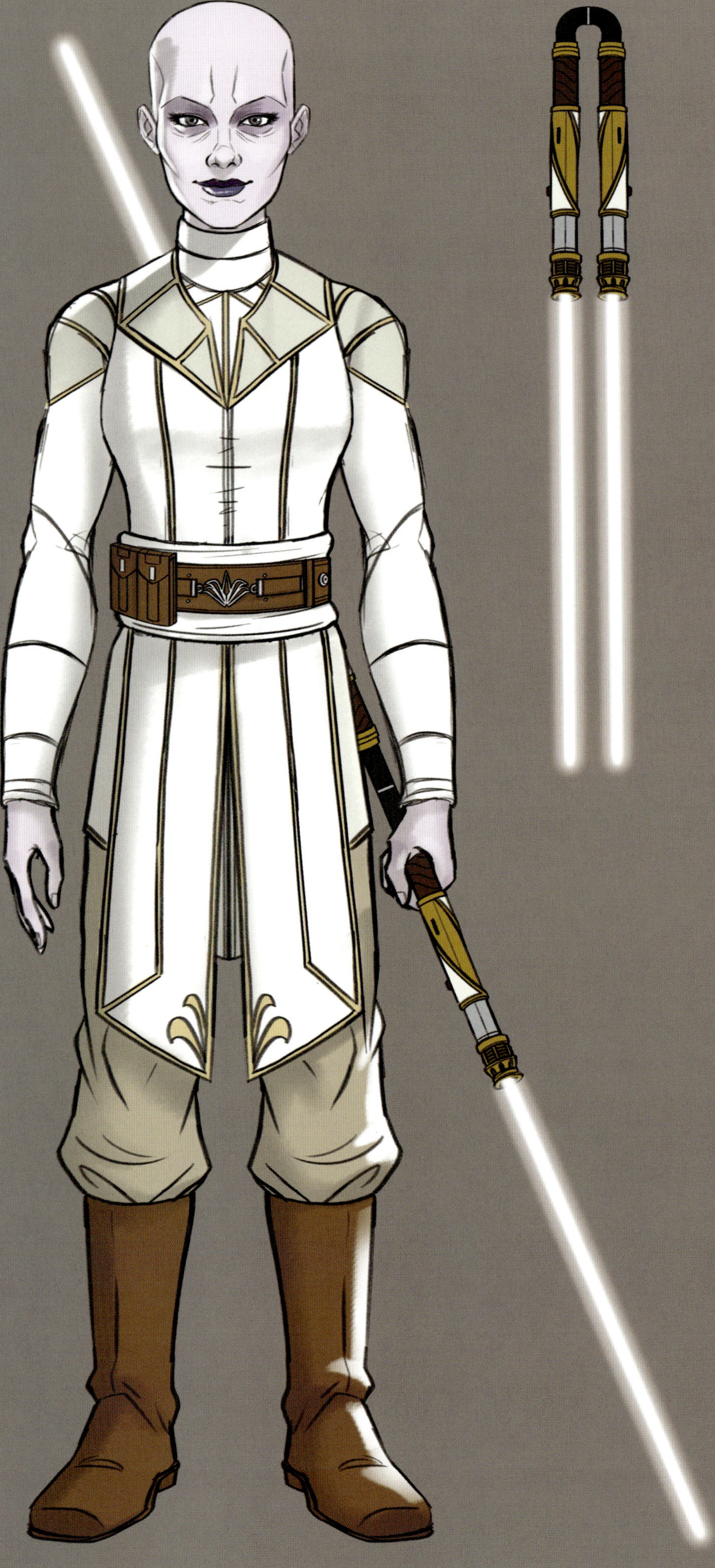

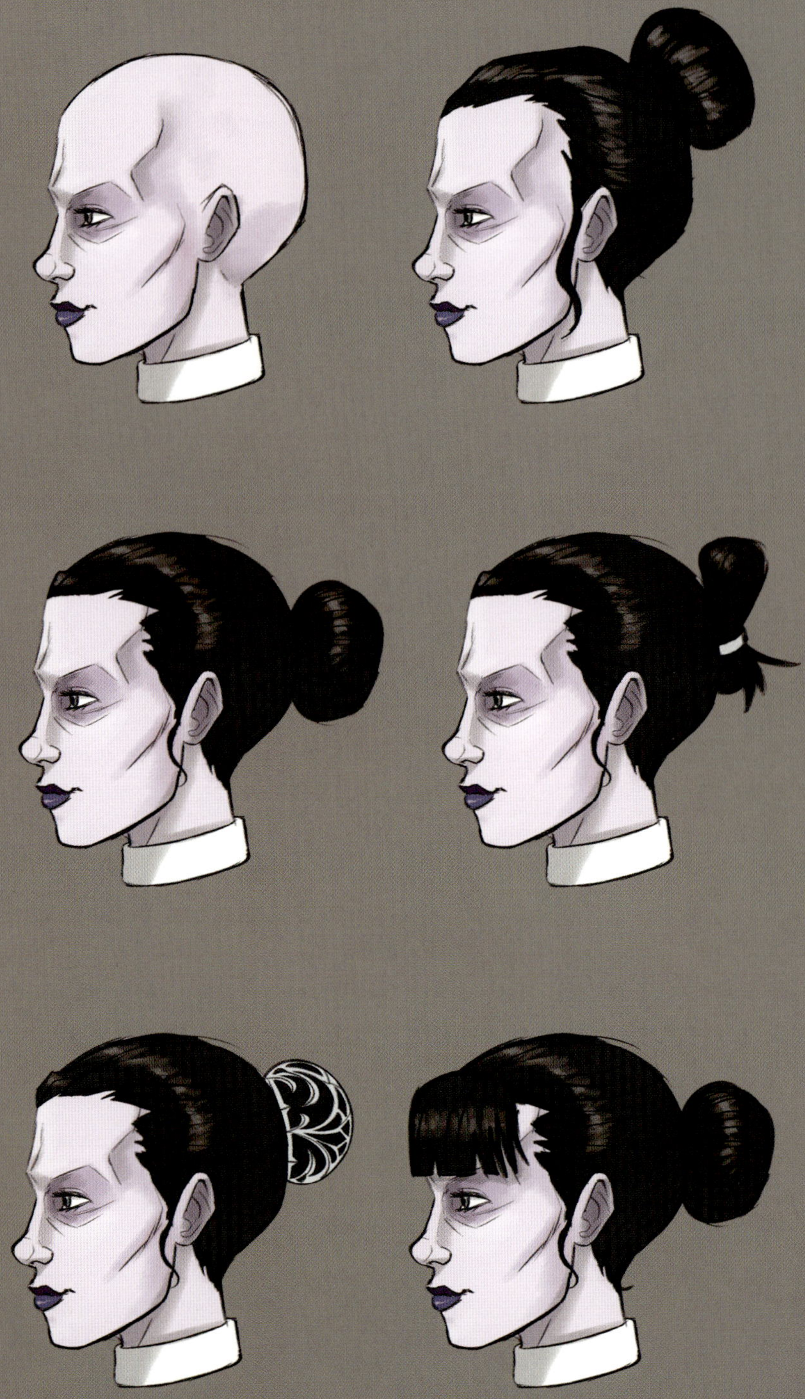

▸ Early concepts of Orla Jareni, January 2021 "They wanted her bald initially, but when I started drawing her, I liked the way that she looked with hair. I got a couple facts and a screenshot of what the [Umbaran] species looked like. I pretty much nailed it right out the gate.

"I didn't realize how Rey's lightsaber in that Dark Rey sequence [from *The Rise of Skywalker*] was supposed to work, so I came up with the idea of it being a flexible cable thing that was in the center. This is the first version, which has the flexible cable, and then we added a hinge." THOMAS

▸ Final design for Orla Jareni THOMAS

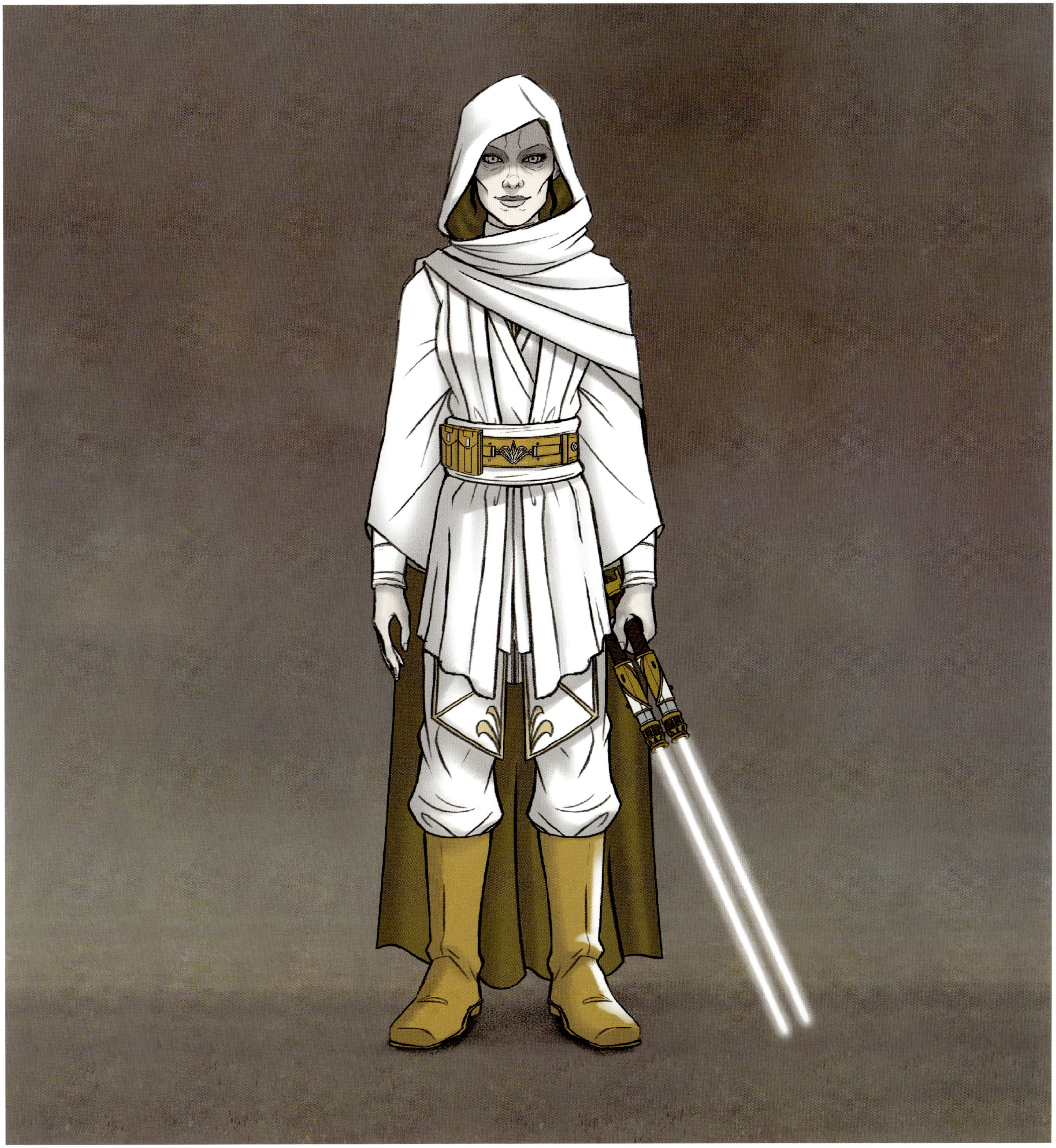

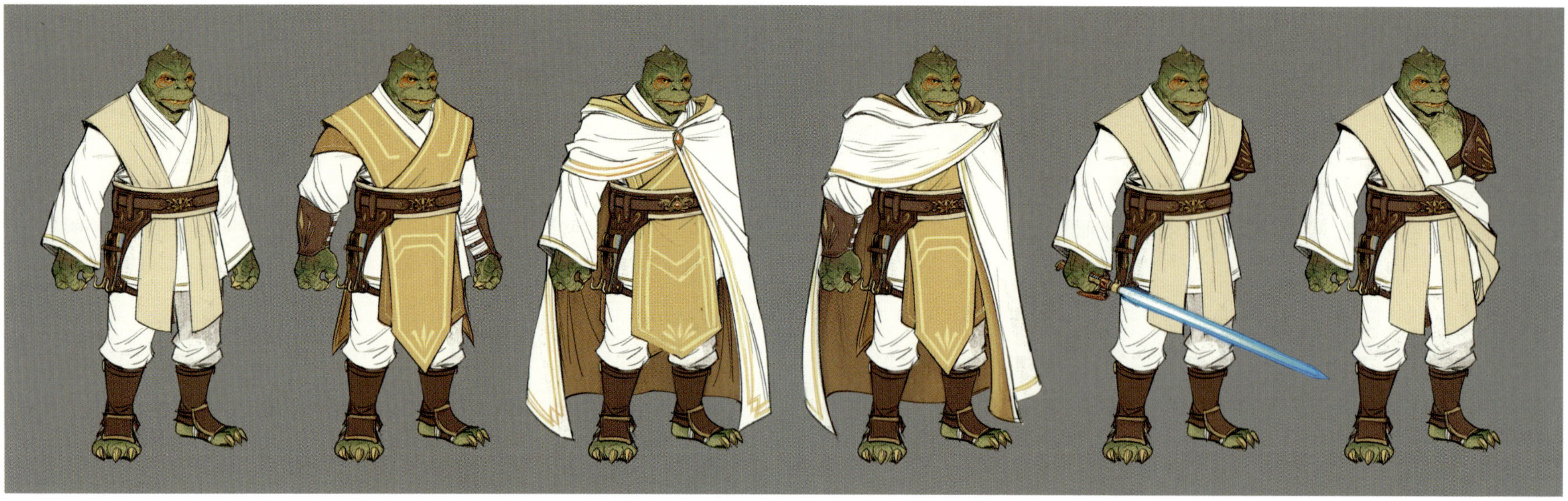

▲ Jedi Master Sskeer in temple attire SAITO

Sskeer's appearance visually hints at the passage of time when his arm is lost in battle but grows back anew due to his Trandoshan genetics.

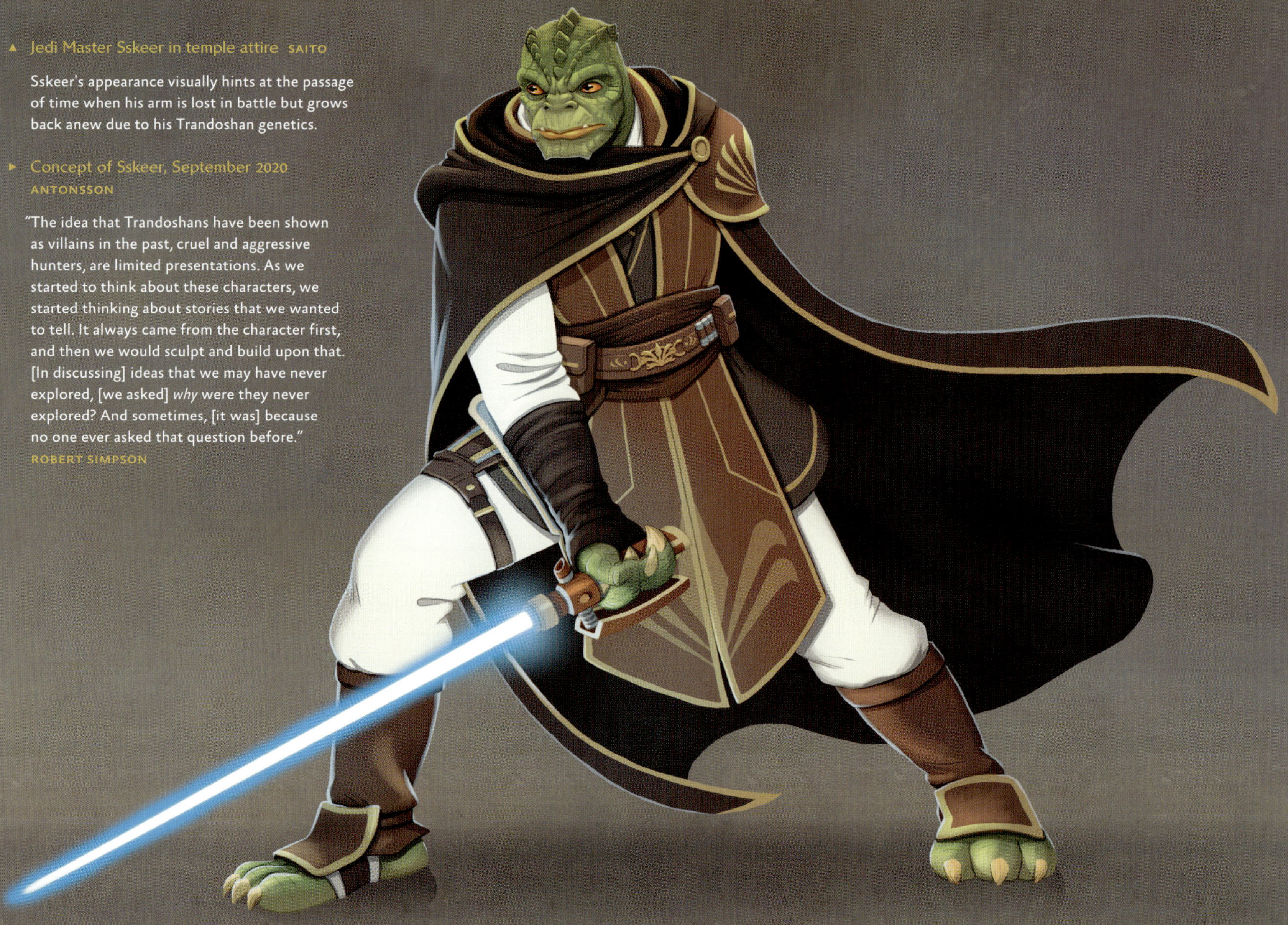

► Concept of Sskeer, September 2020 ANTONSSON

"The idea that Trandoshans have been shown as villains in the past, cruel and aggressive hunters, are limited presentations. As we started to think about these characters, we started thinking about stories that we wanted to tell. It always came from the character first, and then we would sculpt and build upon that. [In discussing] ideas that we may have never explored, [we asked] *why* were they never explored? And sometimes, [it was] because no one ever asked that question before."
ROBERT SIMPSON

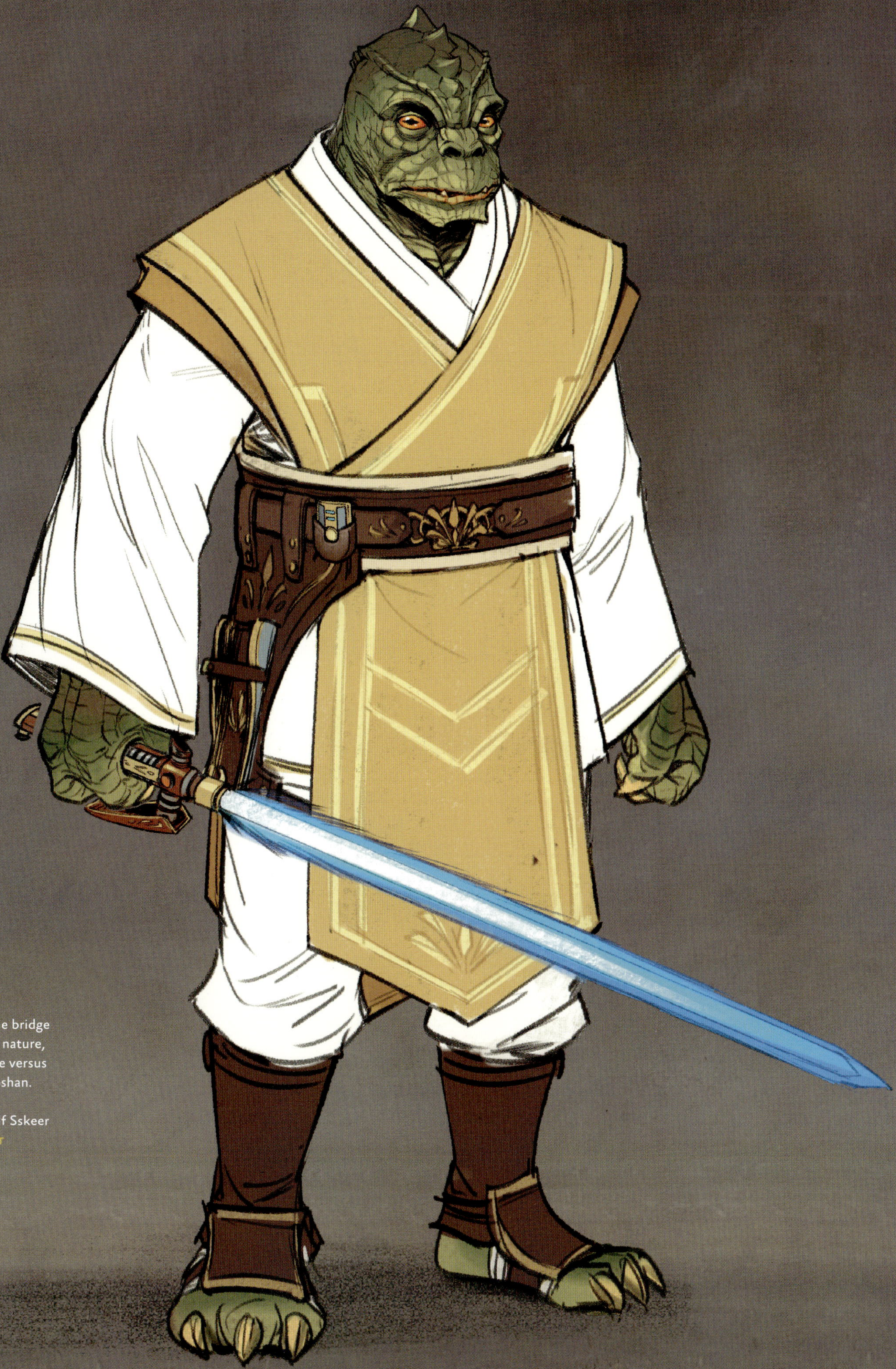

▸ Final design of Sskeer in temple attire SAITO

"A Trandoshan Jedi is like seeing a Klingon on the bridge of the *Enterprise*. It just seemed so against their nature, so I wanted to explore a character who is nature versus nurture. He wouldn't consider himself a Trandoshan. He's always been a Jedi.

We wanted Sskeer to be a tank, you know? If Sskeer was in front of you, you wouldn't argue." SCOTT

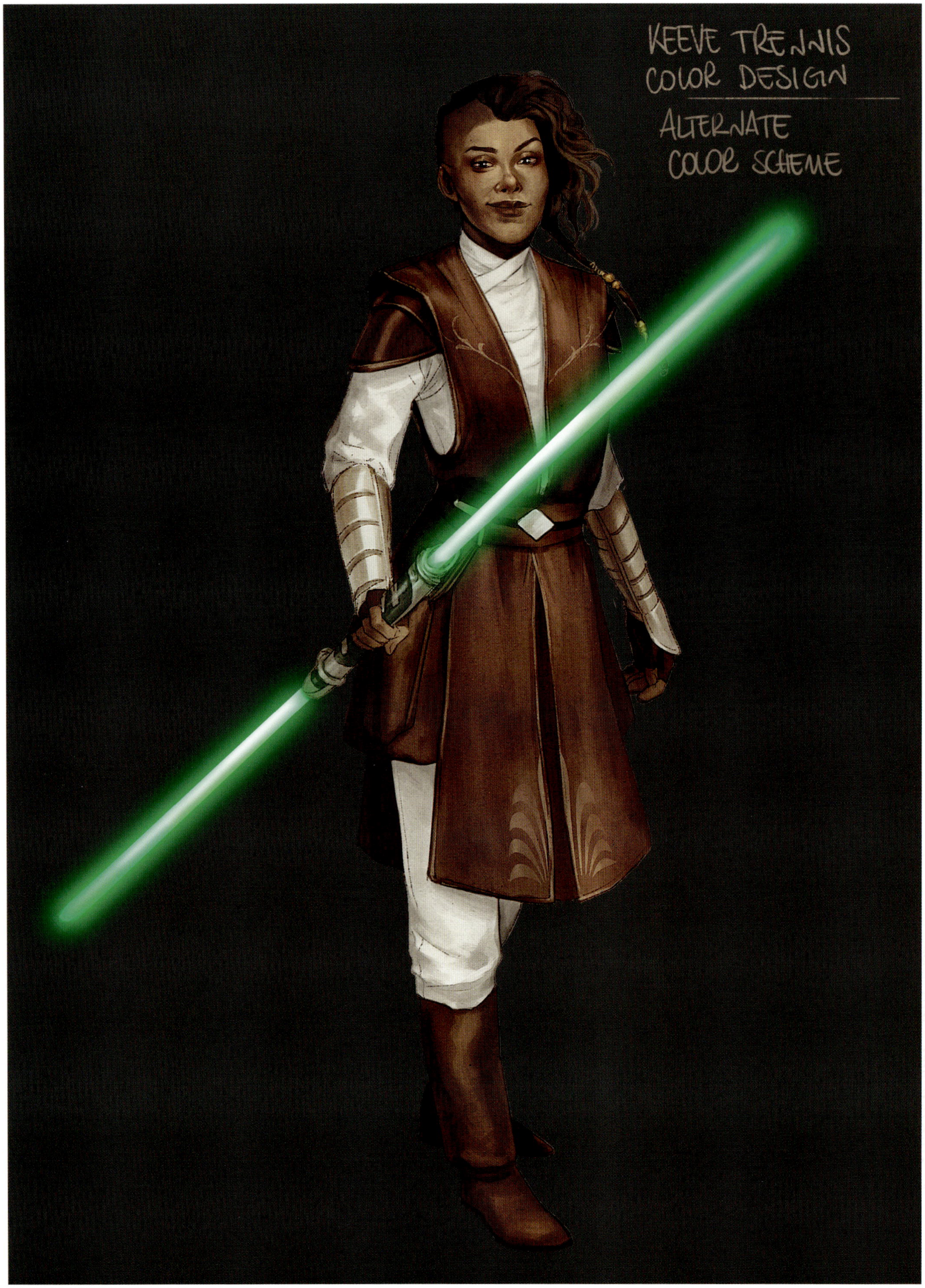

◂ Color design concept of Keeve Trennis SERIO

▸ Keeve Trennis in mission attire SAITO AND BROWN

"There was a moment where Keeve's hair looked drastically different. It was straightened; in some of the early concepts that Phil [Noto] did, her hair looked very relaxed. It was processed and flattened. And both [Lucasfilm graphic designer] Leigh Zieske and I looked at that and were like, 'That doesn't really look like what a Black woman's hair would look like.' We went on a photo search of different hairstyles and created a mood board, and there was an active conversation of wanting to depict her realistically. I mean, she's a soldier. She's a warrior. She's a peacekeeper. She's constantly on the move. [So we explored] how best to represent that in her clothes, her attire, her hair, and just be as realistic as possible." SIMPSON

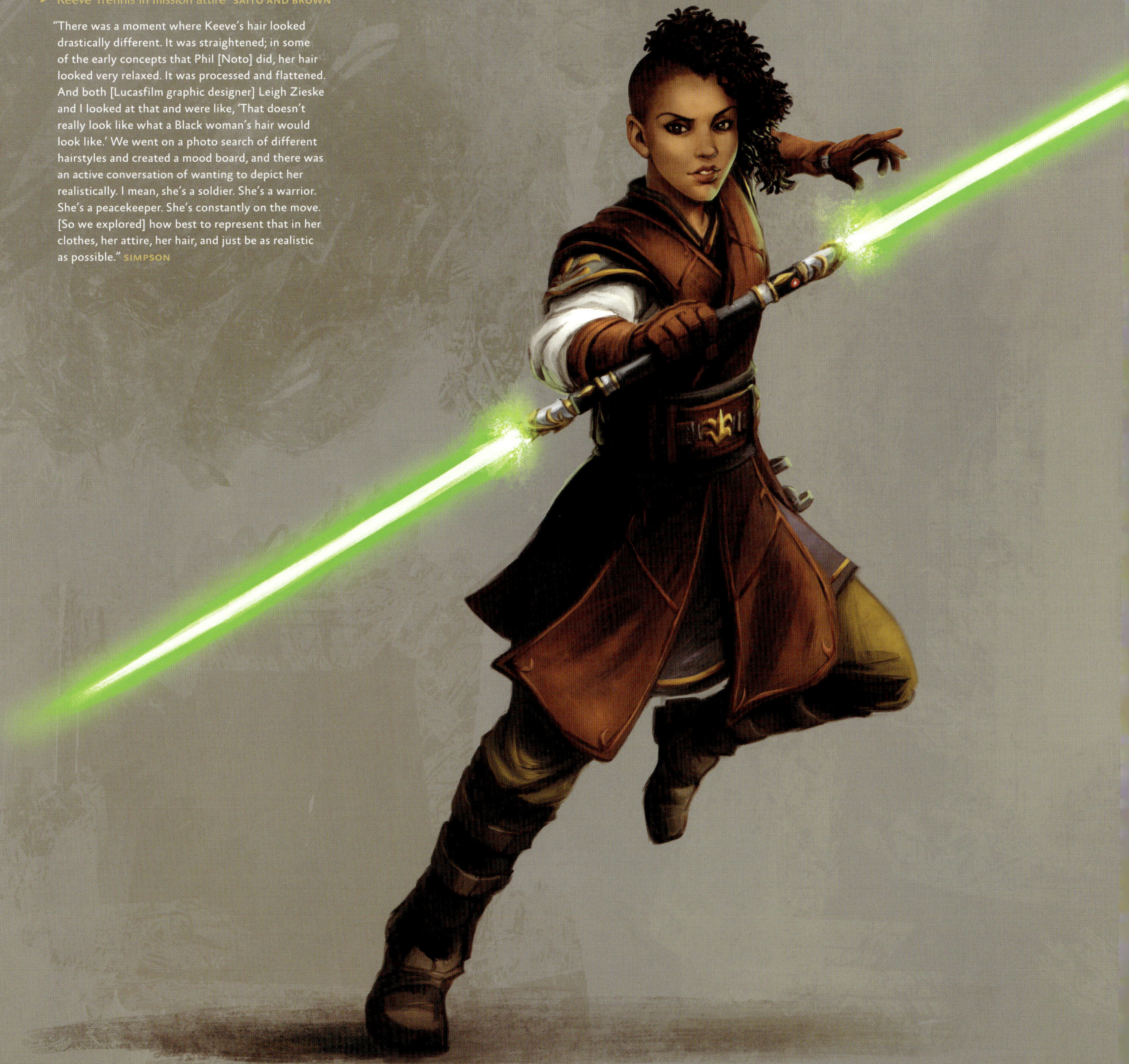

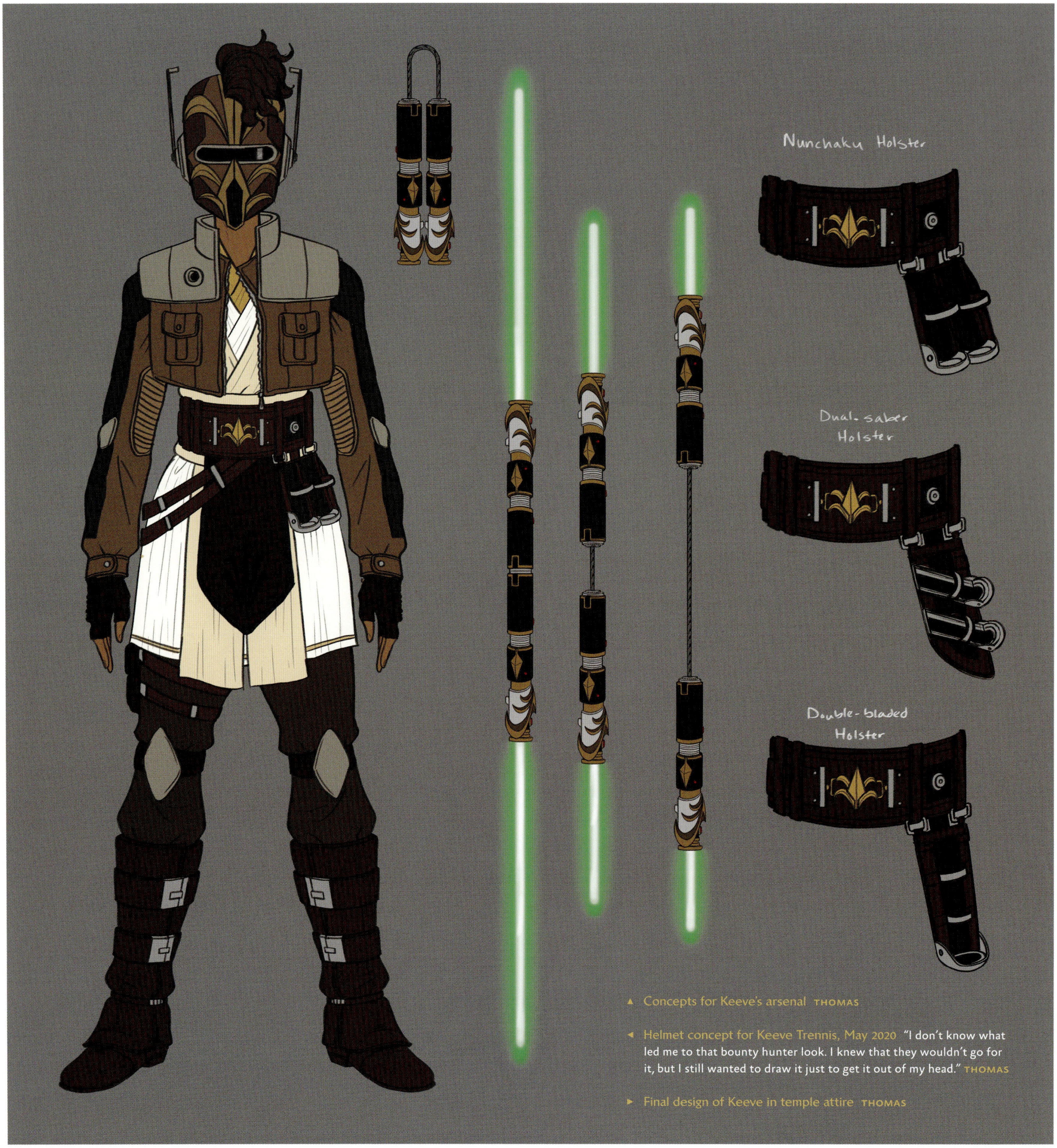

▲ Concepts for Keeve's arsenal THOMAS

◄ Helmet concept for Keeve Trennis, May 2020 "I don't know what led me to that bounty hunter look. I knew that they wouldn't go for it, but I still wanted to draw it just to get it out of my head." THOMAS

► Final design of Keeve in temple attire THOMAS

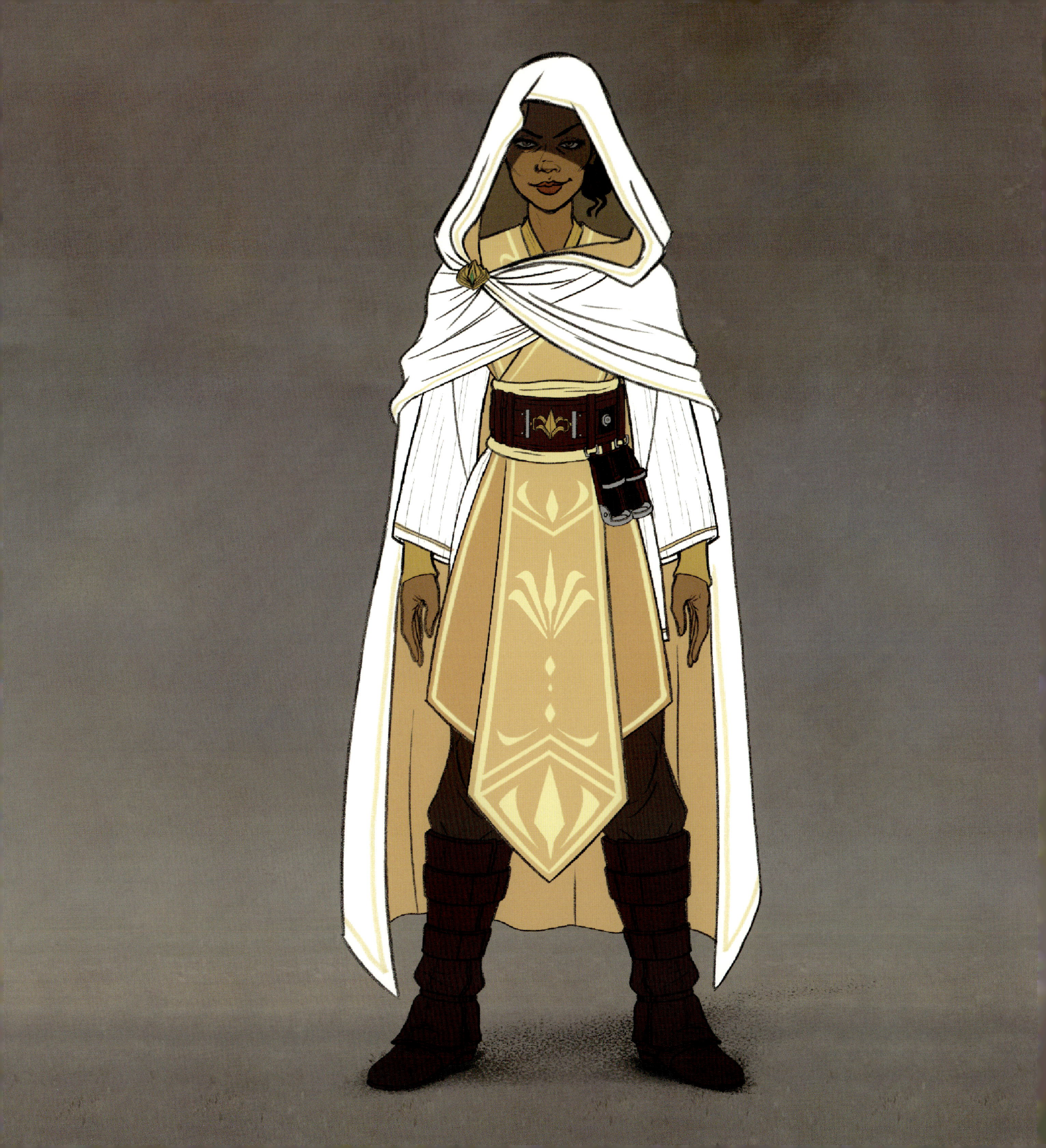

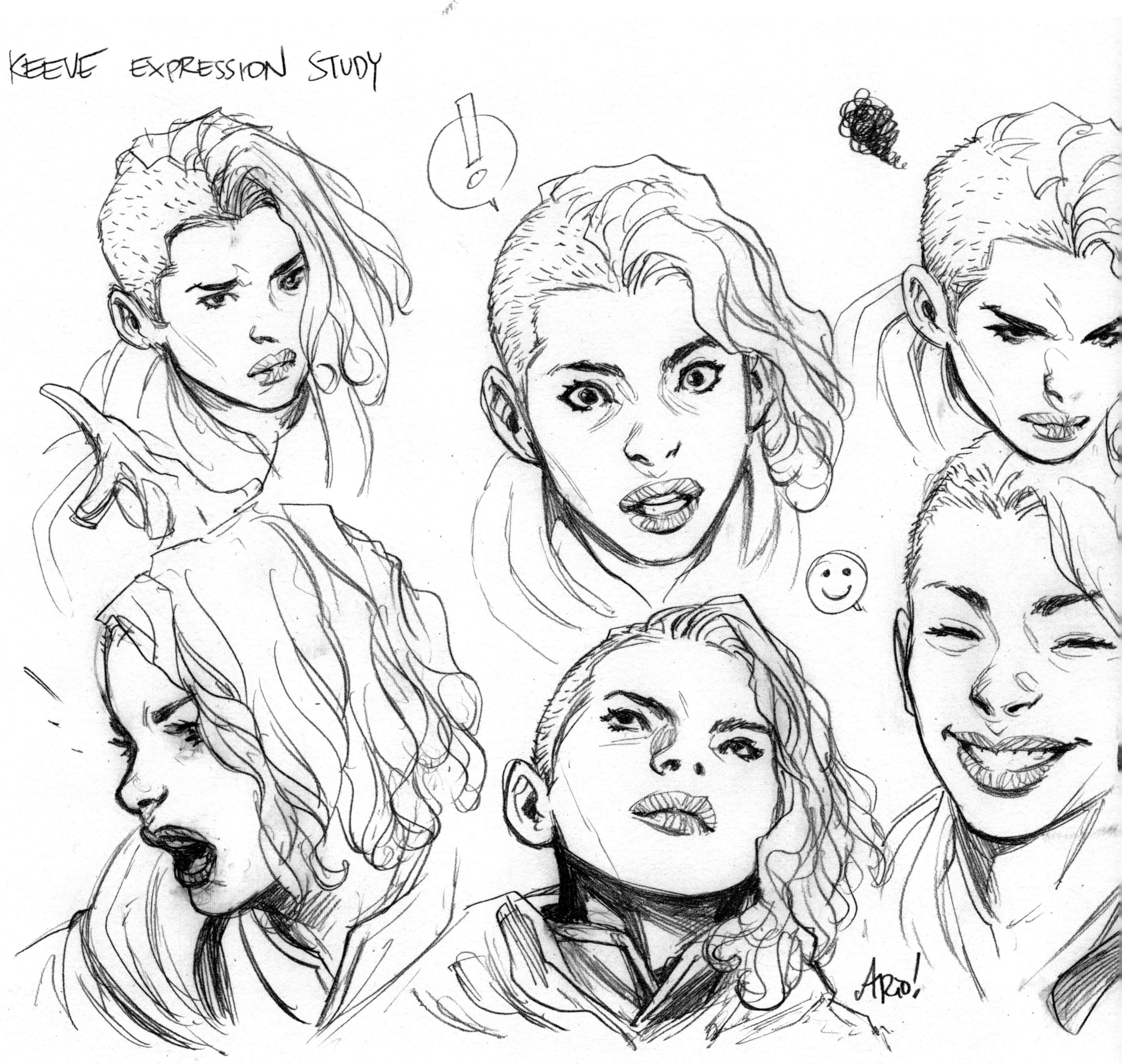
KEEVE EXPRESSION STUDY
!
ARIO!

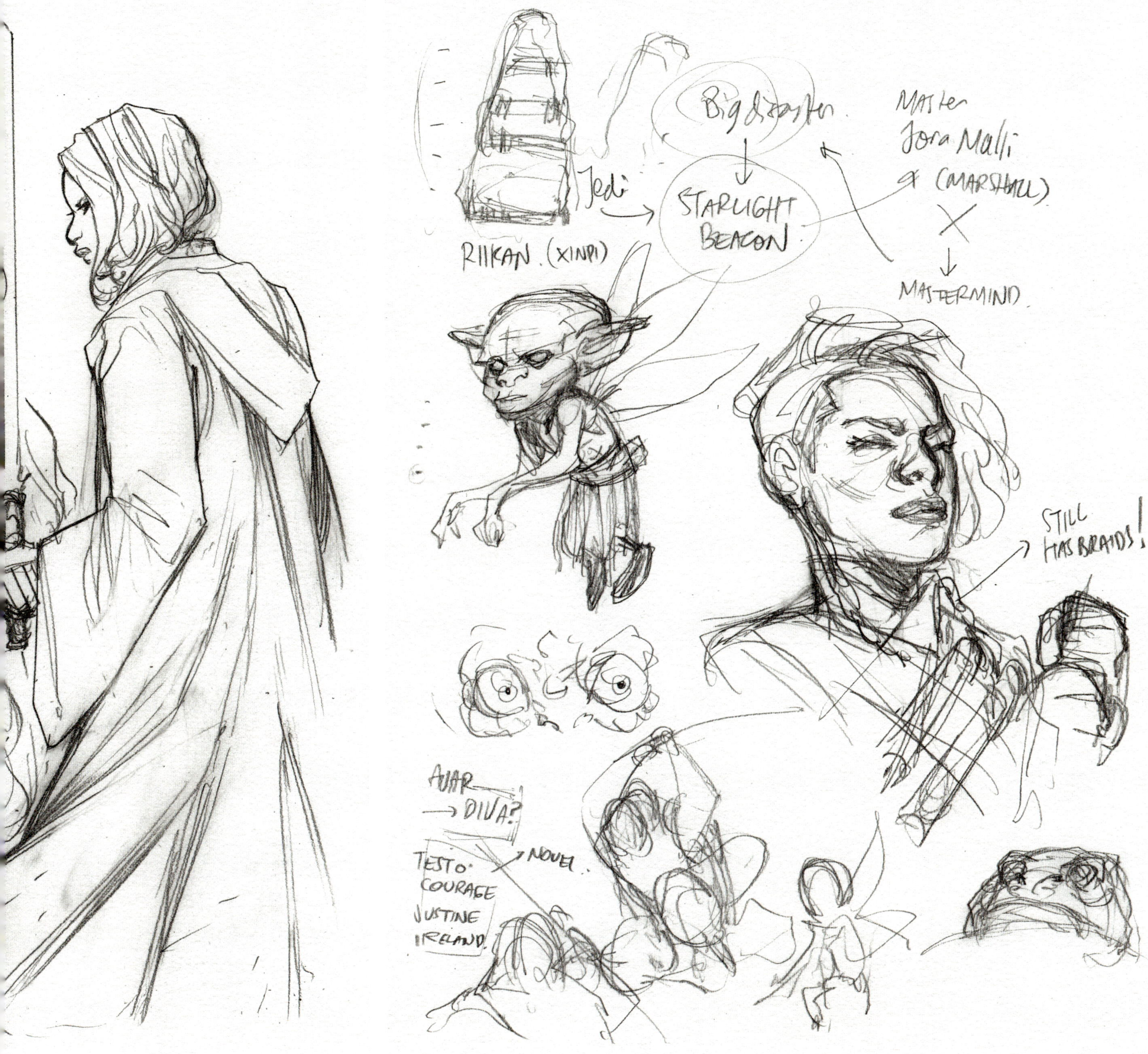

▲ Keeve expression study, July 2020 "Cavan and I both have a huge responsibility to make Keeve relatable and lovable. Cav is responsible for her characteristics, and I am responsible for how the characteristics project in a visual way. If I draw Keeve unsympathetically, then the reader might not feel that she's relatable." ANINDITO

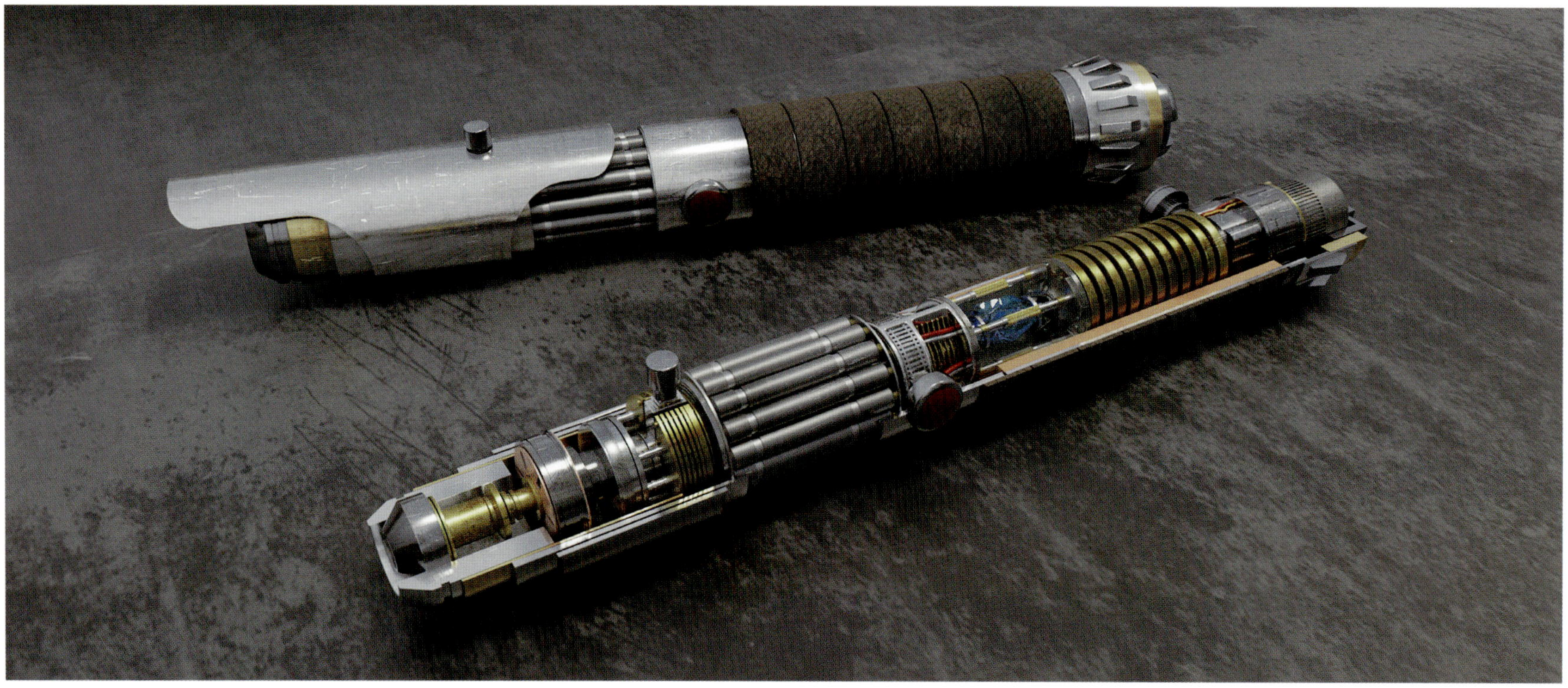

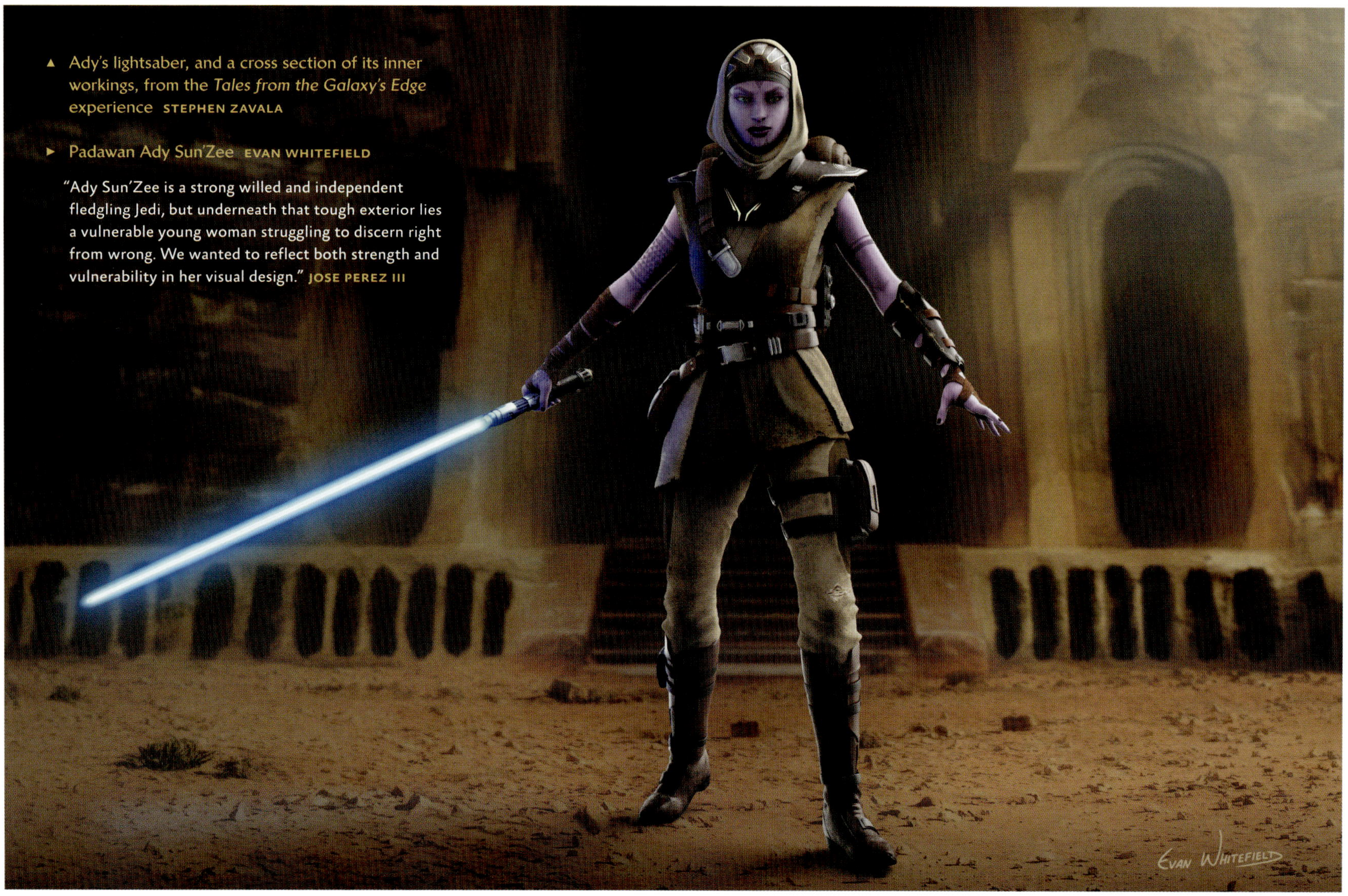

▲ Ady's lightsaber, and a cross section of its inner workings, from the *Tales from the Galaxy's Edge* experience **STEPHEN ZAVALA**

► Padawan Ady Sun'Zee **EVAN WHITEFIELD**

"Ady Sun'Zee is a strong willed and independent fledgling Jedi, but underneath that tough exterior lies a vulnerable young woman struggling to discern right from wrong. We wanted to reflect both strength and vulnerability in her visual design." **JOSE PEREZ III**

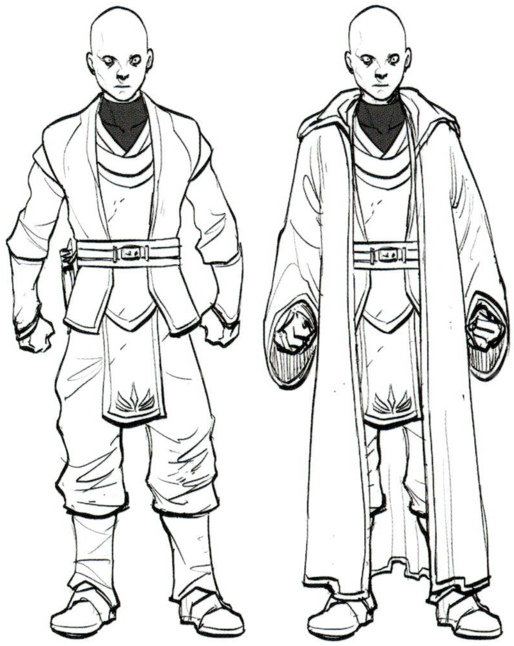

▲ Concept design for Terec and Ceret in mission attire, October 2020 ANINDITO

Creating the look for the Kotabi bond-twins' mission gear brought to mind the look of late 1990s boy bands, who often wore similar apparel with slight variations to showcase individuality. "It's all the same shape, but the color is different because they are basically the same. There's two, but they're one," Anindito said with a laugh. "I decided to incorporate a lot of leather because they need to be protected, and I put this metal chest protector on them, just for the sake of the boy band [aesthetic], because it's all incorporated in the design. Even on the chest plate you get to see two parts of it with one line separating it. The design is basically a lot of replication."

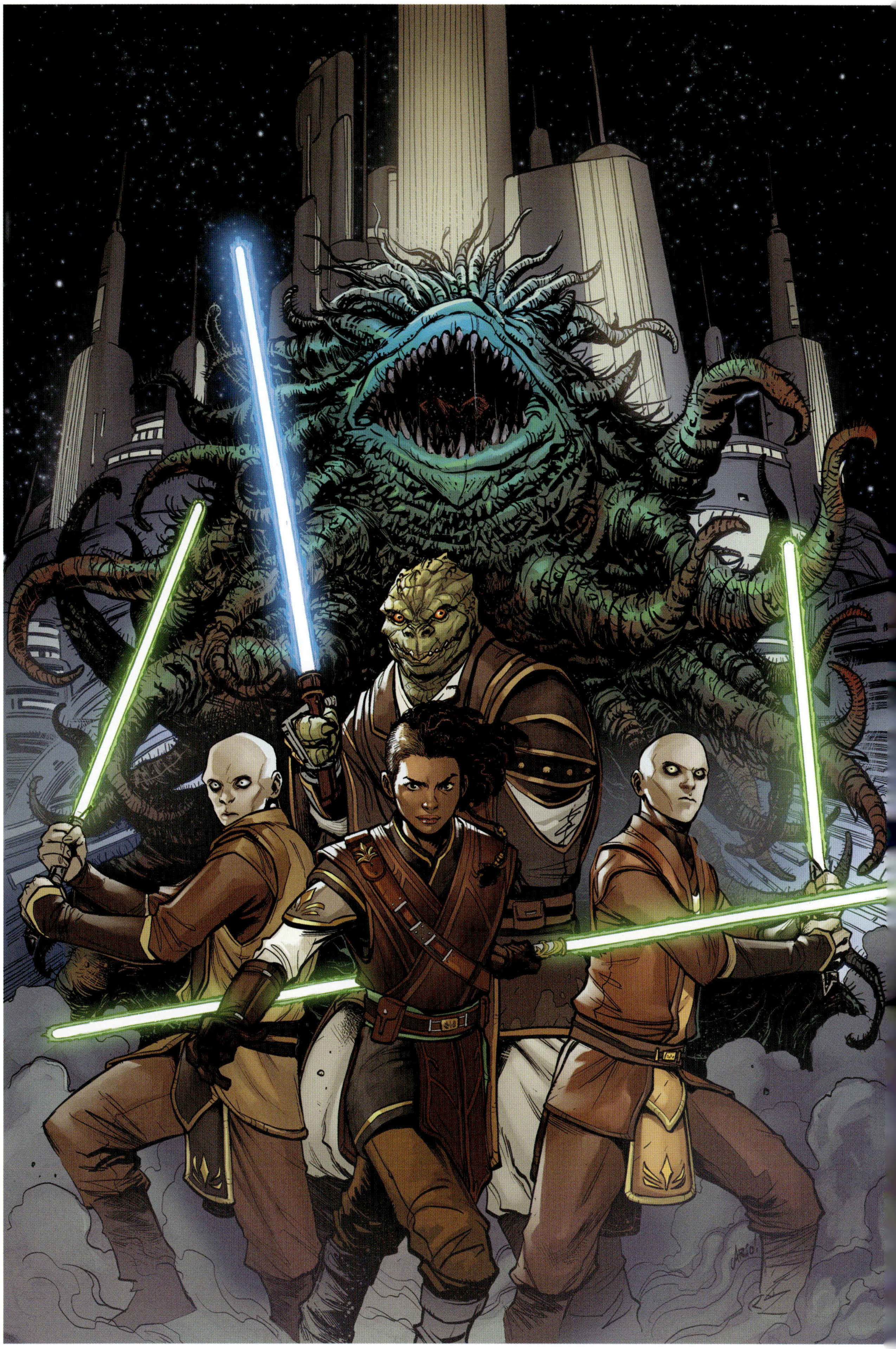

► Final design of Keeve, Sskeer, Terec, and Ceret as seen on variant cover B of Marvel's *Star Wars: The High Republic* #1 ANINDITO (PENCILER) AND RAIN BEREDO (COLORIST)

"We changed the Drengir's color from purple and pink to green and blue to be more menacing. I deliberately made Keeve's lightsaber cropped on the right because I want to push the reader to open the page." ANINDITO

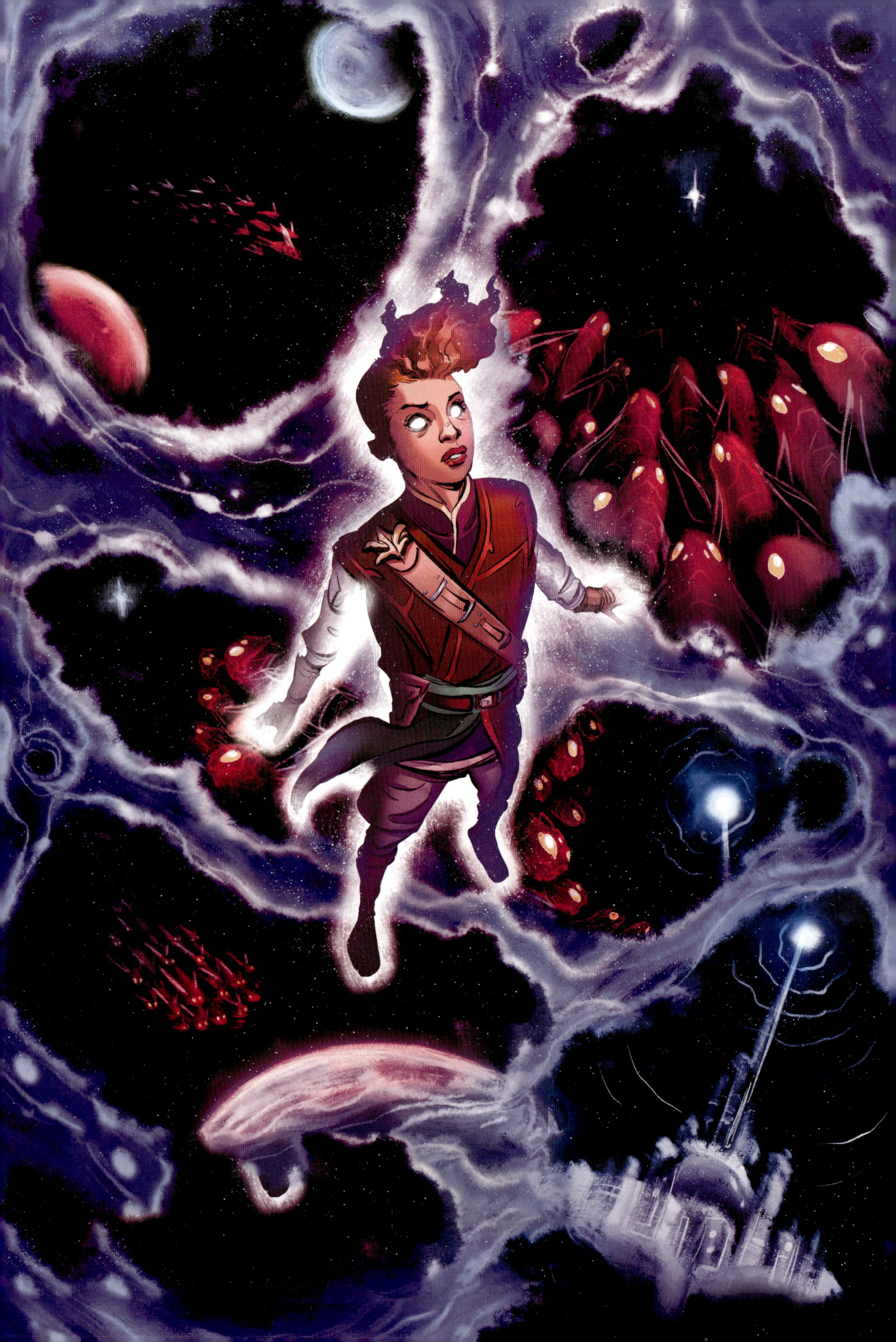

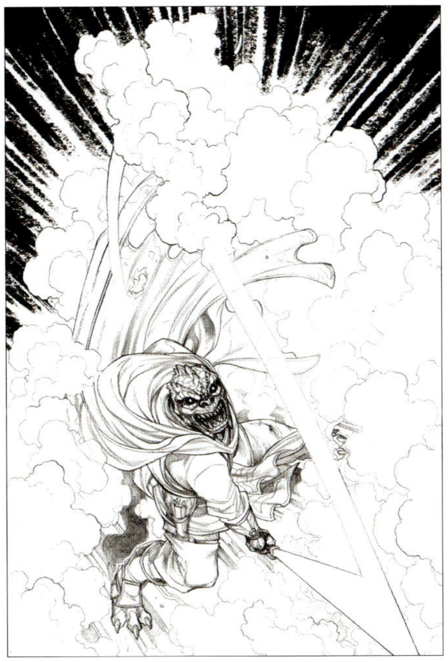

▲ Preliminary pencils for an interior from Marvel's *Star Wars: The High Republic* #2, later used as a second printing cover ANINDITO

► Final designs for Sskeer out of control and under the influence of the Drengir for the second printing variant cover of Marvel's *Star Wars: The High Republic* #3 ANINDITO (PENCILER), MORALES (INKER), AND LEONI (COLORIST)

"The first time we get to see Sskeer out of control and letting his animalistic side come out because he's frustrated that he's losing the Force, it doesn't really look like him. It looks evil. It looks like you [shouldn't] trust him anymore. I think most of it is the eyes.

"When he's being controlled by the Drengir, you can see that he is more zombie-like instead of a raging monster. You don't feel scared, but you want him to be OK. You want him to be free. And in a way, it is also scary because you don't know what he is capable of doing under the Drengir's influence. And also there are Drengir behind him, so it's a situation that you don't want to meet at the end of a tunnel." ANINDITO

◄ Concept design of the Force as seen by Keeve Trennis from Marvel's *Star Wars: The High Republic* #1 ANINDITO (PENCILER), MORALES (INKER), AND LEONI (COLORIST)

"I want [Keeve's experience of the Force] to feel very cosmic. This is the Force that connects everything. It is very ethereal. I had a hard time imagining the pages before I made it, but once I started, I don't know what happened to me. Maybe the Force is strong with me. [*Laughs*] This is the most powerful visual that I've ever done for *Star Wars*." ANINDITO

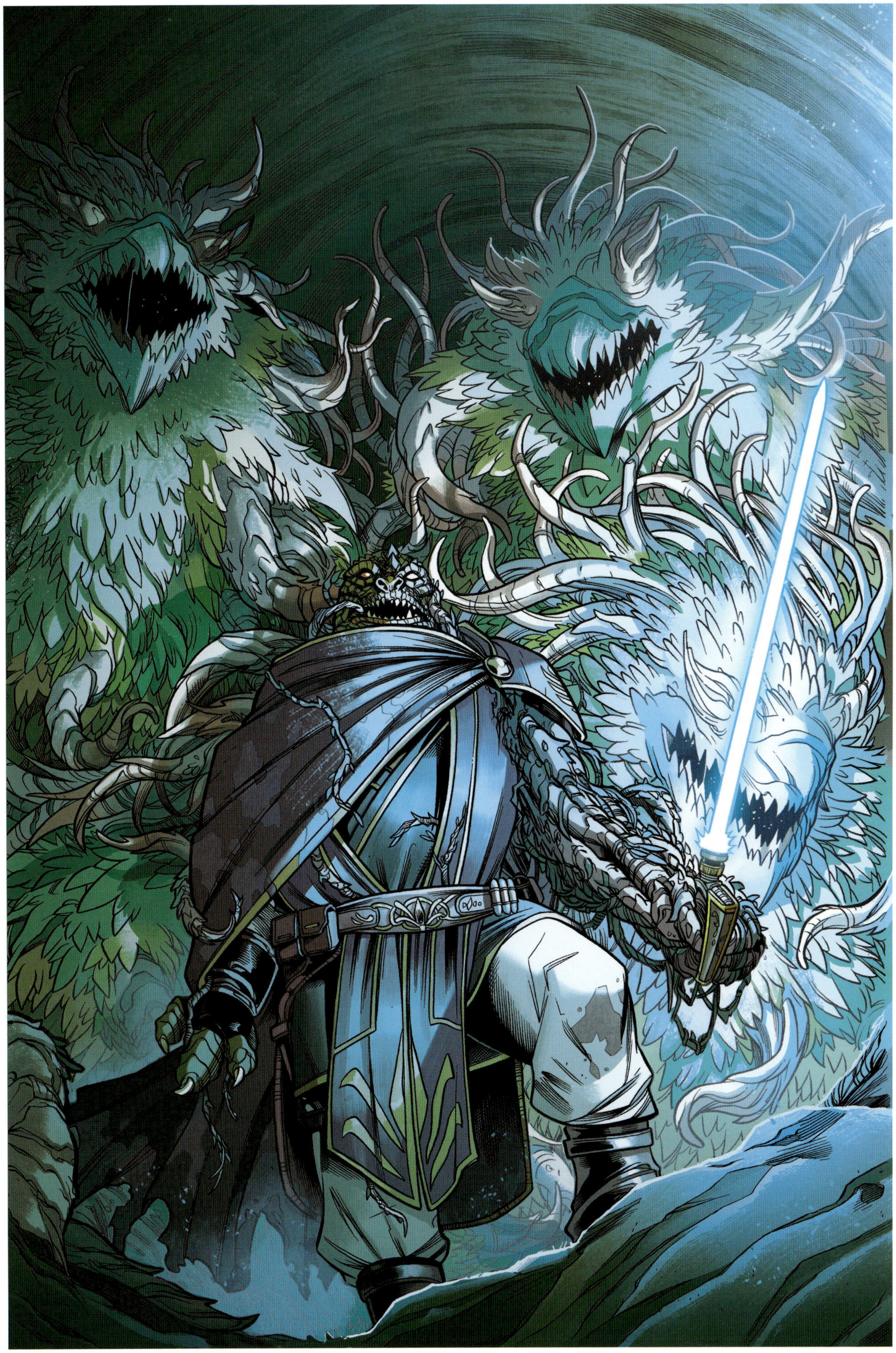

▸ Initial concepts for Porter Engle

"He was skewing a little Hellboy-ish with his horns, and he wasn't as jolly as he should have looked; he looked kind of evil and mean, so we got rid of the color in his hair, giving it more of a Santa Claus-like base." THOMAS

Thomas was watching a lot of *MasterChef* during the time he was designing for *Star Wars*. Gordon Ramsay's attire inspired the master-duelist-turned-cook's sleeveless chef's jacket and made Engle one of his favorite characters to design. "I just love the idea of a really badass Jedi that just wants to cook," he said. "He loves cooking. He retired to become the chef. I think that's so cool."

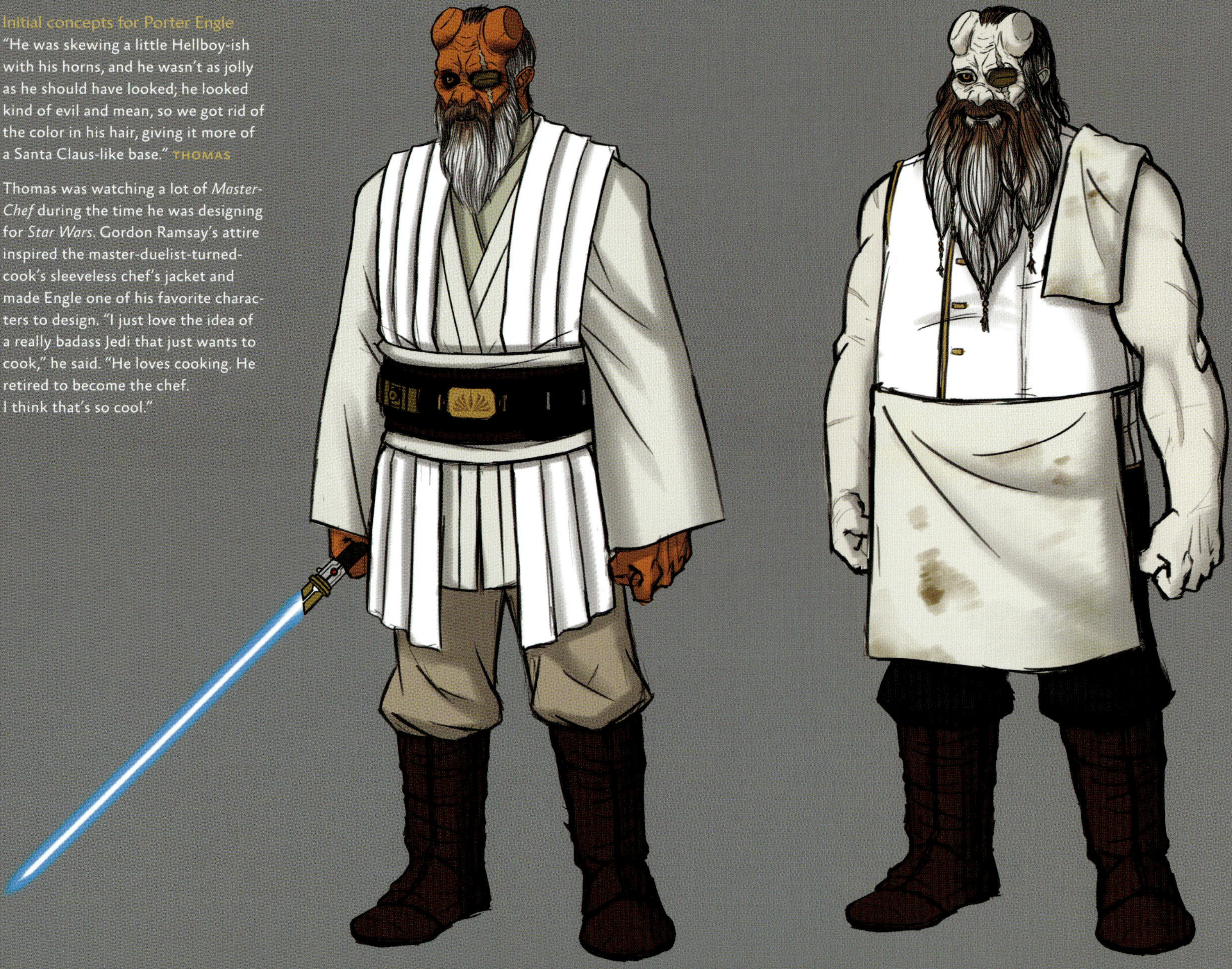

▸ Concepts for Engle's lightsaber

"Count Dooku's lightsaber, you know, it's made for his fighting style; he's like a fencer-duelist. I thought that Engle should have a curved handle, too." THOMAS

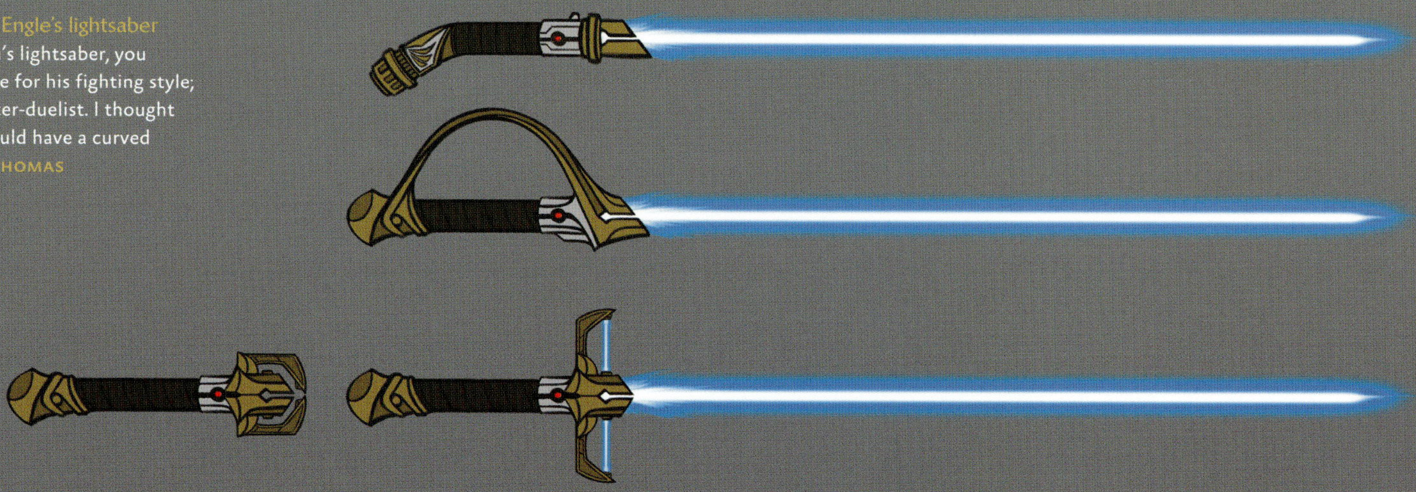

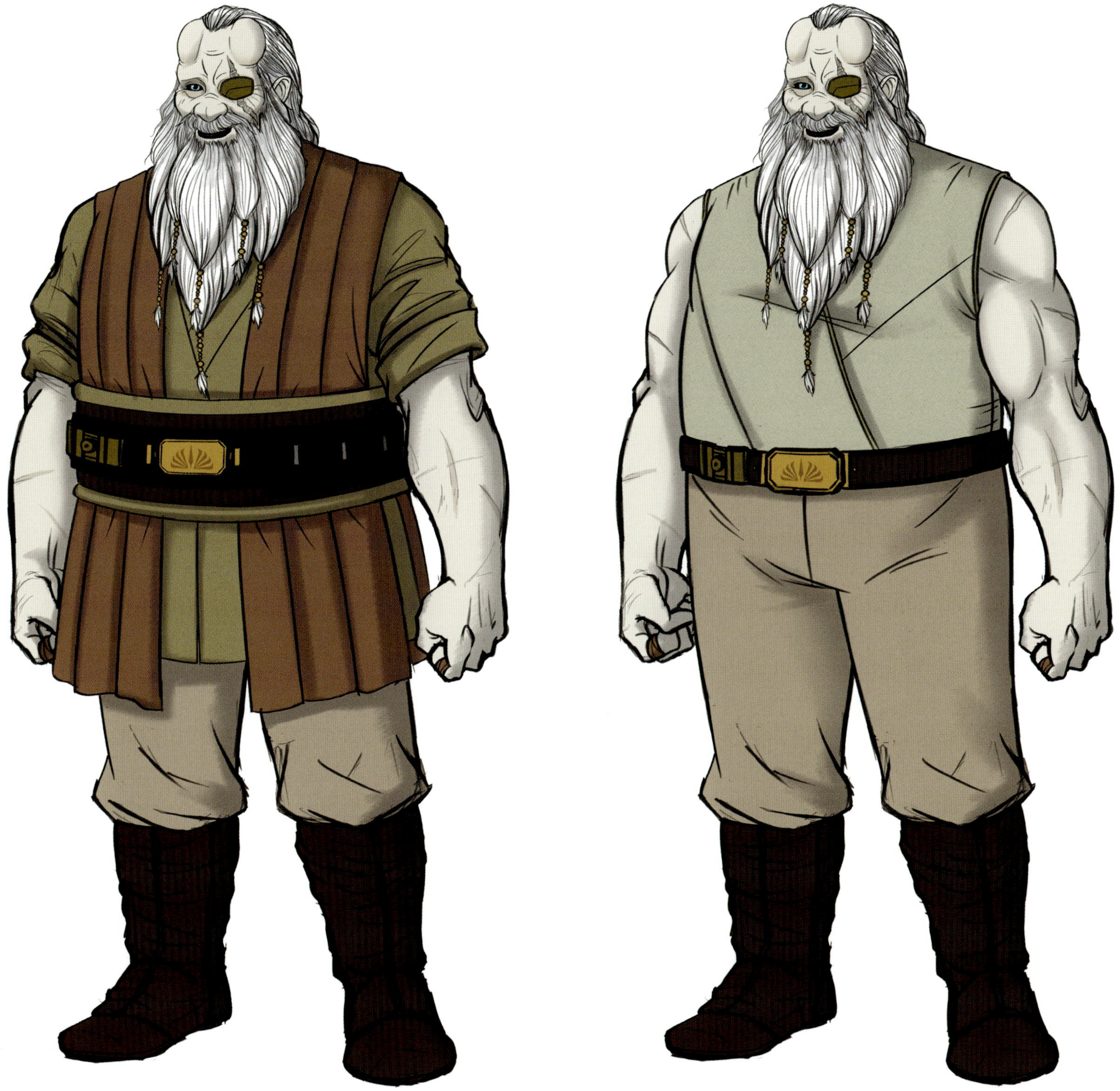

▲ Final design for Porter Engle, May 2021
THOMAS

"Porter Engle wants to be friends with you, but it's hard for people to get close to him, and he finds it hard to get close to other people, and it's very isolating. He's a character who I love, and I think his design reflects that.

He's more beard than man, but he's this Jedi that has been part of the Order for 300 years and has done everything. He's an utter legend. When he gets reactivated in the story because the Nihil come calling, he becomes absolutely terrifying. I don't think you want to be anywhere near a guy like that when he is [in active combat]. The sad thing about Porter Engle is that he knows that. There's a reason he decided to go be a cook . . . I wanted [him] to feel like the happy cook because that's the version that he really wants to be. And that's the version I think people really connect with." SOULE

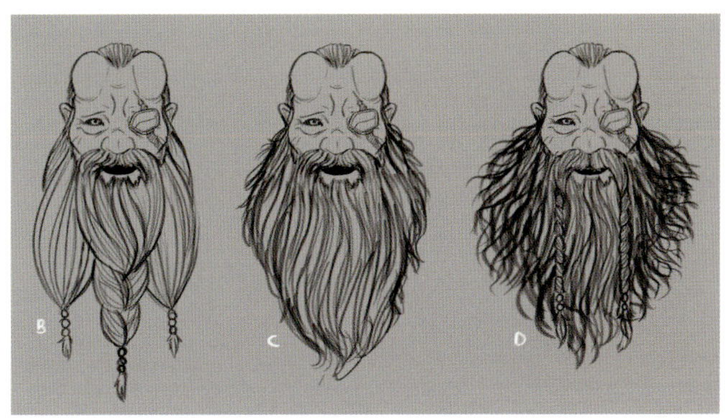

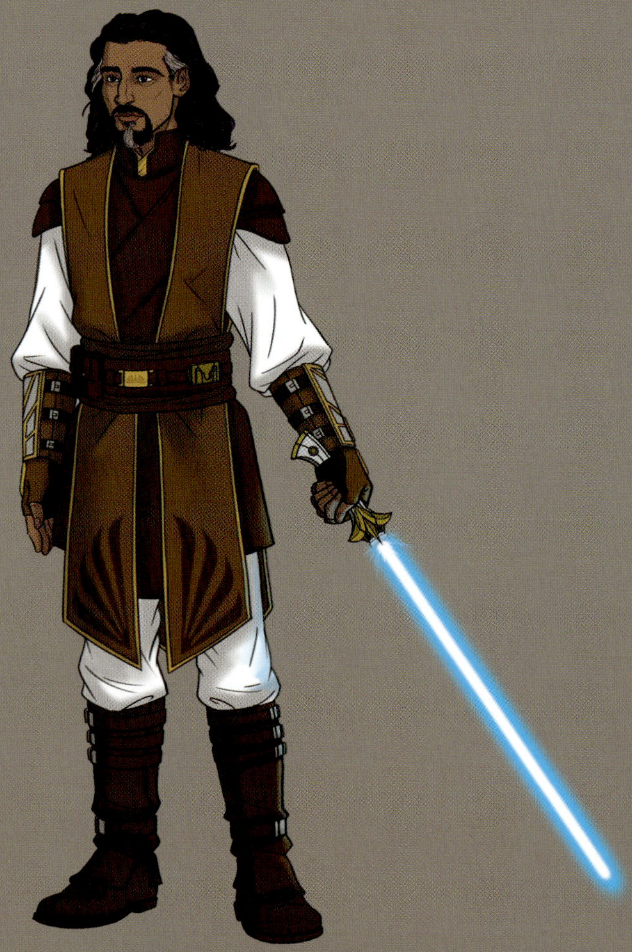

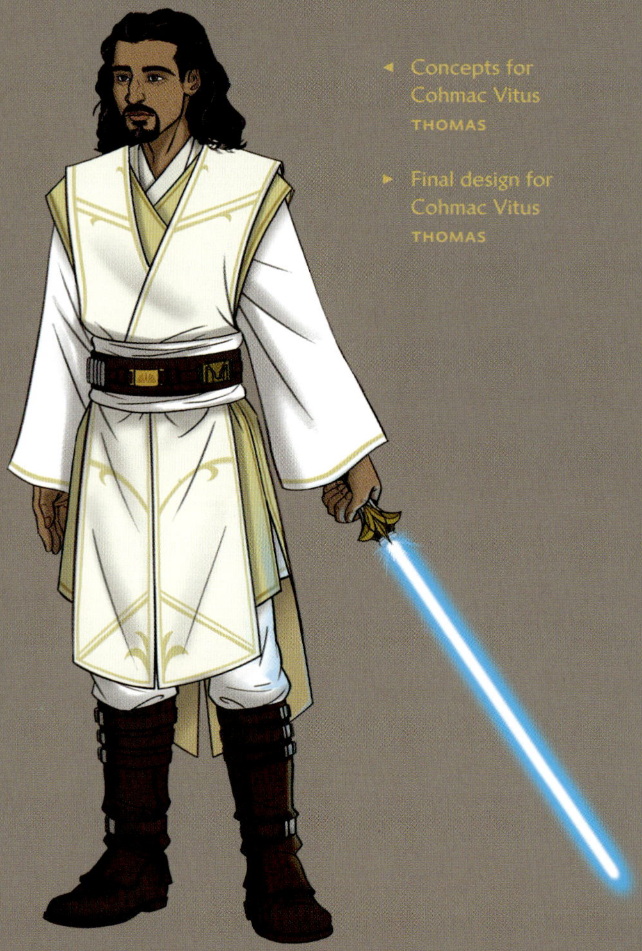

◄ Concepts for Cohmac Vitus
THOMAS

► Final design for Cohmac Vitus
THOMAS

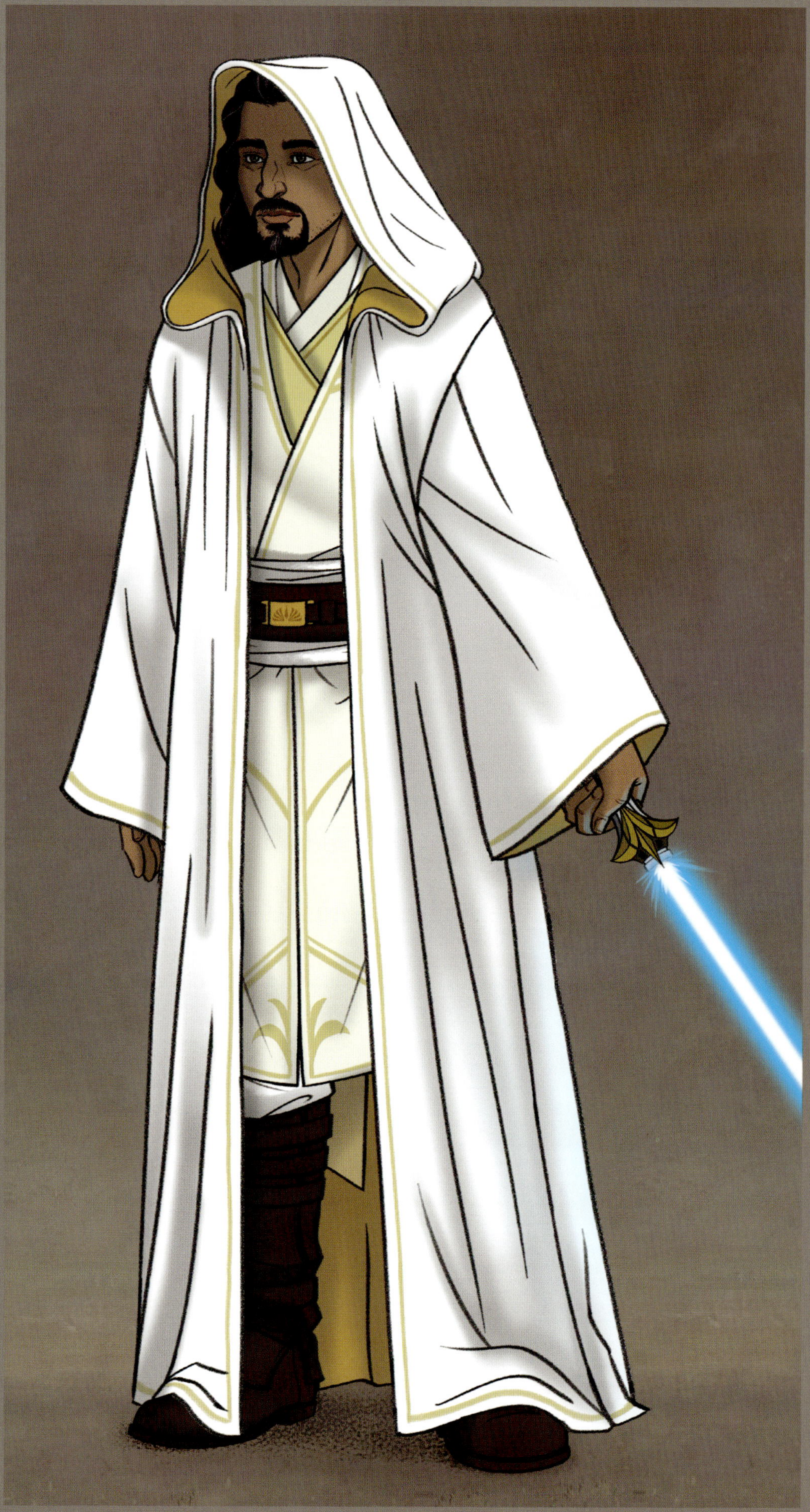

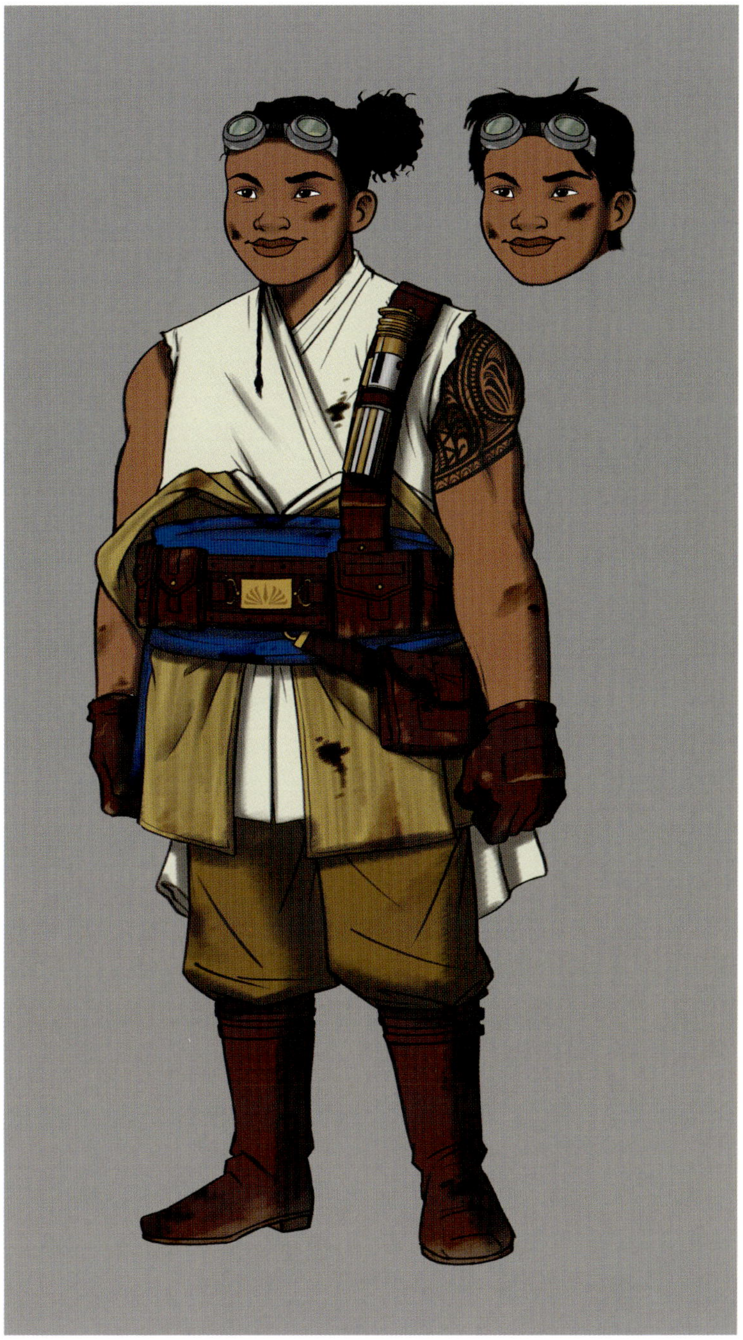

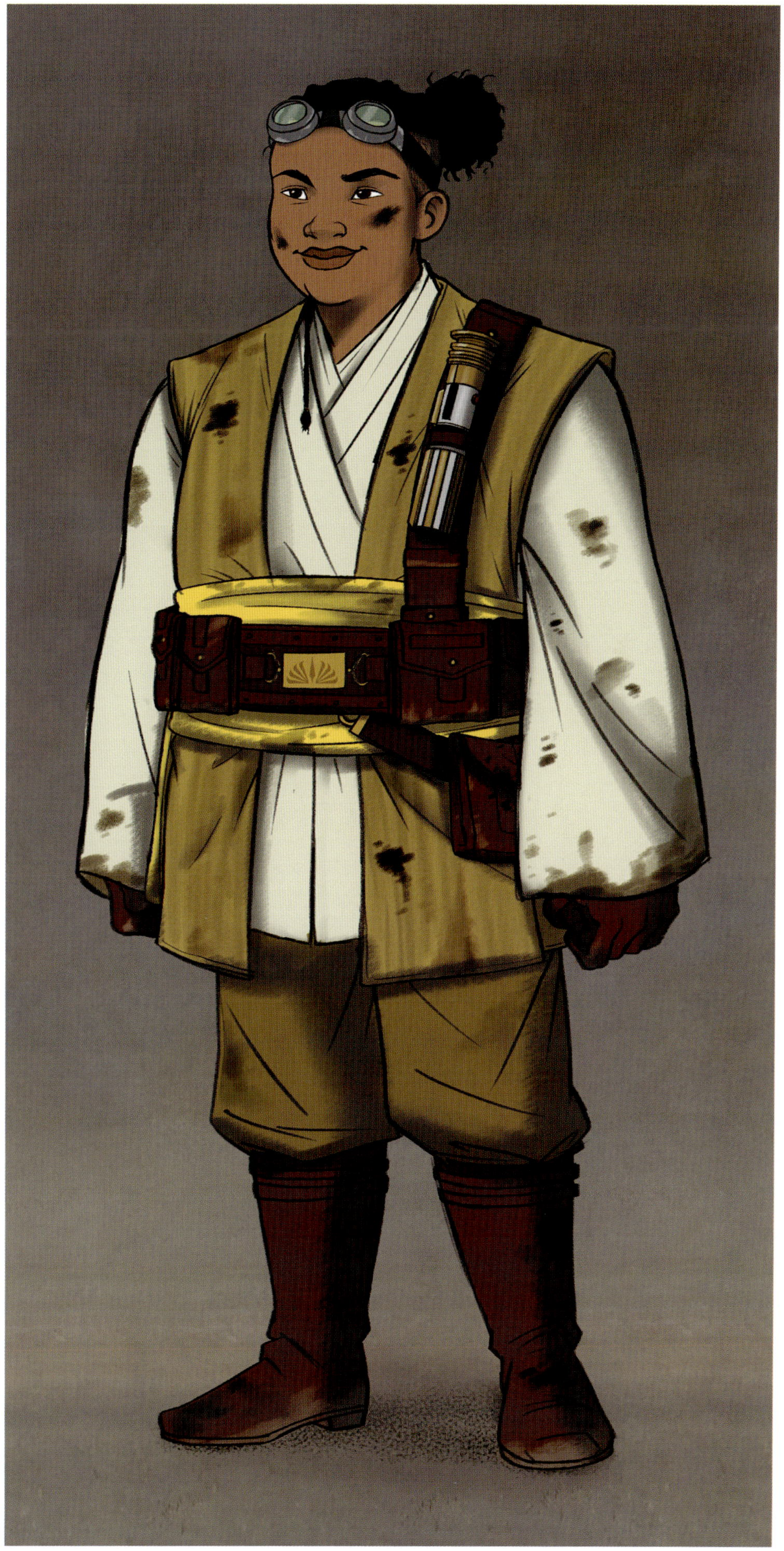

▲ Concept for Ram Jomaram THOMAS

"I really wanted Ram to be a bigger kid. I wanted a Jedi that was not interested in the trappings of being a Jedi, but his connection to the Force is really through mechanics. That's how he understands the world, and that's all he wants to do. He doesn't want to be on stage. He wants to fix stuff. And that's what he enjoys doing. He's a very utilitarian Jedi Padawan." OLDER

Early designs for Ram included a tribal shoulder tattoo as a nod to the character's Polynesian inspiration, but it was ultimately removed for sensitivity.

► Final design for Ram Jomaram THOMAS

At the hip, where most Jedi carry their lightsabers for easy access, Thomas instead placed pouches for Ram's tool kit, a nod to the utilitarian Jomaram's priorities. "I figured his tools were his go-to weapon, what he's passionate about. And his lightsaber, the Jedi part of him, isn't too far away from that," Thomas said.

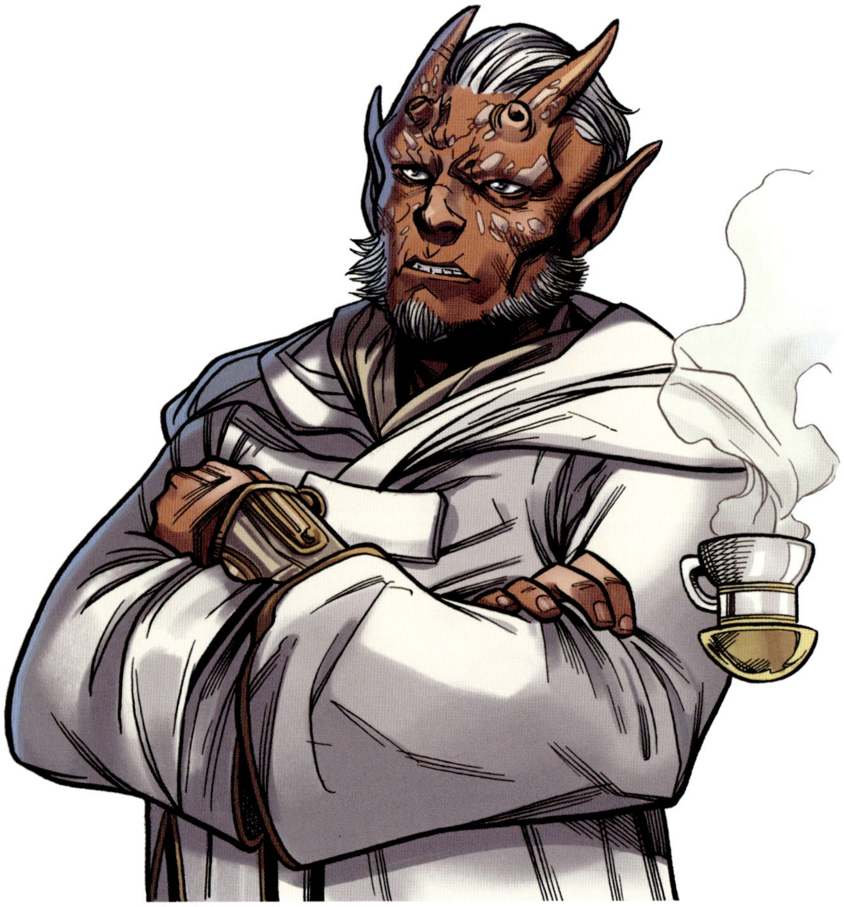

▲ Jedi Estala Maru from Marvel's *Star Wars: The High Republic #3* ANINDITO (PENCILER), MORALES (INKER), AND LEONI (COLORIST)

"Maru was a Twi'lek right up to the last few minutes of us designing him." SCOTT

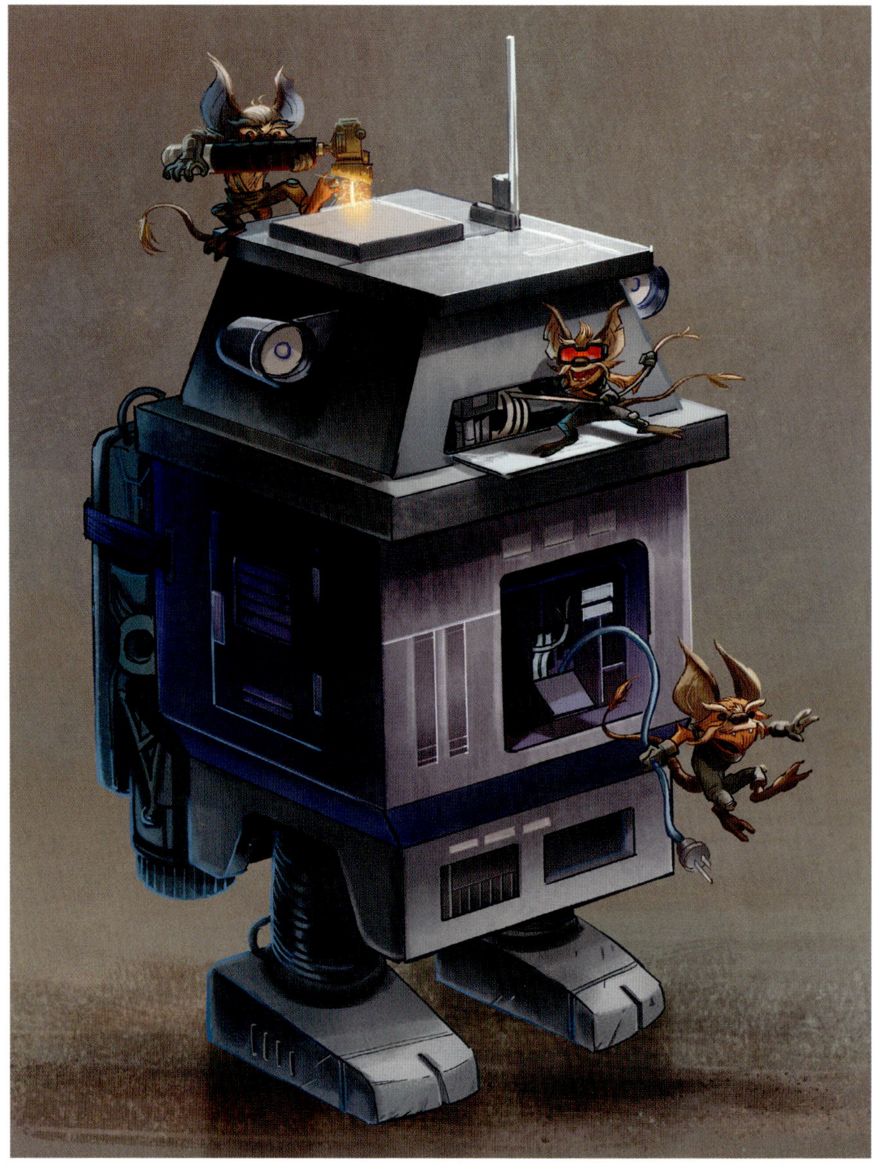

▸ V-18 and bonbraks ANTONSSON

By making some special modifications himself, Ram transformed an old droid, V-18, into something more. "V-18 is like a box. Ram has to paint him purple so that he doesn't [get mistaken for a crate and] keep getting traded away," Older said.

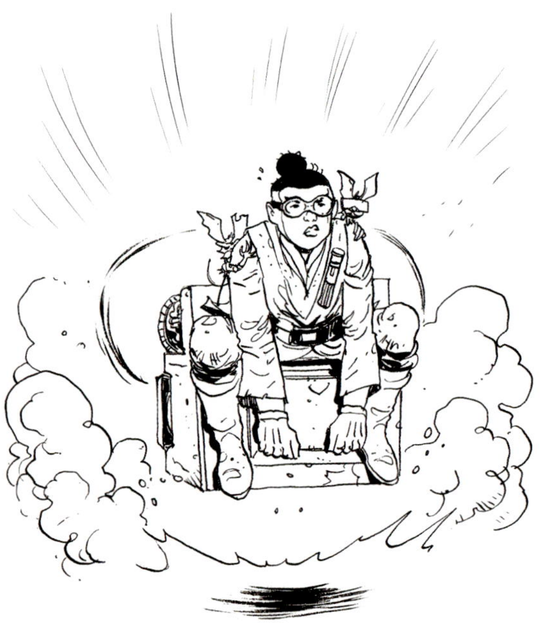

▲ Ram flying on V-18 NICK BROKENSHIRE

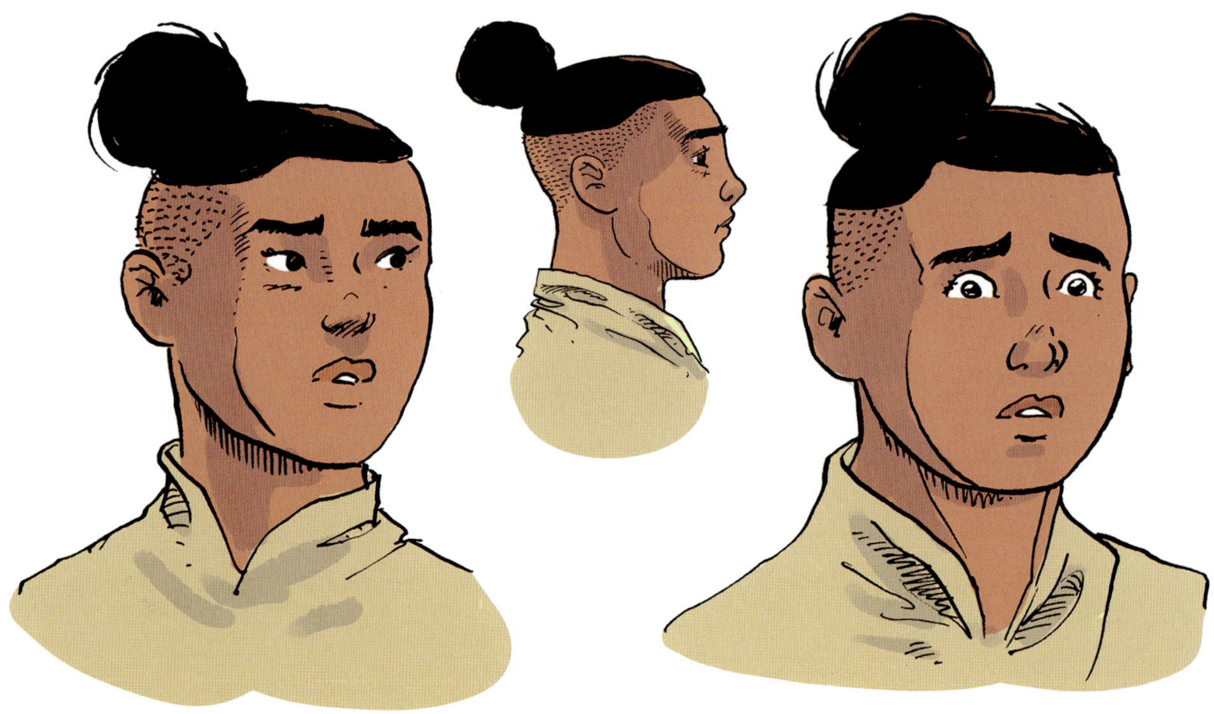

▸ Facial study for Ram Jomaram BROKENSHIRE

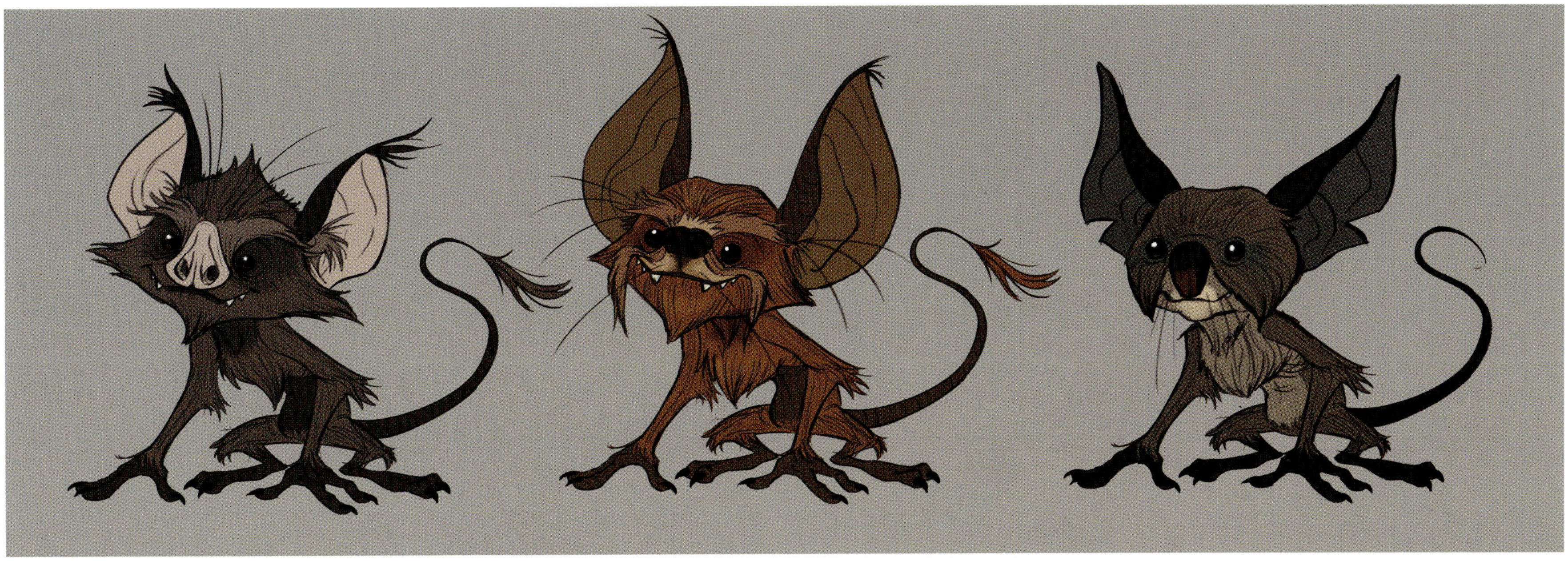

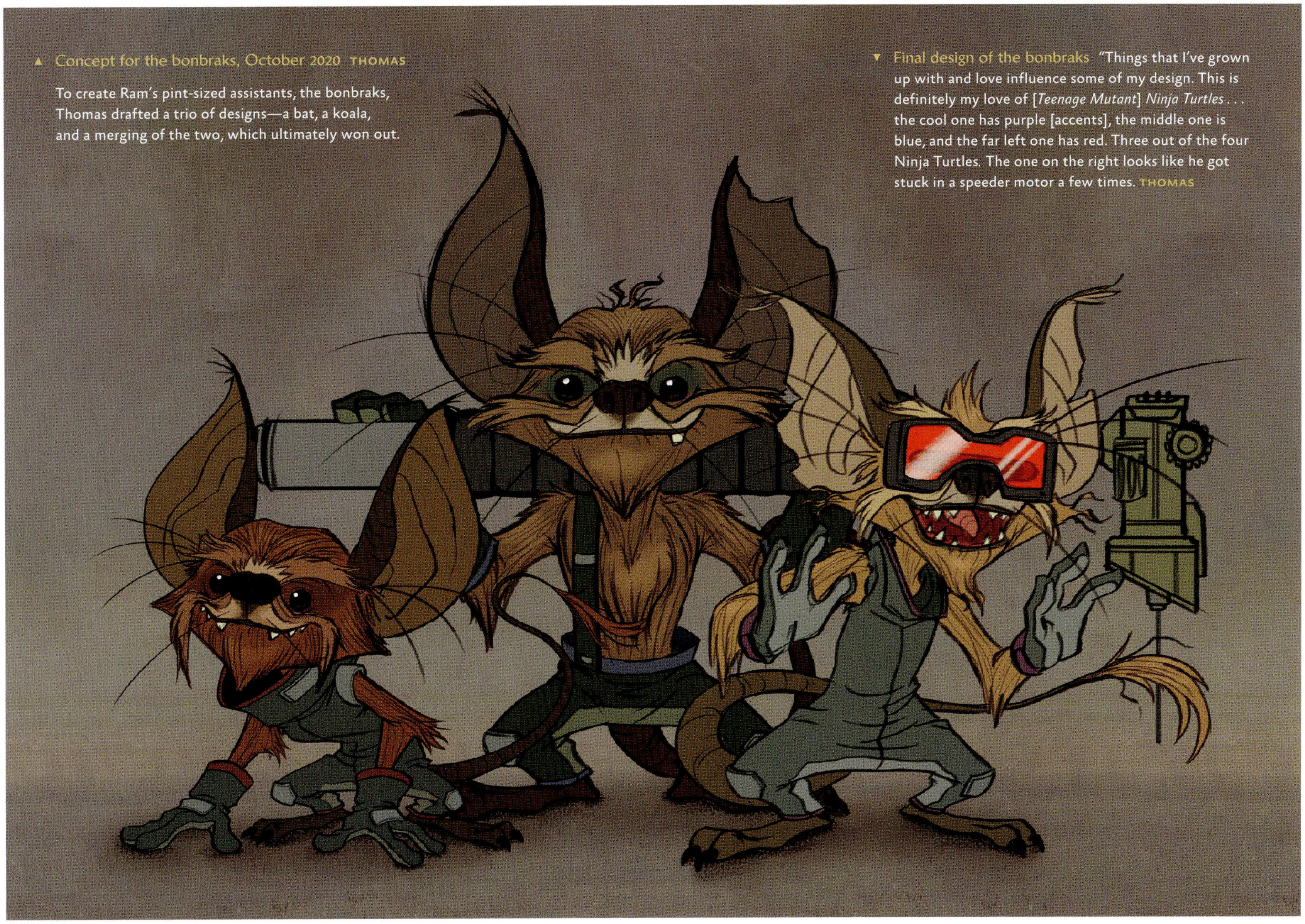

▲ Concept for the bonbraks, October 2020 THOMAS

To create Ram's pint-sized assistants, the bonbraks, Thomas drafted a trio of designs—a bat, a koala, and a merging of the two, which ultimately won out.

▼ Final design of the bonbraks "Things that I've grown up with and love influence some of my design. This is definitely my love of [*Teenage Mutant*] *Ninja Turtles* . . . the cool one has purple [accents], the middle one is blue, and the far left one has red. Three out of the four Ninja Turtles. The one on the right looks like he got stuck in a speeder motor a few times. THOMAS

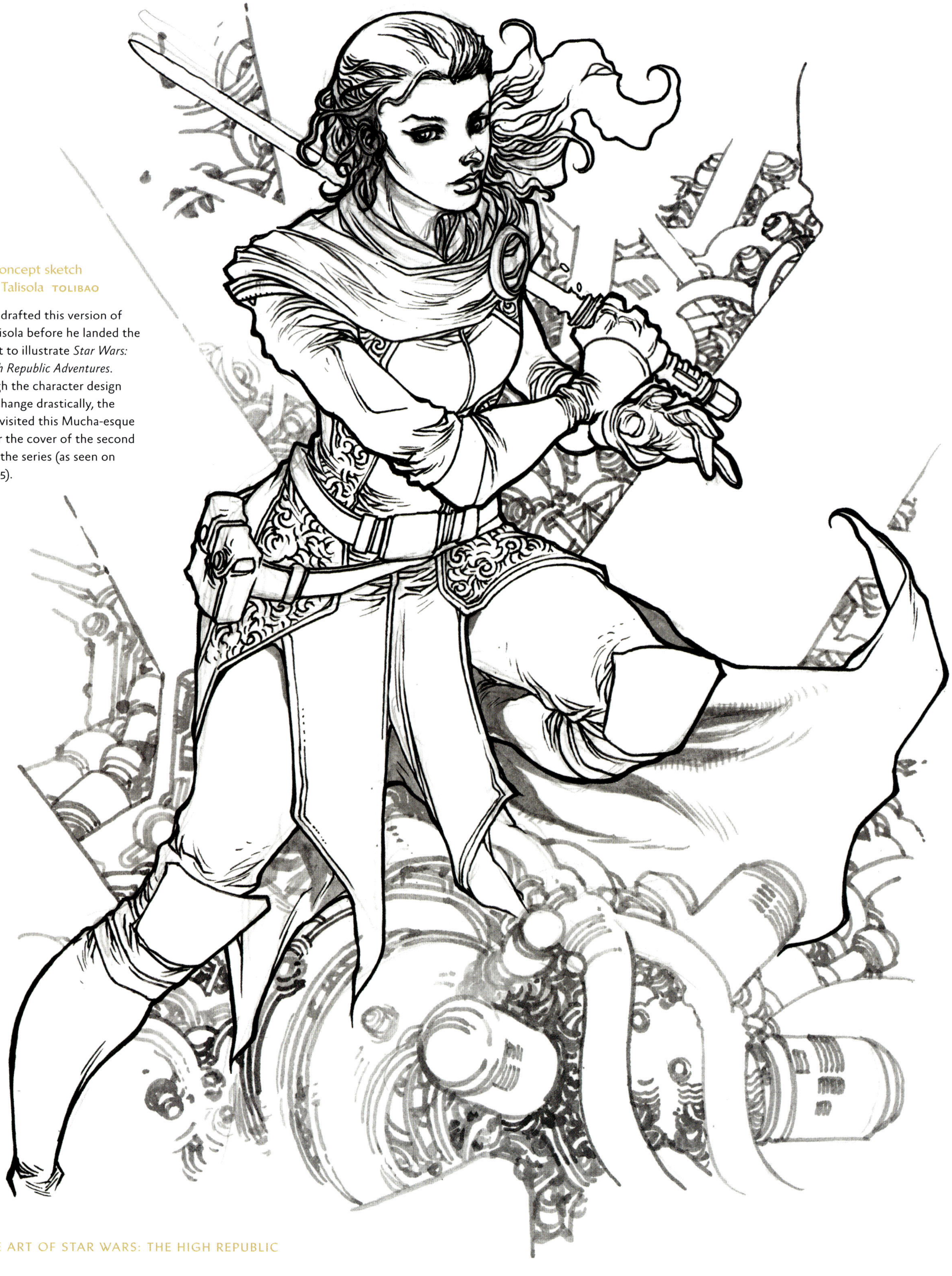

Initial concept sketch of Lula Talisola TOLIBAO

Tolibao drafted this version of Lula Talisola before he landed the contract to illustrate *Star Wars: The High Republic Adventures*. Although the character design would change drastically, the artist revisited this Mucha-esque pose for the cover of the second issue in the series (as seen on page 205).

▸ Initial designs for Farzala, "Quort," and Lula MAX DUNBAR

An early design for Qort added an extra vowel to his name and envisioned his bony face covering as a skull-like plague doctor's mask with a series of feathers affixed along the crown. The first incarnation of Lula Talisola appeared older and wore her hair in loose curls instead of her trademark dreadlocks. But Farzala remained largely the same, a protective older brother figure who was inspired by the character Kambei from *Seven Samurai*, the Akira Kurosawa epic that was an important influence on George Lucas when he initially envisioned his space opera. "When you watch that one, there's one character who is like the big brother of everyone," Tolibao said. "He's the toughest one. And that's my Farzala."

▾ Sketches for the cover of IDW's *Star Wars: The High Republic Adventures #1* TOLIBAO

As Tolibao refined Qort's mask, the facial covering's softer edges took on the recognizable shape of a triceratops' bony frill. "When I designed it, for me, it's a mask. And I always think that there's a kid behind it. There's a kid inside this mask," Tolibao said, noting the mysterious nature of the character's bandage-covered body. A Jedi in training, this Padawan doesn't speak Galactic Basic, a fact that brings to mind a loyal Wookiee. "For me, he's like Chewbacca."

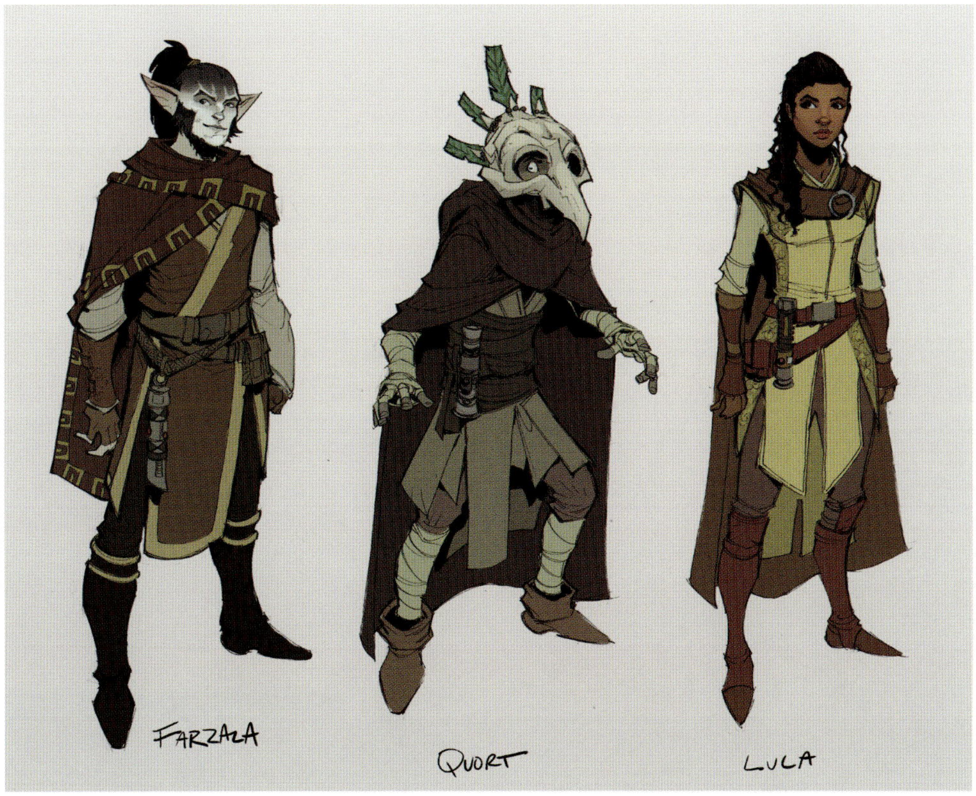

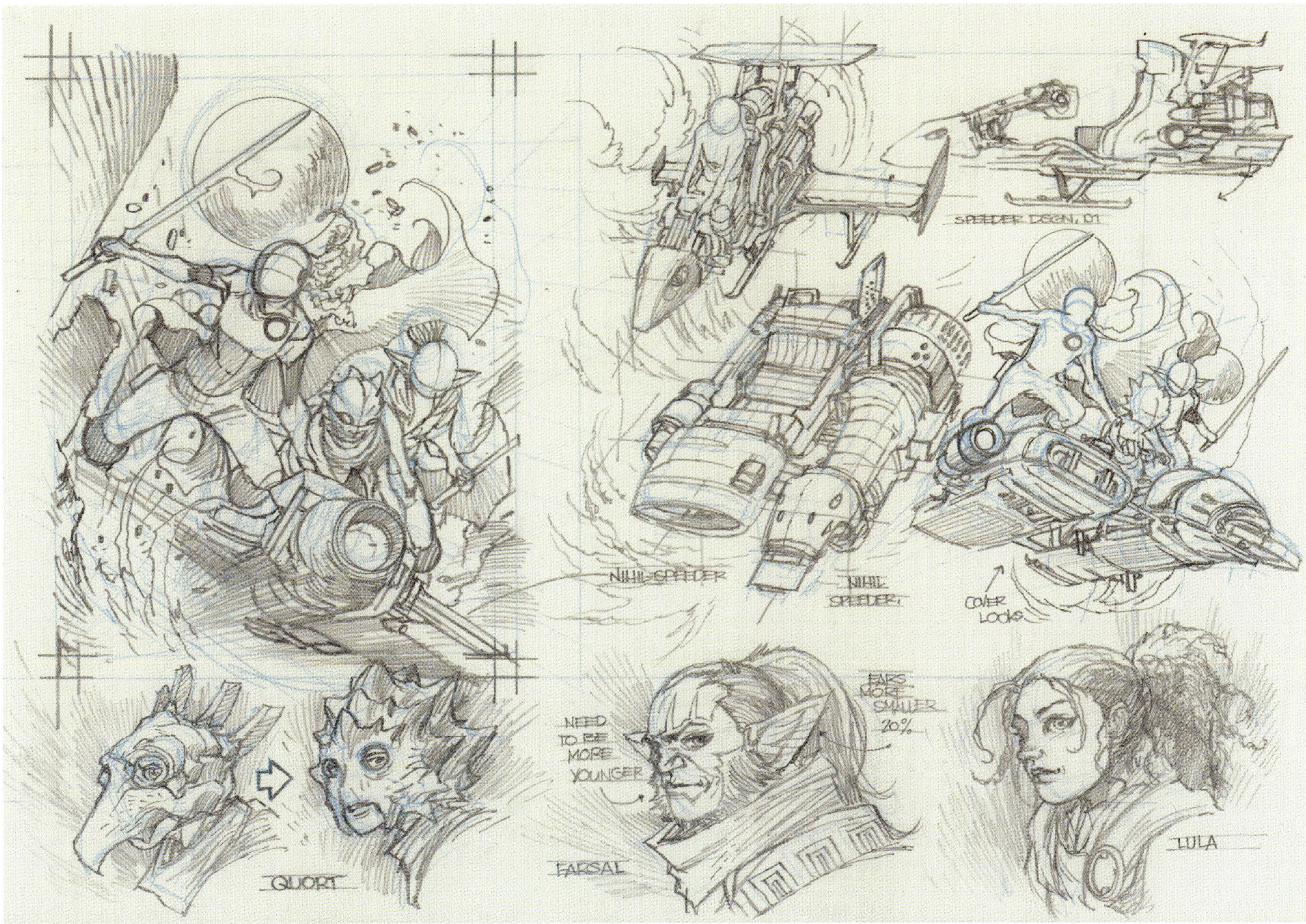

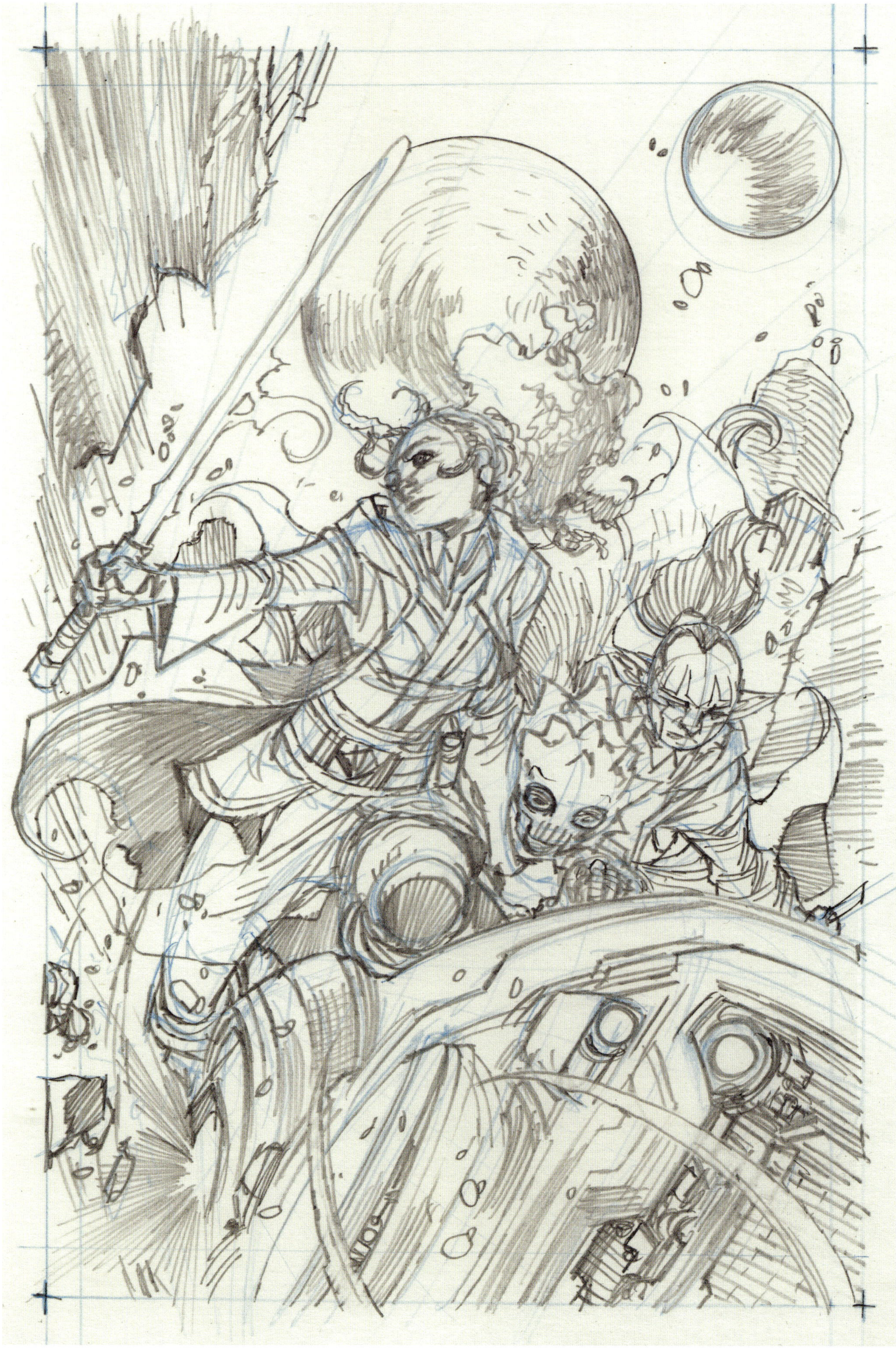

◂ Sketch for the cover of IDW's *Star Wars: The High Republic Adventures* #1 TOLIBAO

▸ Sketches for the cover of IDW's *Star Wars: The High Republic Adventures* #1 TOLIBAO

Tolibao took inspiration from a prequel-era speeder design (as seen on page 169) as he designed the Padawan's speeder.

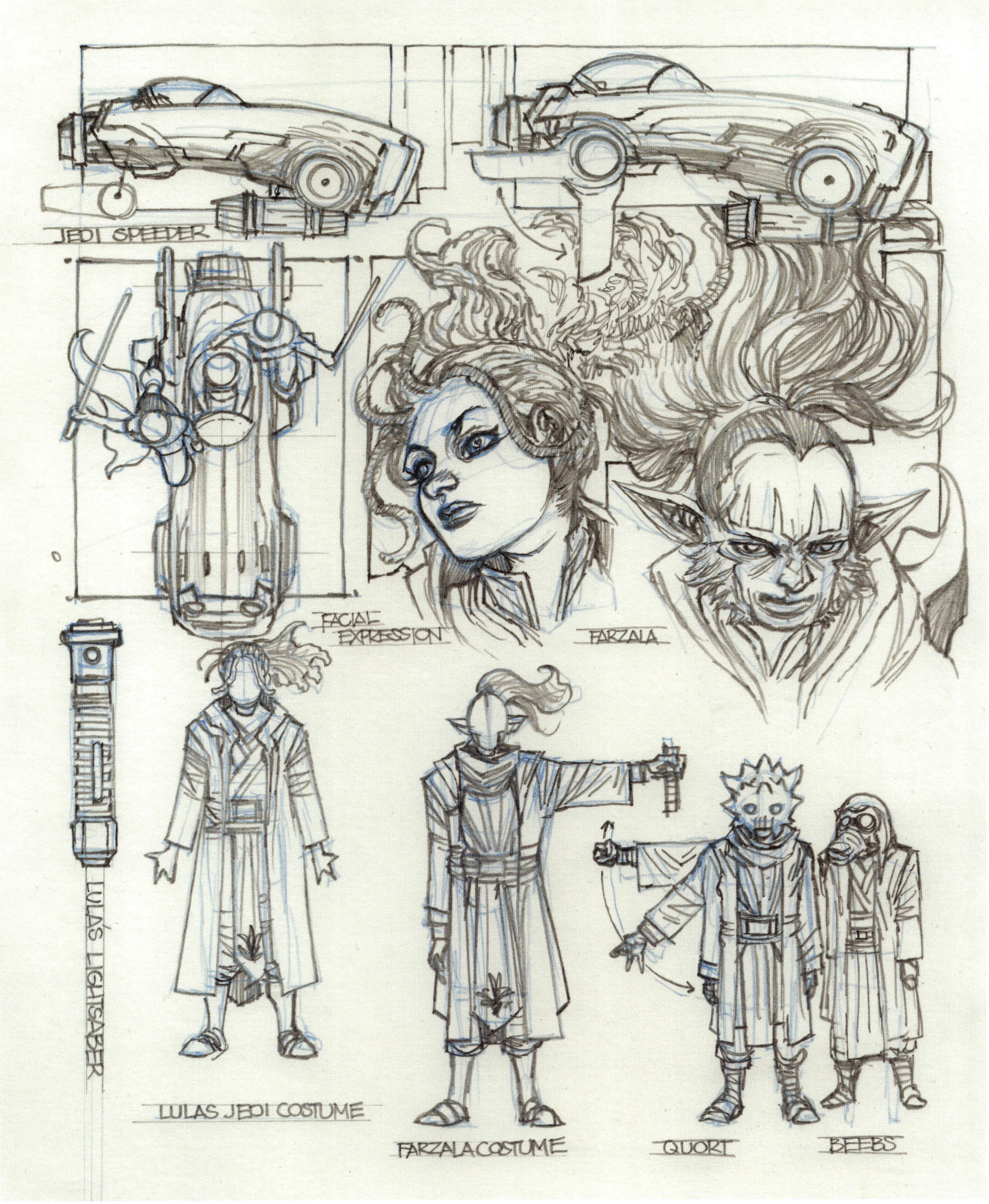
JEDI SPEEDER
FACIAL EXPRESSION
FARZALA
LULA'S LIGHTSABER
LULAS JEDI COSTUME
FARZALA COSTUME
QUORT
BEEBS

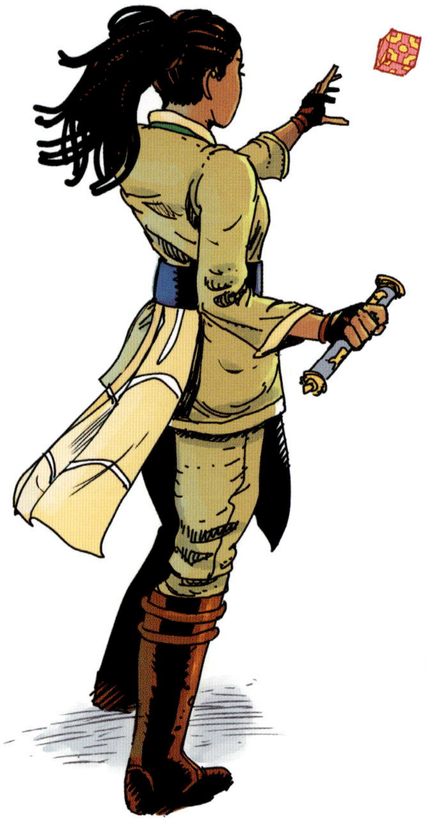

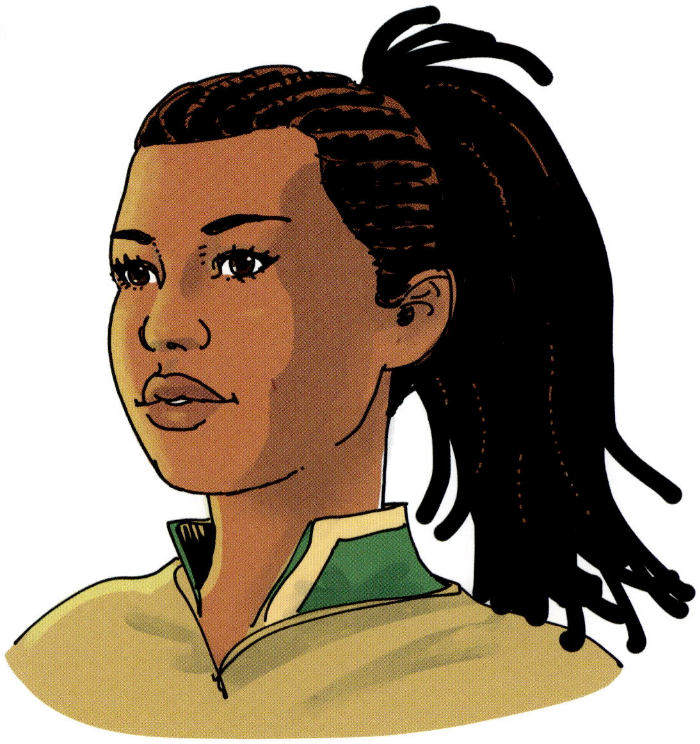

▼ Action study for Lula Talisola BROKENSHIRE

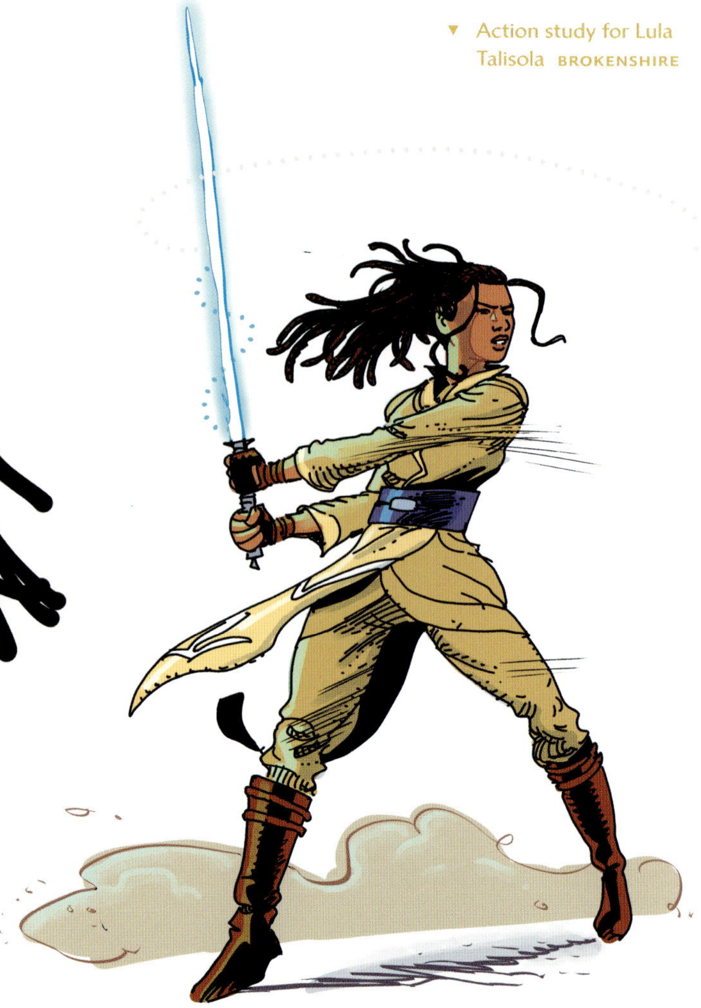

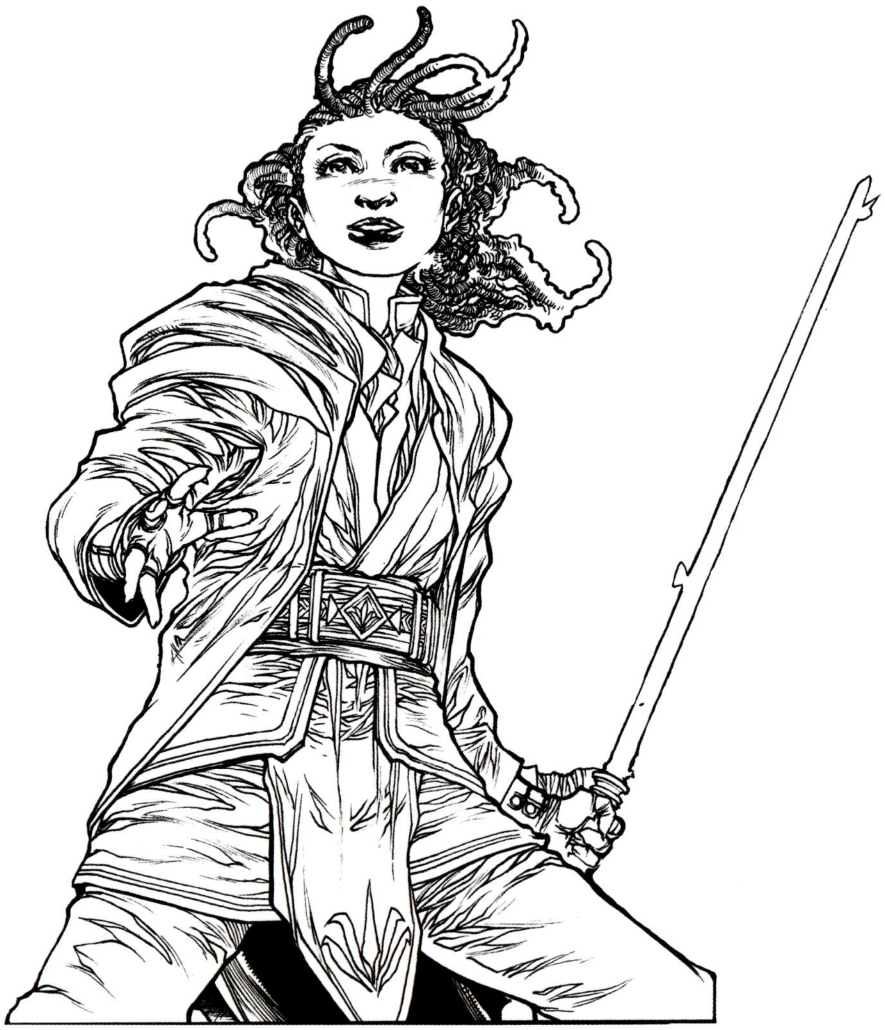

▲ Inks detail of Lula Talisola from IDW's *Star Wars: The High Republic Adventures* #1 TOLIBAO

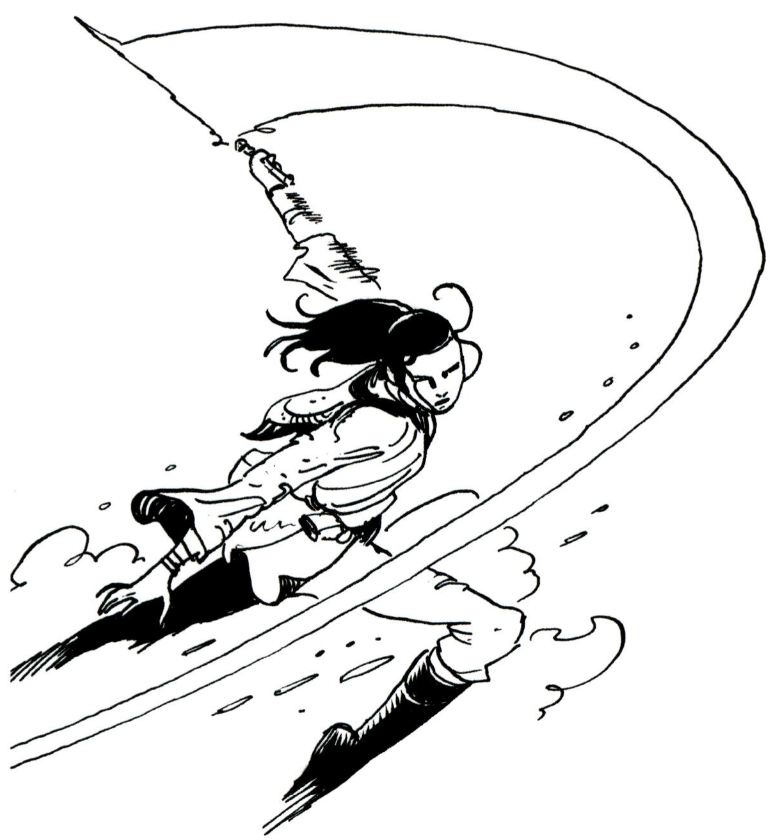

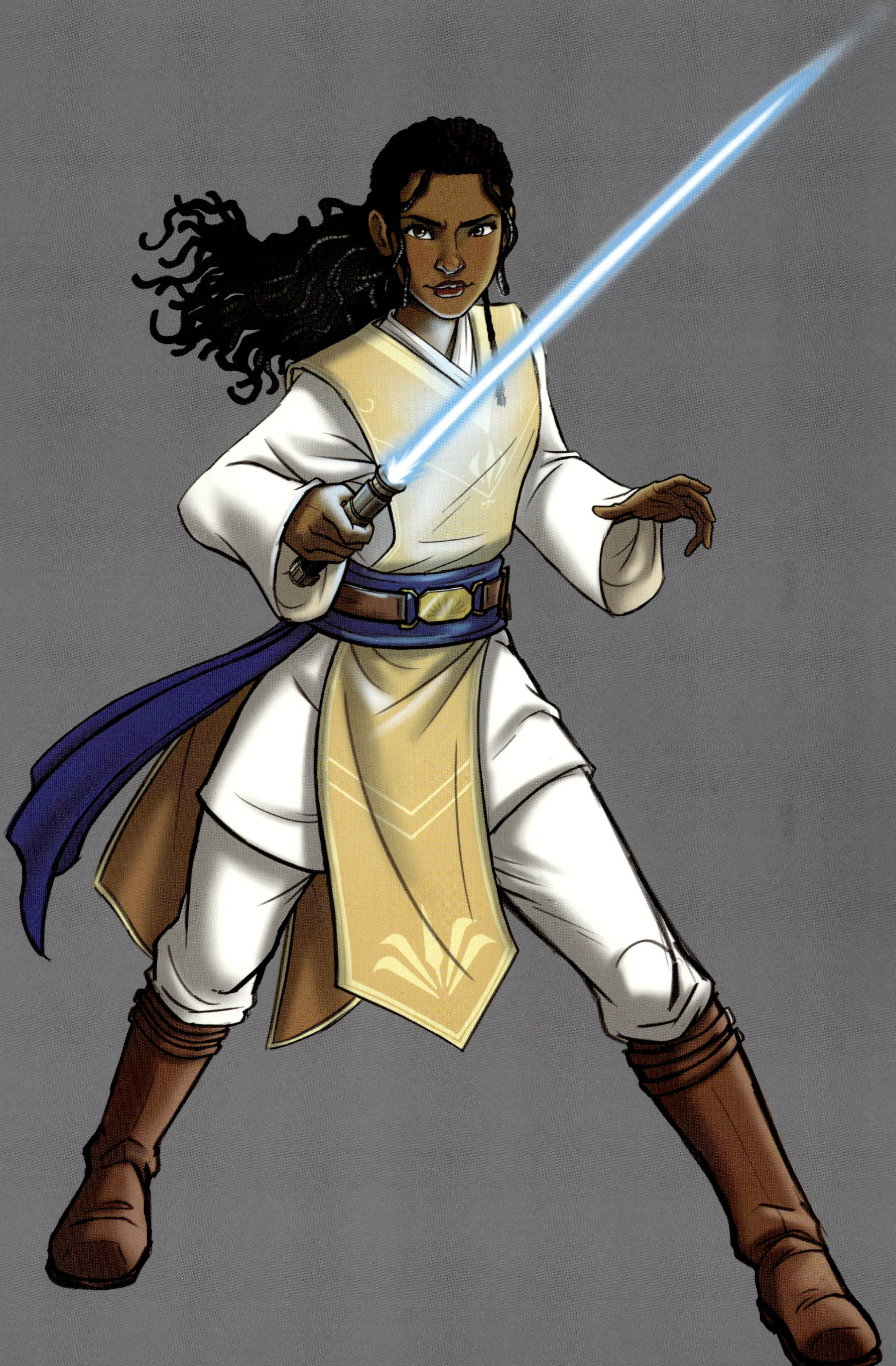

Final design for Lula Talisola in temple attire THOMAS

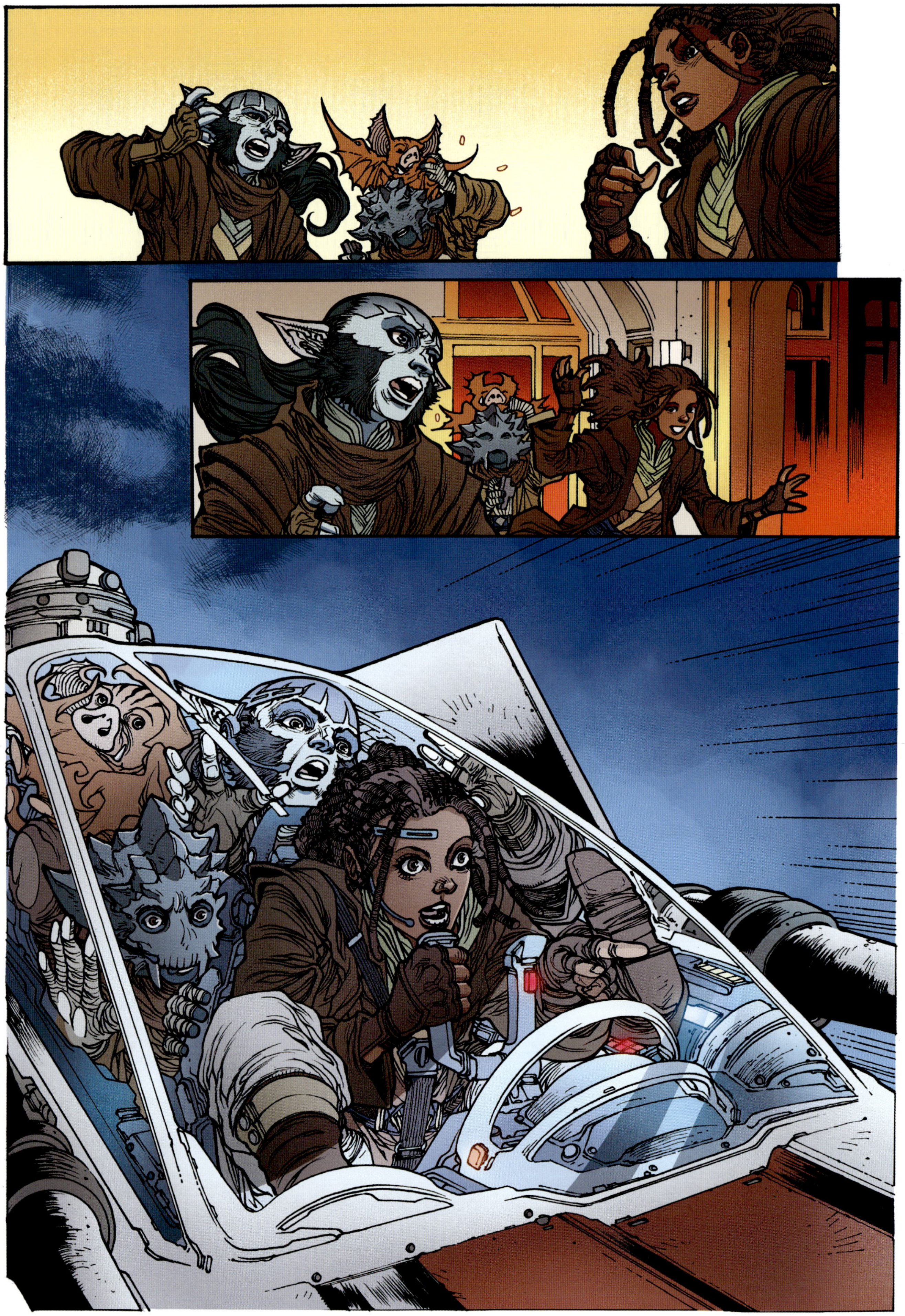

◂ Page from IDW's *Star Wars: The High Republic Adventures* #4
TOLIBAO (PENCILER) AND NALTY (COLORIST)

This moment of comic relief was inspired by Mr. Bean, Tolibao said.

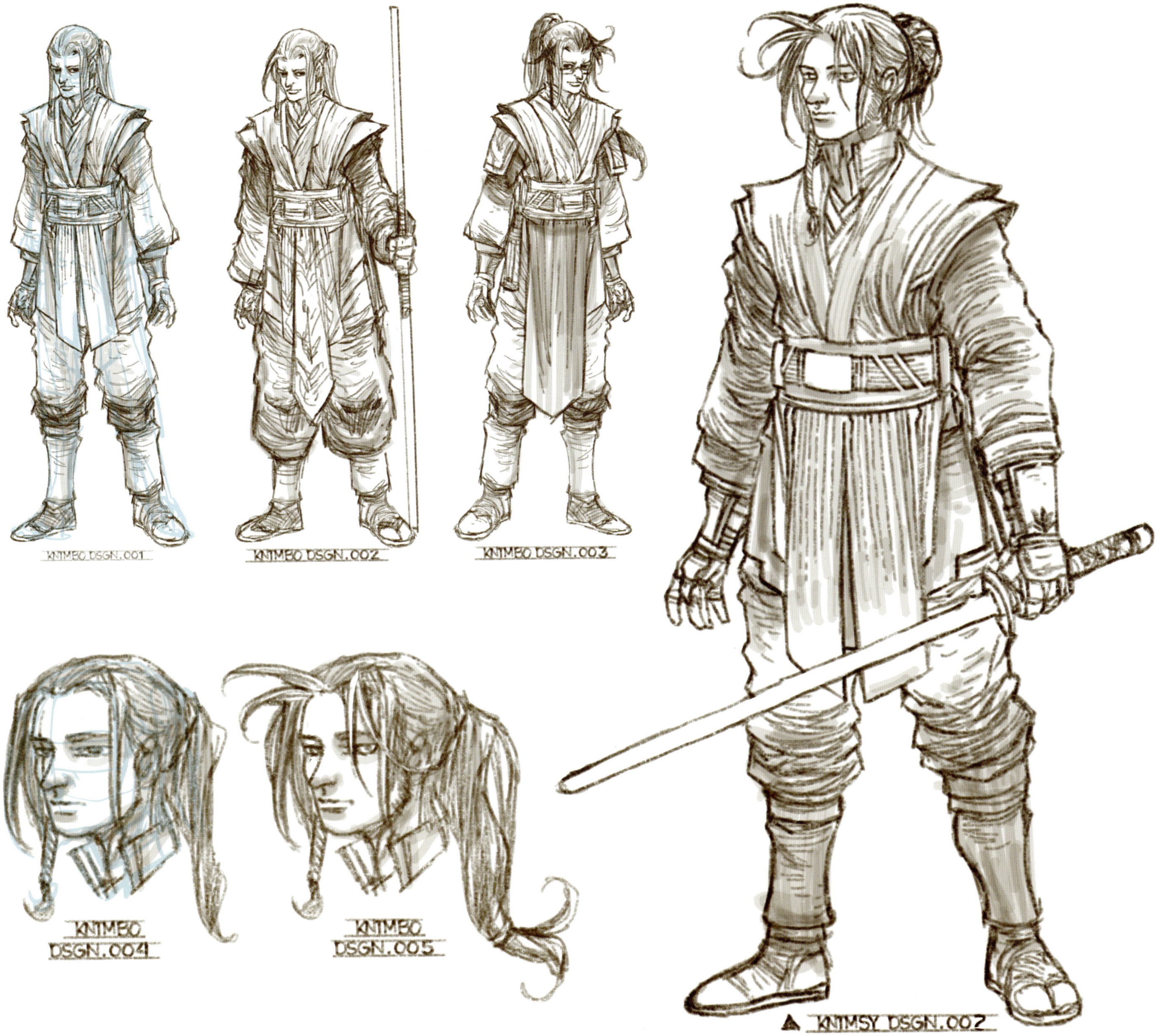

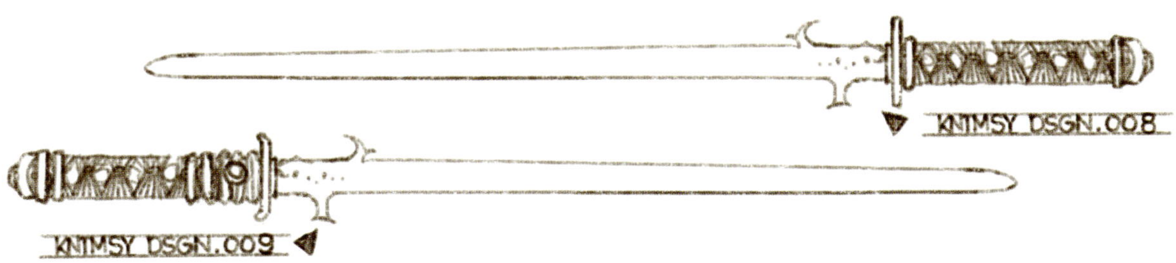

▲ Early Kantam Sy concepts TOLIBAO

The look of the Jedi initially named Kantam Bo is inspired by Japanese culture, made clear through the design from their Samurai-like bun to their sandaled feet. The character holds special meaning for Tolibao, whose grandmother was Japanese and married his Filipino grandfather.

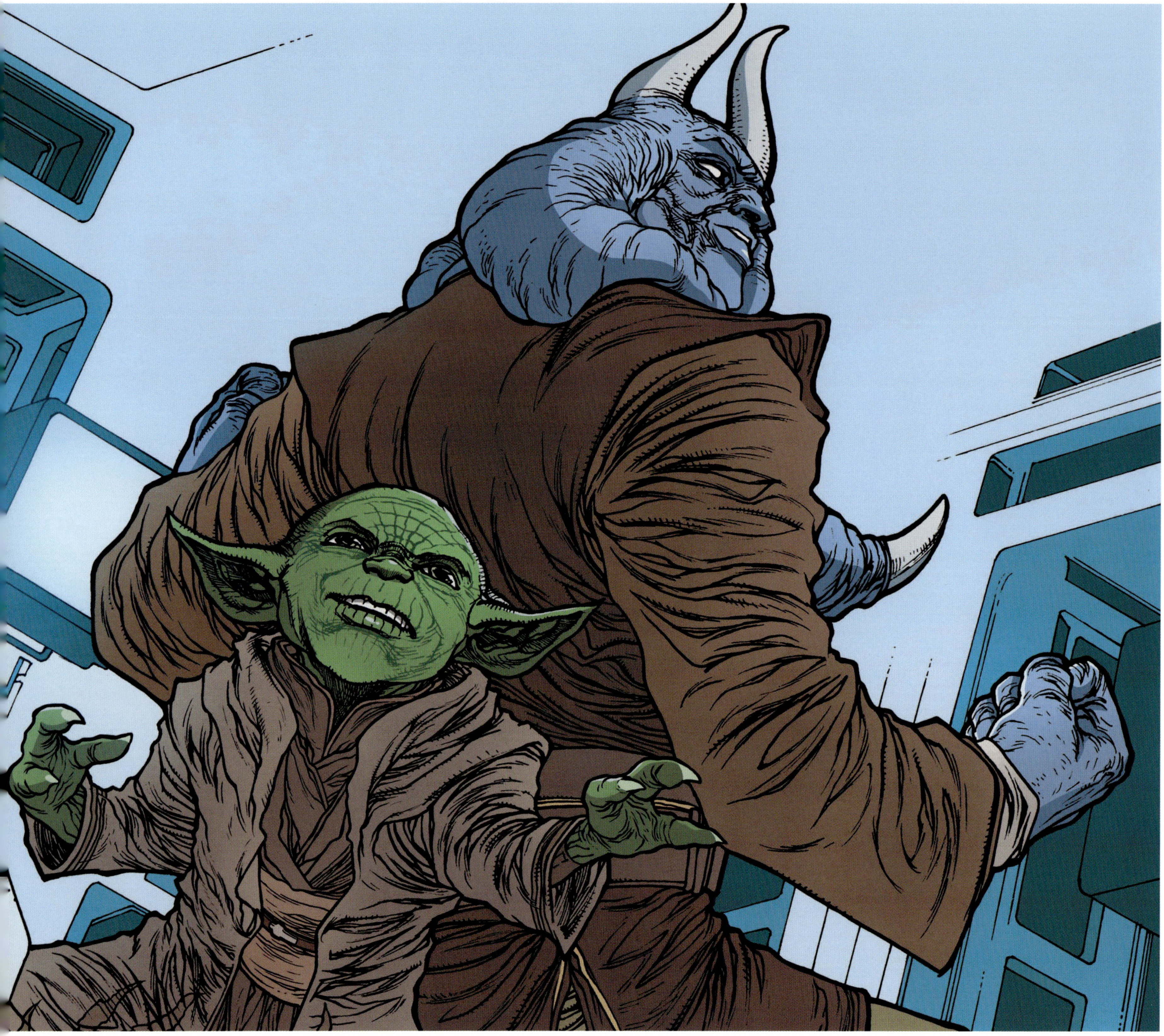

▲ Final design of Torban Buck, seen with Master Yoda in a panel from *Star Wars: The High Republic Adventures* #1 TOLIBAO (PENCILER) AND NALTY (COLORIST)

Jedi Master Torban Buck—aka Buckets of Blood—is a study in contrasts, a hulking Chagrian who wants to heal people, not fight with his lightsaber. "There's a new fan base just for this guy. This is the healing guy, so the way he is dressed is different from the other Jedi, like a doctor. And the way he holds his lightsaber is different from the others," Tolibao said.

"The fundamental schism in him is that he just has a gory name, but he wants to heal people," added Older. "It doesn't even occur to him that people are going to be freaked out by the name."

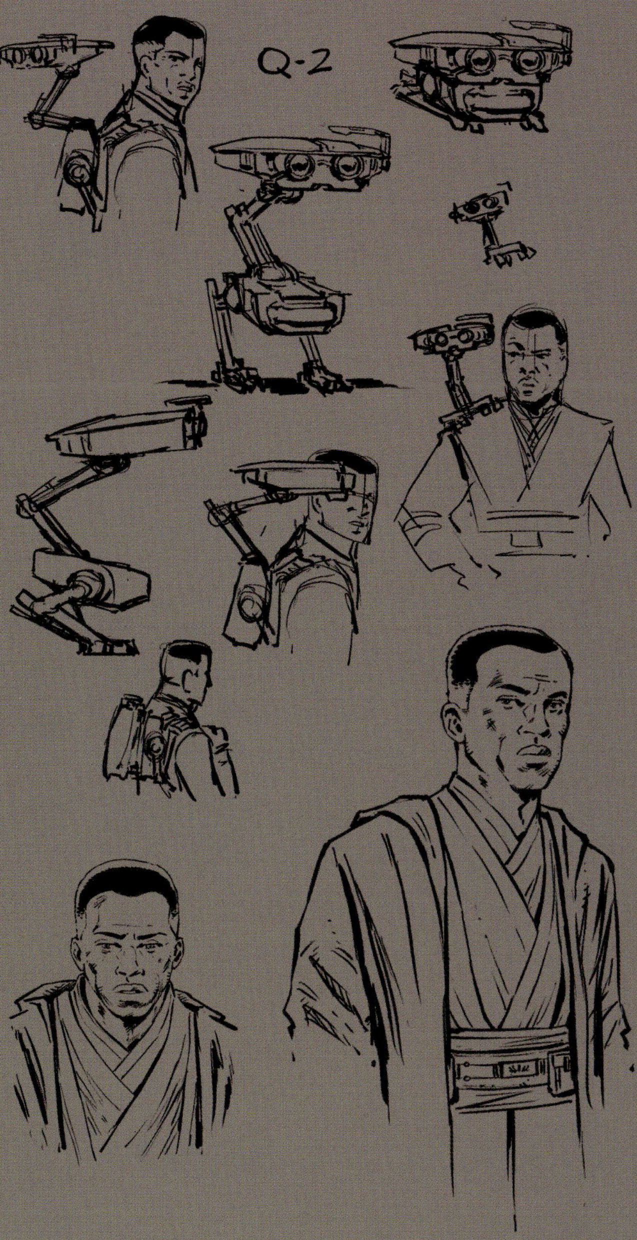

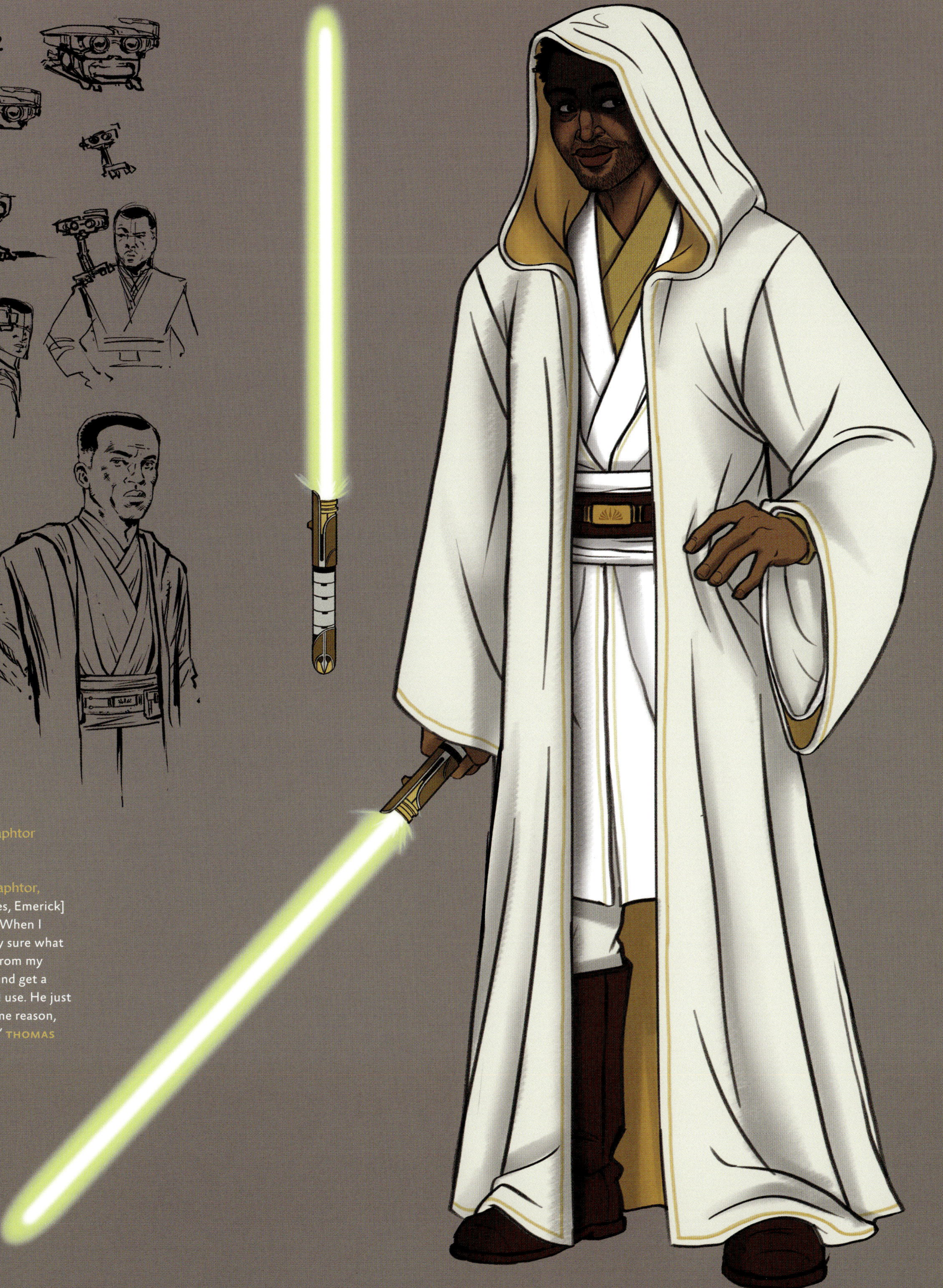

▲ Concept sketches of Emerick Caphtor for *Trail of Shadows* WACHTER

► Early concept of Jedi Emerick Caphtor, April 2021 "[Of the two detectives, Emerick] was supposed to be the calm one. When I design a lightsaber, I'm not entirely sure what it's going to look like. I just draw from my knowledge of lightsabers and try and get a sense of what the character would use. He just made me think 'minimalist' for some reason, so he has a very simple, clean one." THOMAS

CHARACTER CHART

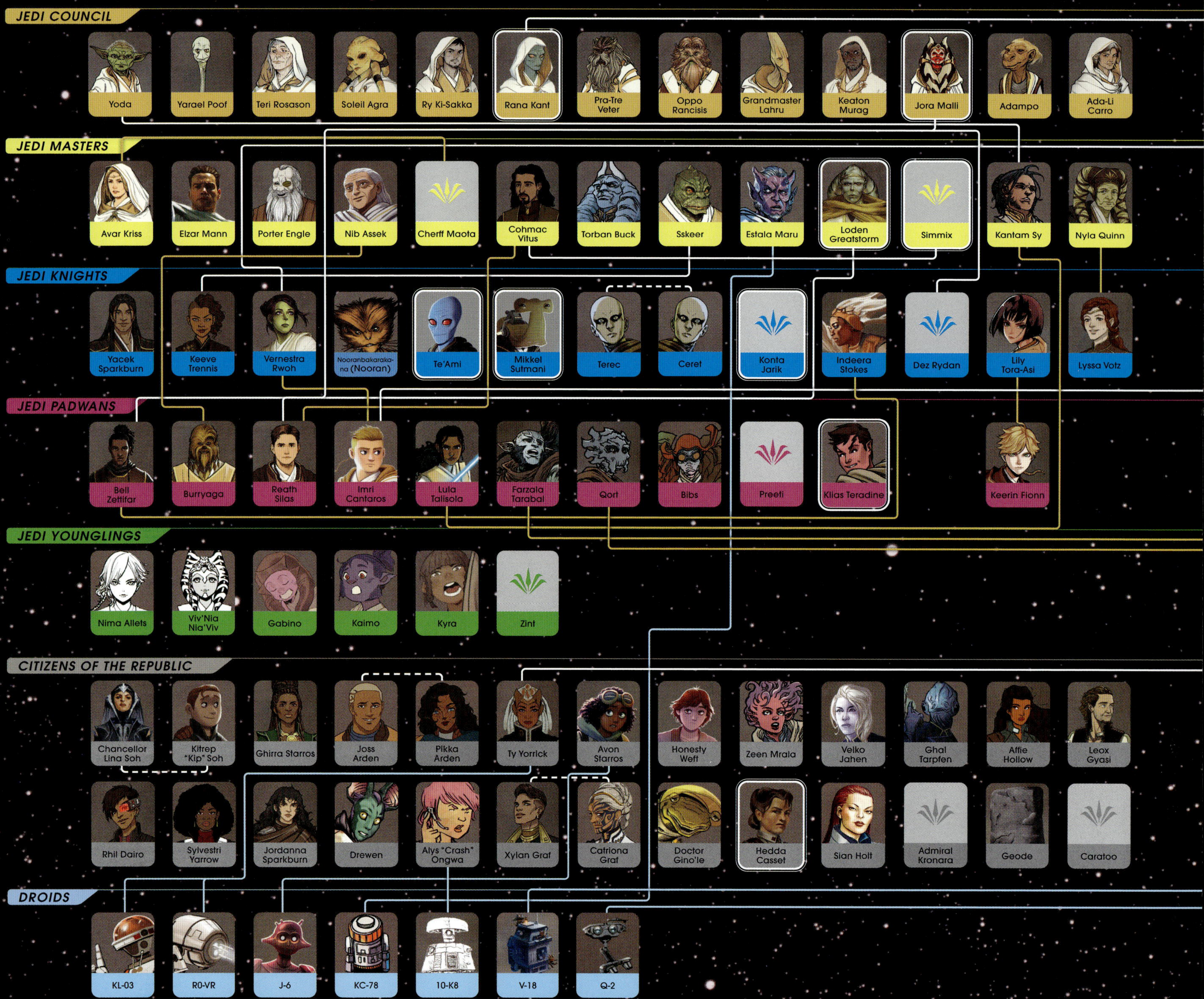

STAR WARS
THE HIGH REPUBLIC

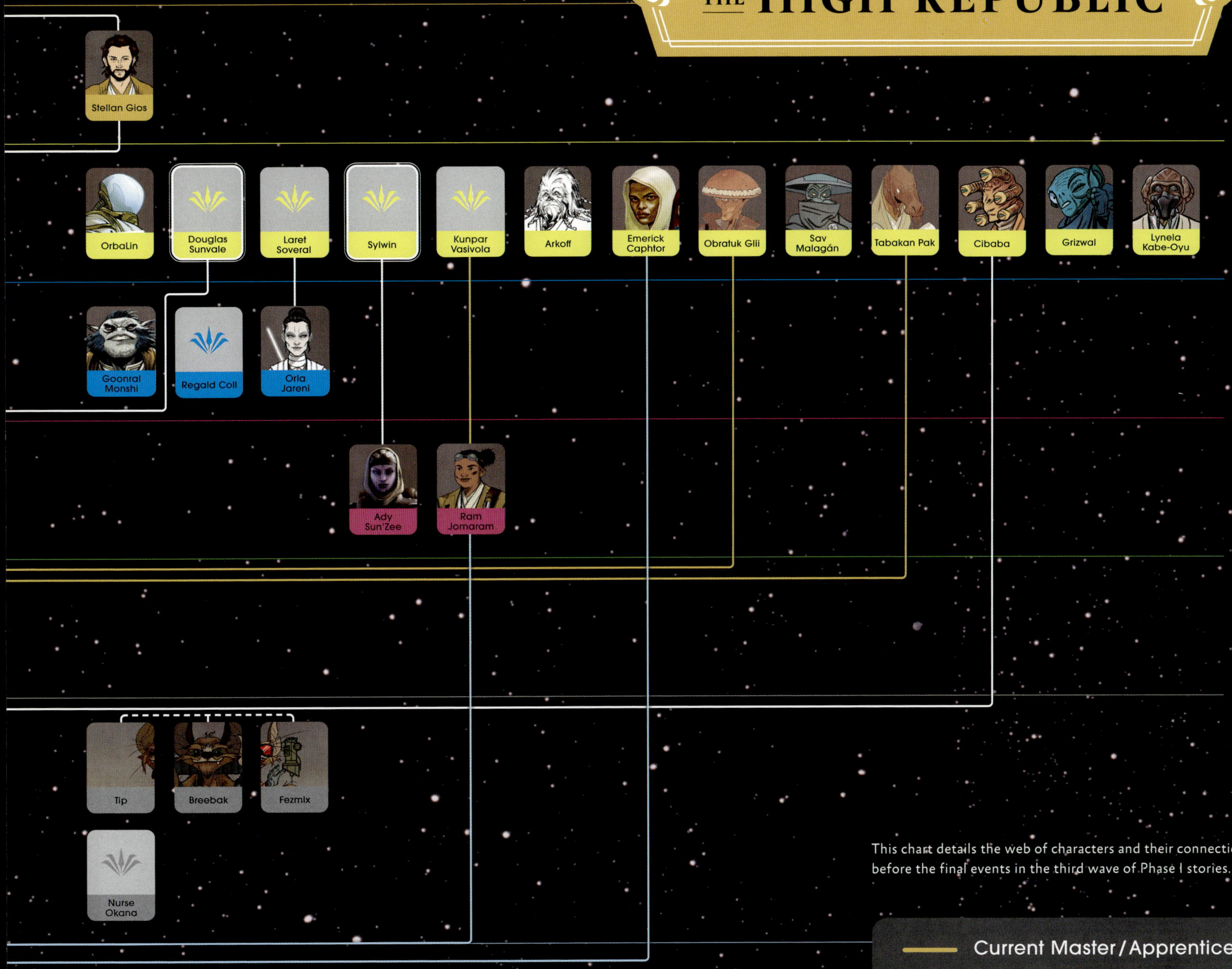

This chart details the web of characters and their connections before the final events in the third wave of Phase I stories.

- Current Master / Apprentice
- Former Master / Apprentice
- Family relation
- Droid partner
- Deceased

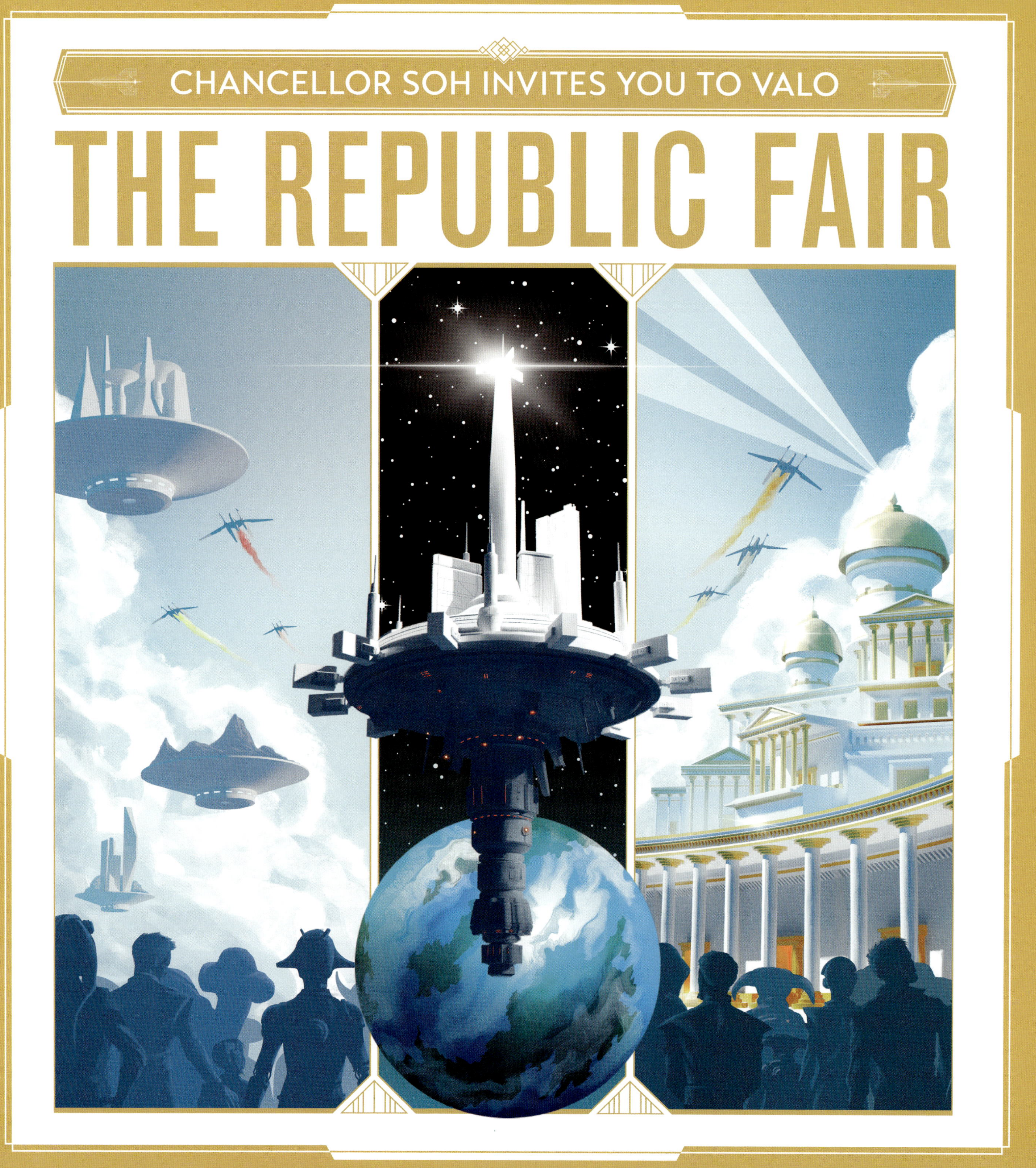
CHANCELLOR SOH INVITES YOU TO VALO
THE REPUBLIC FAIR

CHAPTER 3
CITIZENS OF THE REPUBLIC

THE RISE OF THE EMPIRE—seen in the *Star Wars* prequel films and in *The Clone Wars* animated series and its spinoff, *The Bad Batch*—showed us what it takes to bring a fragile democracy to ruin. The regal High Republic was an opportunity for storytellers to showcase the inverse: a government and a galaxy enjoying prosperity and, most importantly, embodying the ideals to which every era after would strive to return.

Led by Chancellor Lina Soh, creators of *The High Republic* envisioned a time of innovation, with hyperspace lanes connecting Outer Rim Territories to more urbanized Core Worlds like Coruscant. "What's been missing from some of our storytelling is [something to] remind us: What *is* this galaxy worth fighting for?" said Lucasfilm Story Group senior creative executive Pablo Hidalgo. "When people say we want to restore the Republic, what is the ideal?"

"Everyone's always talking in such glowing terms about the Republic," added author Justina Ireland. "It had to have been a functional government that people enjoyed and felt safe under at some point. But we hadn't seen it yet." Creating an idyllic governing body added a new challenge for storytellers, a discussion that Ireland estimated lasted nearly two weeks as they puzzled out: "How do we still make it interesting? Because when things are going well, that's usually when it's the least interesting, right?"

If the Jedi of the period evoked the Camelot of myth, Soh's bid for unity was inspired by the so-called Camelot of the John F. Kennedy White House and the space race that that allowed Neil Armstrong to take the first steps on the moon. "There were a lot of publications put out by the U.S. government in the 1960s as we're building up to the moon landing to try to get people excited about the possibilities of space," said author Charles Soule. "Those have this really awesome feel of 'anything is possible,' and an elegance to the design. There were concept designers in that era who were trying to inspire, who were trying to make people think about things differently. It was a time when many things were possible and things were changing and, hopefully, in ways for the better. Certainly, America had ambition."

The High Republic is aspirational, with a hint of western expansion, this time in the Outer Rim, populating the galaxy with an array of complex characters with a variety of motivations and backgrounds. "I think what was exciting was the kind of optimism of it all," said James Waugh, Lucasfilm's vice president of Franchise Content & Strategy. "We wanted to be really careful with the idea of trying to have this noble, bright Republic that's going to somehow bring its greatness to these Outer Rim places. Evoking colonialism was not the intent. Instead of an age of discovery, we wanted it to be about connection."

Soh and her political allies and adversaries were a given, as well as hardscrabble frontier explorers, smugglers, simple farmers, and rogues like author Claudia Gray's eccentric pilot Leox Gyasi. "He wound up about 75 percent pre-political Matthew McConaughey, 25 percent The Dude from *The Big Lebowski*," said Gray. "He has a healthy sprinkling of both, with a lot of beads. I wanted a pilot with a little bit of a roguish thing, but I didn't want him to just be Han Solo—or worse, Diet Han Solo. The minute Matthew McConaughey [popped into my head] I was like, 'That's it.' That guy is on his own wavelength. I think Leox would 100 percent be behind naked bongo-ing."

Ireland found the average denizens of the High Republic particularly intriguing. "We started off talking about the Jedi so much, but I am endlessly fascinated by just regular

◂ Poster art for the Republic Fair MATT GRIFFIN

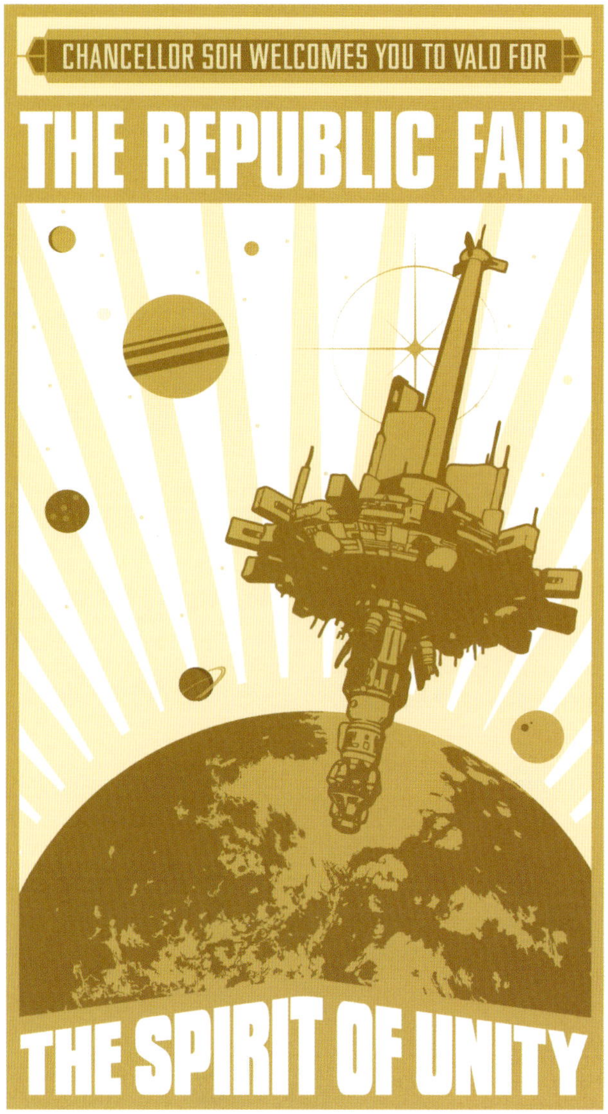

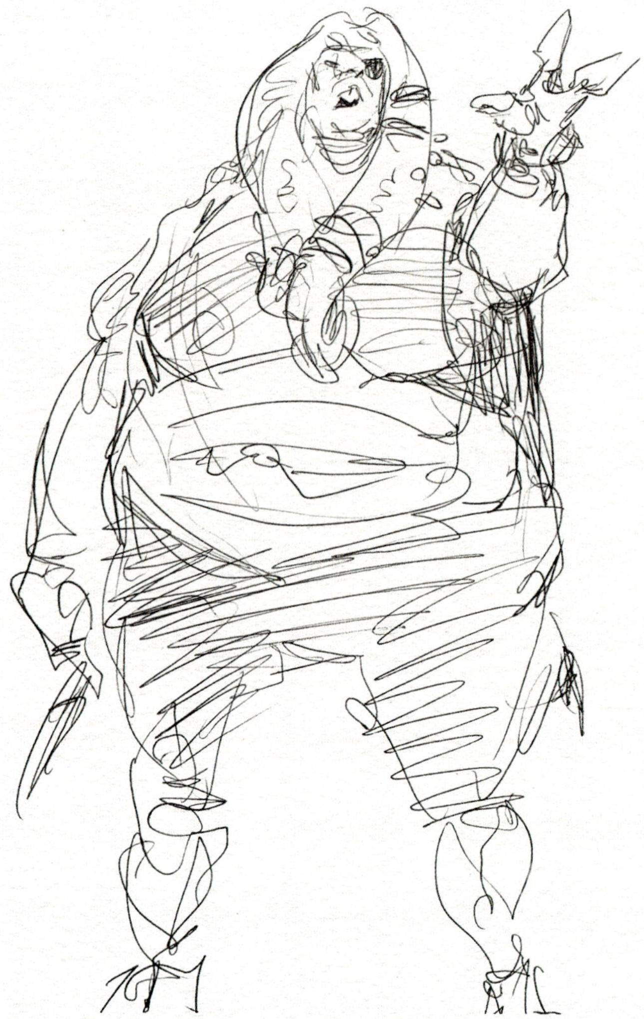

people," Ireland said. "Like, the guy who was the janitor on the Death Star. The regular people around superheroes are what make superheroes compelling. How are they going to take care of those people? And what are those random people going to teach them? That's how [heroes] reveal their humanity." Ireland's aspiring inventor Avon Starros helped provide a counterpoint to the Jedi tasked with watching over the senator's daughter, while Sylvestri Yarrow and her ex-girlfriend Jordanna Sparkburn were constructed in opposition to their own kin, the scientist Chancey Yarrow and the San Tekka clan. "Sylvestri is very concerned about making a living. She is focused on the goal," Ireland said, a trait that informed her description and the resulting design of the no-nonsense pilot. "You have someone who's a spaceship captain, very capable and self-assured, and they aren't going to necessarily worry about braiding their hair, because that's the least of their concerns! She just needs to make sure that the Nihil don't take over her ship." In contrast, her mother was more fanciful and oddly carefree. "It's a very powerful thing to just walk around without shoes," Ireland said. "If you think about the connotation, [Chancey is] not afraid to get her toes stomped. She's not going to be walking anywhere where it's not going to be safe."

For Jordanna, Ireland was adamant that the character retain some stereotypically feminine traits after initial concept art came back showing the young woman "really butch," she said, and outfitted as if she was ready to join up with the Empire. "Just because she's a lesbian doesn't mean she's evil," Ireland said with a laugh. "She's just a teenage girl. And I think it's important to show that this is a queer character. Notice how she looks just like all of our other characters?"

The era's dedication to representation remains one of its defining characteristics, heartily embraced by fans. "I think it's important that we show our fictional worlds are just as diversely populated as our real worlds," Ireland said. "Sometimes it's hard to get people to break out of those molds, which is kind of the fun part of the High Republic. We came up with the types of characters we wanted to see in the world. Obviously we have the Jedi, but who are we following on the Republic side? Some government officials are obvious; the chancellor is a no brainer. But who are our ambassadors and our senators and all those other people who round out the government? When we're creating those characters, they are inclusive. You have Xylan Graf and his family, who are definitely what we consider in our world people of color. We've seen a lot of white women who are also brunette, but we

▾ Republic Fair poster
LEIGH ZIESKE

In-galaxy posters promote the Republic Fair on the planet Valo, a spectacle in the style of the World's Fair.

▴ Sketch of a Twi'lek citizen, July 2019 "I always wanted a giant Twi'lek. I'm always asked to draw all these beautiful dancing ones. I thought, let's have a one-person mosh pit."
McCAIG

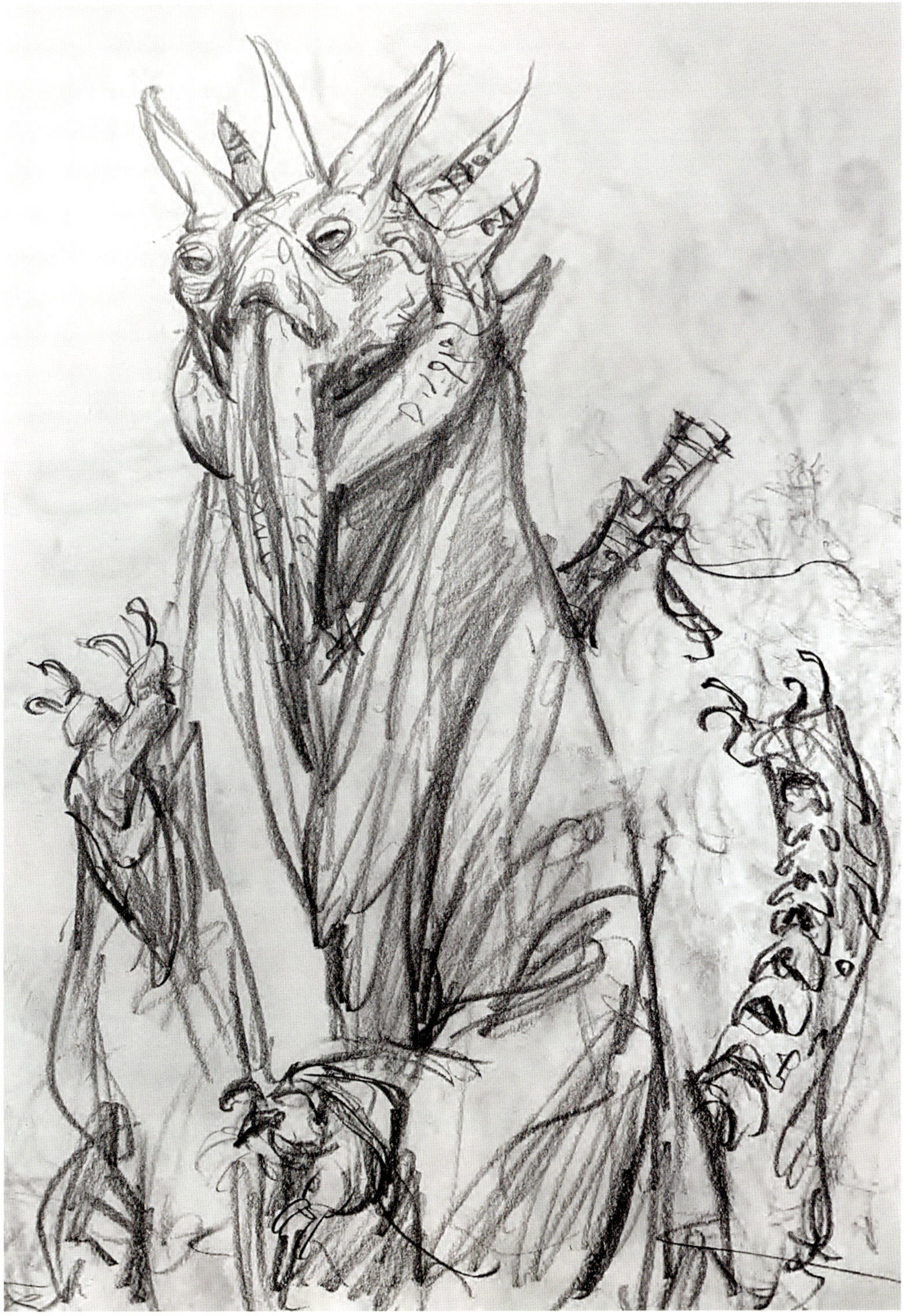

haven't seen a lot of Black women. It's about being inclusive and making sure that all of our characters don't look one degree away from somebody we've already met. And I think it's especially important visually."

The collaborative storytelling continued as new characters took shape. Chancellor Soh, in particular, is the product of no fewer than five creators. Iain McCaig's drawing of a regal woman with two catlike creatures was birthed without a name, but quickly inspired Soule to resurrect a character from his original pitch known then as "the Good Chancellor." Concept artist Grant Griffin refined the black-and-white sketch with his painterly style and a wash of vibrant primary colors. "I didn't know what those two tiger creatures were, but Daniel [José Older] really likes animals, so Daniel ended up naming their species," Soule said. "Then Cavan [Scott] gave them actual names, Matari and Voru [after Coruscant gods]. The art inspired us to be creative and pull all these different elements together."

▲ Early sketch of a galactic citizen, July 2019 McCAIG

As the leader of the Republic at the time, Soh is emblematic of the period's aesthetic, an extension of the art nouveau–inspired decadence glimpsed in *The Phantom Menace*. "*Star Wars*, for whatever reason, exists in a universe where the templates of how things look have existed for a very, very long time. But you can say this age has its own personality, its own look, its own energy," said Gray. "This was an era where people could care about aesthetics. They had the wealth and the luxury to do that. By the [age of] the Empire, nobody has that. The Empire's appearance is very much about function, about being scary and intimidating and depersonalized."

Concept artists capturing the grandeur of the Republic's varied citizens looked to the upper echelons of Naboo, as seen in *The Phantom Menace* and *Attack of the Clones*, and the city among the clouds in *The Empire Strikes Back*, adhering to George Lucas's philosophy on finding recognizable themes and personalities from our own world, but skewing them to exist uniquely in a different time and space. "George always said *Star Wars* is real life with a little twist," said concept artist McCaig. "If you go too far one way, you're just doing our world and it's not *Star Wars*. If you go too far the other way, you're doing pure science fiction. So, it's walking that line."

At its core, the High Republic is populated by relatable characters and living creatures whose human nature shines through in the story and design. "This isn't like the original trilogy where you really only have three or four or five main characters," said Ireland. "We have so many cool characters, and that's one of the nice things about this initiative, [which] is that we've been able to build out the galaxy in a way that feels big."

Yet thematically, the High Republic continues to echo all that came before it. "An element that I think is fundamentally *Star Wars* is that choice between being selfish or selfless," said Waugh. "We wanted the storytelling to definitely fit within those themes, and I think the Republic's intent is to do more selfless [acts to] the betterment of all."

"You go back to those early conversations about *Star Wars* and it's about 'a new hope,'" added Lucasfilm senior editor Robert Simpson. "It's a story of a boy growing up wanting to leave home, learn more about his father, and find his place in the world, that has absolutely nothing to do with laser swords and spaceships. It's a story that everybody can identify with. And there are things going on in the High Republic that ask those same kinds of questions and put those characters in the same kinds of situations. They make hard choices about how they're going to live their lives, how far they're going to go for what they care about, what they'll do to protect the people that they love. You know, the laser swords and the spaceships are fun and add to it and make it so much greater, but it's already pretty great just telling those stories of those characters."

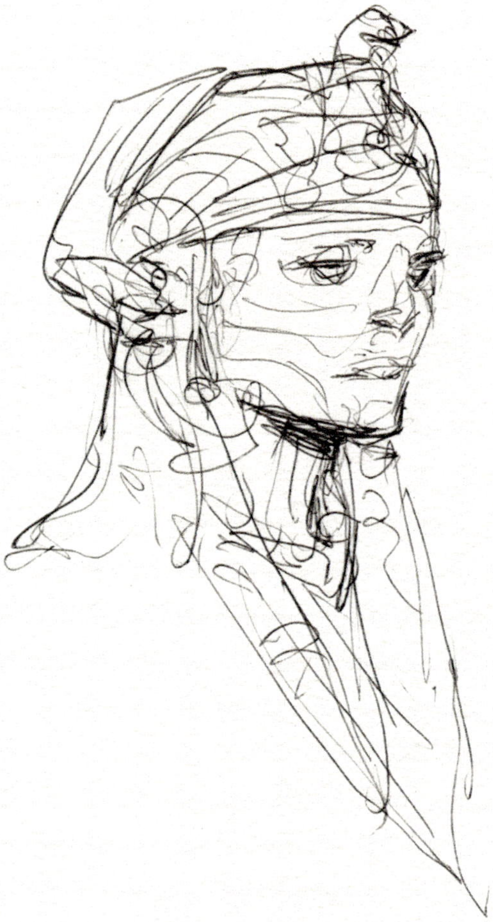

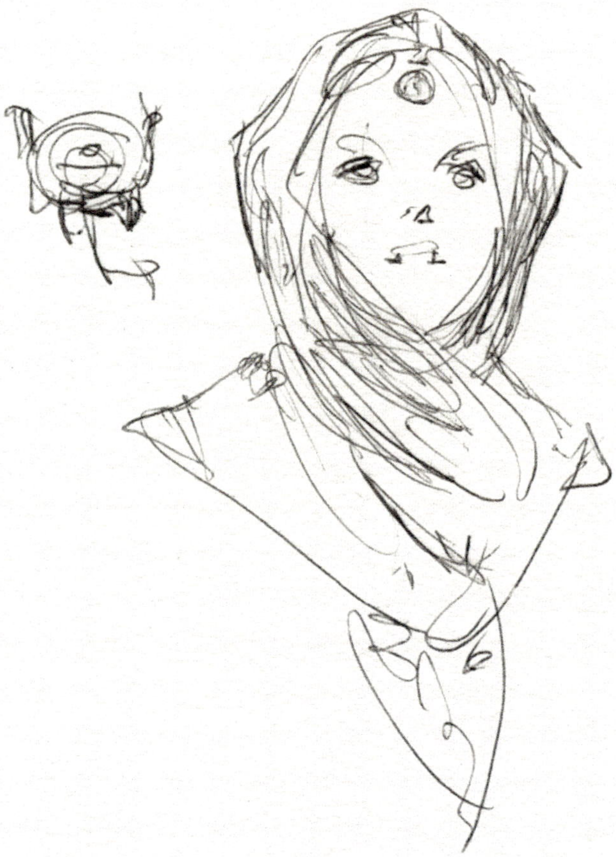

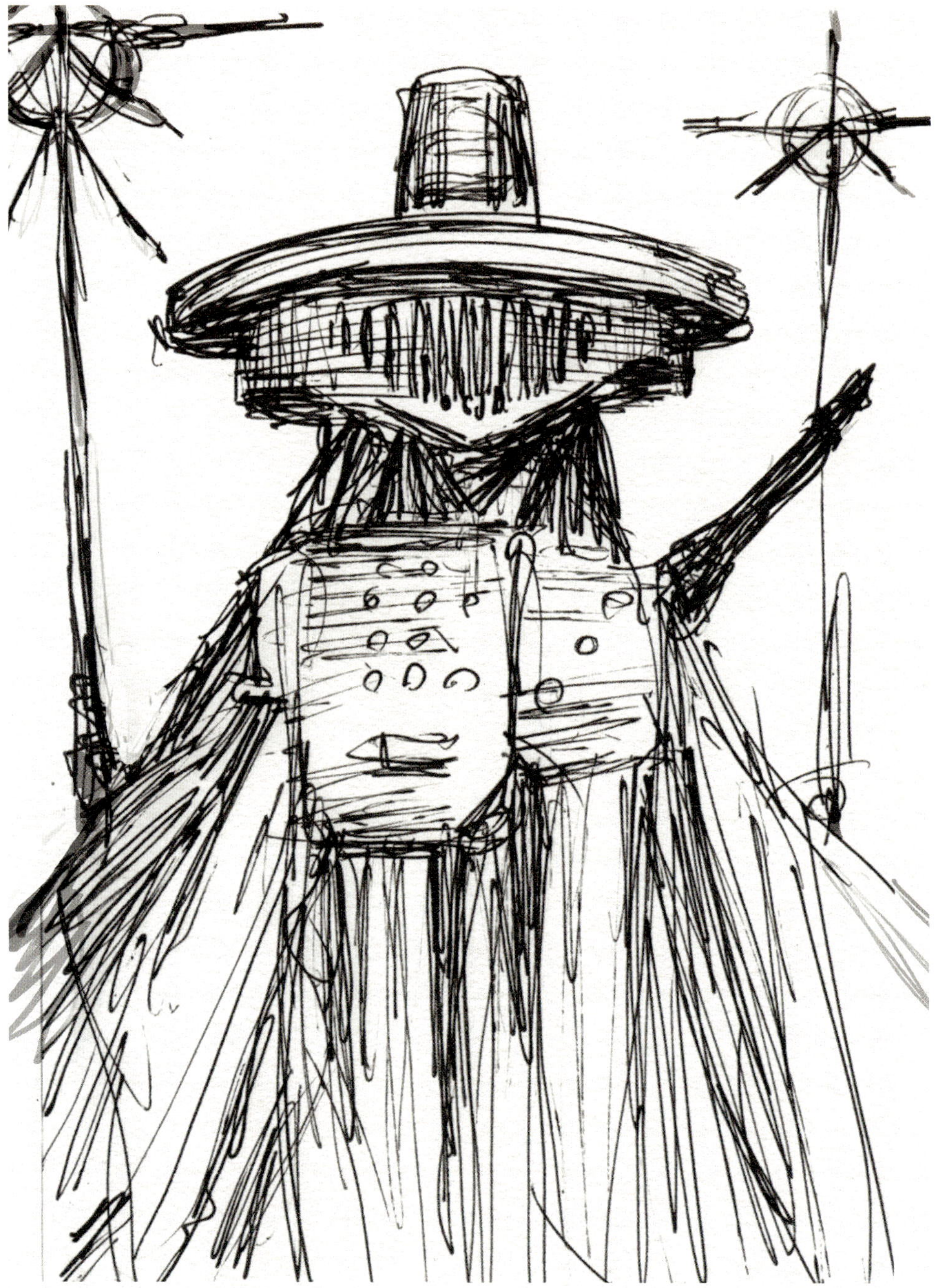

▲ Concept sketch of a religious droid, July 2019 "I wanted a real fundamentalist, fanatical religious order. So I took my French press lid [*laughs*] and put it in a cloak. A droid religious order is what I had in mind. And the armor plating? That's my garlic press. My secret sauce of weird, wonderful ships and robots is the kitchen. I just raid the drawers." McCAIG

◄ Early sketches of galactic fashion, July 2019 "I'd just been to an Egyptian exhibition, and I was blown away by the statues and the headdresses. Because it's old sandstone, you're never sure where one part starts and the other ends. It can either just be a shape or it can become a creature, and that can tie into the mythology of the story you're telling. They're all story seeds." McCAIG

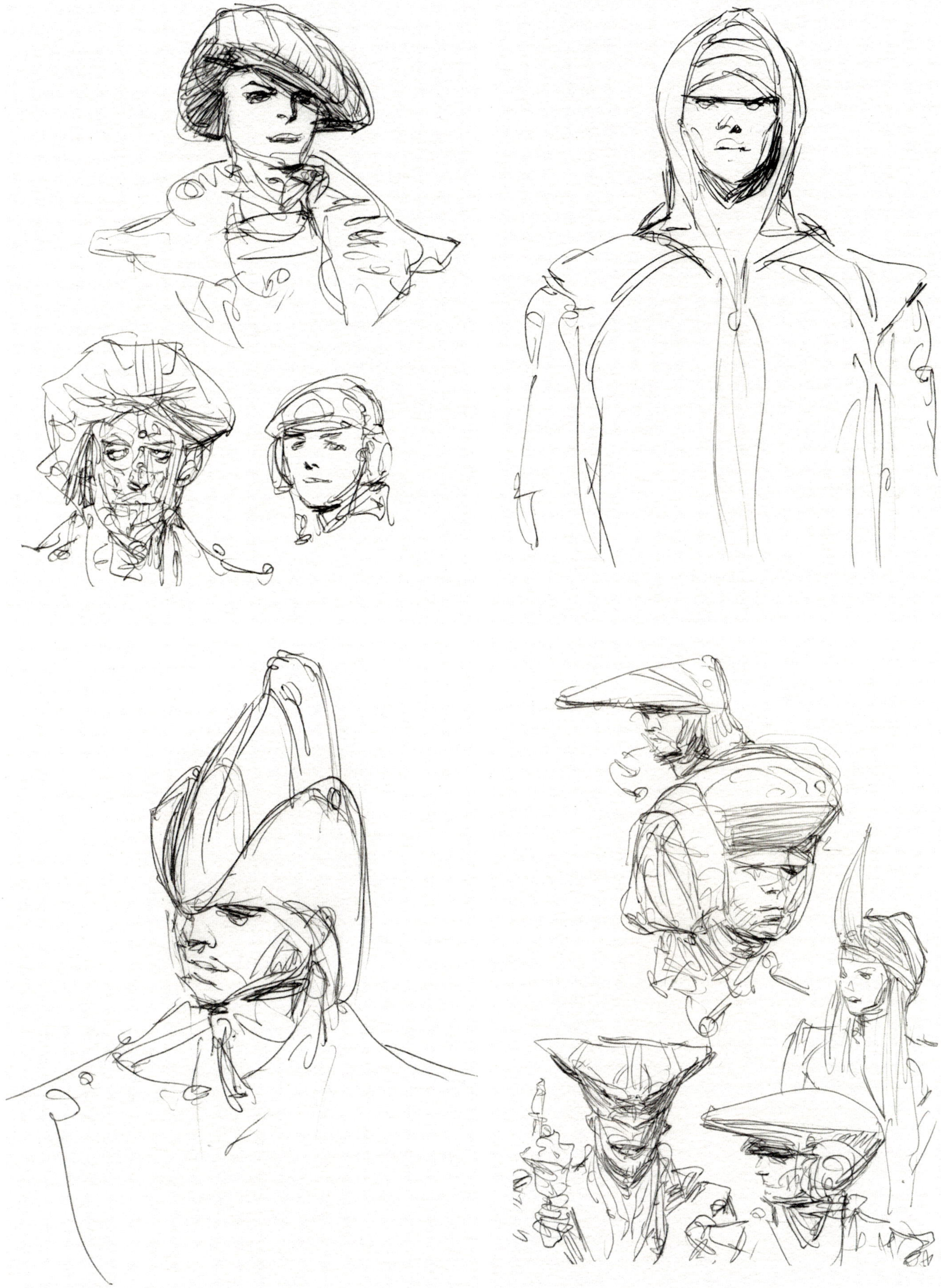

▸ Early sketches of Republic fashion, July 2019 "I wanted to know what the ordinary people felt like. And also, if I'm trying to establish a fashion that's raging through this world, why not hats? Even for ordinary citizens, hats are the rage. Creating fashion creates a sense of history." McCAIG

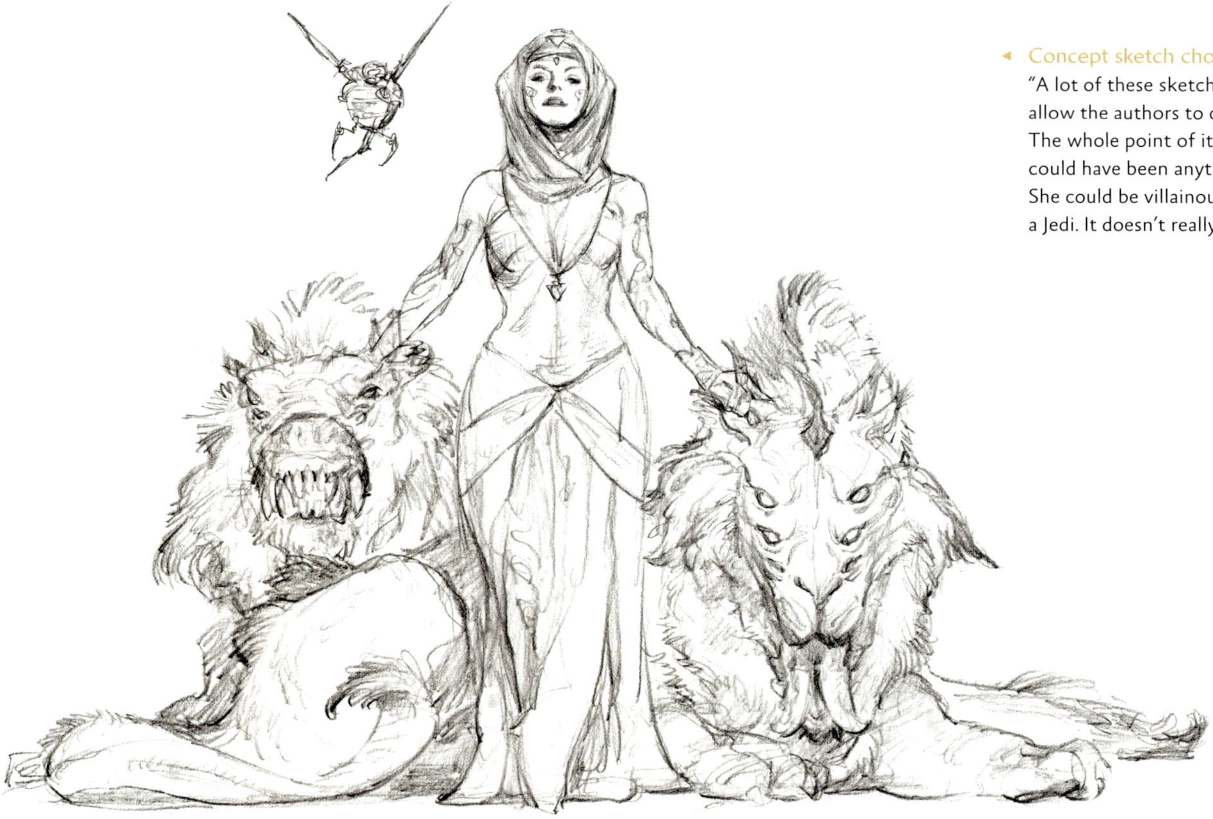

Concept sketch chosen for Chancellor Lina Soh

"A lot of these sketches were deliberately mysterious to allow the authors to come in and [tell their own stories.] The whole point of it is to inspire rather than to tell. She could have been anything, right? She could be benign. She could be villainous. She could be a Sith. She could be a Jedi. It doesn't really matter." McCAIG

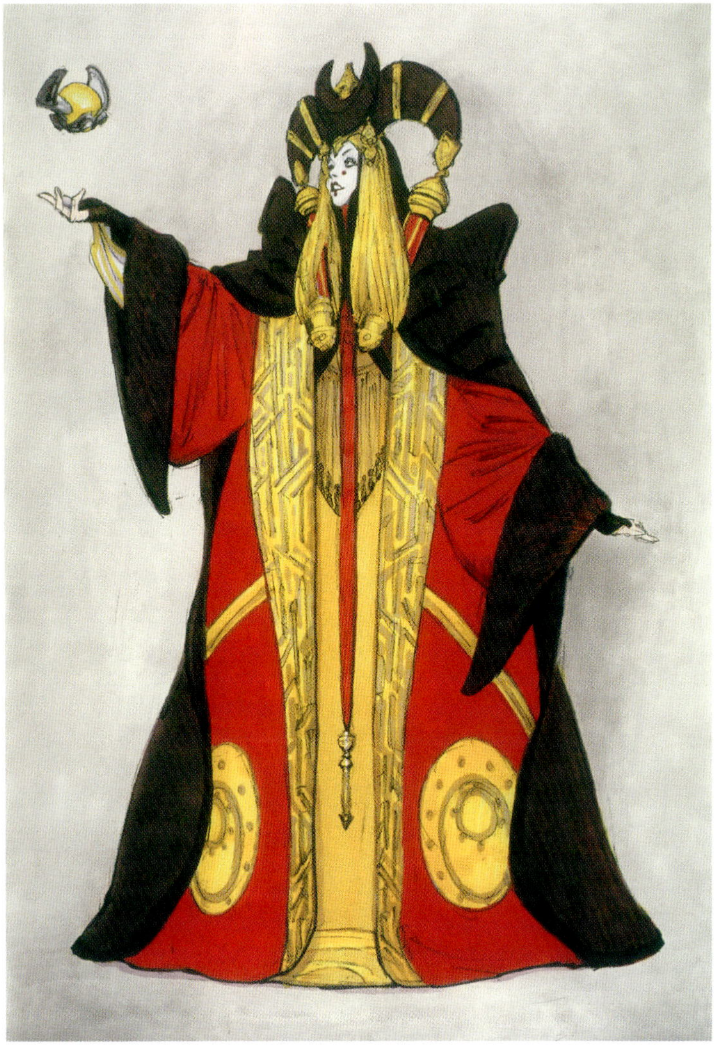

Costume concept for Padmé Amidala for *The Phantom Menace*
McCAIG

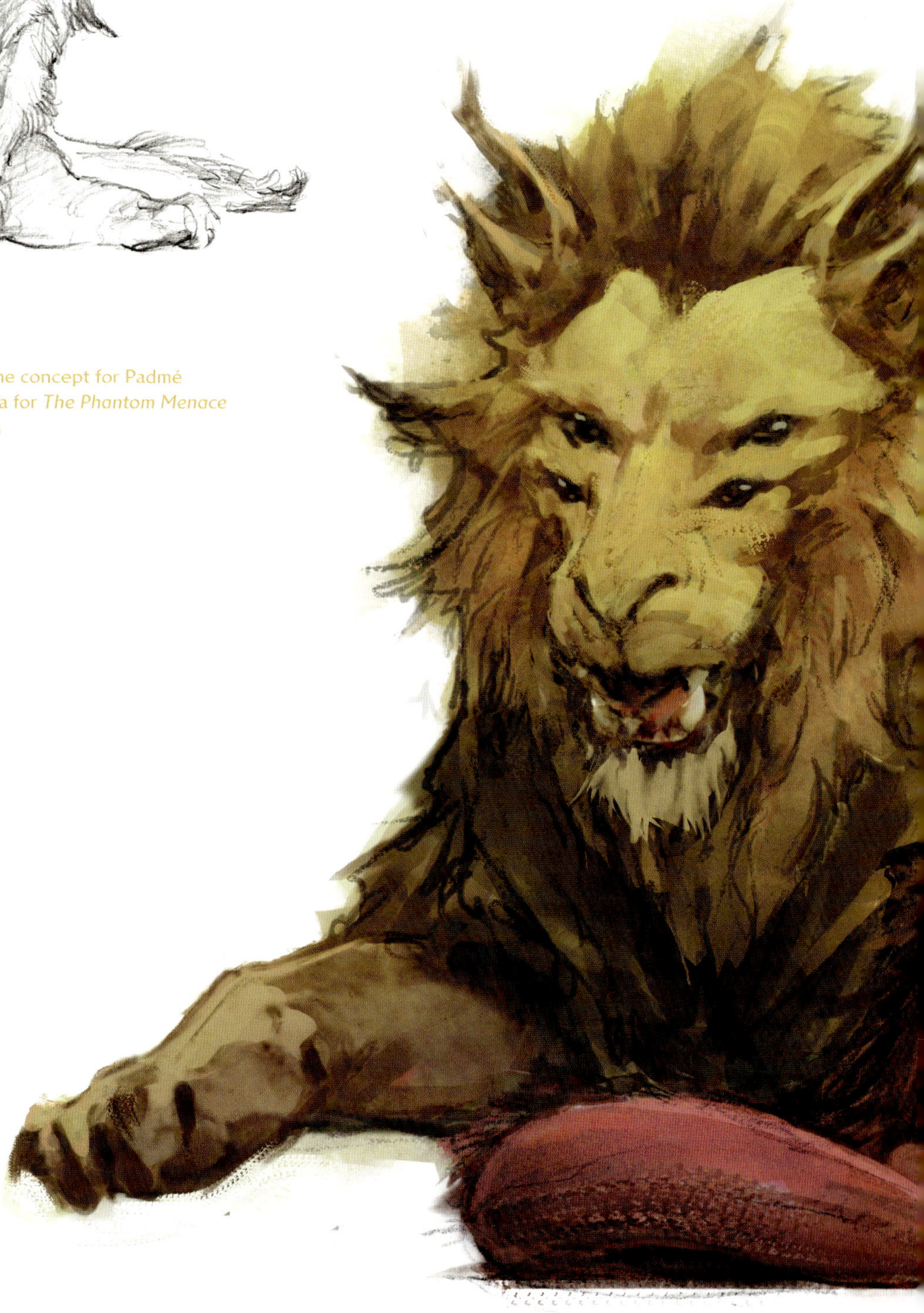

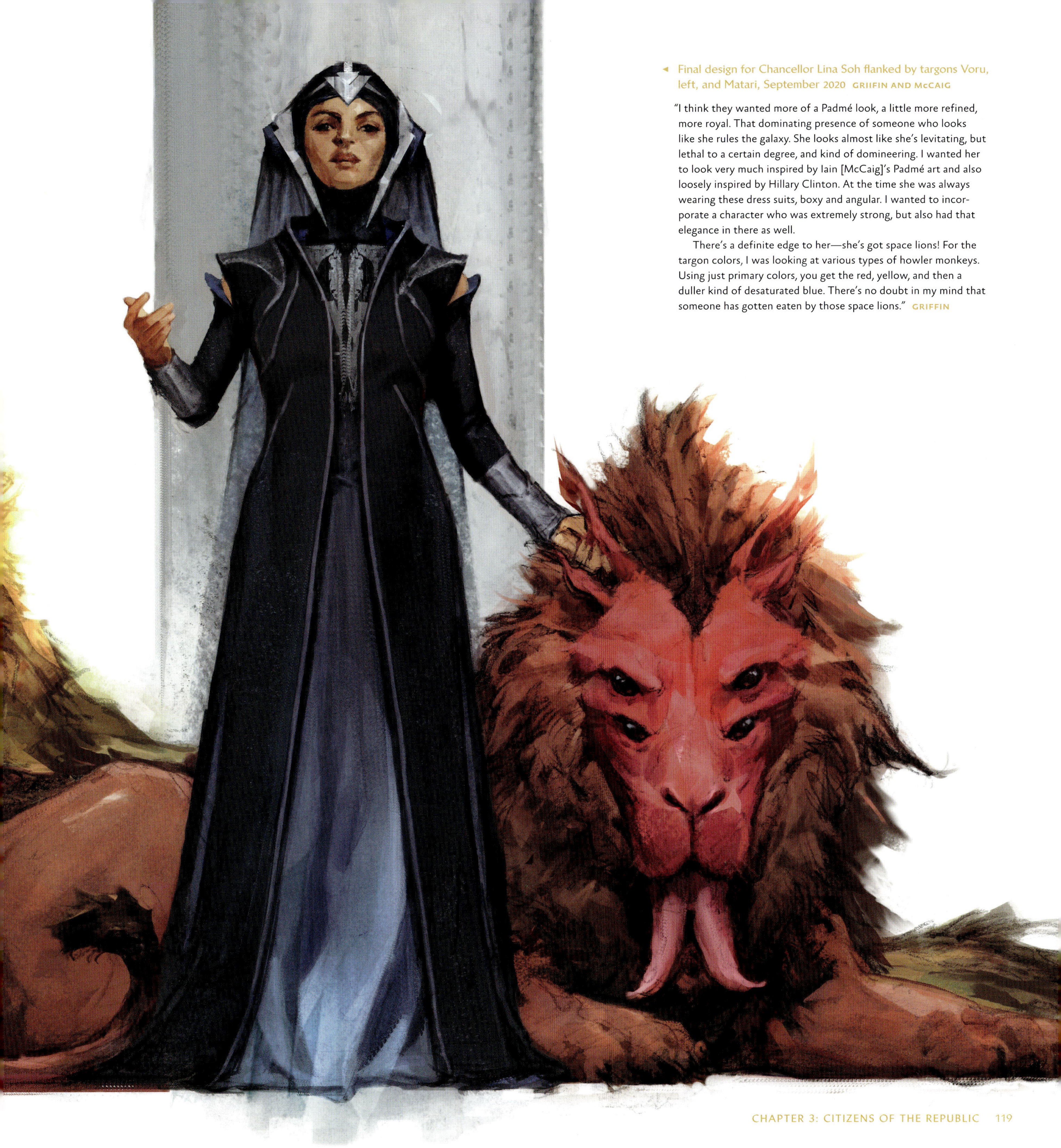

◂ Final design for Chancellor Lina Soh flanked by targons Voru, left, and Matari, September 2020 GRIIFIN AND McCAIG

"I think they wanted more of a Padmé look, a little more refined, more royal. That dominating presence of someone who looks like she rules the galaxy. She looks almost like she's levitating, but lethal to a certain degree, and kind of domineering. I wanted her to look very much inspired by Iain [McCaig]'s Padmé art and also loosely inspired by Hillary Clinton. At the time she was always wearing these dress suits, boxy and angular. I wanted to incorporate a character who was extremely strong, but also had that elegance in there as well.

There's a definite edge to her—she's got space lions! For the targon colors, I was looking at various types of howler monkeys. Using just primary colors, you get the red, yellow, and then a duller kind of desaturated blue. There's no doubt in my mind that someone has gotten eaten by those space lions." GRIFFIN

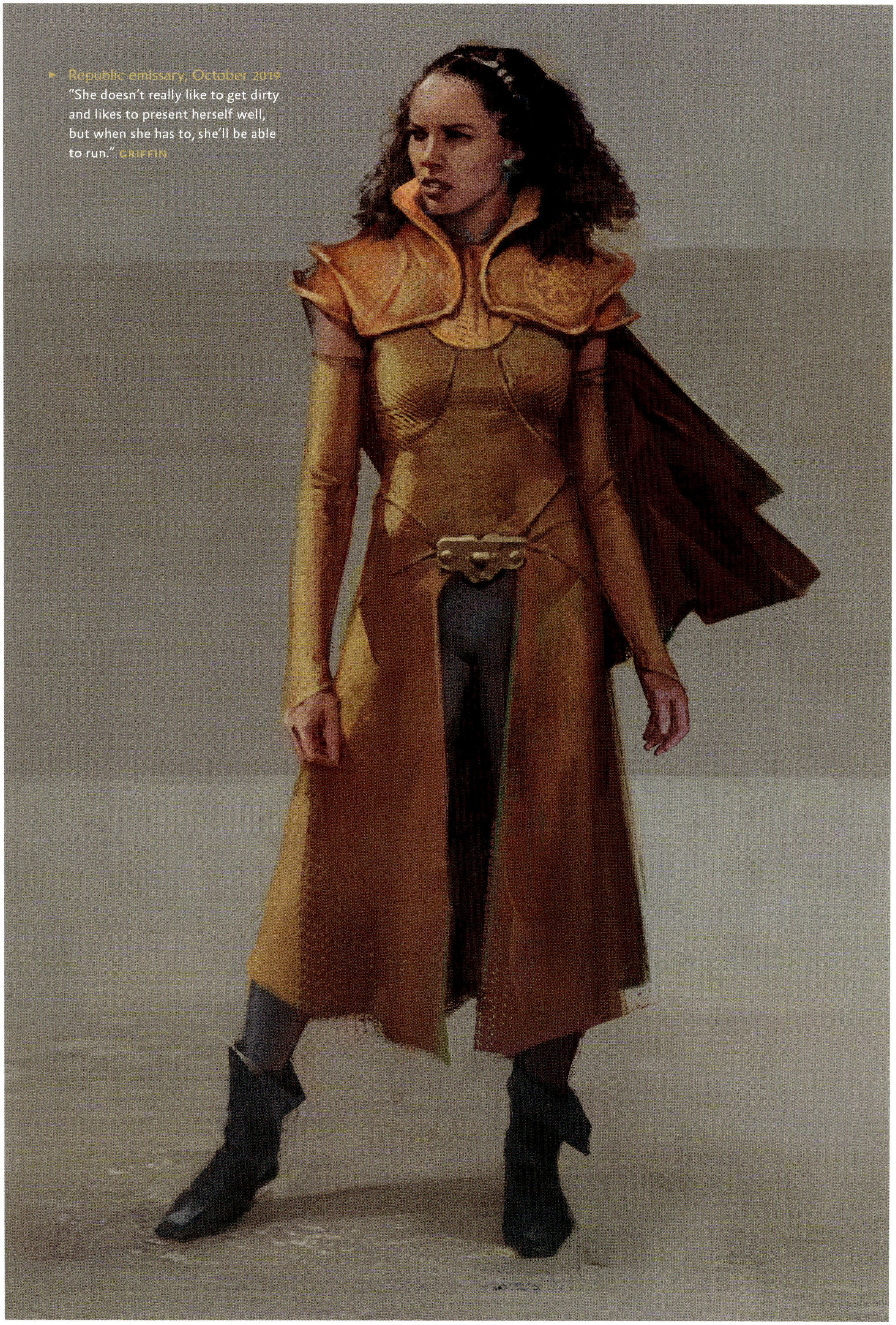

▸ Republic emissary, October 2019
"She doesn't really like to get dirty and likes to present herself well, but when she has to, she'll be able to run." GRIFFIN

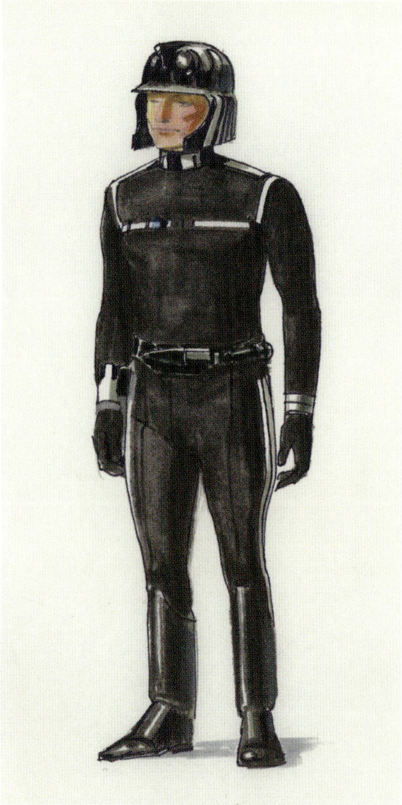

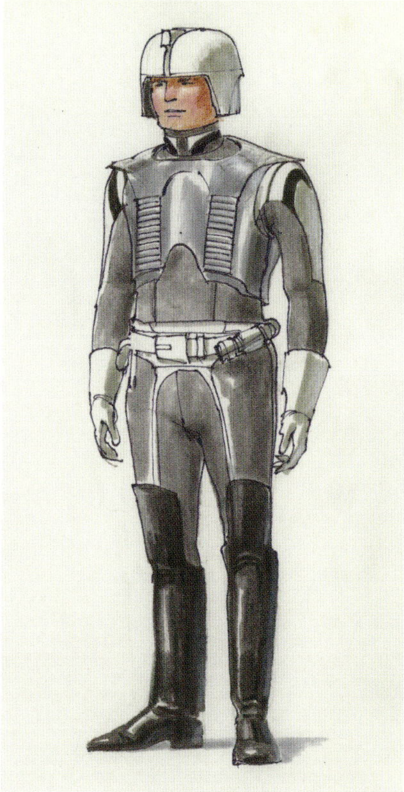

▴ Costume concept for Imperial guards
McQUARRIE

Costume designs for *Return of the Jedi* were used as mood board inspiration and were referenced when designing the citizens of the Republic and the overall aesthetic of the metropolis of Coruscant in the High Republic's heyday.

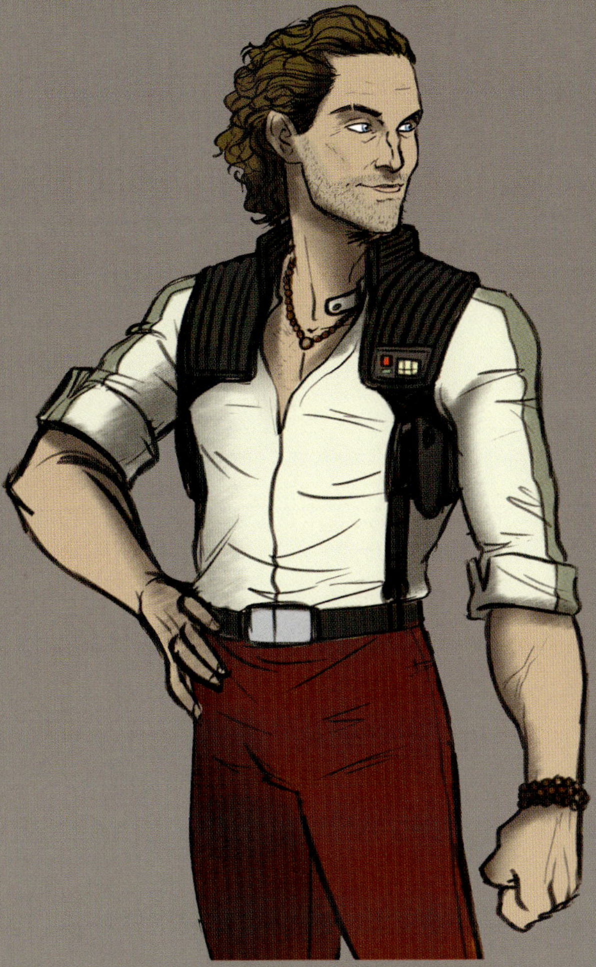

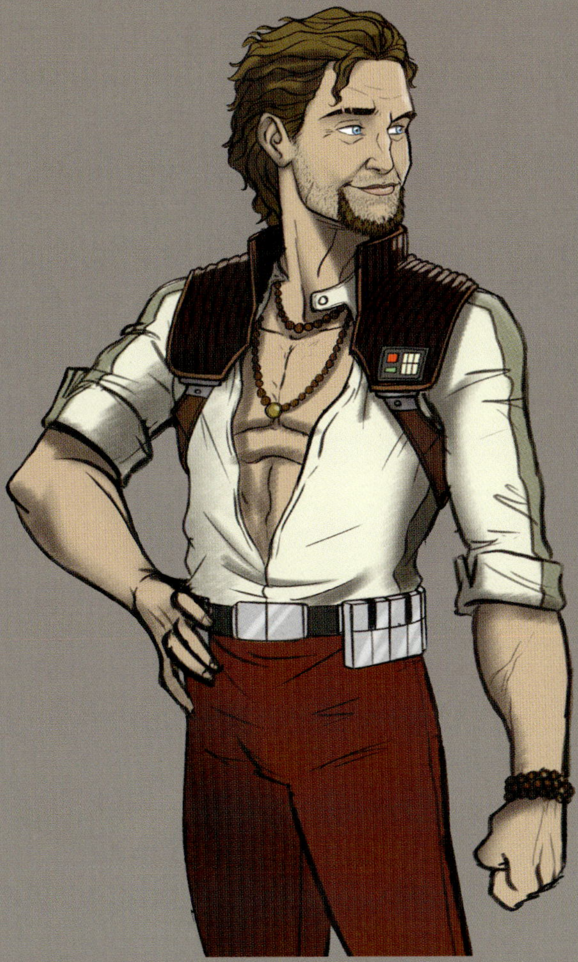

◂ Early concepts for Leox Gyasi THOMAS

▸ The final look of Leox Gyasi THOMAS

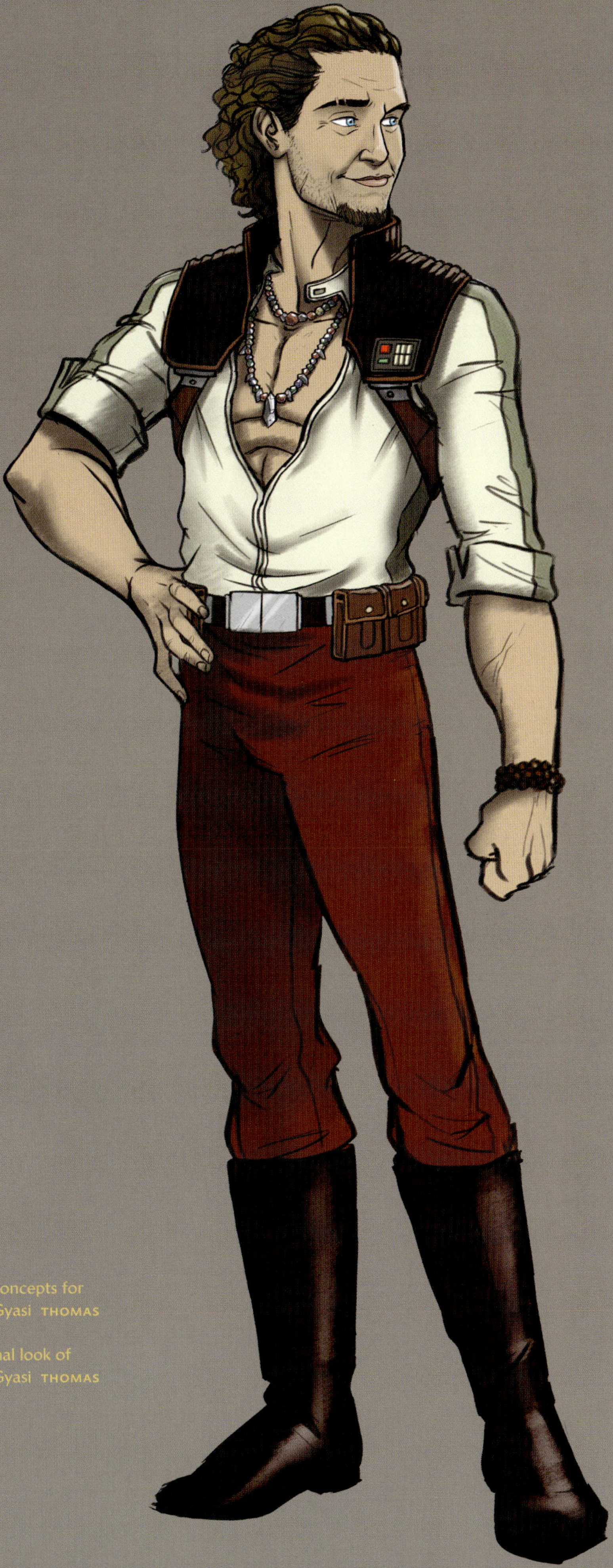

▸ Initial Geode concept, version 1, September 2020 THOMAS

"Mike sent me art of Geode. 'Does this look right?' And I was like, first, it is hilarious that we're looking at art for a rock. Second, this is wrong. It was really pointy, and it's not even roughly rectangular. He was a little too broad. He has to be able to move through the ship. We never see him move through the ship, but he does move through the ship. He had ragged edges; he should be smooth, like water has worn him smooth. Geode goes with the flow. I did not know there were so many points that would be vital about his appearance. But he's plinth-y now." CLAUDIA GRAY

▾ Early Geode concept, version 2 "He's not supposed to have any discernible face, and I kept trying to put too much visible character into him. It's not a face, but the holes and cracks almost *look* like a face." THOMAS

▴ Early Geode concept, version 3 "He looks like his wife left him [*laughs*]. I had plenty of opportunity to curve the mouth up so it didn't look so depressed, but I thought it was so funny." THOMAS

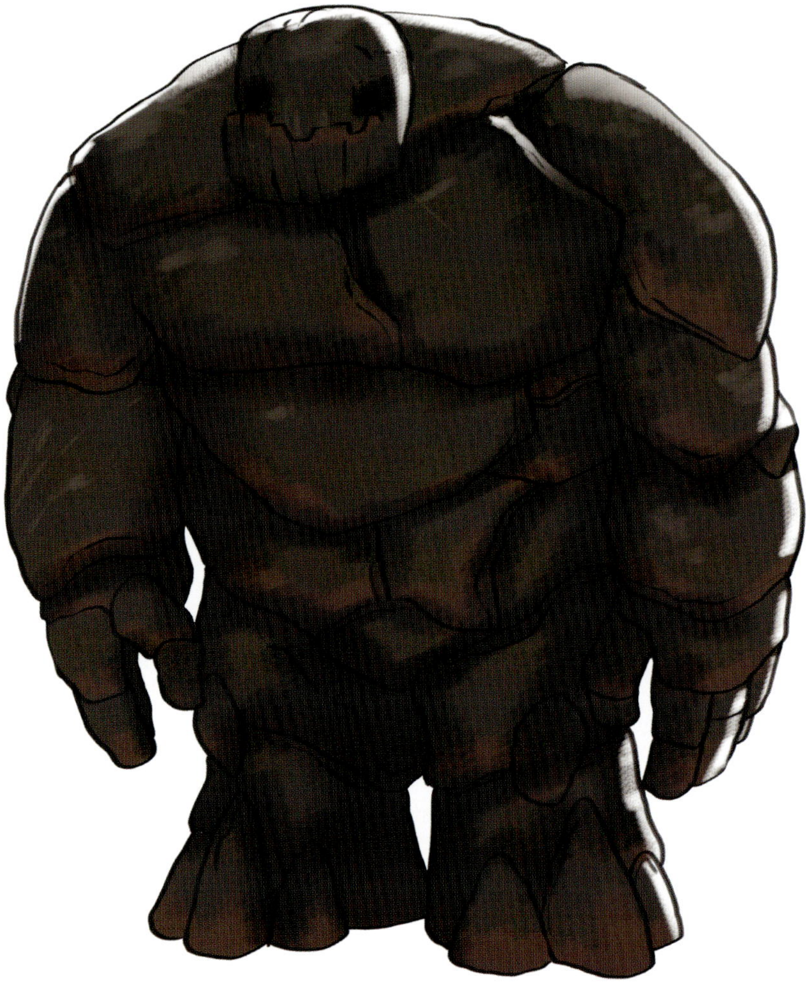

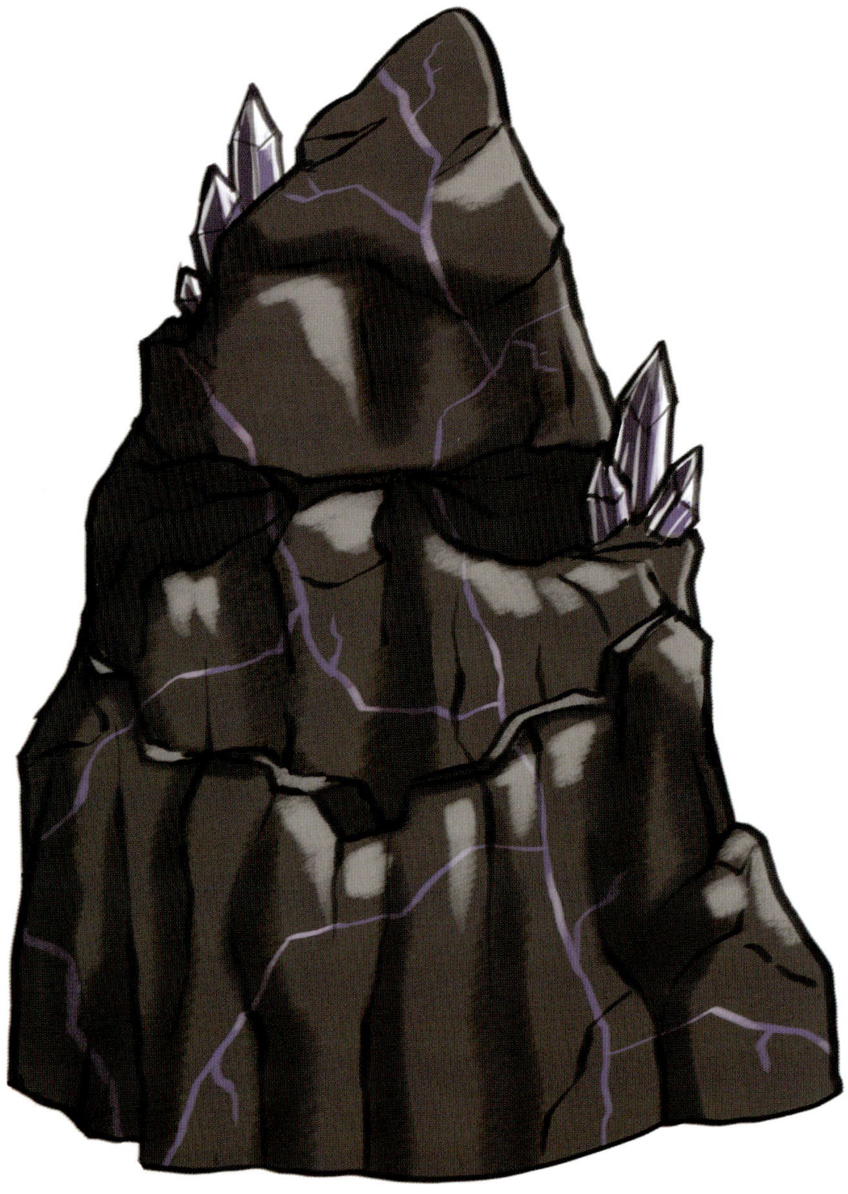

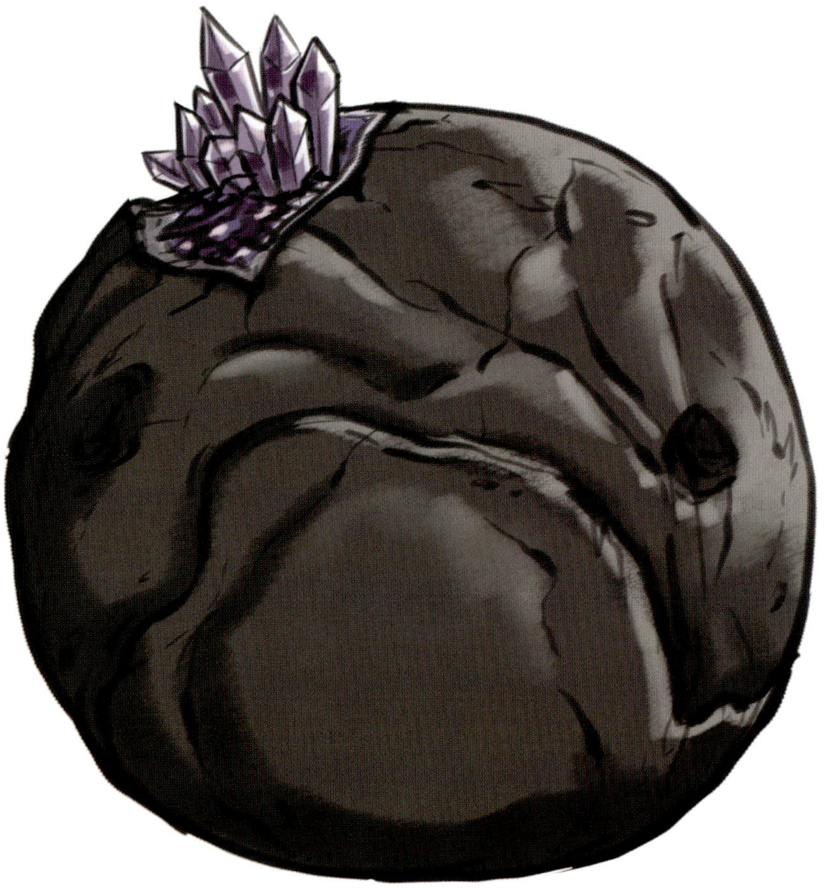

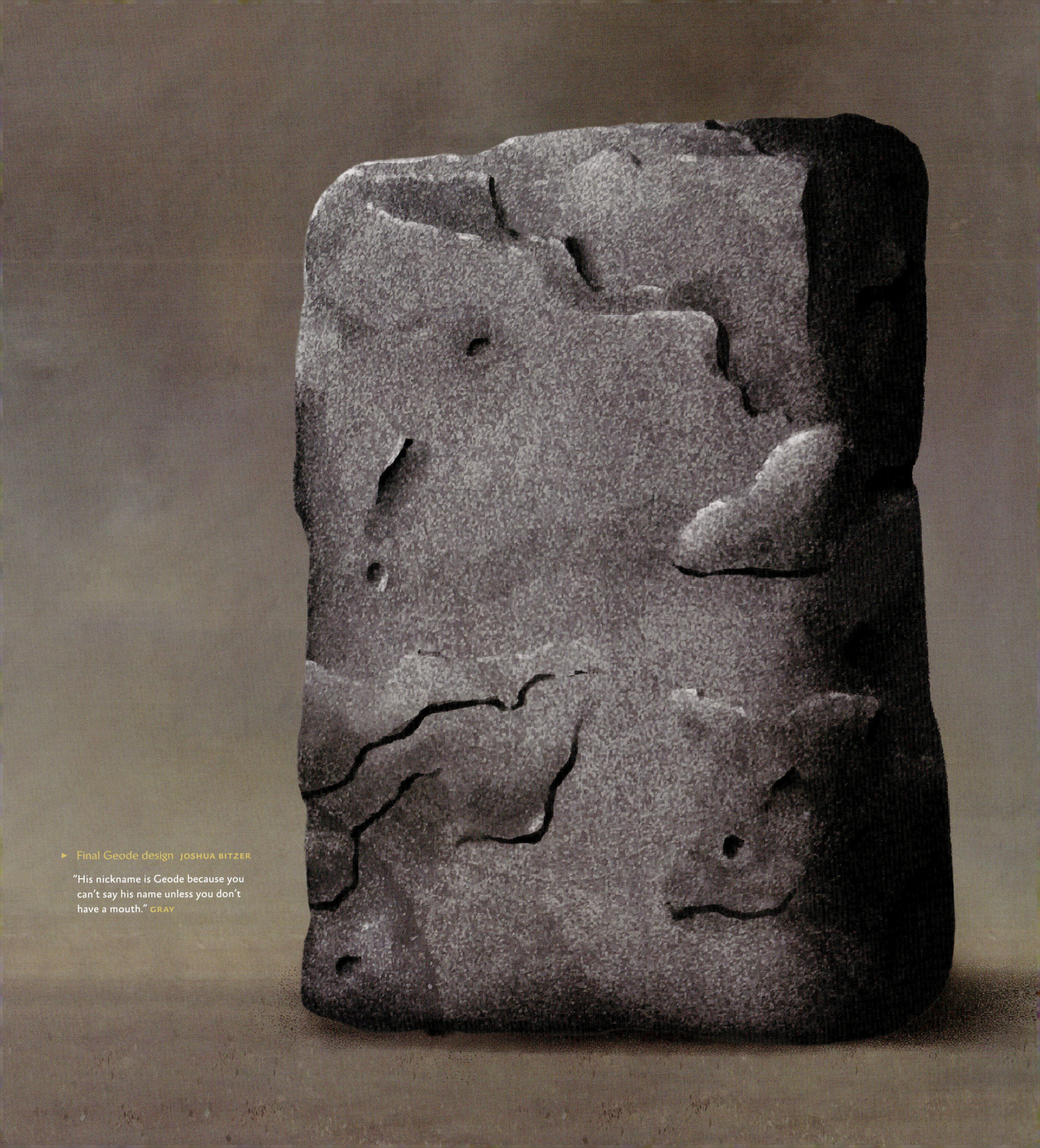

► Final Geode design JOSHUA BITZER

"His nickname is Geode because you can't say his name unless you don't have a mouth." GRAY

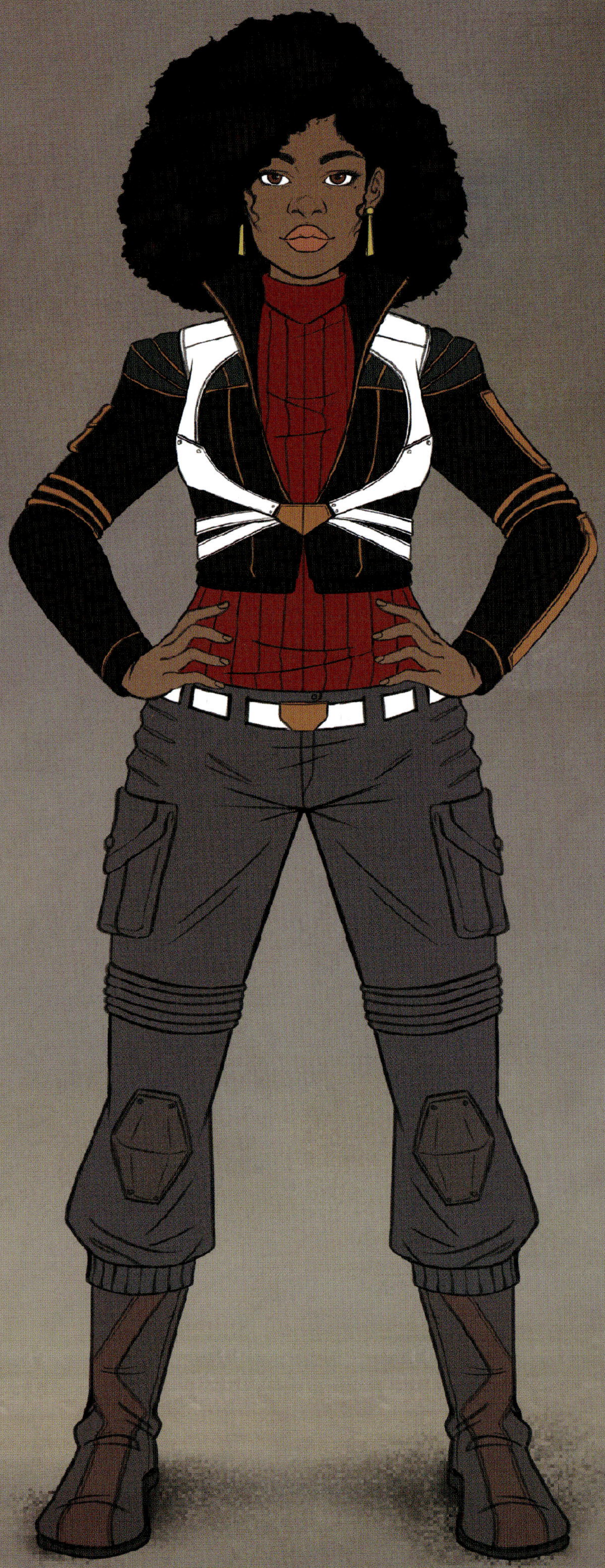

◂ Final design for Sylvestri Yarrow THOMAS

Sylvestri Yarrow was designed for the cover art of Justina Ireland's *Out of the Shadows*, the YA novel that first introduces the no-nonsense pilot. "We didn't have concept art created already, so it was a collaboration between the author, me, and our editor Jennifer Heddle," said Lucasfilm designer Leigh Zieske. "I pulled different things from the manuscript, but a lot of it was just thinking, 'If I was eighteen and I was the pilot of the ship that I got from my mom, what would I wear?'"

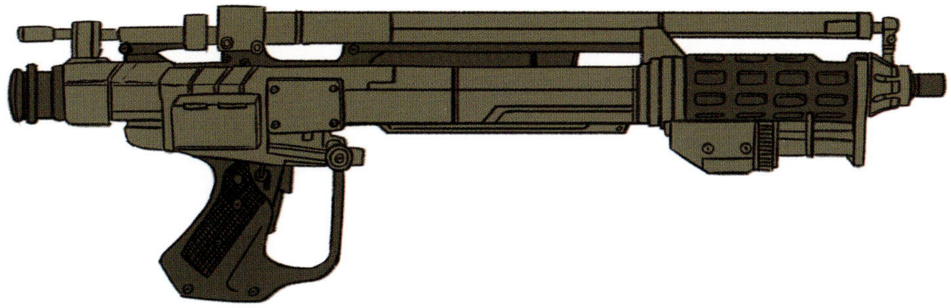

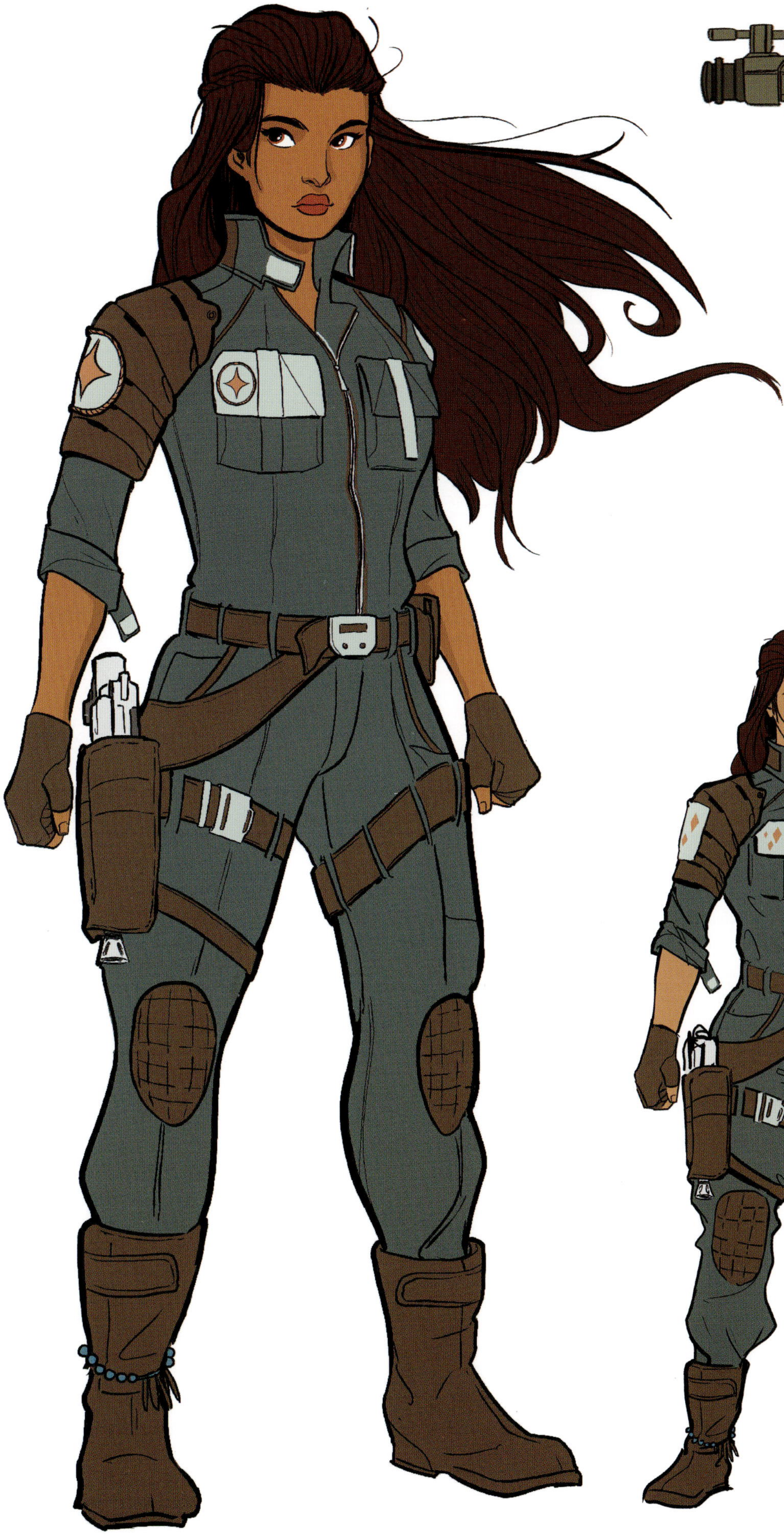

▲ Design for "Beti" THOMAS

Sylvestri's blaster, named after a childhood doll, is often concealed in a unique holster slung across her back.

◀ Final version of Affie Hollow MANNY MEDEROS

▼ Early sketches of Affie Hollow MEDEROS

"The first art for Affie made her look like she was about twenty-eight or so. And I was like, 'OK, we actually have to take this character and de-age her a little bit' because in your head [and on the page], you can do that." GRAY

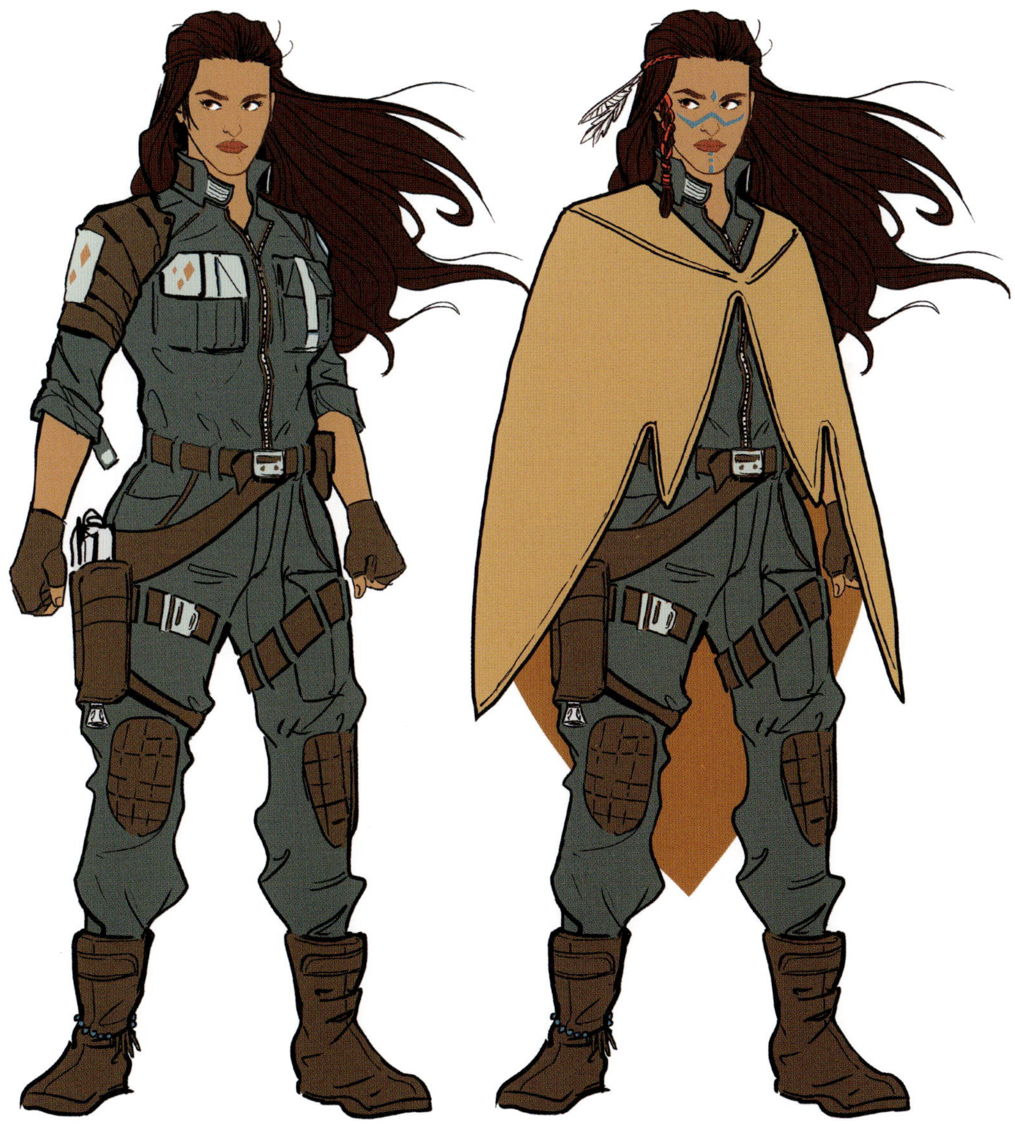

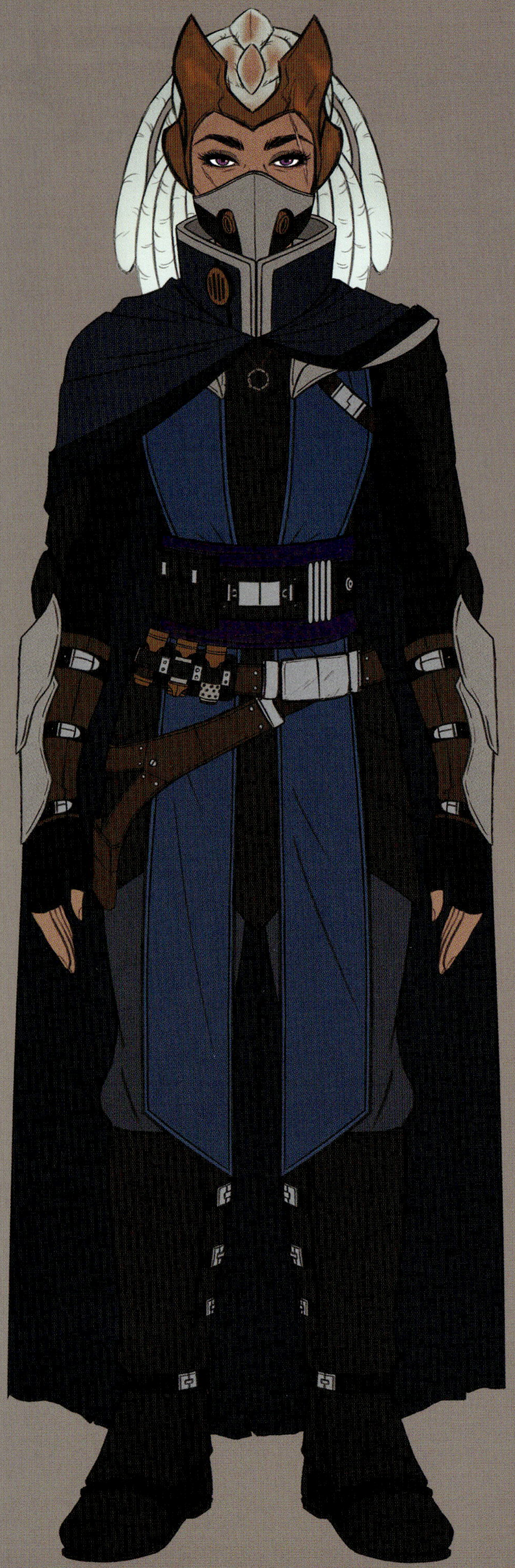

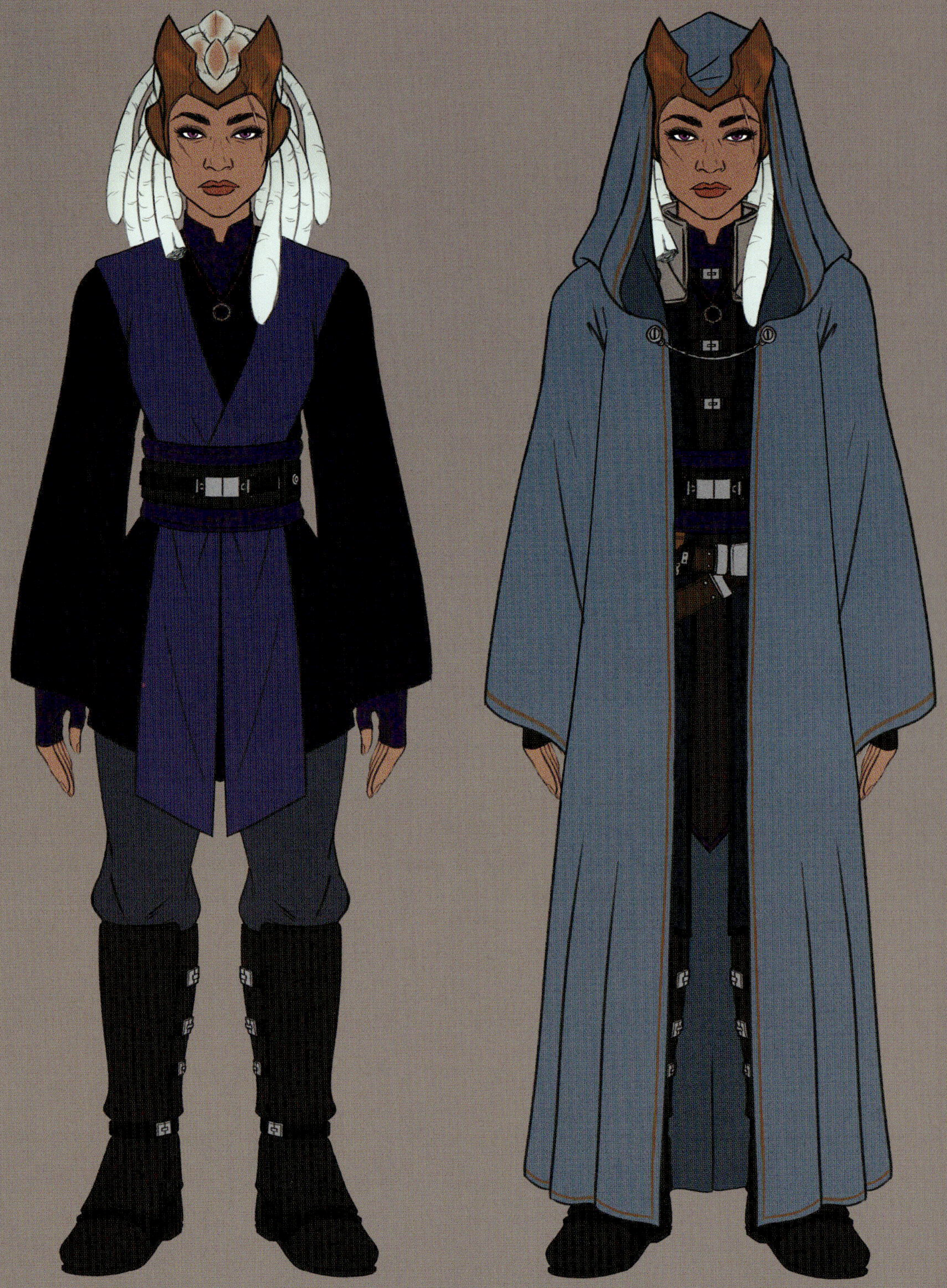

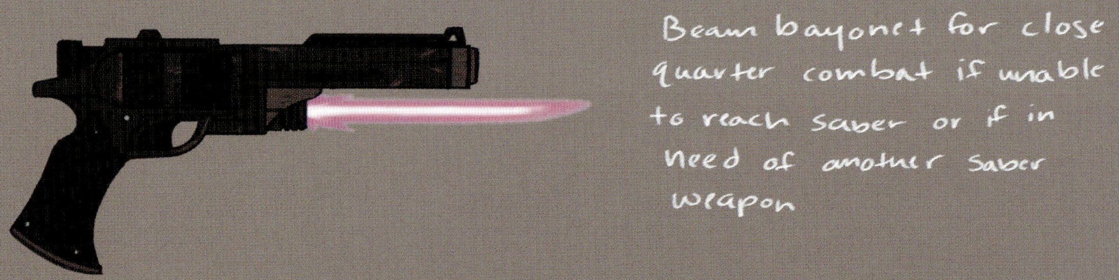

▲ Early designs for monster hunter Ty Yorrick THOMAS

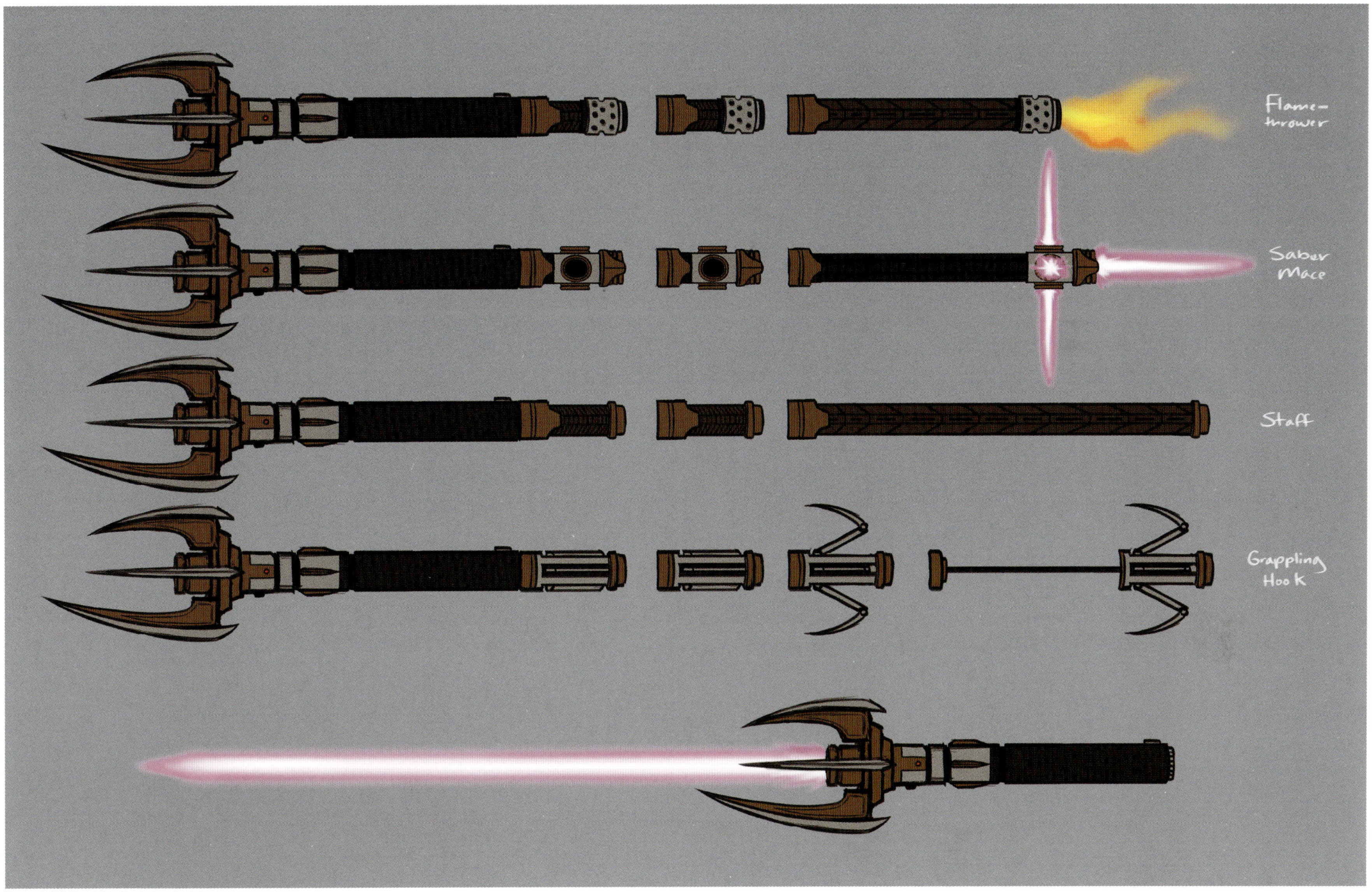

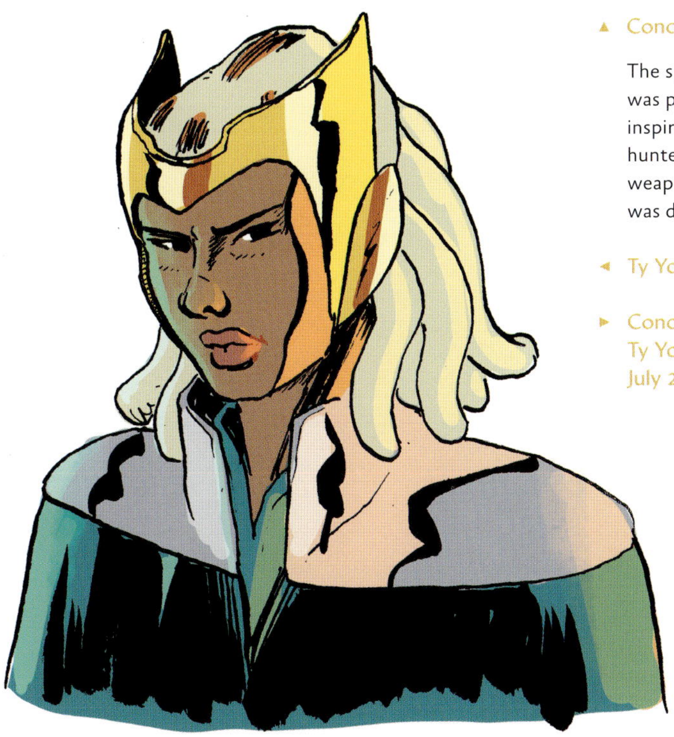

▲ Concept for Ty Yorrick's arsenal THOMAS

The spiked hilt of Ty Yorrick's lightsaber was part of the original concept art that inspired the character, but the monster hunter's arsenal of attachments and other weaponry, which ultimately went unused, was designed by Thomas.

◄ Ty Yorrick study BROKENSHIRE

► Concept sketch to engineer Ty Yorrick's lightsaber, July 2020 THOMAS

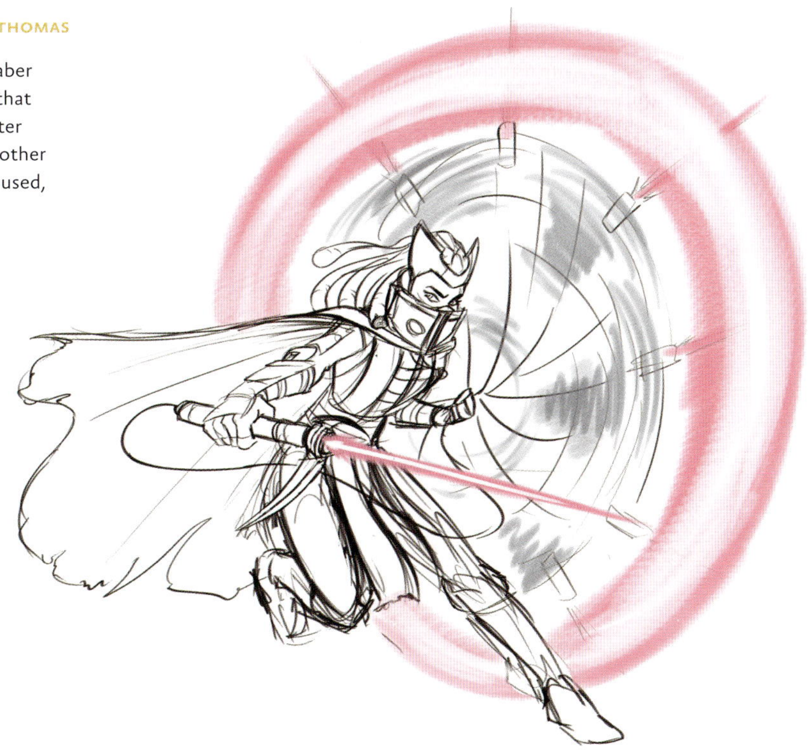

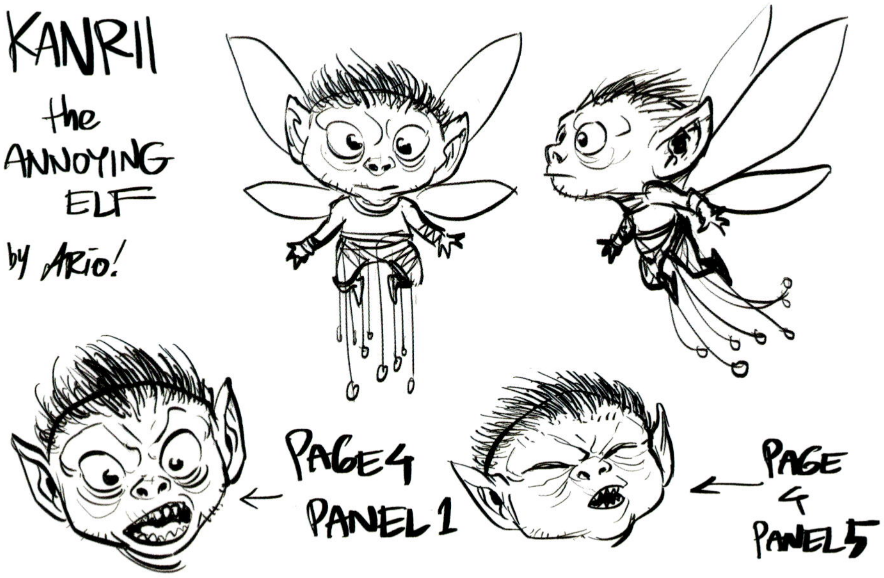

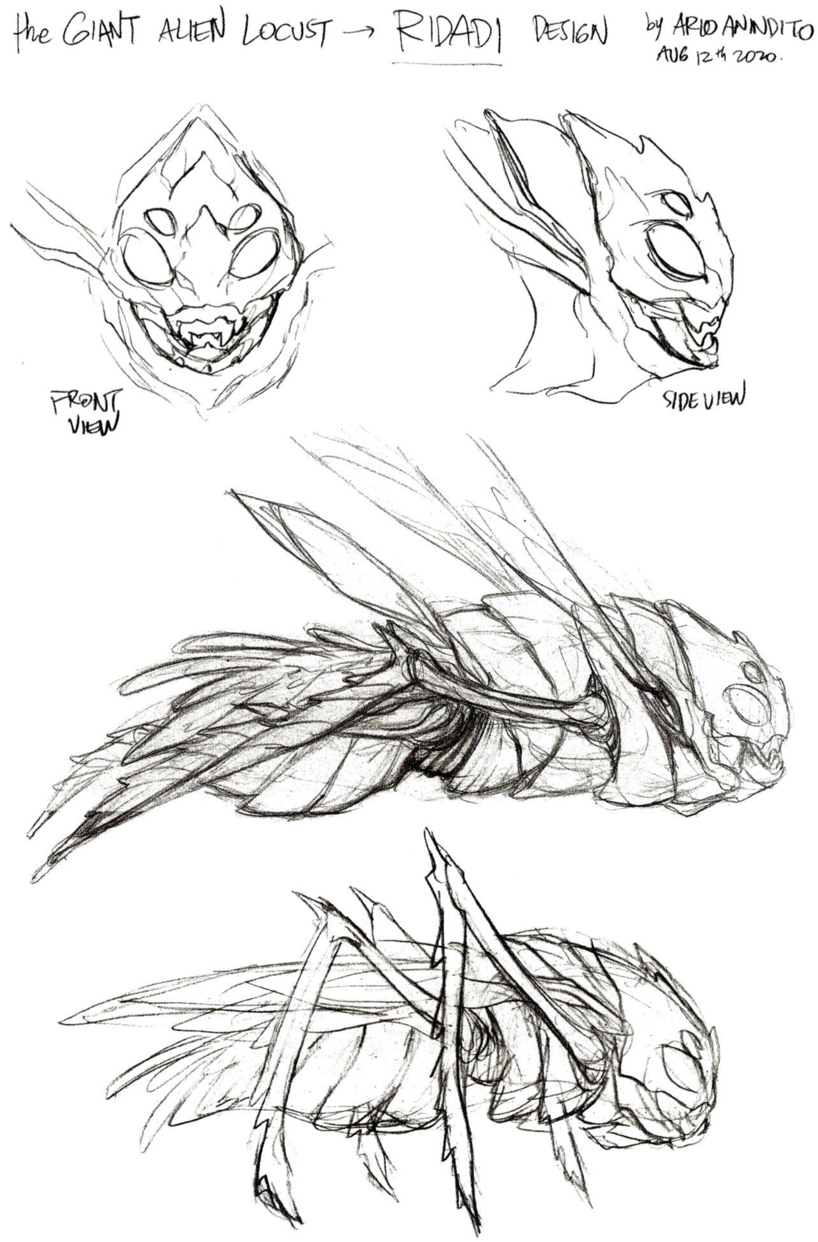

▲ Character study of Kanrii the Ximpi
ANINDITO

Although the Ximpi species already appeared in comic form in Marvel's *Lando* #1, Anindito's exploration of Kanrii's grating personality is evident in his design for the character. "I kept the dangling things on its belt and, of course, the wings," Anindito said. "One thing that I needed to emphasize on the design is it needs to look like it wants to know everything. For the hair, I imagine it as if it were in live action. The hair is going to be very soft and wavy, and it made you want to punch the Ximpi more."

▼ Early concept for Cham Cham "This is the first character we designed. I told Daniel, 'I'm a big fan of Jar Jar Binks. It's a very big part of my life.' And he said, 'I have something like that. His name is Cham Cham!' It's cute, but it's dangerous. We really worked everything into the smallest detail: the tail from a scorpion, the wings from a bat, but he's like a piggy. Daniel sent me a video of a wolverine, and that's our Cham Cham when he gets angry." TOLIBAO

► Early sketch for the ridadi, August 2020
ANINDITO

Anindito pulled from his childhood love of the Japanese manga superhero Kamen Rider and insects like the grasshopper to create this scary-looking, but ultimately misunderstood, creature attracted to the light source of the Starlight Beacon like a moth to a flame. The posterior of the creature, however, resembles a chicken's feathery tail. "In my imagination, it sees a different way," Anindito said. "The upper set of eyes can detect heat and the lower eyes see like a fly, with faceted eyes."

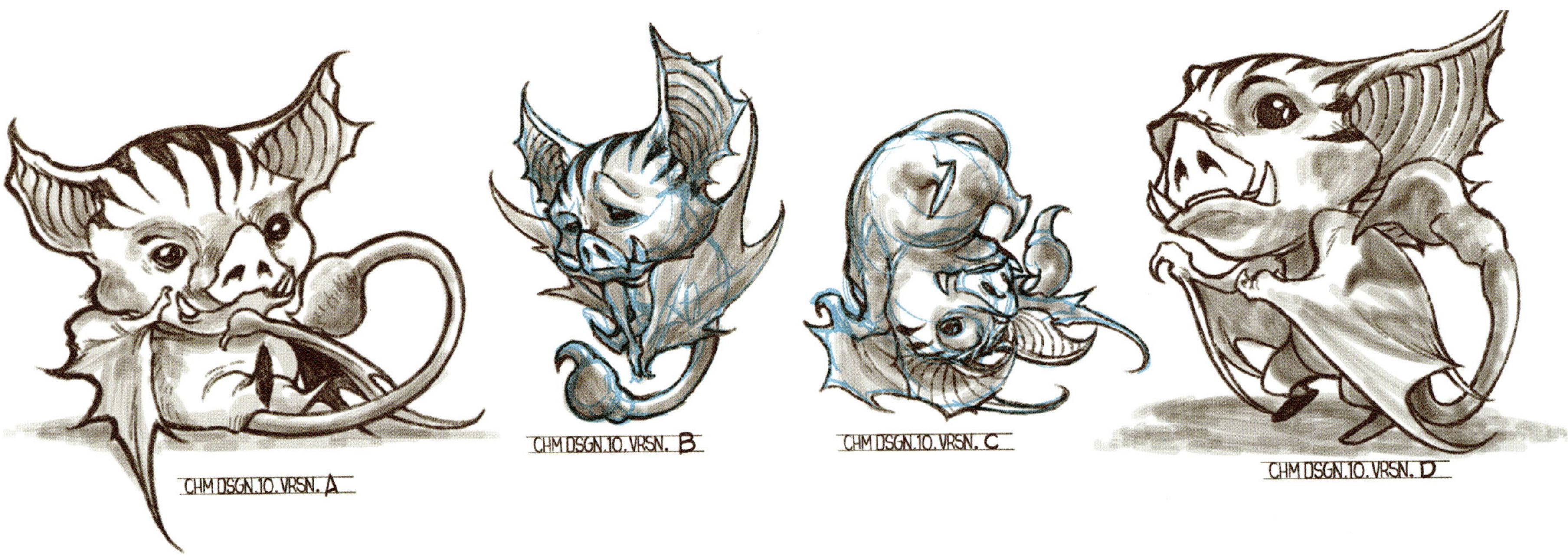

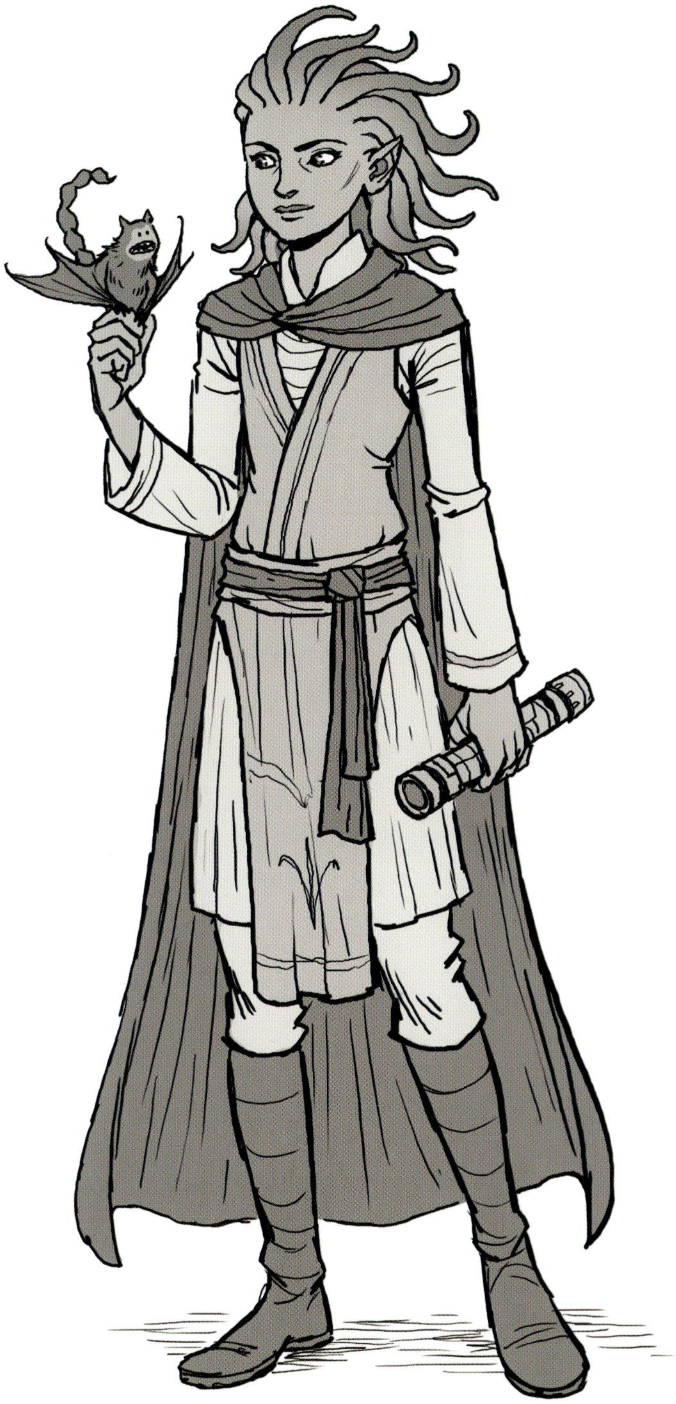

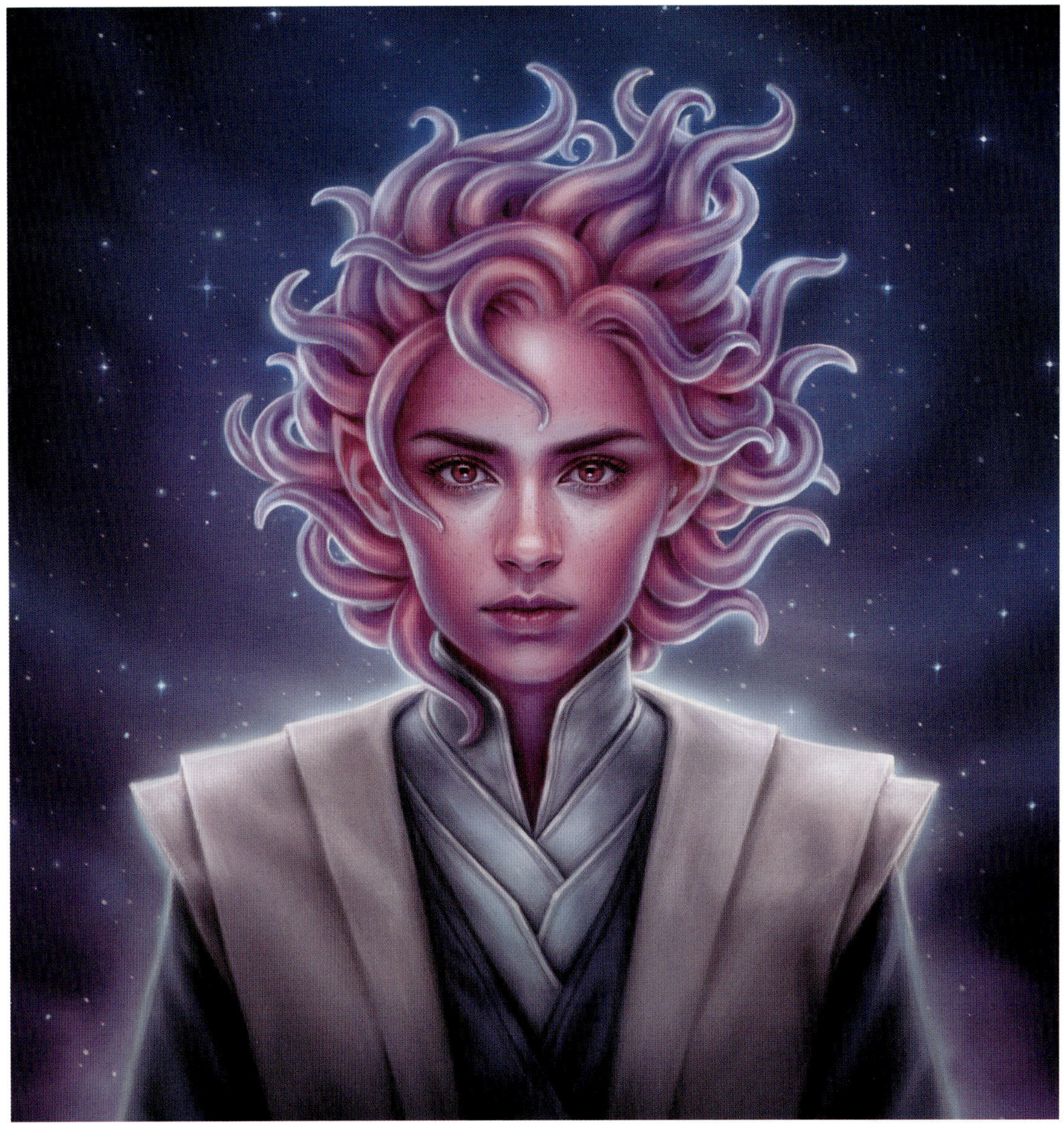

▲ Zeen Mrala ANTONSSON

◄ Zeen Mrala featured on a variant cover for *Star Wars: Midnight Horizon* TARA PHILLIPS

► Facial study of Zeen Mrala BROKENSHIRE

"For me, the moments of humanity come from these huge decisions that they make that really matter, like Zeen saving everybody knowing that it's at the cost of her best friend and the secret that she's harboring for her whole life. It's a huge moment for her where she shows this generosity of spirit that is gigantic. And she doesn't even think that hard about it. She just does what has to be done. So that matters. But it's also the small moments of her just caring about a little creature named Cham Cham that also make her feel like a real teenage girl." OLDER

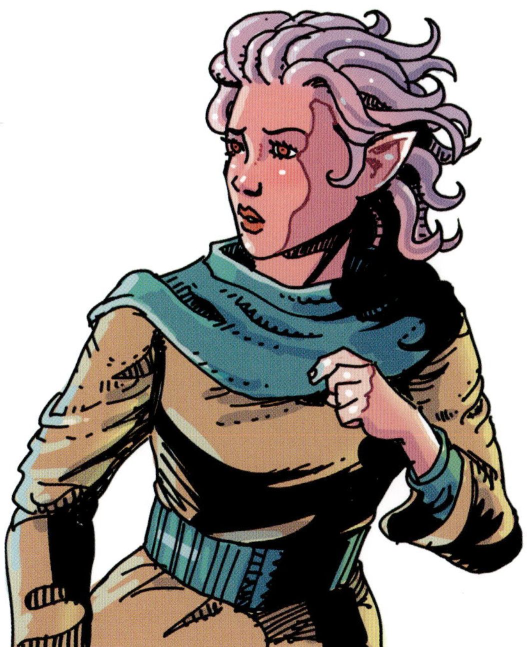

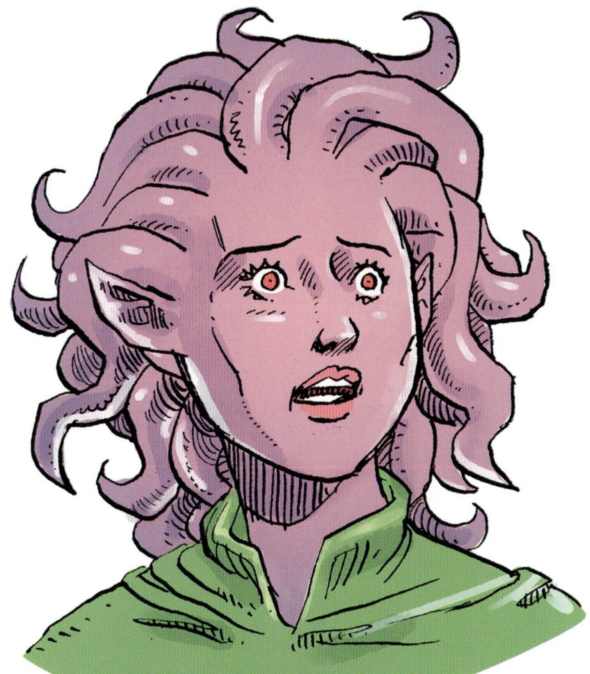

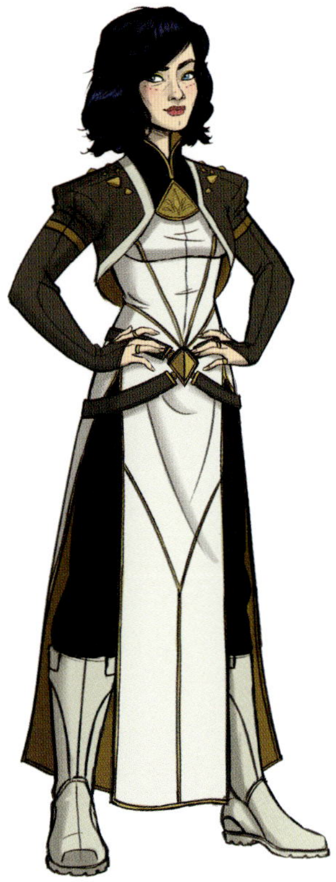

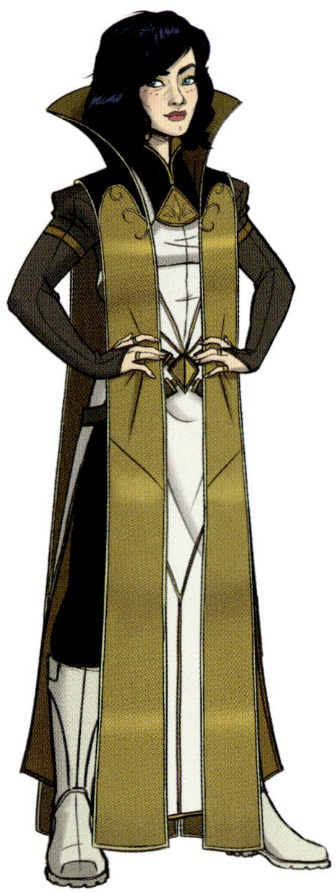

▲ Early concepts of Detective Sian Holt, April 2021 "Sian felt a little ornate in my first [drawing] and they wanted to make her a redhead and to play up the more regal colors, like blue or purple, so I remember simplifying her outfits, but still giving her a kind of over-the-top robe option and adding some of that color to it." THOMAS

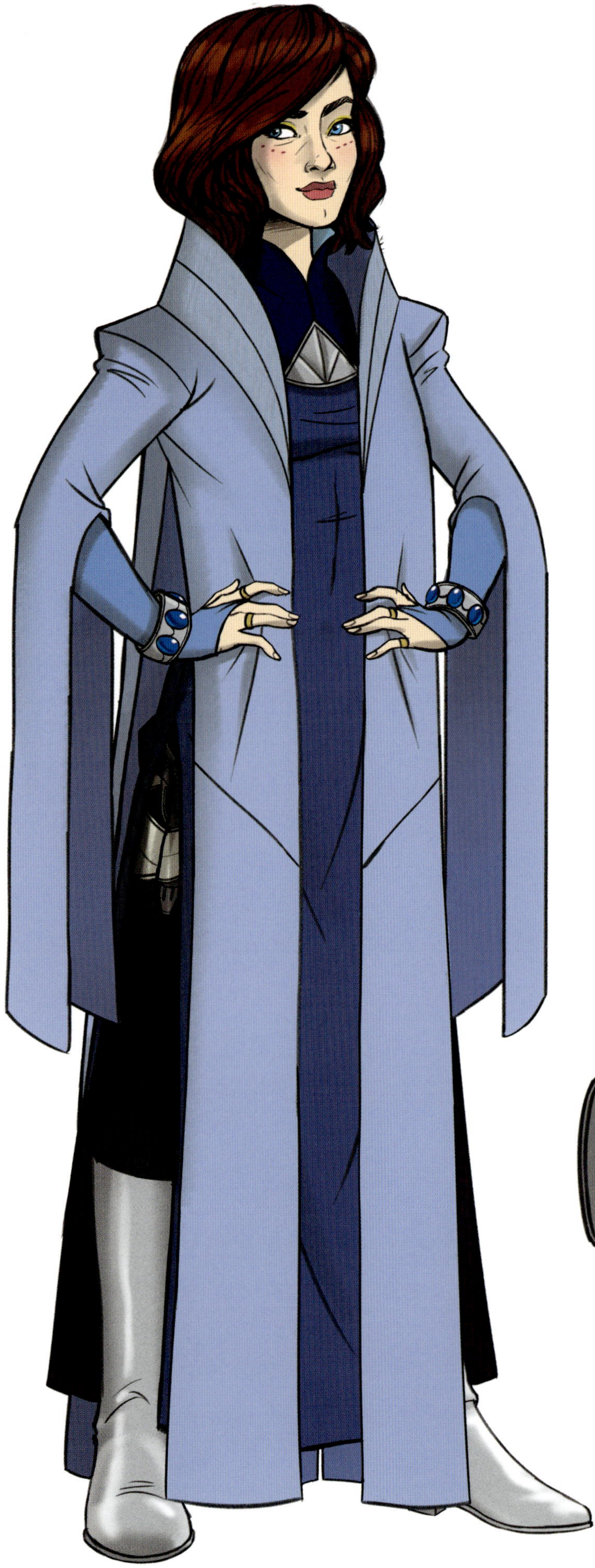

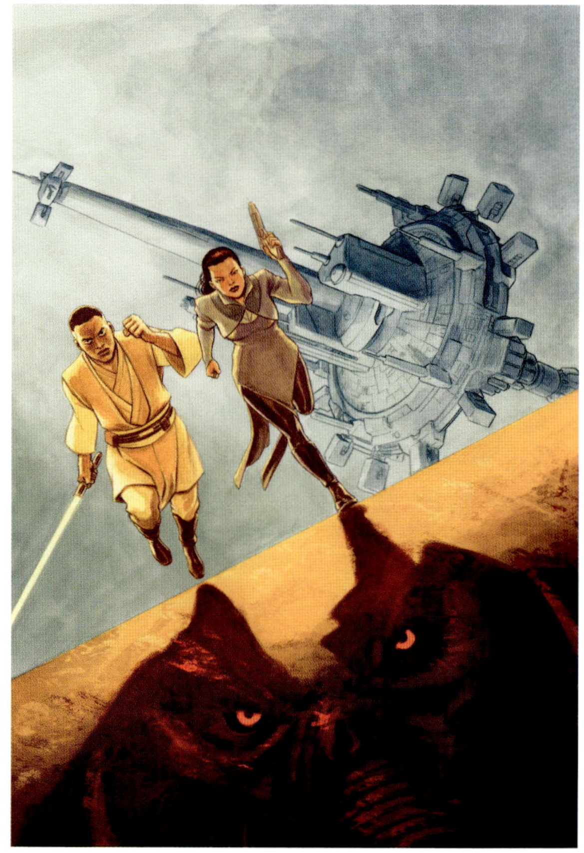

▲ Variant cover for Marvel's *Star Wars: Trail of Shadows* #2 DAVID LÓPEZ

◀ Final concept of Detective Sian Holt, April 2021 "She's supposed to be kind of the unknown badass, and I wanted to implement that in some of her gear. I remember really liking the idea of the hidden pistols and concealed blasters in her fancy bracelet." THOMAS

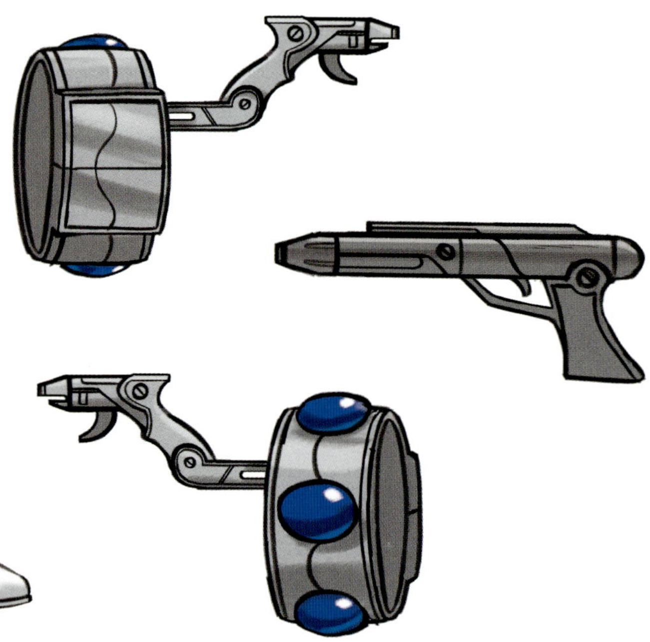

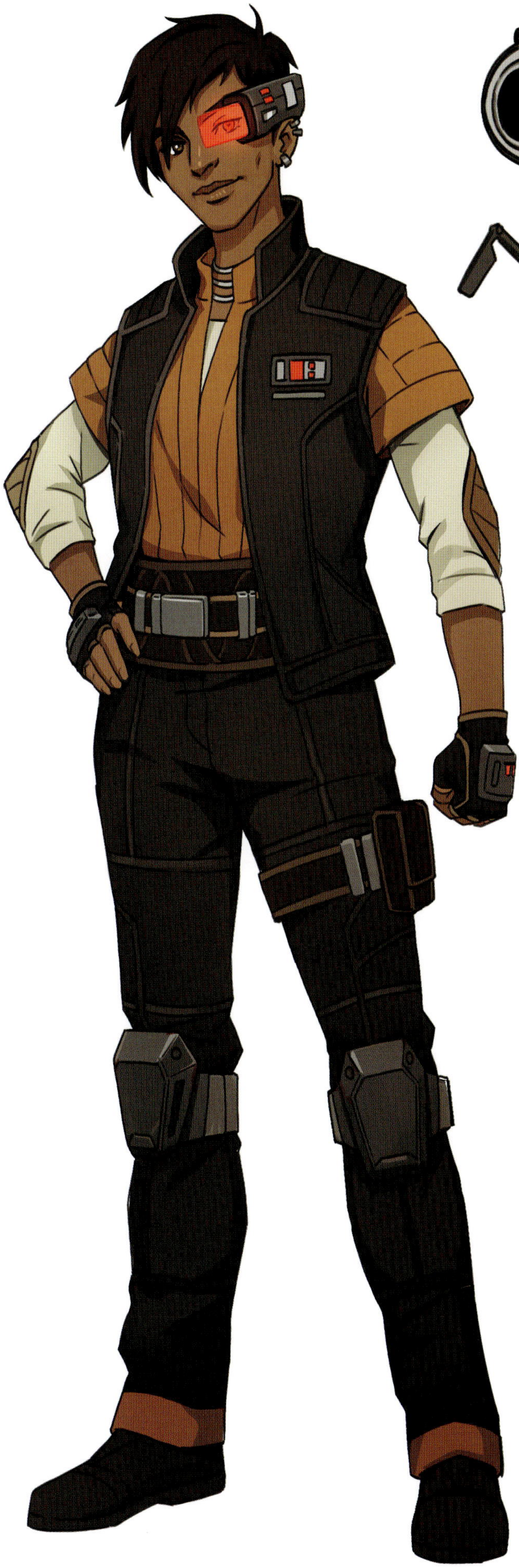

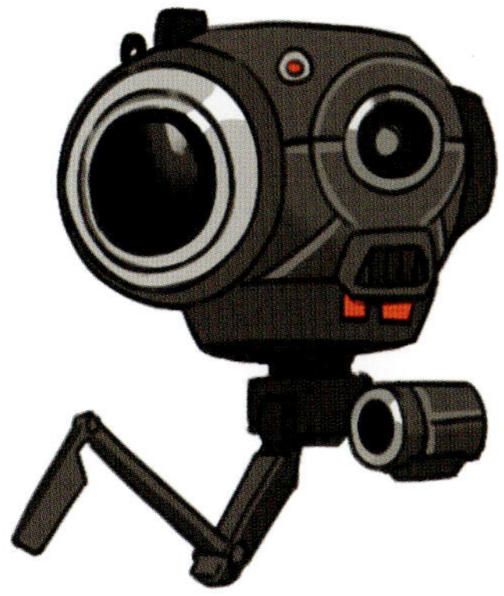

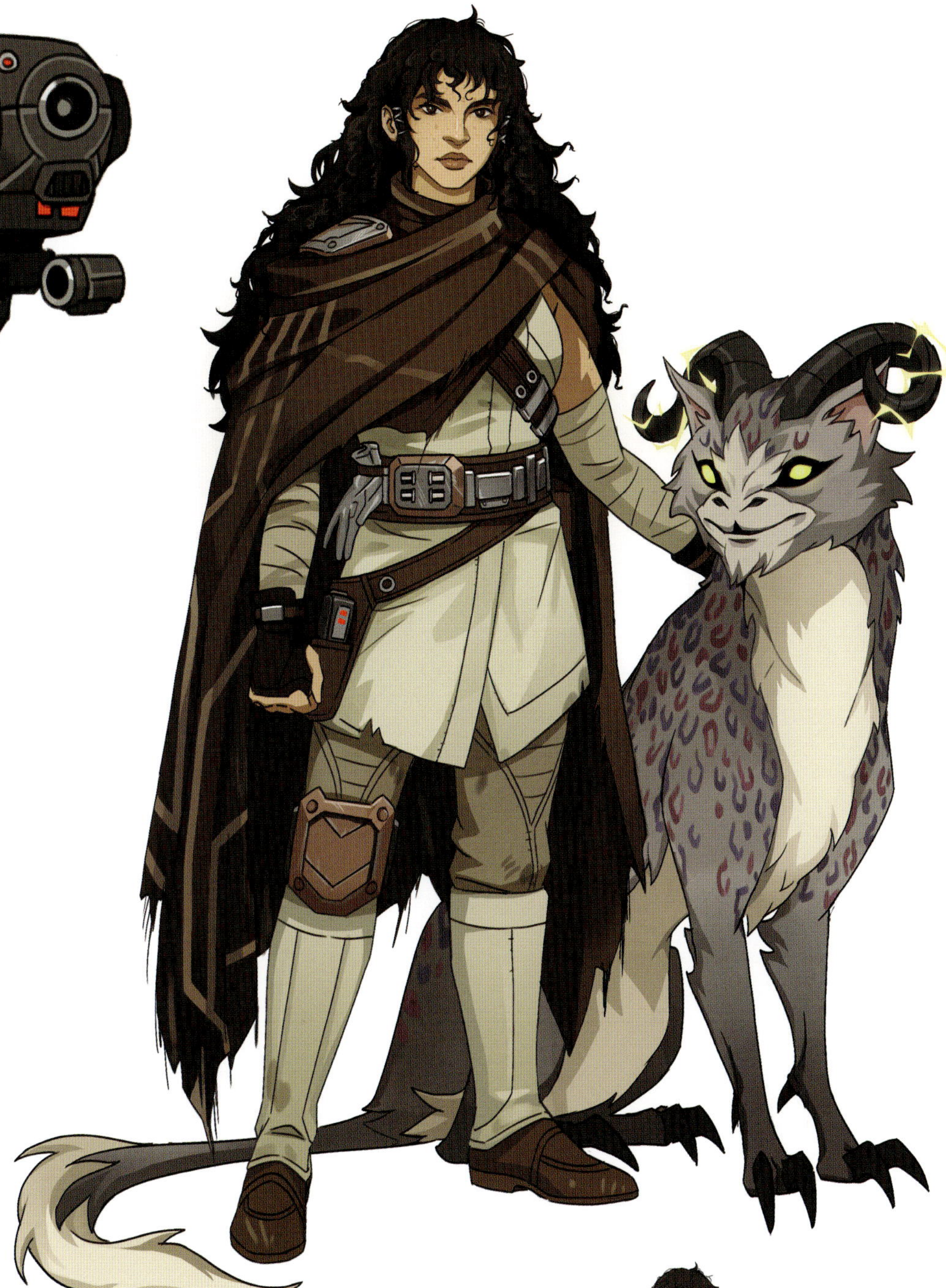

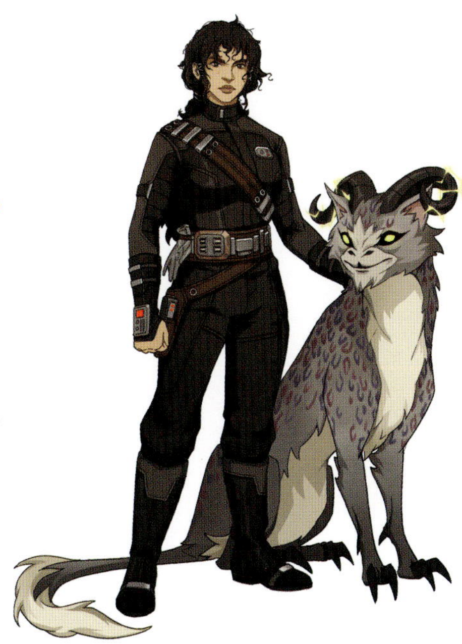

▲ Jordanna Sparkburn and Remy the Vollka MINJI YOON

◄ Rhil Dairo and VT-9 YOON

"She's like if Lobot and the photography team from *The Hunger Games* were combined into one *Star Wars* character. She's this on-the-ground battle reporter, but she's in the story to do this puff piece on the Republic Fair. And then the Nihil come, and she has to go back into war correspondent mode. There's Jedi, of course, being heroic left and right, but it's crazy to see this one small woman making this huge impact and trying to get communications out. It really shows you that you could always be waiting to be saved or you could do something about it. And she's one of those people that is a doer." ZIESKE

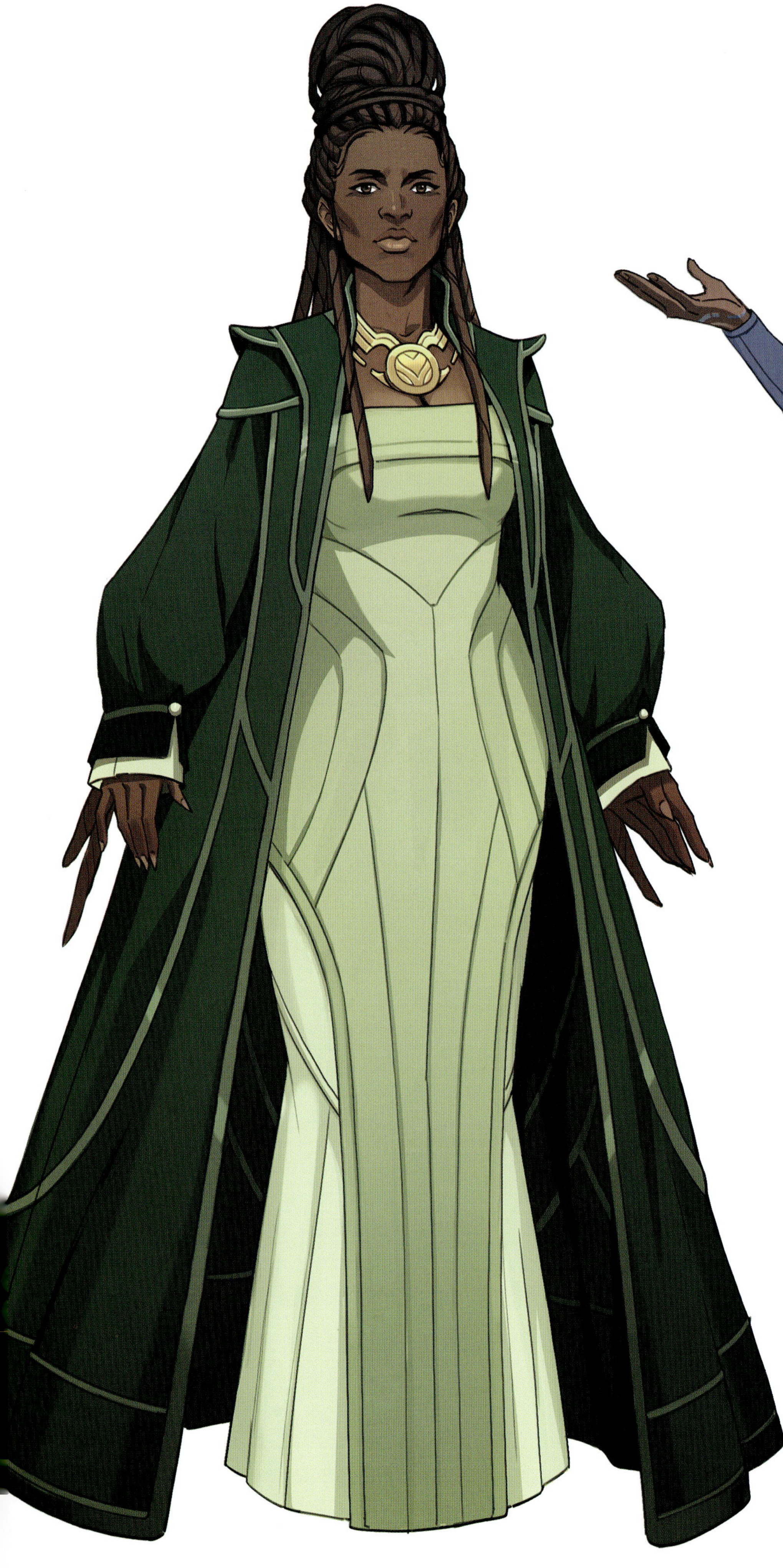

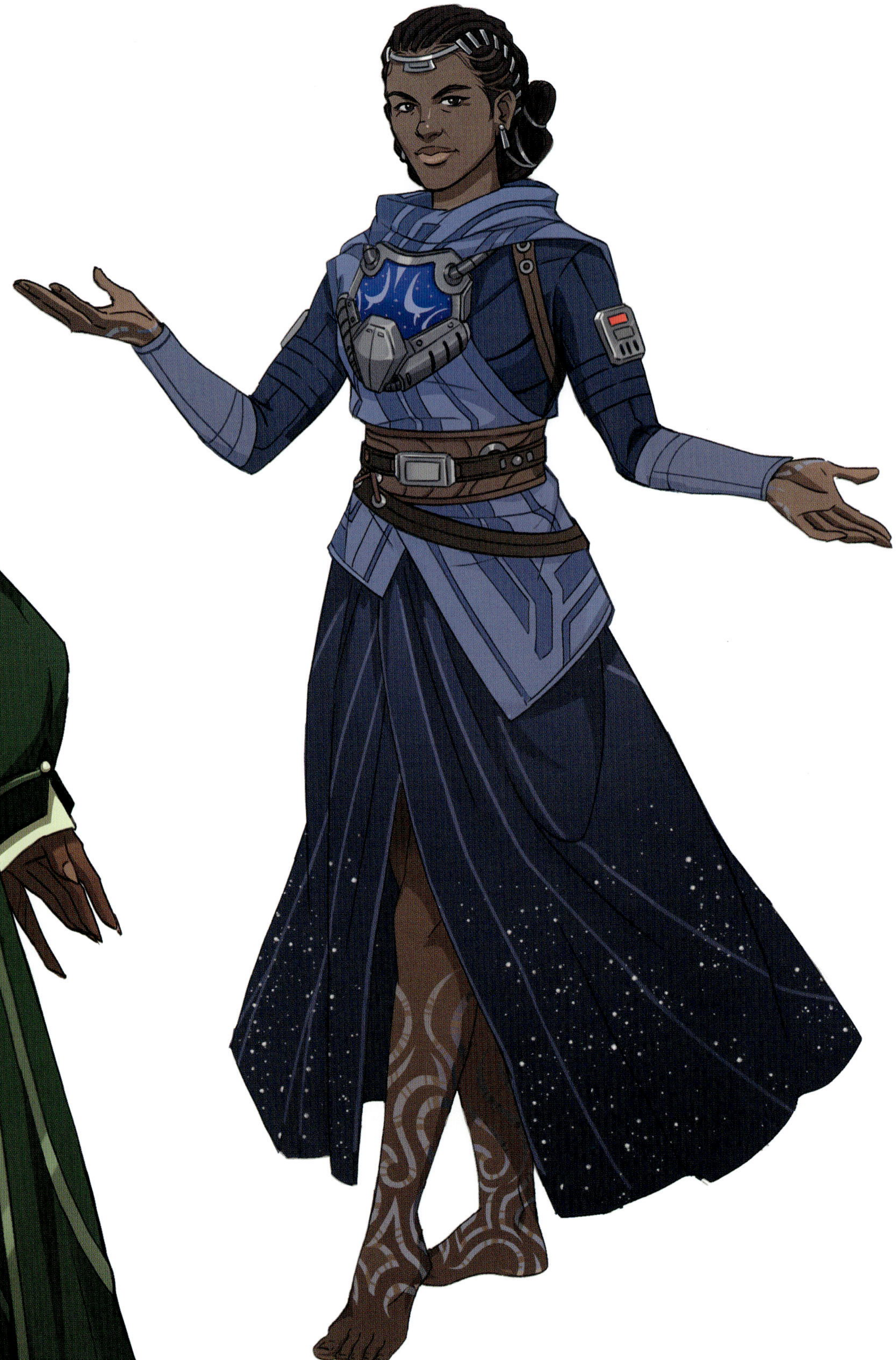

▲ Concept for Chancey Yarrow YOON

◄ Concept for Ghirra Starros YOON

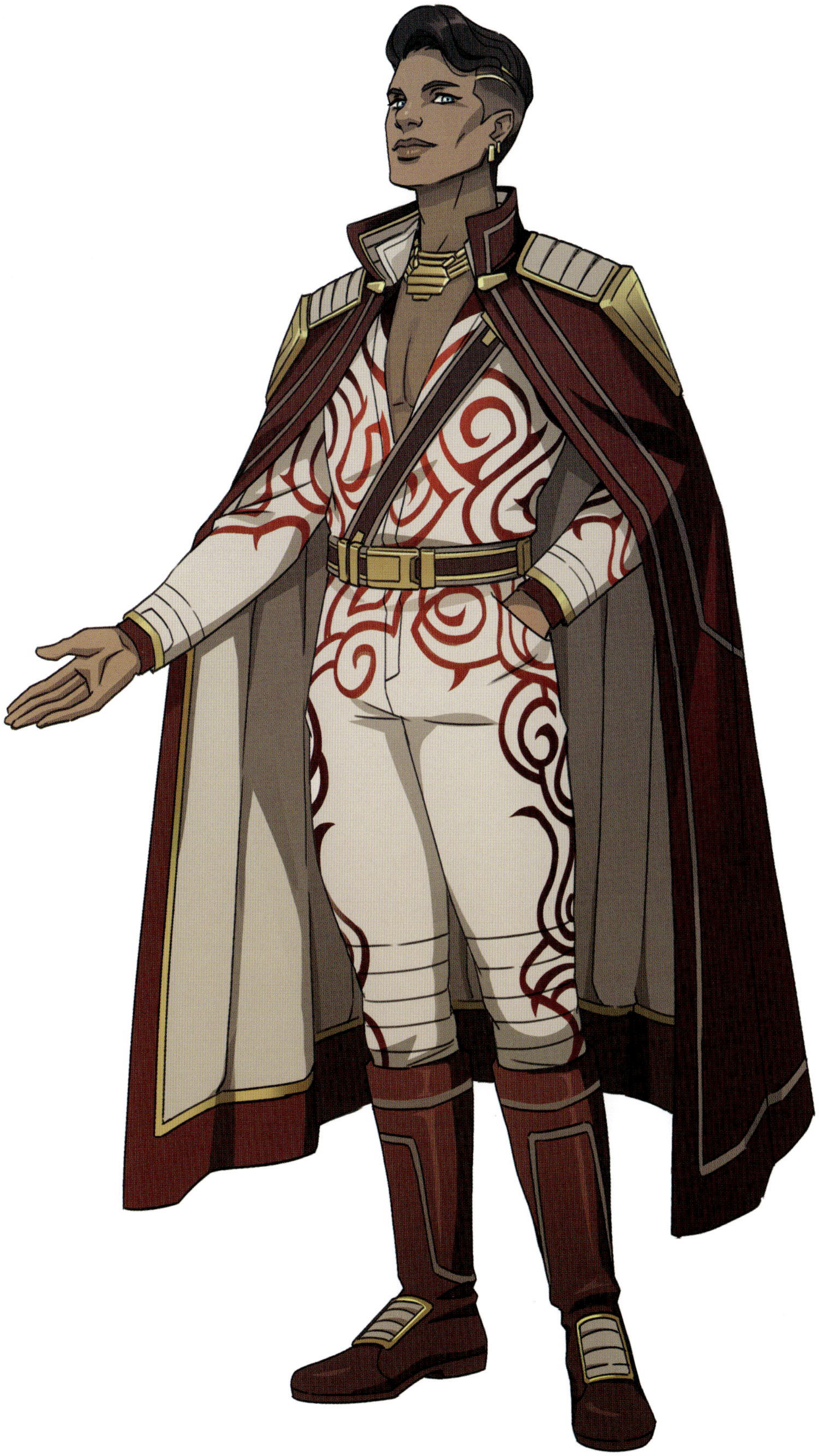

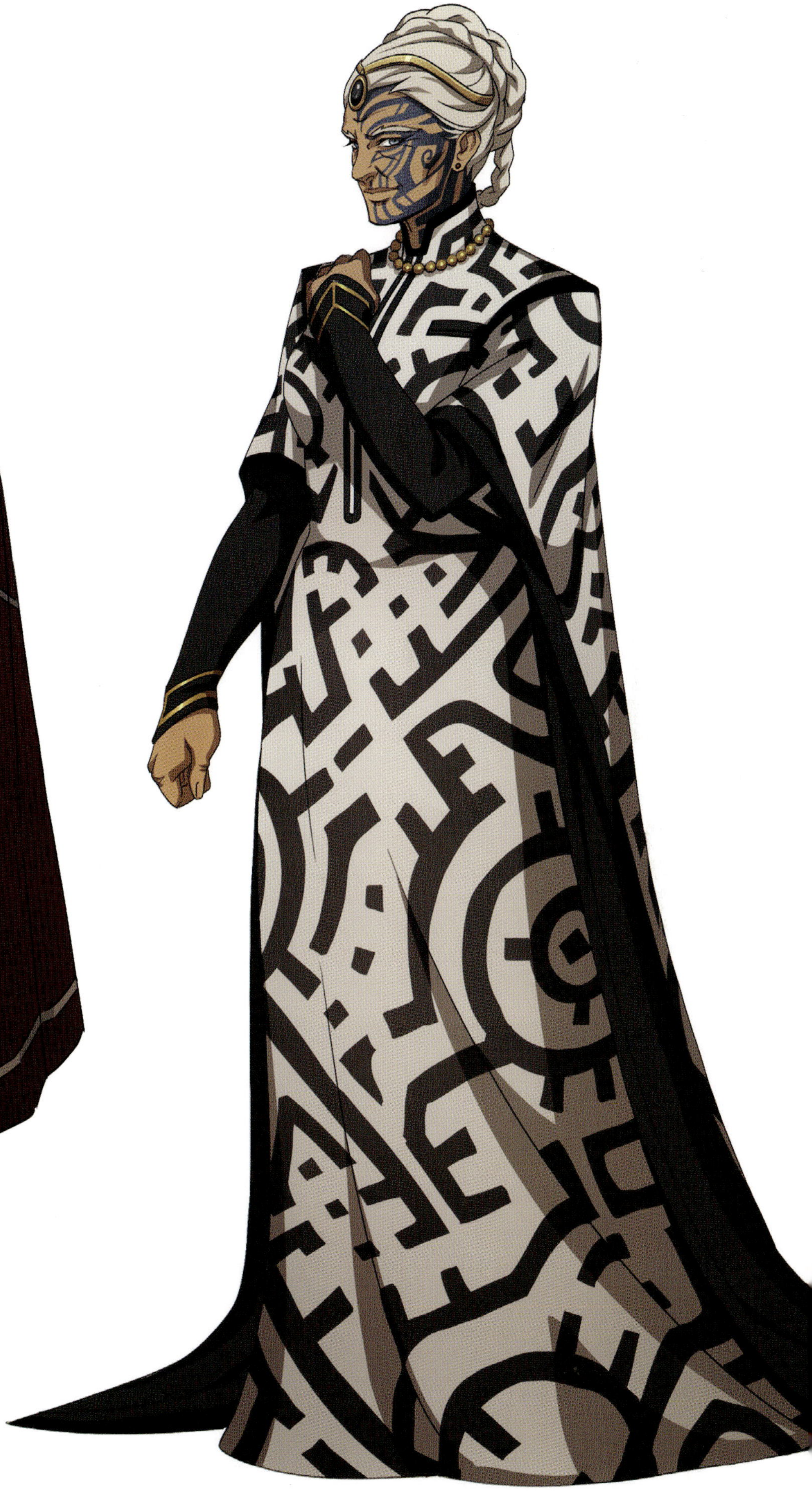

▲ Concept for Xylan Graf YOON

► Concept for Catriona Graf YOON

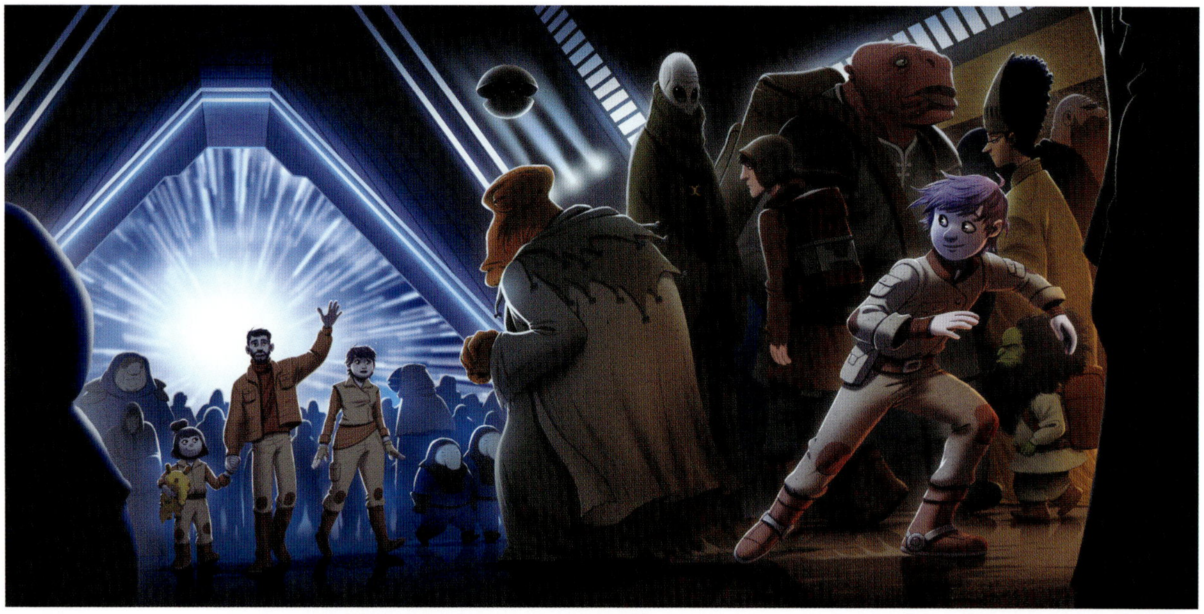

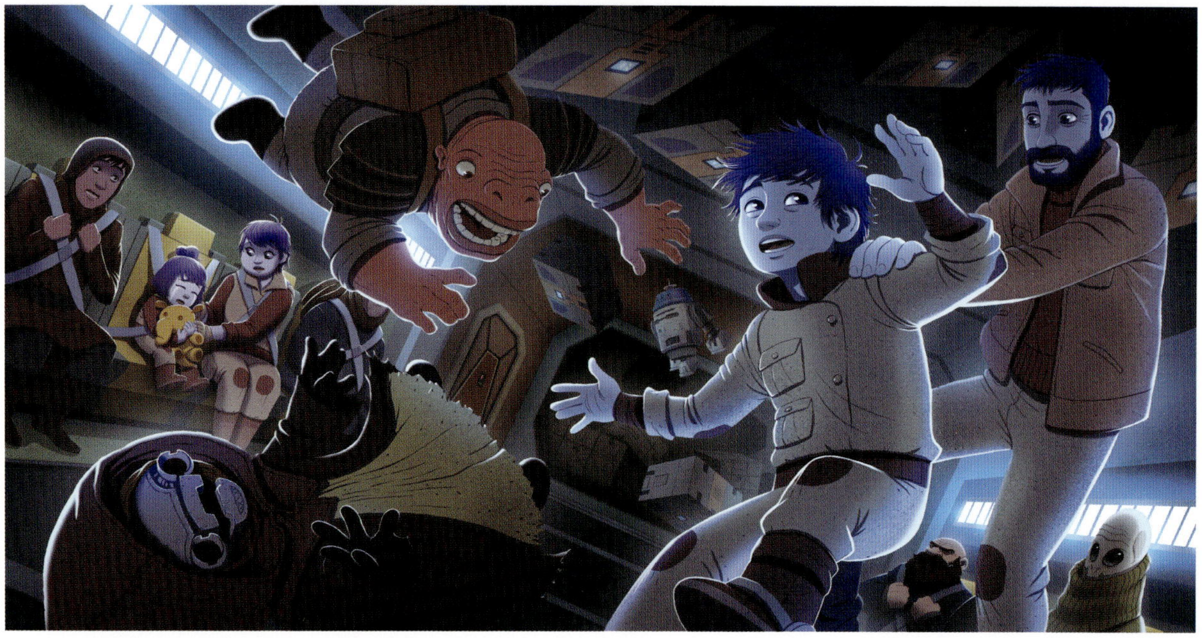

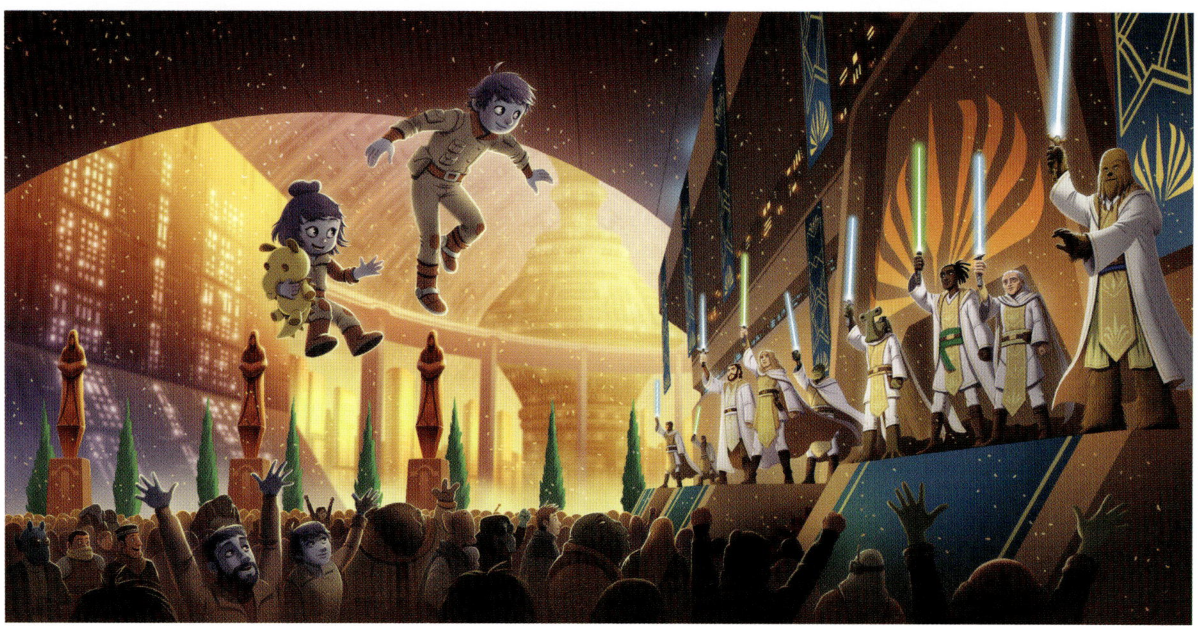

◂▸ Unused art for *The Great Jedi Rescue*
ANTONSSON

"Cav originally centered *The Great Jedi Rescue* storybook on a young boy named Tox, his sister, and their parents, all of whom were looking for a better life on the frontier. They were passengers on the *Legacy Run* when the Great Disaster struck, which would've enabled readers to see the main events of *Light of the Jedi* through Tox's eyes. But in order to include all of the story points about the Great Disaster *and* the Jedi's response in a mere twenty-four pages, we had to cut Tox's story. Hopefully we'll be able publish the extended versions of all three of our 8×8 storybooooks, because there's definitely more art—and story—left on the cutting room floor." MICHAEL SIGLAIN

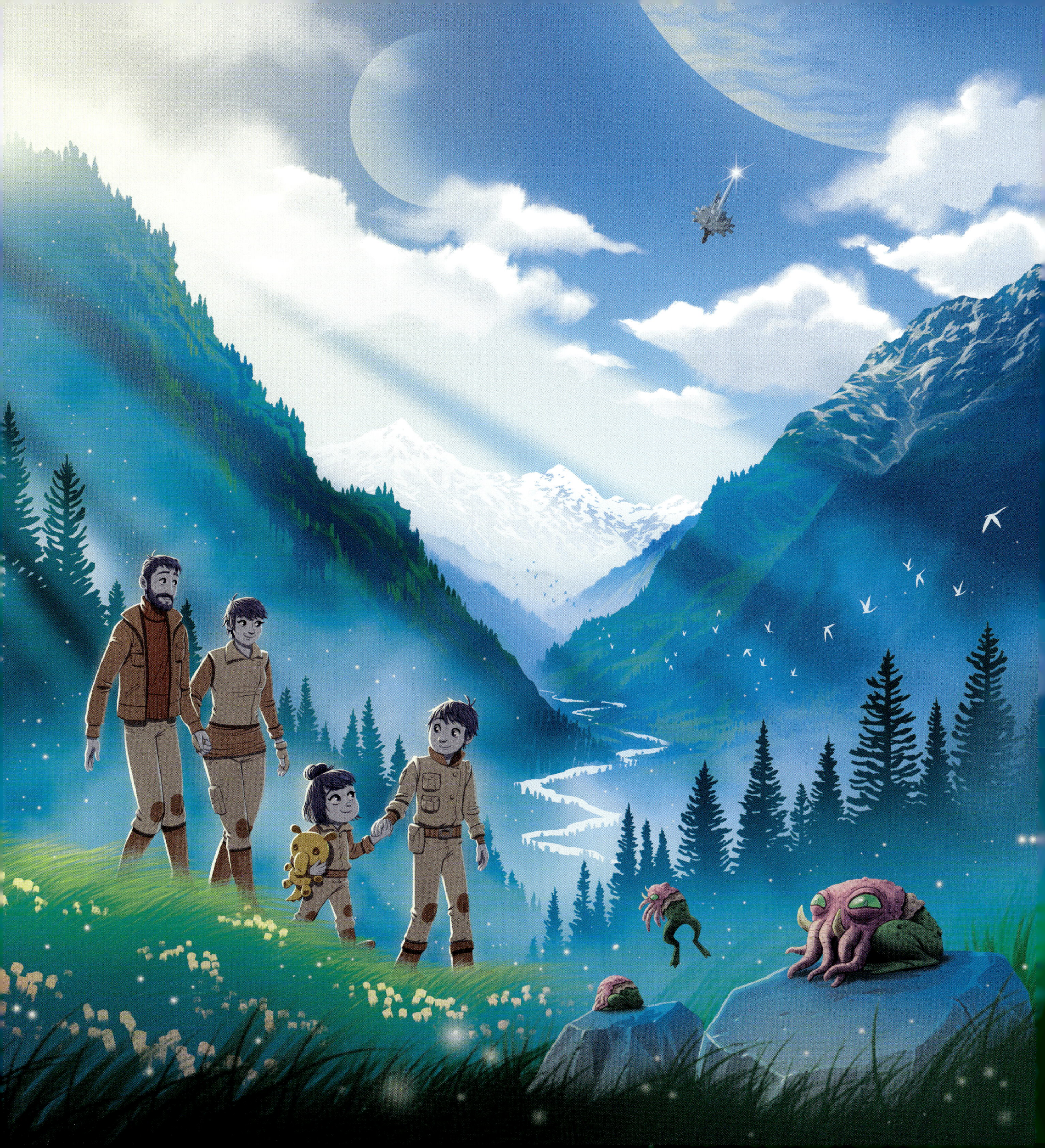

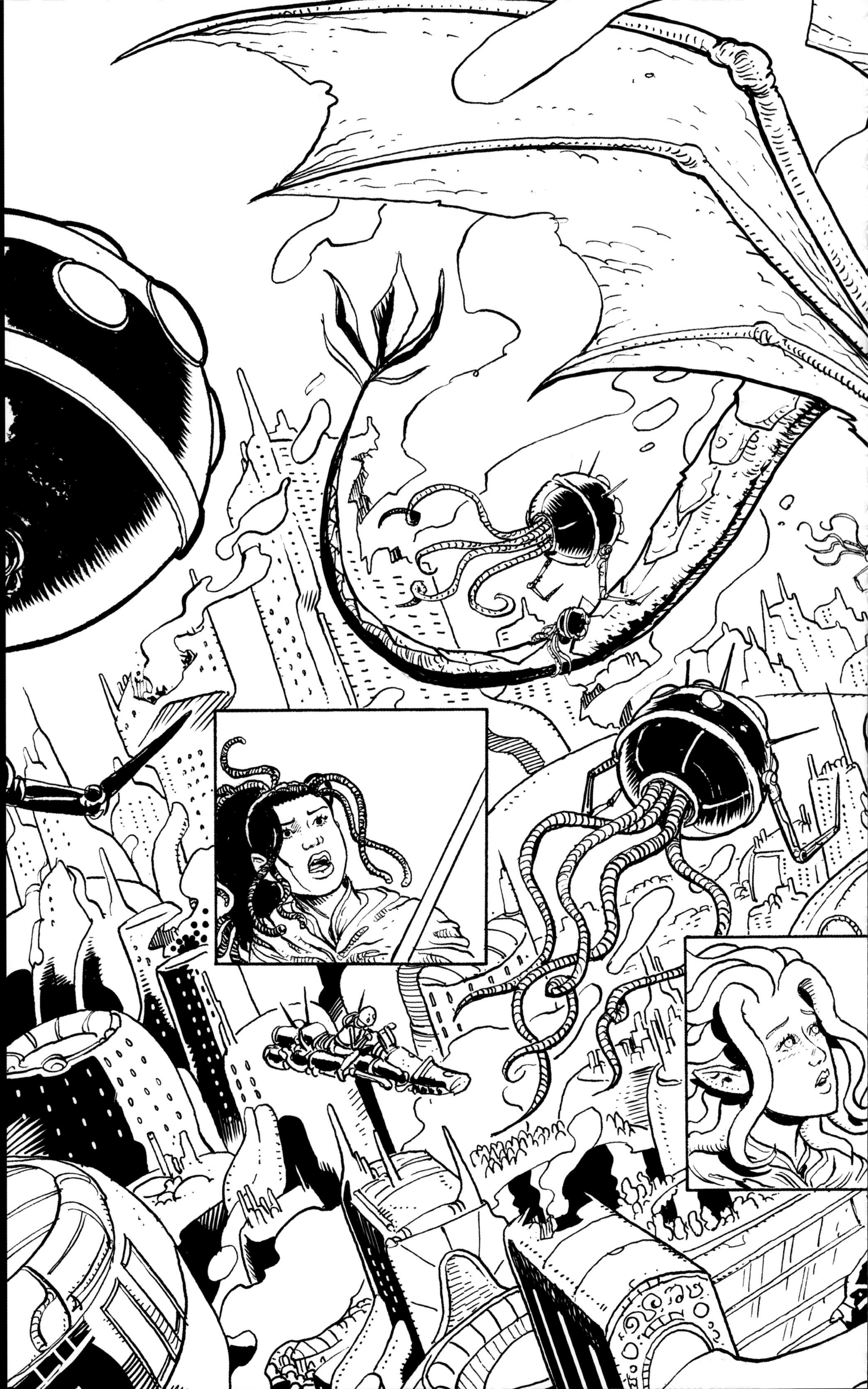

Attack on the Republic Fair, from IDW's
Star Wars: The High Republic Adventures
Free Comic Book Day 2021 BROKENSHIRE

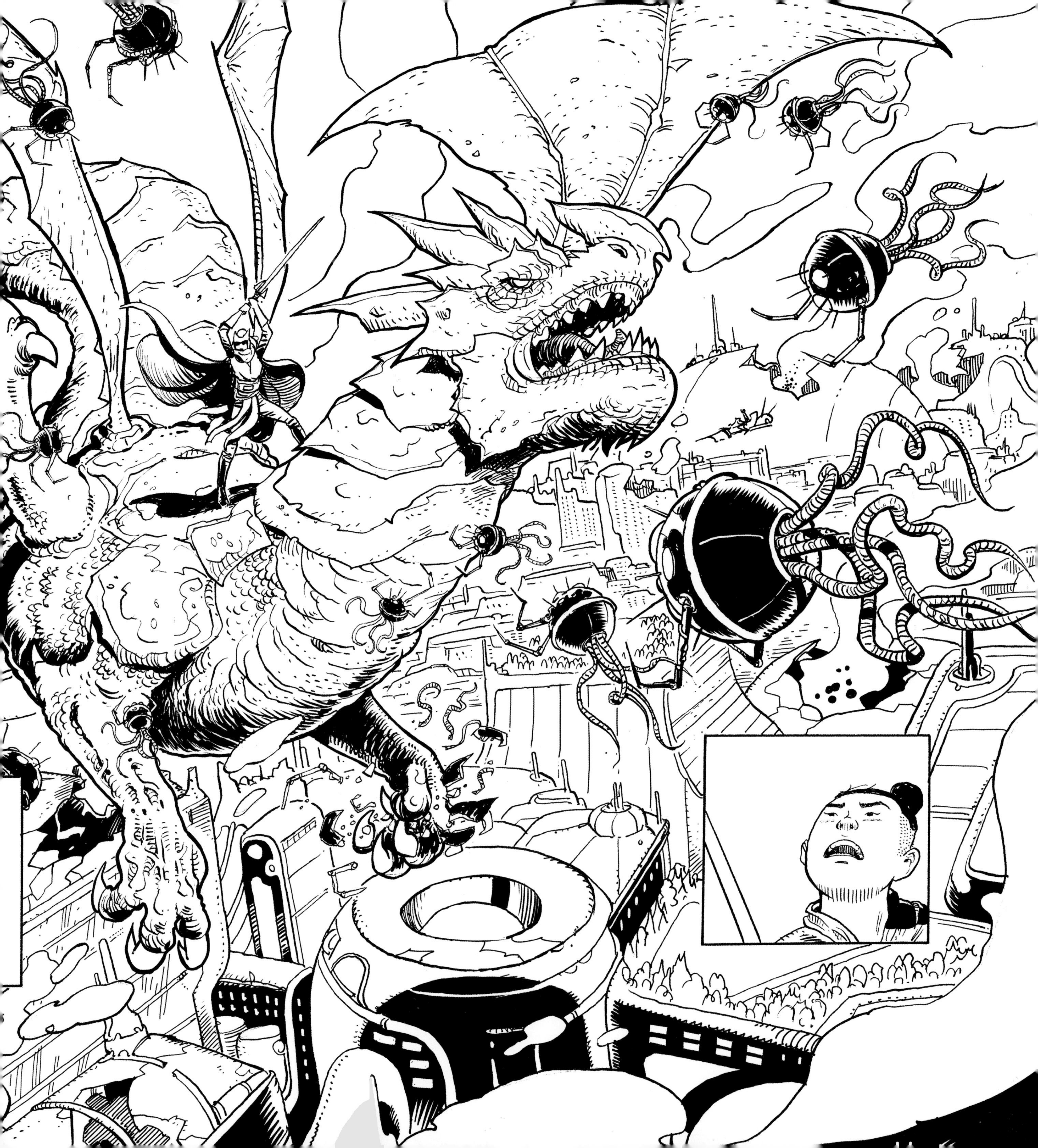

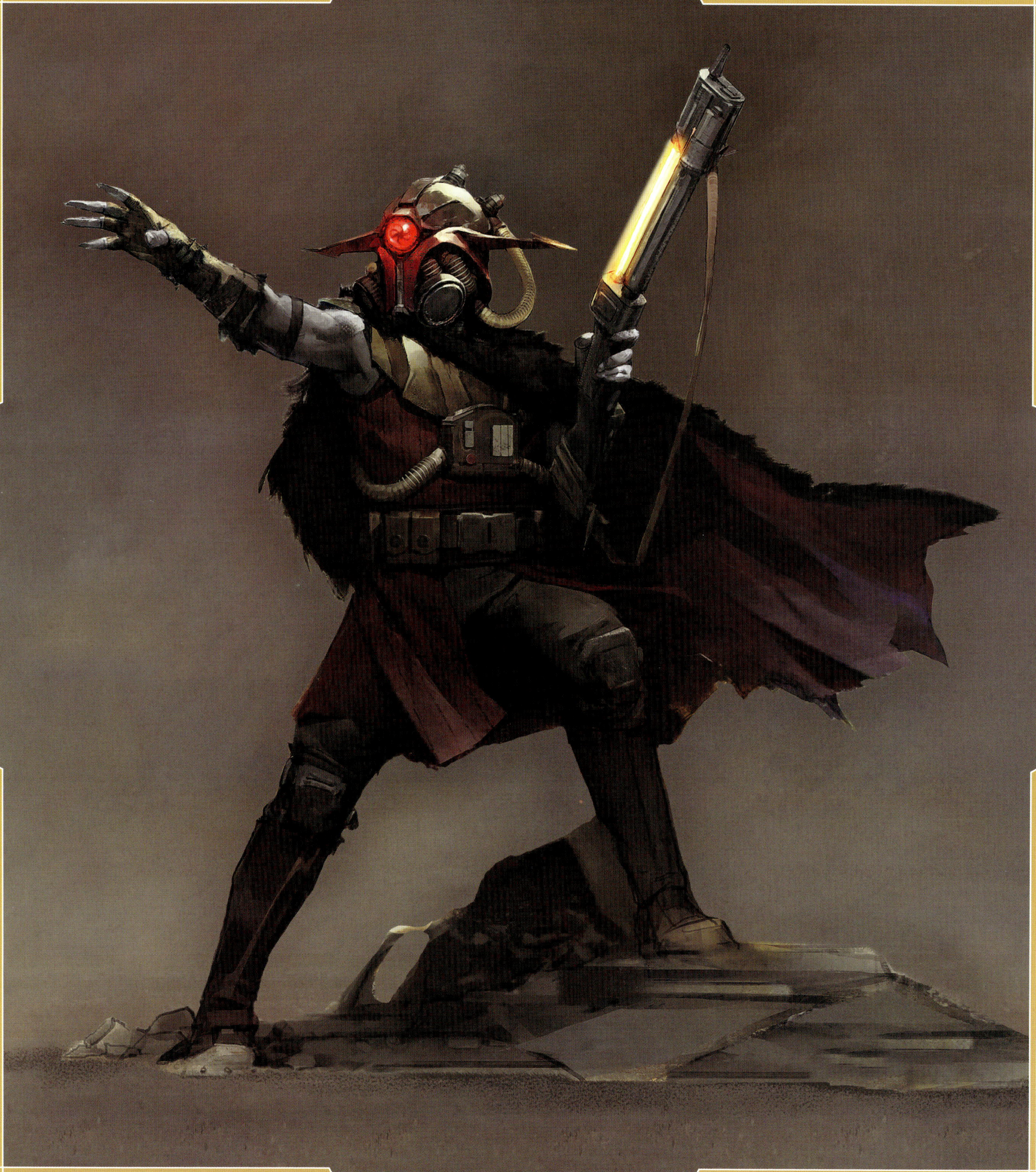

CHAPTER 4

ENEMIES OF THE LIGHT

IN THE ABSENCE OF WAR, there is still the potential for anarchy.

Star Wars continuity dictated that the High Republic's (Phase I) placement 200 years ahead of the prequels meant it was about 800 years too late for another full-scale war. But good storytelling calls for some form of conflict even in a time of peace. "The storytelling of *Star Wars* that we've all grown to know and love has been about the defending and the reclaiming of hope," said Lucasfilm Publishing's senior editor Robert Simpson. "*The High Republic* begins in an era where hope is abundant, where harmony is abundant. The people in the original trilogy era are longing after something that's been gone for a very long time. And in the High Republic, it's not gone yet, and then it starts to be taken away little by little by forces that confuse and frighten and terrify common people and Jedi alike. So I think the hope that's growing out of this story is: how do we preserve what we love?" The same sentiment has been echoed on-screen by Rose Tico in *The Last Jedi* and behind the scenes by director Irvin Kershner as he was filming *The Empire Strikes Back*.

The Drengir sprouted from an Iain McCaig sketch originally intended as a design for another unnamed foe, inspiring the dark side-aligned plant species that could blend with native flora while in stasis only to be awoken, hungry and muttering one word: "Meat." It was one of the easiest designs to finalize, said senior designer Jason Wojtowicz. "The whole thing was based off of a sketch, which more or less came out fully formed." In author Claudia Gray's skillful hands, the rustling of thorny tendrils gave way to a galactic Hydra-like beast, an invasive species that returned with a vengeance with each frantic slash of a lightsaber. In comic book form, author Cavan Scott and illustrator Ario Anindito brought the carnivorous, amorphous sentients to the masses, providing the first visuals of the creatures' brutal harvest, controlling and sucking the life force from their victims until they were little more than husks.

"What I love about monsters, and this actually relates a lot to *Star Wars*, is that we take the terrible things in us, and we like to think they're in other people instead so we can burn them in windmills [like in *Frankenstein*] and we can blame everything on them," McCaig said. "So, what monsters actually do in stories is they allow you to experience the monster inside you, and now you experience what it's like to go there. And for the first time, you have some empathy for the monstrous side. All you have to remember is, you just say 'no.' *Return of the Jedi* is the story of Luke overcoming the monster in him. He says 'no' to the Emperor, 'I won't kill my father.' And with that little word, he has total power over this monster and changes the heart of a monster."

While the Drengir were nightmarish, the main villains of the time were something more blatantly and consciously nefarious: the Nihil, a roving band of barbaric marauders in kitbashed ships, unscrupulous heathens led by the Eye, Marchion Ro. After launching the initiative with *Light of the Jedi*, author Charles Soule had the final word on Ro in Phase I with Marvel's *Eye of the Storm*, a pair of comics unraveling the origin story of the initiative's most menacing character to date. To put it simply, "You wouldn't leave your dog with Ro," Soule said.

Populated by an eclectic blend of alien species including Ortolans, Dowutins, and Gungans, a June 2019 design brief on the Nihil positioned them as literal nihilists, "punk rock space Vikings" opposing the law and rule of the Jedi and Republic, a drug-fueled cohort united by a shared desire to

◂ Final Marchion Ro concept, October 2020 GRIFFIN

steal their way to riches, leaving a trail of terror, uncertainty, and violence in their wake. Visually, the Nihil are the polar opposite of the polished Republic and its knights, chaos personified from their haphazard uniforms scavenged from previous victims to their mismatched ships, recognizable by hulking Path engines. The design aesthetic of the paramilitary War Boys in *Mad Max: Fury Road* and Negan and the Saviors from *The Walking Dead* were early influences, with iconography that celebrated the 1970s British punk rock movement mixed with the fearfulness of World War II–era Europe that preceded it, when a planetwide conflict left everyone from soldiers to civilian children looking deeply inhuman behind lifesaving gas masks.

"One of the things I was trying to challenge the writers to explore early on was, what do [the Nihil] say about the state of the galaxy? What's the antagonists' thematic resonance?" said James Waugh, Lucasfilm's vice president of Franchise Content & Strategy. "And what we ended up with is, if this is a time of high civilization and the potential of a Republic, of people working together, who are the people against or who oppose the system? From that core fantasy perspective, the Nihil are basically sticking a middle finger up at the world."

Even amid the chaos of the Nihil, there is a discernible hierarchy of Strikes, Clouds, Storms, and Tempest Runners, the meteorological symbolism a reflection of the galaxy itself, with a mysterious old crone, Mari San Tekka, the key to their success, and Marchion Ro in control. "A spiral galaxy looks like a hurricane as seen through space," Soule said. Grounding the metaphor, Ro's mask design came to reflect the churning, seething squall where his face, and more importantly his eyes, should be. Initial costume briefs from Soule compared Ro to a Yakuza enforcer, with a spattering of blood marring an immaculate dark suit and slim tie, later traded for a fur cloak that once belonged to his father. "He's got a lot of daddy issues, as many people in *Star Wars* do," Soule said.

Concept artists began piecing together Ro's appearance in late 2020, an alien with an otherworldly complexion and shark-like eyes that would be hidden away behind a mask like so many classic *Star Wars* villains that came before. "I spent enormous amounts of time, many rewrites and lots of calibrating so that [Marchion Ro] would land properly," said Soule. "As the main villain, he needed to stand up alongside Darth Vader, Emperor Palpatine, and Kylo Ren."

Despite Soule's detailed exploration of Ro in text, capturing his look in visual design was a challenge. "He took more design passes than almost anything else we did," Soule said. "And there was a lot of discussion. We had two very clear camps [among] the writers. One thought that he should read as an alien, basically very inhuman, and then the other camp, of which I was a strong proponent, thought that he should be somebody who you can identify as a human." After some spirited debate in a weekly call among the five authors and Siglain, Ro snapped into focus as they found a real-world animal counterpart. "Ro is essentially the *Star Wars* version of a great white shark, and that's what brought everyone together," said Siglain.

Soule took the sharklike villain and ran with it, infusing the Eye of the Storm with a twisted sense of righteousness and a decidedly unhinged view. "Hannibal Lecter is scary because he's us, you know?" Soule said. "He looks like us, but there's something that's off behind his eyes. I have this term for people that you meet in your life who are just off: spider people. That was my inspiration. But they can also kind of turn on the charm when they want to, like flipping a switch, and it's very unsettling and very creepy. The other word for them is sociopaths. So I wanted Marchion Ro to be somebody who you have this sense of unease when you're around them, but you can have a beer with them. It's more just like the minute that you're out of the room, their face goes blank." And like the best characters, whether alien or human, there's an element that we can't help but recognize. "What's important for a villain is that you can relate to his motivations and his choices. This is somebody that you're going to understand and identify with in some horrible way."

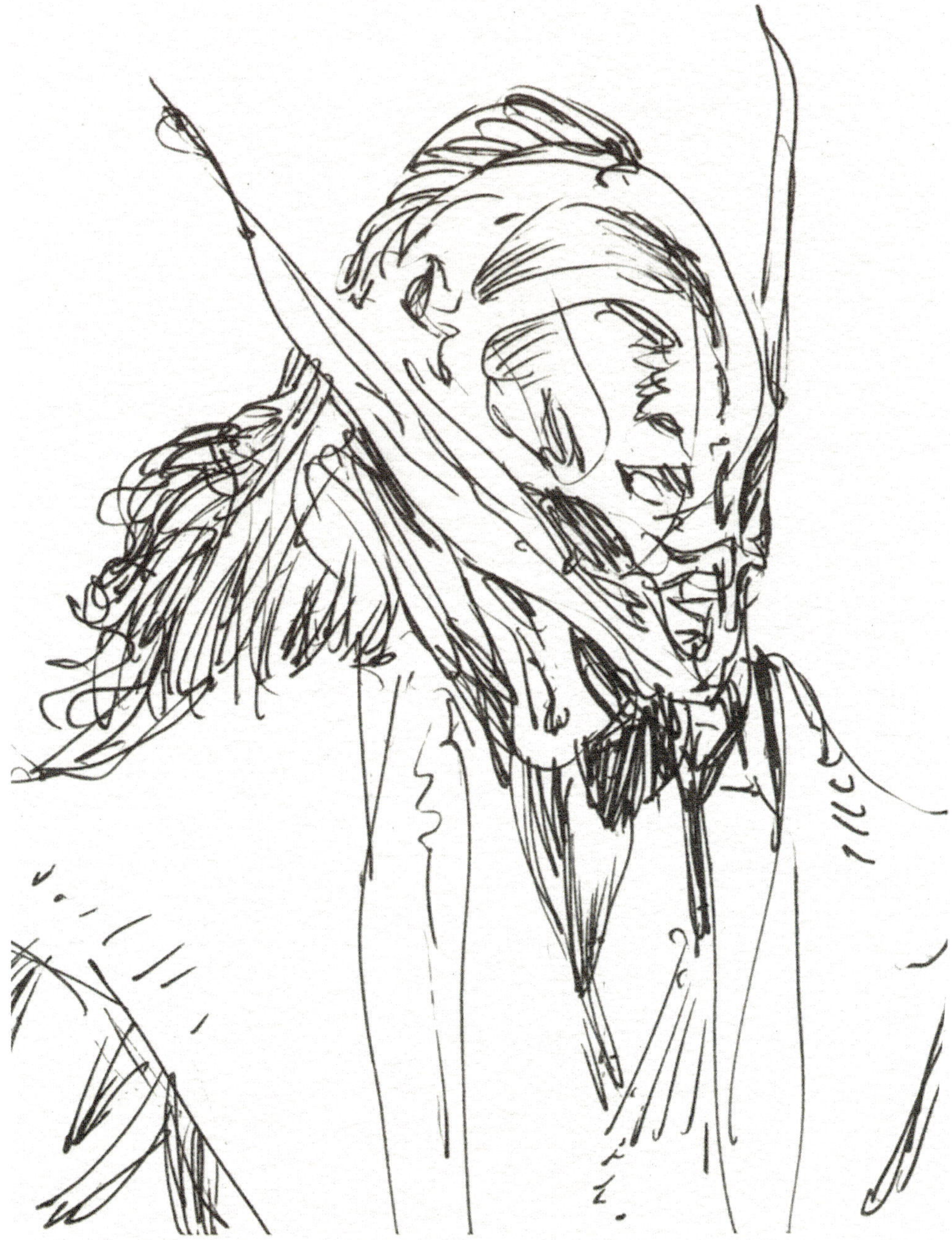

▲ Sketch of proto-Marchion Ro, July 2019 **McCAIG**

McCaig has a collection of skulls he uses for inspiration. For the head or helmet of this character, he took the arches around one creature's cheekbones and loosened them. "Let them fly and it gives you a weird, winged head," McCaig said. "I think it's a helmet, but it doesn't have to be. I don't always know; when I draw, I draw shapes."

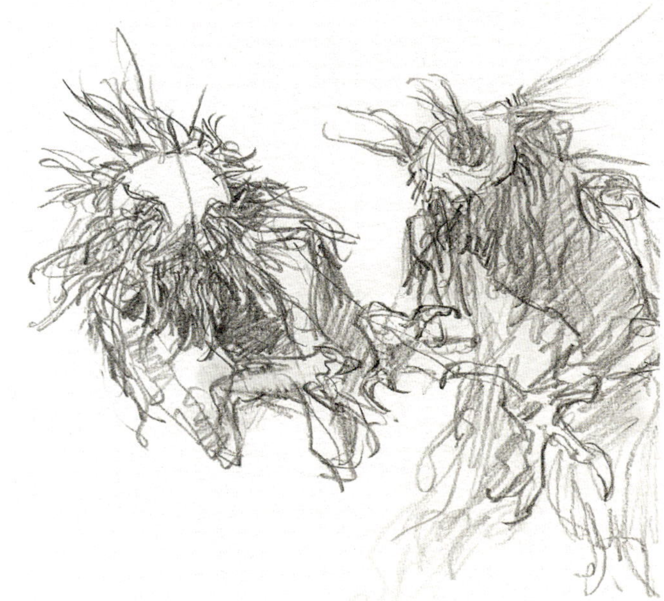

▲ Sketch of a parasitic infestation, July 2019 "There's a mushroom, a fungus, that can take over [insects'] brains. They grow inside and they actually go through part of the ants, and what they do is they mind control. They're terrifying to look at. Disease scares us. I might even have made a COVID-19 creature if I'd known about COVID back then. It's a really beautiful object, and it's terrifying what it does." McCAIG

▼ Drengir sketch, March 2020 ANTONSSON

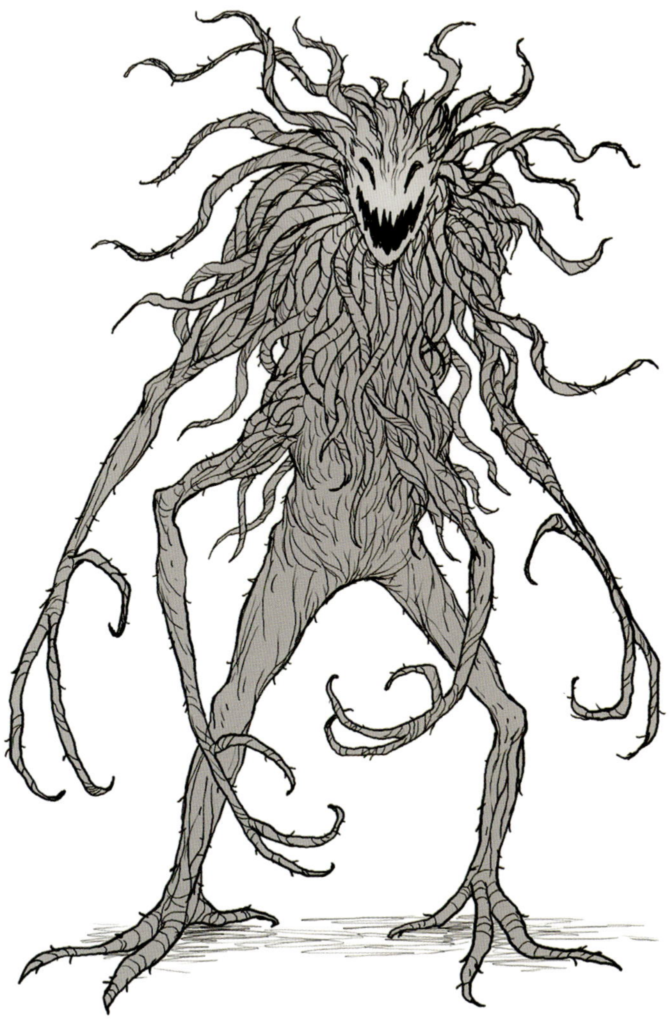

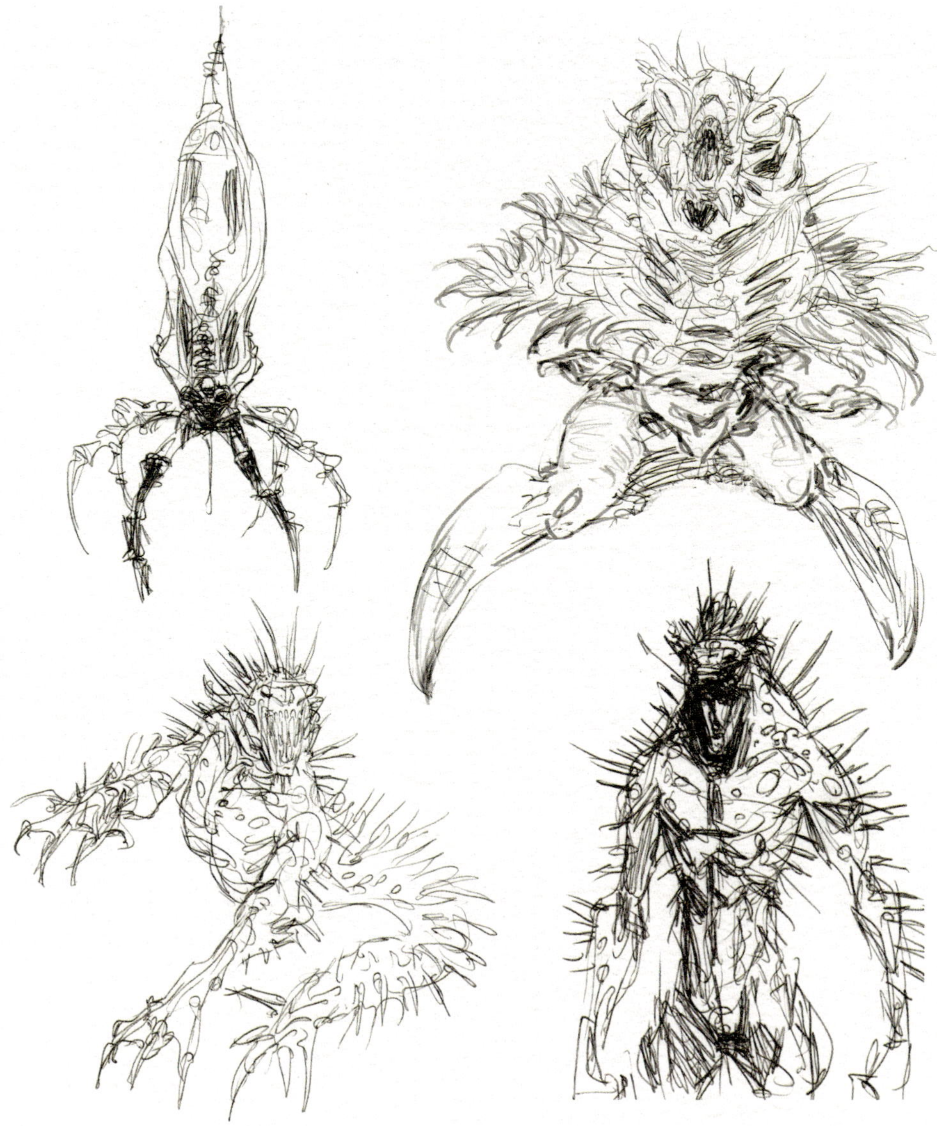

▲ Life cycle of a creature, July 2019 "I was always impressed with *Alien*. It's an egg, and then it launches a facehugger, and then it plants something inside you that bursts out of you and then grows into an alien. So the little thing hanging down is the egg form of it all, and then it eventually grows to the one in the middle as the junior version, and then evolves into this beautiful spiky merman creature. I think the one on the bottom right corner is where I started. And I thought, *No, you know what, no, let's do something better than just a humanoid thing.* So I left him there and then did the others around that." McCAIG

► Concept of a corpse flower creature, July 2019 "In the San Francisco Conservatory there's a corpse flower plant, and it smells so bad when it [blossoms]. So I wanted something that was like that but with a grinning skull-like face. In my mind, it grows this amazing flower out of the top of its head, usually after it's fed on something human, and it stinks to high heaven, but it looks so beautiful." McCAIG

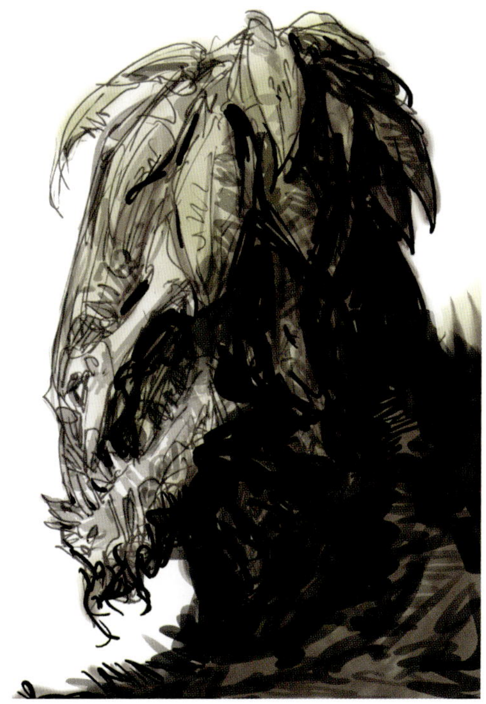

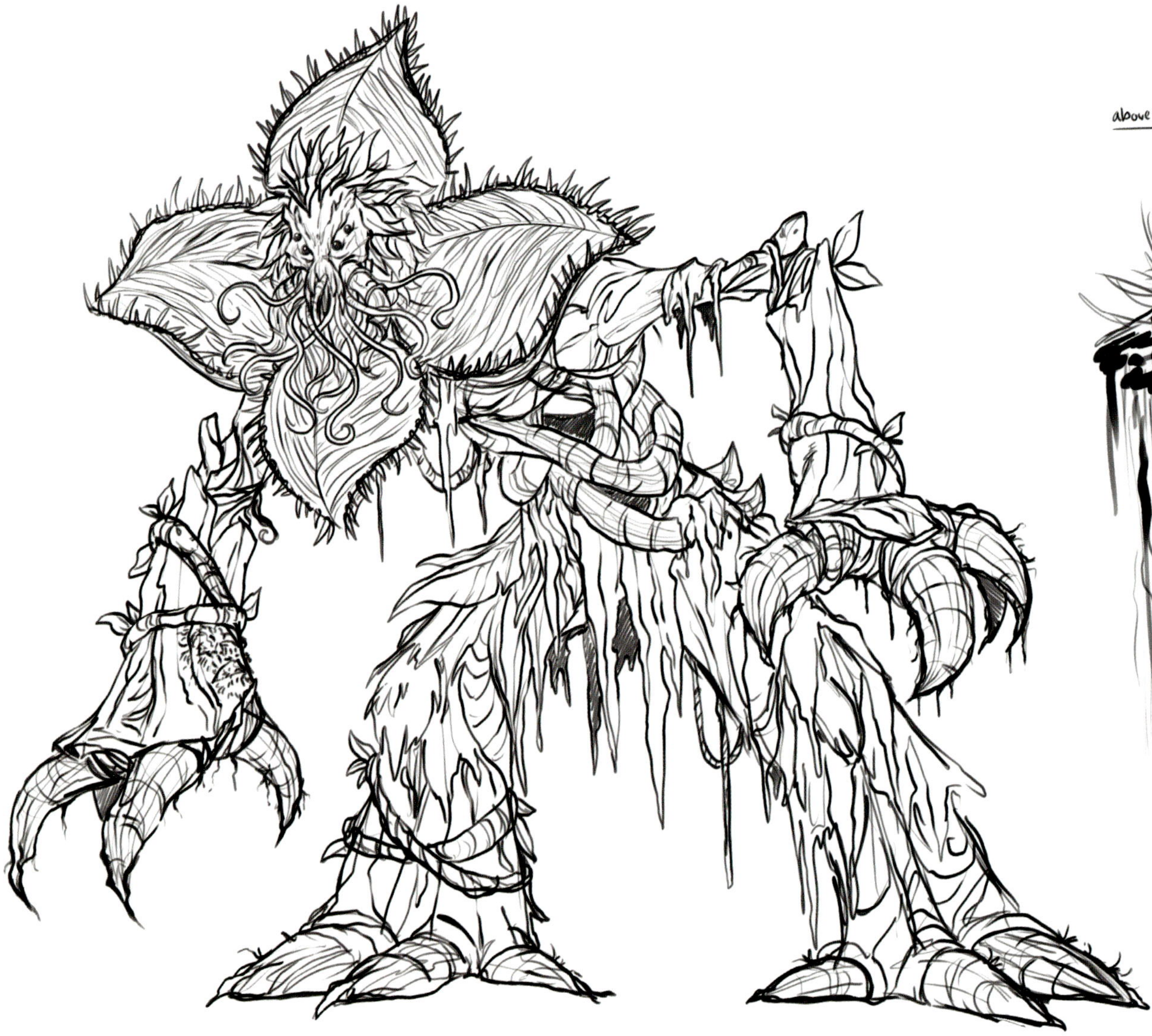

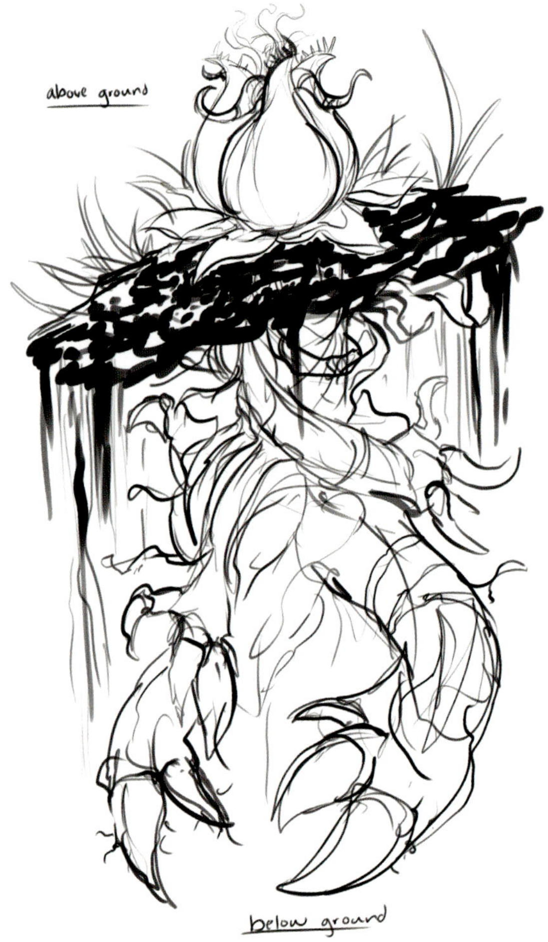

▲ Drengir sketch, February 2020 "It kind of made me think of Audrey II [from *Little Shop of Horrors*]. The monster's head was inside the beautiful flower." THOMAS

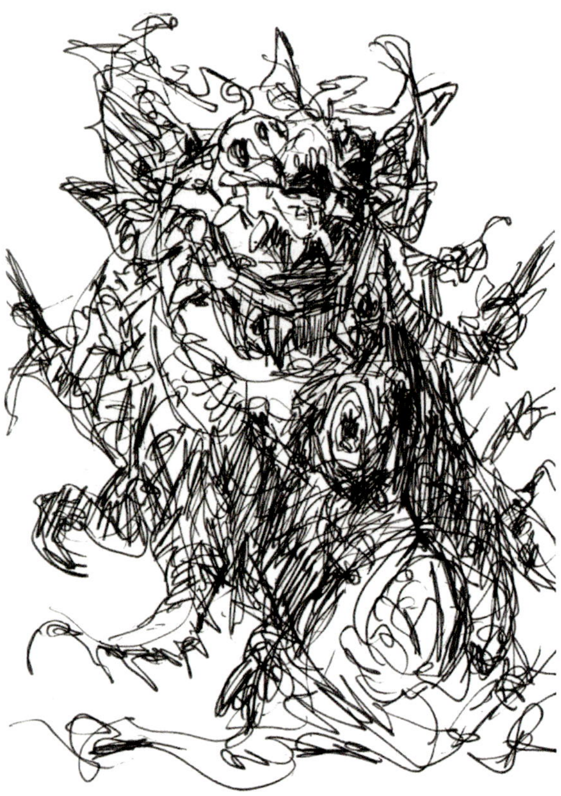

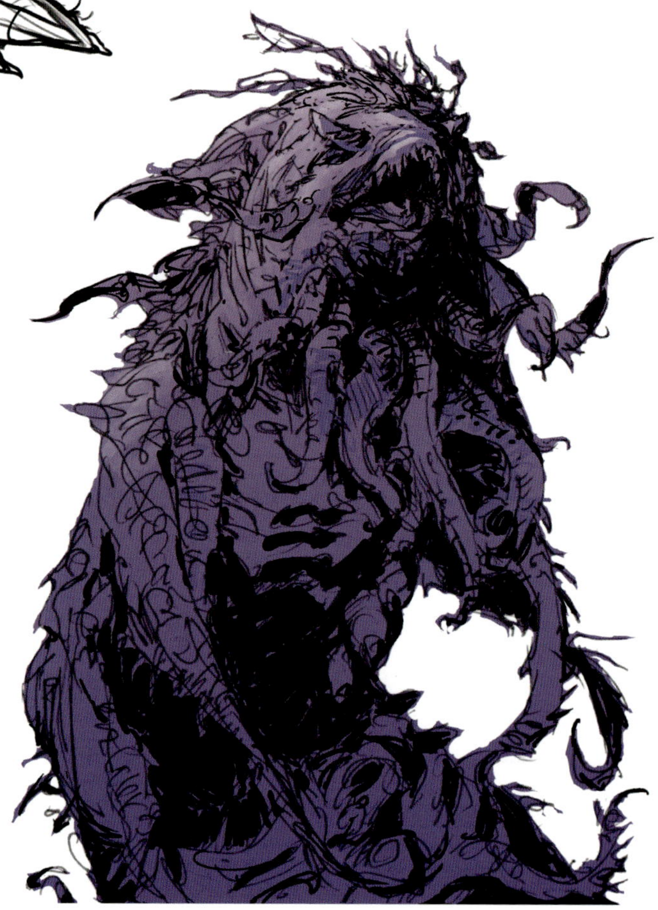

◄ Rough sketch that became the Drengir, July 2019 McCAIG

► Concept sketch of the Drengir, July 2019 "I wanted something that had a lot of arms and a monstrous face and was rising up out of the ocean, the swamp, the galaxy. At the same time, I'm really not a fan of things that are scary *because* they're just ugly, so there had to be a beauty to this, too. And the beauty for me, always, is trees. The history of its life is shown in the way it looks. There's a rhythm to trees; they grow partly in response to their environment. I wanted to put that into this creature, so it wasn't just an ugly thing. It could also, from a distance, be a beautiful tree." McCAIG

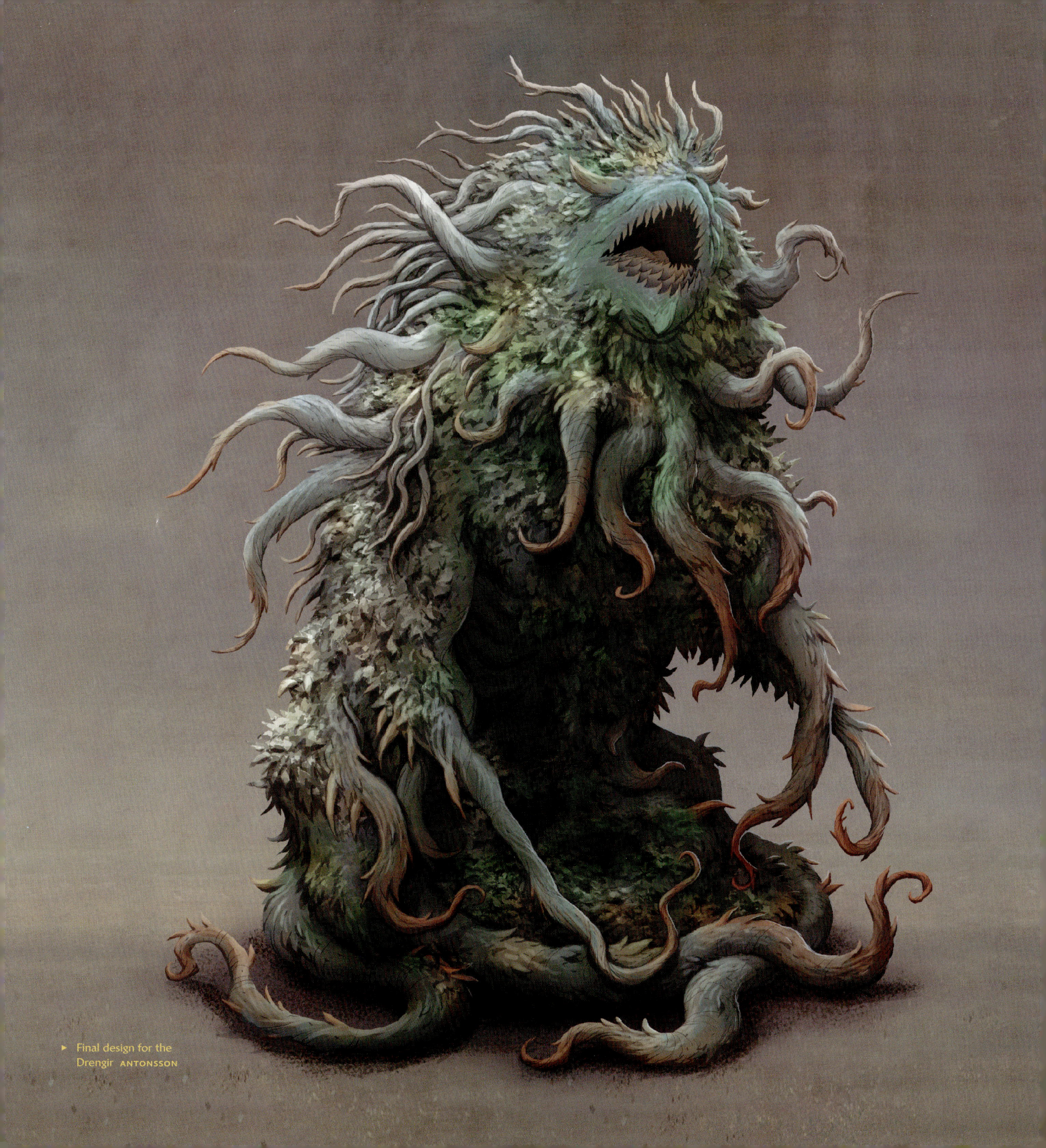

▸ Final design for the Drengir ANTONSSON

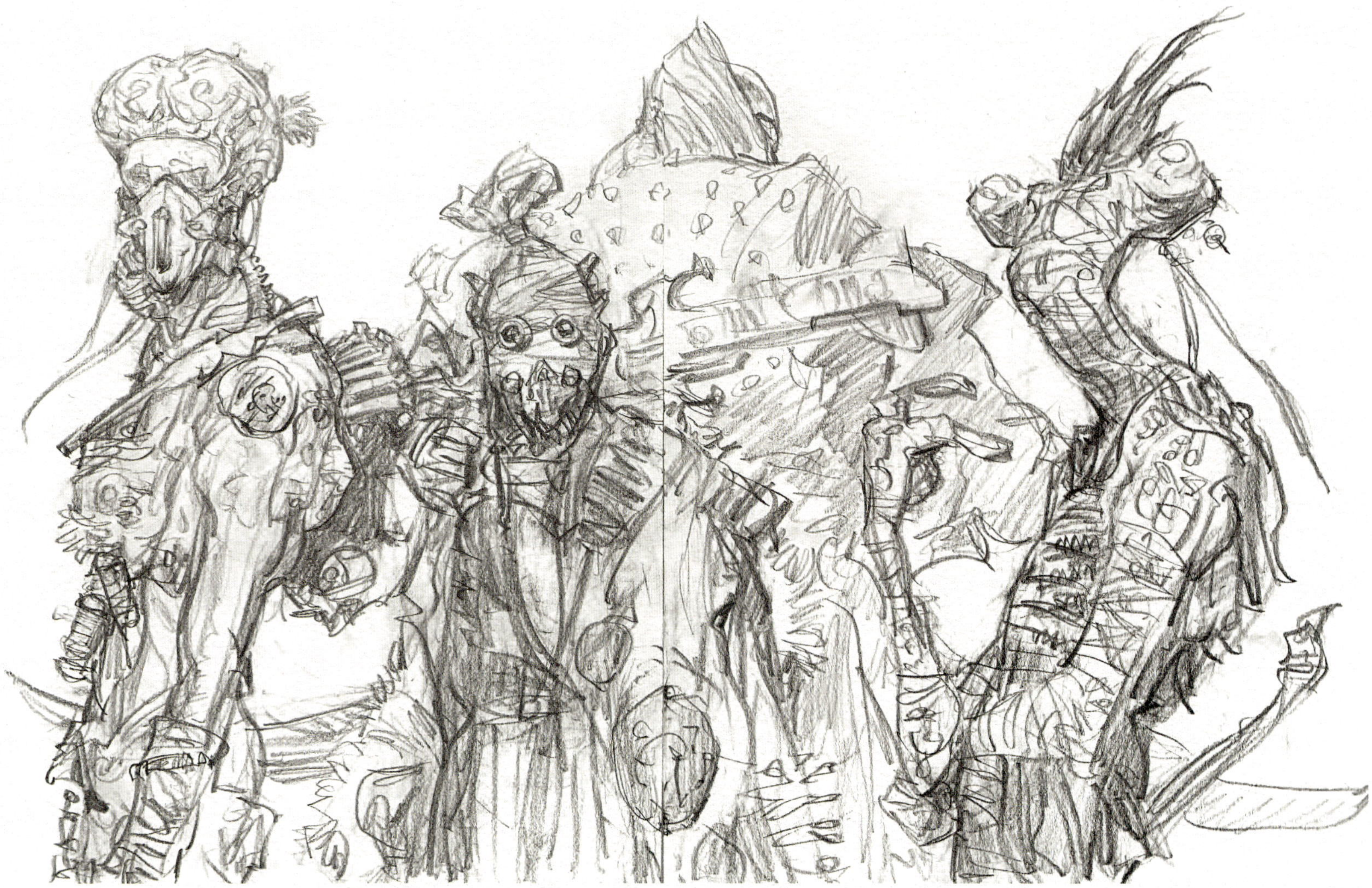

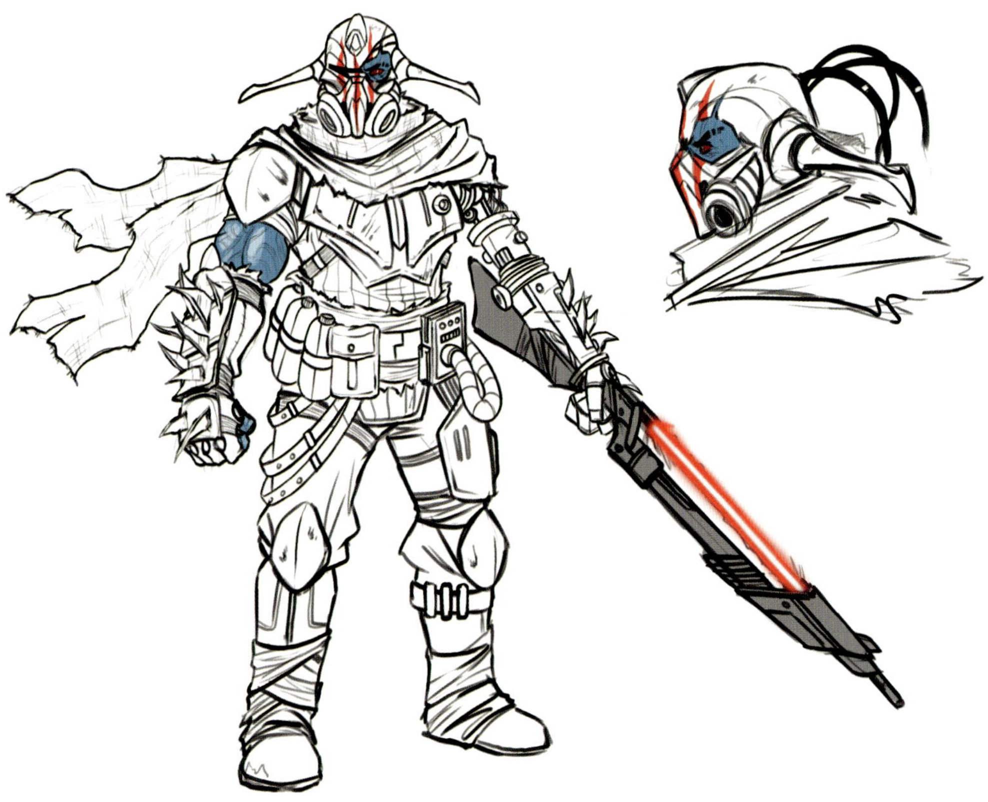

▲ Initial sketch of the proto-Nihil, July 2019 "This is probably the first stab at the Nihil ever, because that's the first time I heard this group was going to be in there. We needed a gang, a really tough gang. The one I like best is the one that's got his back to you. He won't even pose for the drawing." McCAIG

◄ Early Marchion Ro concept, January 2020 "For my first pass of Marchion Ro, the helmet silhouette was something that they wanted me to carry over, but they gave me free rein to design him how I wanted. One of the big differences about this initial design compared to the final design was I also had control over his species. Since I love Admiral Thrawn and how cold and calculating he was, I originally wanted Marchion to be a Chiss. That didn't stick. However, something that did stick from this initial design was Marchion Ro's saber rifle. As a warrior, I pictured him as a deadly sniper who preferred not to get his hands dirty, but if some unsuspecting Jedi were to get the drop on him, he would be able to hold his own in saber combat. The rifle I designed in my very first attempt stuck with the character." THOMAS

► Initial Marchion Ro design, January 2020 "This was the lead up to Marchion, one of the early [iterations] where there were no building blocks. It was just the bad guy for the Nihil, the first take on the leader. This may have been a building block for the concept art that I got later—my prior baby may have been handed off to another artist and then came back to me looking like this other thing. And then I took it and added to it." GRIFFIN

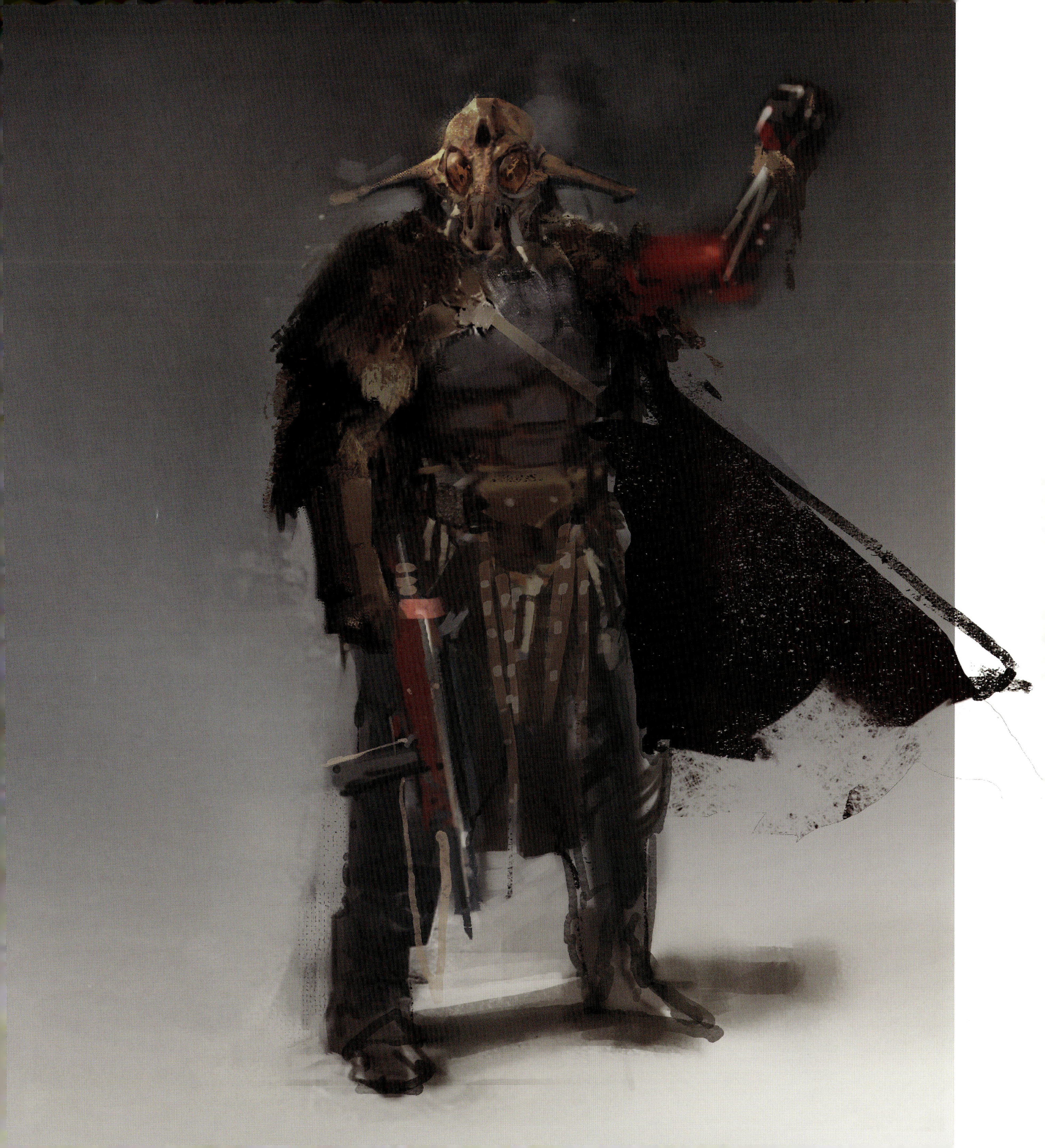

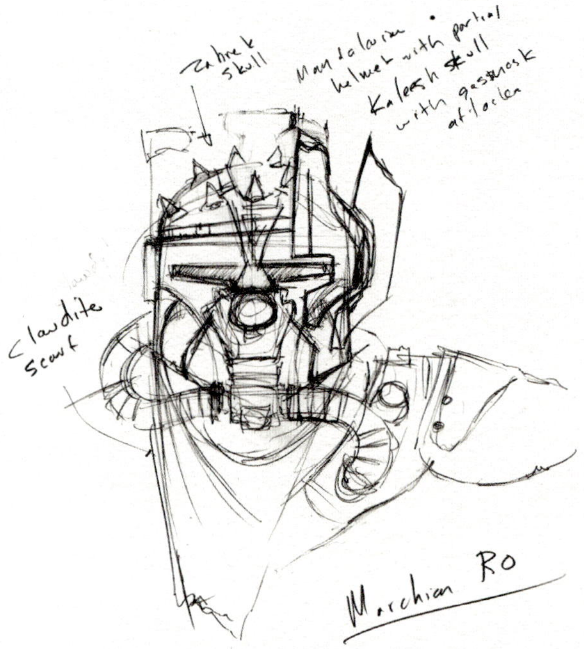

▲ Early Marchion Ro concept, February 2020 HARTMAN

► Early Marchion Ro sketch, March 2020 ANTONSSON

▼ Kylo Ren concept art used for Marchion Ro inspiration GLYN DILLON

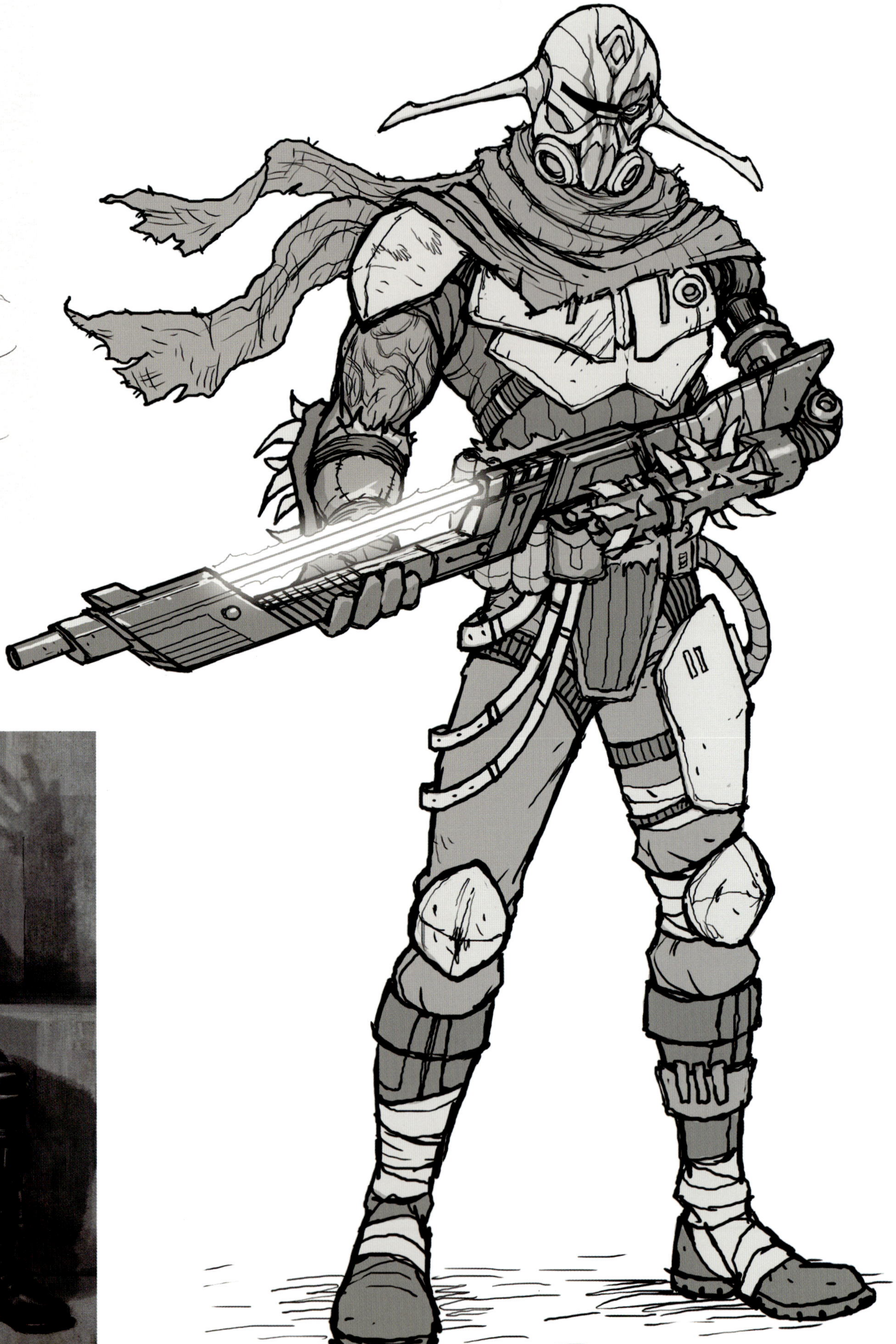

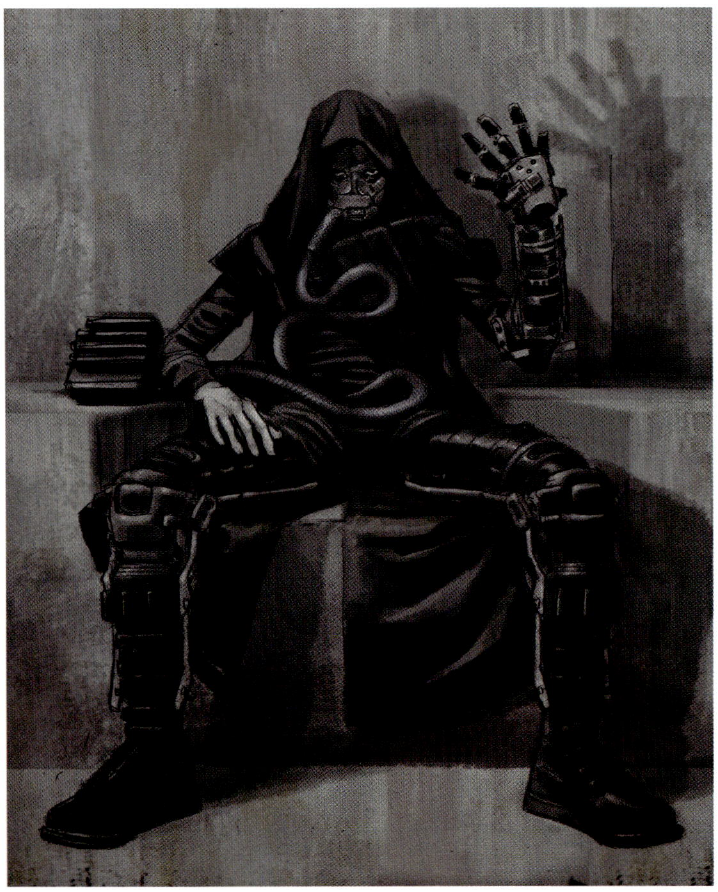

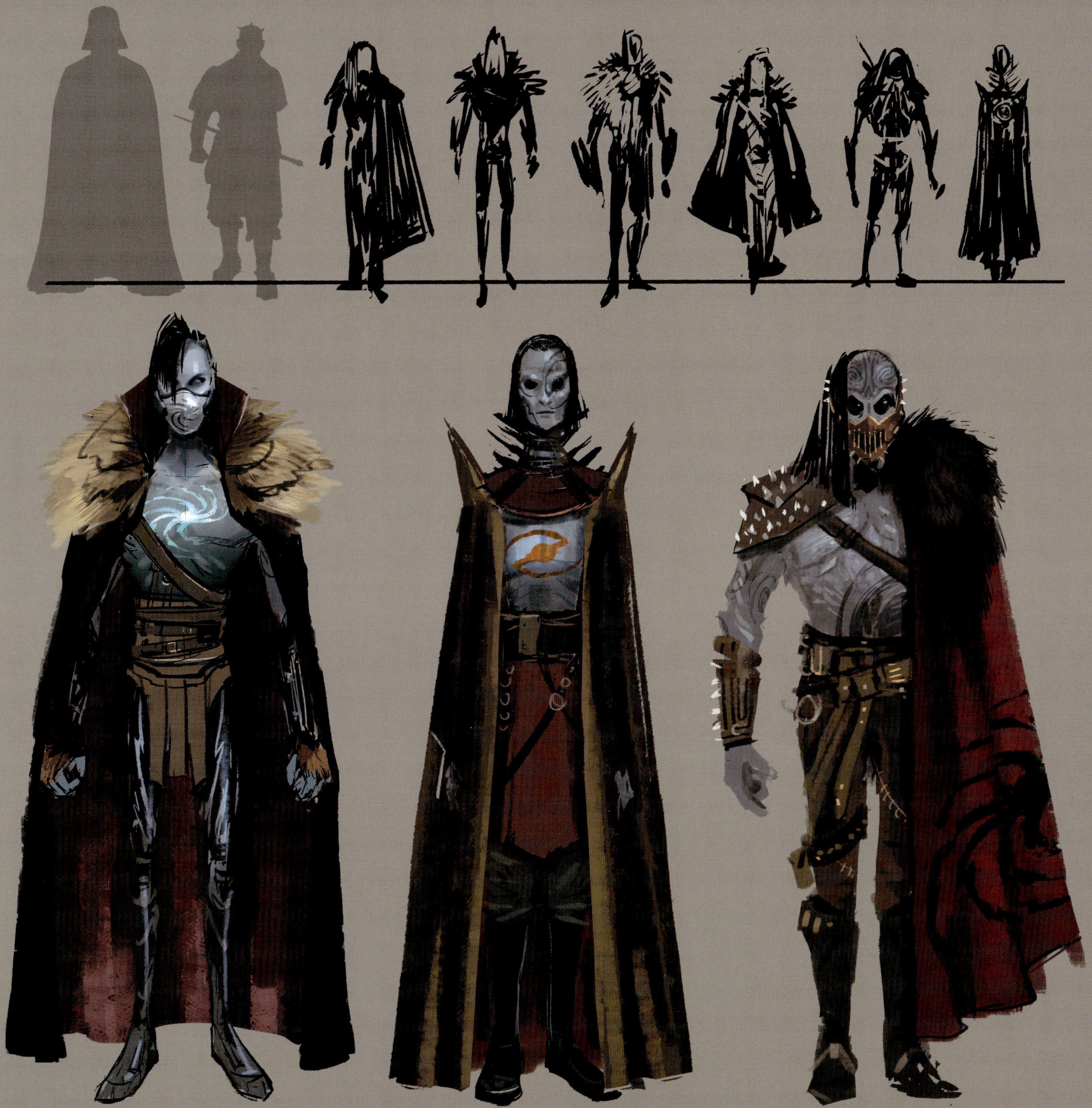

▲ Marchion Ro concepts, June 2020 LEE

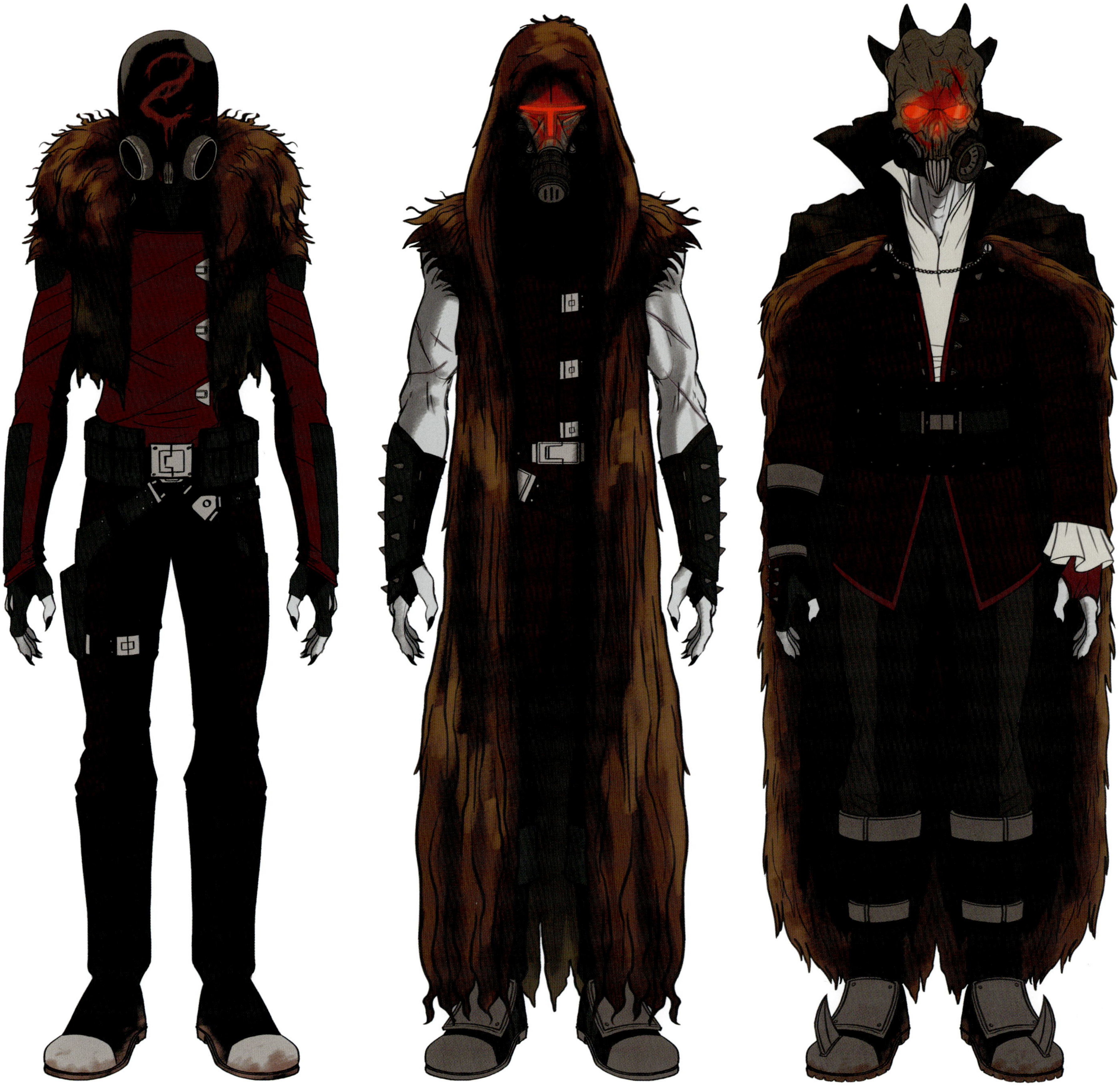

Thin Marchion Ro concepts, June 2020 THOMAS

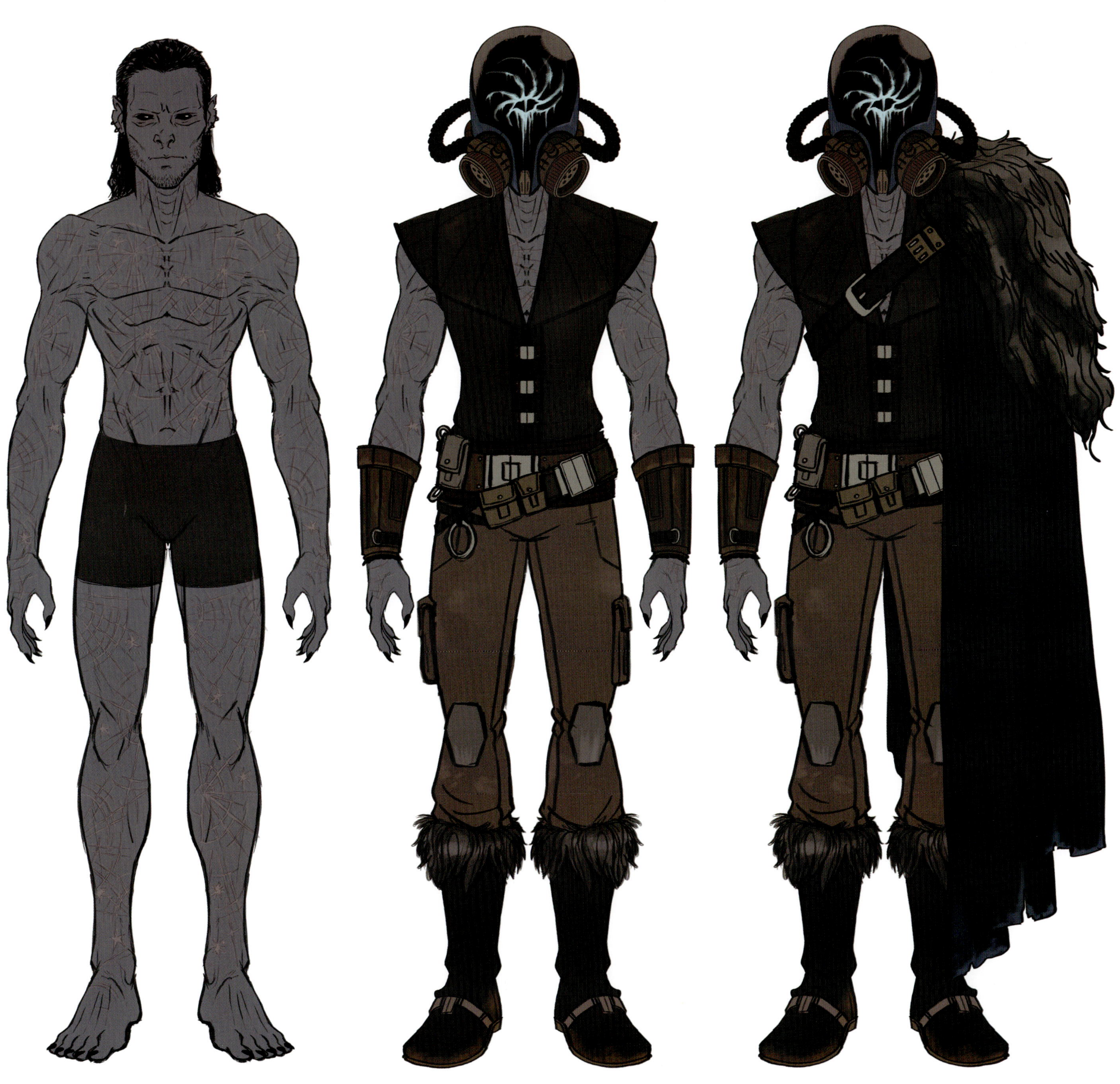

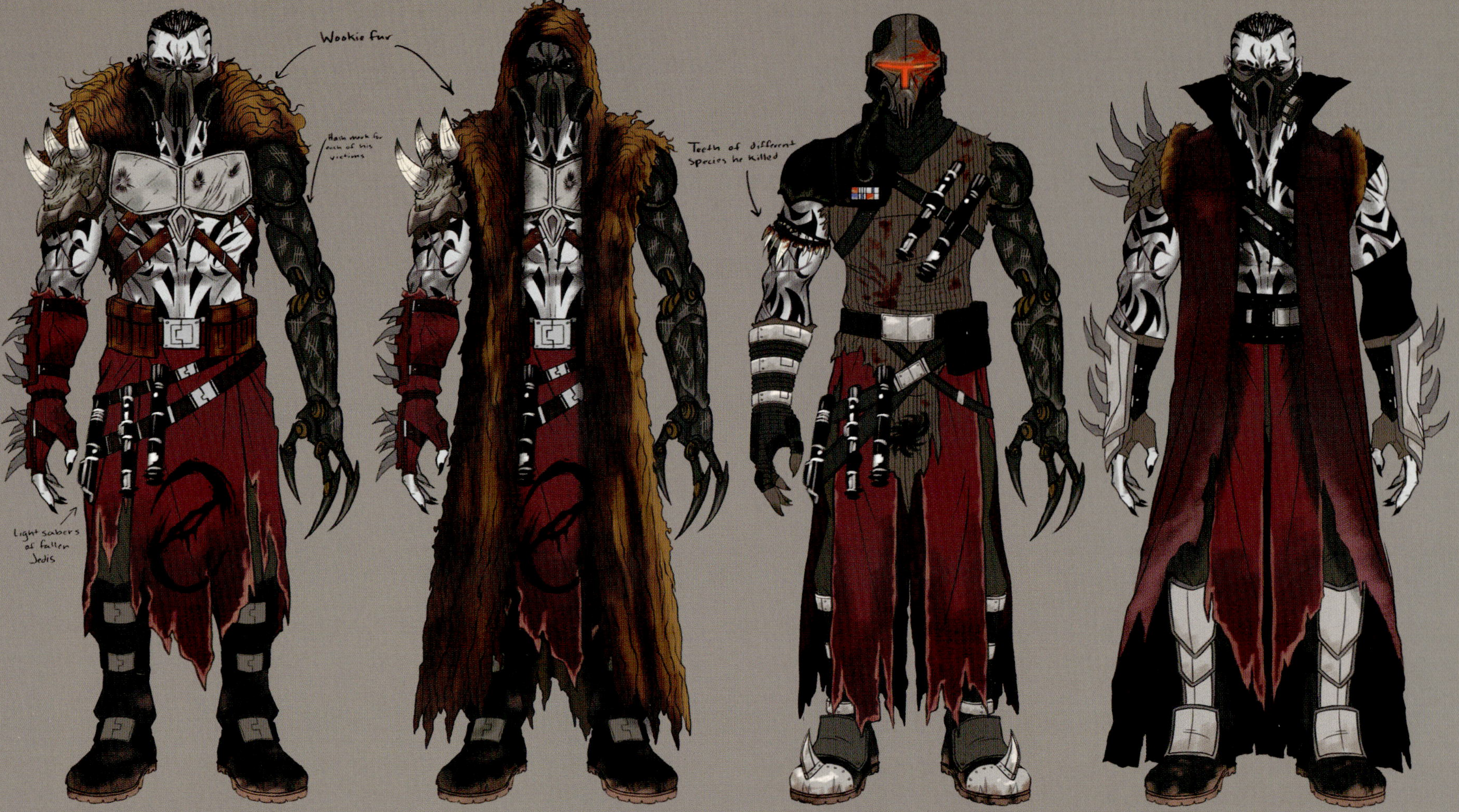

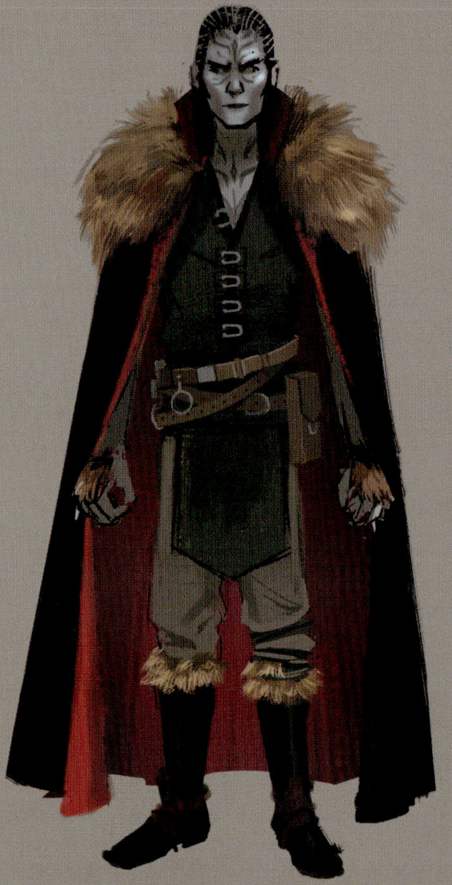

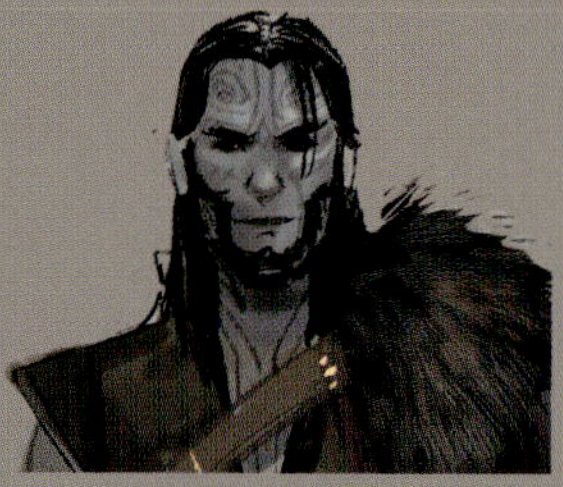

ORIGINAL HEAD

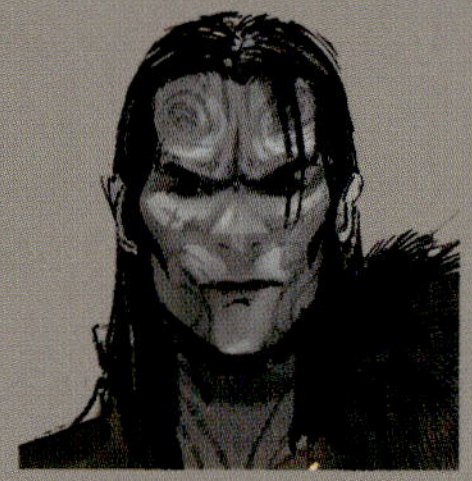

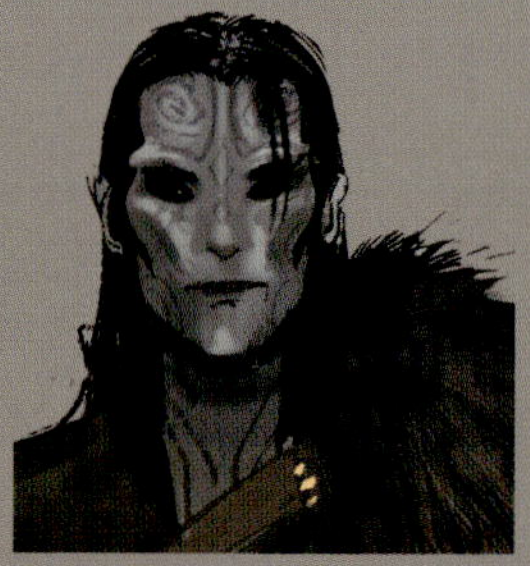

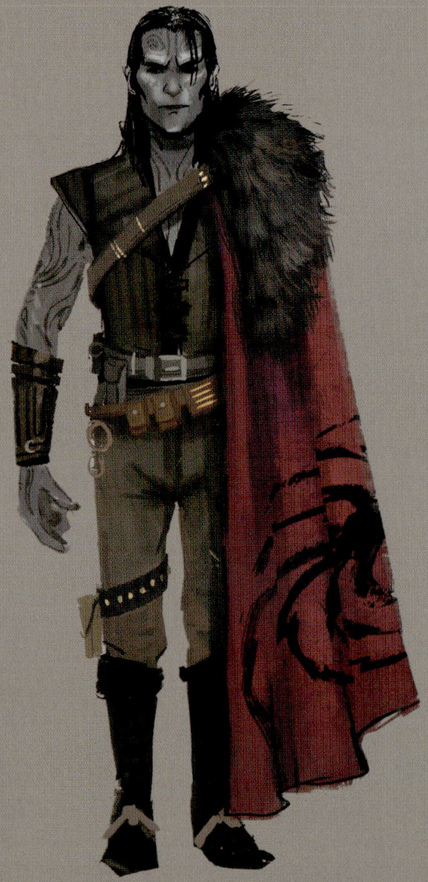

▲ Marchion Ro species and costume study, June 2020
THOMAS

Before Ro's species was defined, Thomas experimented with a light-skinned alien with black tattoo-like markings. "There wasn't a species, yet. Just gray skin and black eyes like a shark," Thomas said. This version called for a robotic arm, cluttered with hash marks counting every time he'd killed with the appendage.

"I made him carry a lot of trophies of the people he'd killed, like the lightsabers of all the Jedi he bested [in a nod to General Grievous]. On one, he has an armband that has the teeth of the different species he's killed. Apparently in my version of Marchion, he's a crazy homicidal maniac. His gauntlet was made up of shards of different ships he'd taken over."

One design in particular, with an Imperial-like shoulder piece [third from left], was inspired by Starkiller's design in *The Force Unleashed* video game.

► Concepts of Marchion Ro, June and July 2020 LEE

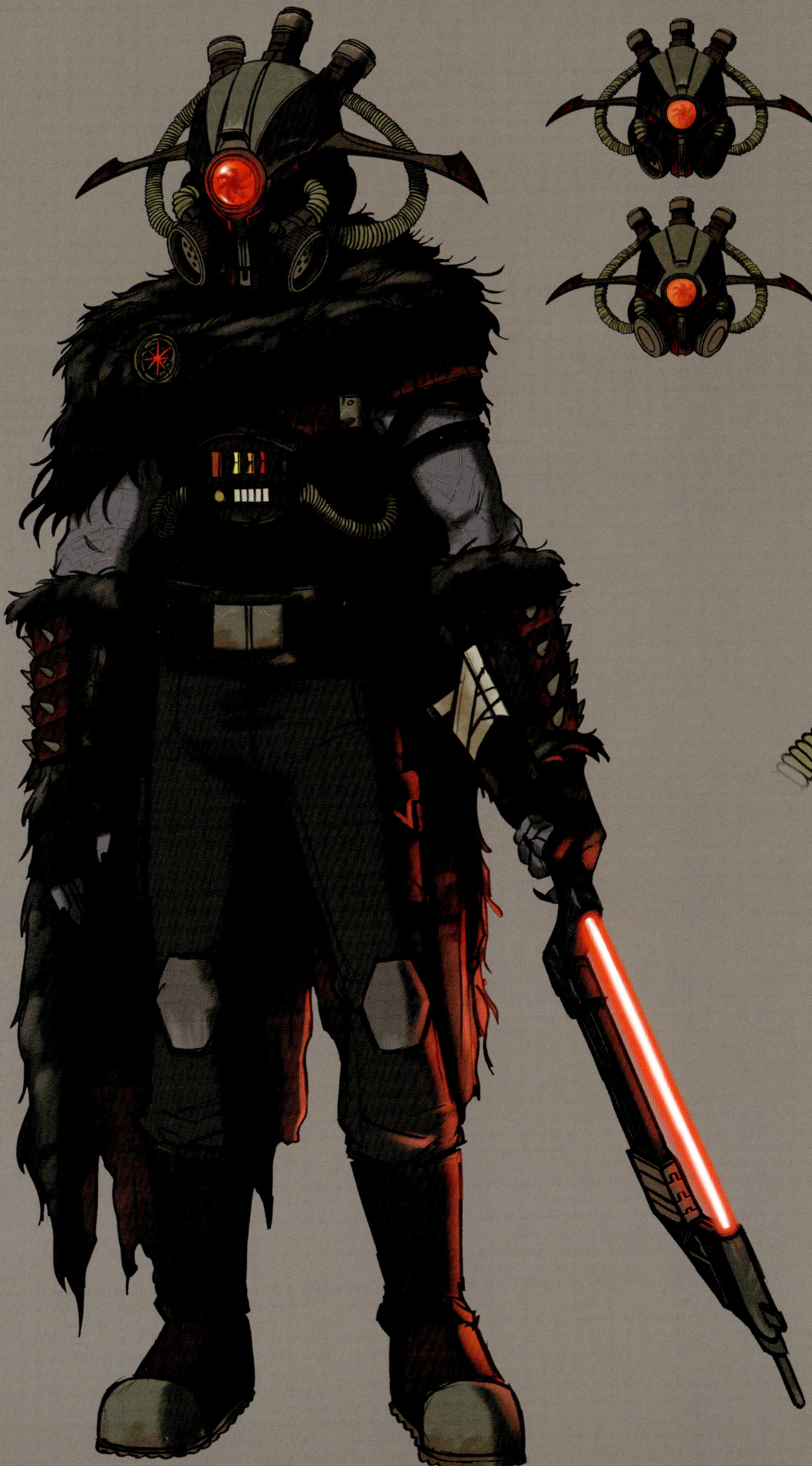

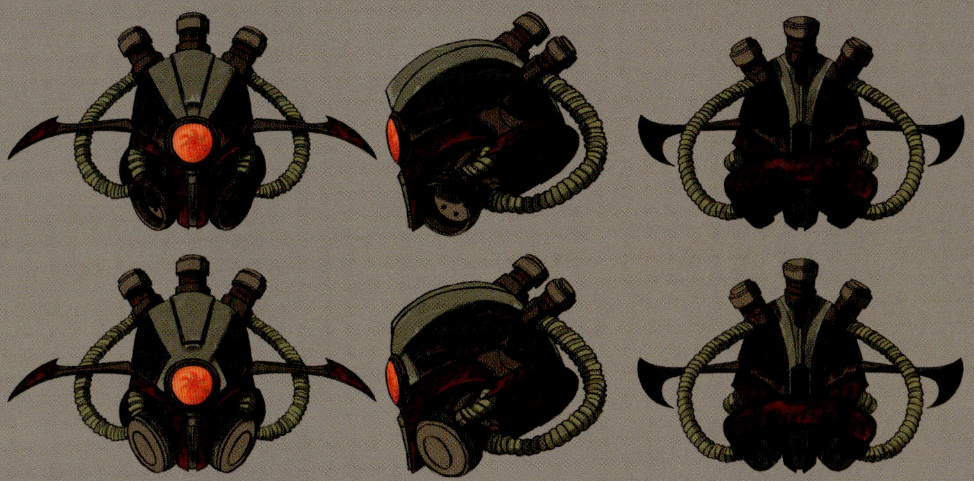

▲ Final Marchion Ro helmet turnaround, April 2020 THOMAS

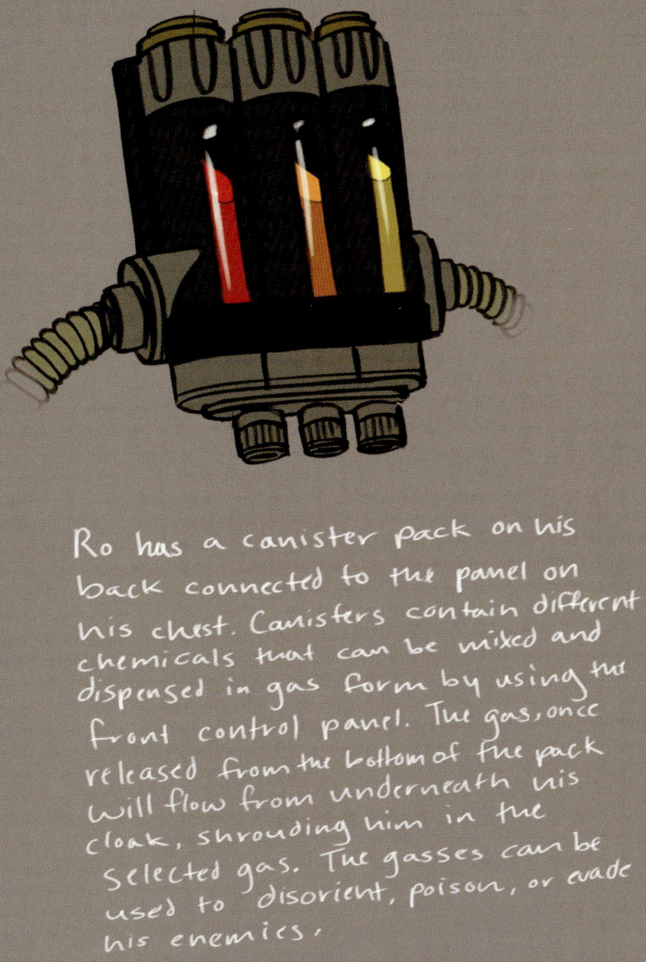

▲ Study of Marchion Ro chest box, August 2020
"His chest box allows him to mix different chemicals to form different gases that you can dispense while fighting, so this is kind of breaking down how his gas delivery system works. I pictured him entering a room and then a cloud of poisonous gas comes out from underneath his cloak." THOMAS

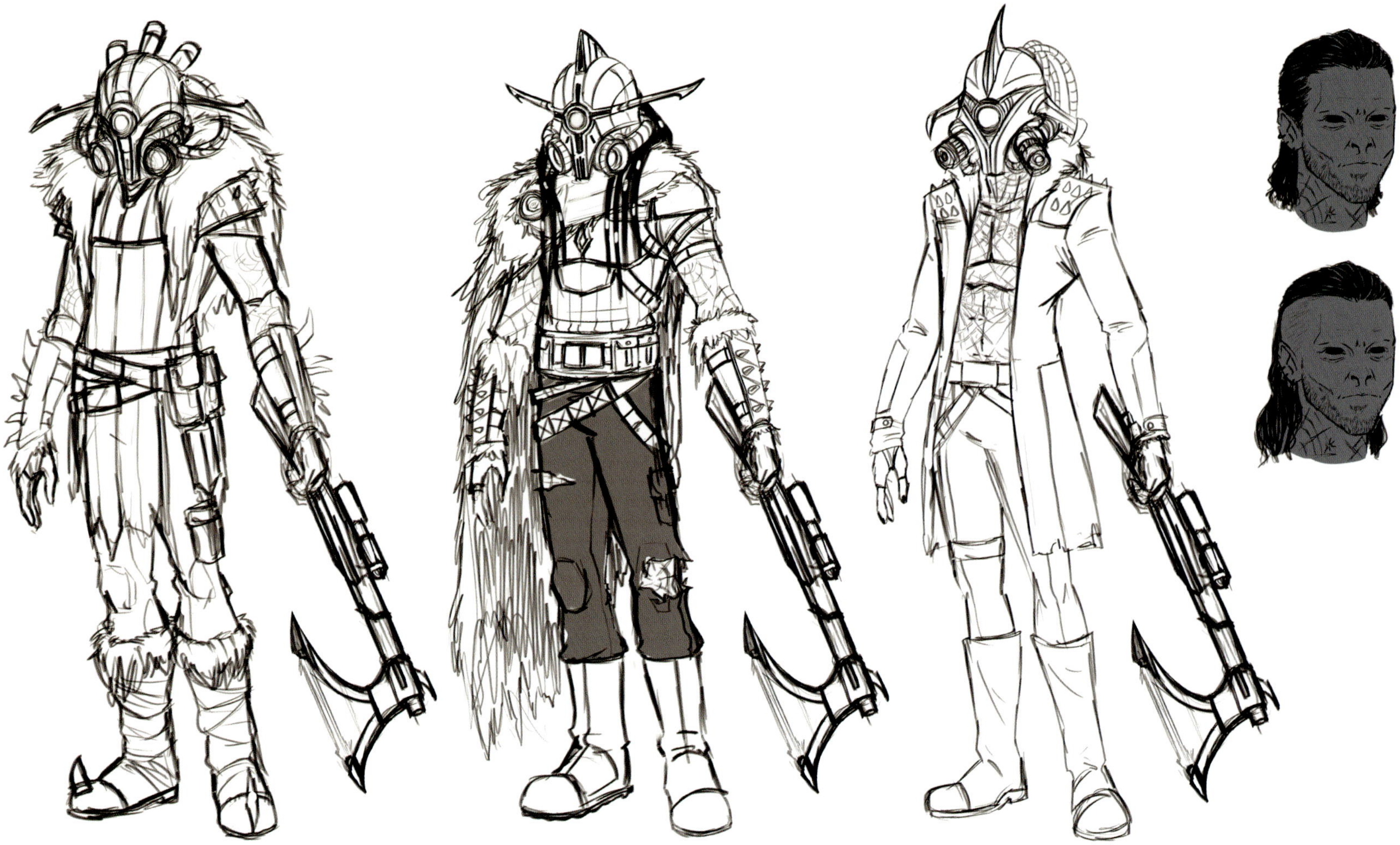

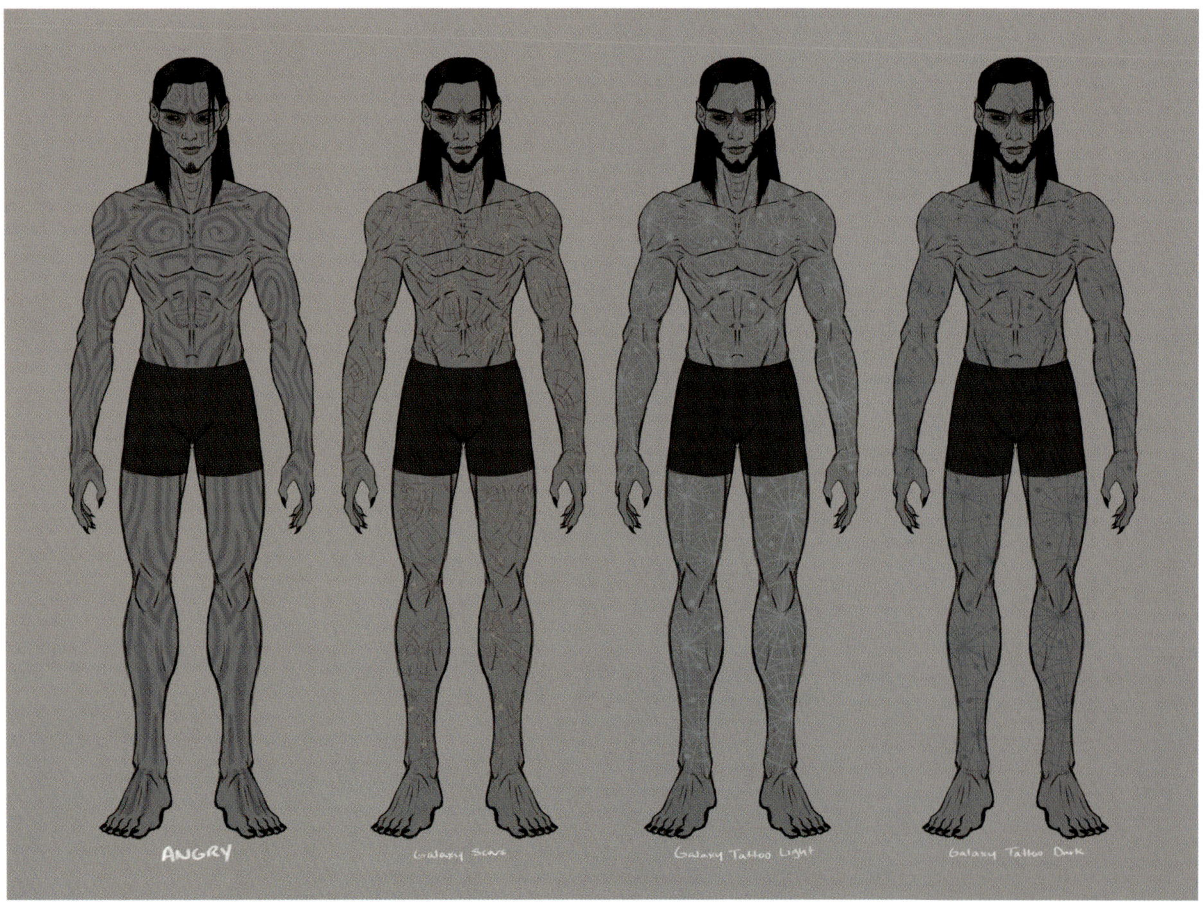

▲ Marchion Ro costume lineup, August 2020 **THOMAS**

Elements of this trio of sketches became the final design for Marchion Ro's costume, combining the helmet of the first figure and the cloak and chest plate of the second.

◄ Concepts for Marchion Ro skin texture, July 2020 **THOMAS**

Random tattoo markings on Ro's skin eventually merged into a new idea: constellations. "I'm exploring him having star maps carved into the skin," said Thomas. "There was a lot of back and forth on his species' appearance."

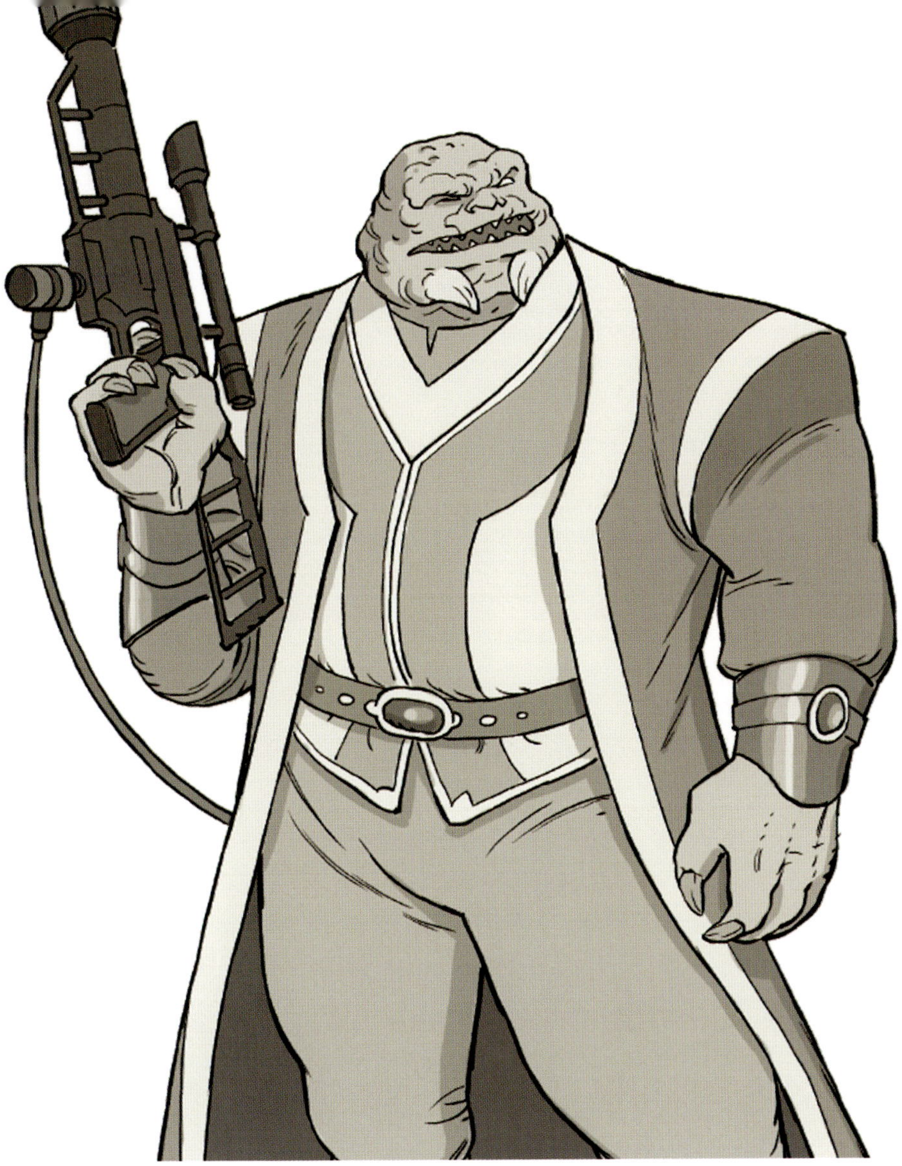

◄ Concept for Pan Eyta TOMATOFARM

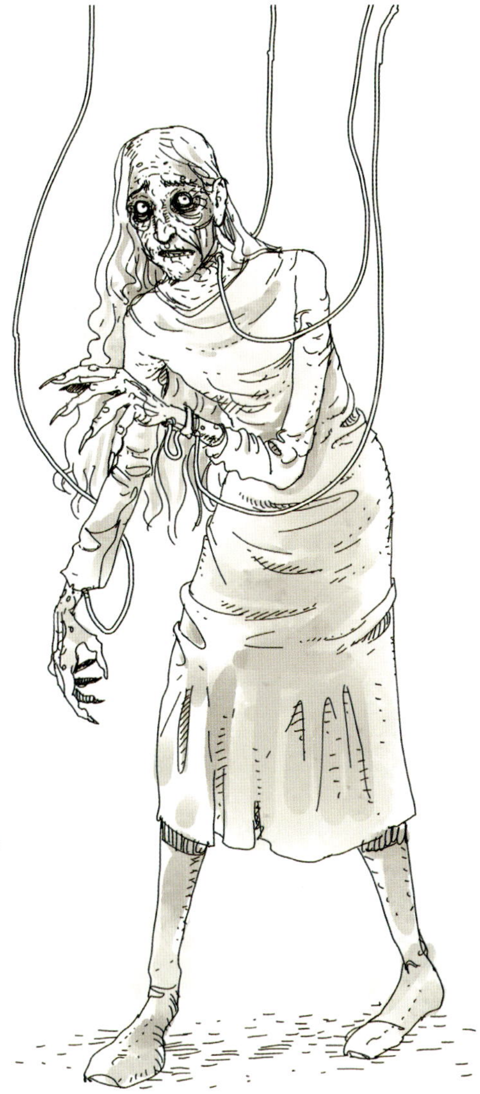

► Final design for Mari San Tekka
"I originally envisioned Mari creeping out to make her declaration to Uttersond [warning of the emergence of more debris from the Hyperspace Disaster in *Star Wars Adventures* #6]—until it was pointed out to me that she would still be in her life support tube! I was attempting to convey a very old woman connected to machines that kept her alive staggering due to her advanced age. By putting her in silhouette, I hoped to make her look kind of scary and zombie-esque. Zombie-hyperspace-oracle-lady!" BROKENSHIRE

▼ Concepts of Doctor Uttersond
"The first iteration of the doctor was my first response to the description of him. Overweight, grubby, with a messed-up eye.

"Version two certainly has more menace but is perhaps a little too strange. The cocktail glass was my attempt to add some quirky Peter Lorre vibes along with his unsettling droopy eyes. In the end, we pulled it back and settled on version three, which translated a bit better in the small panels he appears in." BROKENSHIRE

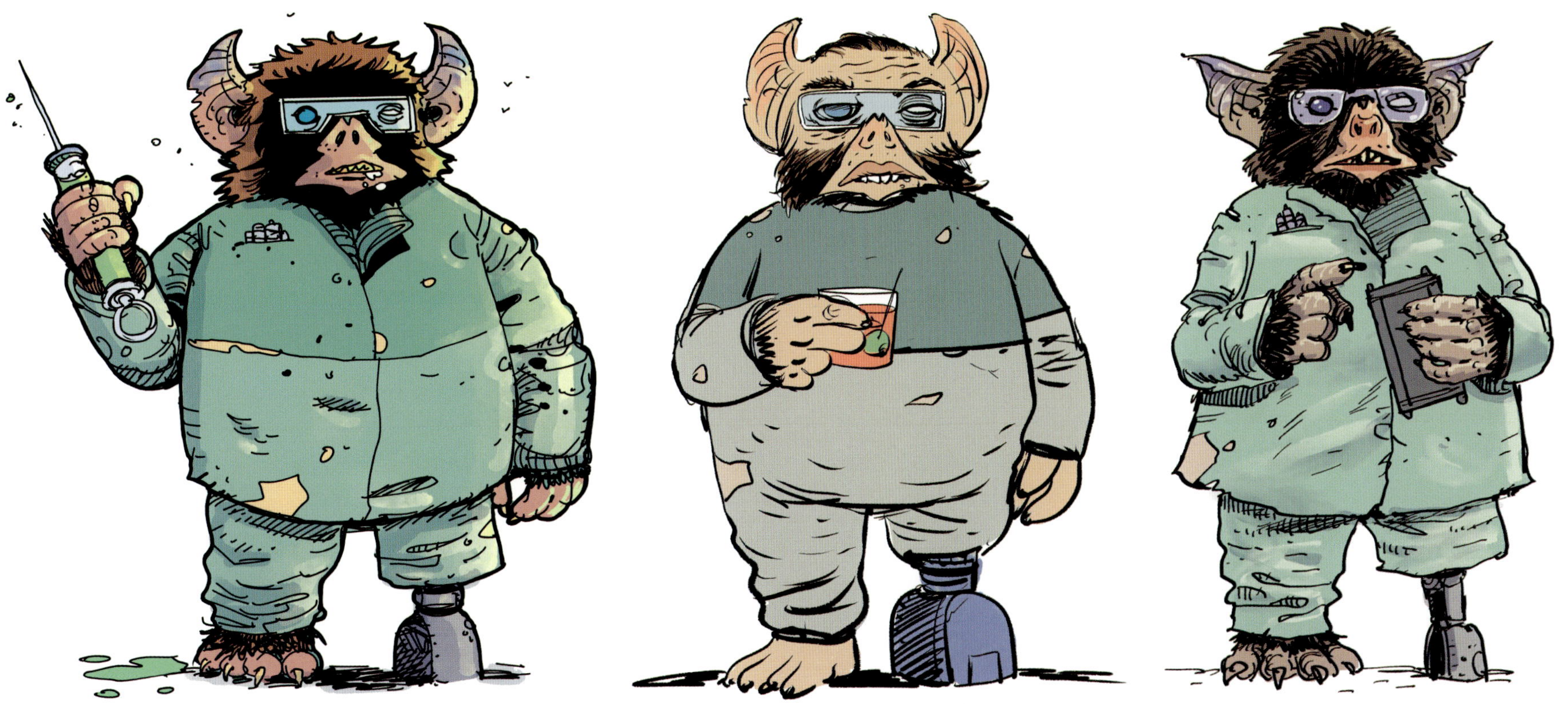

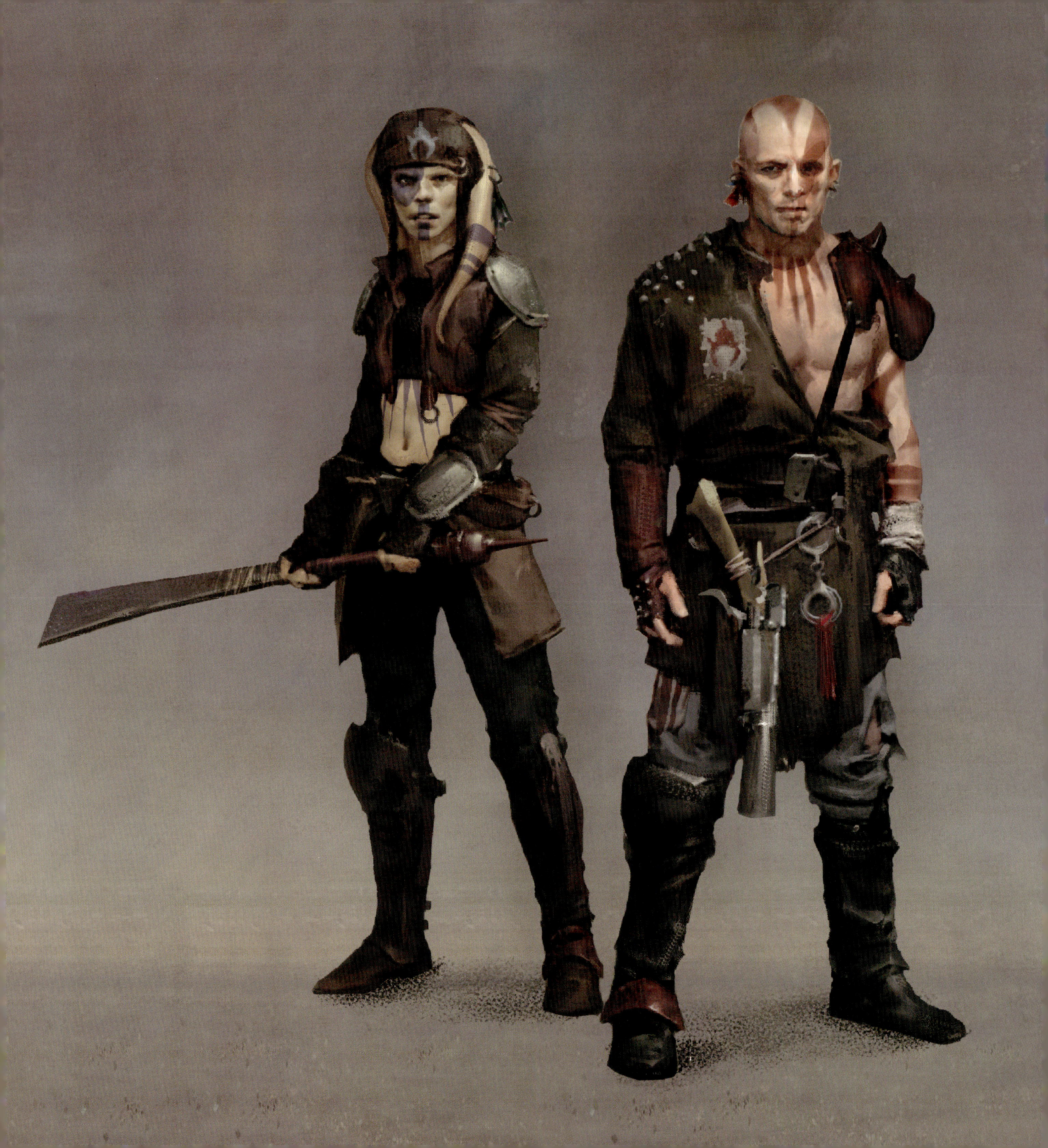

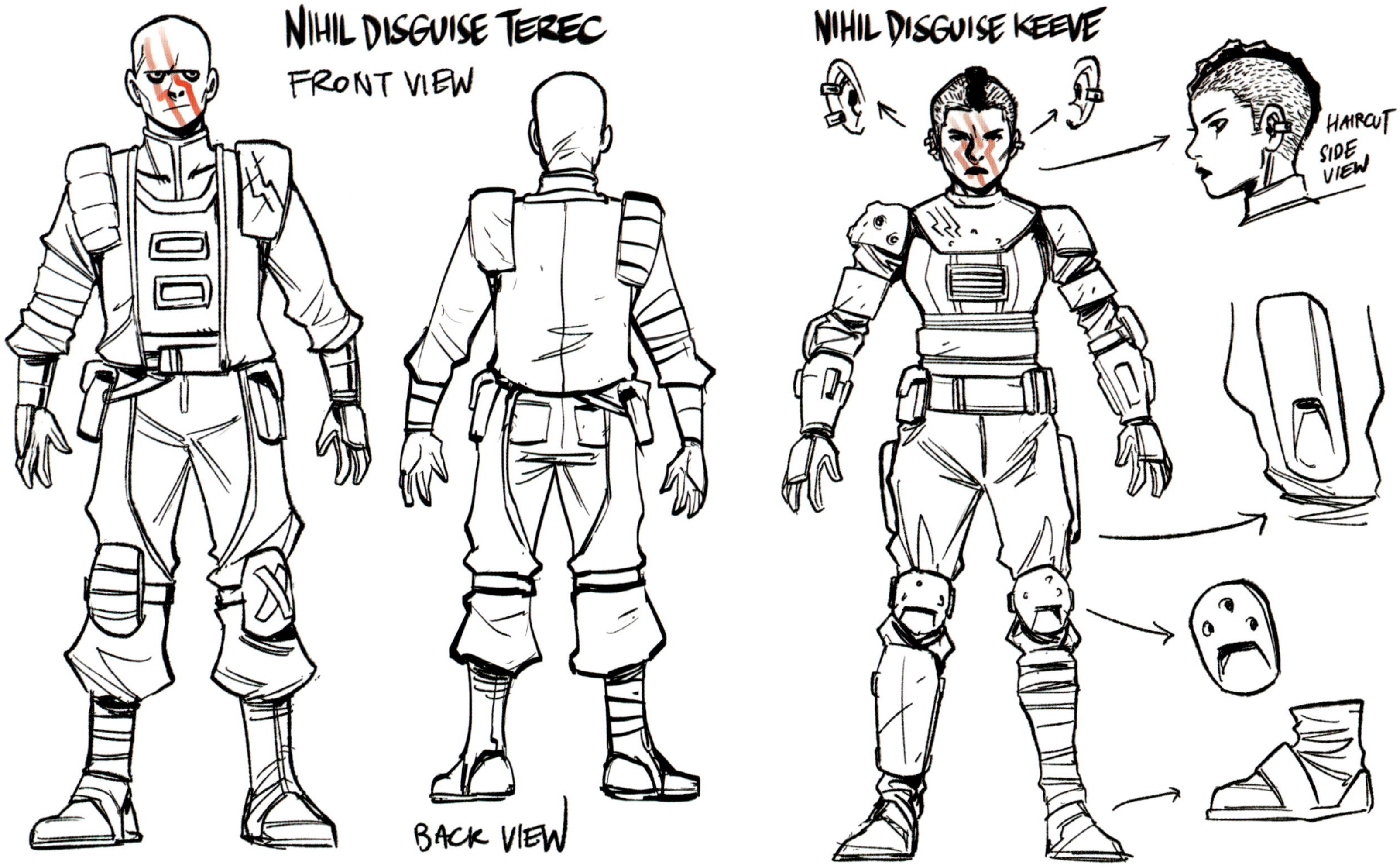

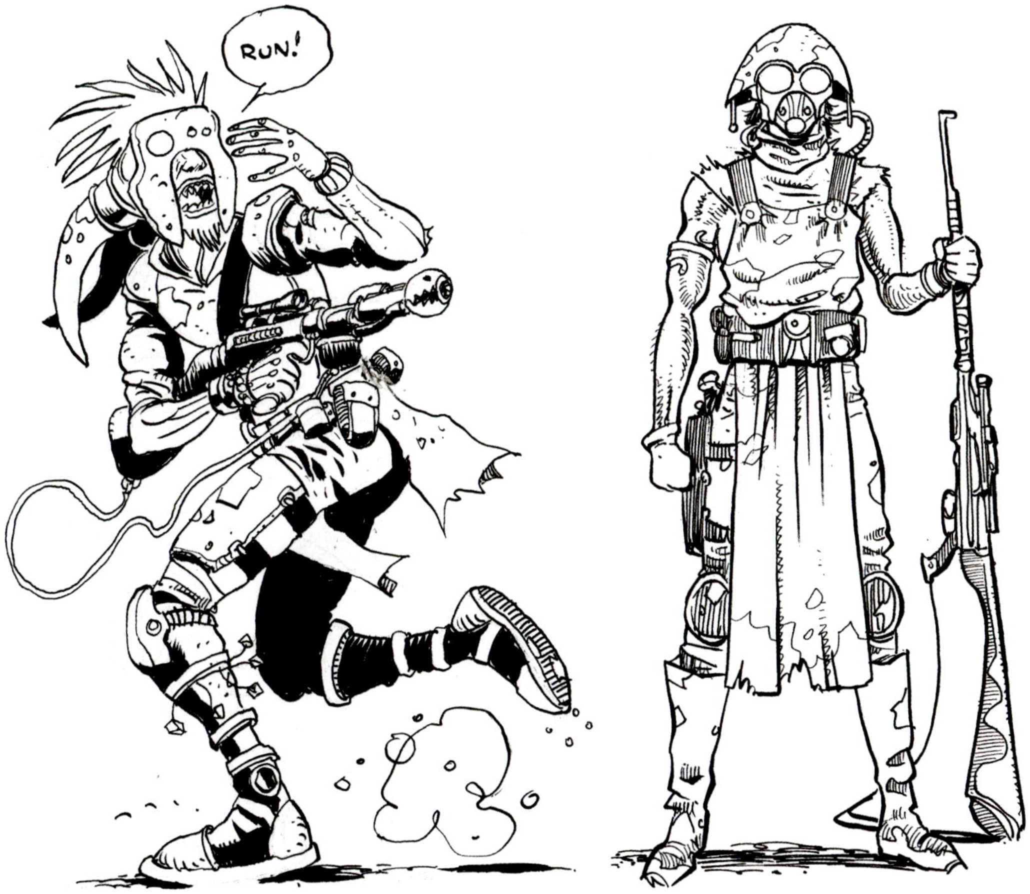

▲ Keeve and Terec Nihil disguise concepts
"I took most of the armor from Phil Noto's design on the cover because he made the cover before I made the pages. We need to respect that. But [on the cover], Phil drew Keeve with the old hairdo. In the pages, I decided to go back to the early concept of Keeve before she was Keeve, that Phil Noto drew with the mohawk [as seen on page 21]. It's the same." ANINDITO

"One of the reasons she changed her hair to go undercover is that her image was all over the place when she was at the dedication [of the Starlight Beacon]." SCOTT

◄ The Nihil "I was thinking of terrorism in general, how it works. [The Nihil] are no match for a Jedi one on one, but they pop up and terrify everyone. They instill that fear. All their weapons are either for close combat or blunt-force trauma. Maybe you get a few of them together, and for an untrained Jedi or a young one, there's a fear factor there." GRIFFIN

► Sketches for Nihil gang members BROKENSHIRE

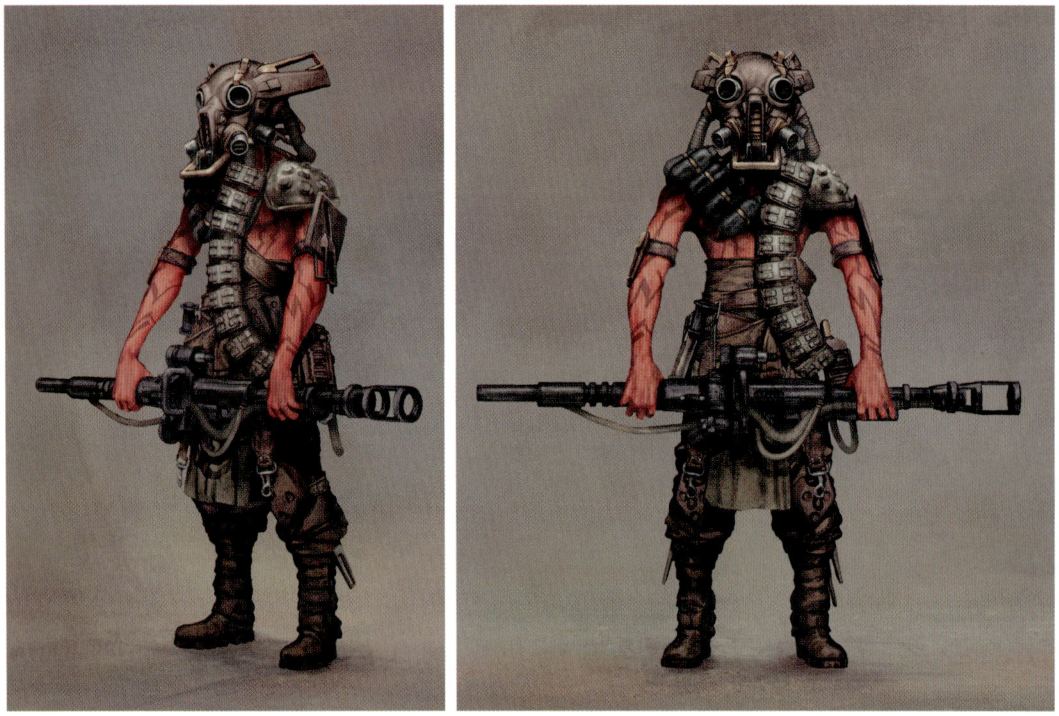

◄ Early concept of male Nihil, February 2020 BLANCHÉ AND KENNY

► Initial concept for Lourna Dee BLANCHÉ

"We did push back on one concept of Lourna Dee wearing a tube top. We were like, so the Nihil don't wear clothes?" JUSTINA IRELAND

▼ Early concept of Lourna Dee, May 2020 BLANCHÉ AND KENNY

"I was never given a specific character's name, I was more exploring the style for the Nihil: space pirates, with a *Mad Max* approach. I think the team was really fond of my design style with complex tubing and kitbash armor." BLANCHÉ

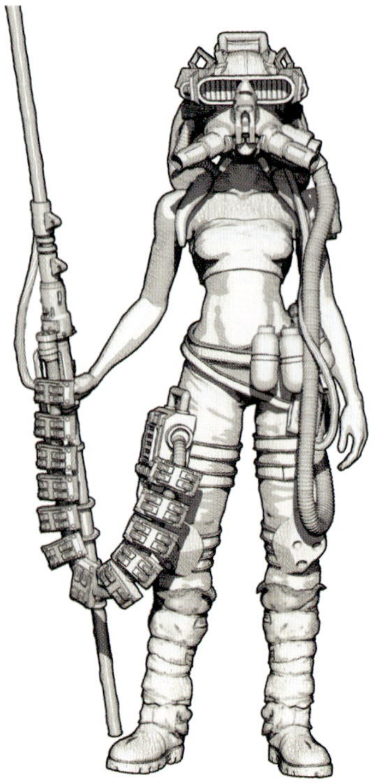

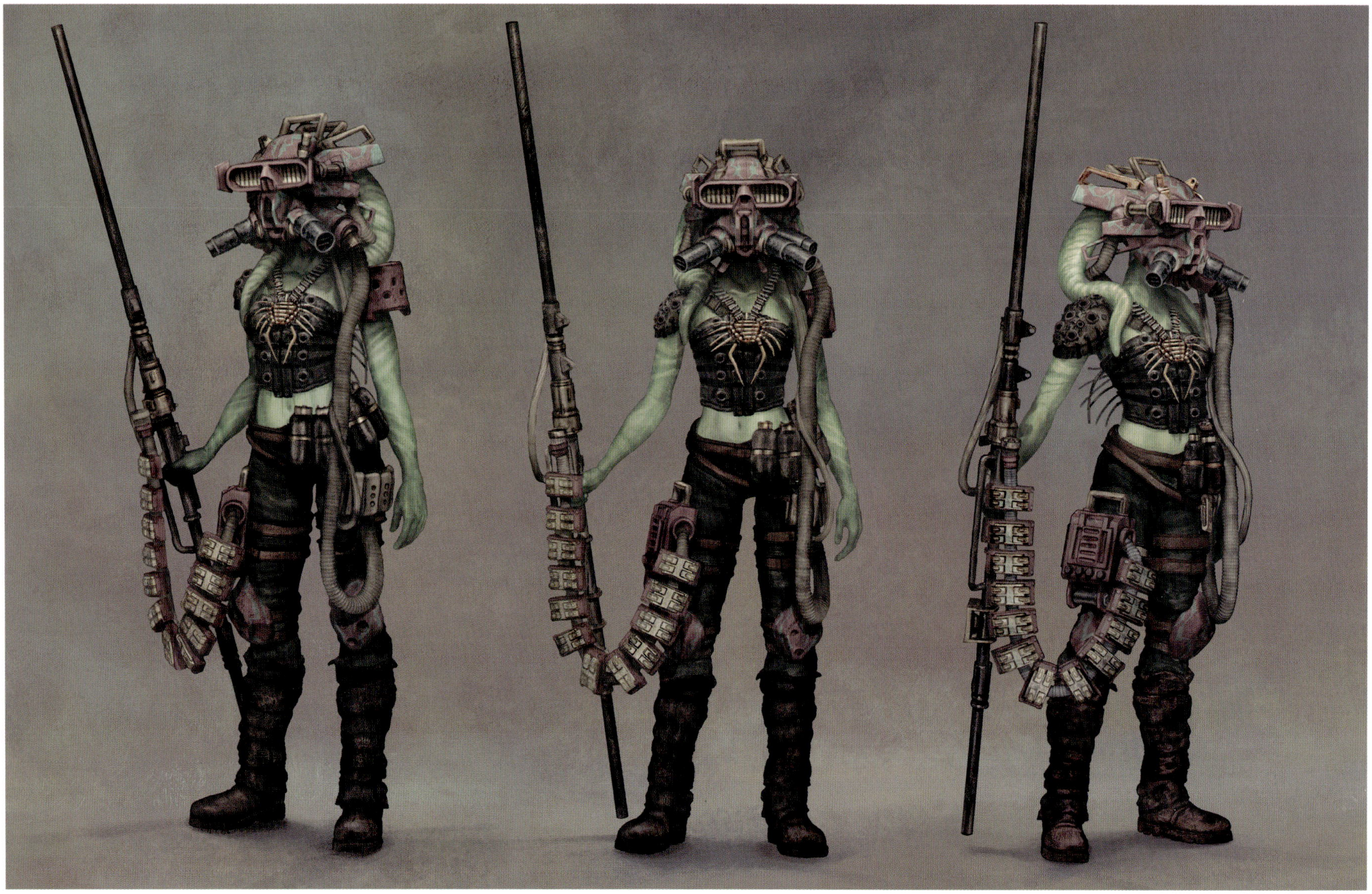

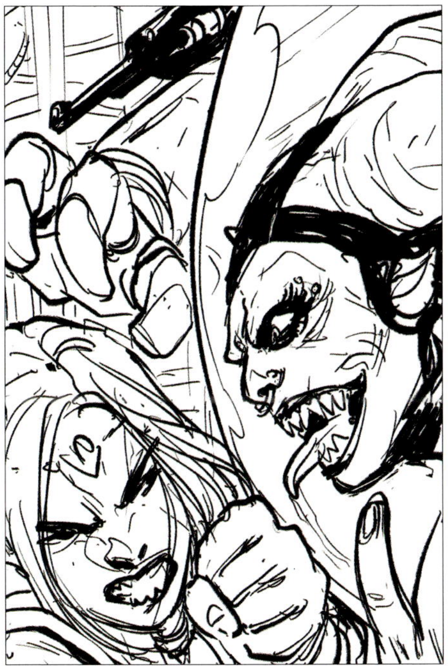

▲ Sketch for variant cover of Marvel's *Star Wars: The High Republic* #13 ANINDITO "I wanted to pay tribute to *Aliens*, you know, the image where we see the Xenomorph and Ripley. We can see from outer space that [Avar is] disgusted with what's coming. Lourna took over the power suit from Zeetar, and she's about to unleash all hell on Avar Kriss." ANINDITO

► Concept sketch for Lourna Dee without her Nihil mask "The only note that [Cavan Scott] sent me was 'She files her teeth so they're all sharp.' What a lady! [She has facial piercings, and] I wanted to incorporate a BDSM leather strap. And when she takes off her mask, there's going to be a lot of sharp points on it so it scratches her chin. She's fine with it. She's used to the scratches.

In my head, I just found her face. It's scary. And I can even already imagine how she talks and how she moves and how intimidating she will be. That's her secret. She's always angry." ANINDITO

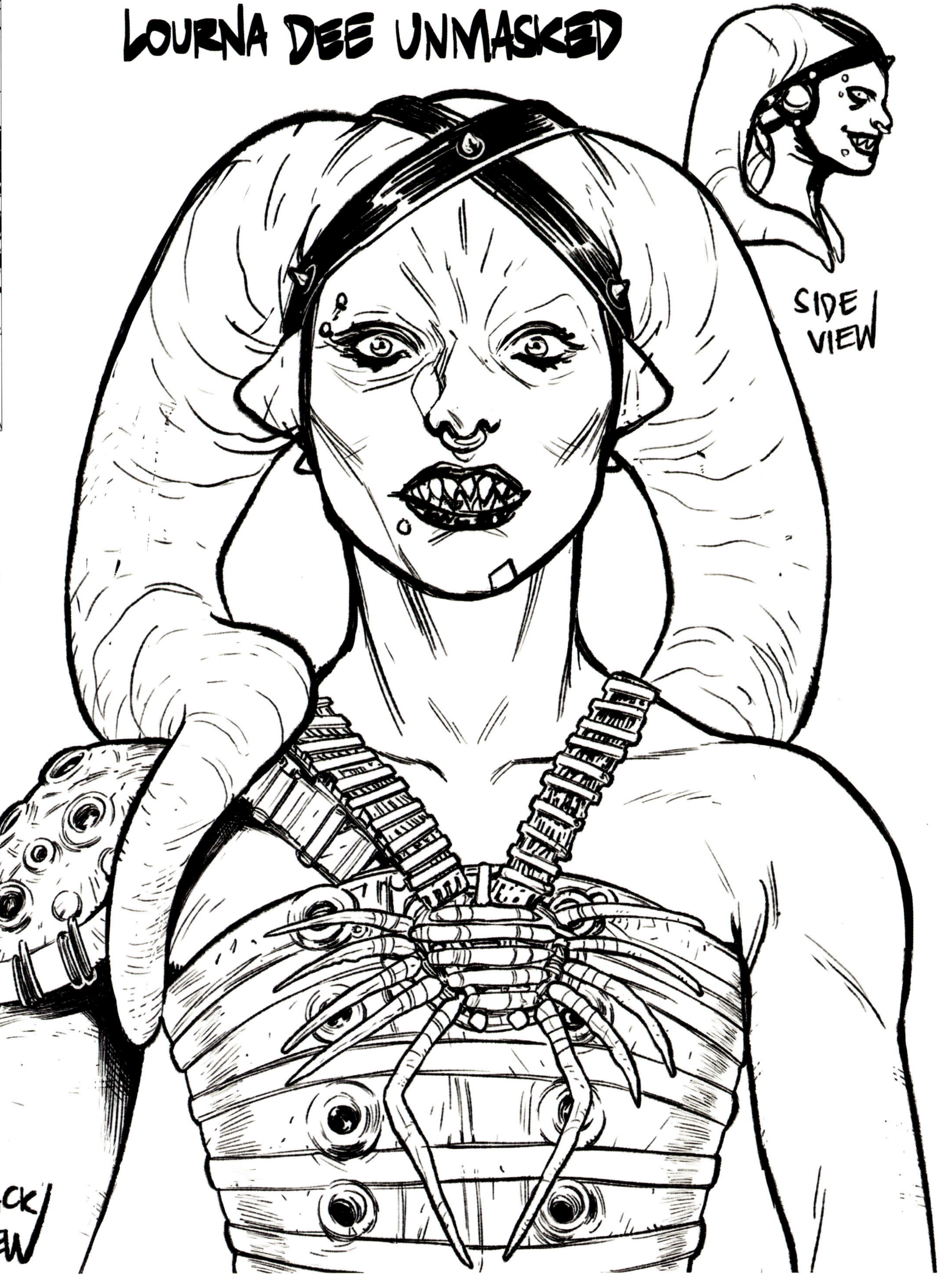

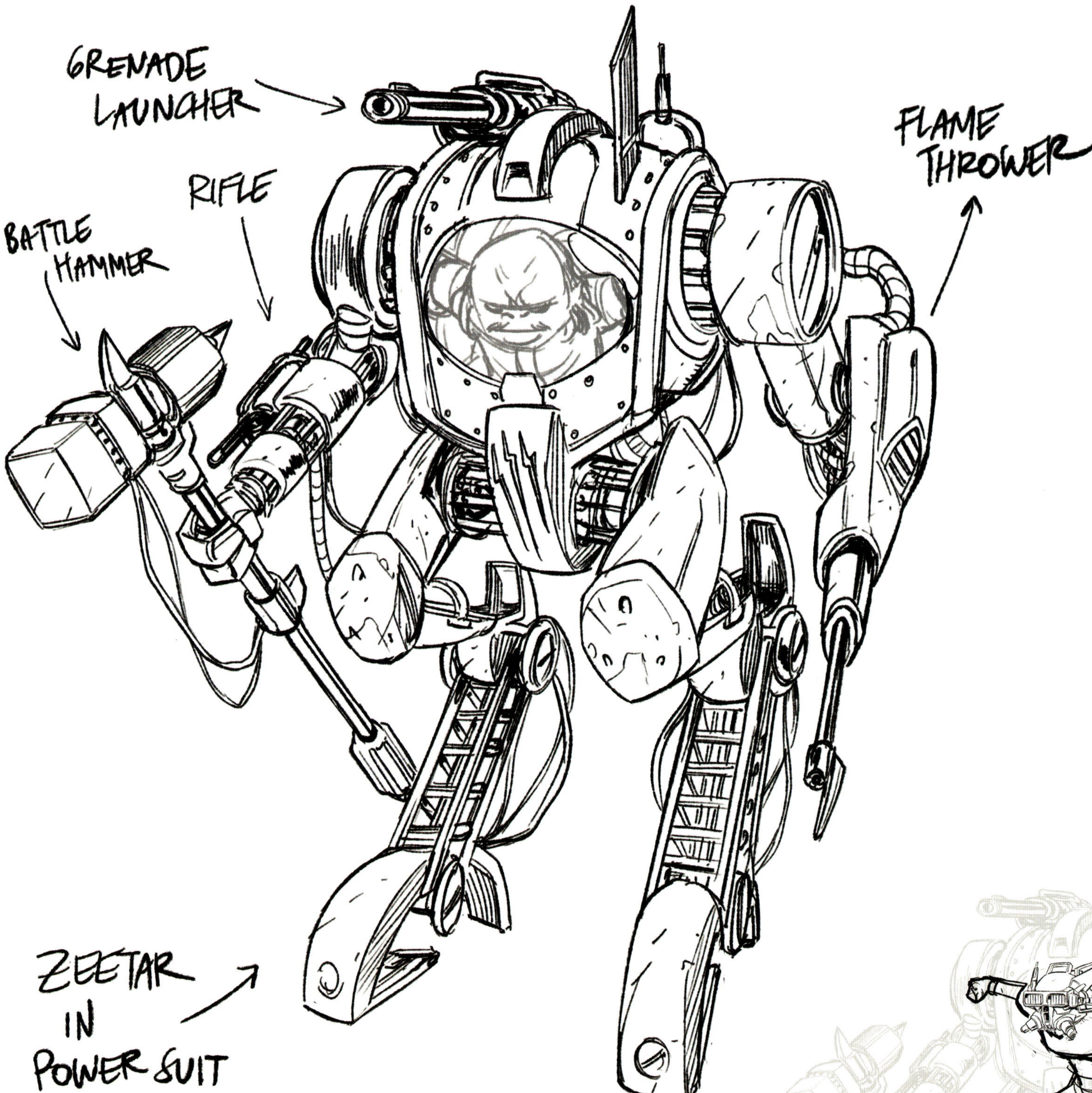

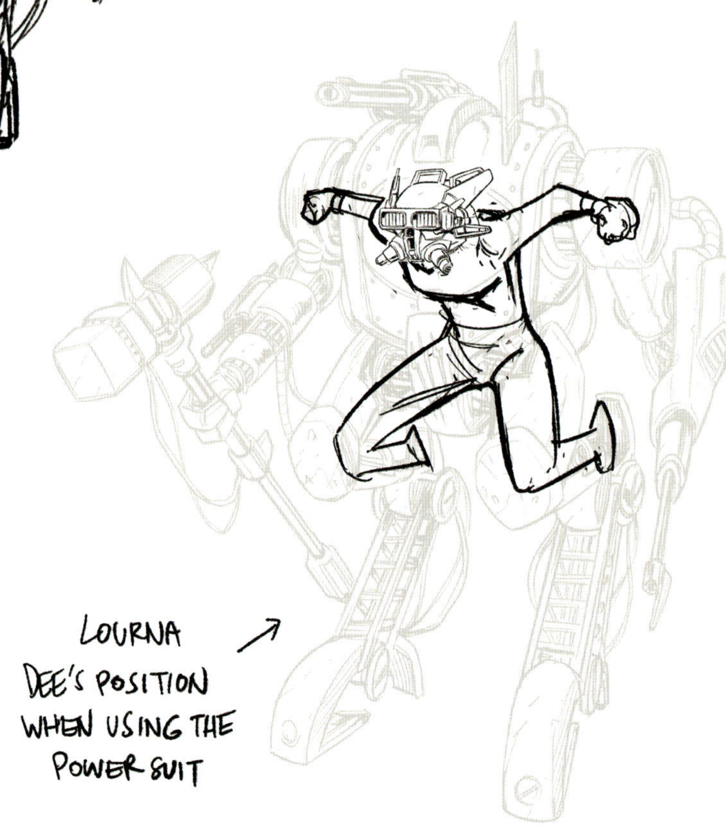

▲ Design for Zeetar's power suit, July 2021 "It was my intention to make it as weird as possible. Like the first *Iron Man* armor, the one Tony made from scraps. That's what I had in mind. I want him to look menacing, like a Nihil robot, incorporating some elements from Marchion Ro's helmet: the round eye from the mask and a lot of tubes and cables. As for the weapons, Cavan told me he's going to have a flamethrower, a rifle, a grenade launcher, but then I got to put in the details. The flamethrower will need gas or something like that, so I put a canister in the back, which can be used as a tool to destroy the power suit itself. Anything can happen. I just want to put something that can be his kryptonite." ANINDITO

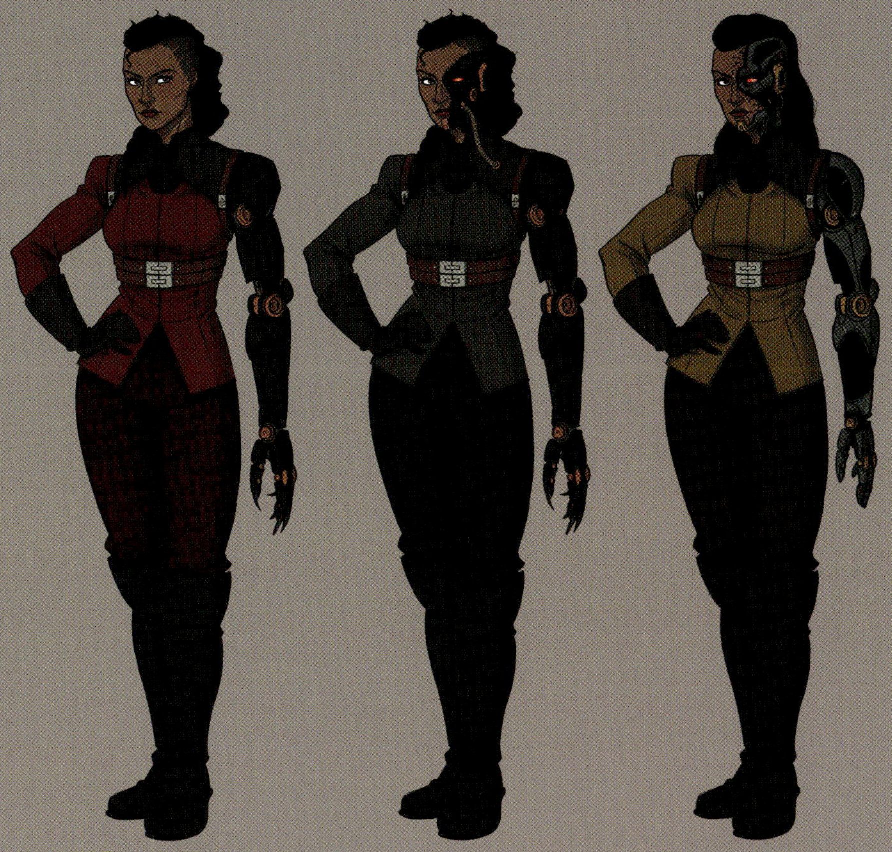

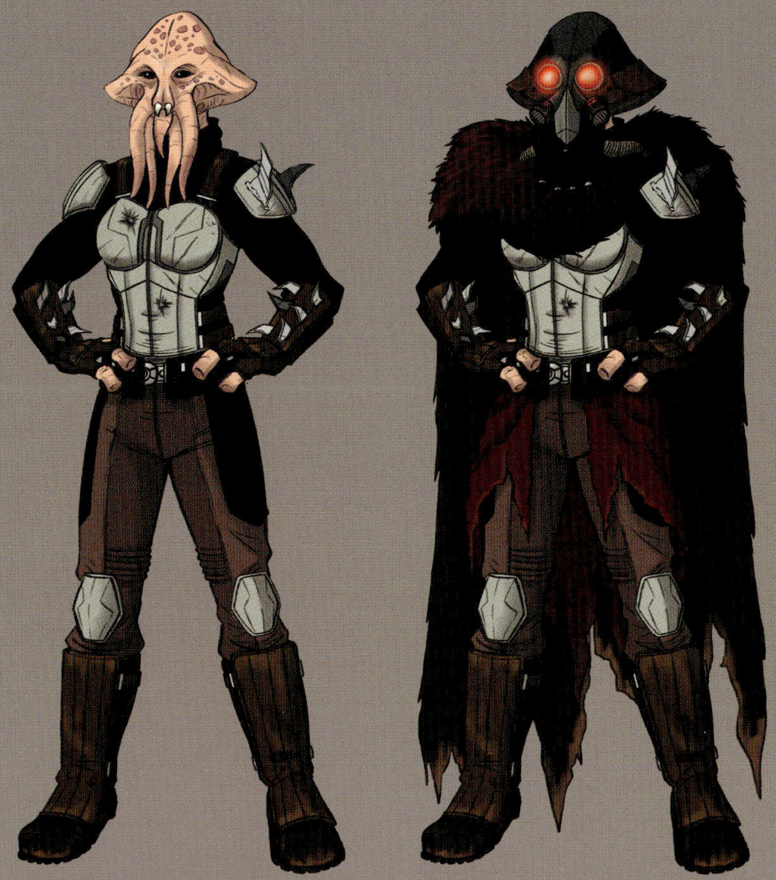

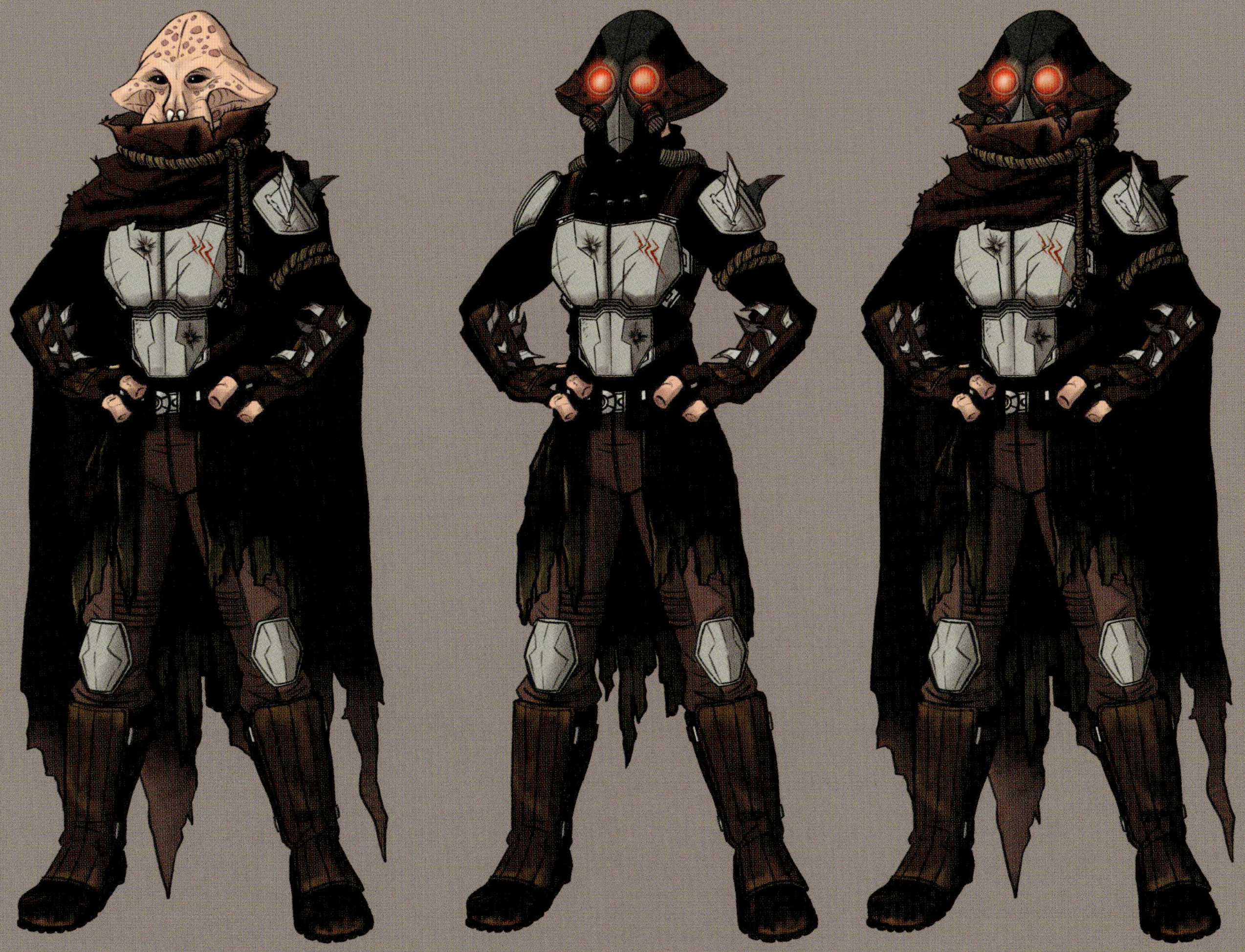

▲ Early designs for Zadina Ukampa, June and July 2021 THOMAS

Early designs for the cyborg doctor call to mind the *Terminator* franchise, a little more machine than man.

◄ Early concepts for Tempest Runner Kara Xoo, July 2021

"It makes me think of Black Manta from the *Aquaman* comics where he had a big black helmet with the red eyes. Even though it's like a weirdly shaped helmet, it just feels really menacing." THOMAS

► Final design for Tempest Runner Kara Xoo THOMAS

To differentiate from the Eye—Marchion Ro—Xoo's furs and shredded skirt were replaced with more nautically themed garb. "I'm putting on a torn-up sailcloth that's tied with rope that she uses to conceal her face," Thomas said. "And I'm also turning her little skirt into seaweed pieces."

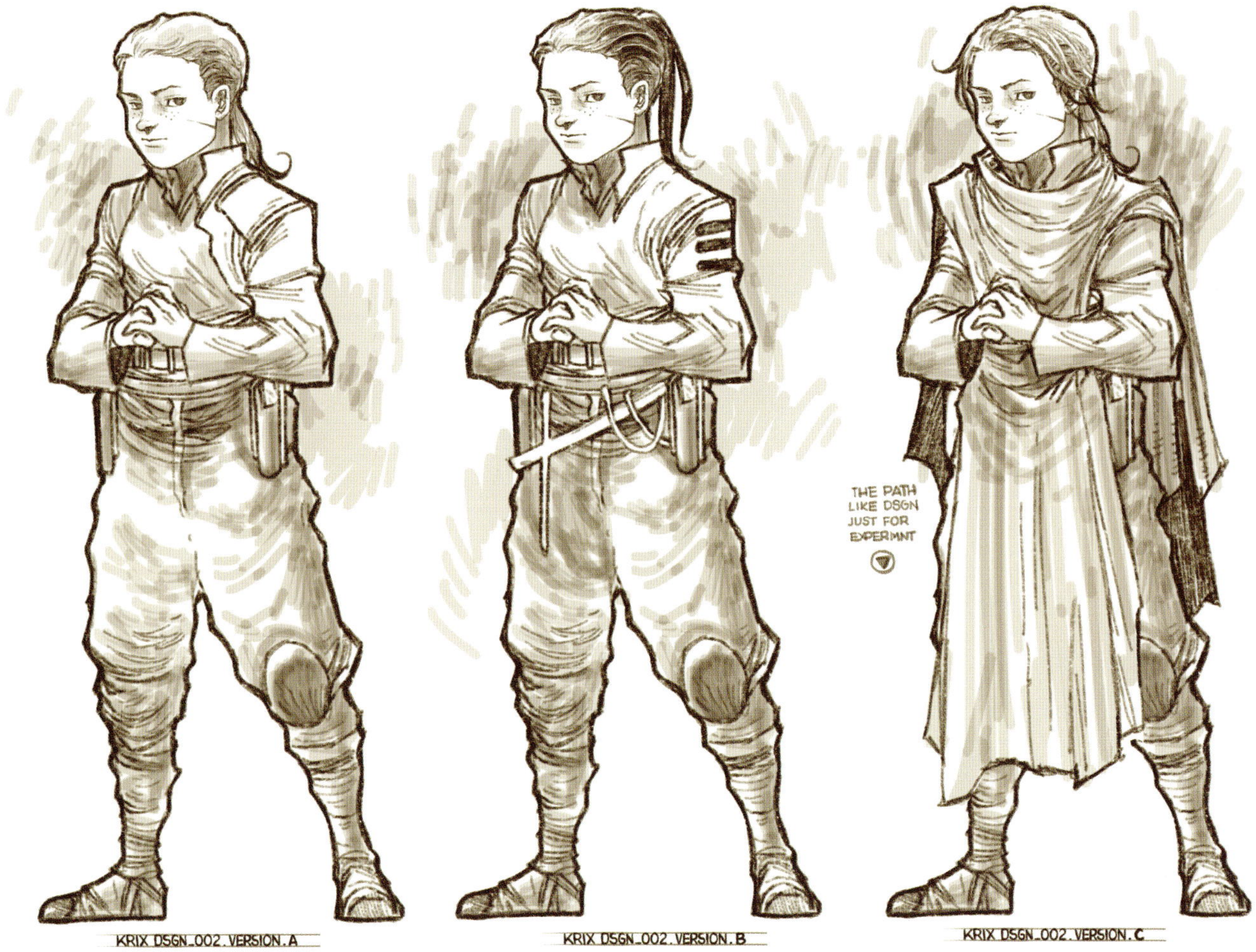

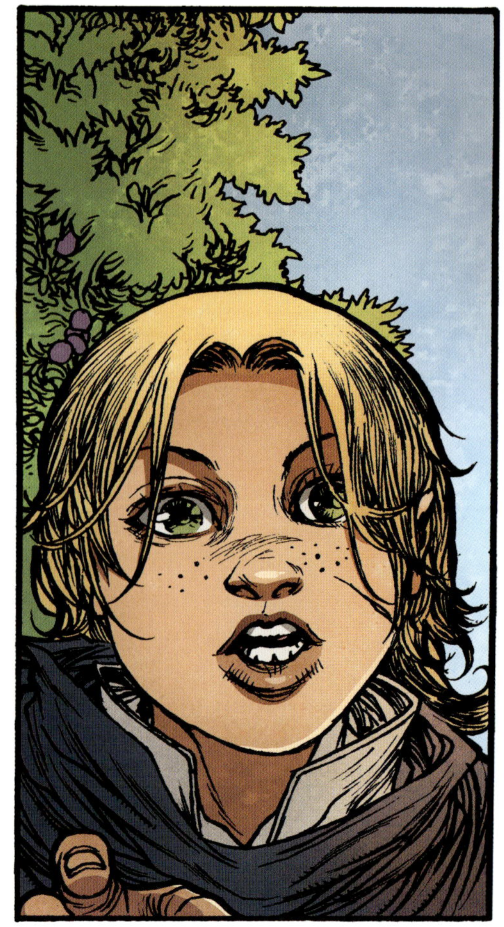

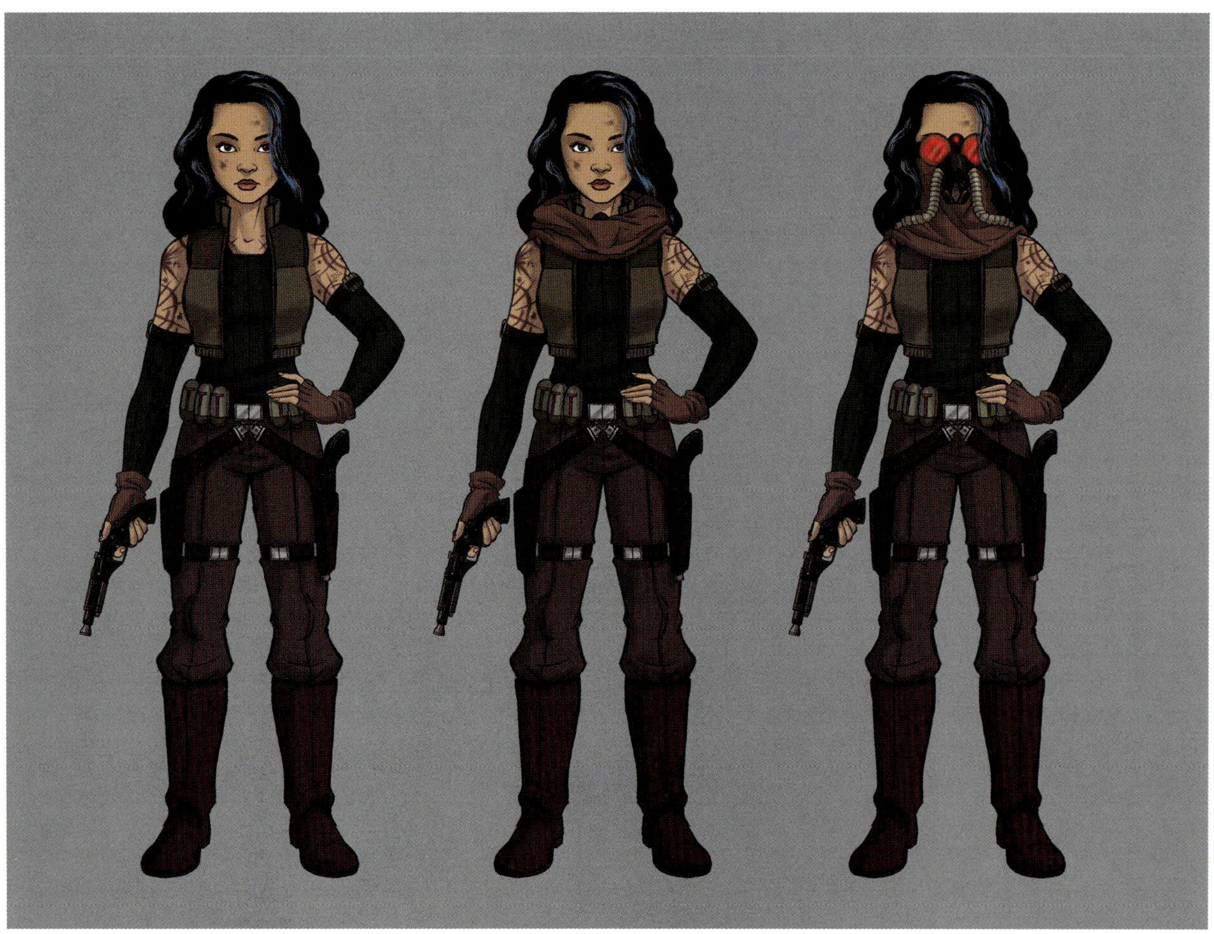

▲ Panel from IDW's *Star Wars: The High Republic Adventures #1* TOLIBAO (PENCILER) AND NALTY (COLORIST)

▼ Early Krix Kamerat concepts
"Krix is my Kylo Ren. In my design, he doesn't know that he's turning into a bad guy, but he's really a good guy. He's been saving Zeen all this time. He has a scar, so that means he's been fighting his whole life. He's been through a lot." TOLIBAO

"In the comics, where Ro gives Krix a helmet, it looks [similar to] the one he wears. There's a lot of visual storytelling that happens between Ro and Krix, and he's kind of stepping up to become the next Ro." DANIEL JOSÉ OLDER

◄ Early concept for Nan THOMAS

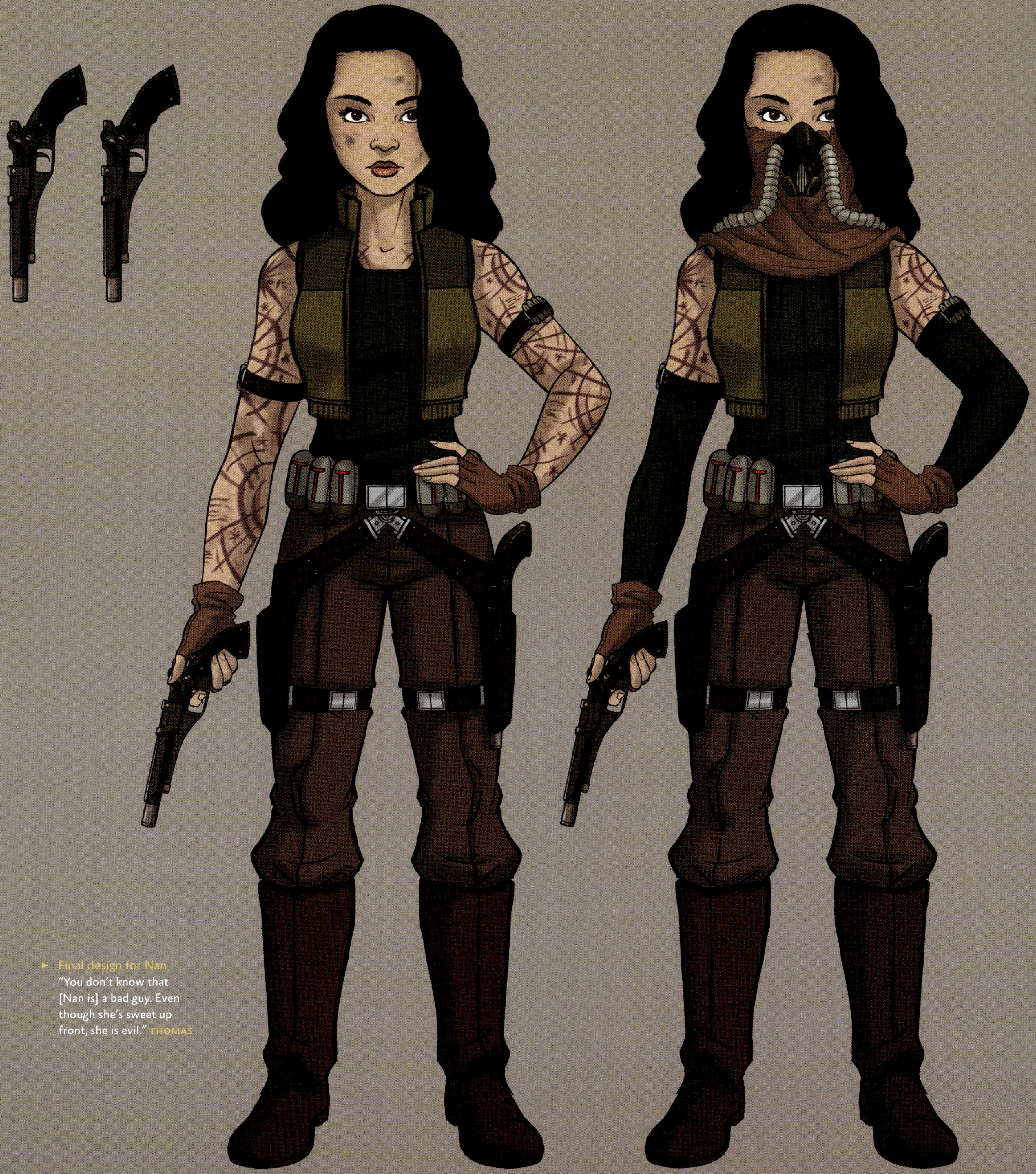

▸ Final design for Nan
"You don't know that [Nan is] a bad guy. Even though she's sweet up front, she is evil." THOMAS

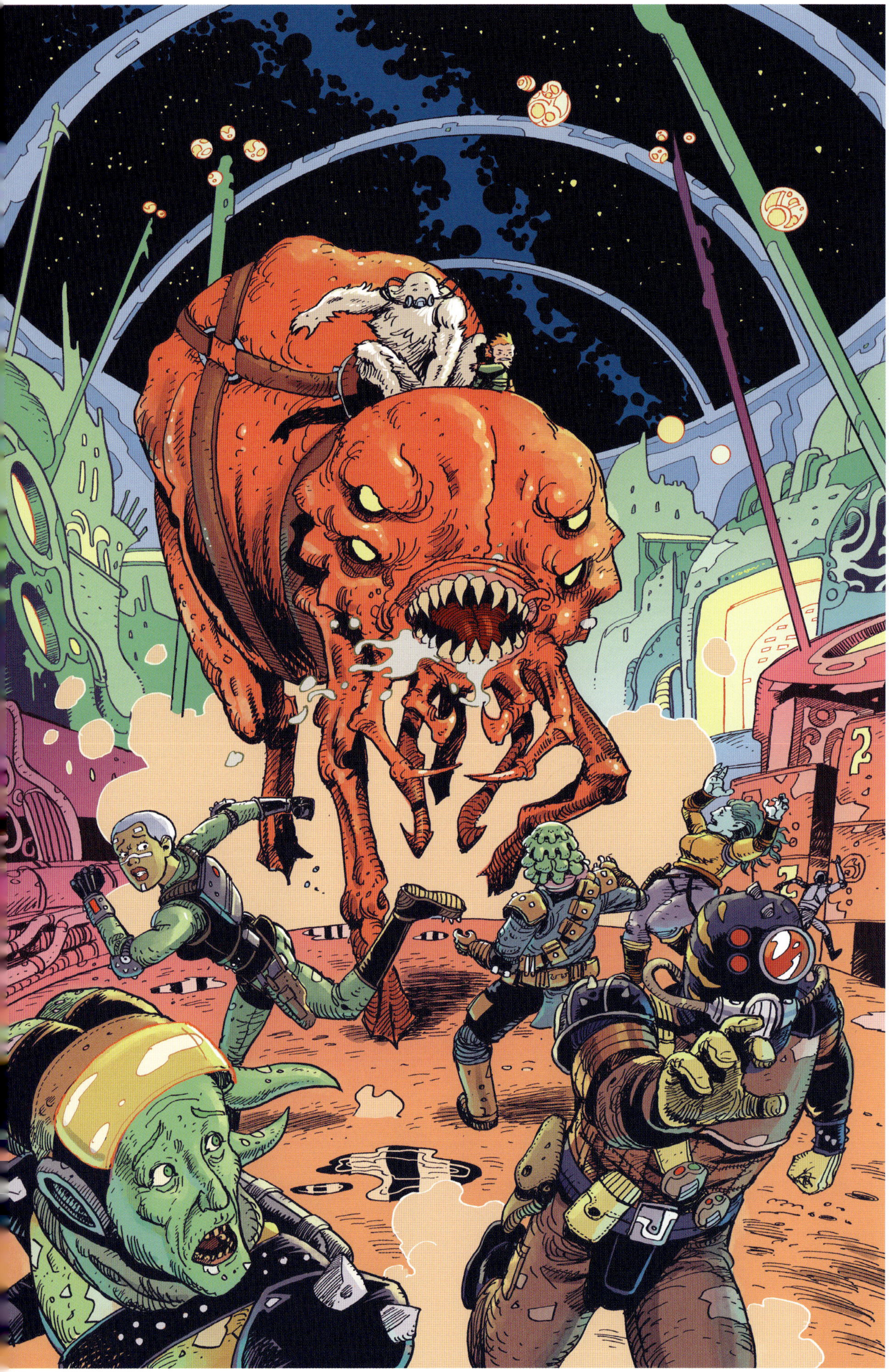

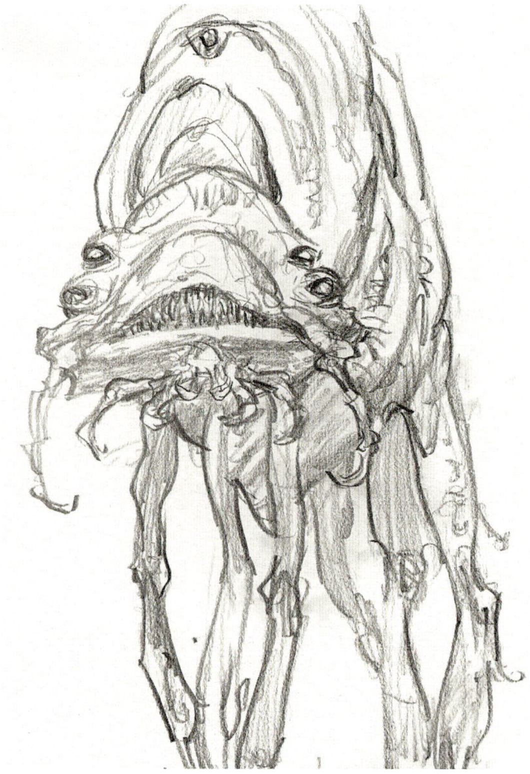

▲ Early sketch of the bogaranth, July 2019 "This one is inspired by an electron microscope photograph of one of the [tardigrades] that we never get to see. I couldn't believe how much it looked like some sort of giant beast that would walk along right next to a tauntaun." McCAIG

◄ The bogaranth rampaging on the *Gaze Electric* in IDW's *Star Wars Adventures #6* BROKENSHIRE

► Concept of bogaranth and Nihil "It reads like a biological AT-AT. In my mind, [bogaranths] were this terrifying monster on sight, but [in reality] it's this docile being that's probably just eating some sort of vegetable in the desert, and that the Nihil have captured and beaten into servitude. I was thinking of a stubborn donkey or cow, but extremely friendly and less threatening. And termites! Just anything that makes your skin crawl. I remember specifically looking at microscopic termites and some other gross parasite-type elements to really capture those fly hands. Anything that is unsettling. So naturally, the evil that is the Nihil would commandeer these gentle pastoral creatures and then use them for their fearsome aesthetic." GRIFFIN

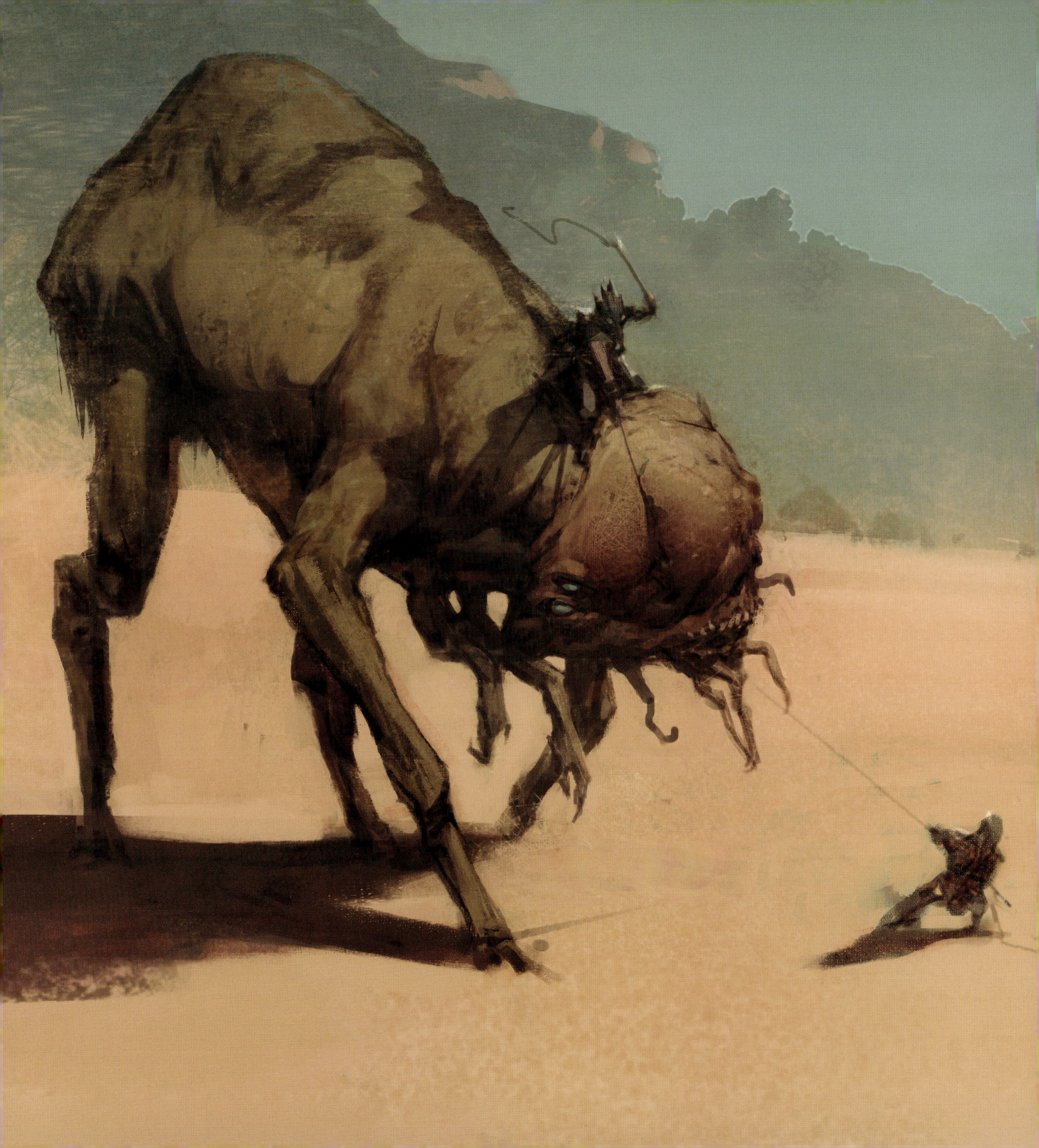

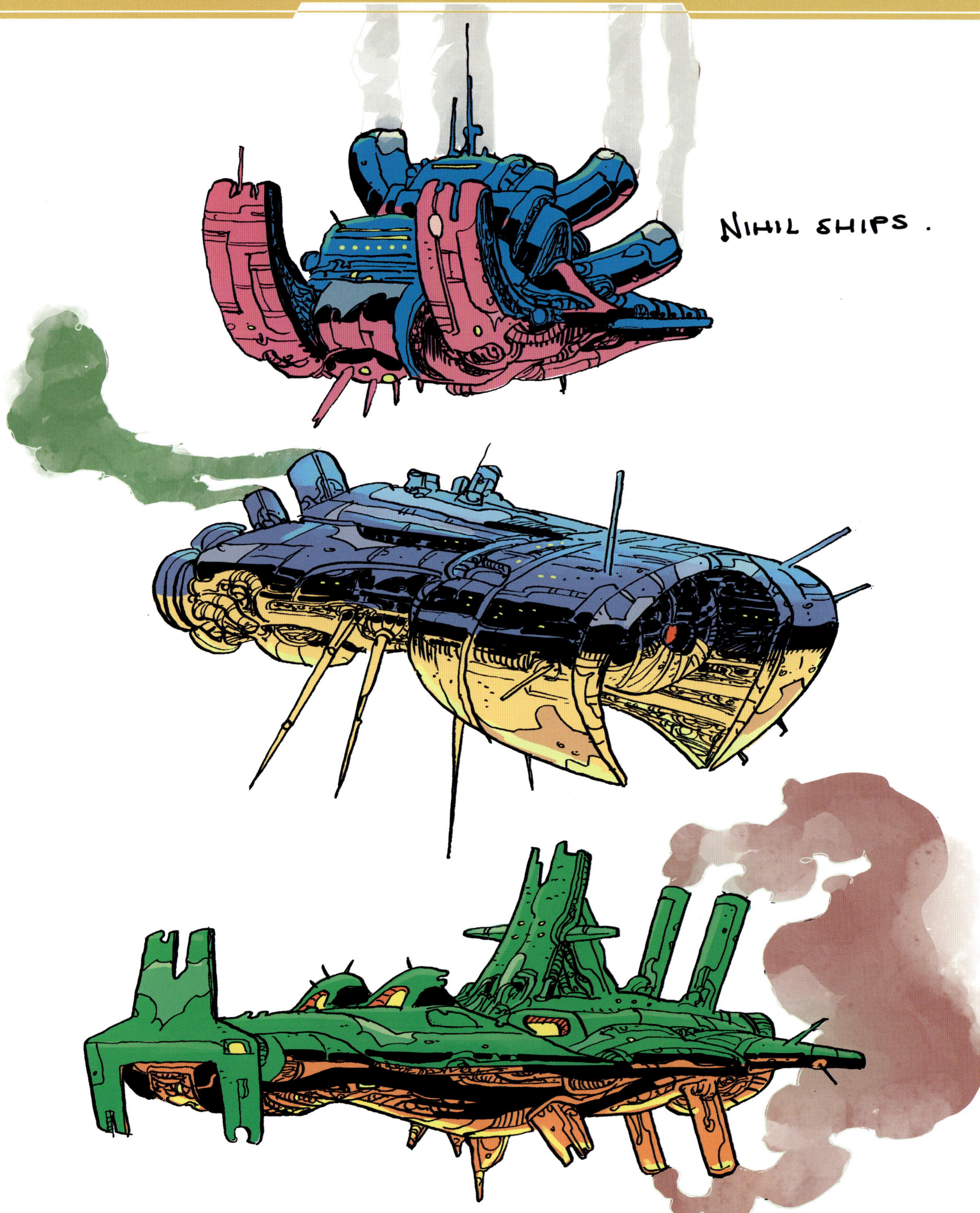
NIHIL SHIPS.

CHAPTER 5

SHIPS AND VEHICLES

THE HISTORY OF *STAR WARS* design is inherent in every aspect of The High Republic, but nowhere quite so keenly as in the ships and vehicles of the period.

Designers often go back to the roots, be it referencing Ralph McQuarrie's sketches, utilizing Lucasfilm's vault of unrealized concepts, or taking in the filmography and mythology that inspired George Lucas to create the galaxy in the first place. When Lucasfilm creative art manager Phil Szostak was called in to provide unused concept art for the Nihil and other antagonists in the series in late September 2019, he'd already pulled together some of the same archival art among the thousands of pieces delivered to director and executive producer Deborah Chow, whose *Obi-Wan Kenobi* series was in preproduction at the time. Looking through Lucasfilm's treasure trove of designs for creatures, aliens, vehicles, and locations is a staple in every new production or project, as creators look for inspiration and study the shape language and grit that give *Star Wars* its distinctive appeal. Alongside Lucas, supervising director Dave Filoni incorporated many previously unrealized designs and McQuarrie concepts into *Star Wars: The Clone Wars*, and later *Star Wars Rebels*, *The Mandalorian*, and *The Book of Boba Fett*, imbuing each project with its own identity while ensuring that the newest tales remain a part of the fabric of the greater galaxy.

In a small office space at the Letterman Digital Arts Center at the northern tip of San Francisco, editors, Story Group members, and art directors met regularly to review the first designs generated for the initiative throughout late 2019 and early 2020, before the pandemic sent workers scattering to their homes to shelter in place in March 2020. However, with time and money already dwindling on February 7, 2020, the archive of concepts became a lifeline to realizing an integral facet of *Star Wars* storytelling: the starship. A conversation among art director Troy Alders, Story Group senior creative executive Pablo Hidalgo, and Szostak spurred the idea.

Instead of simply using the wealth of concept art as a guideline for new designs, storytellers were given freedom to lift from the roughly 25,000 pieces of previously unused illustrations generated across forty-five years of *Star Wars* history.

"A quality that is one of, if not *the*, main thing that made *Star Wars* work in '77 that was unlike any other science-fiction movie is that it wasn't polished," Alders added. "It was used. It was weathered. It was the detail and aesthetic that made people think, 'Wow, this is real.'"

Beyond the McQuarrie works that set the tone for *Star Wars: A New Hope* and everything after, each new production calls for fresh ideas and designs, employing a small squadron of artists and illustrators. But this time, mining the unrealized designs allowed authors to cherry-pick a gleaming prequel-era starfighter to become the Jedi Vector and a McQuarrie speeder fit for monster hunter Ty Yorrick, with little need for retrofitting. A small fleet of podracers intended for *The Phantom Menace* made for perfect Nihil crafts with a slight modification, while a piece from original trilogy artist Joe Johnston spoke to author Charles Soule as the visual representation of the Nihil's homebase, the *Gaze Electric*. "It really clarified in my mind immediately that it was this big kind of empty place," Soule said. "Like a cathedral in Europe or something like that, it has this cavernous quality. That's what Marchion Ro's ship feels like."

The used-future feel of the galaxy far, far away is replete with designs that suggest eons of technological discovery and evolution, allowing creators to pull from more recent designs for the sequel trilogy of films as well. A prime example is

◂ Sketches of Nihil ships BROKENSHIRE

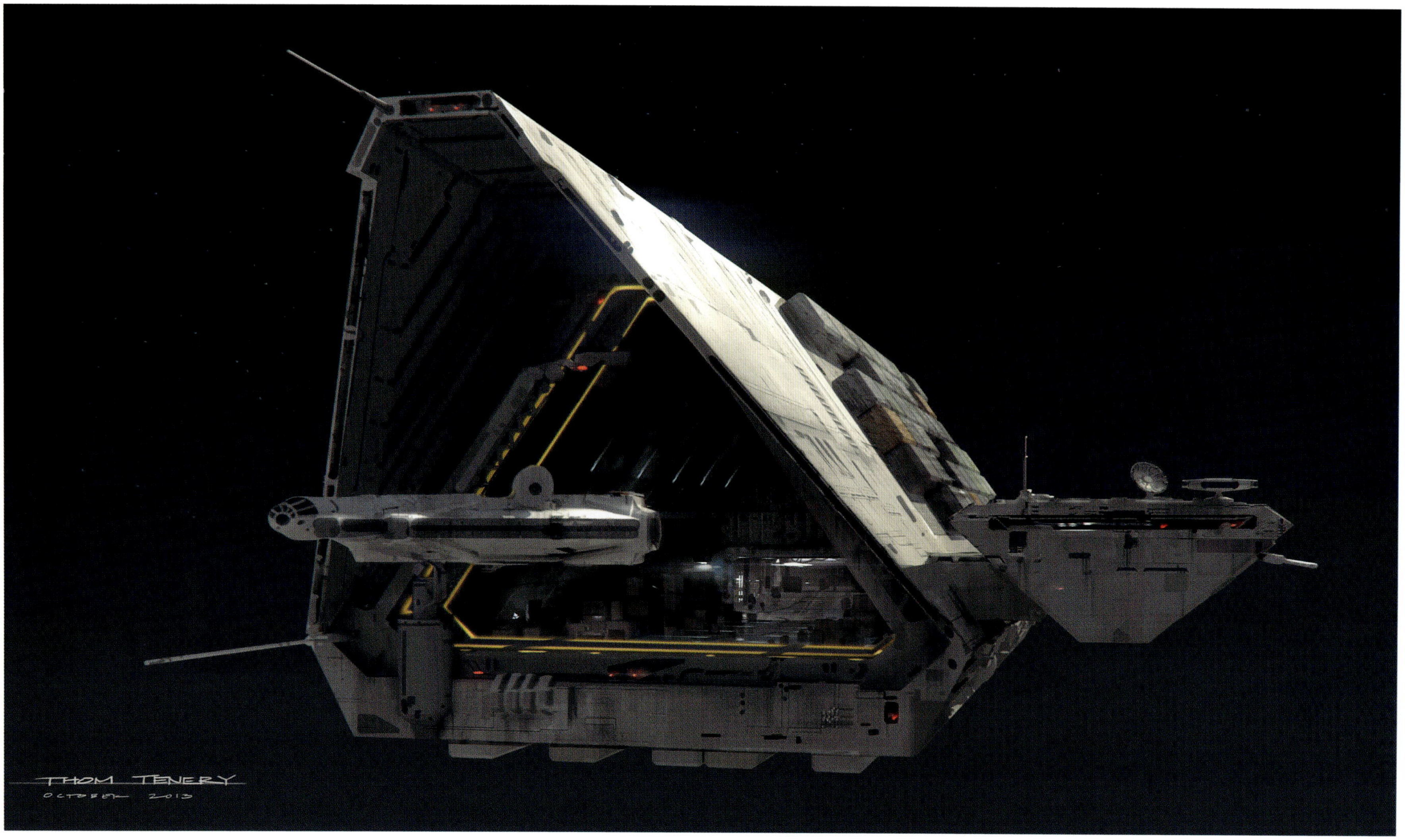

▲ Unused freighter concept
THOM TENERY

"The *Legacy Run* was derived from an unused design for Han Solo's freighter [the *Eravana*] in *The Force Awakens* that I always liked. There's a blunt simplicity to it: a flying box of boxes. It tells a story that this isn't a luxury passenger liner, but it's all some people can afford. In this case, it didn't matter that it came from the Resistance/First Order era, because this design is likely hundreds of years old. *Star Wars* designs are shaped more by culture than they are by innovation, so this is much more a working ship." PABLO HIDALGO

the *Legacy Run* freighter. First envisioned for Han Solo's home away from home in *The Force Awakens*, its decrepit hull added to a feeling of age. "We don't know how old that ship is. It could be hundreds of years old unto itself. And it's not of a particular era," said Szostak. "Oftentimes, the artists are not really reflecting back to other *Star Wars* societies, they're reflecting back to Ralph [McQuarrie,] Joe [Johnston,] and Nilo [Rodis-Jamero], those original designers. It's all coming from the same place, and it's a kind of *Star Wars* shape language. It's not so much reflective of a time as it is just reflective of *Star Wars*."

"The prequels were very helpful because they were chasing that handcrafted 'gilded age' of *Star Wars*," said Hidalgo, "the more artisanal age, as opposed to the boilerplate, machine-stamped-on-a-conveyor-belt Imperials."

The main restriction across the board was avoiding an origin story for an iconic design, like a C-3PO-model protocol droid or the prototype Imperial TIE fighter. "But everything else is fair game as long as it just feels appropriate," said Szostak. "*Star Wars* is historical by nature. It's not futuristic, and continuing the design language is something that feels of a culture versus something that's just wildly fantastical."

A key tenet in *Star Wars* design requires every hero, villain, ship, and place to be readable at a glance and easily replicated by a child capable of sketching only the most basic shapes. The densely populated worlds are often explored at a breakneck pace, with little time to stop and stare. Behind the scenes, those working on vetting the designs for The High Republic adhered to a three-second rule, "understanding at a glance," Szostak said. "Everything's got to be good or evil and it has to read clearly," added concept artist Grant Griffin.

Since *Star Wars* is space fantasy, not science fiction, there's still generous creative freedom to stretch the boundaries of our own physical world. "We don't want anything too outlandish," said Lucasfilm senior editor Robert Simpson, "but it is kind of fun to see how far afield we can go with certain ship designs." And storytellers did not have to factor in the added expense of making their chosen designs a reality—at least not yet. "There were no budget restrictions to putting certain aliens or certain effects in a book because, you know, you don't have to make it real," said Hidalgo. "Your imagination makes it real, and that has no budget."

But the wealth of concept art for ships and other designs in this initiative speaks to a general scarcity in the publishing industry. "It's rare that we have art for stuff that only exists in a novel unless that novel is being translated into a visual medium," said Hidalgo. "If a character ends up appearing in a comic book or appearing in a video game, that's when they get their visual identity. It's super rare for that to come first."

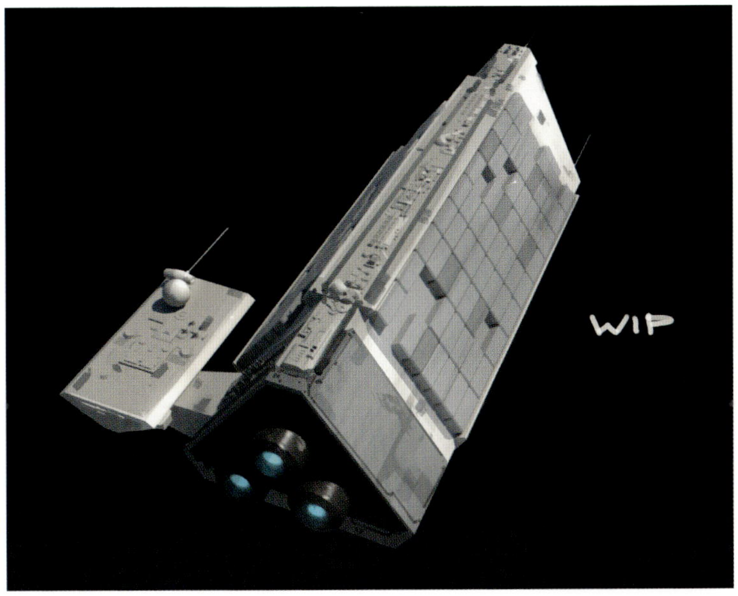

▲ Unused freighter concept TENERY

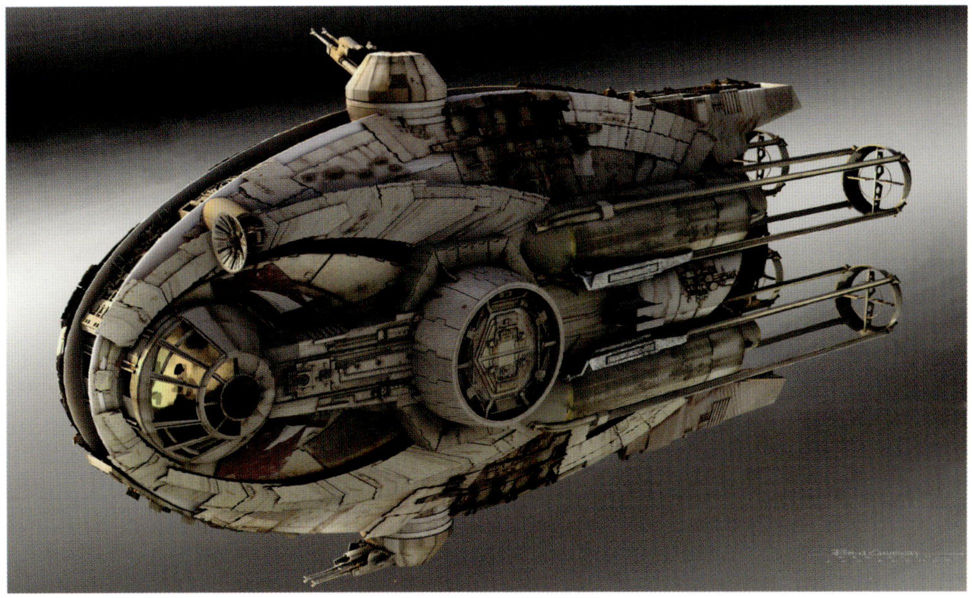

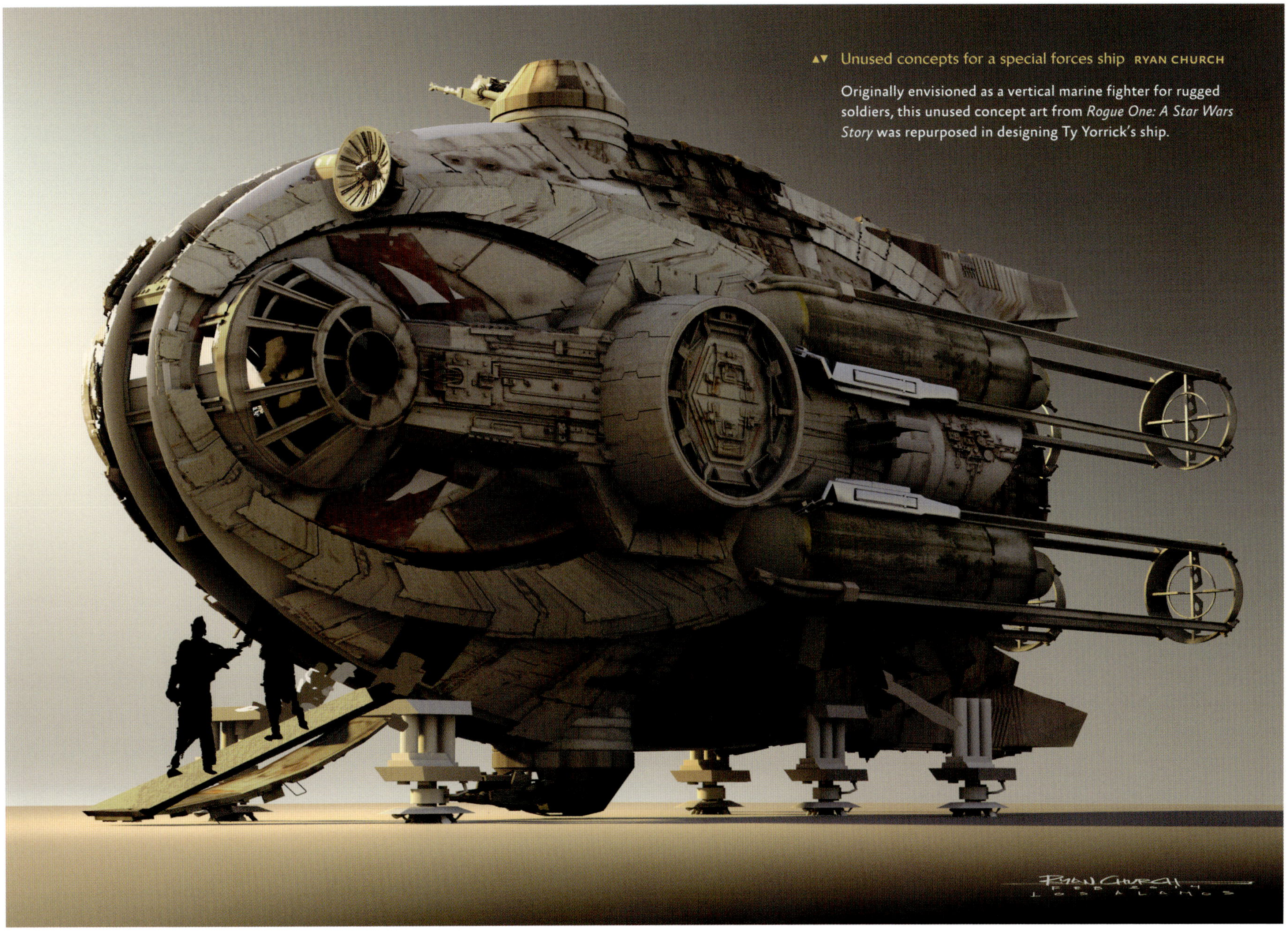

▲▼ Unused concepts for a special forces ship RYAN CHURCH

Originally envisioned as a vertical marine fighter for rugged soldiers, this unused concept art from *Rogue One: A Star Wars Story* was repurposed in designing Ty Yorrick's ship.

▼ Unused *Return of the Jedi* speeders McQUARRIE

Created by Ralph McQuarrie for *Return of the Jedi*, these previously unseen speeder bike concepts have become the design inspiration for Ty Yorrick's agile craft.

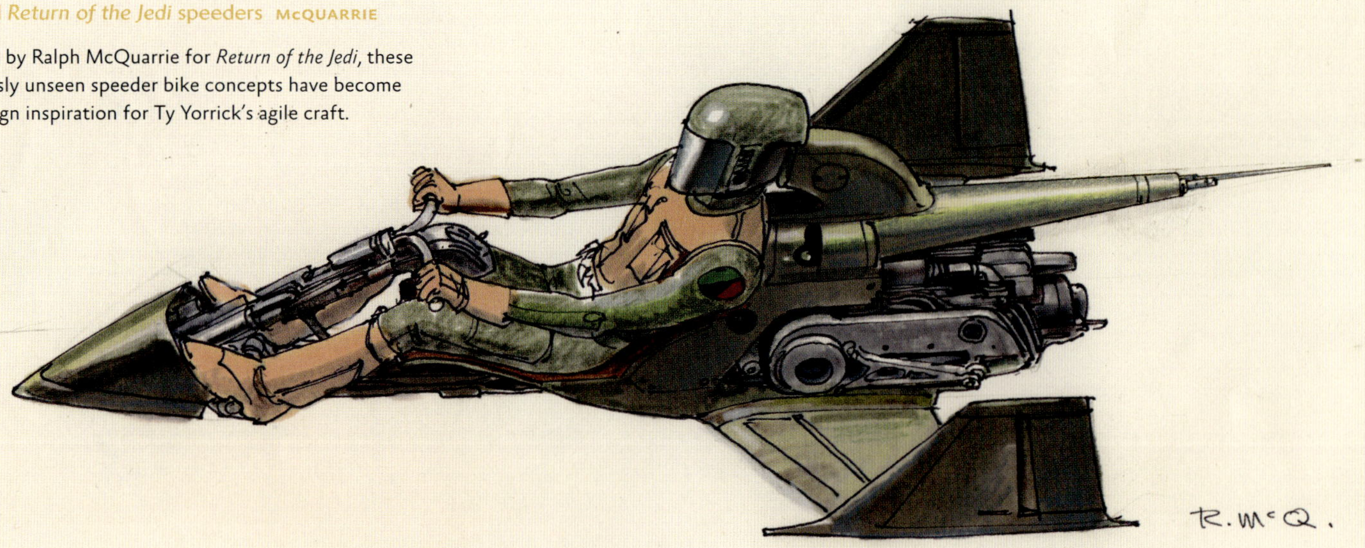

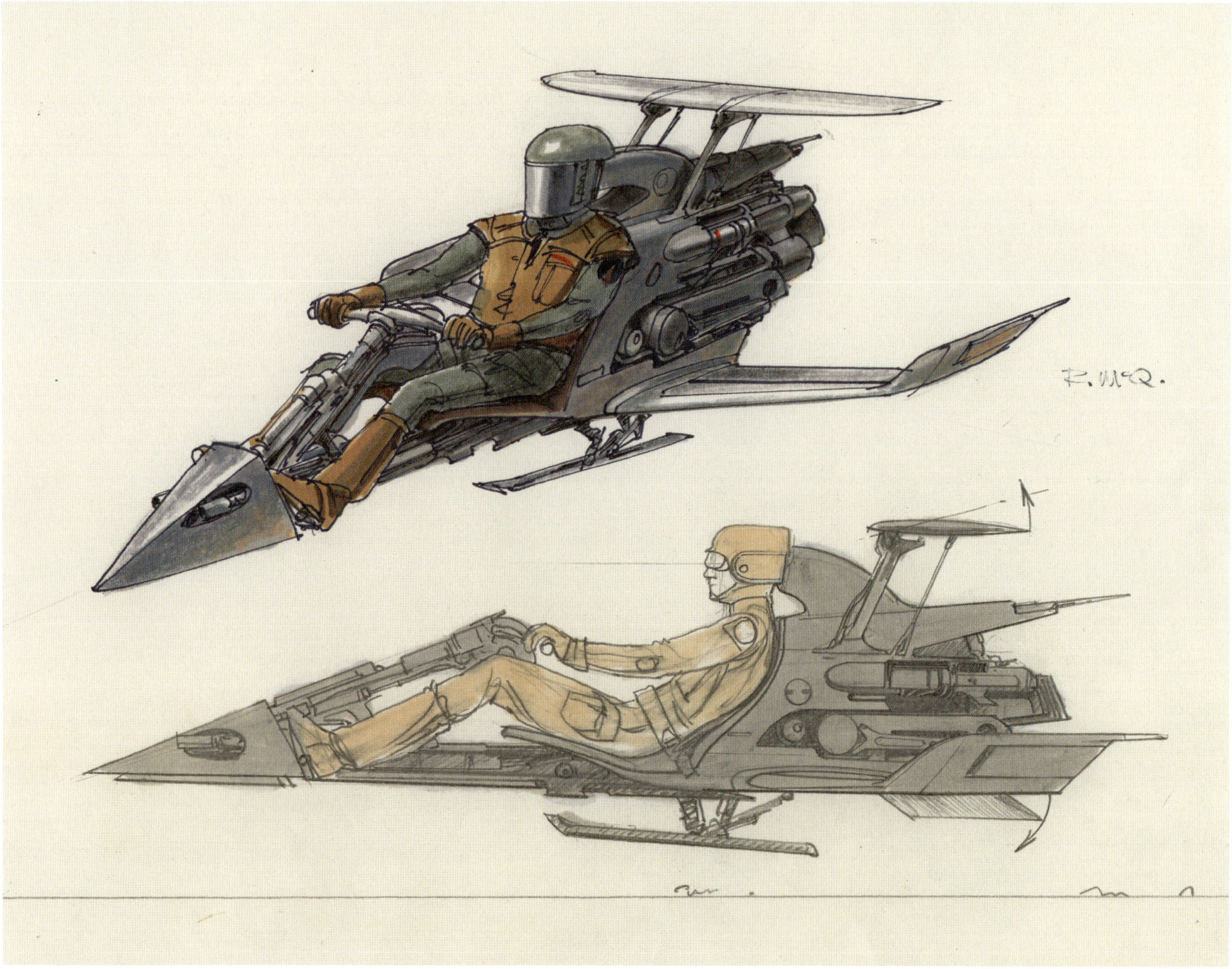

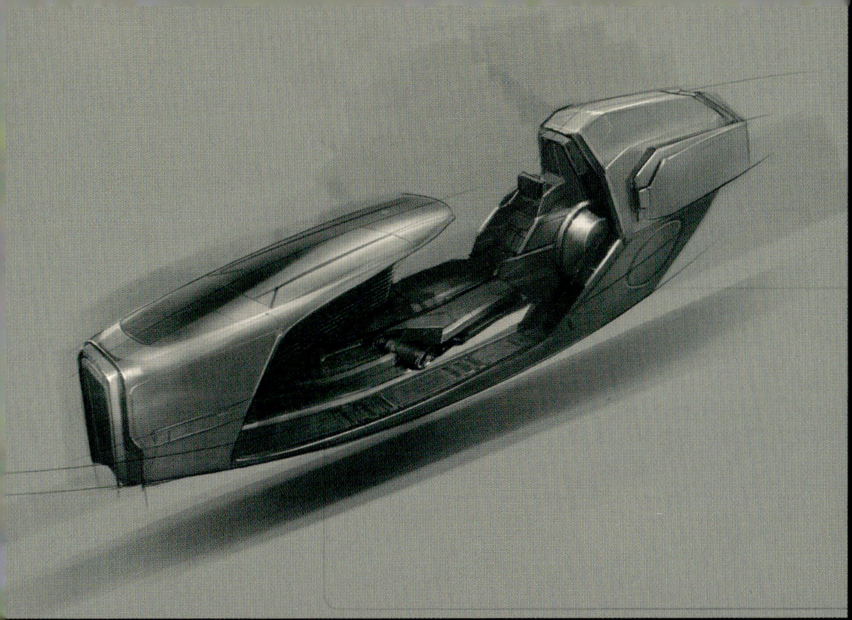

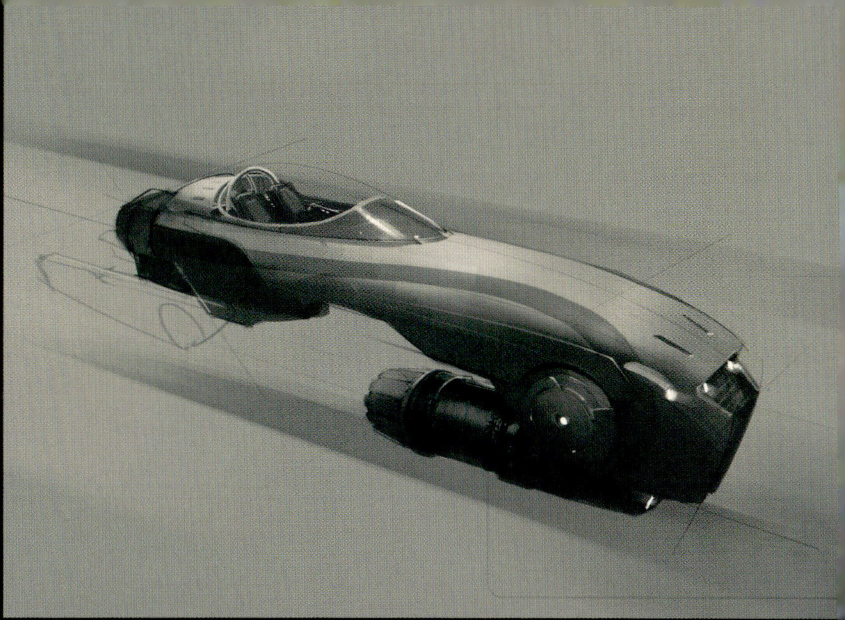

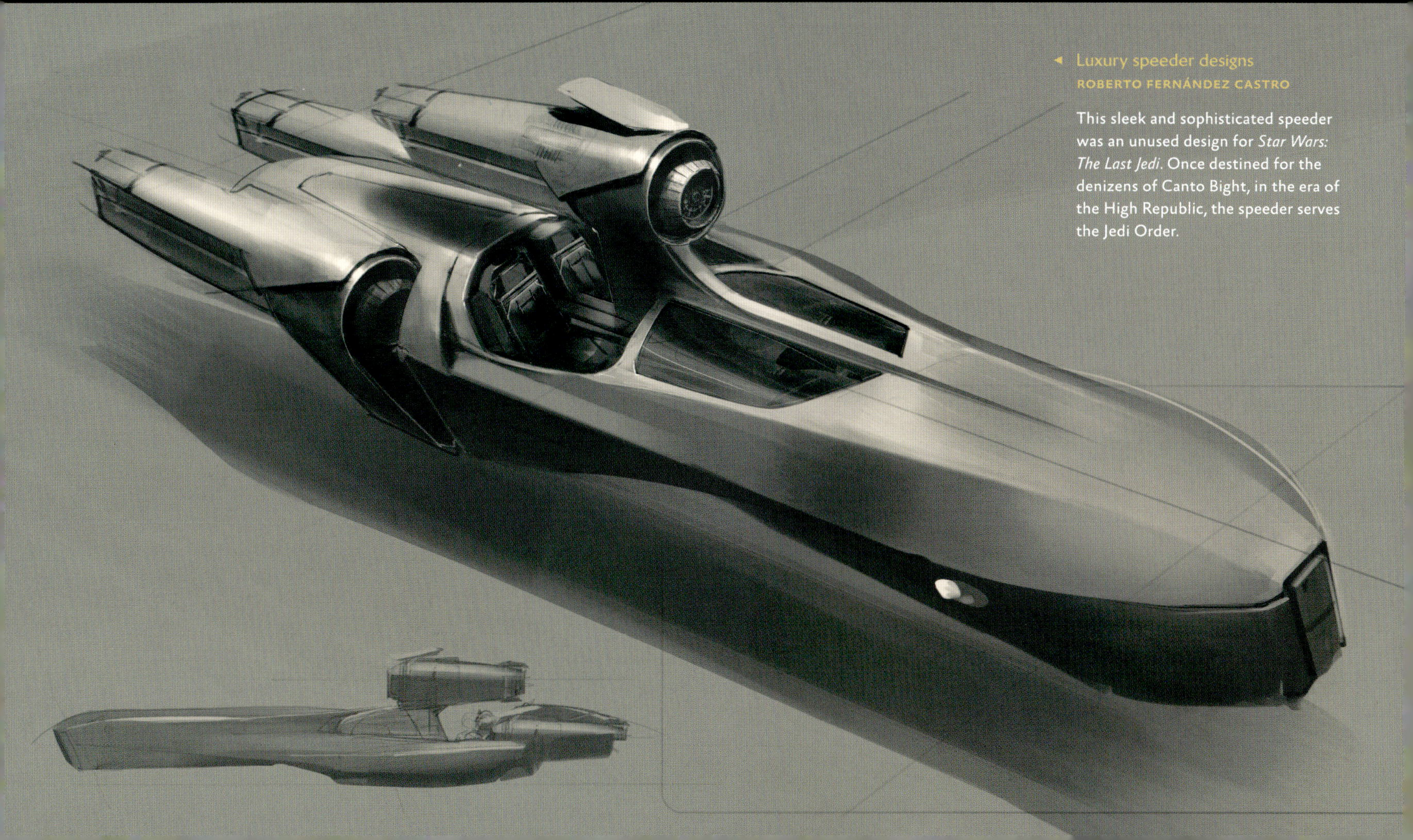

◂ Luxury speeder designs
ROBERTO FERNÁNDEZ CASTRO

This sleek and sophisticated speeder was an unused design for *Star Wars: The Last Jedi*. Once destined for the denizens of Canto Bight, in the era of the High Republic, the speeder serves the Jedi Order.

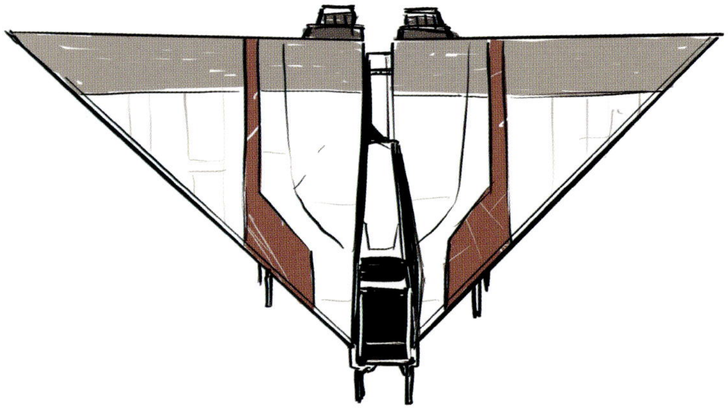

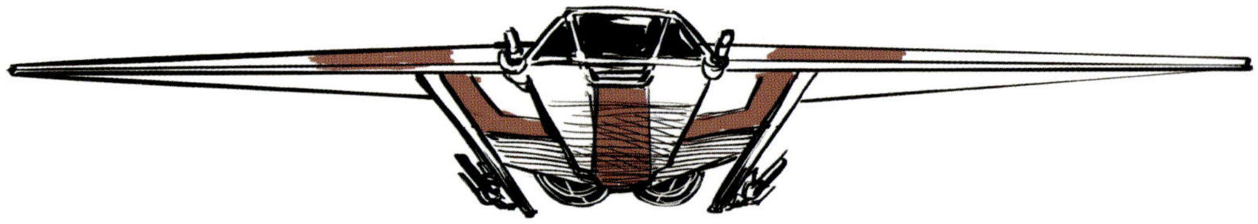

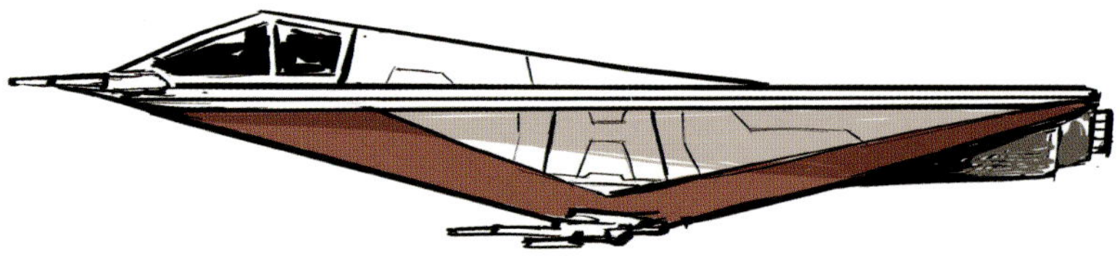

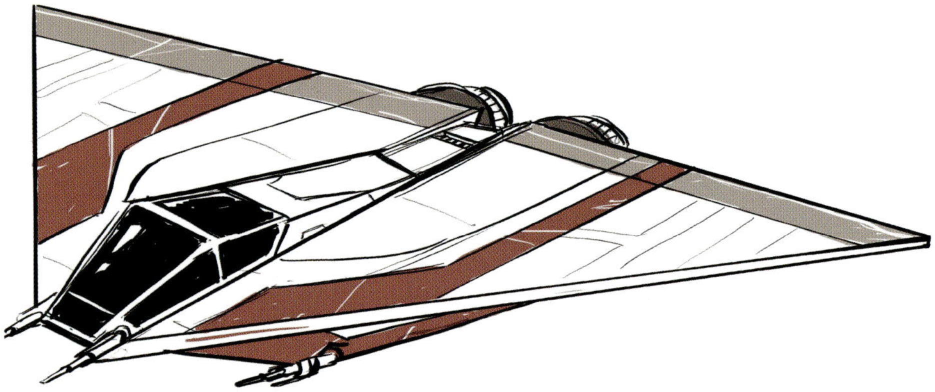

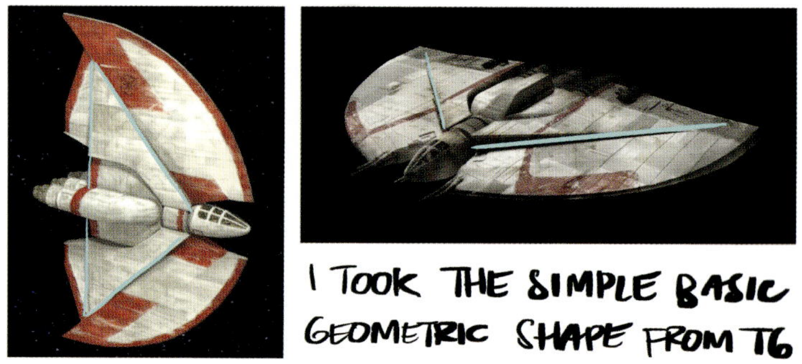

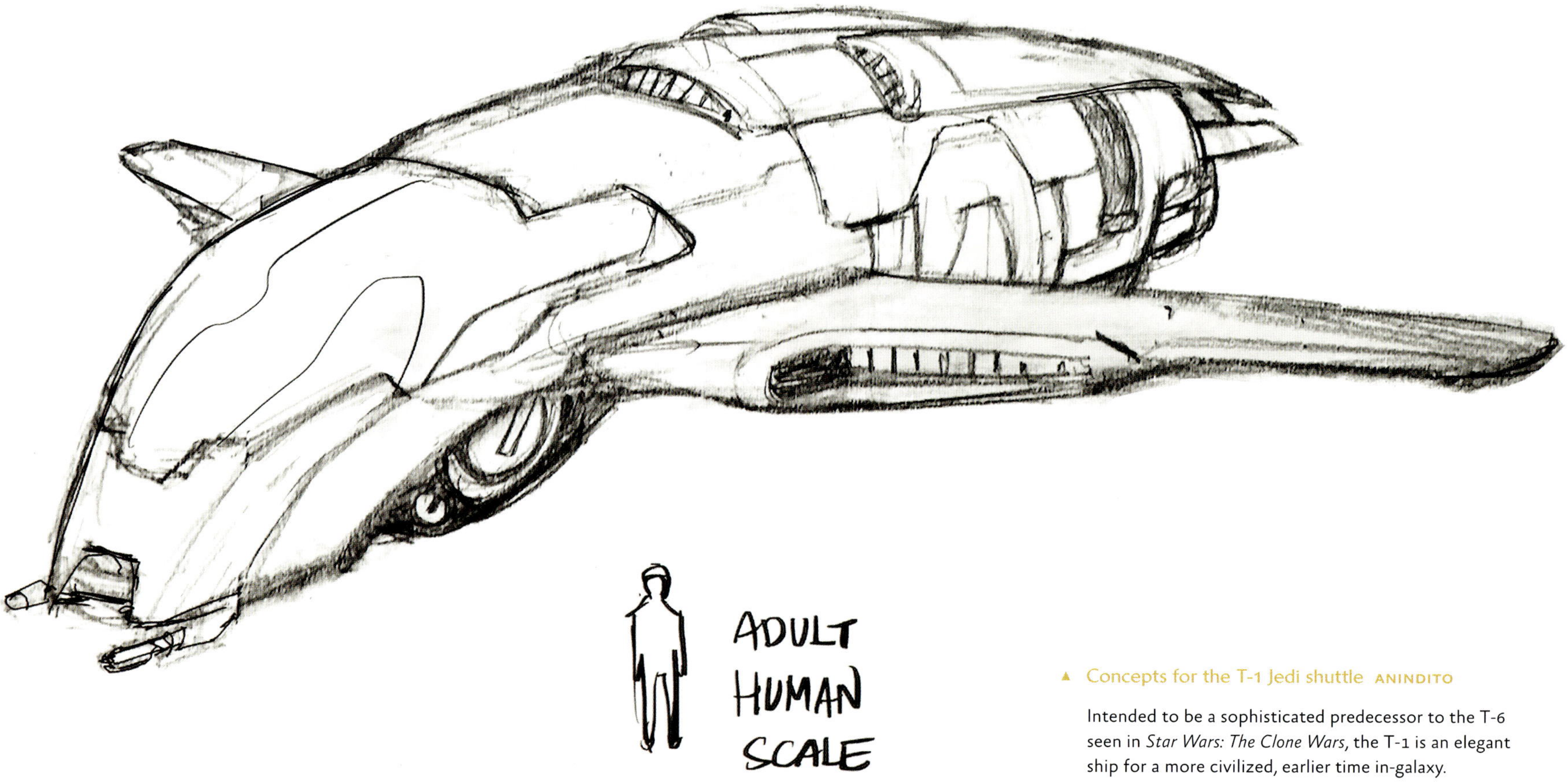

▲ Concepts for the T-1 Jedi shuttle ANINDITO

Intended to be a sophisticated predecessor to the T-6 seen in *Star Wars: The Clone Wars*, the T-1 is an elegant ship for a more civilized, earlier time in-galaxy.

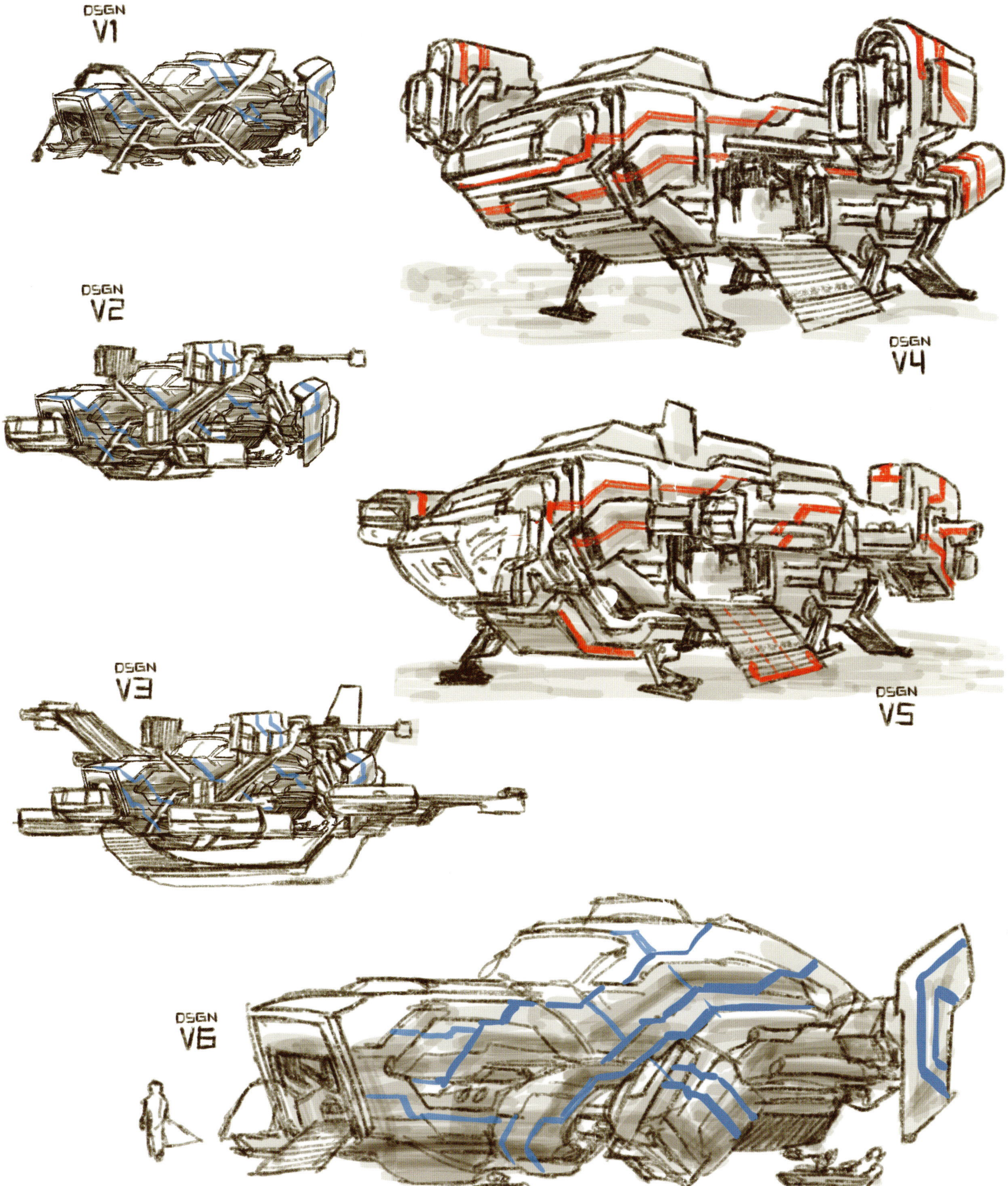

▸ Jedi medical frigate TOLIBAO

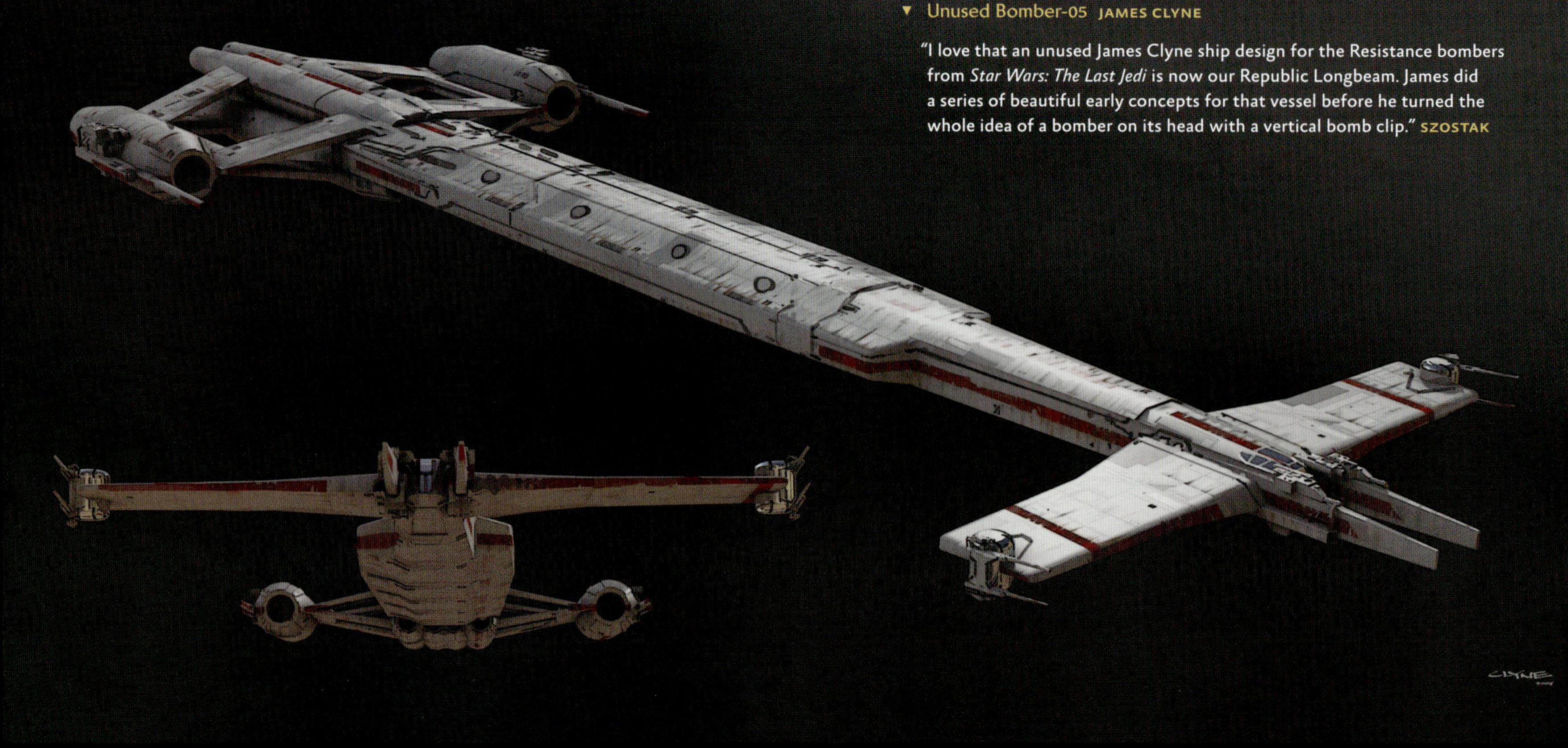

▼ Unused Bomber-05 **JAMES CLYNE**

"I love that an unused James Clyne ship design for the Resistance bombers from *Star Wars: The Last Jedi* is now our Republic Longbeam. James did a series of beautiful early concepts for that vessel before he turned the whole idea of a bomber on its head with a vertical bomb clip." **SZOSTAK**

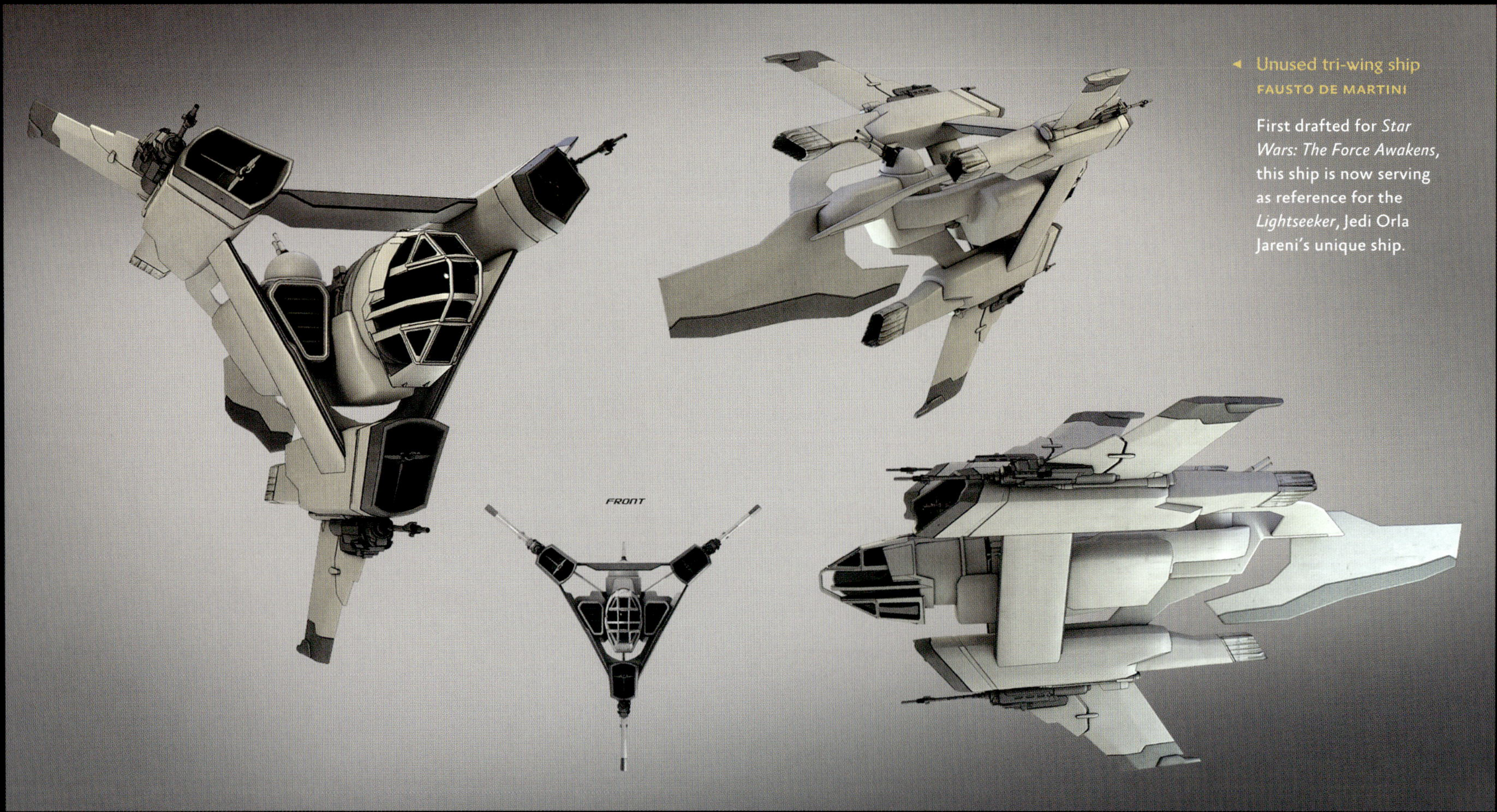

◄ Unused tri-wing ship **FAUSTO DE MARTINI**

First drafted for *Star Wars: The Force Awakens*, this ship is now serving as reference for the *Lightseeker*, Jedi Orla Jareni's unique ship.

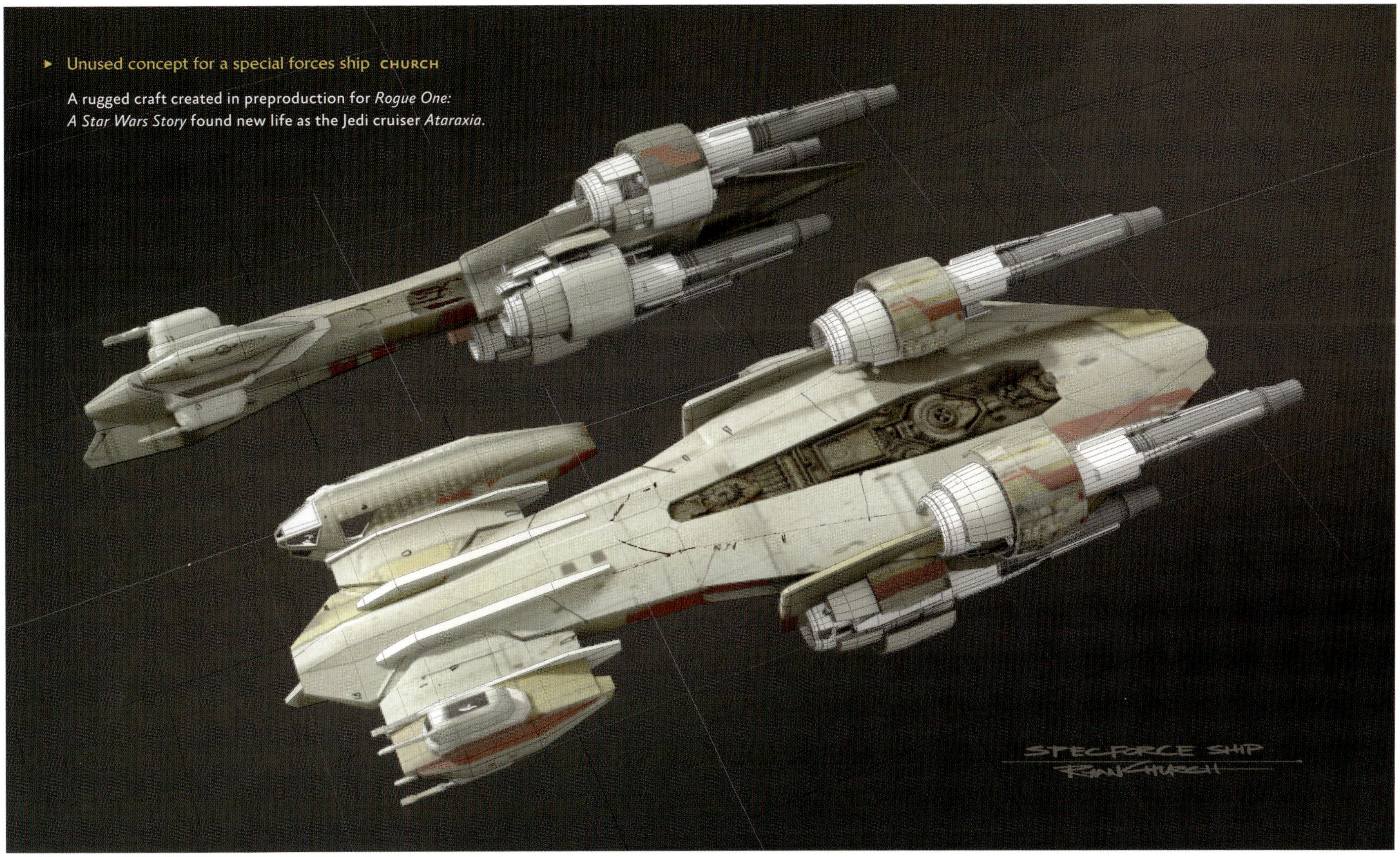

▸ Unused concept for a special forces ship **CHURCH**

A rugged craft created in preproduction for *Rogue One: A Star Wars Story* found new life as the Jedi cruiser *Ataraxia*.

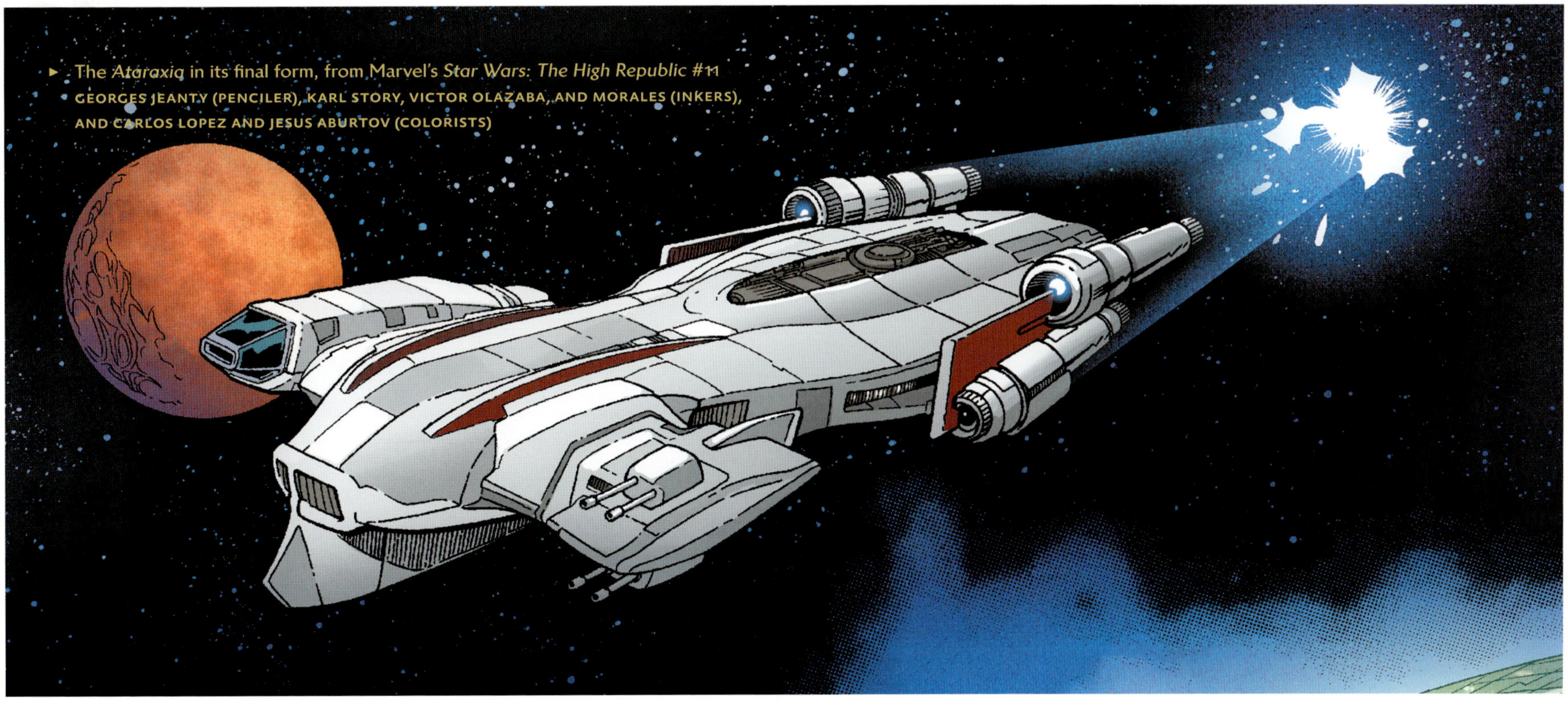

▸ The *Ataraxia* in its final form, from Marvel's *Star Wars: The High Republic* #11
GEORGES JEANTY (PENCILER), KARL STORY, VICTOR OLAZABA, AND MORALES (INKERS), AND CARLOS LOPEZ AND JESUS ABURTOV (COLORISTS)

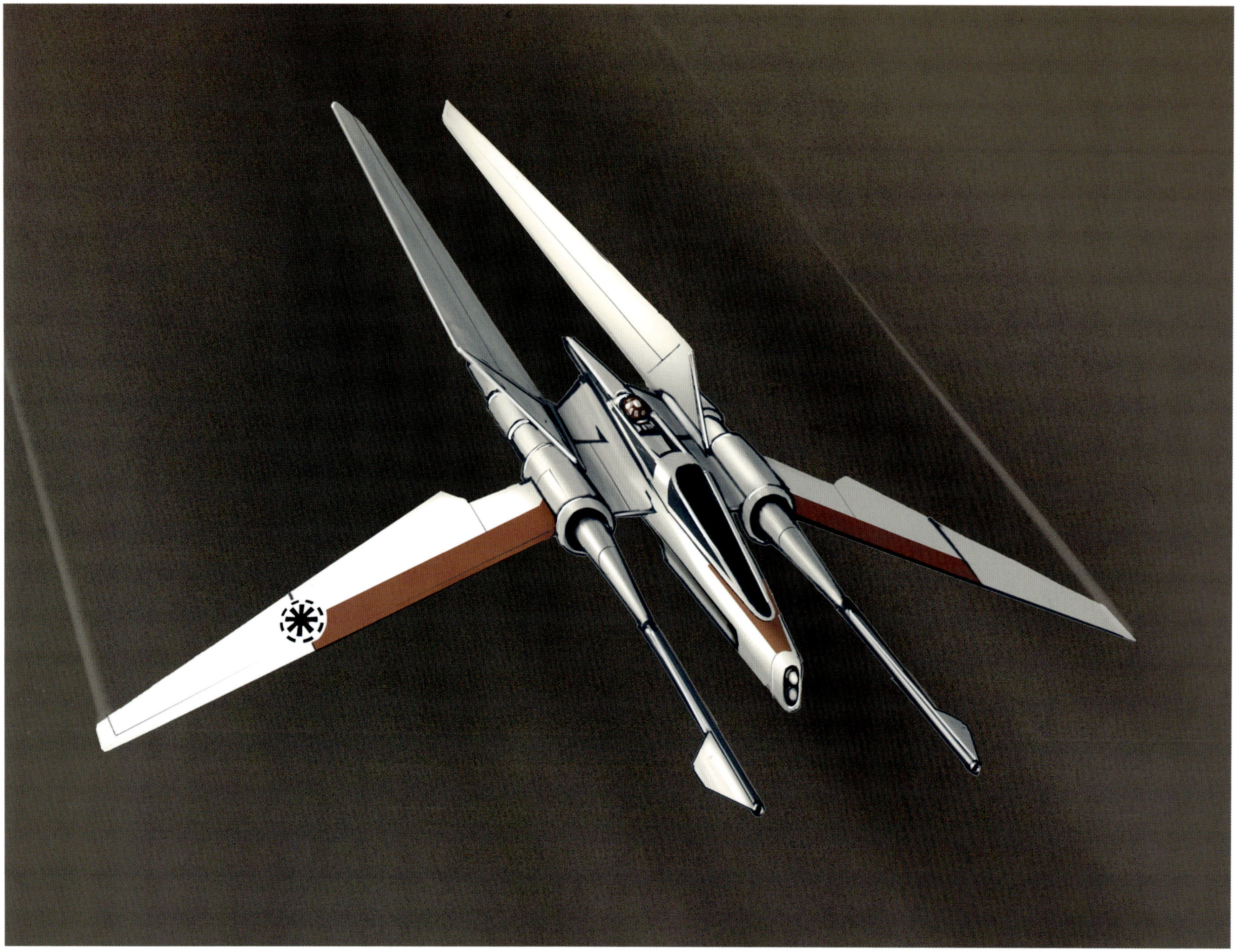

▲ Republic Clone skyfighter WARREN FU

Created for *Star Wars: Revenge of the Sith*, this sleek starfighter was the inspiration behind the Jedi Vector, with one small change. Instead of a socket for an astromech droid, the cockpits of the Vectors are elongated to allow room for Jedi masters to travel with their apprentices. "The Jedi, especially in this era, aren't necessarily looking for a starfighter that's going to be suitable for war because there is no war, no enemy that they're fighting," said Szostak. "It's a time of peace. And so, I think a ship like the Vector is kind of appropriate for this time. You see it from a distance: here come the Jedi. You know, it's not just the some boxy, utilitarian ship."

▸ Jedi *Star Hopper* TOLIBAO

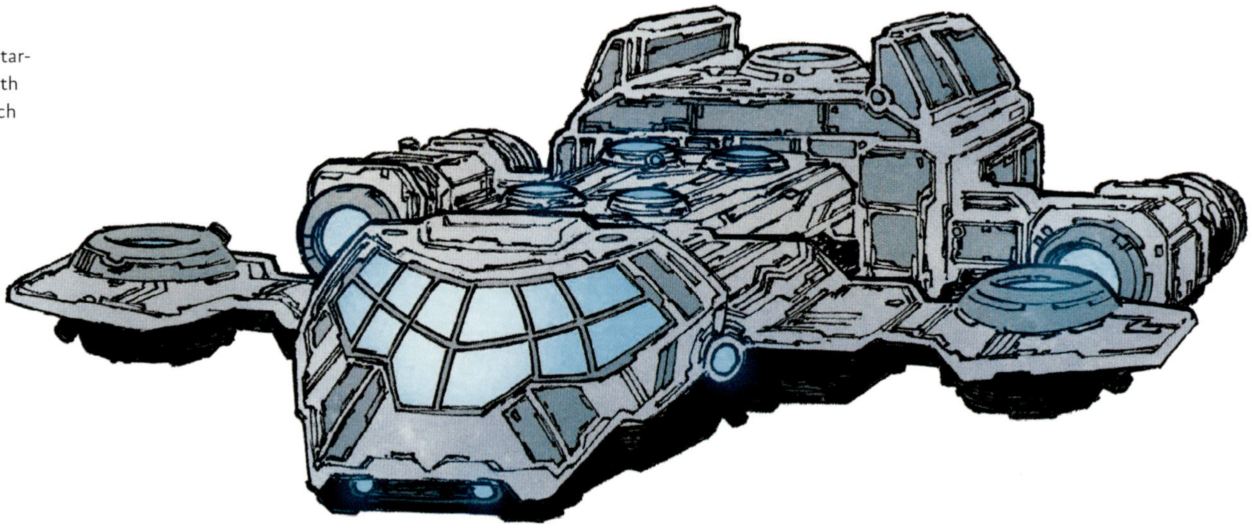

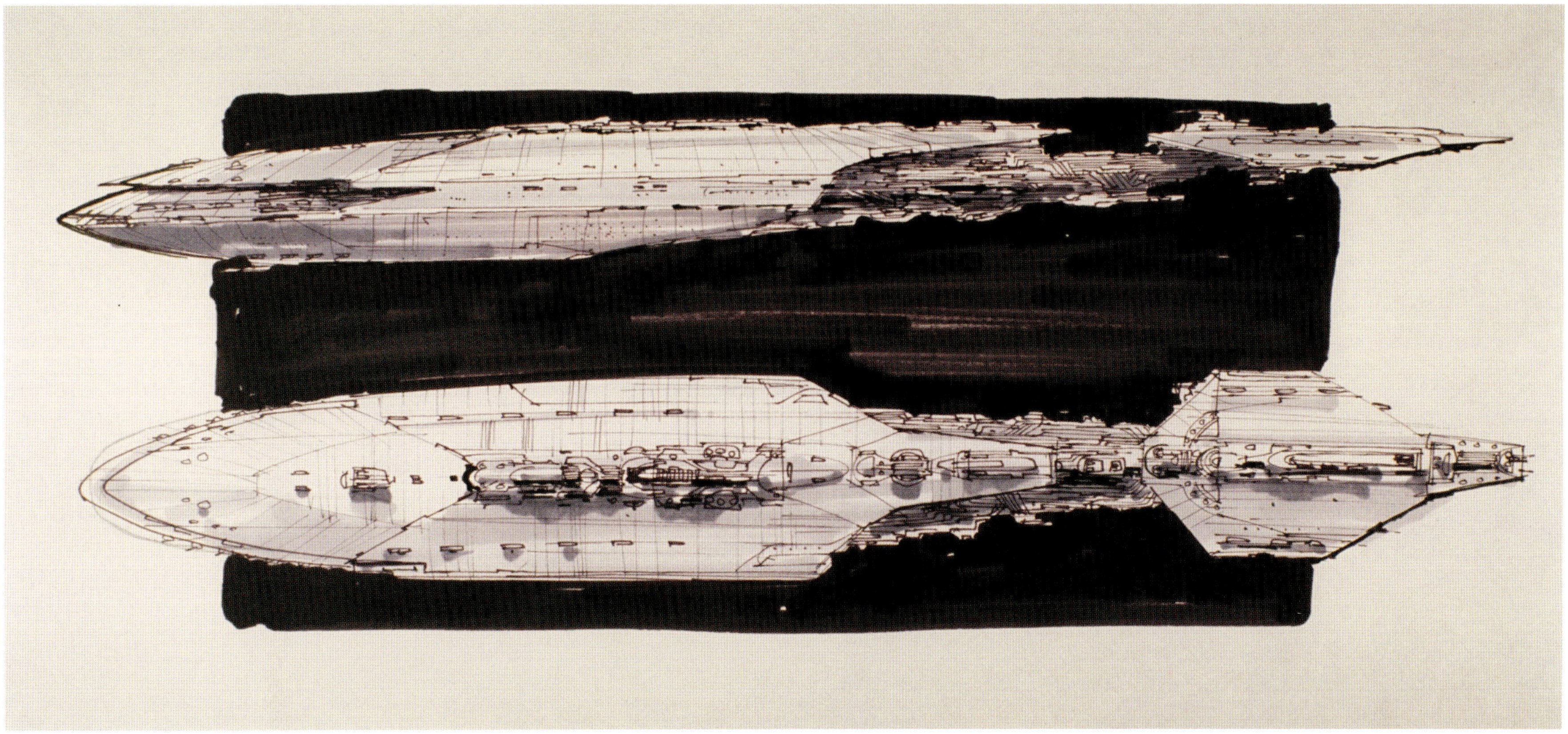

▲ Unused starship JOE JOHNSTON

A concept design from *Star Wars: Return of the Jedi* was the inspiration behind the first ideations on the Nihil's command vessel the *Gaze Electric*.

► Sketch of Nihil ship BROKENSHIRE

▼ Final design for the *Gaze Electric* from IDW's *Star Wars Adventures* (2021) #6 BROKENSHIRE

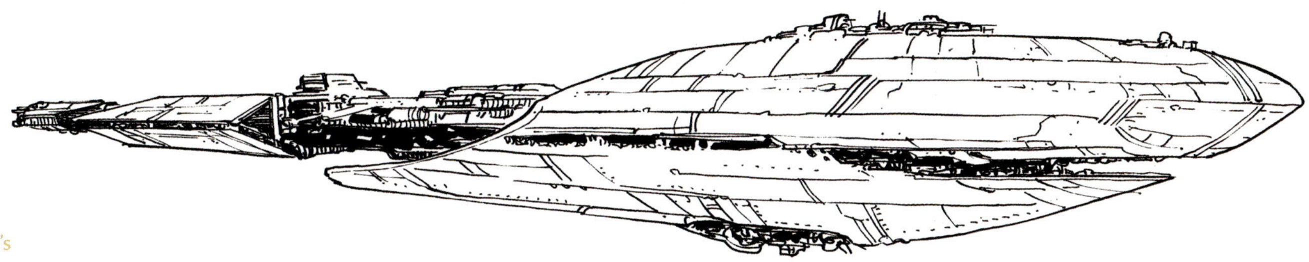

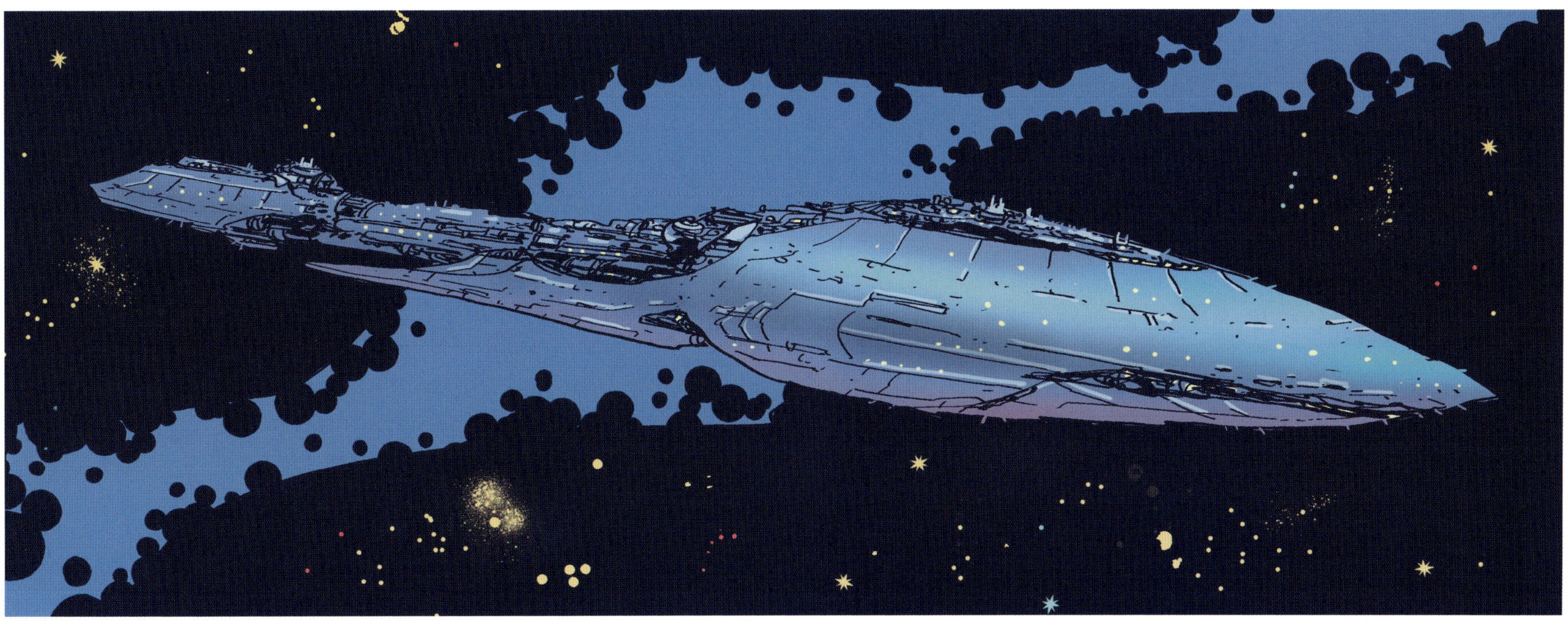

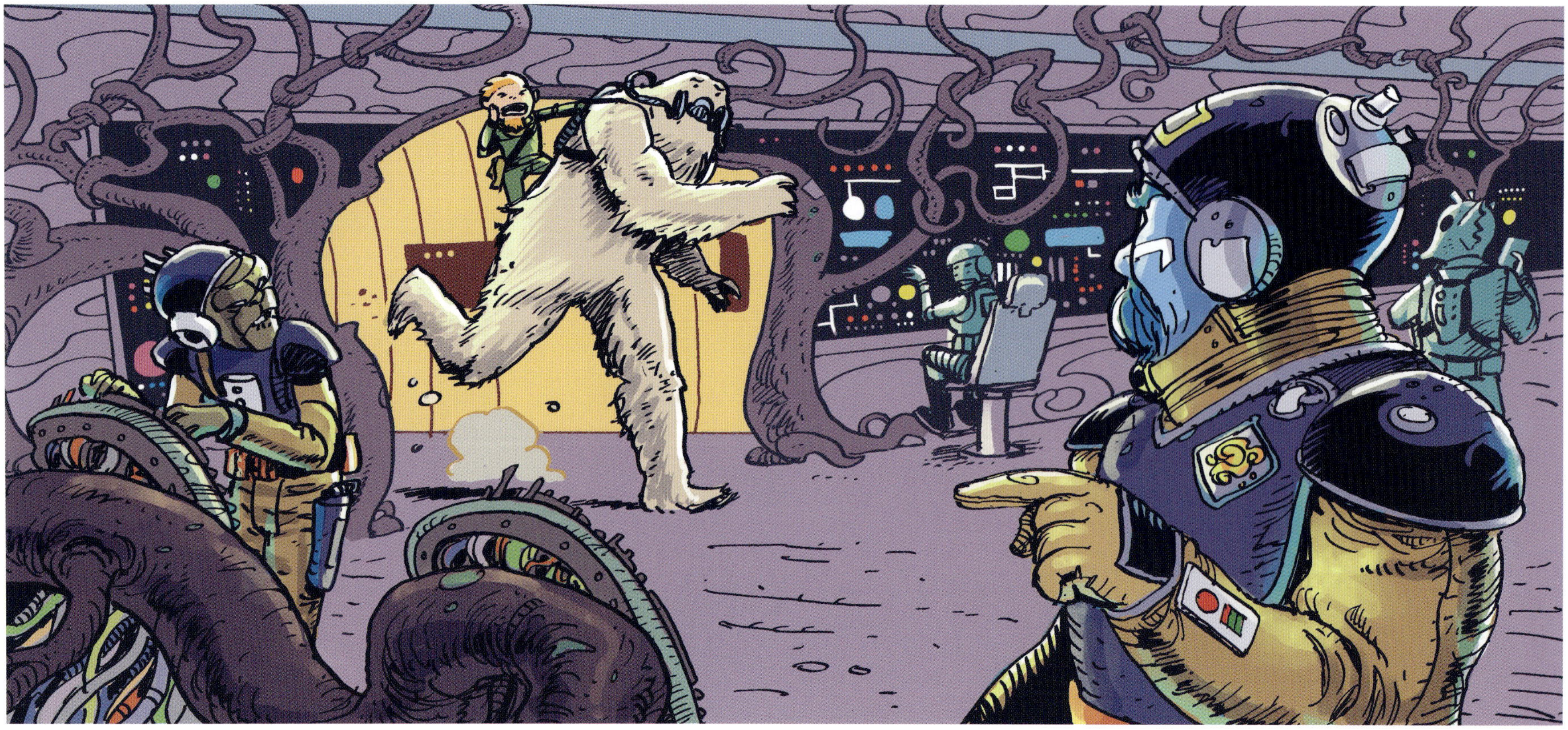

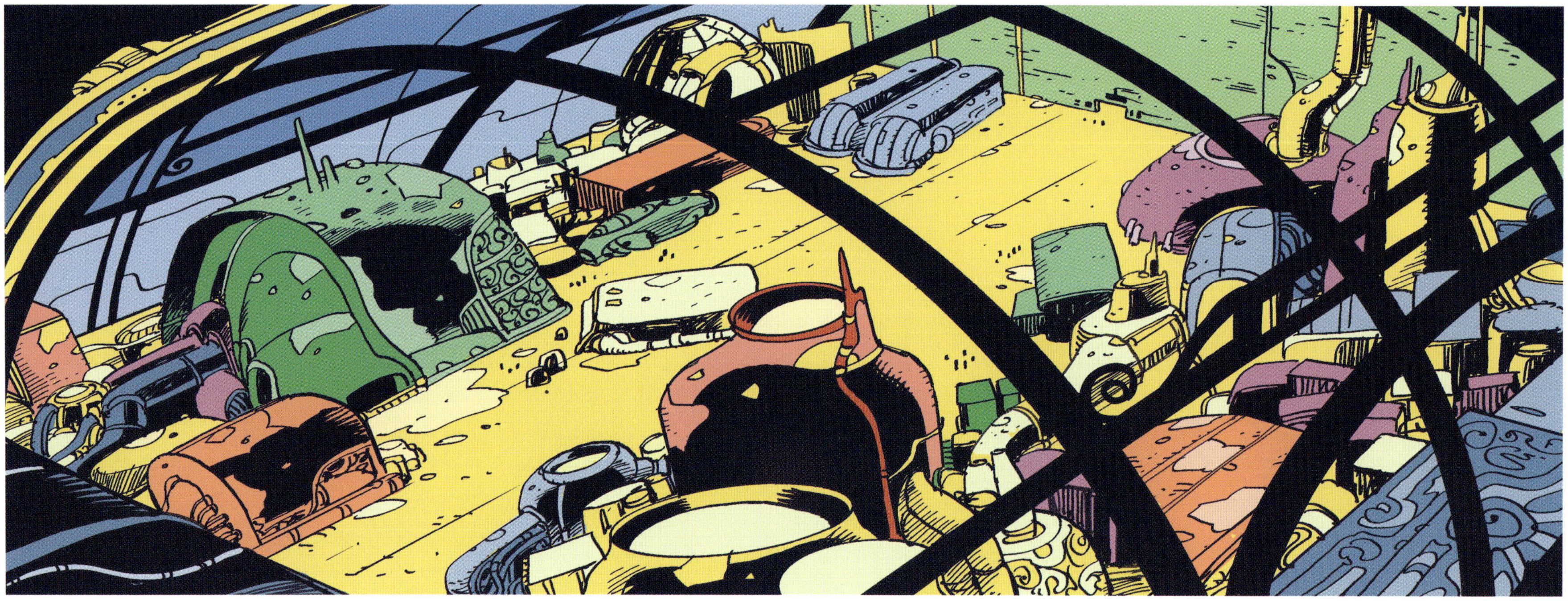

▲ Interiors of the *Gaze Electric* from IDW's *Star Wars Adventures* (2021) #6 "The *Gaze Electric* interiors were tricky to design. The folks at Lucasfilm asked me to look at the design of the *Cygnus* from the movie *The Black Hole* and that led to me employing this wobbly art deco latticework. I liked the idea of being able to stand in the hallway and look up through these vast windows out into space. As for the colors, I like to reference the *Star Wars* comics of the '70s and '80s. In those days, color choices were based on using the limited color technology to make images pop and not to try and imitate reality. Sometimes Vader's armor would be green, and Chewie would be pink. It all depended on what the image was trying to accomplish. I very much subscribe to that approach in everything I do.

The bridge of the *Gaze Electric* was described as being made out of a wroshyr tree from Kashyyyk, and when I colored it originally it looked too much like the Drengir had overrun the ship, so we employed the old-school sensibility and colored it purple, because why *not* purple?" BROKENSHIRE

► Final design for the *Gaze Electric* from *Star Wars Adventures* (2021) #6 BROKENSHIRE

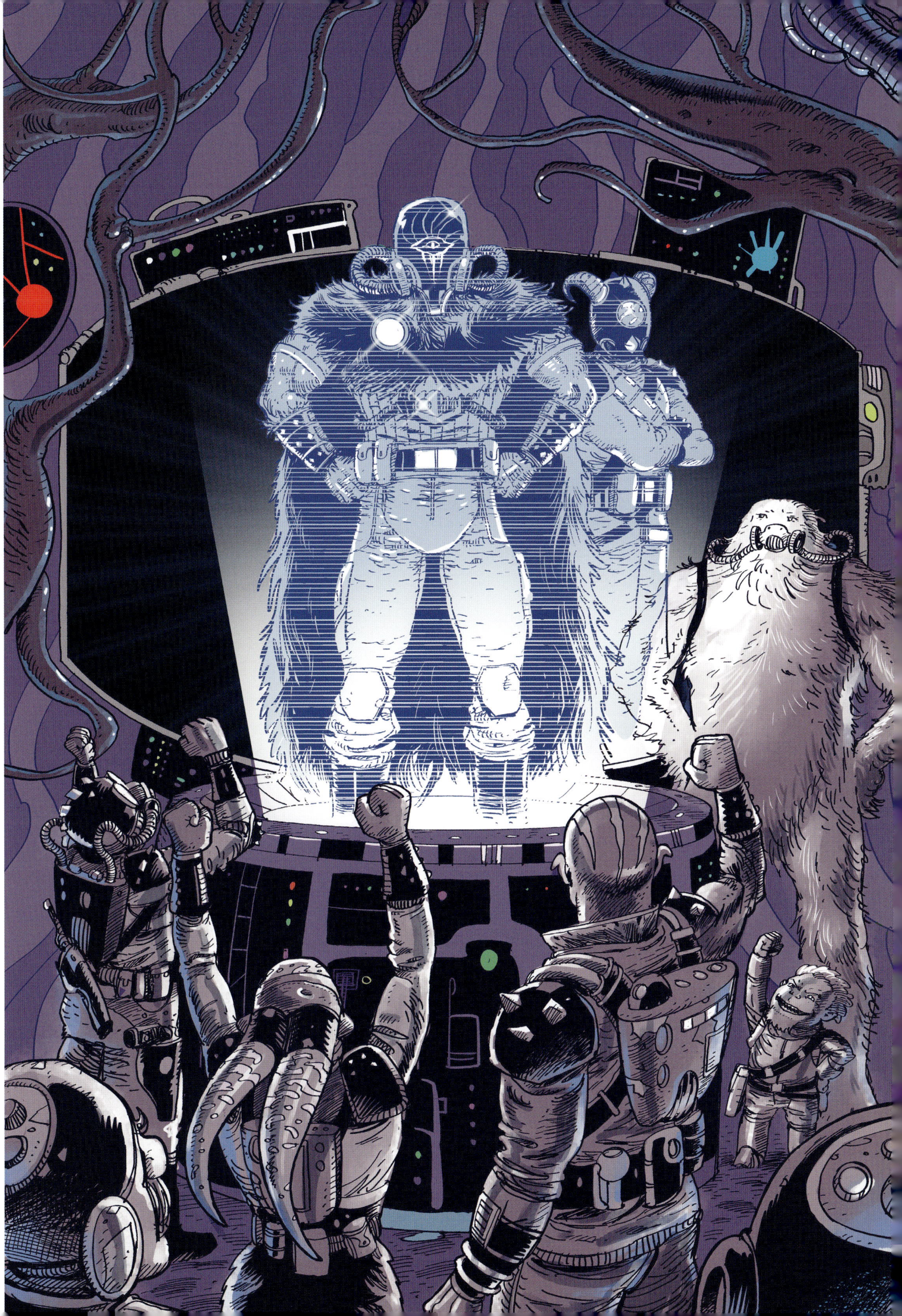

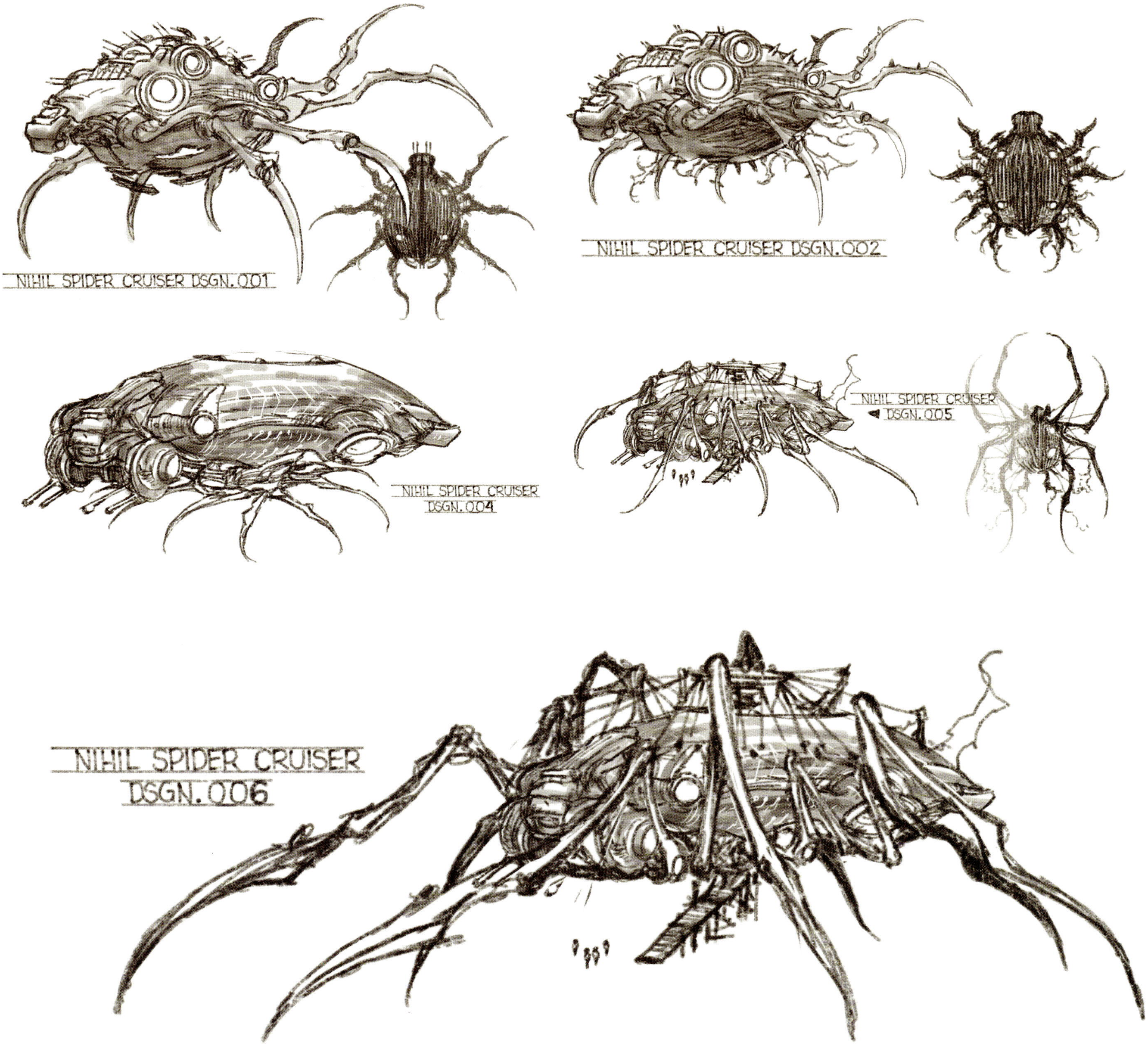

▲ Nihil Spider Cruiser designs 1, 2, 4, 5, 6 (final) TOLIBAO

"A lot of people tell me 'Harvey, you got that one from [the Will Smith film] *Wild Wild West*!' [*Laughs*] The spider represents a lot of things because spiders are smart in trapping insects and even birds in their web. For me, the Nihil is a different kind of race. They always betray the people that they do business with; these guys are not honest. The same with the spider; the spider's web is beautiful, and the insects get trapped and they get eaten. I wanted the feeling of an unfinished ship."

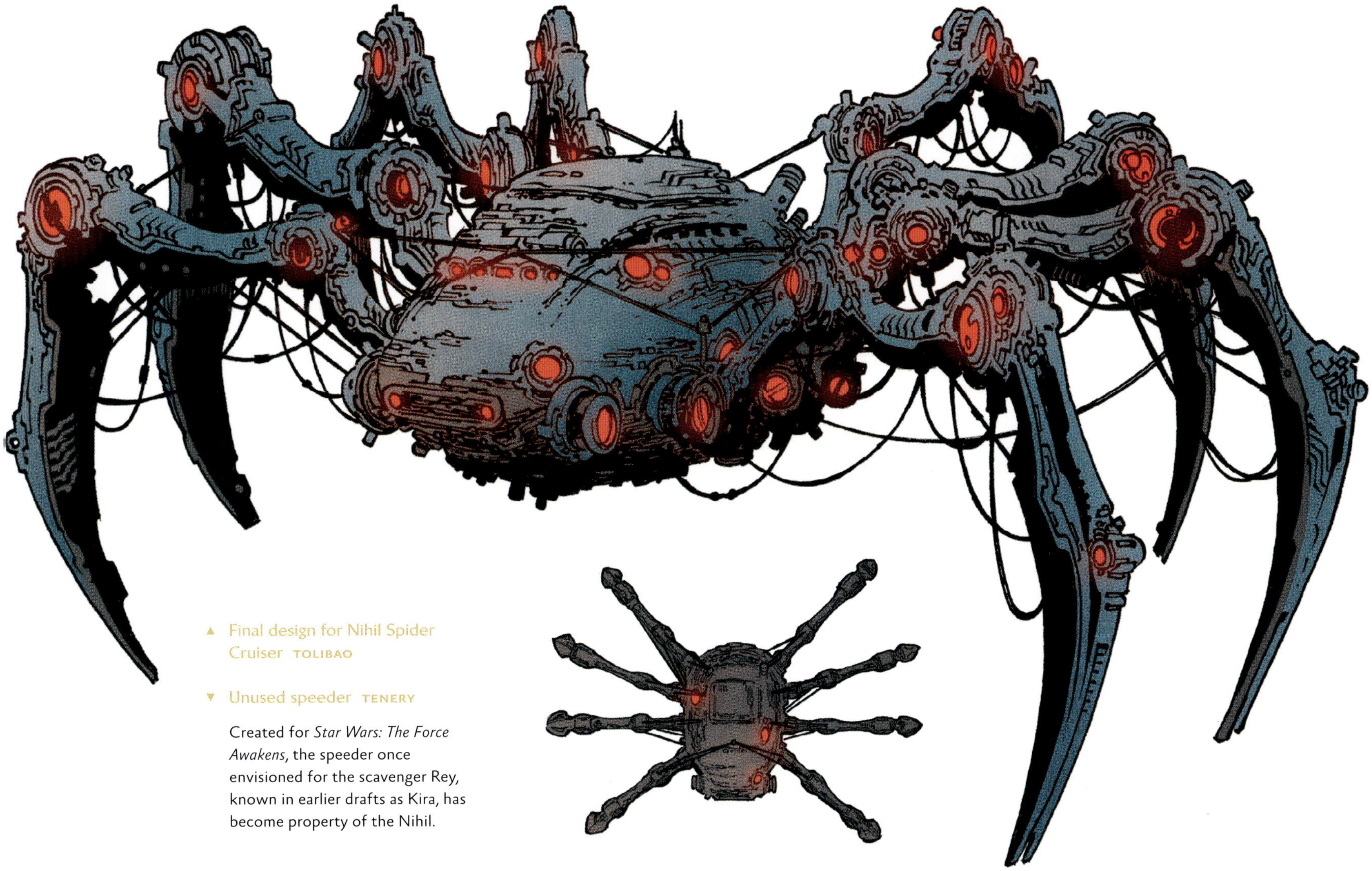

▲ Final design for Nihil Spider Cruiser TOLIBAO

▼ Unused speeder TENERY

Created for *Star Wars: The Force Awakens*, the speeder once envisioned for the scavenger Rey, known in earlier drafts as Kira, has become property of the Nihil.

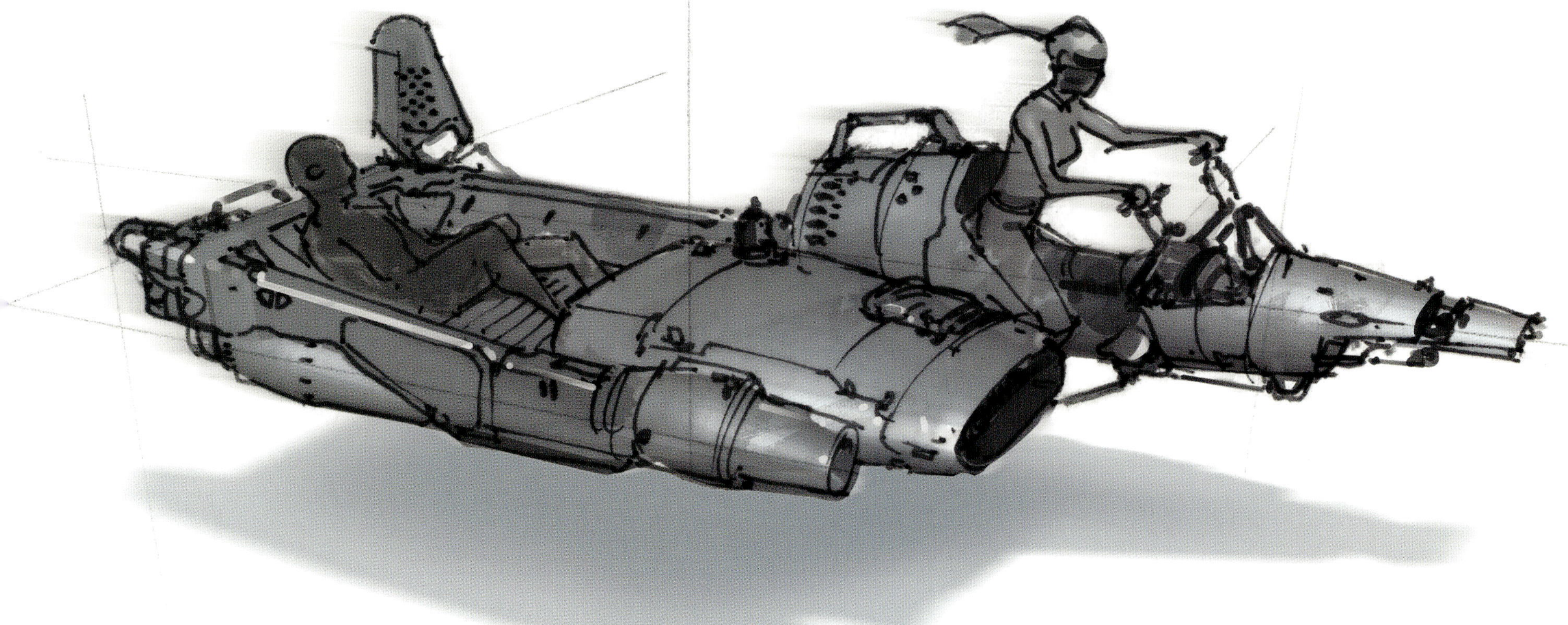

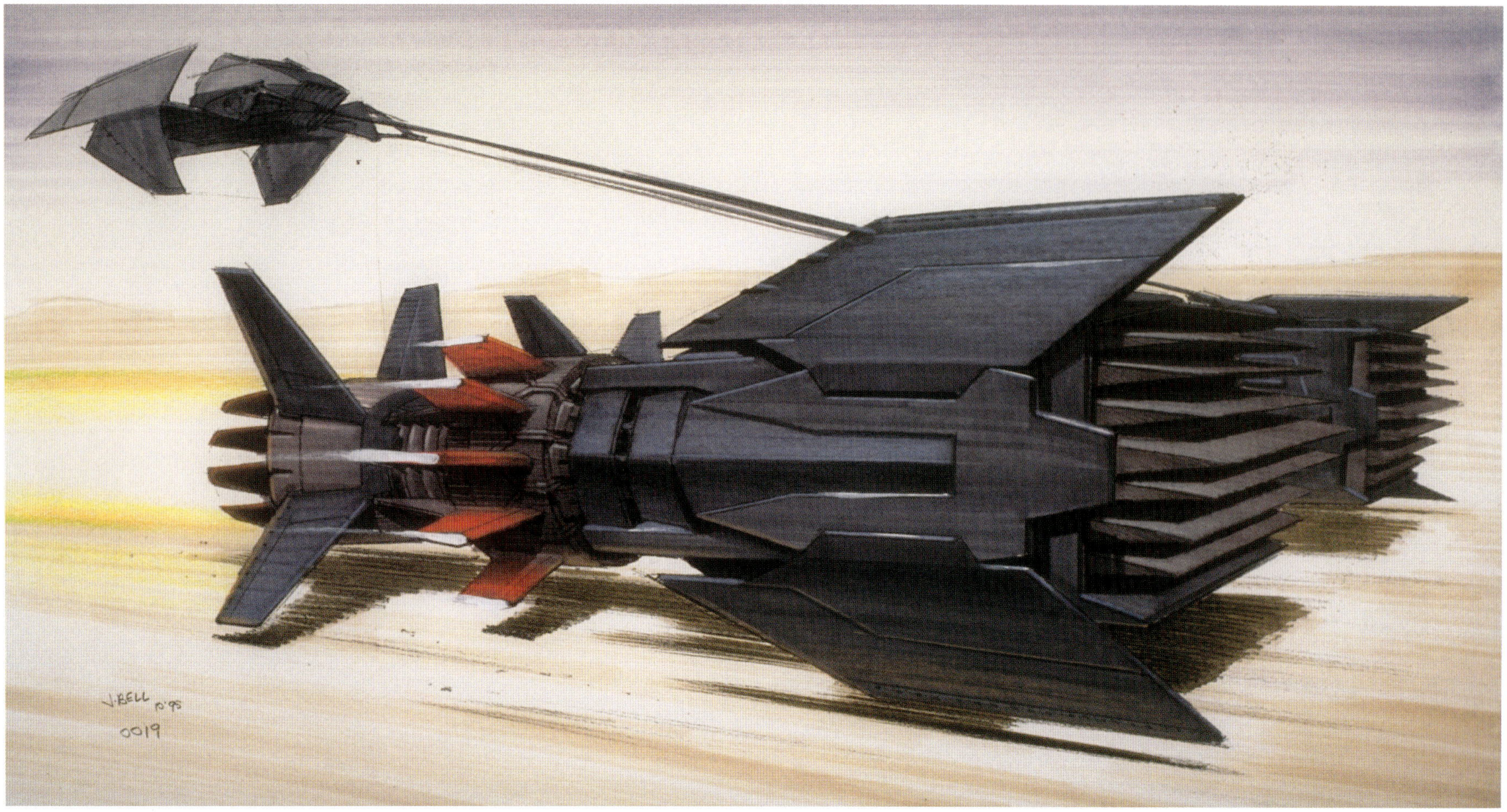

▲ Unused podracer design JOHN BELL

The spiky and aggressive feel of this early podracer design created for *The Phantom Menace* made an ideal concept for the Nihil stormships once the pilot's small pod was severed from the hulking engines and discarded.

► Sketch of Nihil ship BROKENSHIRE

▼ Sketch for Keeve Trennis's Nihil ship, the *Ransacker* "Because it's a Nihil stormship, I decided to make the front, the main hull or cockpit, look like Marchion Ro's mask with the round blue eye, with a round window. And I want it to be red because I want it to be like the one red eye coming at you is scary." ANINDITO

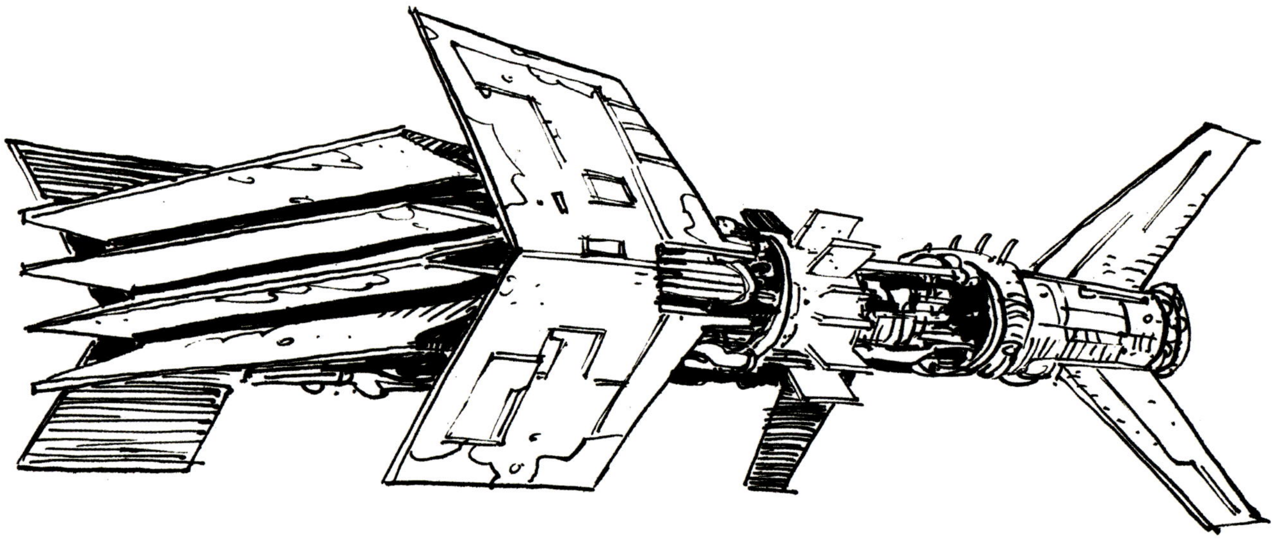

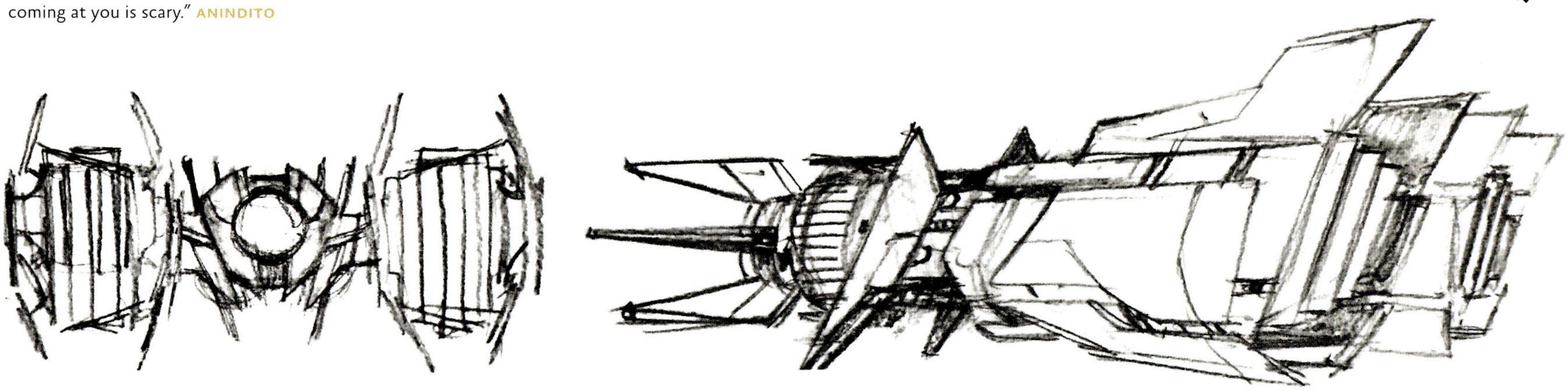

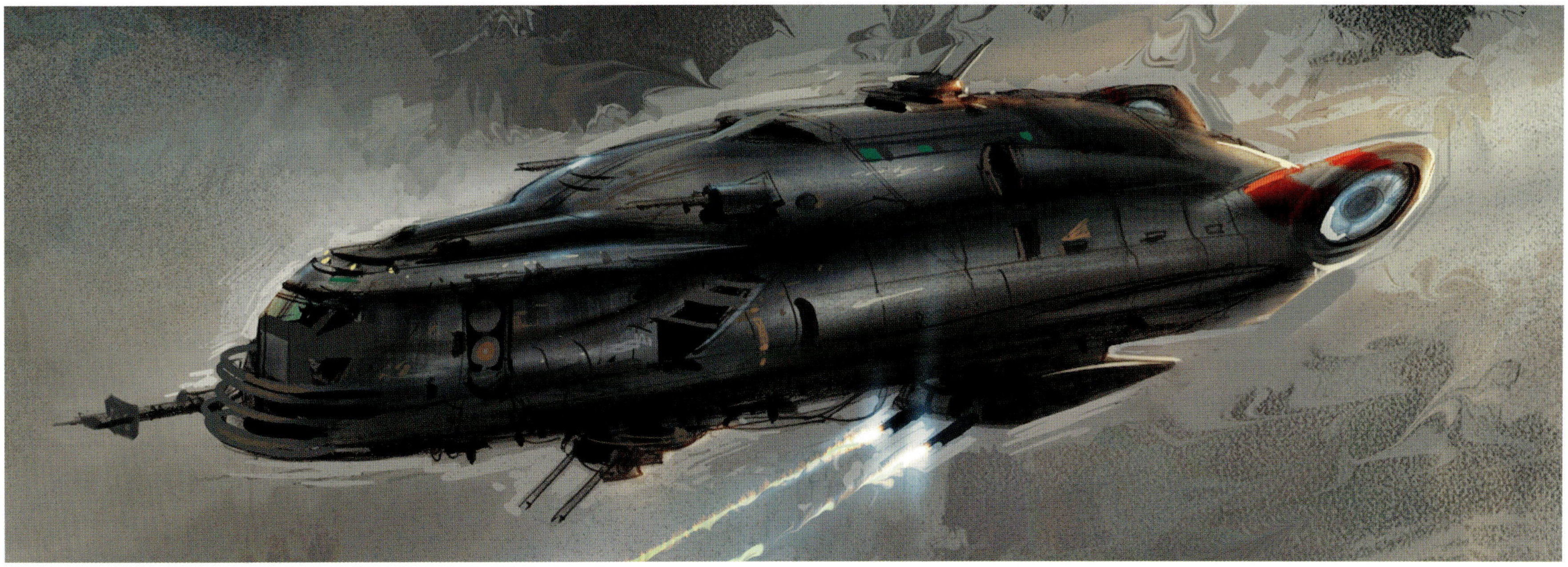

▲ Unused Republic gunship concept ERIK TIEMENS

Illustrated in 2002 during preproduction of *Star Wars: Revenge of the Sith*, an early design for the Republic warships now serves as the Tempest Runner Pan Eyta's ship, the *Elegencia*.

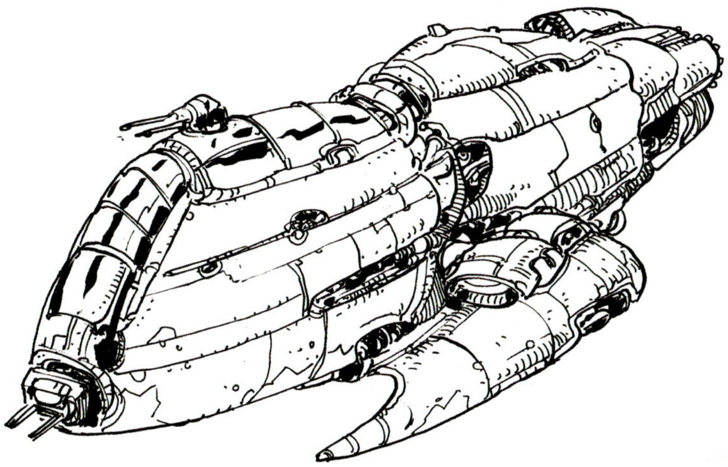

◄ Sketch of Nihil *New Elite* ship BROKENSHIRE

▼ Unused Republic gunship concept TIEMENS

Another unused gunship design became the *New Elite*, Nihil Tempest Runner Kassav Milliko's ship in *Light of the Jedi*.

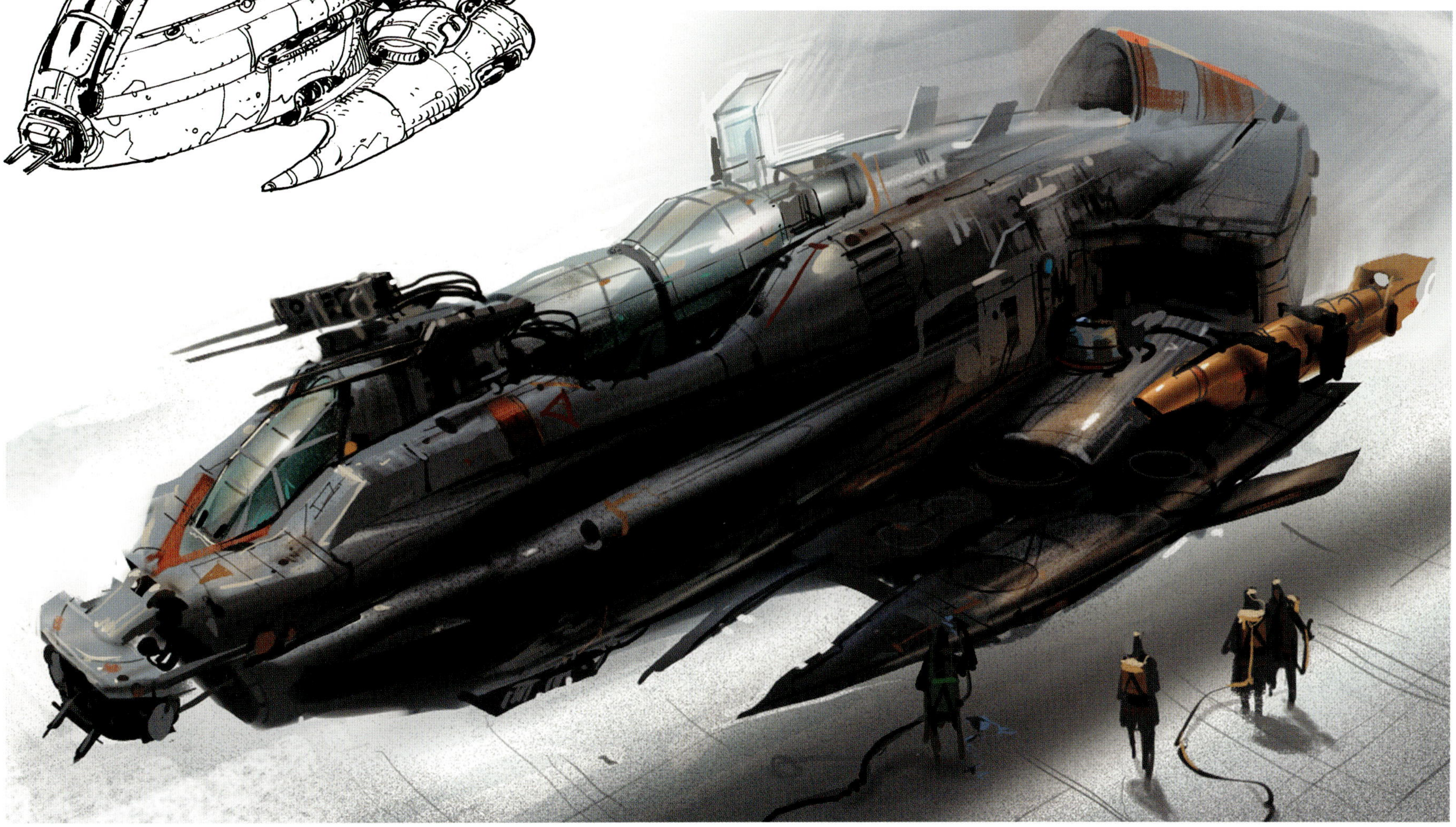

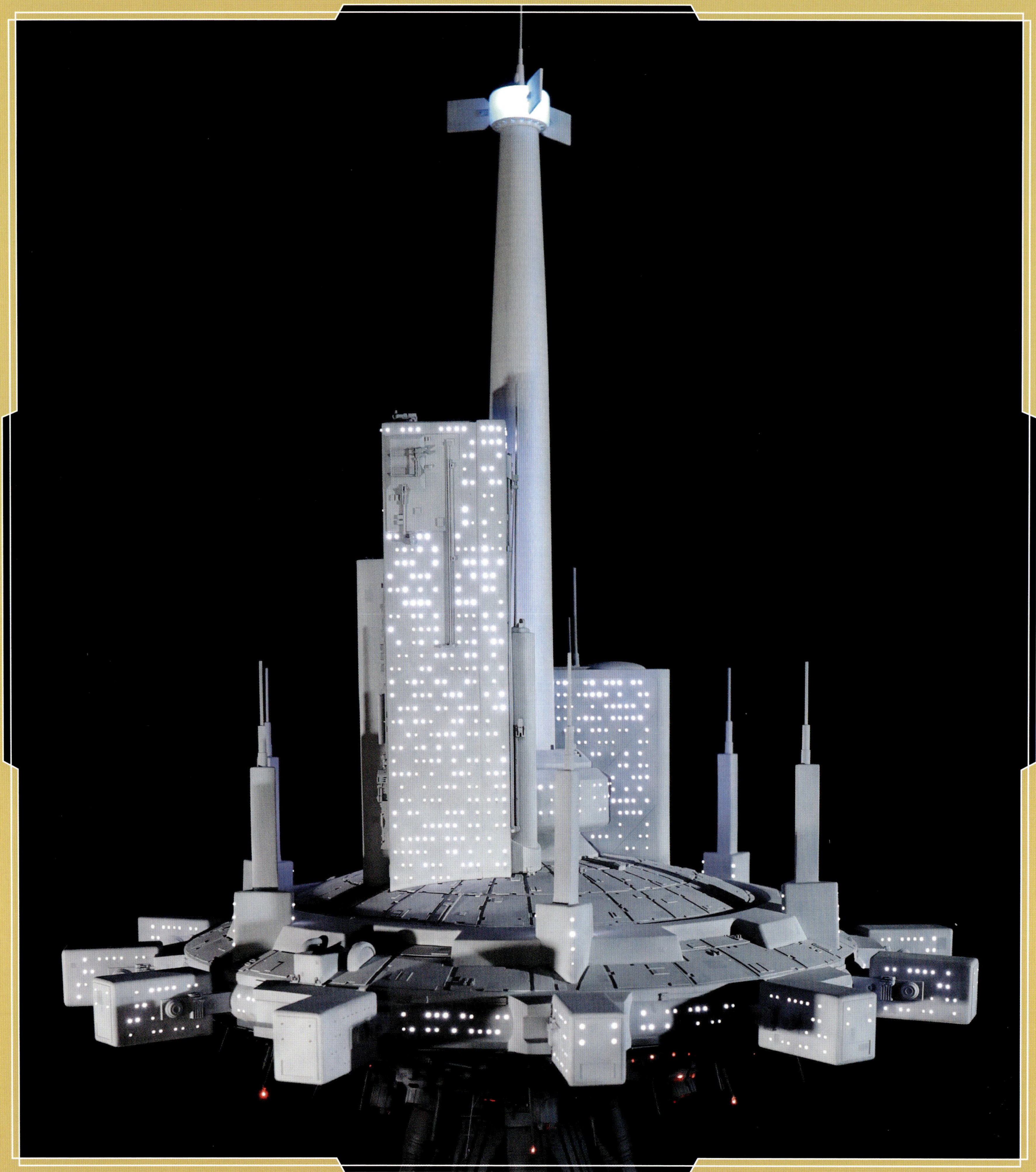

CHAPTER 6
LOCATIONS

THE STARLIGHT BEACON, jewel of the Republic, is a potent symbol of the era in which it launched.

While the Death Star was a space station of the Empire's making, hell-bent on destruction, the Starlight is a tangible representation of the Republic's prosperity and the Jedi's strength, conceived as a literal beacon of hope in the inky and vast expanse of space. It's simultaneously a guiding light for wayward travelers, a way station for refugees, and a symbol of innovation. "Building a new era, where we could tell stories while drawing on the legacy of *Star Wars*, we were coming from a place where it was kind of a blank slate," said Lucasfilm senior editor Robert Simpson. "We could tell any kind of story with any kind of characters and really take a look at the sector of the galaxy that they're in through fresh eyes. These stories didn't have to take place on Tatooine. They didn't need to take place on Coruscant. They didn't need to take place on any planet that we'd ever been to before."

Creators introduced the lush, tree-covered planet of Trymant IV; Hetzal Prime, seated in the agricultural cradle of the Hetzal system where the most pervasive crop was an essential ingredient in newly discovered bacta; the frontier world of Shuraden; and Valo, home of the Republic Fair, while also reimagining Coruscant and Corellia. However, as the foremost location present across the entirety of Phase I, which started with its delayed dedication and ended with the station's fiery destruction, Starlight's design was the product of the most careful consideration of them all. "We started with the iconography in the shape language of both the temples on Coruscant and lightsaber structures, and that became the foundational basis for designing [the Beacon]," said Steve Blank, Lucasfilm's director of Franchise Content & Strategy. That brought creators to the point where they could ask, "What's an expression of that within this other era? How would they have used those same design principles a couple hundred years ago to build this new outpost?"

"The Starlight Beacon is a good example of a design telling a story," added Lucasfilm Story Group senior creative executive Pablo Hidalgo, who helped define what different sectors of the station would contain, including the Jedi quarters and the ship hangar. The spires of the top half echo the Jedi Temple on Coruscant, a monument to the power of the Force and its practitioners. "It has the spires reaching to the heavens, and that's in all the Jedi temples that we create," added Lucasfilm creative art manager Phil Szostak. Meanwhile, the underbelly is pure utility, hidden in shadow, an industrial foundation that lacks a pleasing façade but is nonetheless essential, form meeting function. "It's the plumbing," Hidalgo said.

Those two halves comprise the whole, like the light and dark side, symbolic symmetry working in tandem. "It represents the Force in so many ways," said Szostak, "as a beacon of hope and a literal, physical beacon in the darkness of space." Even in design, the Starlight Beacon, like the Force itself, is all about balance. "Those who are allied to the ideals of the Republic can look at it as an inspiration, an example of balance, of working together," said Hidalgo. "Those against the Republic can get riled by what they see as a statement of class and divisions."

Similar themes ripple through the storytelling, a mix of humor and trauma, light and life versus darkness and death. "The flavor of *Star Wars* is really found in the balance of *Star Wars*," said author Daniel José Older. "There's a very particular balance of darkness and light, humor and adventure, risk and politics, and fun. All those things are always weighed

◂ Model of the Starlight Beacon JASON EATON (ARTIST) AND KYLE KAO (PHOTOGRAPHER)

in the balance of each other in whatever *Star Wars* movie you find, [although] sometimes it tilts more one way or another."

Illustrator Pascal Blanché was brought onto the project in October of 2019 to sketch the basis of the Starlight Beacon design, while concept artist Gonzalo Kenny was hired afterward to add color to the blueprint-like sketches. "From the very first moment, I had this vision of it floating near a planet, illuminated by a beautiful sunrise and glowing in the middle of space," Kenny said. "It was an image that appeared almost immediately in my head."

Artists were given a mood board dominated by the lush paintings of original *Star Wars* concept artist Ralph McQuarrie, with scenes from the first designs for the Death Star and Cloud City used to evoke the clean lines and clinical appearance of the new construction. After completing a piece that showcased the upper decks, Kenny turned his attention to the operational underbelly. "In the upper part of the satellite, I tried to show the prosperity of the city and its administrative sectors, represented by light and cold tones, something very similar to what we see in Cloud City in *The Empire Strikes Back*. For the lower part where the industrial section is located, I used warmer and darker tones, with steam [vents] and chimneys lit to represent the operation of power plants, processing plants, and maintenance machinery." The beacon itself was the final segment to be designed, with a series of test concepts produced for variation.

ON MARCH 22, 2021, model maker Jason Eaton was hired on to create a scale replica of the station for the *Star Wars: The High Republic Show*, a bimonthly online video program produced by StarWars.com. Over the course of four months, Eaton painstakingly created the three-dimensional model using a mix of 3-D printing and fabrication by hand. Relying on a computer alone may have made the model too perfect. "All the *Star Wars* physical models, including some of the costume pieces like the stormtrooper helmet, have built-in asymmetries," said Szostak. "It doesn't look right if you make it perfectly symmetrical. Those little imperfections give it a human quality and a design quality that makes it feel more real than something with all the rough edges smoothed out."

"I printed the model in subsections, working on each section as the next in line printed, and once all that was done, the *real* fun began, adding styrene plating and model kit parts in the traditional ways," Eaton said. "This is where, as a builder, I feel closest to how it may have been in the model shop, and I utilized many 'signature parts' from kits that ILM loved to use."

Eaton designed the backside of the station, not previously illustrated. "Part of his responsibility was to effectively take what you see on the front side in the concept art and extrapolate," Szostak added, "and that's challenging because you're trying to not only continue the forms that you see, but also make it aesthetically pleasing and integrated." In some cases, Eaton added his own details, like a pair of small ships placed to give the hangar and the Starlight itself a better sense of scale. "A favorite detail by far is that landing bay, as it not only sells [the] scale, but it scratches an itch I always have to build little worlds inside of worlds," Eaton said. "Anyone that looks into the landing bay is rewarded with little ships, doors, and lighting." The craft he chose to represent were Professor Huyang's ship, the *Crucible*, a training vessel first seen in *Star Wars: The Clone Wars*; and Eaton's personal favorite Easter egg, the re-creation of the *Dowager Queen*, a ship seen as detritus and debris in Mos Eisley. The intact version was a digital model drawn by Eaton's friend Stinson Lenz, based on an original sketch by artist John Barry, who provided a smattering of ink concept designs in 1975 during preproduction on *Star Wars: A New Hope*. "This is a colony ship, and could have existed in the High Republic timeline, so that is a warm shout-out to the original *Star Wars* production team in Tunisia," he said.

Throughout the process, Eaton was in regular contact with Hidalgo and Szostak for guidance on the design. When his first beacon test had the emblematic light turning too rapidly, Szostak steered the artist toward an animated short on the station and advised him to match the speed from there. "He's creating it as if it's going to be a filmed model, as if the *High Republic* was live-action," Szostak said. "That's the level of detail and the quality of the work." To further incorporate Lucasfilm history, Eaton constructed a preliminary lighting test using an inflexible neopixel ring, the same kind used by John Goodson on the *Razor Crest* model for *The Mandalorian* and finished the build with pieces of mesh screen left over from an ILM model maker who had used the same material on TIE fighter models. "Those pieces of screen material in the lower inner spire area are actually unused pieces of TIE Fighter wing 'Kool Shade' bronze louvers," Eaton said, "gifted to me from an ILMer that worked in the shop from late '75 onward."

Fittingly, Phase I launched with the dedication of the Starlight, a ceremony nearly waylaid by the Great Disaster and the ensuing Emergences, when the destruction of the *Legacy Run* at lightspeed sent debris and terrified survivors hurtling across the galaxy and ended with a bang as the Nihil succeeded in infiltrating the Beacon and setting off a series of explosions that tore the majestic feat of engineering in two. With the same careful consideration creators took to manifest the Beacon, author Claudia Gray worked closely with Hidalgo to assess the best way to successfully reduce the station to rubble in the final adult novel in Phase I, *The Fallen Star*, originally greenlit under the working title of *Starlight Down,* which was ultimately deemed to be too much of a spoiler. "We had the design of the Starlight Beacon, and a series of *Star Wars Insider* stories set aboard it, so already there was thought as to the geography of the station," Hidalgo said. "Based on what we were going to do for *The Fallen Star*, I painted over art of Starlight Beacon defining how major areas of it were used and, broadly, how its unseen infrastructure distributed power, and I shared this with Claudia. Then we talked on a call about the kind of things you would have to do to knock it out of orbit and what would be required to try to keep it from falling, so all that action followed a physical framework."

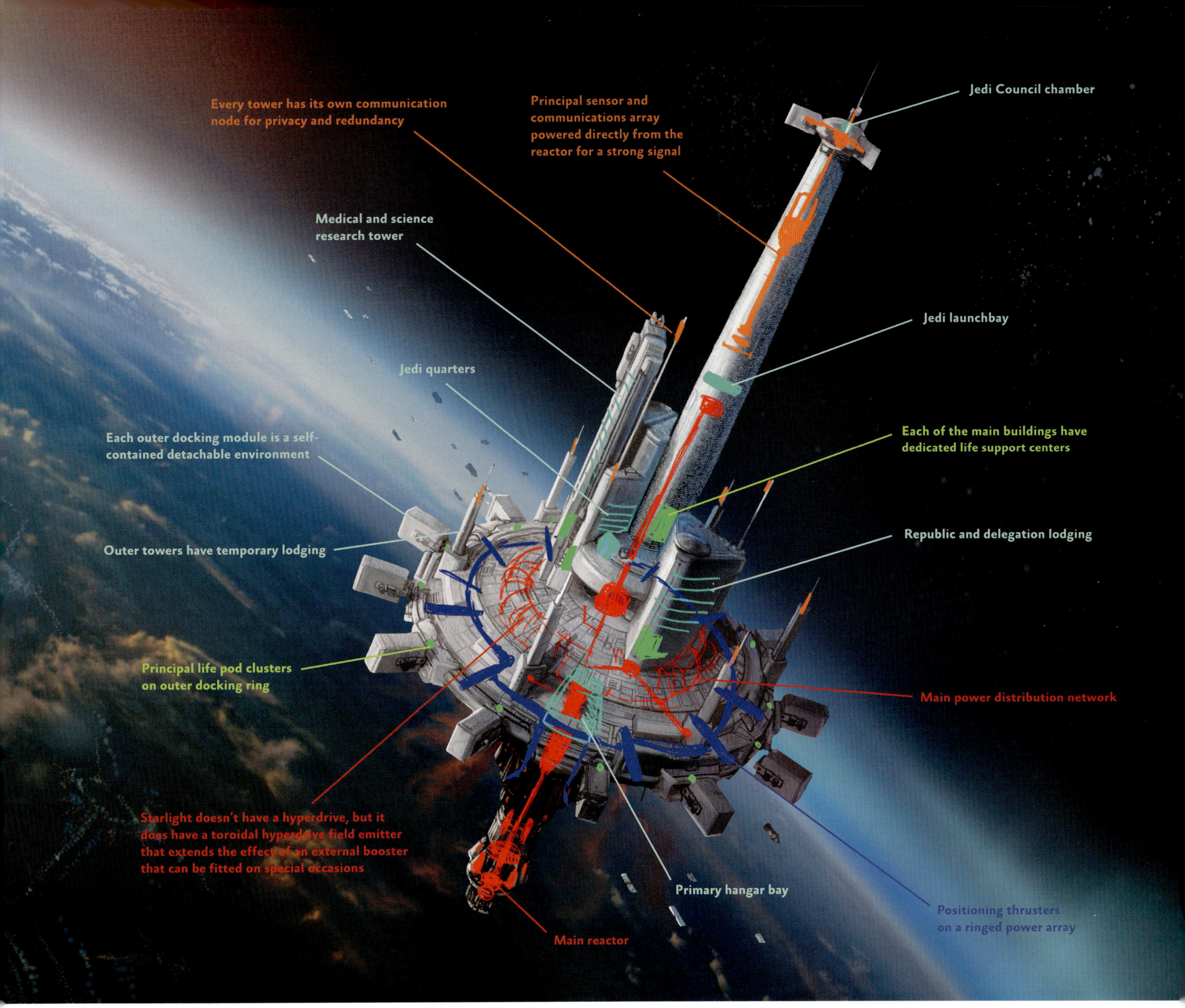

▲ Annotated notes on the Starlight Beacon PABLO HIDALGO WITH ARTISTS BLANCHÉ AND KENNY

Hidalgo worked closely with Gray to determine the exact layout of the Starlight Beacon to help with plotting key story points in *The Fallen Star*.

During the second Summit, Gray was granted a few hours to spend in the Skywalker Ranch library, paging through books on mythology, philosophy, art, and design, curated to help storytellers of all kinds harness ideas. "I remember I found really old little notes [in a book] that had clearly been used for another production. And from the notes I could tell it was from *Star Wars*." She also read early drafts of the *Star Wars* script, which bear little resemblance to the story as we know it today. Reading those initial ideas helped Gray in her approach to The High Republic and ultimately led her to a cliffhanger ending in the spirit of *The Empire Strikes Back*. "George Lucas may not have come up with the singular plot [for *A New Hope*] yet, but he knew [the *Star Wars* galaxy.] He knew it and what it ought to look like and how it ought to feel," Gray said. "And that's really the main thing when it comes to this sort of project. Can you imagine that world? Can you imagine yourself being there? Can you help somebody else imagine it? That's really, fundamentally what it comes down to."

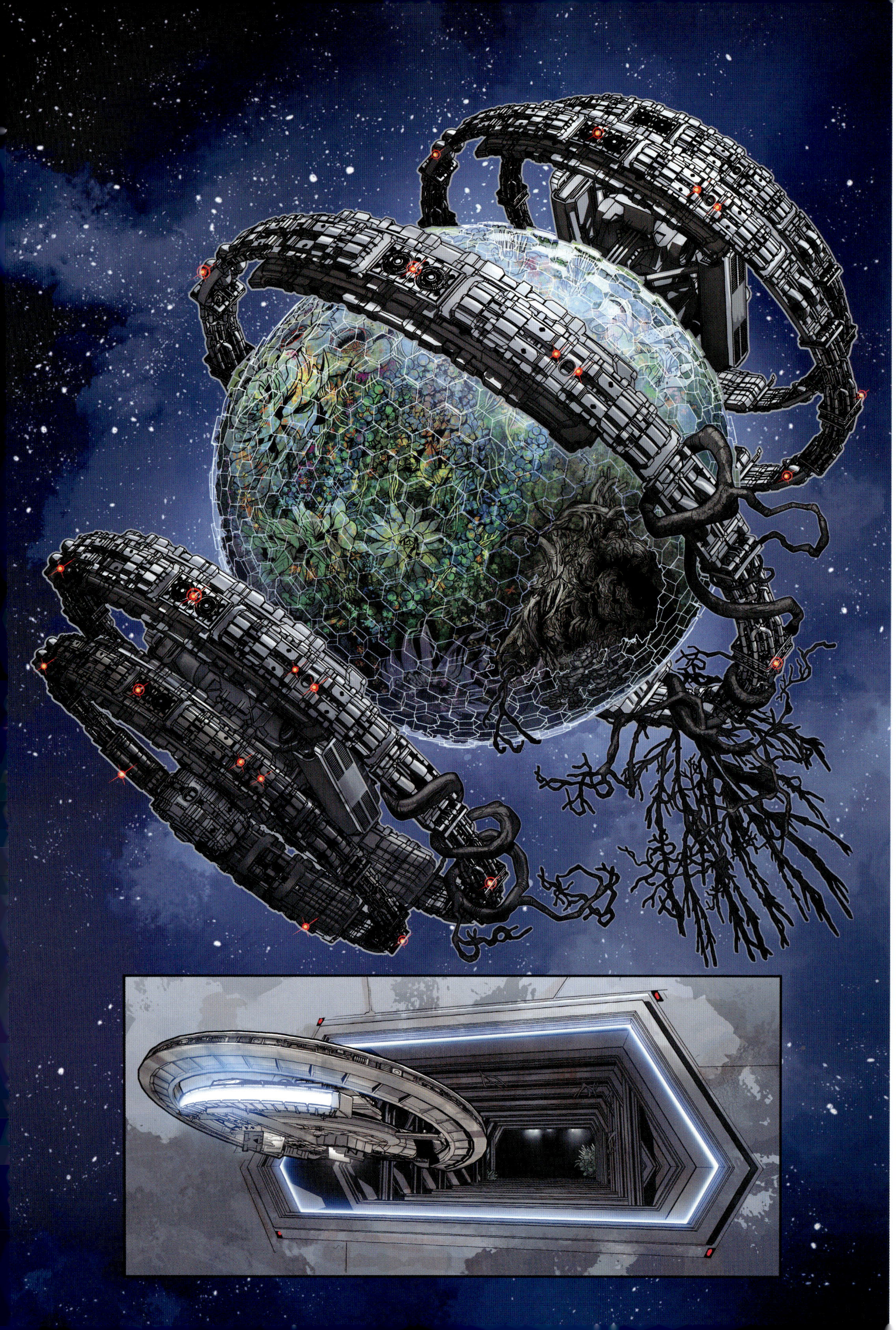

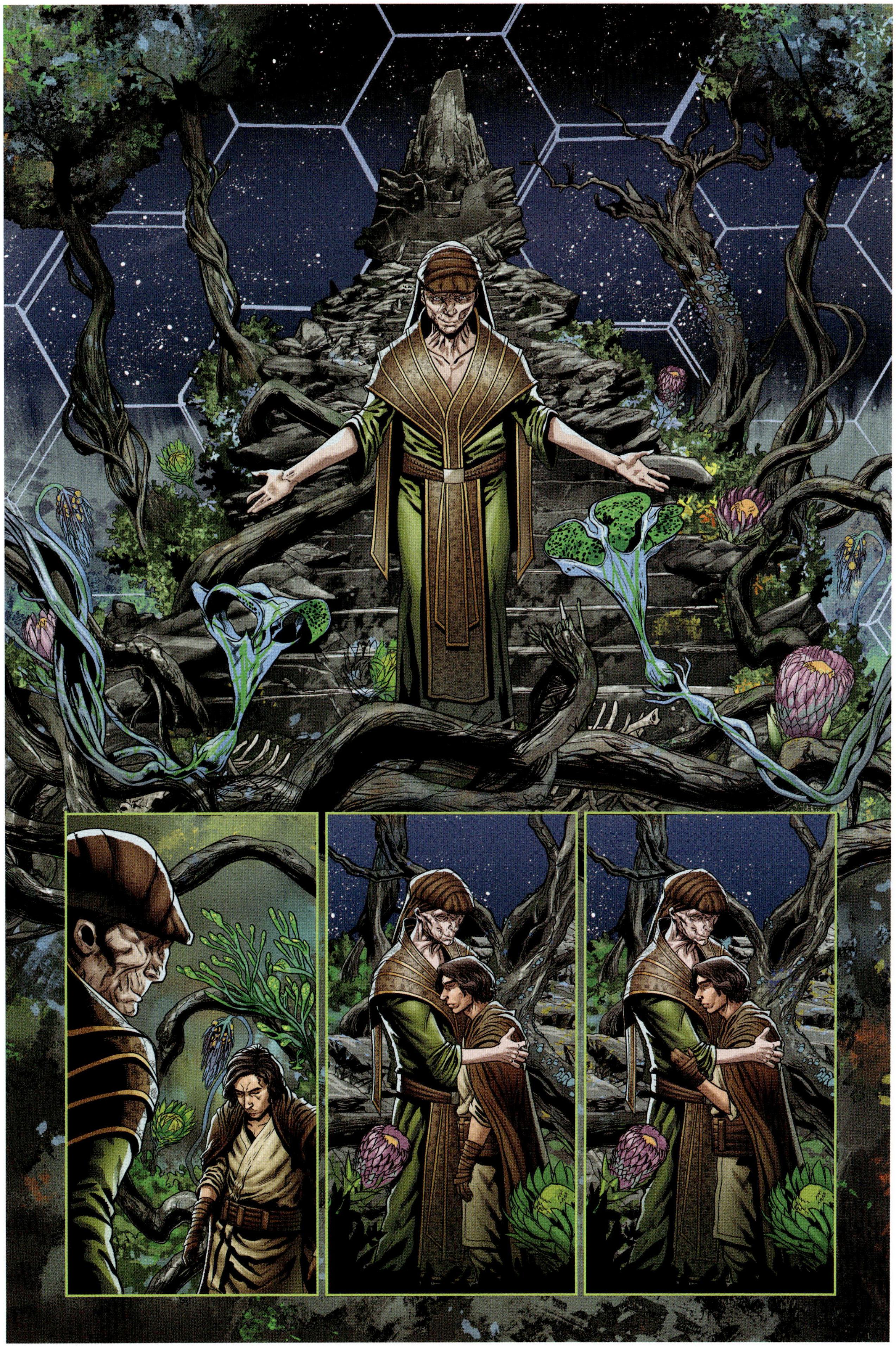

◂▸ The Amaxine Station, as seen in Marvel's *Star Wars: The Rise of Kylo Ren* #1 WILL SLINEY (PENCILER) AND GURU-EFX (COLORIST)

"I was working on the idea for this station. I had it being an arboretum and we realized it can be the same station. It was a backstory that fit well with what Charles [Soule] does with it later. That was a happy moment. One of the things about working on *Star Wars* is there's this incredible well of design work that goes back decades, some of the greatest artists in the world have been working on this for more than forty years. And so there's this wealth of stuff to dive into. It was more recent, but still, it was one of those things that was just there waiting to go, yes, this is the thing you use and it makes it perfect." GRAY

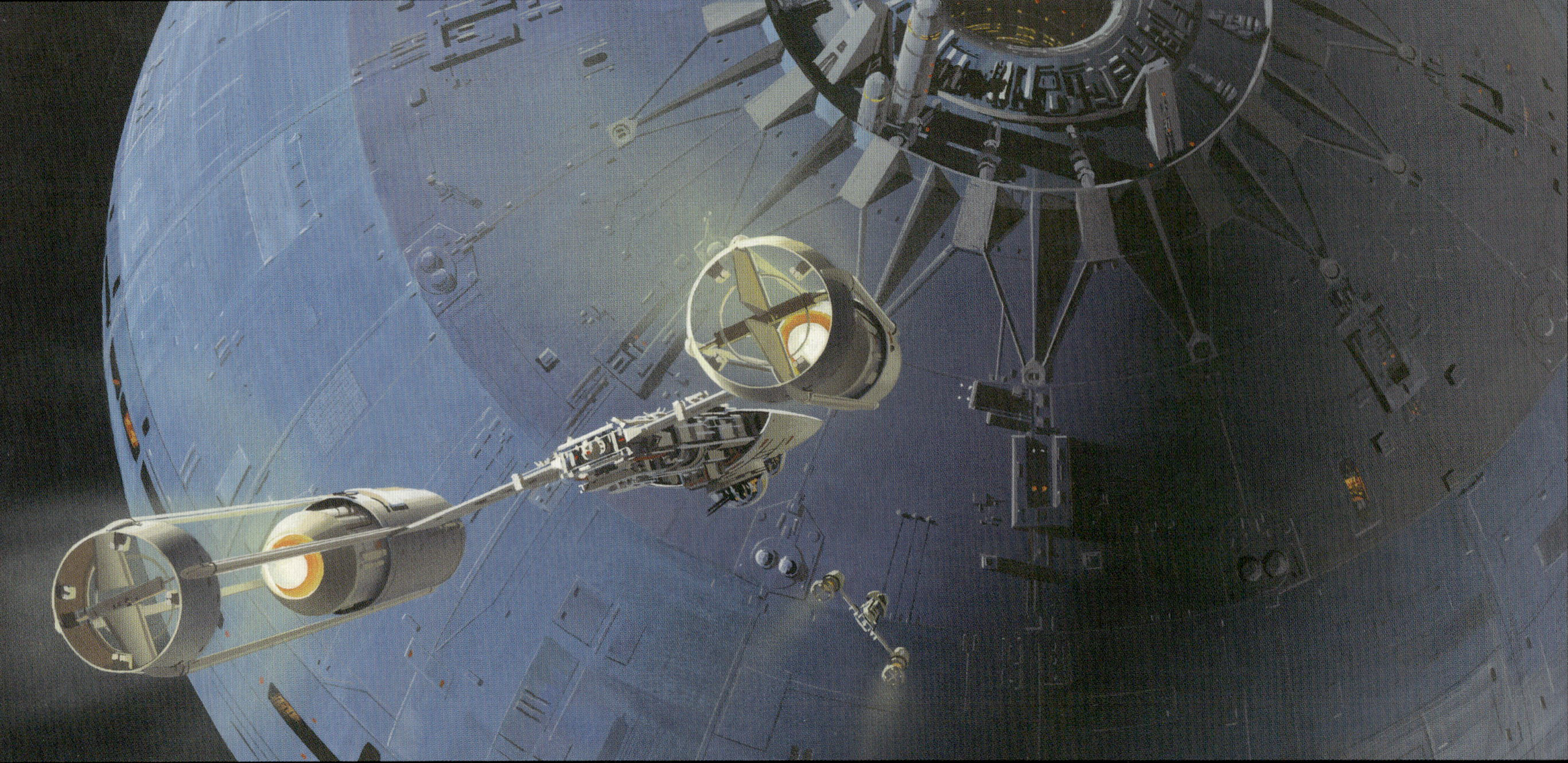

▲ Y-wing approaching the Death Star MCQUARRIE

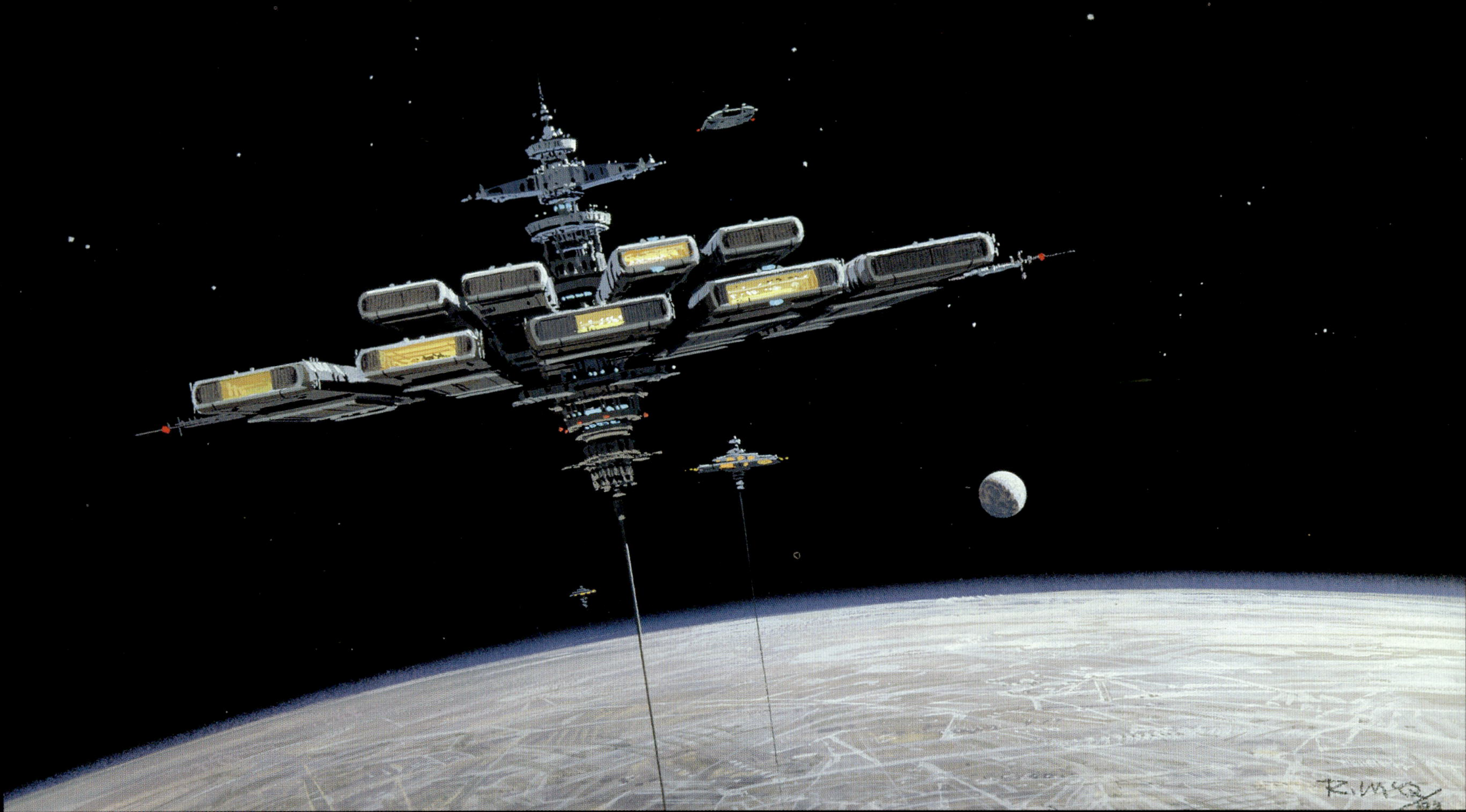

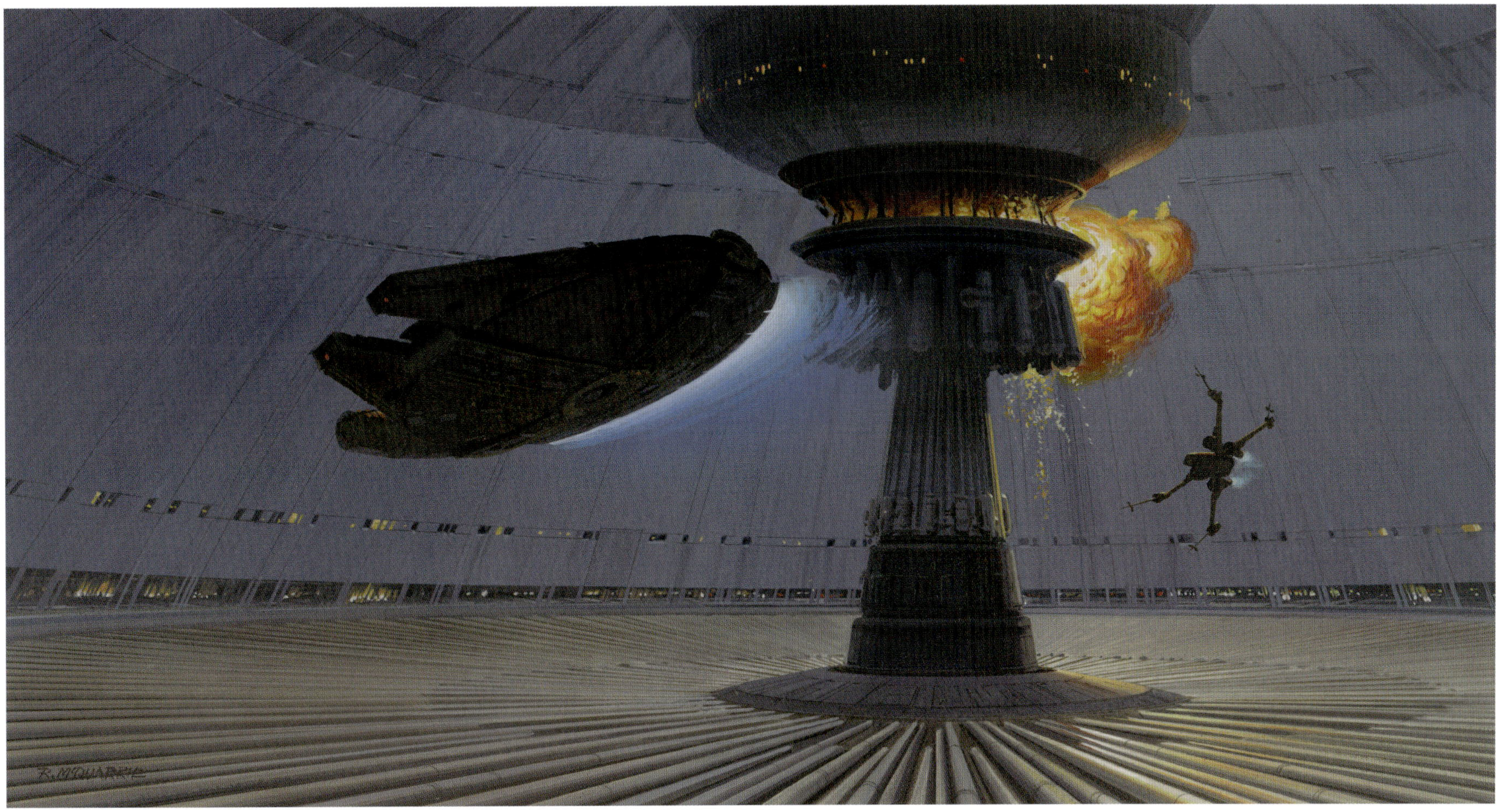

▲ Rebel attack on the central reactor core of the second Death Star McQUARRIE

▼ Death Star interior McQUARRIE

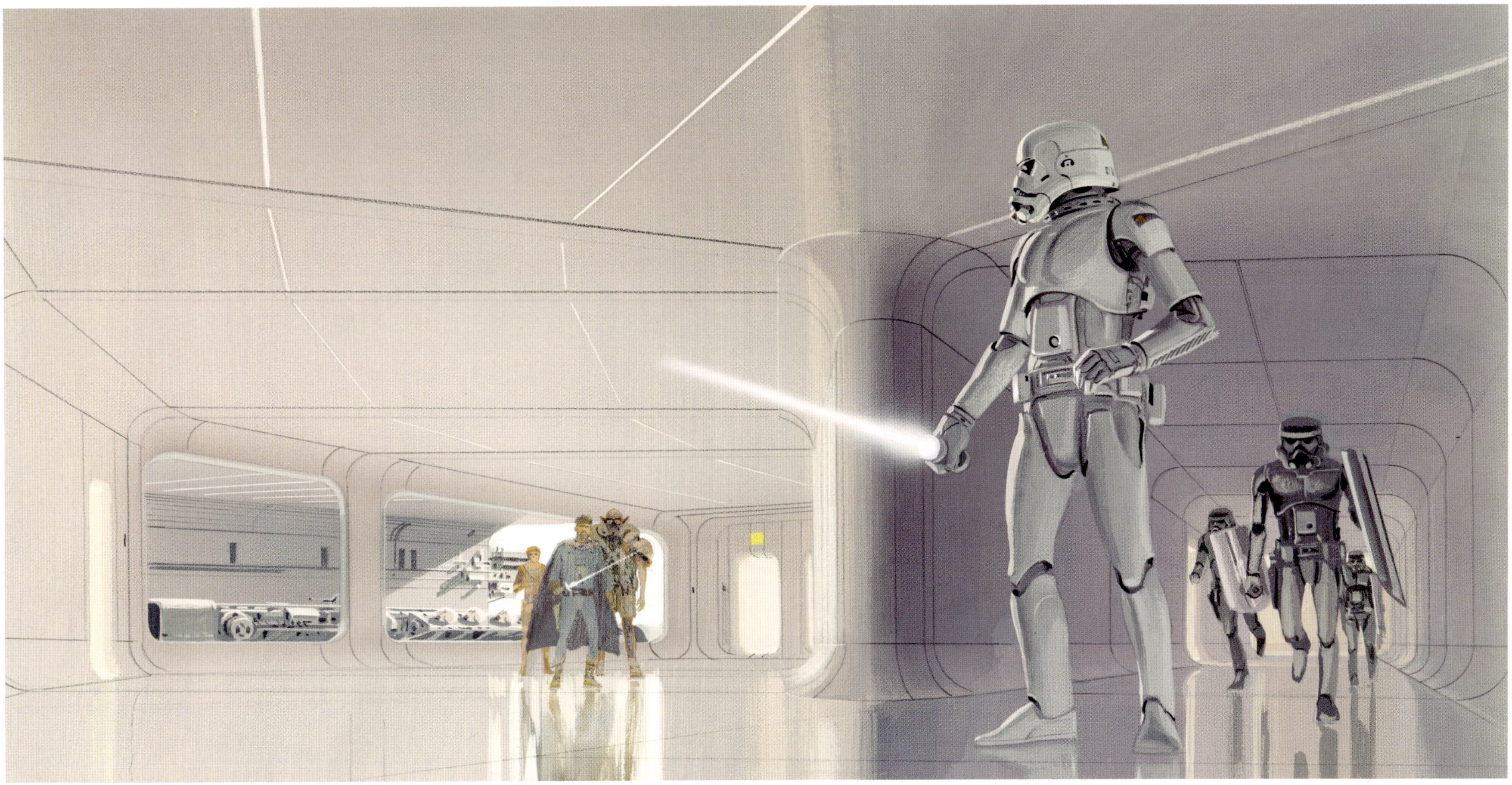

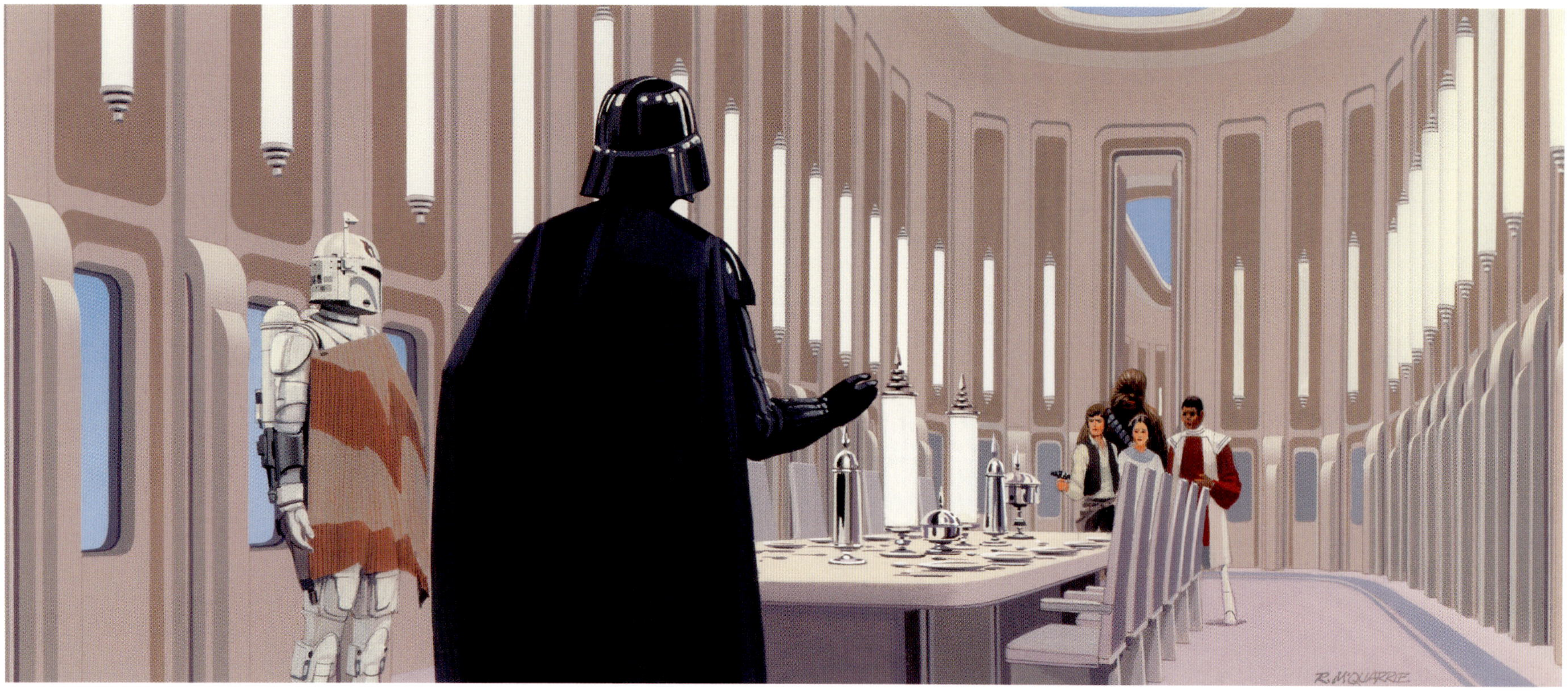

▲ Cloud City dining room McQUARRIE

▼ Cloud City lower decks McQUARRIE

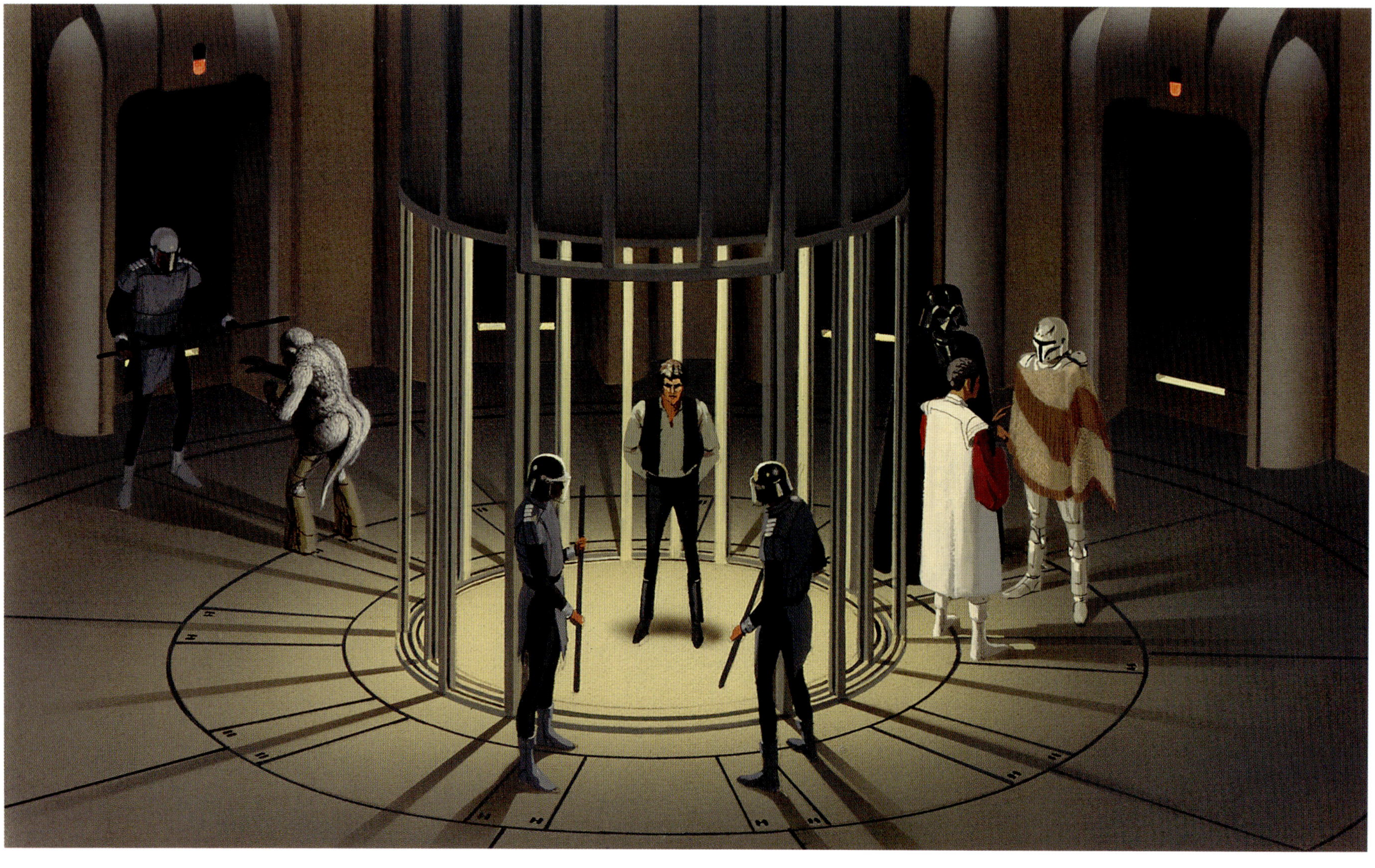

▸ Page from Marvel's *Star Wars: The High Republic* #1 ANINDITO (PENCILER), MORALES (INKER), AND LEONI (COLORIST)

While illustrating Marvel's *Star Wars: The High Republic* #1, Anindito was surprised to learn that not only was there no concept art for the interior of the Starlight Beacon, but the editors invited him to create the look and feel of the space station's corridors and halls. The assignment allowed Anindito a rare chance to use some of the skill he acquired as a college student studying architecture. "I've been wondering all this time, am I ever going to use this architecture major? And voila, this is the reason," he said. "It's like God is telling me, 'This is why you studied architecture back in college, Ario. Because you're going to end up designing the Starlight Beacon's interior.'"

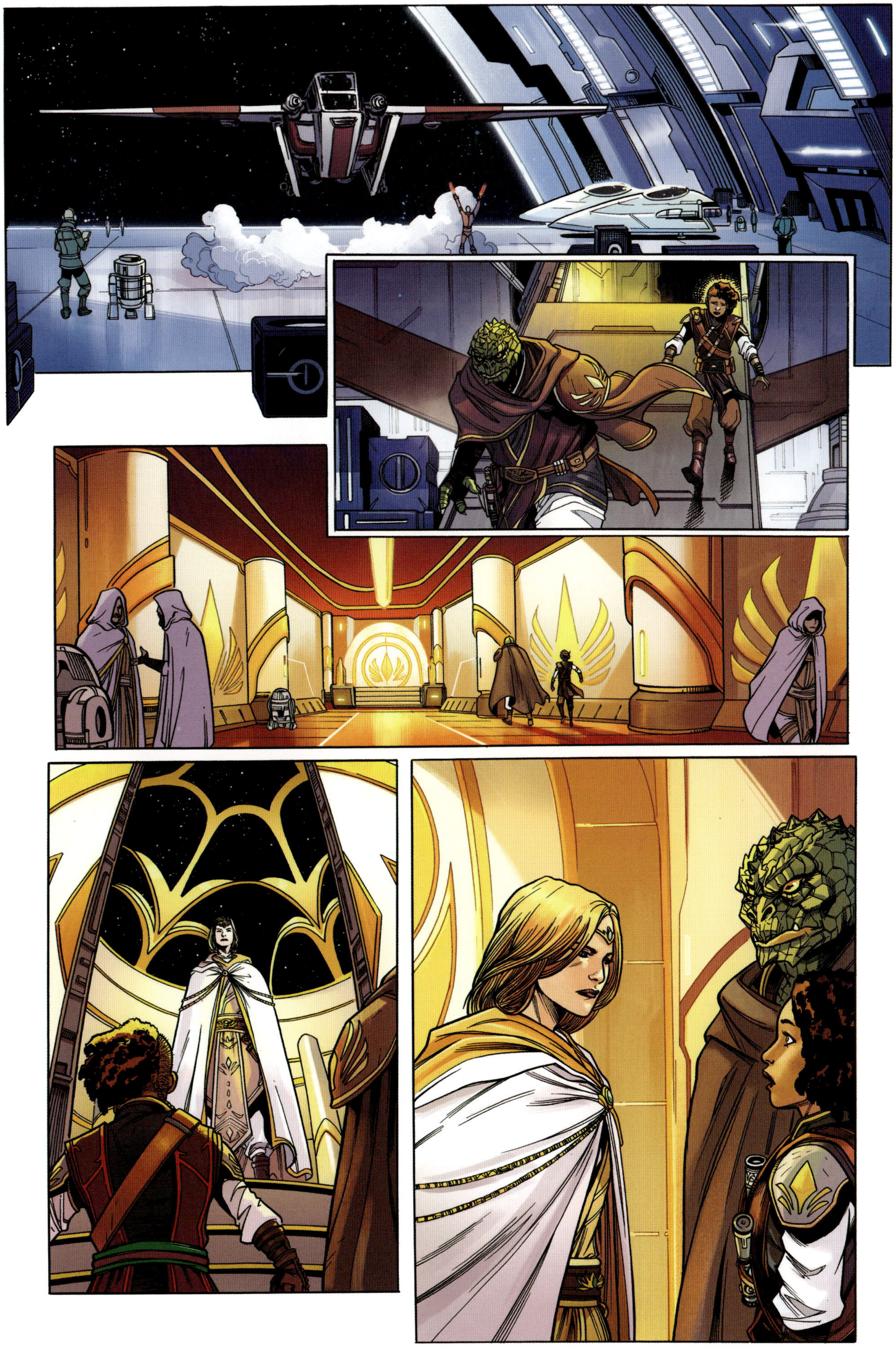

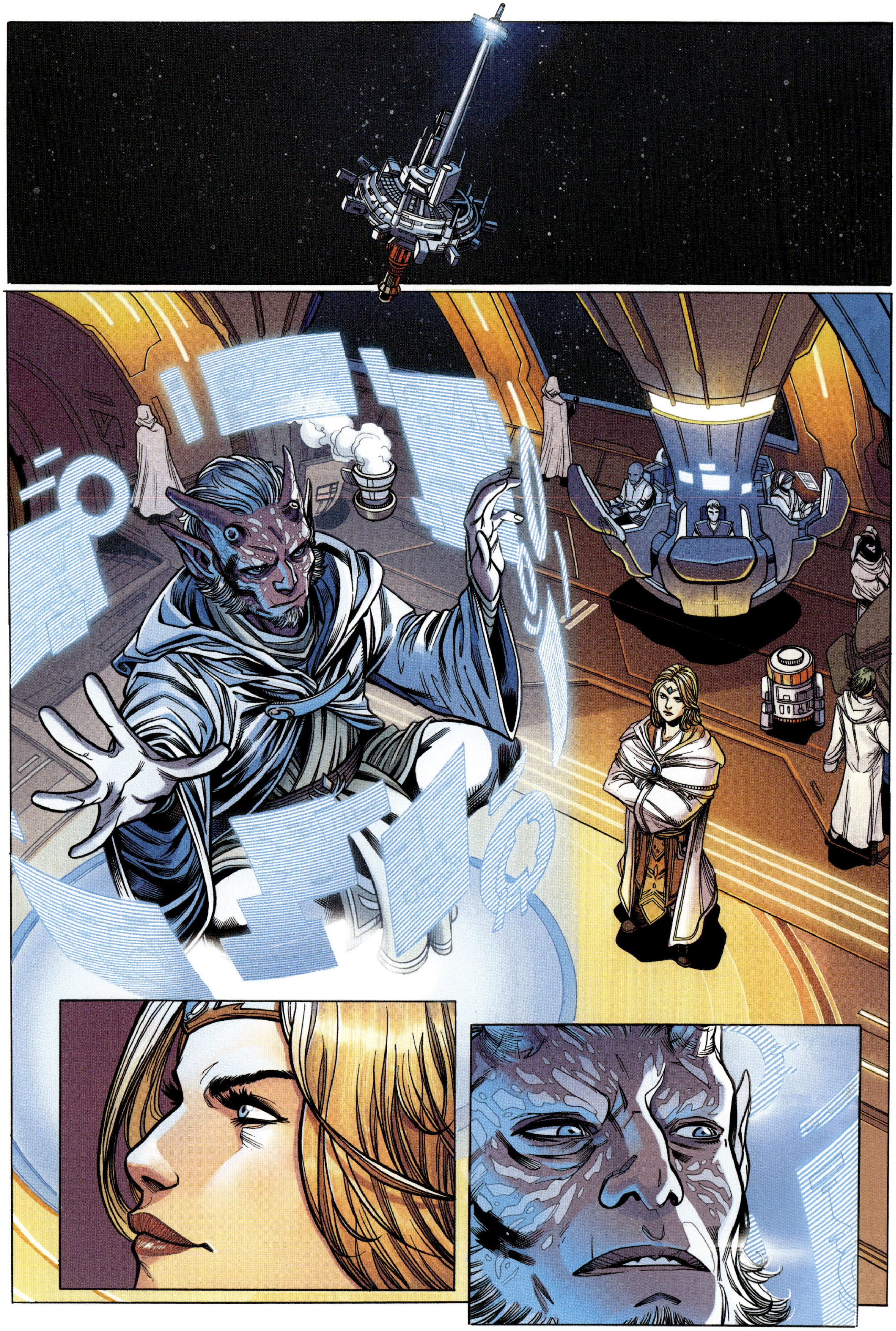

◂ Estala Maru, interior of the Starlight Beacon data chamber, from Marvel's *Star Wars: The High Republic* #1

ANINDITO (PENCILER), MORALES (INKER), AND LEONI (COLORIST)

Anindito was tasked with not only designing Kessurian Jedi Estala Maru, but also coming up with the look of his information chamber aboard the space station. Rotating pods are reminiscent of the Galactic Senate chambers, while Anindito also pulled inspiration from the Jedi Archives of the prequel era. "Basically, I wanted to create something that is new because this is the golden age of the Jedi, but I need to keep it in check that this still belongs in *Star Wars*. It's still identifiable, and yet it's new. That is the guideline that I keep in my head all the time. But if you ask, what is the limit of *Star Wars*? Well, there is no limit."

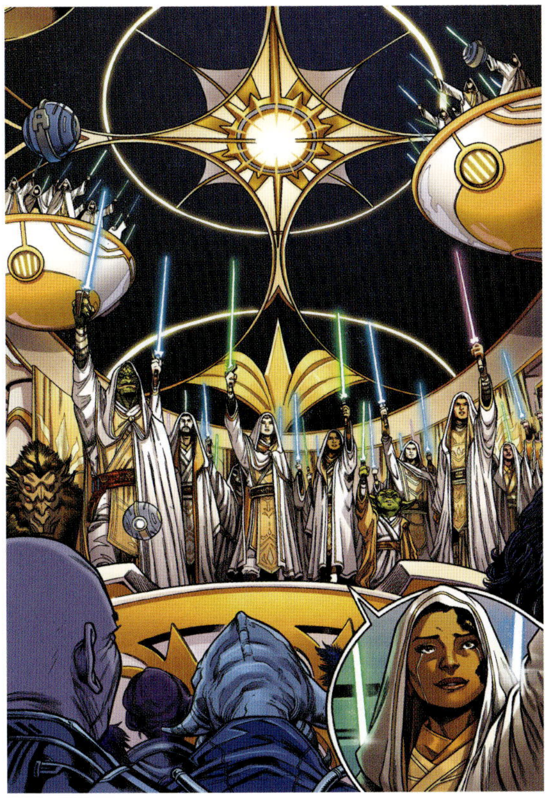

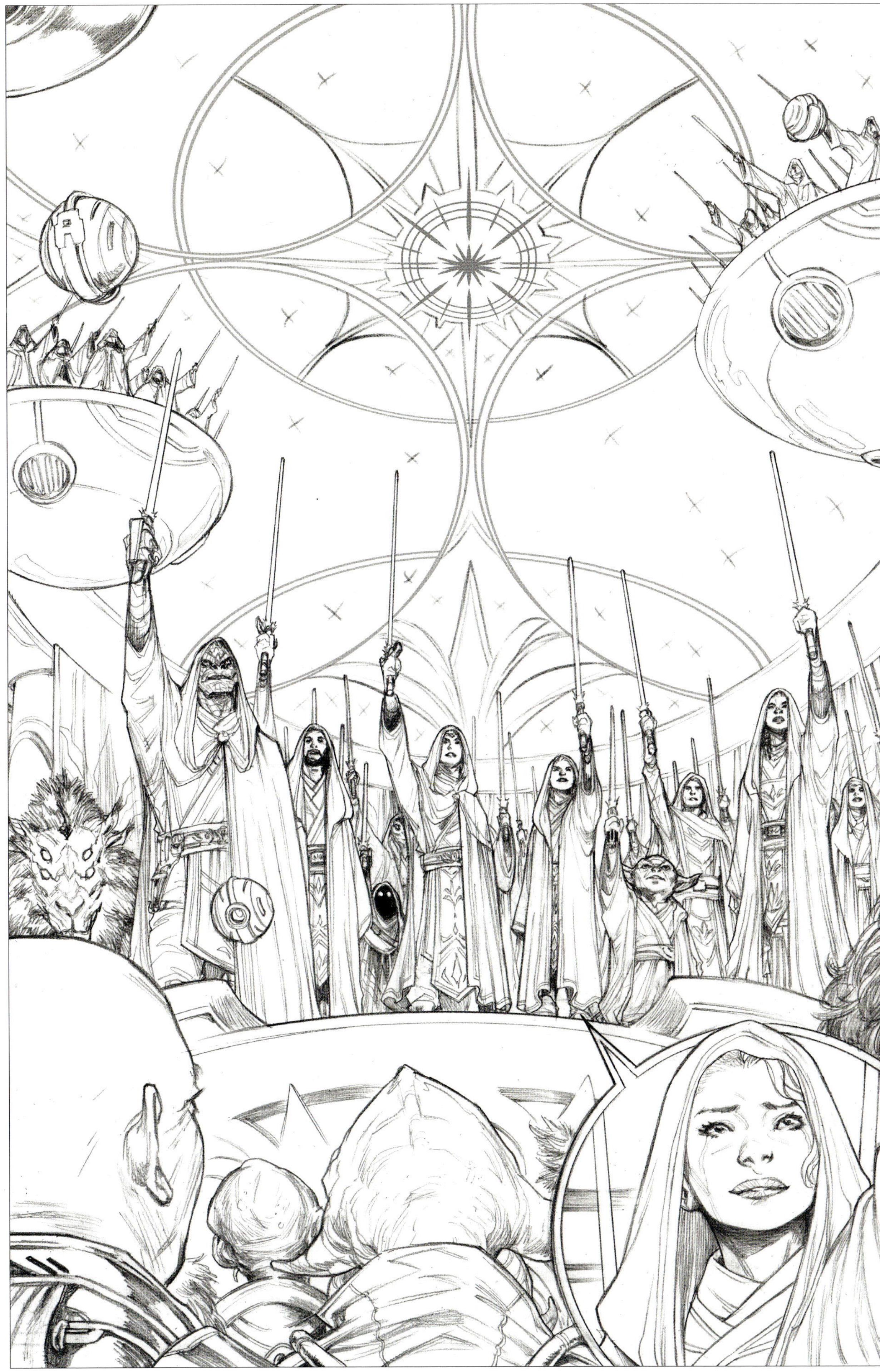

▲ Page from Marvel's *Star Wars: The High Republic #1* ANINDITO (PENCILER), MORALES (INKER), AND LEONI (COLORIST)

► Pencils for the interior of Starlight Beacon ANINDITO

Cavan Scott and Anindito conspired to include a Jawa Jedi in this pivotal moment, with hopes of planting the background Jedi throughout the comic run. "We did try and sneak in a Jawa Jedi," Scott said with a laugh. "The plan was that we were always going to see the Jawa in the background of things and never know what he was doing. I don't know why. But that was removed." [Note the Jawa's absence in the final art above.]

For the golden accents and filigree in the ceiling, Anindito incorporated elements of the logo for the High Republic era and other symbols to create the appearance of a bright star at the top of the great hall where the Jedi stand in solidarity after the Great Disaster. But he was also inspired by standing inside Dok-Ondar's chamber at *Star Wars*: Galaxy's Edge in Disneyland, a very different kind of space that nevertheless made him feel as if he were stepping into the galaxy. "For me, the key is to imagine we are there," Anindito said. "I wanted to make sure that if we are there, we will be in awe looking at the ceiling. It's magical. It's wonderful. This is the golden age of the Jedi."

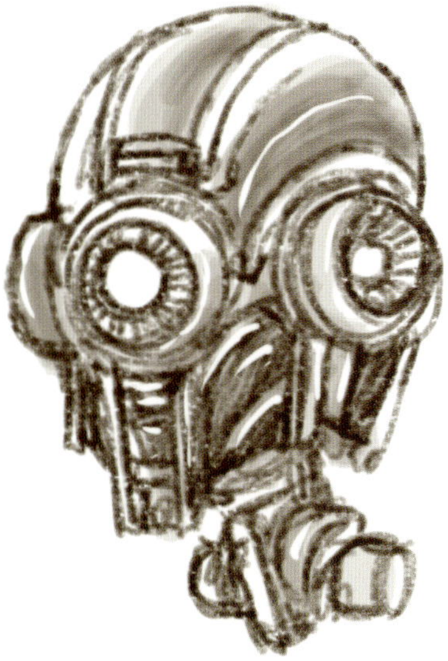

DROID V4

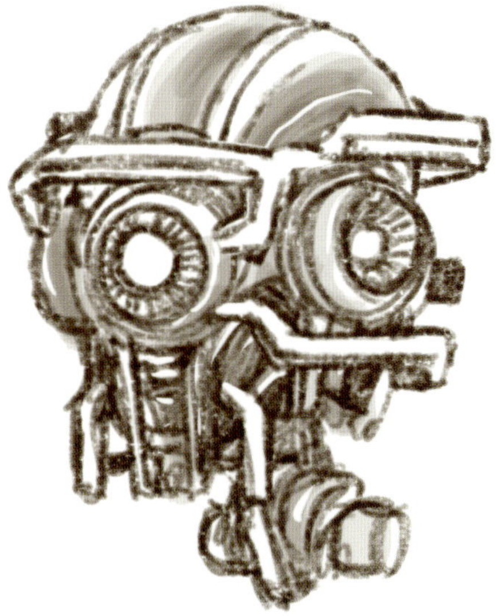

DROID V5

► Early concepts for a Starlight Beacon droid "L3-37 was the influence for this one. We were designing something for the background of part of Starlight Beacon, but we never used him." TOLIBAO

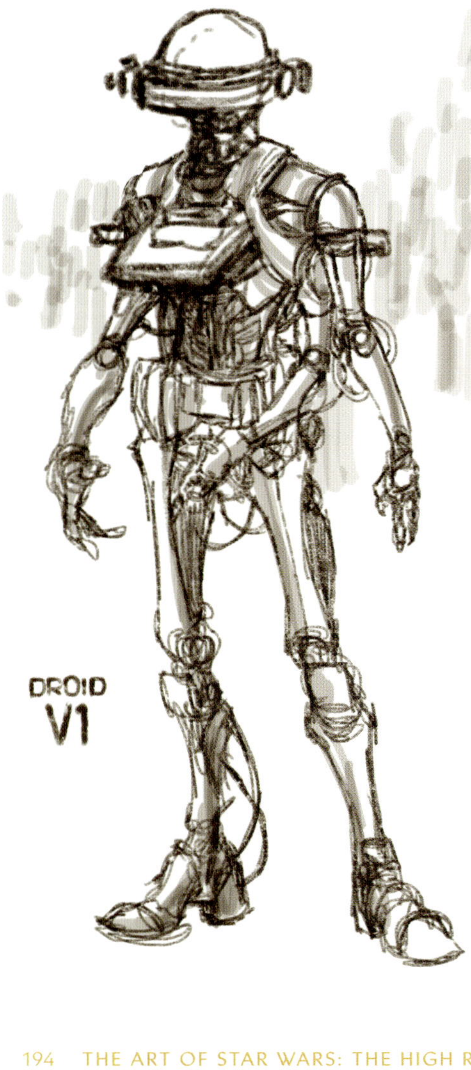

DROID V1

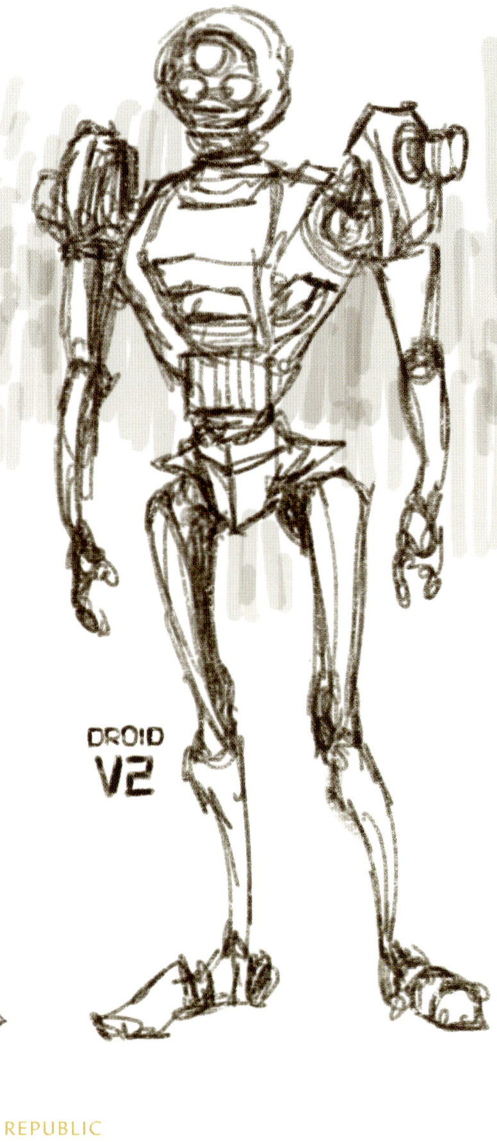

DROID V2

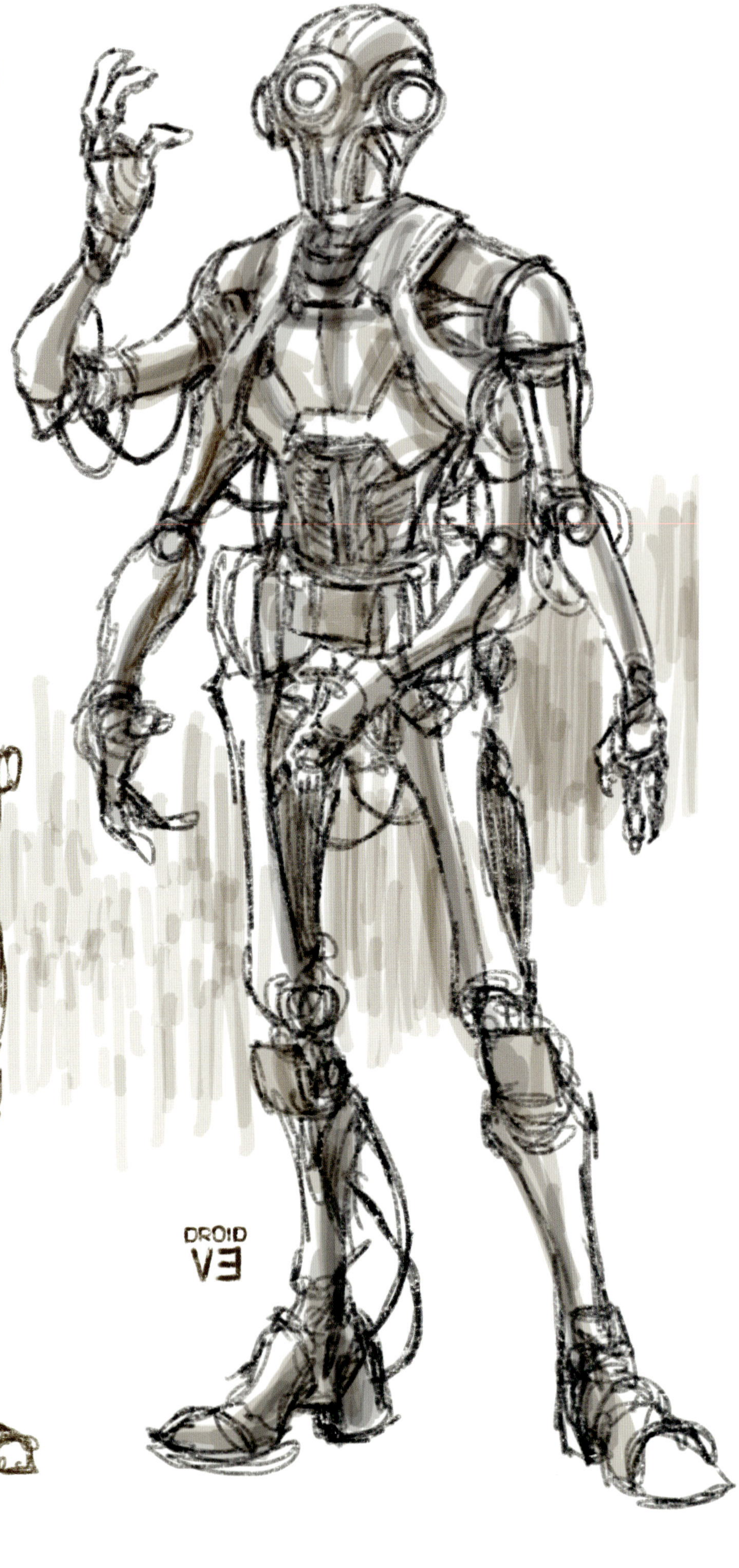

DROID V3

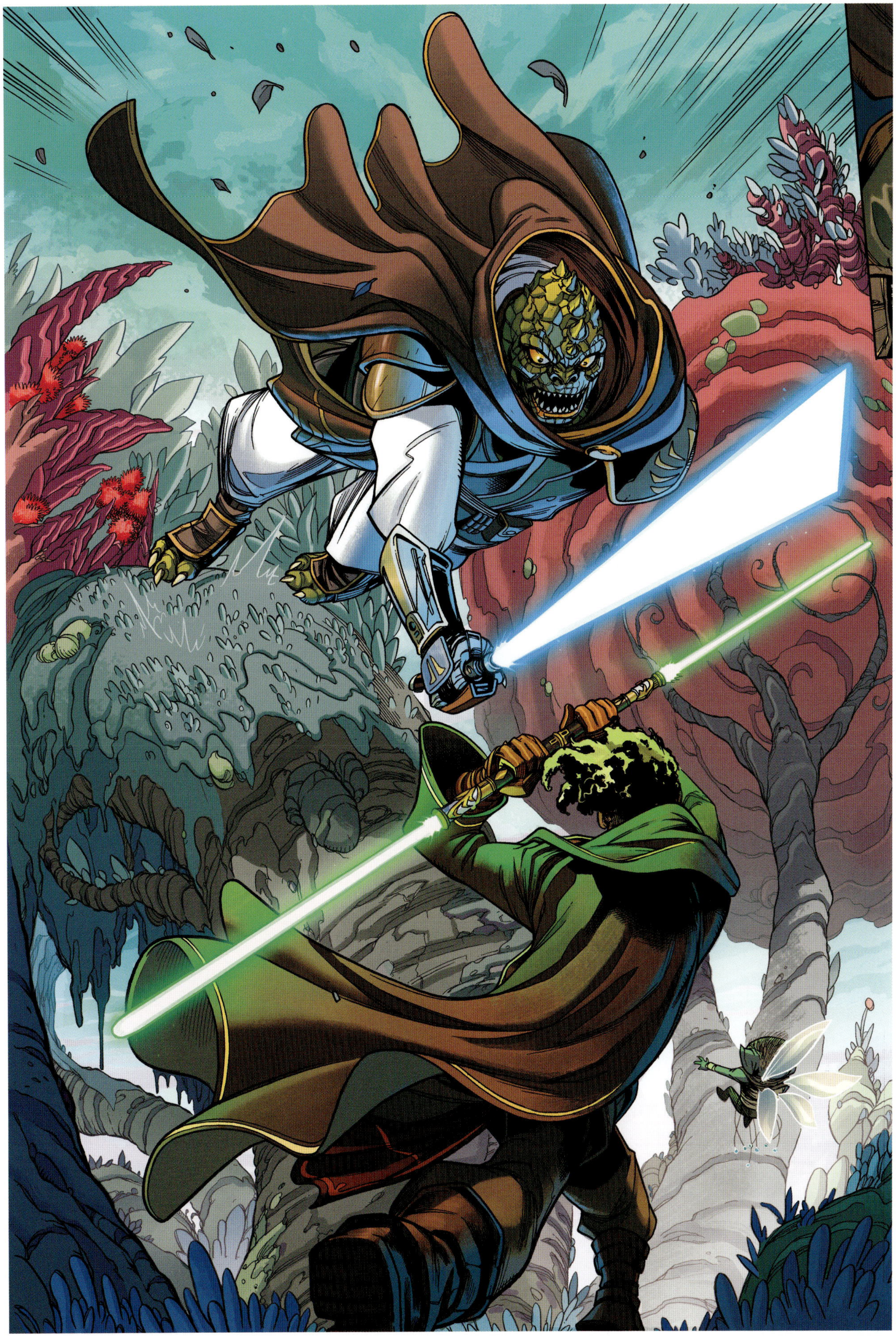

▸ Shuraden from Marvel's *Star Wars: The High Republic* #1 ANINDITO (PENCILER), MORALES (INKER), AND LEONI (COLORIST)

"I love to imagine planets. [This is the place] that I go to whenever I'm bored, whenever I'm sad. I walk in between those trees. So in a way, it's like introducing my imagination into this book. I get to show people my imaginary planet. Of course, I have different colors in my head, but [Leoni and I] worked together to deliver a planet that is different from what we see on Earth.

"I always imagine a movie scene if I draw a page in a comic, especially action pages. So when I got the script, I put the camera near the ground to be able to capture the whole thing. I want the reader to feel as if they are peeking in between the trees to see what's happening with these two characters, but to make it more menacing, you're not just peeking, you're also ducking." ANINDITO

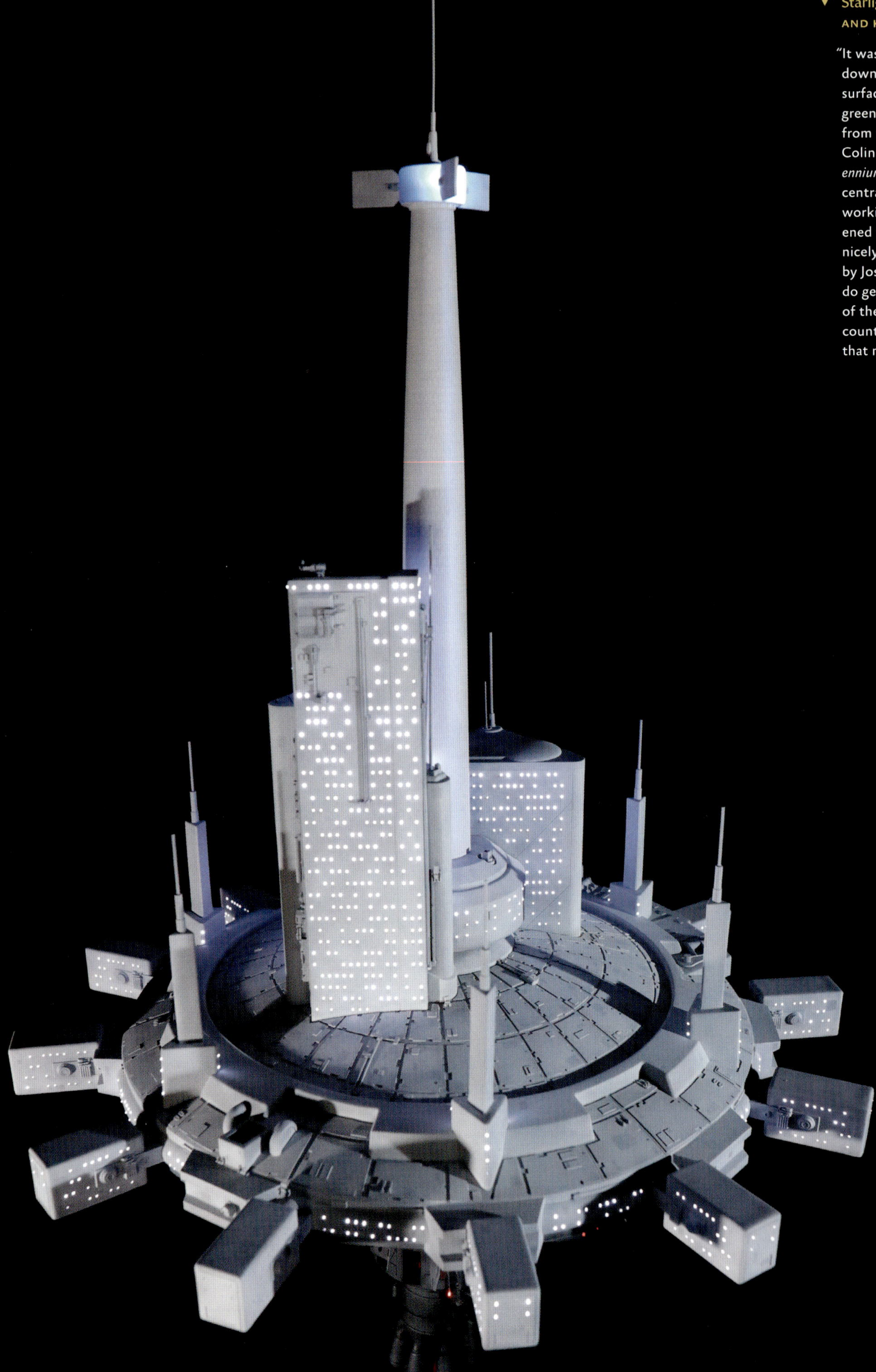

▼ Starlight Beacon model **EATON (ARTIST) AND KAO (PHOTOGRAPHER)**

"It was incredibly gratifying to be able to lay down model kit parts, piping, plating, and other surface details of my own choosing and get a green light for its look and feel. There is a part from the Airfix Hurricane that appears on the Colin Cantwell skyhopper, the five foot *Millennium Falcon*, and elsewhere that I added to the central lower spire, so I get a kick out of that working so well in this design. I was also heartened to see the final rotating beacon diffuse so nicely once the assembly [built and programmed by Josh Maruska] was put into place. And I do get a kick out of knowing it joins the likes of the Death Star, sail barge, *Razor Crest*, and countless one-man fighters as a ship or station that met a fiery destructive end!" **EATON**

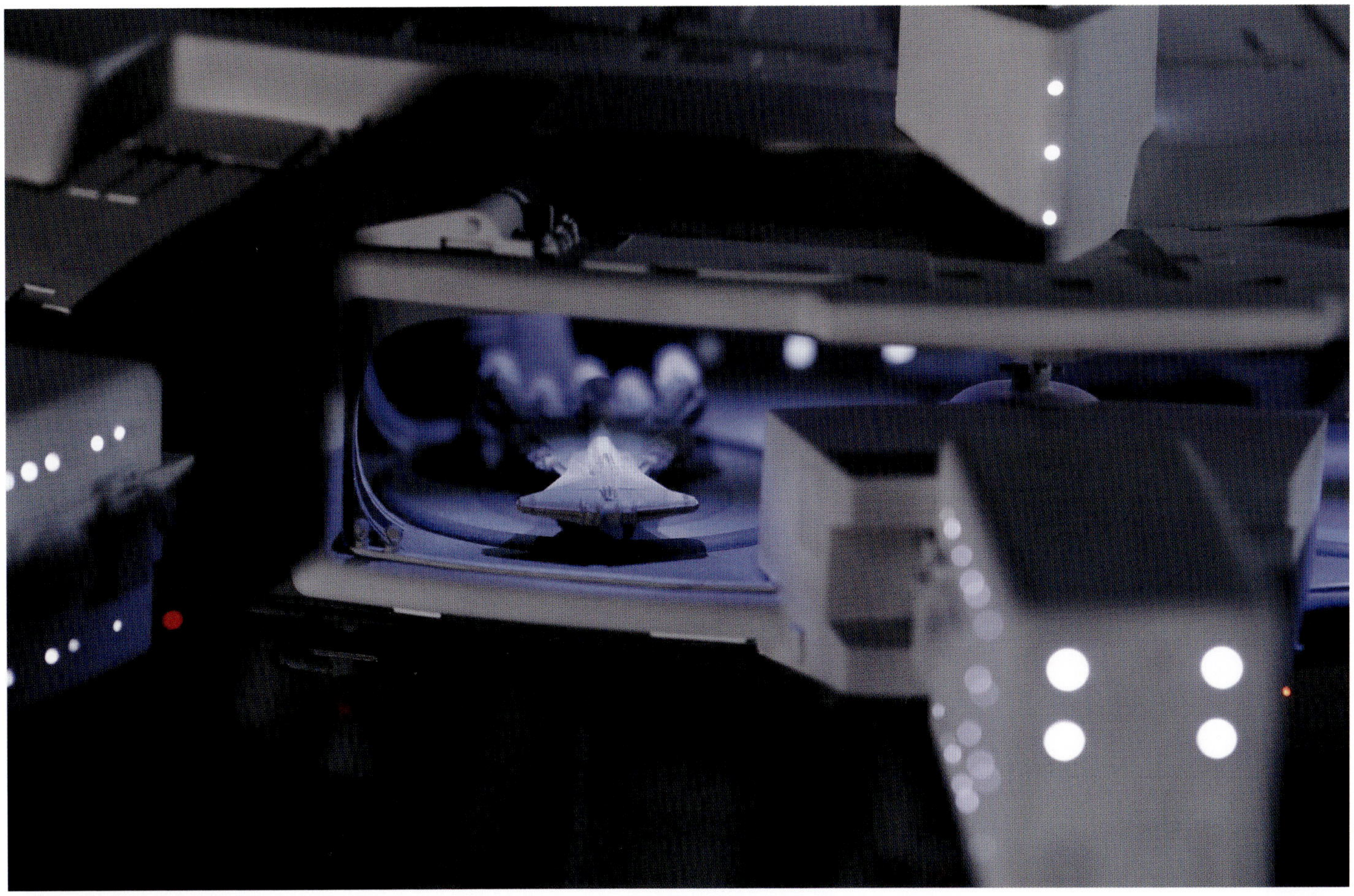

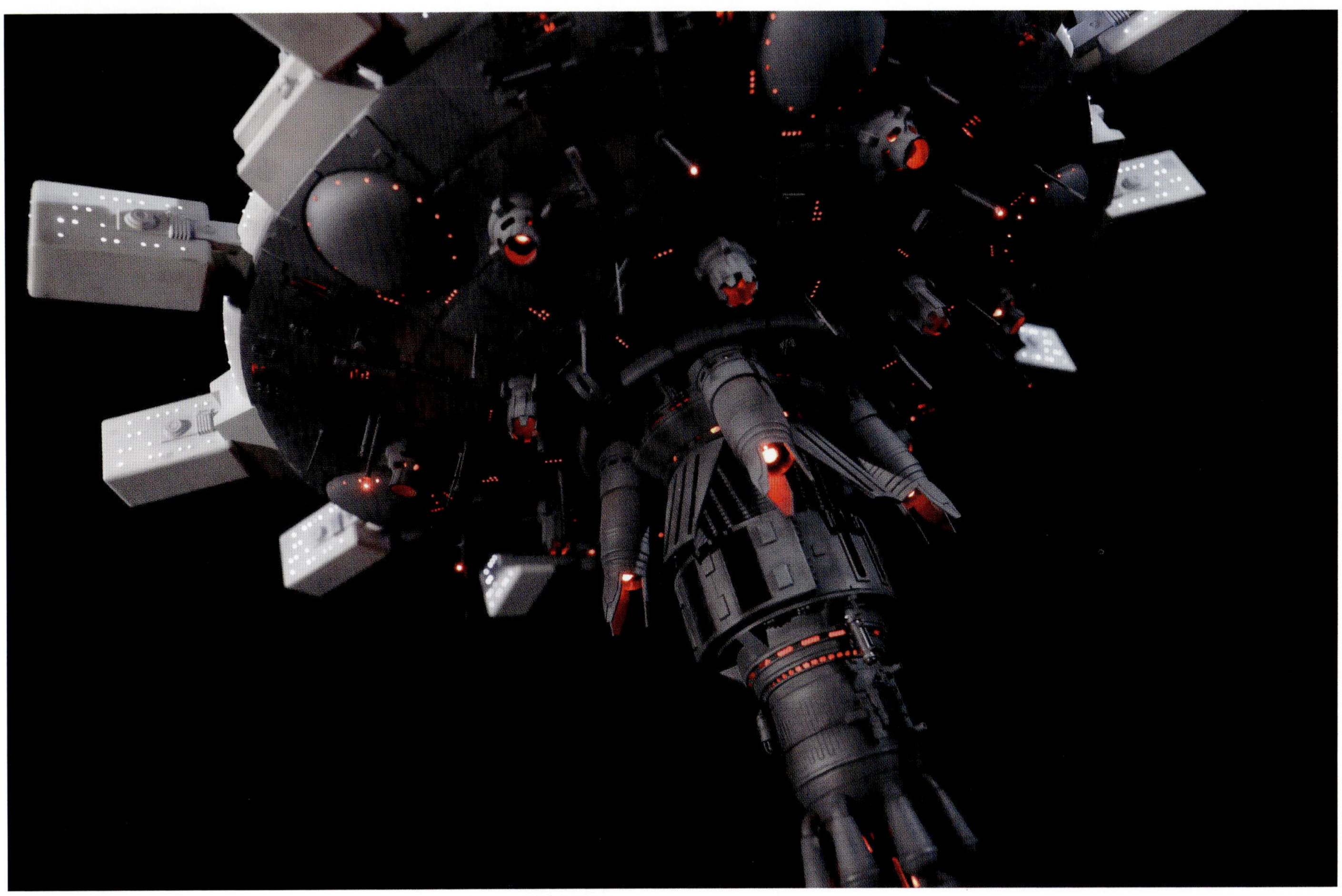

▸ Details, Starlight Beacon model EATON (ARTIST) AND KAO (PHOTOGRAPHER)

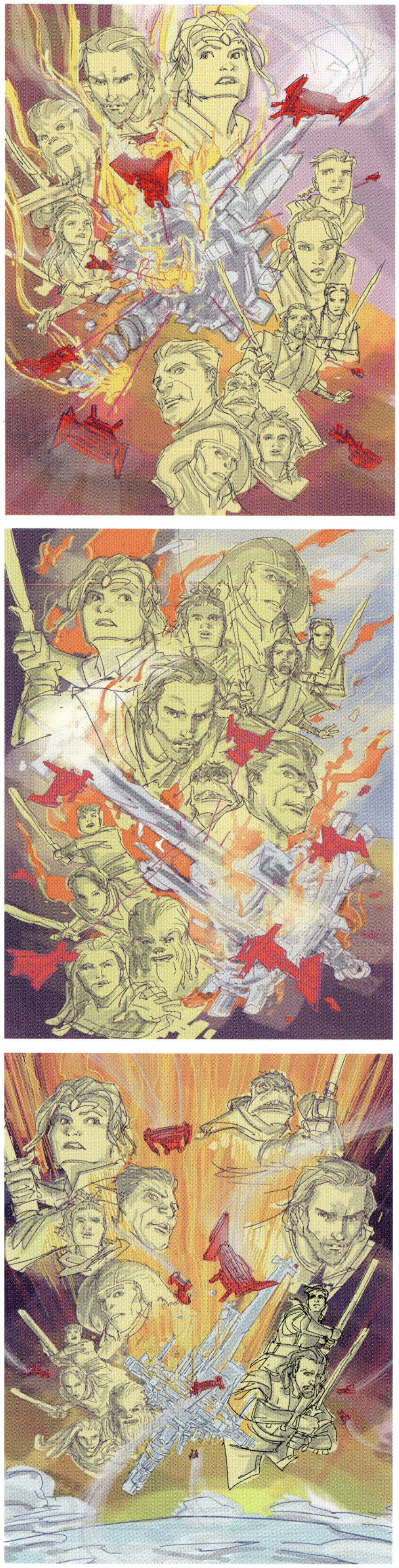

▲ Sketches for the disaster poster STEVE KURTH

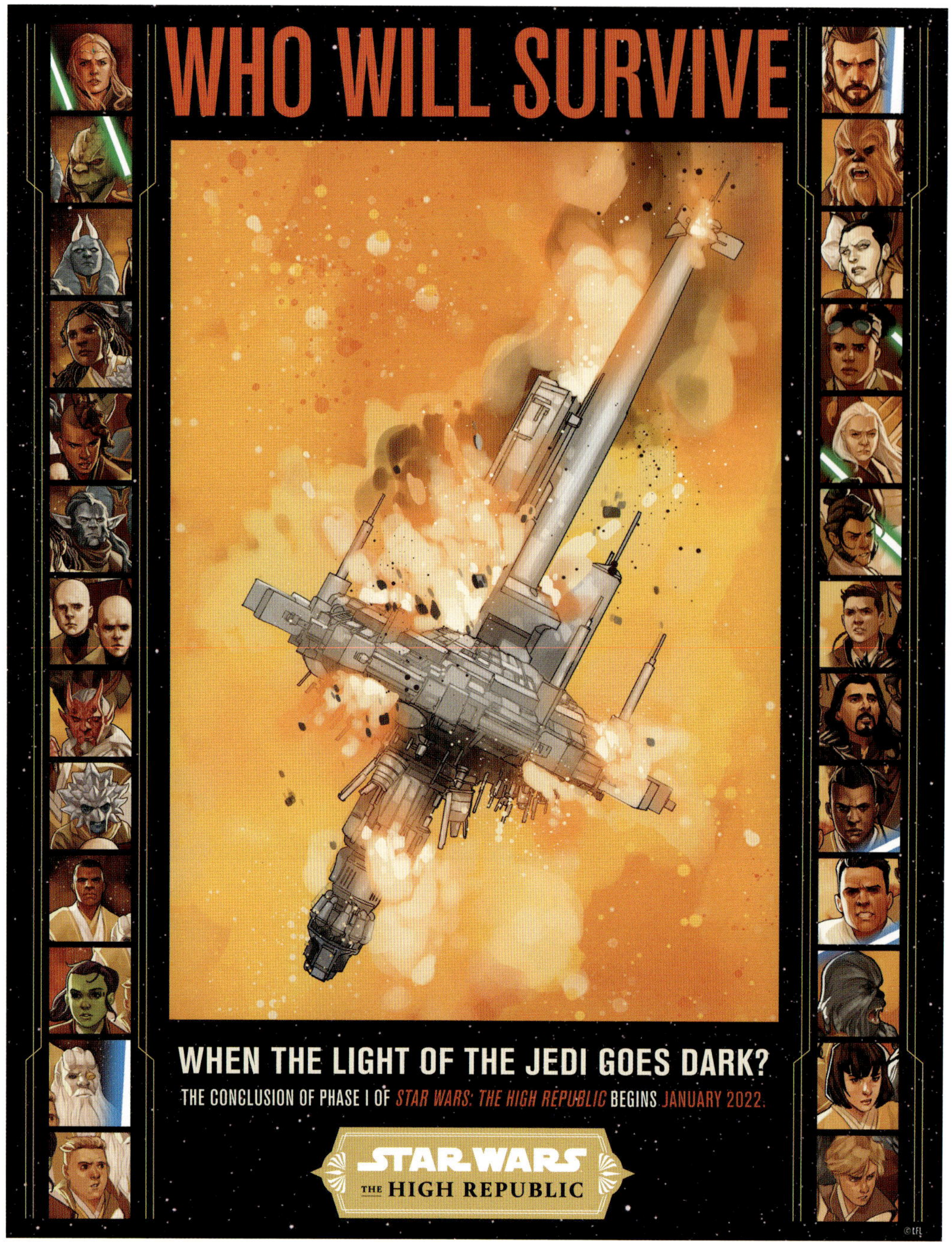

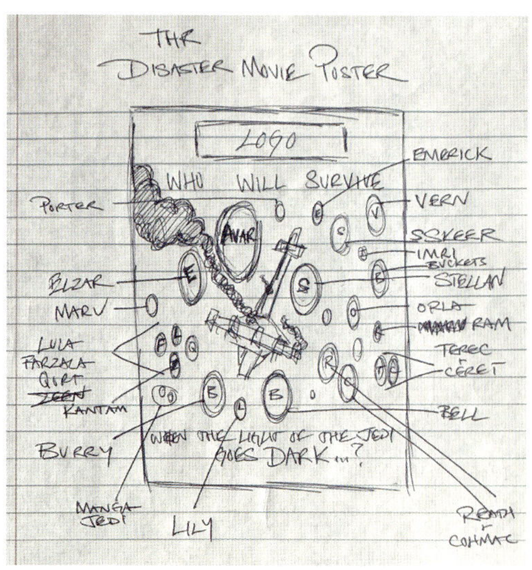

▲ Promotional poster for Wave 3 inspired by cinematic poster art NOTO

To mark the release of the first books and comics in The High Republic initiative in January 2021, the authors gifted Siglain an original production poster of *The Poseidon Adventure* with a simple note: "To our captain from your grateful crew." The film heavily influenced the final act of Phase I's storytelling, including this version of the teaser art directly inspired by the 1972 film poster.

◀ Initial sketch for the disaster poster MICHAEL SIGLAIN

▶ Final concept for the disaster poster NOTO

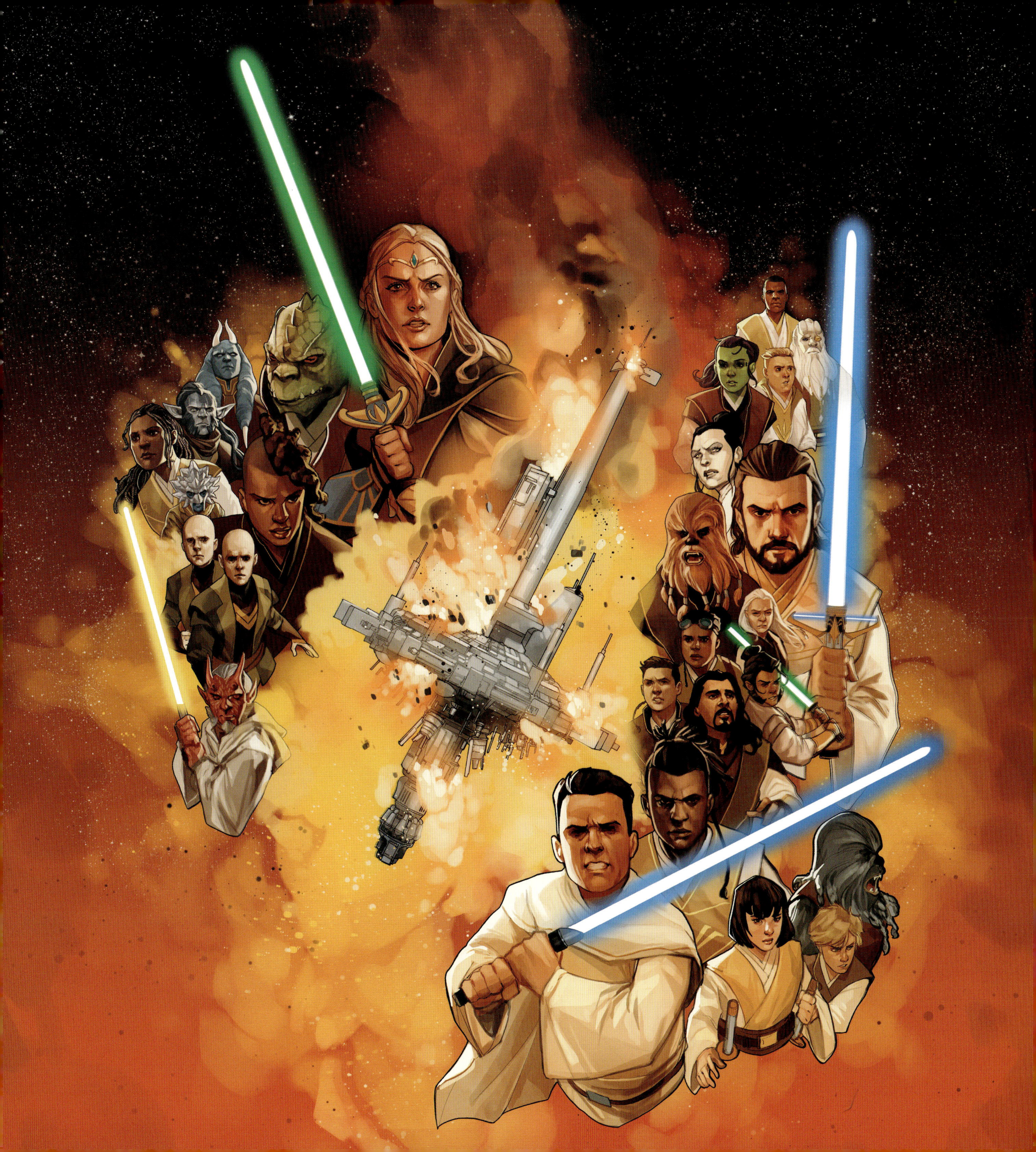

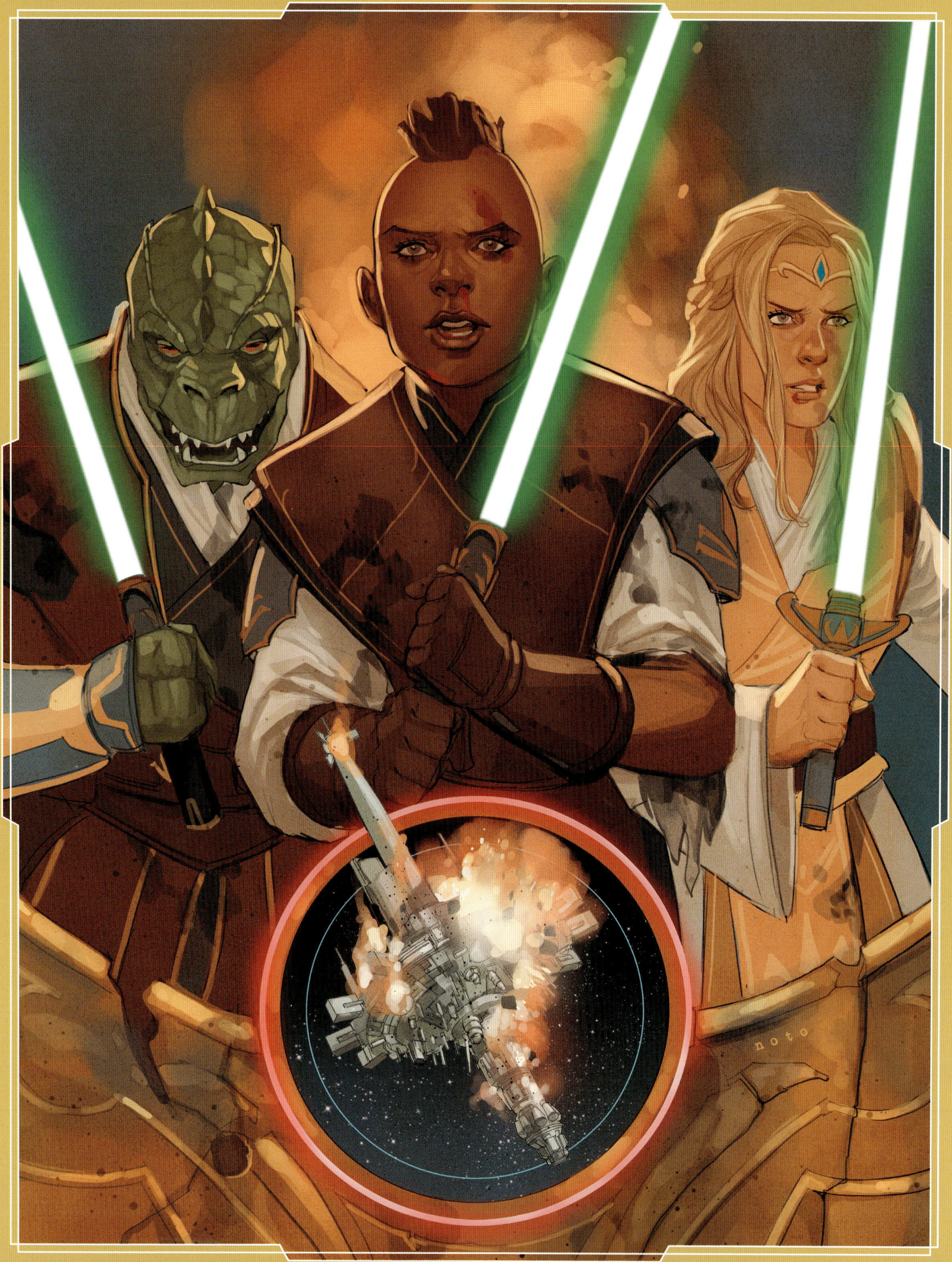

CHAPTER 7
THE SERIES

WHEN *THE HIGH REPUBLIC* ARRIVED in 2021, it debuted in an uncertain time, launching stories of triumph and trial as the real world was grappling with the first nine months of a global pandemic that would stretch into years.

First slated to release on August 25, 2020, with the publication of the novel *Light of the Jedi* and a select few other titles just ahead of *Star Wars* Celebration Anaheim, as the spread of COVID-19 forced hospitals to capacity and left medical workers scrambling for personal protective gear, the convention was canceled, production schedules for future *Star Wars* feature films were pushed, and *The High Republic*'s debut was delayed by five months.

But the success of the initiative upon its arrival spoke to the need for this story of hope and unity, trauma and perseverance. For centuries, stories have been a safe and gentle avenue for humanity to examine larger issues and face their greatest fears. "It's actually the purpose of stories, particularly the ones that are set on far-off worlds and strange fantasy lands," said concept artist Iain McCaig. "Number 1: We want to escape in hard times. Number 2: We want to have fun again and remember that there's fun in the world. And *Star Wars*, always at its best, was fun. And Number 3: We actually *do* want to talk about everything going on, but we can't do it directly. So, if you do it inside a story, it can't possibly be talking about you, yet it is exactly talking about everything—pandemics and genocides and destroying planets—in this world. You don't have to be offended by it right away. You can enjoy it first, which is a good way to teach anything."

Although many of the first stories and characters were written or conceived of before the pandemic surfaced, the global event had an undeniable impact. Author Charles Soule was in the revision stage of *Light of the Jedi* after COVID-19 locked down his home of New York City. "There are elements in the book that people will not believe that I had in the book before quarantine," Soule said. "But they were there. They're based on the way systems and governments and institutions respond to disasters, but I do think they will resonate much more strongly because of the shared experience literally everyone around the world [had]. They will find themes that will be resonant because of the time in which it's coming out and because of the time in which it was written."

For months after, Soule received messages from fans echoing Chancellor Lina Soh's outcry: "We are all the Republic." "I think it was the right kind of book to land at that time," Soule said. "It was exactly the story that I wanted to put into the world at that particular time, the message and the tone and the fact that it was introducing this new era, I felt like it was everything I wanted to do creatively."

Light of the Jedi debuted at number 1 on the *New York Times* bestseller list, while Justina Ireland's *A Test of Courage* captured the number 2 spot in middle-grade hardcovers when the two books released on January 5, 2021, along with the children's book *The Great Jedi Rescue*.

"I was blown away by how well it did," said Lucasfilm art director Troy Alders. "It was a gift."

THE NEXT DAY, the first issue of Marvel's *Star Wars: The High Republic* flagship comic hit shelves, spurring six printings of the first issue alone. If not for the pandemic forcing the comic book industry to hit the brakes on the typical speed of production, it would have been a far different story. Writer Cavan Scott said he penned a lost issue in March 2020, a debut titled "A More Civilized Age," which began with the Starlight Beacon dedication, where issue #1 as we know it

◂ Final cover art for Marvel's *Star Wars: The High Republic* #15 NOTO

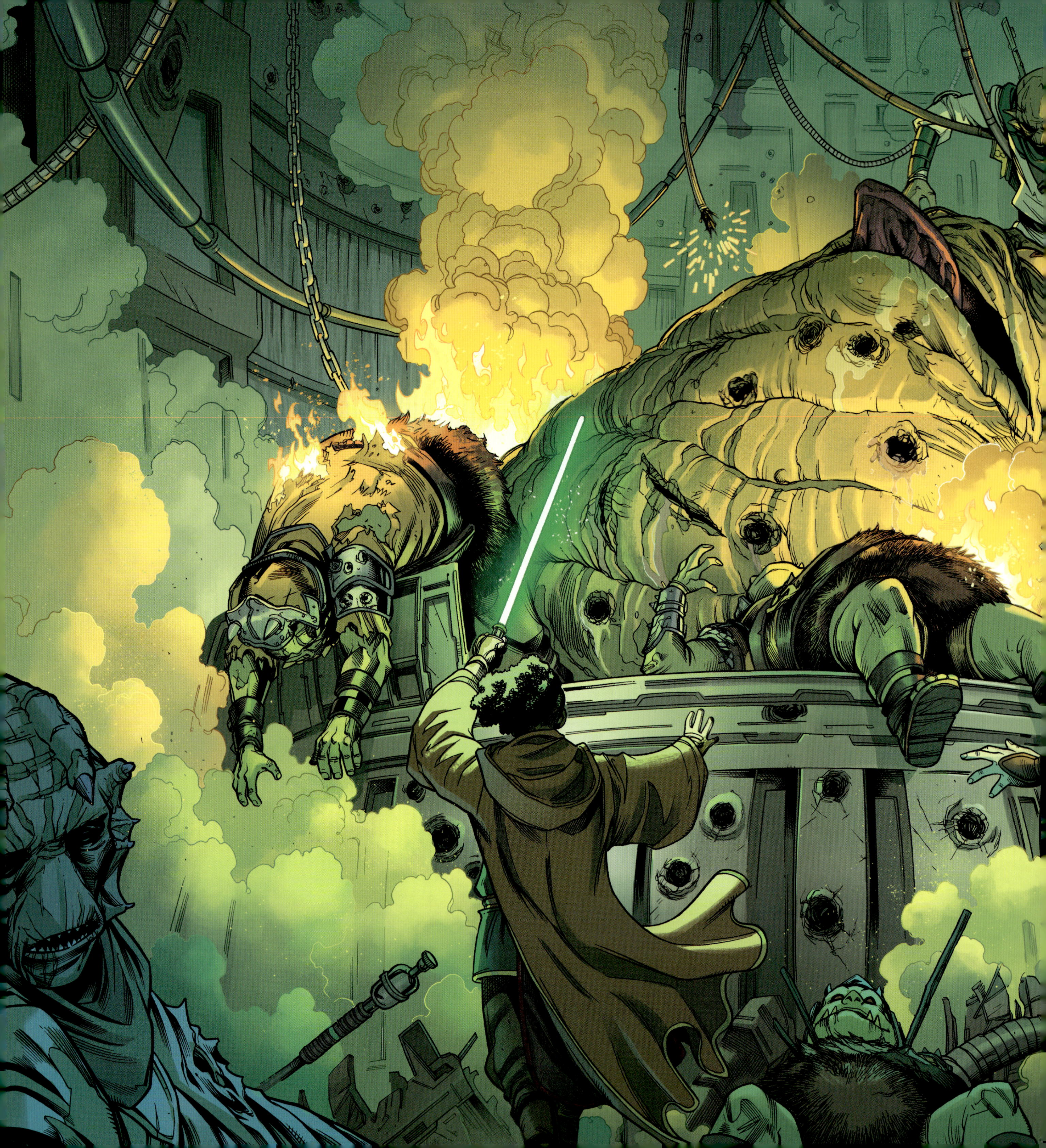

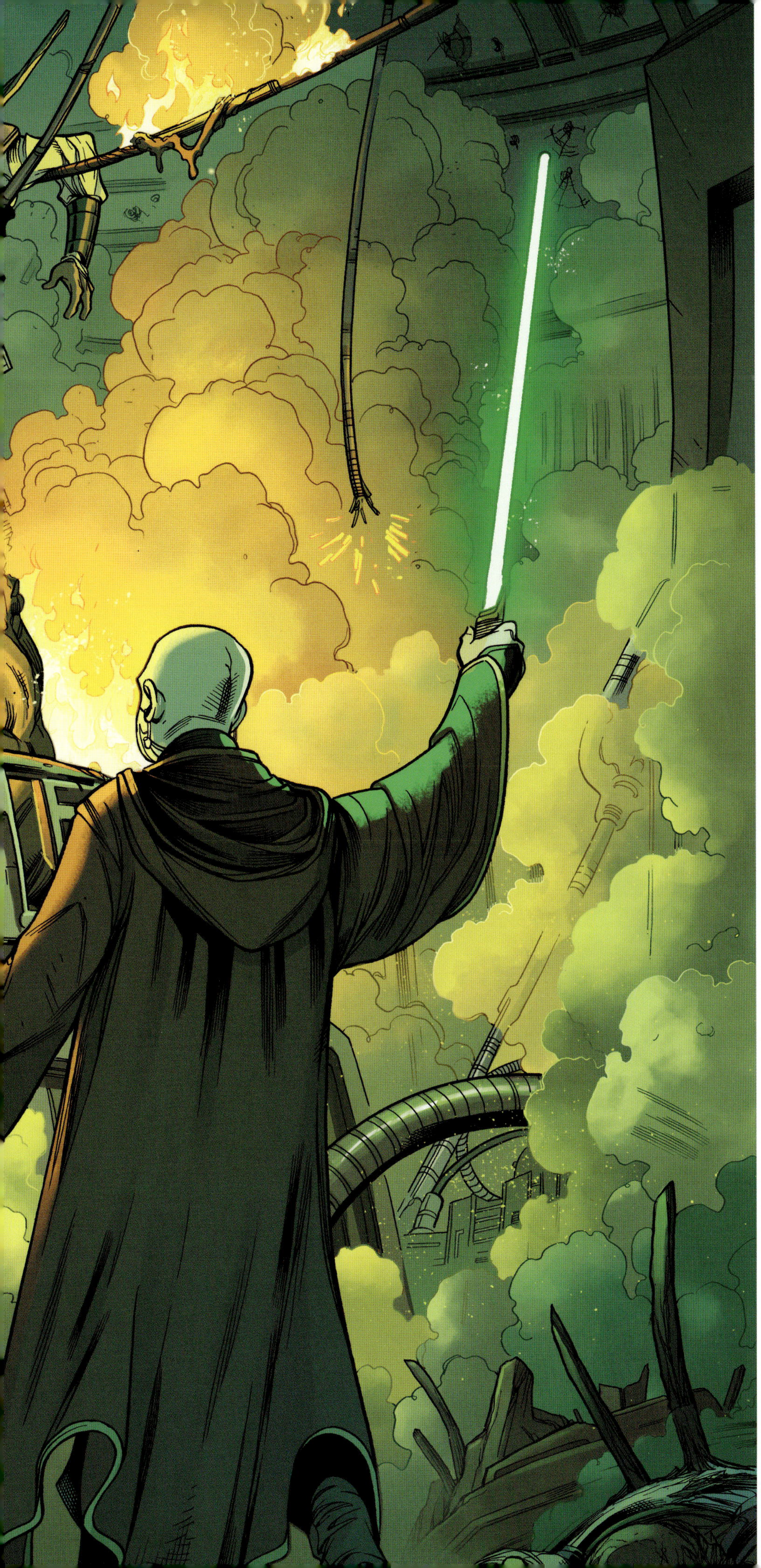

ends. Instead of an apprenticeship to Master Sskeer, the story followed multiple arcs including one thread that saw Keeve Trennis in the company of a Republic contractor named Vane Sarpen, captain of the *Rapscallion's Heart*, as they fought off scavenger droids unleashed by the Nihil. An even earlier draft considered Sarpen as a possible love interest for the young Jedi, a dalliance that was scrapped by the time the script was sent off to the editors. A secondary plot followed Sskeer, Avar Kriss, Imri Cantaros, and Vernestra Rwoh as they defended a planet that was, at that stage, called Carnagra, a world that was crippled in the Great Disaster but still preparing to host the upcoming Republic Fair.

"I sent it in and fretted," Scott said. "It just didn't hang together. There were too many characters, too much going on, and Keeve was getting lost in it all." At one point, that version of Keeve destroyed a Nihil ship, which "while dramatic, just wasn't Keeve," Scott said. "We were hoping that it would show that she still had much to learn, but it wasn't heroic at all. It wasn't Jedi." The subplot leaped into Sskeer's disconnect to the Force, a storyline that would end up in a story released several months after the first issue and introduce a swarm of space locusts in the second issue. "It just felt like action without any heart. It all tied in, but I was finding it hard to care about the characters," Scott said.

When the ramifications of the pandemic put his comic on temporary hold, Scott took advantage of the extra time. "It gave me a chance to take a step back and look at the entire first arc afresh, especially that first issue. I pulled the arc apart, losing the stuff on Carnagra, and bringing the space-locusts into a brand-new issue #1 that would see Keeve taking her trials before jumping straight into the Drengir plot. At the same time, I wrote a completely new bottom-up draft of issue #1, which is pretty much what you see in the published issue," Scott said, now titled "There is No Fear." The *Rapscallion's Heart* and its crew were left on the cutting-room floor, although Vane and the ship turned up in a short piece of fiction for *Star Wars Insider*. "Looking back, it's crazy to me that Sskeer wasn't Keeve's master in that first draft. Their relationship is such a huge part of the comic," Scott said.

◂ The Hutt-slaying interior from Marvel's *Star Wars: The High Republic* #2 and cover art for third printing ANINDITO (PENCILER), MORALES (INKER), AND LEONI (COLORIST)

Scott and Anindito's shared love of horror film can be felt in this ominous moment, which takes inspiration from the scene in *Alien* when the *Nostromo* crew discovers the strange species. "It left a mark on me," Anindito said. "Imagine you go to a spaceship and you find a dead alien just sitting there. What happened? Now I want to deliver that kind of feeling, but in this particular issue, it's not just one alien. It's a massacre."

Equally important to the line art is the color story, awash in greens and vibrant yellows. "This is one of Keeve's first missions as an actual Jedi Knight, so she's very green. And you can see that green in the whole page," Anindito continued. "But I also think of something toxic. The Teenage Mutant Ninja Turtles' ooze is green; the Joker's laughing gas is green. So it's a deadly thing. Green is dangerous. Keeve is green, and green is lethal."

Leoni differentiated the smoke from the fire with pops of yellow. "And we get to play on the layering of the gas itself," Anindito said. "Like this gas is near you and that gas is far away. But you cannot see everything clearly, and that puts more terror in it."

ON FEBRUARY 2, 2021, Claudia Gray's young adult novel *Into the Dark* was released, yet another number 1 *New York Times* bestseller for the initiative, while Daniel José Older's *Star Wars: The High Republic Adventures* #1, an all-ages comic from IDW illustrated by Harvey Tolibao, was released the following day and would become the second-best-selling comic in IDW's history.

The second wave of books arrived in the summer, with Scott's *The Rising Storm* and Older's middle-grade reader *Race to Crashpoint Tower*, debuting on June 29, 2021, followed by Ireland's young adult novel *Out of the Shadows* on July 27, 2021. All three once more topped the *New York Times* bestseller lists.

Just as the onset of the COVID-19 pandemic had altered the first wave of stories and shifted the release schedule, real-world events continued to impact the fictional galaxy. After introducing and killing off several characters in *Light of the Jedi*, *The Rising Storm* heightened the stakes by showcasing that even the Jedi were coming up against something that could leave them paralyzed and powerless. However, the initial plan would have spared Loden Greatstorm at the expense of his Padawan, Bell Zettifar, a turn of events that became unthinkable in the wake of George Floyd's murder and the swell of support for the Black Lives Matter movement. Ireland noted that she was in favor of sparing the Padawan, a young Black man, from the start. But "after George Floyd, I was like, 'You cannot kill Bell,'" she recalled, and the author of the book, Scott, agreed. The trauma of the pandemic and the social issues that erupted during the summer of 2020 had a profound effect on both the storytellers and their art, forcing Ireland to be more conscious of the emotional through line of her contributions. "We were a lot more sensitive about the stories we were putting out because we didn't want to put out as much doom and gloom and despair when the world is doom and gloom and despair," Ireland added. The novel ultimately debuted soon after the one-year anniversary of Floyd's death. "Can you imagine?" Ireland said, reflecting on the potential ire had the original story gone to print killing off Zettifar. "The thing is, we're writing in a fictional world, but it's still being read by people in the real world. And so we still have to be considerate to that."

In between those major drops, the IDW and Marvel comics continued the expansive story, with Scott's graphic novel *The Monster of Temple Peak,* illustrated by Rachael Stott, dropping the first of four installments on August 11, 2021, and his audio original *Tempest Runner* arriving on August 31, 2021. A manga, *The Edge of Balance*, written by Ireland and Shima Shinya, and illustrated by Mizuki Sakakibara, followed on September 7, 2021, with Marvel's *Trail of Shadows*, by Older and illustrated by Dave Wachter, released on October 6, 2021.

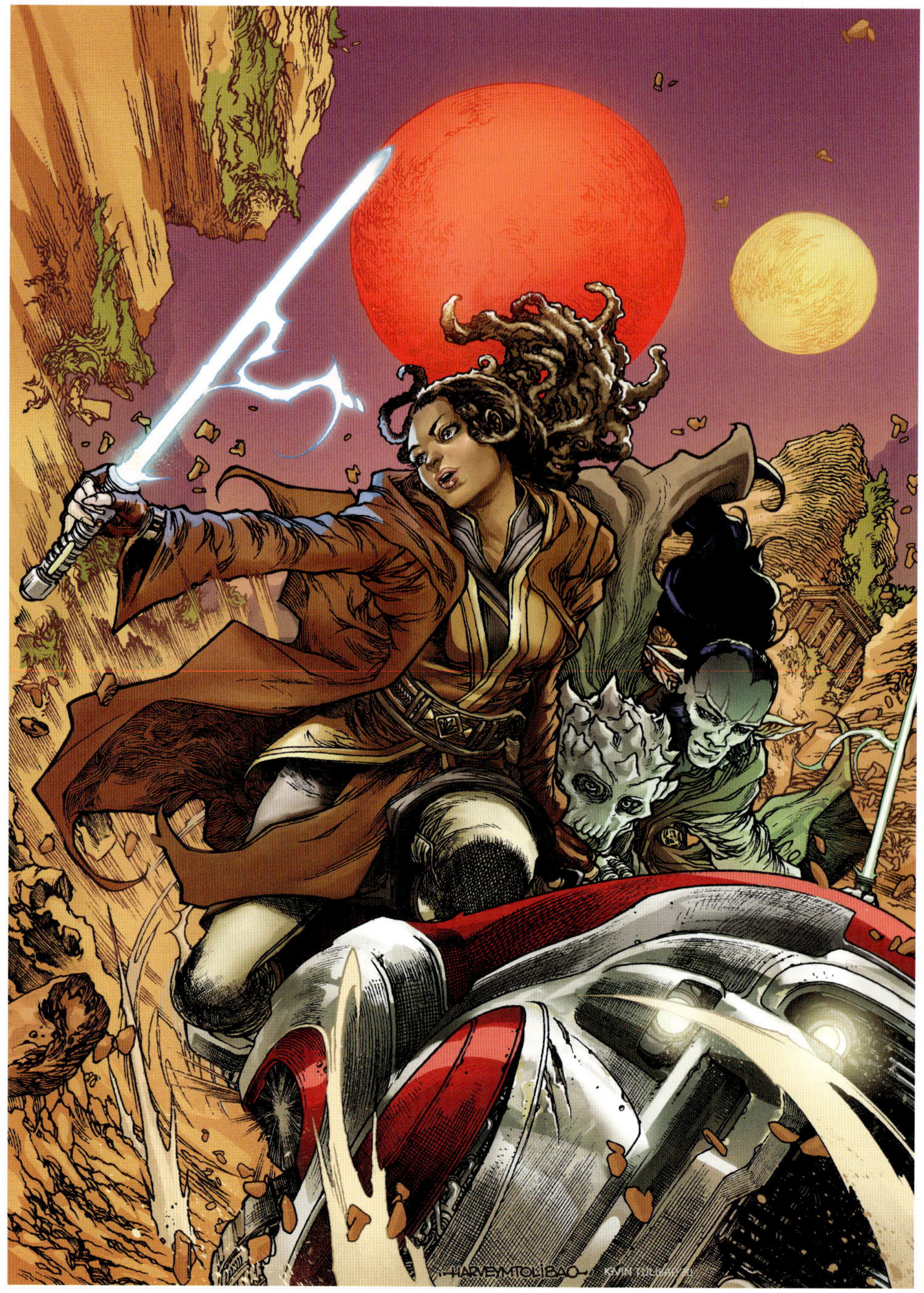

▲ Final cover art for IDW's *Star Wars: The High Republic Adventures* #1 TOLIBAO (PENCILER) AND KEVIN TOLIBAO (COLORIST)

Tolibao's brother, Kevin Tolibao, serves as the colorist on the series' covers.

THE THIRD AND FINAL WAVE of stories in Phase I published beginning on January 4, 2022, with Gray's adult novel *The Fallen Star* leading the charge and once again topping the *New York Times* bestseller list. It was followed by Older's young adult novel *Midnight Horizon* on February 1, 2022, the second installment of the VIZ manga written by Shinya and Older released as an ebook on February 22, 2022 (with the print edition released on May 24, 2022), Ireland's middle-grade reader *Mission to Disaster* on March 1, 2022, and ended with a cliffhanger moment in the second part of Soule's Marvel two-shot, *Eye of the Storm*, Marchion Ro's origin story illustrated by Guillermo Sanna, released on March 2, 2022.

The stories continued to celebrate a rich, diverse galaxy that reflected the multitudes in our own world, while reacting and responding to some of the crises unfolding with the tension after America's presidential election that unseated

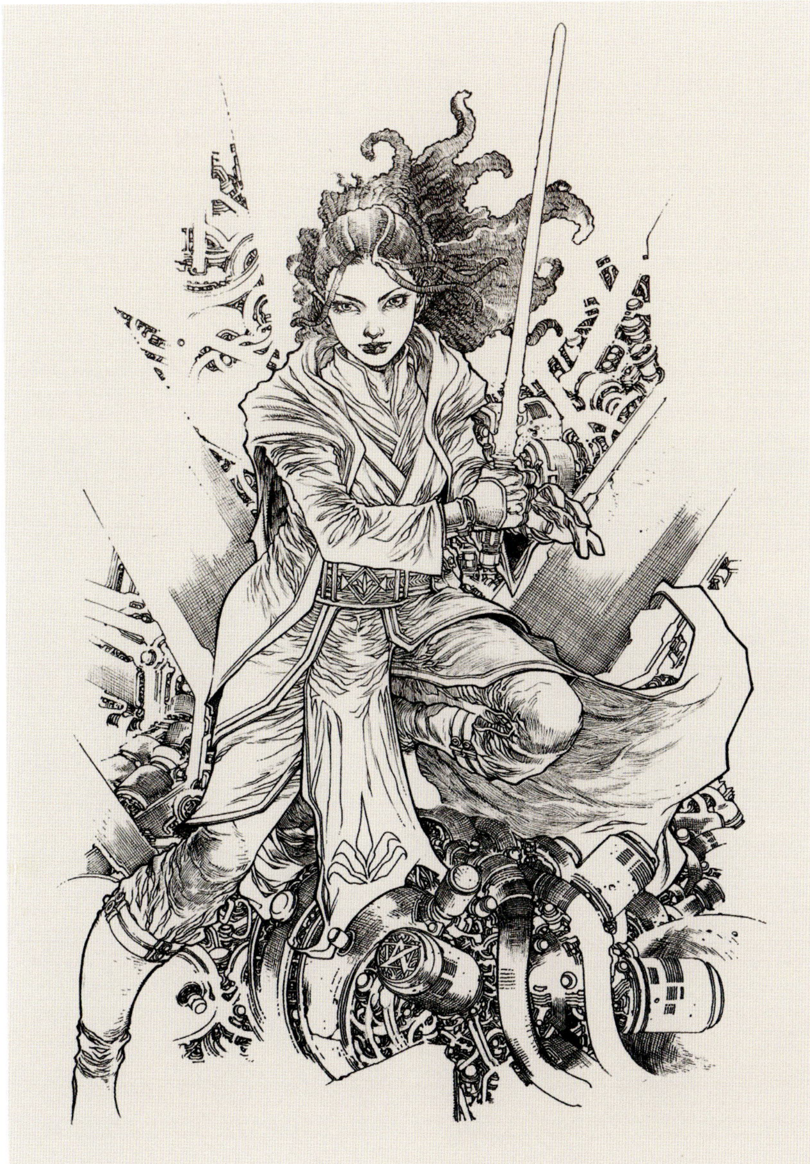

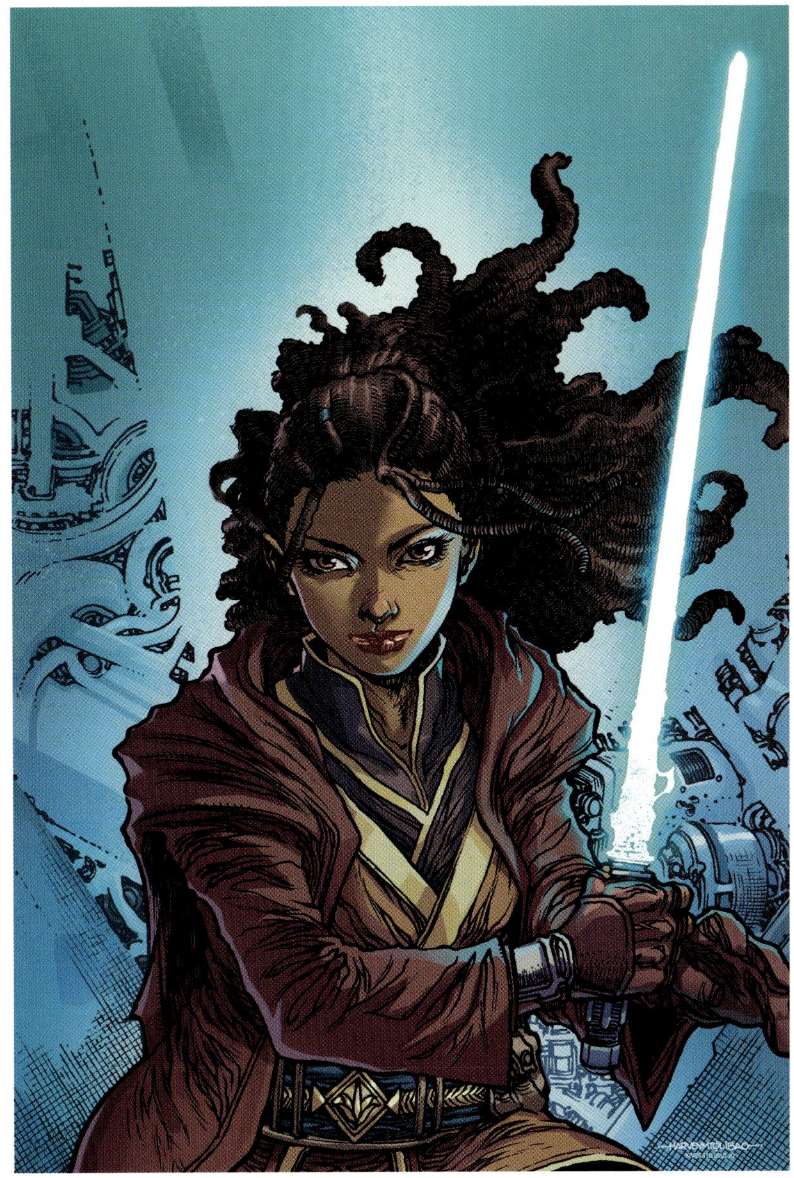

▲ Original line art and final cover of IDW's *Star Wars: The High Republic Adventures* #2 TOLIBAO (PENCILER) AND KEVIN TOLIBAO (COLORIST)

Donald Trump. The insurrection at the United States Capitol on January 6, 2021, directly informed a scene in Older's young adult novel featuring a Nihil masquerade ball in Coronet City, as the upper echelon of Corellia show they are woefully blinded to reality. "It's a place where people are very much not on the lookout for the Nihil. You know, there's just a given understanding that the Nihil are not going to be able to get a foothold that deep into the core of the galaxy. And so they have been lulled into a sense of safety, and because of that, they truly don't see it coming when that exact thing happens," Older said. "That's very much a story about fascism and the rise of fascism anywhere, but including what we were seeing. Very specifically, there is this moment where they throw a big party and it's such a joke to everybody that people dress up as the Nihil—totally out of touch, dressing up as the people that are actually taking down Starlight. And there are actual Nihil infiltrators in that crowd in the party dressed like themselves. They've infiltrated the police. They've infiltrated the politicians. It's actually very easy for them to then just go ahead and rule there. And that's what we saw on January 6th, a very obvious and violent example of that."

For Older, it was a response to the culmination of everything the years of the pandemic had wrought, from the trauma of staggering death tolls and the millions dead to the divisive political upheaval. "There's a moment in there where Ram gets so angry that glasses start breaking around him. It's not really the dark side, he's just really upset. Reath has to come and calm him down, and that's the conversation about balance, right? Whether you've lived through it, really faced down death like Ram has, or you just see it on TV every day or you hear about it over Skype with your family, everyone is going through understanding death on a much more everyday basis than they used to."

With the light of the Jedi dimmed with the destruction of Starlight Beacon and the Republic left in chaos, Phase I ended with the villains emerging victorious. "We're going to pull the rug out and say, 'OK, to be continued,'" said Lucasfilm Publishing's Michael Siglain, with the final stories in Phase I signaling several months of silence in The High Republic initiative. But it's nowhere near the end of the story. "The next time you see the High Republic, it's going to be 150 years in the past."

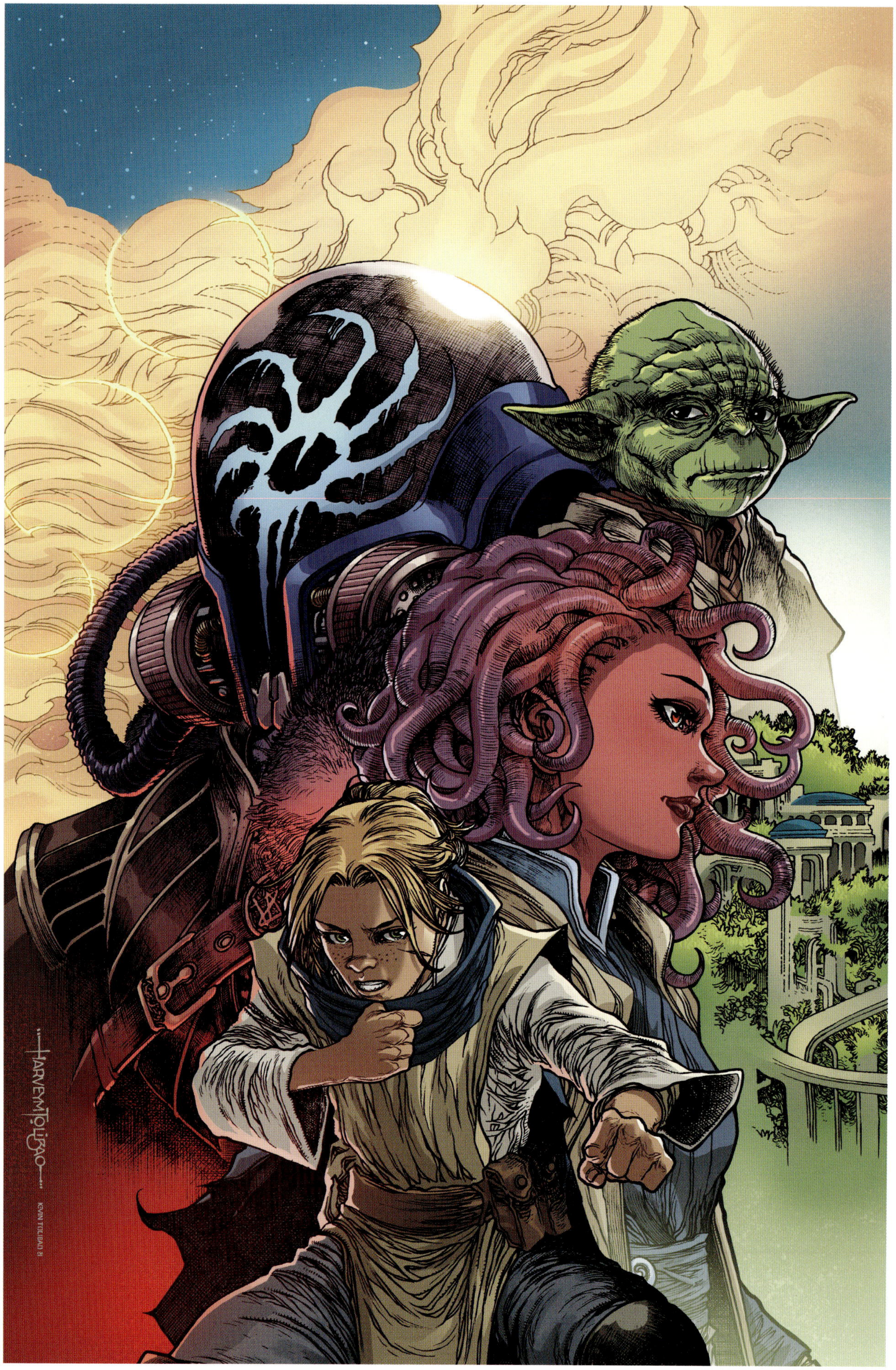

◂ Final cover art for IDW's *Star Wars: The High Republic Adventures* #3
TOLIBAO (PENCILER) AND KEVIN TOLIBAO (COLORIST)

Zeen Mrala, a Force-sensitive Mikkian, is no Jedi, but a hard life has made her precocious in nature. For her hair-like tentacles, Tolibao favors drawing the otherwise limp headtails in motion. "I use it as an expression of her body language," Tolibao said. And the artist often pays homage to his own family in his work. "You always find on my covers a W and Z. That's my sons—Wayne and Zad—so they're always there."

▸ Final cover art for IDW's *Star Wars: The High Republic Adventures* #4
TOLIBAO (PENCILER) AND KEVIN TOLIBAO (COLORIST)

"I always try to insert Cham Cham on the cover because I love the chemistry of Cham Cham and Zeen and Cham Cham and other characters. There's a scene with all the kids, and Cham Cham is playing with the kids, so it means that sometimes he's nice, especially when he knows that it's just part of this family, but when it's the Nihil, he's got to eat them." TOLIBAO

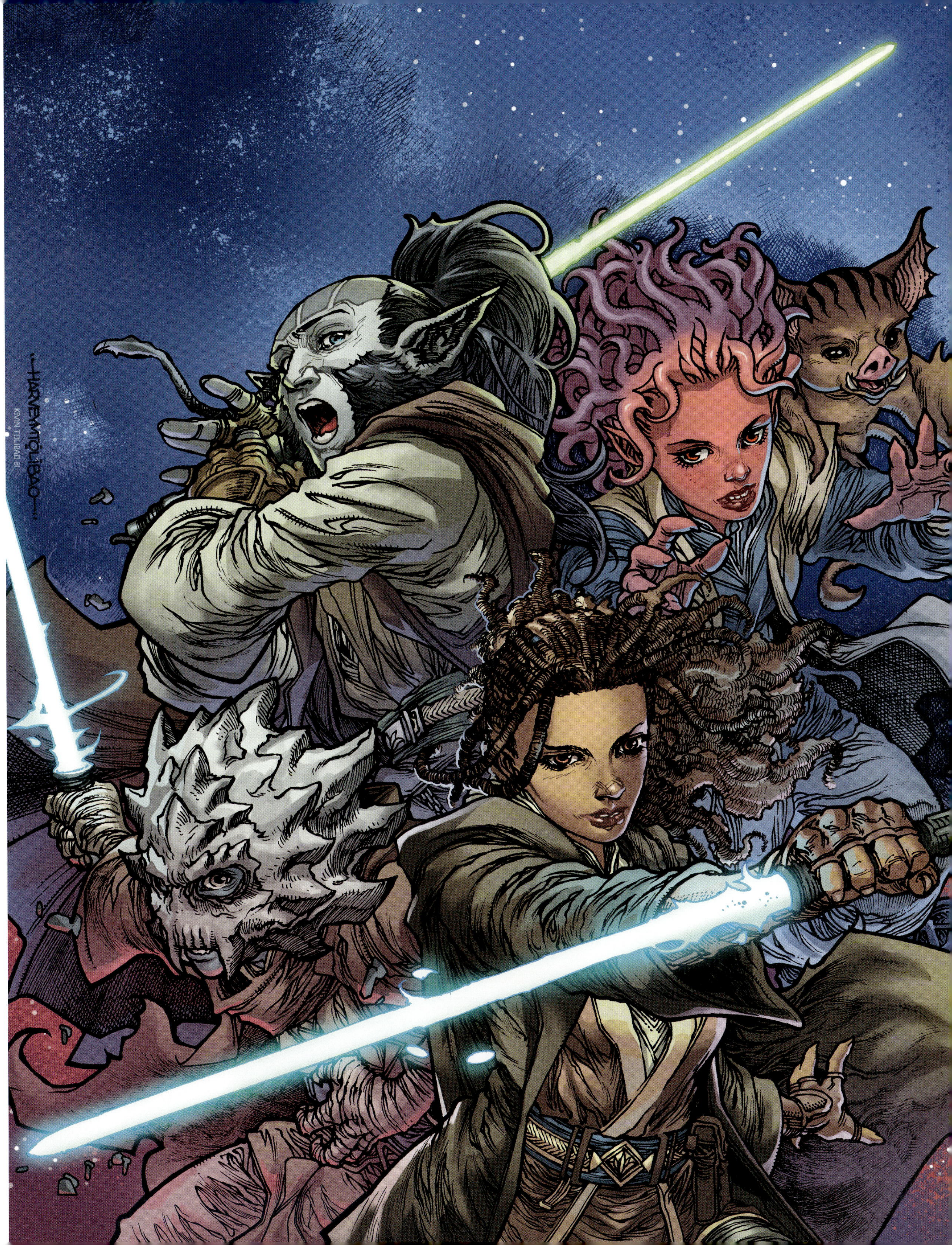

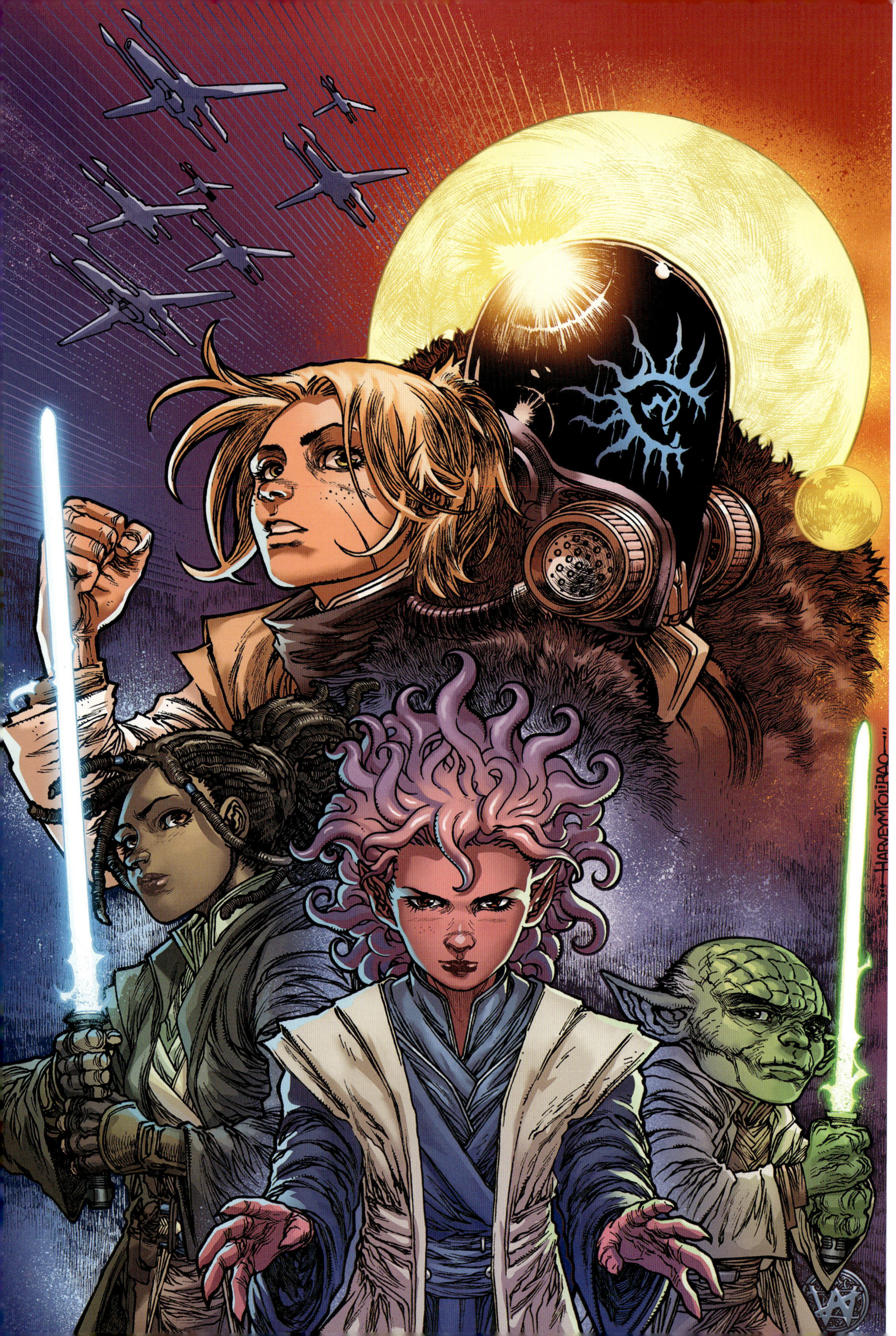

Final cover art for IDW's *Star Wars: The High Republic Adventures #5* TOLIBAO (PENCILER) AND KEVIN TOLIBAO (COLORIST)

"Drew Struzan is a very big influence, and, for me, you can see it here. Krix is starting to turn to another side, and you can see that the body [is blending with] the design of the body of Marchion Ro. There's something happening." TOLIBAO

▾ Cover for IDW's *Star Wars: The High Republic Adventures* #6 from sketch to completion TOLIBAO (PENCILER) AND KEVIN TOLIBAO (COLORIST)

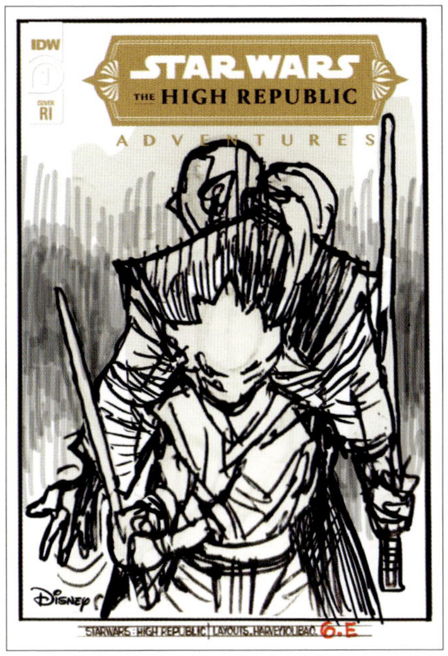

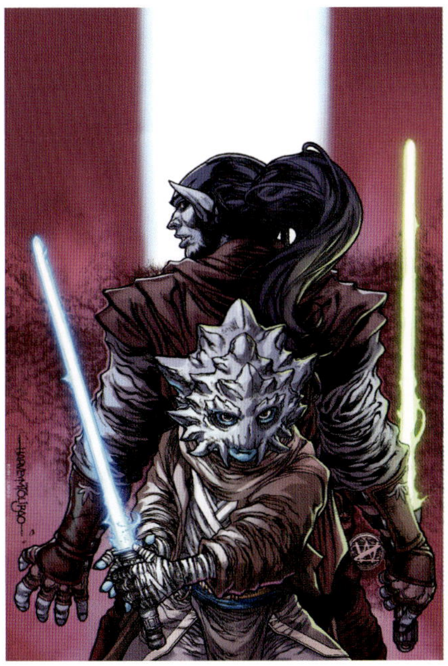

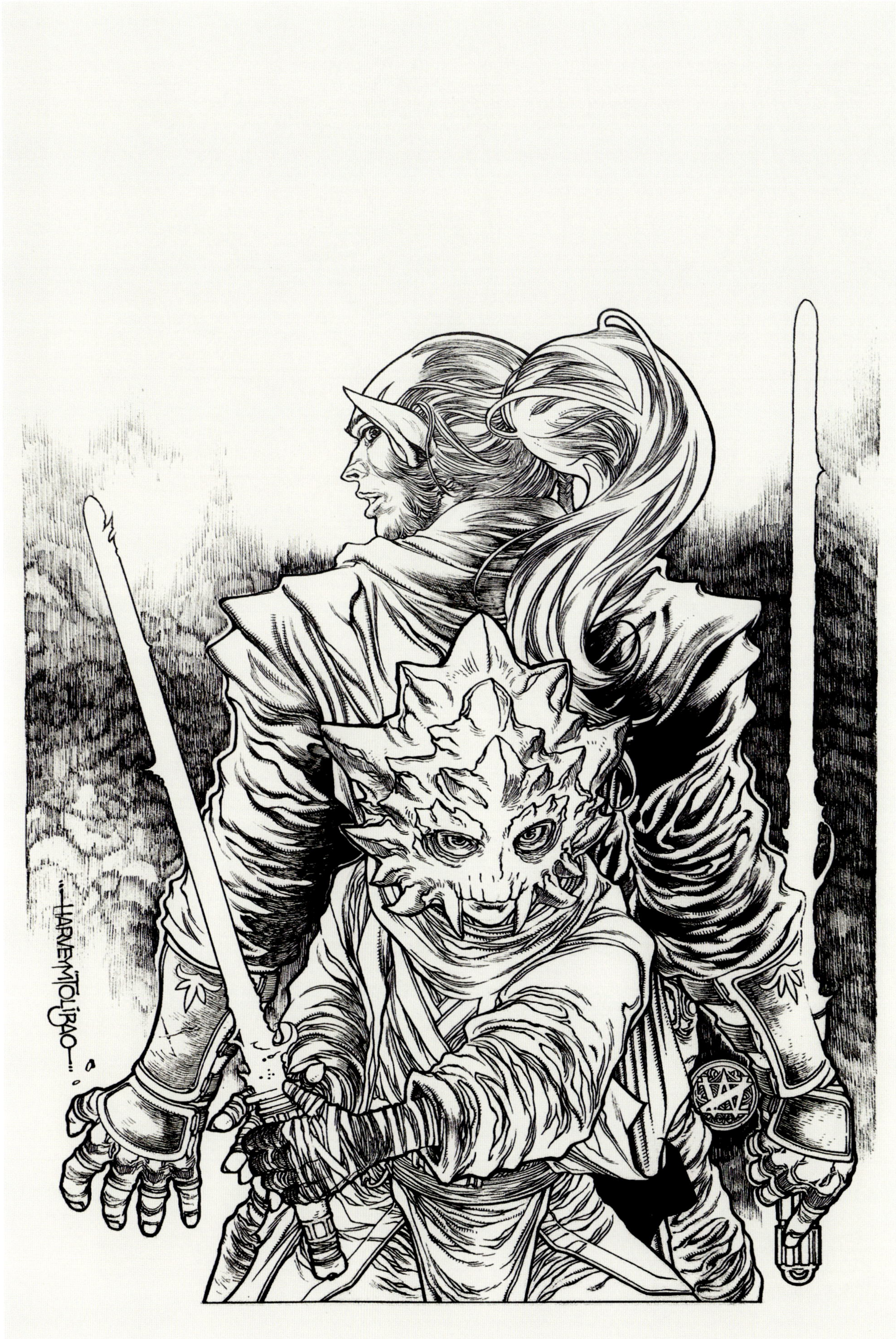

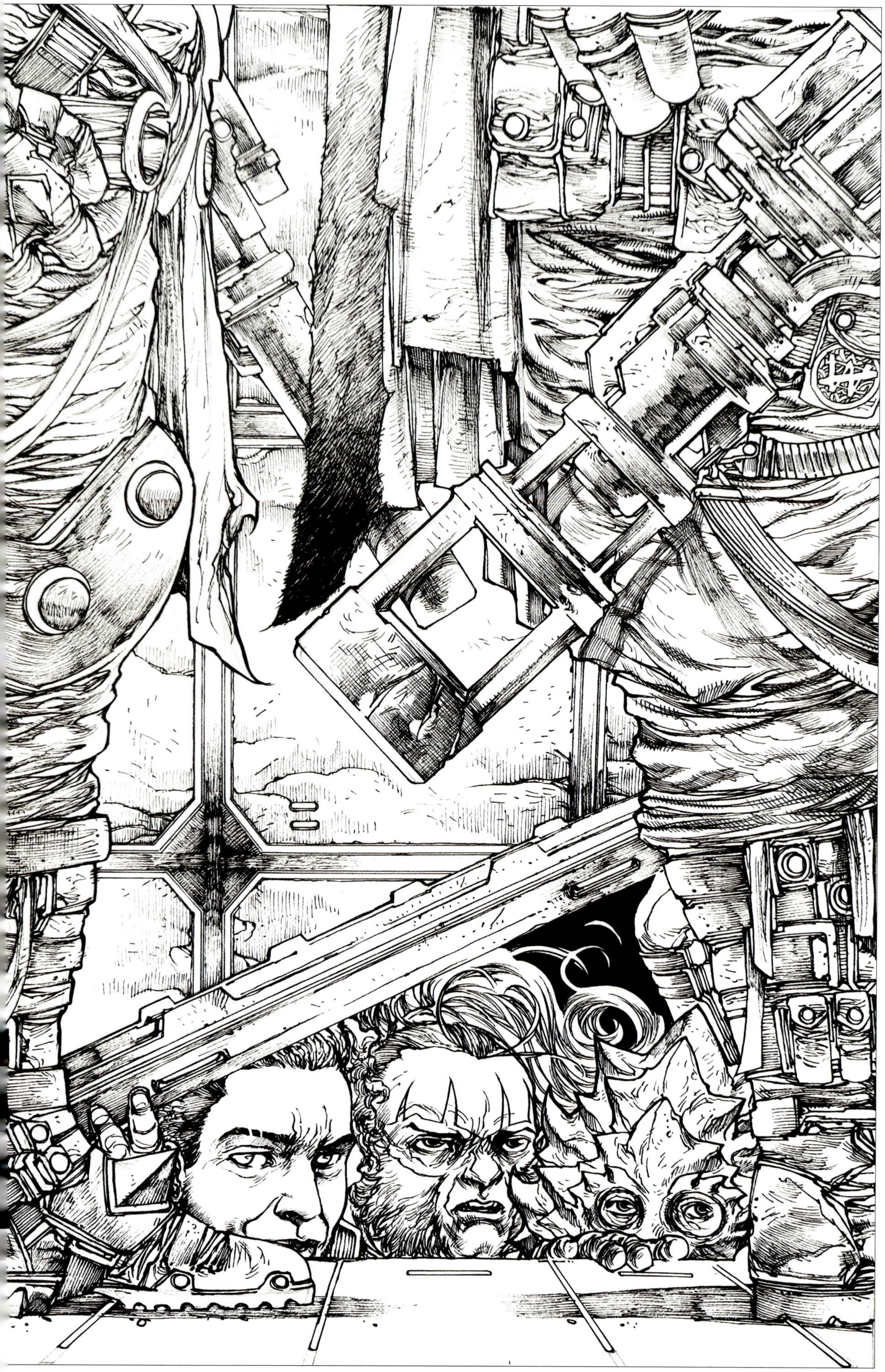

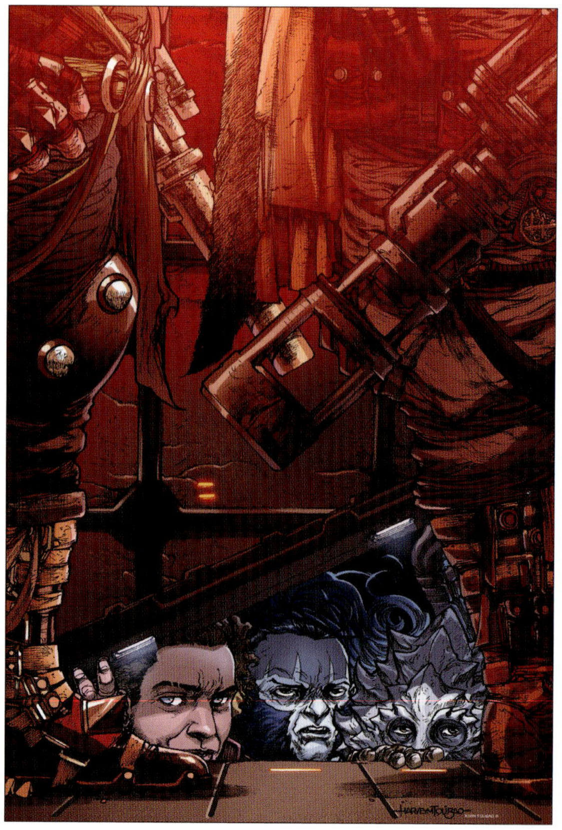

◂ Line art and final cover art for IDW's *Star Wars: The High Republic Adventures* #7 TOLIBAO (PENCILER) AND KEVIN TOLIBAO (COLORIST)

"You can see Farzala's face is like, 'This is a bad idea.' Then Qort is like, 'We have no choice, we have to be here.' And Leox, you know, 'All right, all right, all right. You can do this.'" TOLIBAO

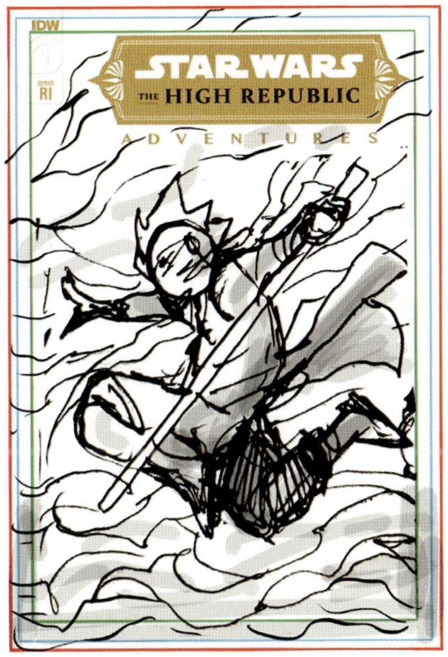

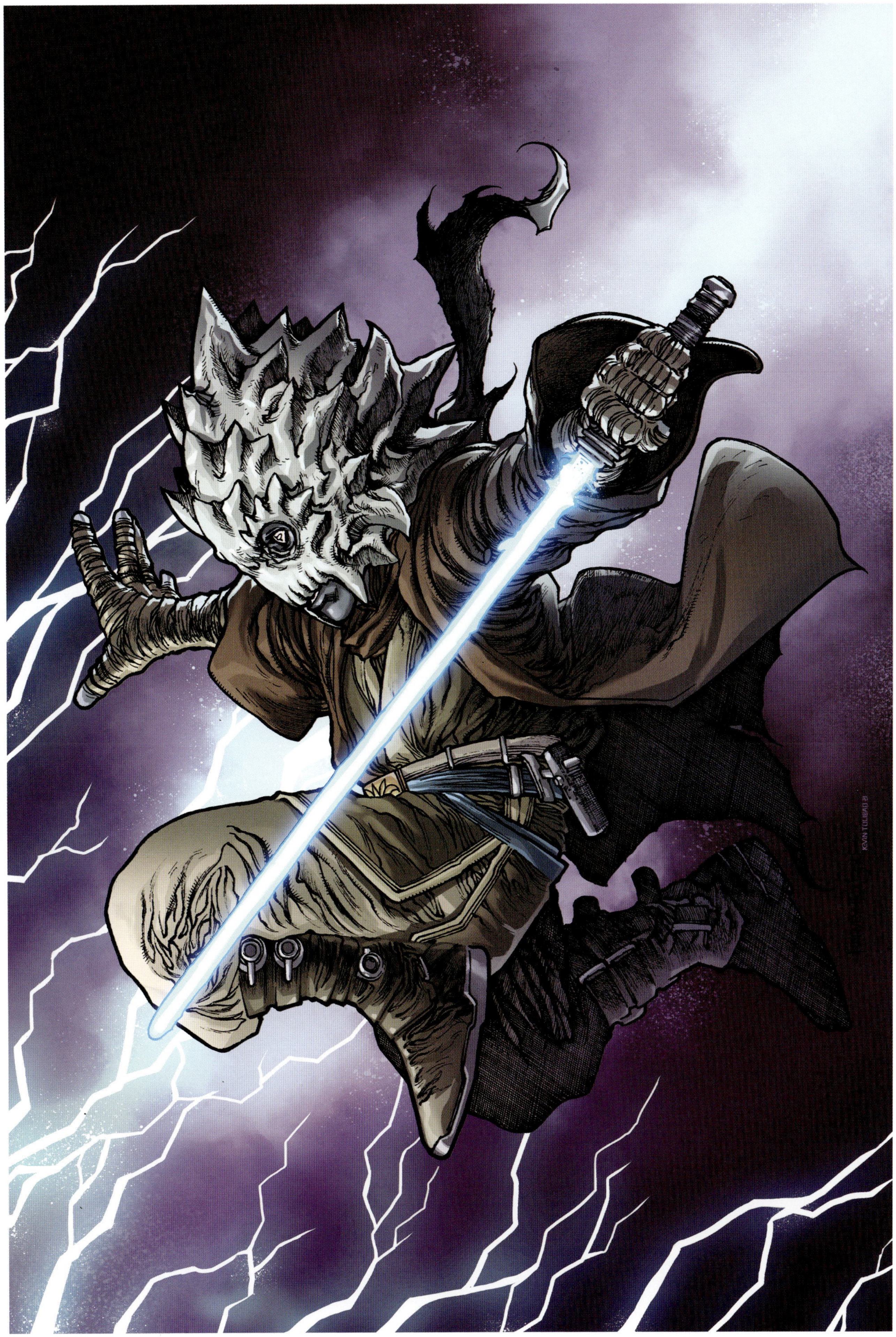

▸ Sketch and final cover art for IDW's *Star Wars: The High Republic Adventures #9* TOLIBAO (PENCILER) AND KEVIN TOLIBAO (COLORIST)

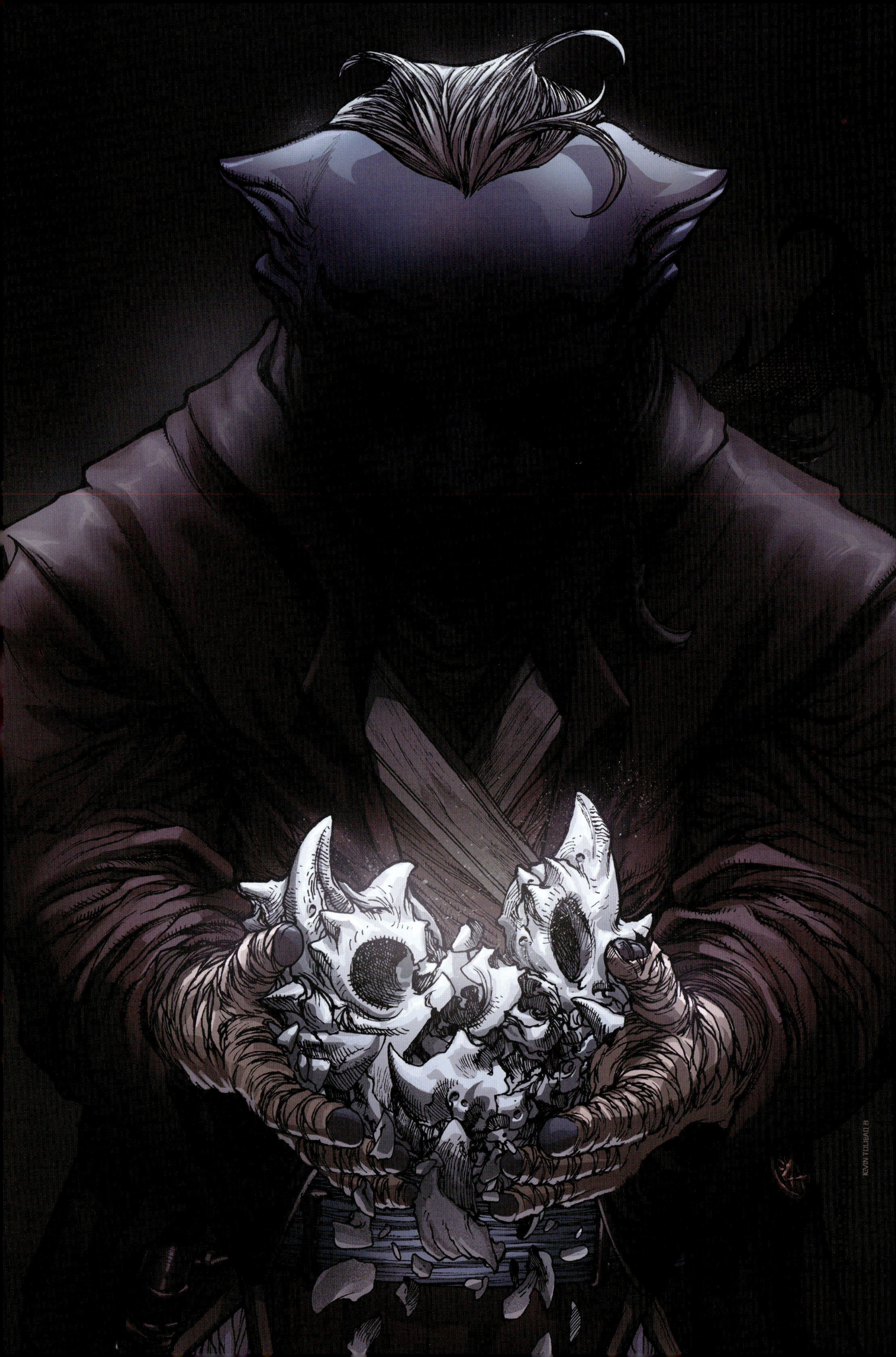

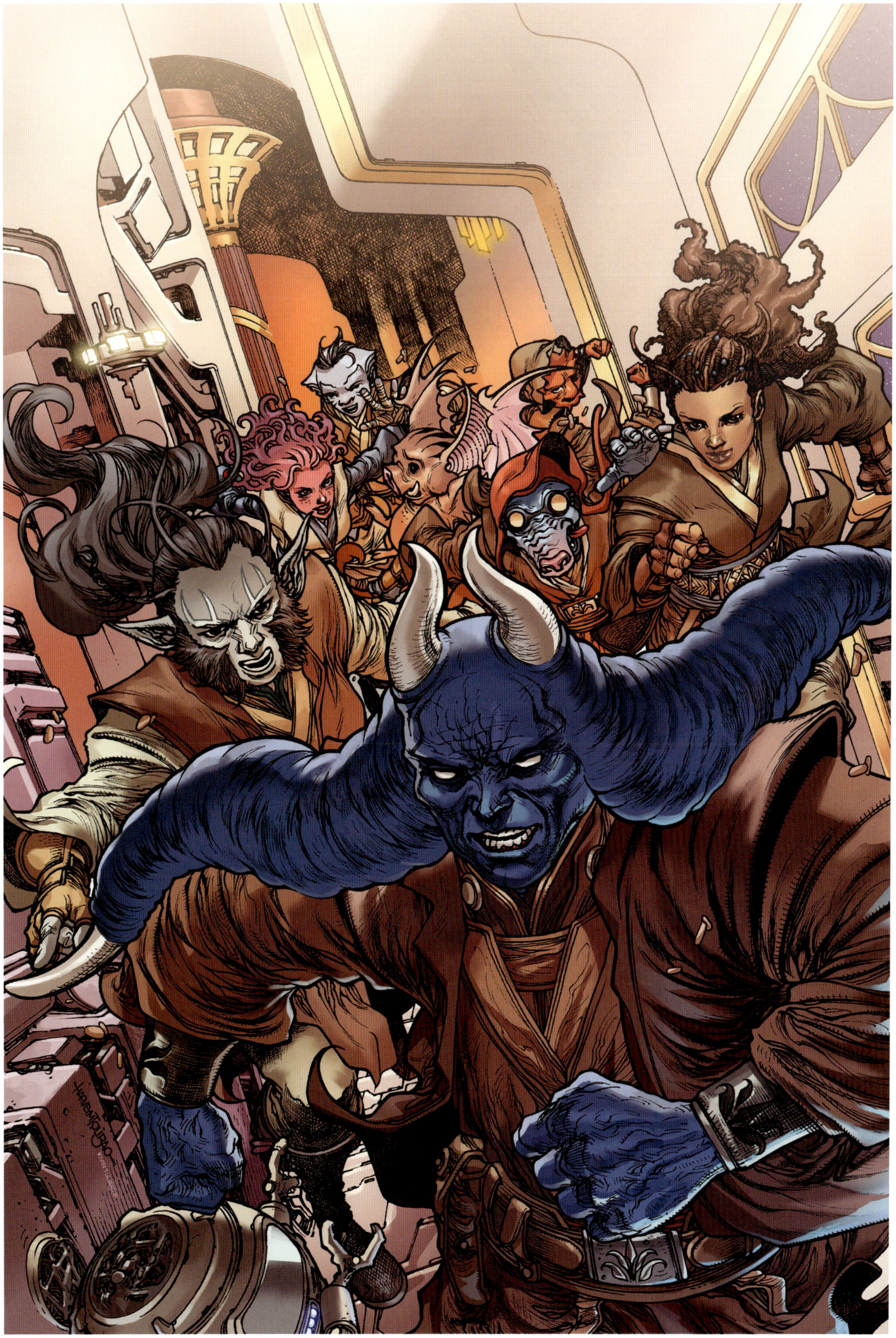

◂ Final cover art for IDW's *Star Wars: The High Republic Adventures* #10 TOLIBAO (PENCILER) AND KEVIN TOLIBAO (COLORIST)

▸ Final cover art for IDW's *Star Wars: The High Republic Adventures* #11 TOLIBAO (PENCILER) AND KEVIN TOLIBAO (COLORIST)

Led by Buckets of Blood, Tolibao's cover for issue #11 envisions the Padawan gang, including a maskless Qort, and their friends sprinting down the hallway of the Starlight Beacon, where the sconce of a light fixture echoes the design of the space station's exterior.

THIS SPREAD Lightsaber, Jedi designs, and final cover illustration from VIZ Media's *Star Wars: The High Republic: The Edge of Balance* manga
MIZUKI SAKAKIBARA

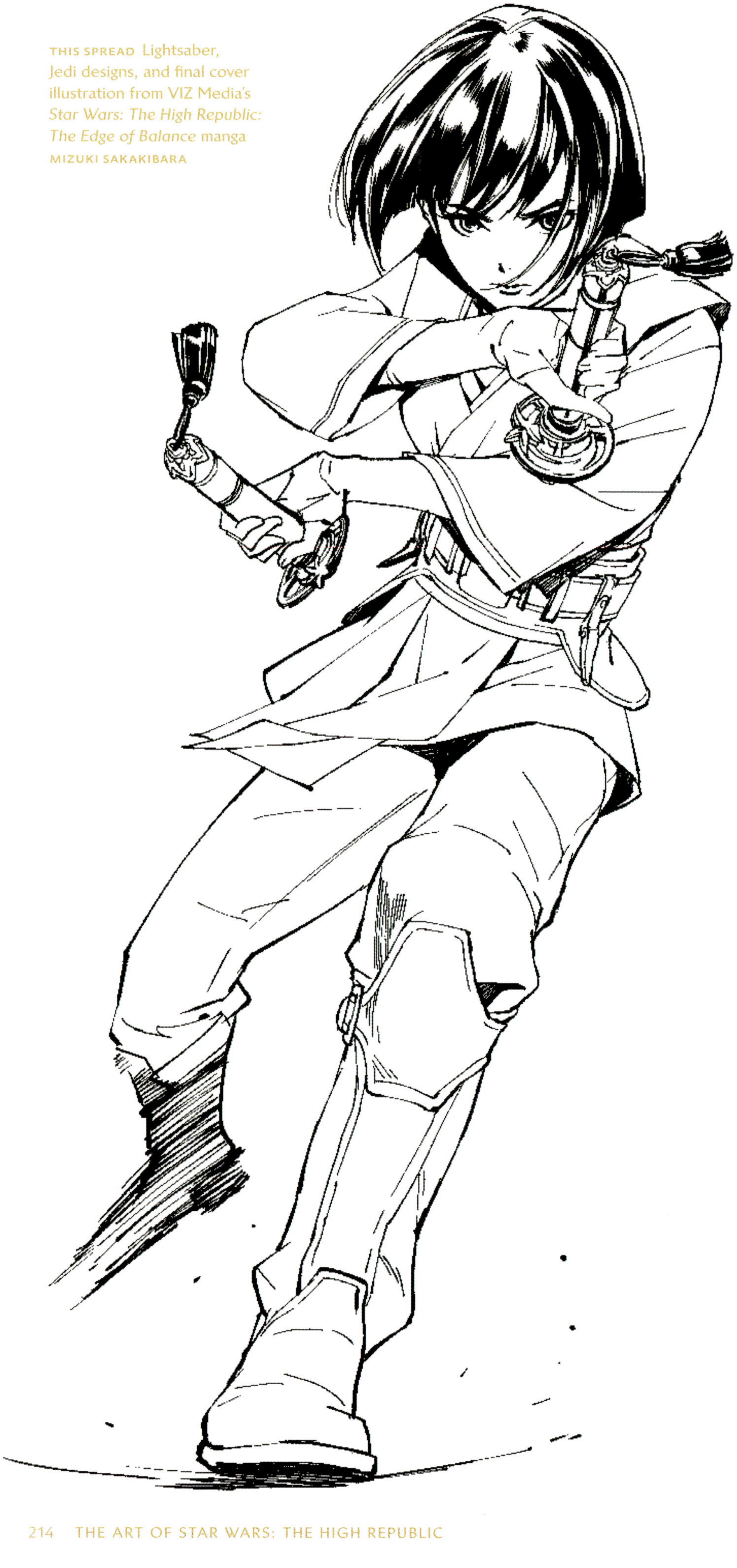

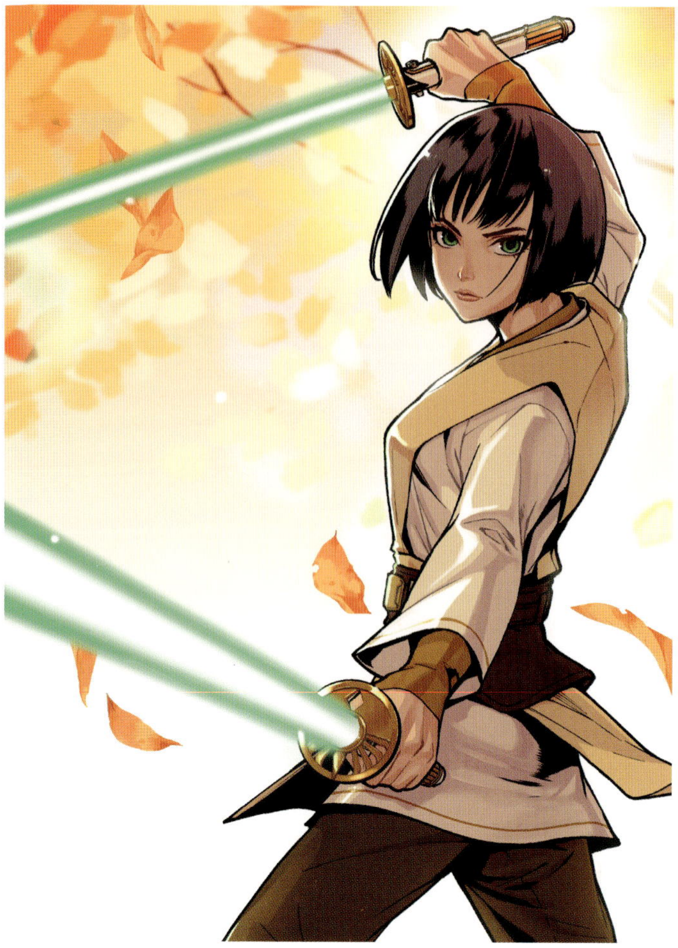

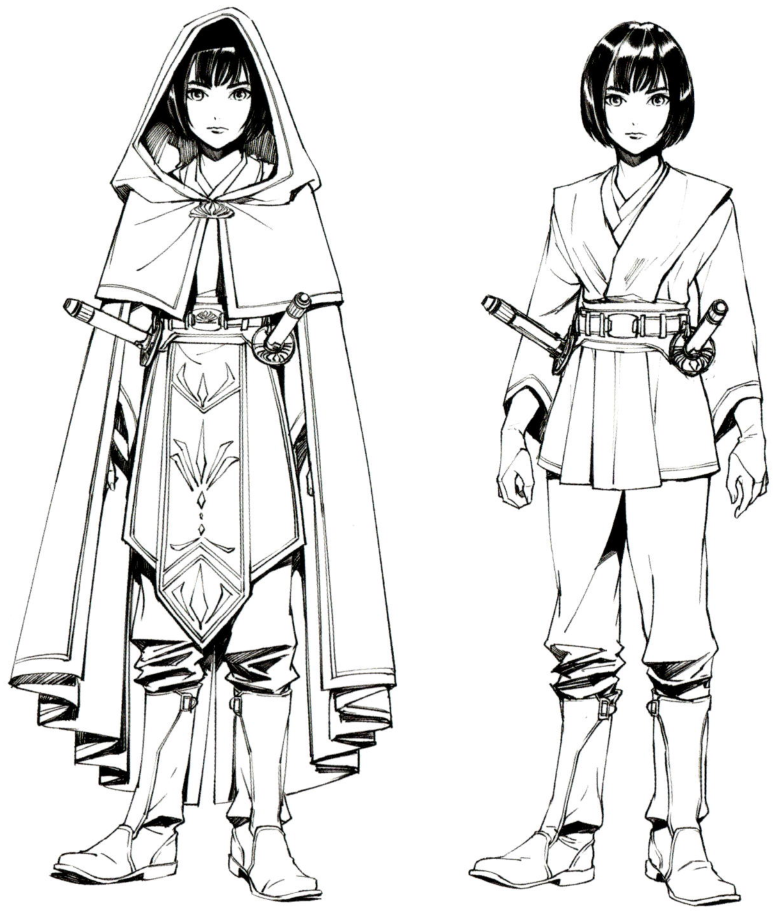

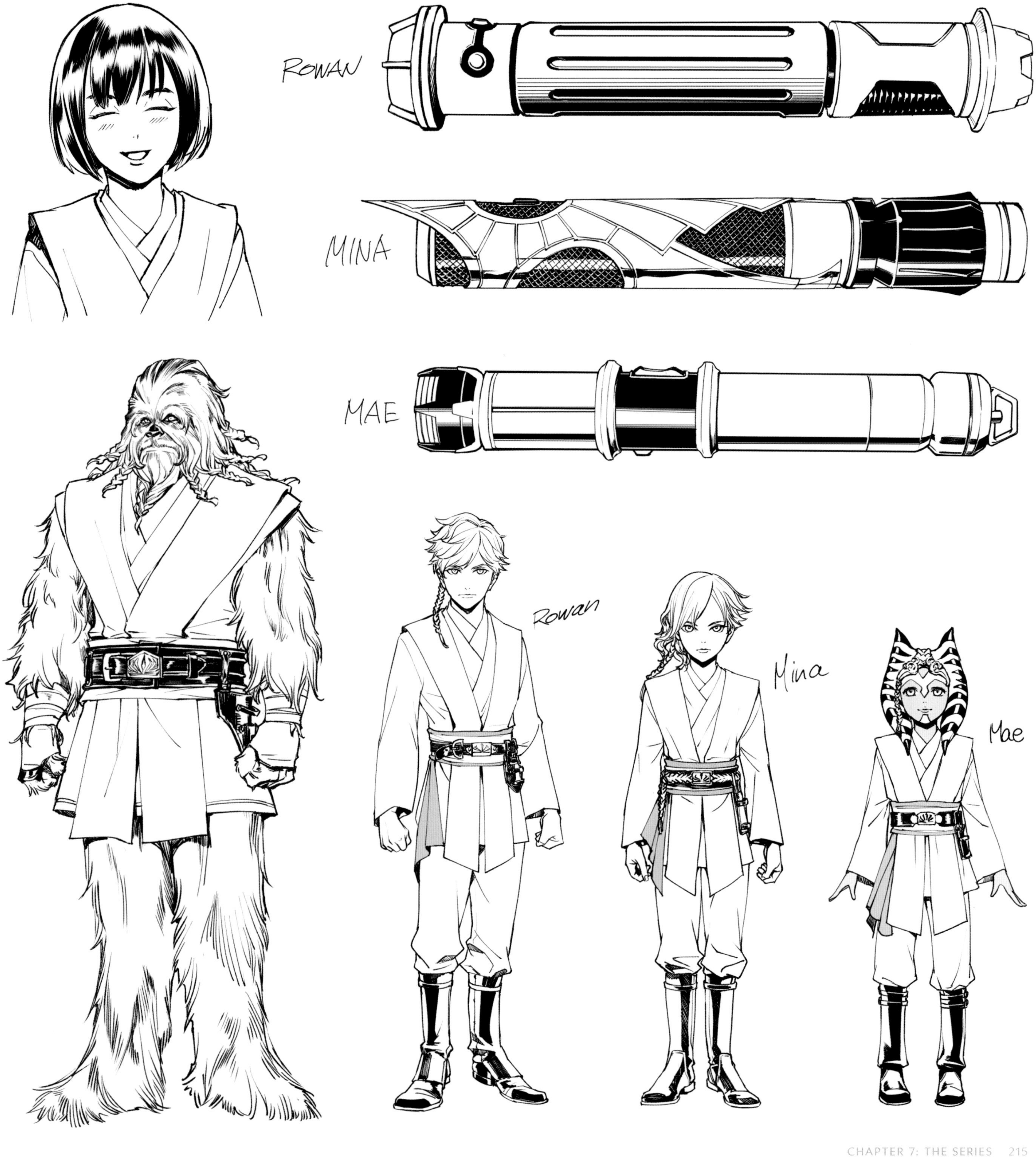
ROWAN
MINA
MAE
Rowan
Mina
Mae

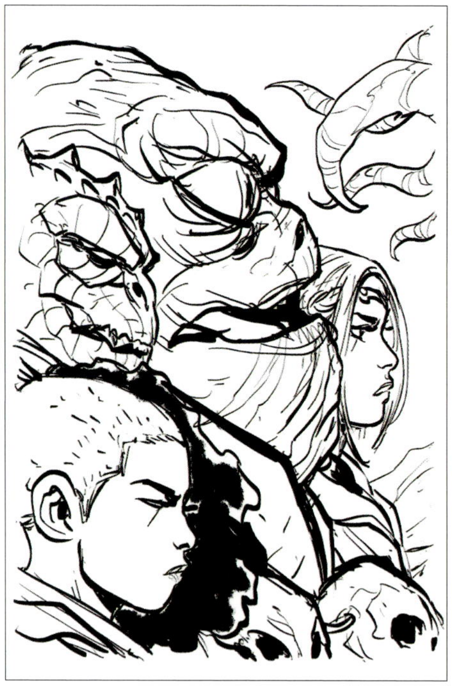

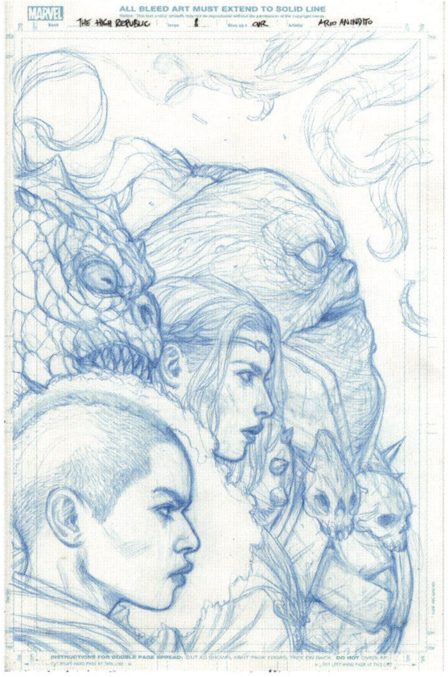

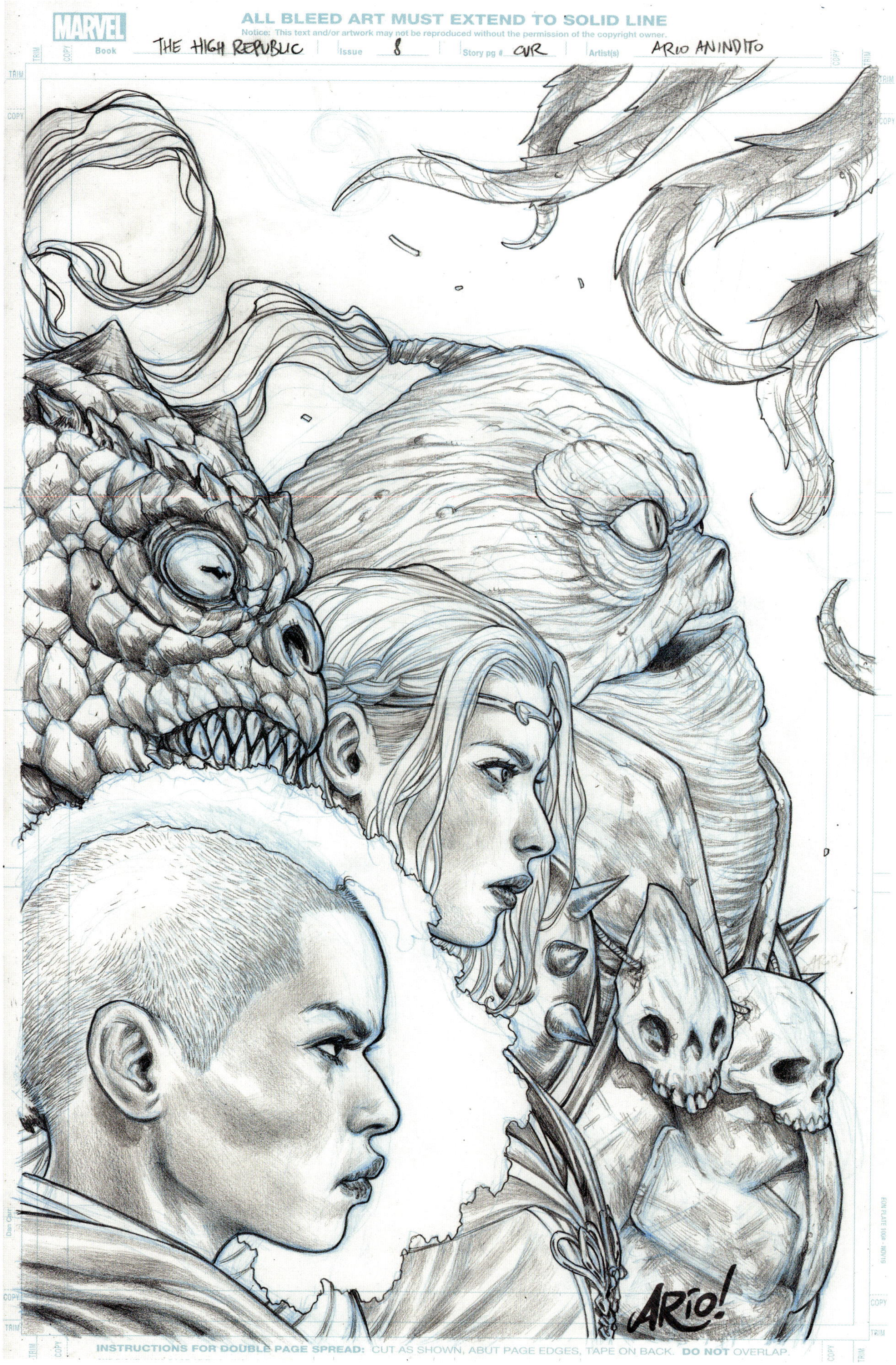

▲ Progression of variant cover art for Marvel's *Star Wars: The High Republic* #8, from sketch to final design "I put Myarga the Benevolent next to the Jedi because, originally, I wanted to show the audience they are now working together. But if we put Myarga too close, it will disturb the title, so I can still show that they are on the same side. It works better this way because we get to see that they are working together, but there's still distance between them; they are not all on good terms, they just have the same enemy. They are standing on the same side looking at the tendrils of the Drengir." ANINDITO

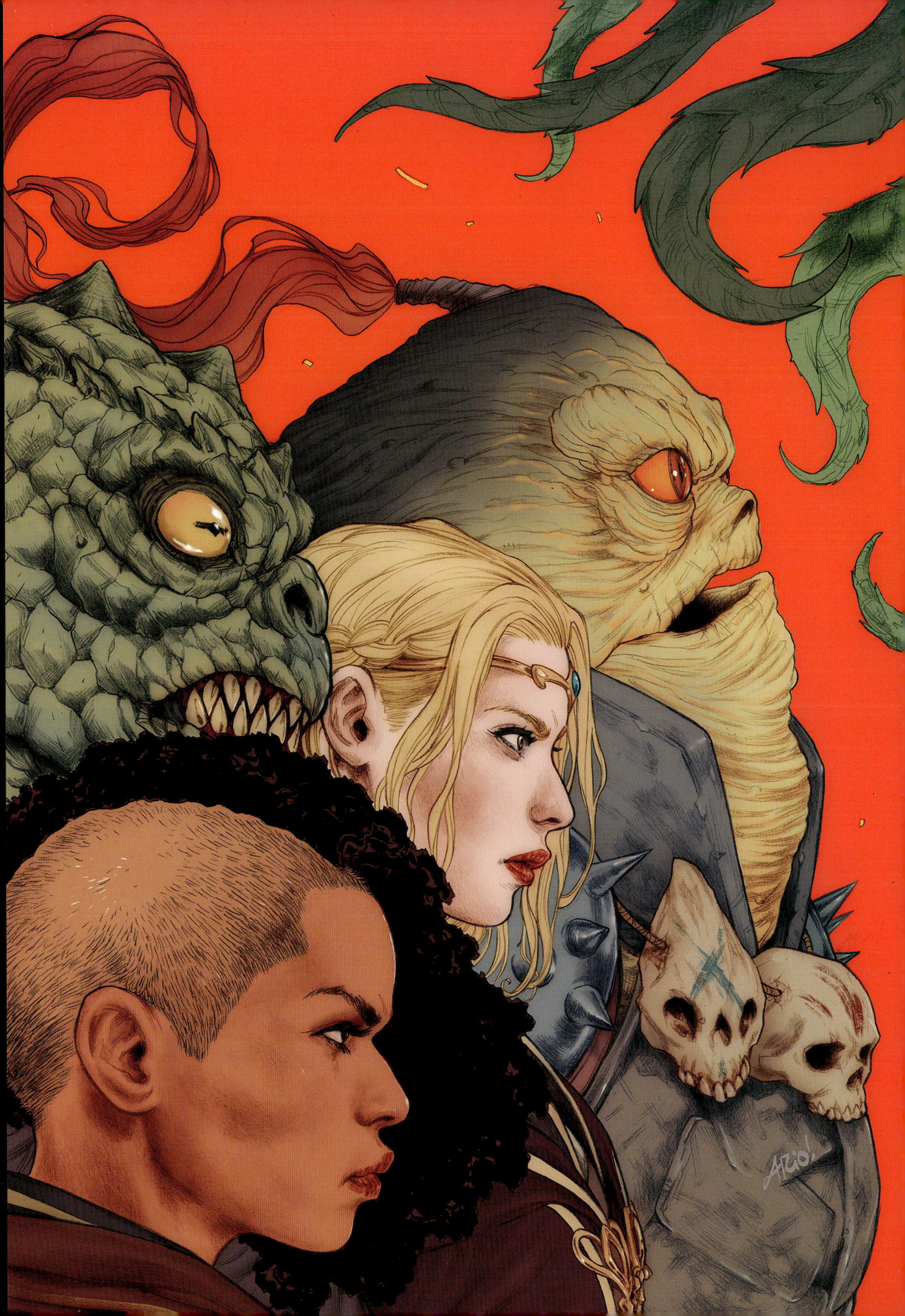

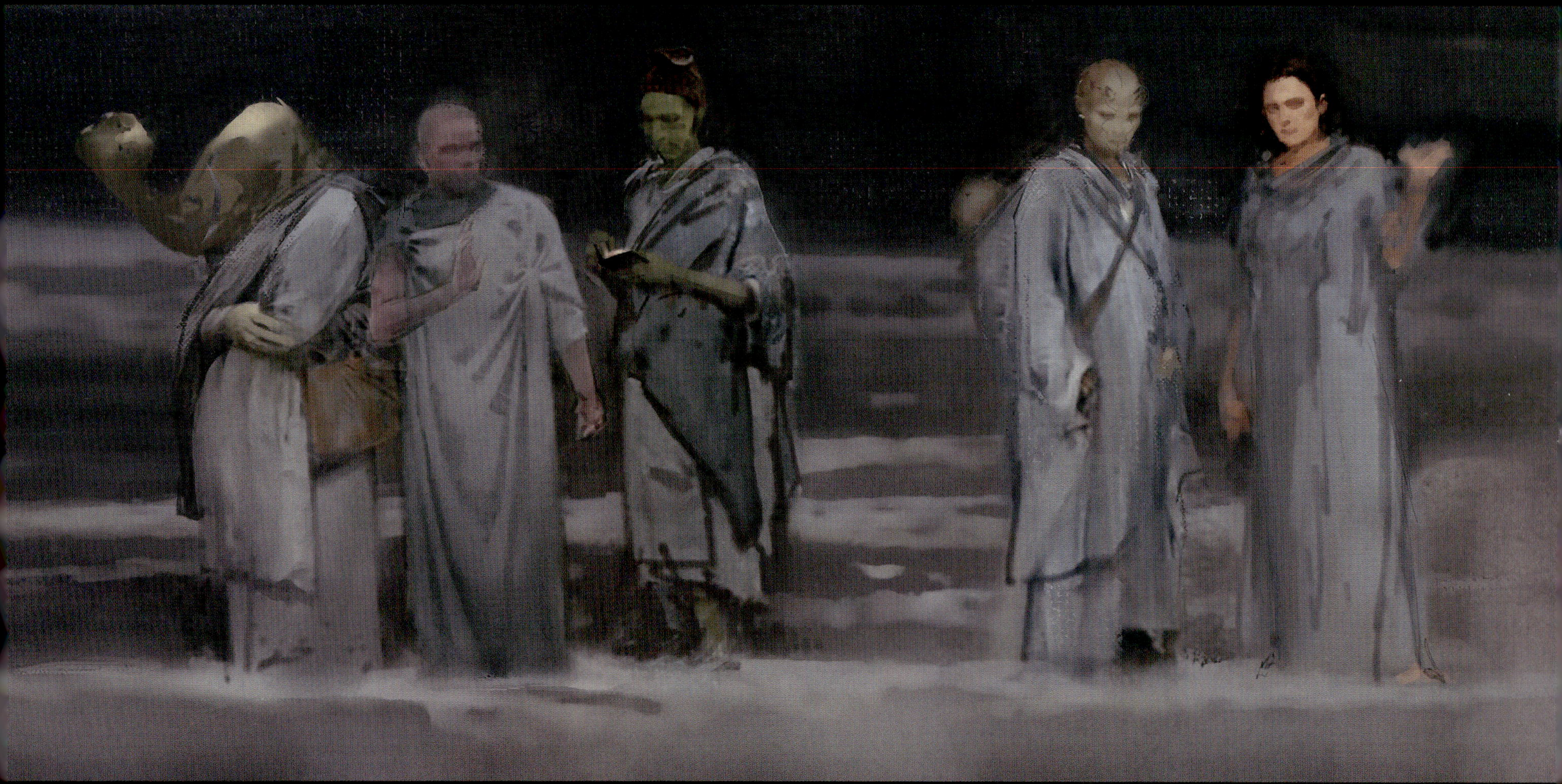

EPILOGUE

IN THE GRAND TRADITION of *Star Wars* storytelling, the next phase in *Star Wars: The High Republic* will step back into the past for a prequel story set a century and a half prior to the events of the Great Disaster and all that followed.

Phase II will introduce an era of frontier prospectors and pioneers, with a few familiar faces, including a younger version of Jedi Porter Engle before he became a cook. In 2021, concept artists had already started to design a mysterious monastic Force cult, known as the Path, at the heart of the new tales. "Phase II: Quest of the Jedi is all about the extremists," said Lucasfilm's James Waugh. "They're all about the imbalance of the Force." And a nameless creature peering out from the final page of Soule's Marchion Ro comic will get a backstory of its own.

"We took a page out of George [Lucas]'s book and said, 'OK, we're going to craft it like the Skywalker saga,'" said Lucasfilm's Michael Siglain. "So, when you're telling the middle, you don't know that it's the middle yet. Nobody knows it's the middle yet. It can't *feel* like the middle; it had to feel really big and really monumental, but at the same time, it has to have the history of what came before." The project will culminate with Phase III: Trials of the Jedi.

And like other *Star Wars* storytelling, the saga of the High Republic was never intended to exist on the page alone. A brief story in virtual reality introduced Padawan Ady Sun'Zee based on a Batuu outpost and fighting alongside Master Yoda as part of ILMxLAB's *Tales from the Galaxy's Edge* in November 2020. Soon after, on December 10, 2020, Lucasfilm president Kathleen Kennedy announced a slate of upcoming *Star Wars* films and series, including the forthcoming Disney+ series, *The Acolyte*, a mystery-thriller focused on emerging dark side powers and set in the final days of the High Republic. Nearly a year to the day later, on December 9, 2021, Lucasfilm Games unveiled plans to produce the first video game set in the High Republic with a cinematic teaser trailer for an intricately branching action-adventure game called *Star Wars Eclipse*. And on May 27, 2022, at *Star Wars* Celebration in Anaheim, California, *Young Jedi Adventures*, a new animated series for kids set during the High Republic, was also announced.

"It was always meant to be an entry point that could go on, if successful, for many years," said Siglain. "We wanted to craft something that felt big and epic. It was always meant to be expansive." But mostly importantly, the High Republic was intended to be a joyride, an epic crusade when brave Jedi Knights defended the freedoms of the galaxy. "We are here with the same goal in mind," Siglain added. "We are all here because we love *Star Wars*. And it's so much fun. The thing about all of this is it should be fun. And it should be for everyone. It's *Star Wars*. It's space wizards with laser swords."

◂ Early concept for The Path of the Open Hand "I love the idea behind this group of devout Force followers who hate the Jedi. That's super fun. Like monks, adopting these layers and long drapery, and looking kind of peaceful. Again, that drapery and simplicity and non-attachment to objects. At one with everything. I'm excited to see how these guys get worked in." GRIFFIN

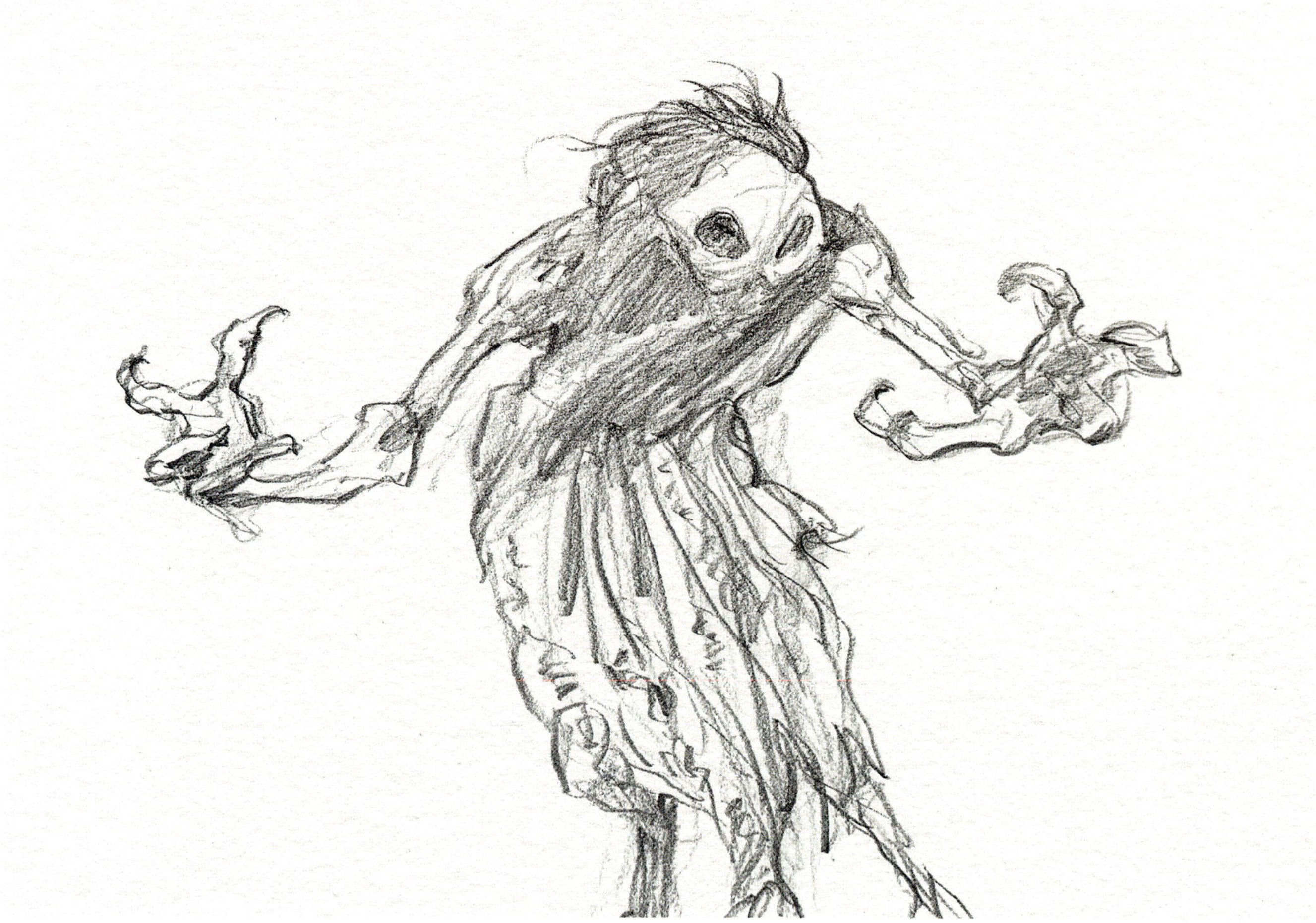

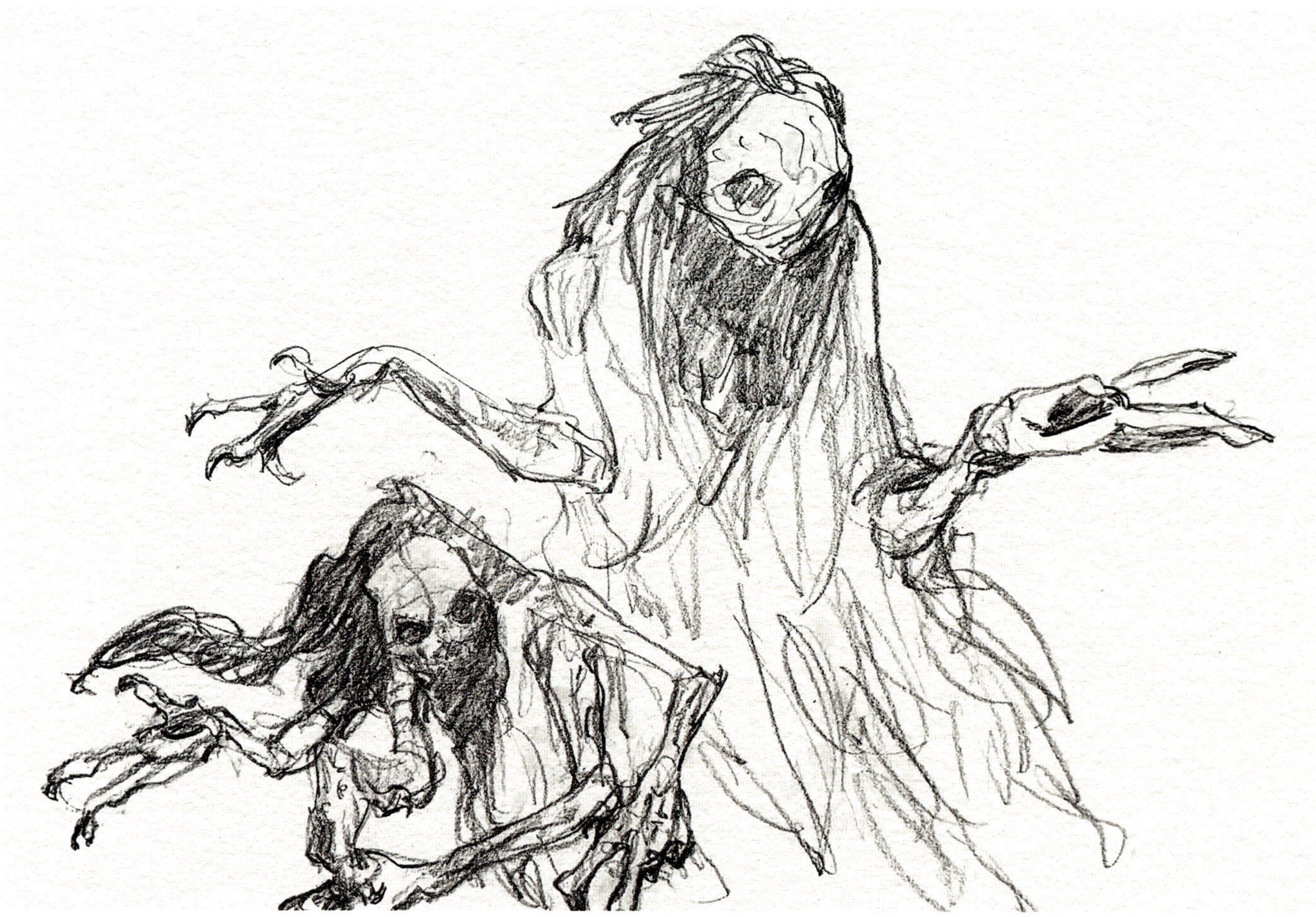

◄ Early designs for "what scares the Jedi," July 2019 "I used to see this character when I was a little kid. It would poke out from behind my brother's bed in the early morning hours before anyone was awake and would wave at me. Scared the pants off me." McCAIG

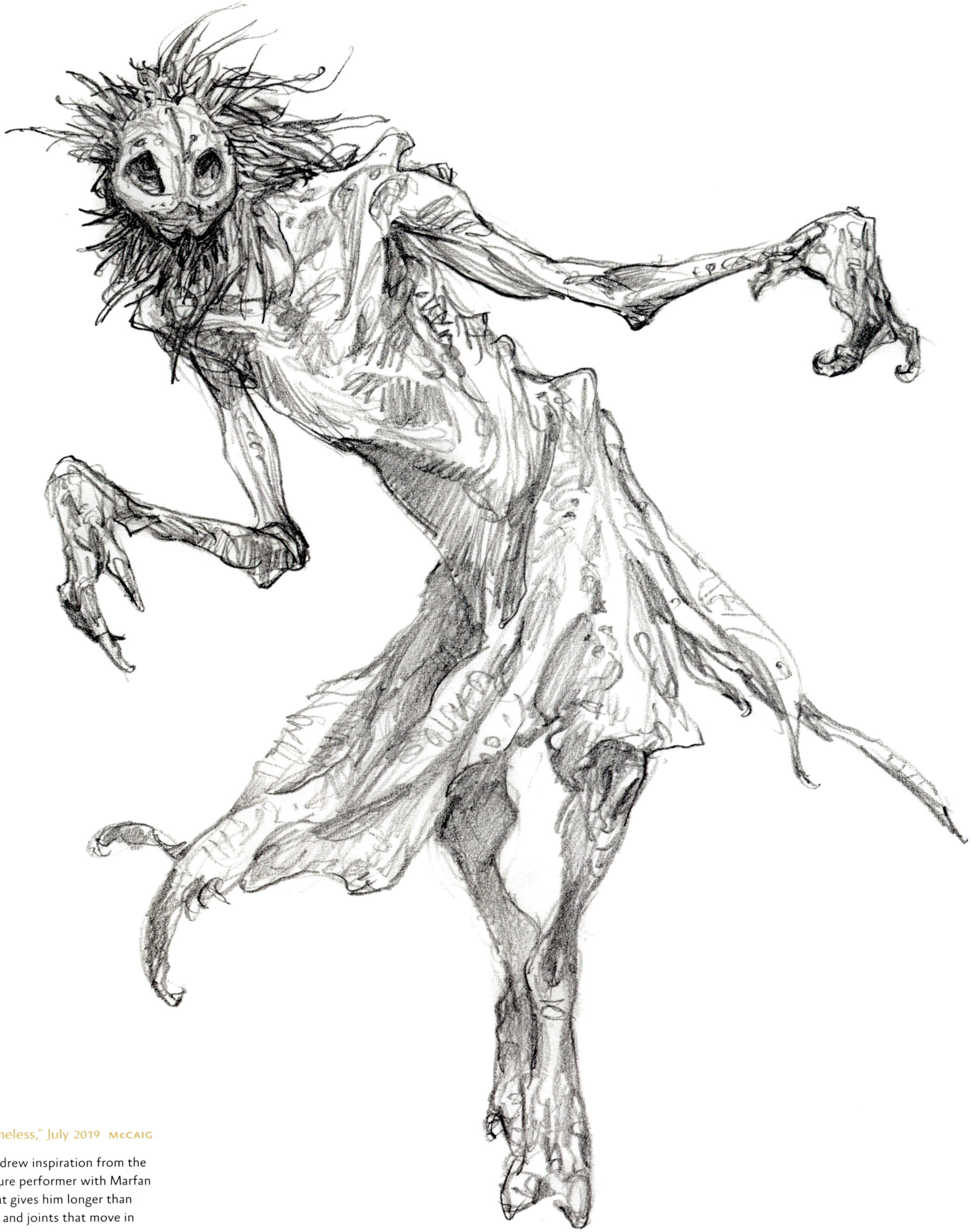

▸ Early sketch of "the Nameless," July 2019 McCAIG

For this concept, McCaig drew inspiration from the actor Javier Botet, a creature performer with Marfan syndrome, a condition that gives him longer than average limbs and fingers, and joints that move in unusual, flexible ways.

INDEX

ACKNOWLEDGMENTS

The High Republic simply would not exist without Cavan Scott, Claudia Gray, Justina Ireland, Daniel José Older, and Charles Soule. Together, you've imagined something truly beautiful. And to all the artists, from Iain McCaig, Grant Griffin, and Phil Noto at the start to Ario Anindito, Harvey Tolibao, and so many others, this book could not exist (and would not be half as beautiful) without you.

My never-ending gratitude to Michael Siglain, Lindsay Knight, Robert Simpson, Lyssa Hurvitz, and the entire *Star Wars* publishing team for not only choosing me for this project, but making it possible. To Connor Leonard, Liam Flanagan, and Eric Klopfer at Abrams, for getting us to the finish line.

For keeping us on course, my humblest thanks to the Lucasfilm Story Group, with special thanks to Phil Szostak, the Jedi Master of *Star Wars* art books, for setting an incredibly high standard of quality in your own work, your invaluable guidance on this project, and your friendship. And, of course, Amy Ratcliffe, Josh Kushins, and J.W. Rinzler, who added to the bedrock that helped inspire this tome.

To Krystina Arielle, who was brought into my life thanks to *The High Republic Show*, for your exuberant love of these characters and the talented people who gifted them to us, your support, and the light you bring into every room. And to Kyle Kao and A.J. Camarillo, Ami Sepahpur and Andrea Reyes—without them, *This Week! In Star Wars* may not have weathered the pandemic.

To my mother, Linda, who ignited my imagination and lifelong love of books and art with a library card and a copy of Paul O. Zelinsky's *Rumpelstiltskin*, and my family—Bill, Heather, Mike, Haley, Ian, and all the rest, especially Michael Lester. To Tina Hess, who made a little girl who wanted to tell her own stories believe that she could.

Thank you to George Lucas for creating this galaxy that's still spawning new stories of hope, and Kathleen Kennedy, who steers the ship in this modern era of storytelling.

And last but not least, to anyone who has entered the era of the High Republic and finally seen themselves represented in the galaxy. People are important. Stories are important. And this one's for you.

FOR LUCASFILM LTD.

Creative Director Michael Siglain
Senior Editor Robert Simpson
Publishing Coordinator Lindsay Knight
Art Director Troy Alders
Creative Art Manager Phil Szostak
Asset Group Chris Argyropoulos and Sarah Williams
Story Group Leland Chee, Pablo Hidalgo, and Matt Martin

FOR ABRAMS

Editor Connor Leonard
Designer Liam Flanagan
Managing Editor Glenn Ramirez
Production Manager Rachael Marks

PAGE 224 Variant cover for *The Fallen Star*
JAMA JURABAEV

CASE Starlight Beacon BLANCHÉ AND KENNY

Library of Congress Control Number: 2022932915

ISBN: 978-1-4197-5655-9

Printed and bound in China
10 9 8 7 6 5 4 3 2 1

ABRAMS The Art of Books
195 Broadway, New York, NY 10007
abramsbooks.com

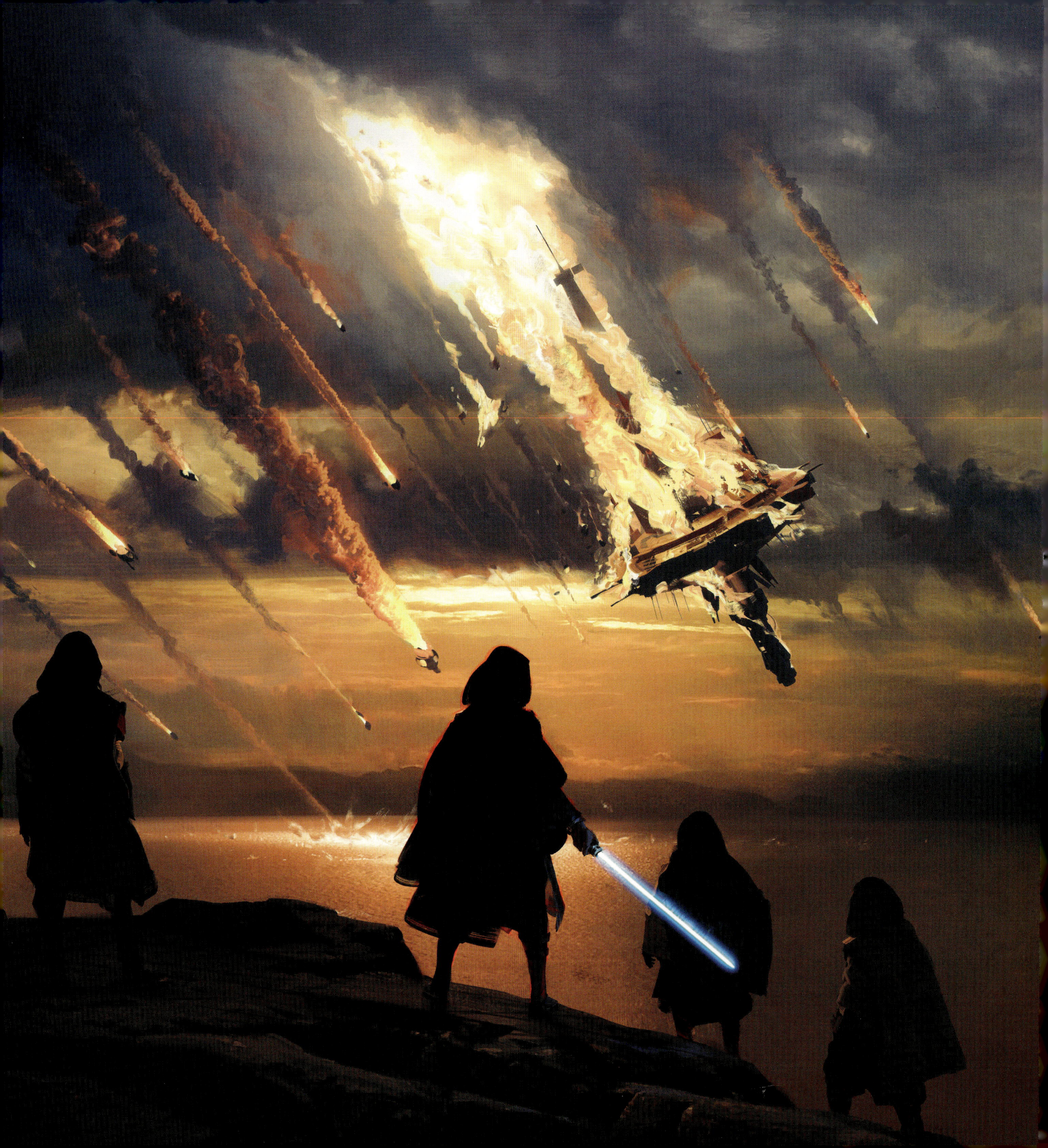